Ex Líbris

Gettysburg

THE SECOND DAY

Harry W. Pfanz

Gettysburg

THE SECOND DAY

The University of North Carolina Press

Chapel Hill and London

©1987 The University of North Carolina Press

All rights reserved

Manufactured in the United States of America

Library of Congress Cataloging-in-Publication Data

Pfanz, Harry W.

Gettysburg—the second day.

Bibliography: p.

Includes index.

1. Gettysburg, Battle of, 1863. I. Title.

E475.53.P48   1987   973.7'349   87-5965

ISBN 0-8078-1749-X

TO

THE MEMORY OF

Letitia Elizabeth Pfanz,

WHOSE

ANCESTORS FOUGHT FOR BOTH

THE UNION AND THE CONFEDERACY

AND WHO SPENT MOST OF HER

SHORT LIFE ON THIS BATTLEFIELD

CONTENTS

MAPS

ILLUSTRATIONS

PREFACE

This is an account of the major action at Gettysburg on 2 July 1863—fought in the three hours prior to darkness on the second day of that enormous battle. It was the assault by the Army of Northern Virginia against the left and center of the Army of the Potomac. Lieutenant General James Longstreet, who commanded two of the three divisions that participated in this Confederate attack, termed the performance of his troops the "best three hours' fighting ever done by any troops on any battle-field." Few would take great issue with his boast. This hard-fought action introduced Little Round Top, Devil's Den, the Wheatfield, and the Peach Orchard to America's historical vocabulary. The mention of these names once quickened the pulses of the survivors of the action and stirred them in pride—and sometimes in defense—of what they and their leaders had done that day. Now the veterans have passed on, and the significance of these places, which was so apparent to them, has faded in man's memory. Such fading is natural, but the veterans of both armies sought to slow its pace. They believed that what they had done at these places was important and sought to preserve the memory of it by erecting memorials on the battlefield and initiating the preservation of the field itself. I hope that this account is a worthy continuation of their preservation effort.

July 2 was a day when many men of both armies performed deeds of great valor and made personal sacrifices that were worthy of the best of their mutual American (and European) heritage. Much of this aspect of the battle is chronicled below. But even the greatest of these men were human and made mistakes. Preparations for the attack—and the defense—began before dawn. There were reconnaissances that supplied incomplete information; there was some indecision and much anxiety; there was misunderstanding if not insubordination in the upper echelons of both armies, and tempers became short. In addition there was hard marching, tiresome waiting, and the usual skirmishing. Finally, the Confederate brigades chosen for the assault stood poised to attack a vulnerable Federal position, and their long-delayed advance began—in accordance with a flawed plan!

Some of the above factors bred discord and two of the most enduring controversies stemming from the war. Major General Daniel E. Sickles, whose Third Corps received the brunt of the Confederates' opening onslaught, sought to shift any adverse criticism that he or his corps might receive to others. He accused his commanding general, George G. Meade, of poor generalship and sought to have him removed from the command of the Army of the Potomac. Sickles opened his attack against Meade before the military campaign was over and continued to refight the battle verbally until his death more than fifty years later. On the Confederate side, after the death of General Robert E. Lee in 1870, some Confederate generals sought to blame General Longstreet for much of the Army of Northern Virginia's lack of success in the campaign, and the ensuing public quarrel extended even into the twentieth century.

These were sad squabbles. They were so much of an appendage to the events presented in this book that I considered preparing a full discussion of them. But sanity or laziness prevailed, and I elected to avoid that morass. Instead I have introduced the substance of the conflicts into appropriate portions of the narrative and used the evidence available for what I deemed it to be worth (which sometimes was not much). I trust that I will not disappoint too many people for taking this higher road.

One of the first decisions that I had to make was whether or not to include the 2 July fighting on Culp's Hill and Cemetery Hill within the scope of this narrative. Although the assaults against the Union right were a part of General Lee's battle plan for that day, they did not begin until the fighting on the Union left and center had virtually ended; then, after a short night recess, they resumed on the following morning. By almost any measure the battles on the Union left and right were separate actions, and so I have omitted coverage of the fighting on Culp's Hill and Cemetery Hill in the expectation that someday someone will give it the full and separate treatment it deserves.

Although I have attempted to be objective in this effort, it is readily apparent that I have written more extensively of the activities of the men of the Army of the Potomac than of those of the Army of Northern Virginia. This is the case primarily because there is simply more information available on the Federal army than on its foe. Indeed, as indicated in the bibliography, for some of the principal Confederate units there are no official accounts of the parts they played in this battle and for many of them there are few unofficial accounts touching on those parts that have any substance. This limits the coverage that their efforts can be given.

I encountered several vexing problems not unique to the study of this engagement but frustrating nonetheless. One is the matter of time. Rarely were participants in the battle in general agreement as to the hour when this or that happened. Therefore, I deemed it wise not to attempt to ascribe specific hours for most events. A second problem is that of changing perceptions and attitudes. In attempting to understand and describe a particular action, I was reminded often of the void that exists in military matters between my generation of soldiers and that of the Civil War. Their methods and mind-sets are rather beyond the reach of our full understanding. Even when they described their doings in detail (and more often than not they assumed that such descriptions were unnecessary and did not give them), it is hard to understand and appreciate what they were describing. A reader of Civil War literature should keep this gap in mind.

I did not shed all of my predilections when I began to prepare this account. I have not followed the current practice of identifying corps by using Roman numerals for two reasons—it was not in use at the time of the Civil War, and for me at least, Roman numerals always require a pause for translation that snags my train of thought. I prefer also to follow a common practice of the Civil War era and use commanders' names to identify divisions, brigades, and batteries. I remember them more easily that way. I am grateful that the Civil War armies had not yet been corrupted by the phonetic alphabet and the computerese that infests the language of our military establishment today.

I took some small liberties with Gettysburg geography. For instance, sometimes Gettysburg savants, with deference to geographic accuracy, divide the high ground that historically is Seminary Ridge into three parts—Seminary Ridge, Warfield Ridge, and Snyder Ridge. It seems practical not to do this, and so I have not. I have taken a few other similar liberties within the text and hope that I shall not confuse the reader by doing so.

I have quoted alleged remarks, conversations, and commands in numerous places throughout the text because they seemed to enhance the narrative and impart something of the spirit of the time. Of course these were initially recorded days, months, or years after they were voiced. Probably many were not recalled verbatim then, and some were tidied up here and there for the benefit of posterity. They should be accepted accordingly.

The action at Gettysburg has had great interest for professional soldiers and students of military history and ought to have some lessons for them as well. The men who fought the battle, by and large, knew their business and probably did it as well as they could under the circumstances and without the benefit of hindsight. However, many if not all of the "Principles of War" (which, as far as I know, were not so neatly set down then as now) were violated by both sides in the course of their preparations for this engagement and during the action itself. Some of these violations will be rather obvious to readers who are interested in the application of these principles. I hope that when possible I have made the reasons for the decisions and deeds of the day—good or bad—sufficiently apparent and urge that anyone making judgments about them do so in the spirit of that day as well as his own.

Conducting a campaign or battle according to certain doctrines is one thing; inspiring men to fight in the face of great adversity is another. The men of both armies who fought in this battle were fatigued when they reached Gettysburg. They had every reason to expect that they might be killed or maimed in the fighting that was to come, but the morale of most men was high and the vast majority tried to do their duty. Some units did not perform particularly well, but most behaved creditably and many fought superbly. It seems to me that while there is some value in understanding why a certain officer did or did not conduct his part of an action according to accepted doctrines of warfare, there is more to be gained from learning why men were motivated to fight poorly or superbly. This knowledge might then be applied with advantage in the leadership of our armed forces today. If nothing else, the knowledge of what was done by our forefathers on this field should provide us with perspective, inspire us to emulate their greatness, and warn us to avoid the weaknesses that led some of them to blunders and tarnished reputations.

ACKNOWLEDGMENTS

I am indebted to many kind people for assistance given to me over the long period of preparation of this study. There were many who helped me in the libraries and repositories listed in the bibliography (and in some others too) whose names I regret that I do not know and who will not be listed here. There were others whose help was more special, perhaps, and whose names are given below.

Foremost among this group were two friends and former colleagues— Robert K. Krick and Edwin C. Bearss. Both of these historians rank among the foremost authorities on the military aspects of the Civil War. Both favored me with advice from time to time, and both read drafts of this narrative and gave me valuable criticisms regarding it. Bob Krick was particularly helpful also in suggesting numerous less obvious Confederate sources for me to examine, in giving me access to those at Fredericksburg National Military Park and in his own collection, and in his unfailing enthusiasm and encouragement, which provided a needed tonic along the way.

I became particularly interested in this portion of the battle of Gettysburg in 1949 when I toured the battlefield with a competent licensed guide. A few months later I prepared a paper on the "Meade-Sickles Controversy" for a history course at The Ohio State University given by Dr. Henry H. Simms. Professor Simms later became my faculty adviser and gave my interest in the Civil War scholarly direction that was helpful later in my professional career and in the preparation of this study. This professional interest was furthered in later years by my association with Dr. Frederick Tilberg at Gettysburg National Military Park.

Civil War officers, when preparing reports, often stated that giving special recognition to a few people within their units would prove invidious but then went on to mention them anyhow. I shall follow their example. Among others on Mr. Krick's staff at Fredericksburg to whom I am particularly indebted are the late David A. Lilly and my son Donald C. Pfanz. Dave called my attention to several Federal sources that I might otherwise have missed. Donald helped me locate materials, checked references for me, and stimulated my thinking with questions and comments during our conversations and tours of Gettysburg and other battlefields.

Colonel Jacob M. Sheads, dean of historians of the Gettysburg area and an old friend and colleague there, helped me with comments and answers to numerous questions about the Gettysburg area. Historians Thomas Harrison and Kathleen Georg Harrison at Gettysburg National Military Park helped me with source materials in their custody and provided me with answers to questions about certain aspects of the battlefield itself.

Others at repositories containing Civil War materials whom I recall with particular gratitude include Dr. Richard J. Sommers and David A. Keough at the U.S. Army Military History Institute at Carlisle Barracks, Pennsylvania; Lucy L. Hrivnak at the Historical Society of Pennsylvania; Russ A. Pritchard and Karla M. Steffan at the Military Order of the Loyal Legion's Civil War Library and Museum in Philadelphia; Marguerite S. Witkop at the Yale University Library; Dr. Oliver H. Orr of the Library of Congress; and Dale Floyd and Michael P. Musick of the National Archives. Two friends, Marshall Krolick of Chicago and John E. Divine of Leesburg, Virginia, aided me with advice and material from their personal collections. I am indebted also to Dr. Edith D. Bancroft of Bryn Athyn, Pennsylvania; William H. Brown of Collingswood, New Jersey; and Levi Bird Duff III of Pittsburgh for generously allowing me use of material from their family papers.

Collecting illustrative material was more difficult than I thought it would be. Among those who deserve special thanks for their help in this are Michael J. Winey at the U.S. Army Military History Institute and photographers Jim Enos of Carlisle, Pennsylvania, and Walter Lane of Gettysburg. I am indebted also to William Nelson, who neatly converted my rough drafts of maps into the finished products within the text.

The world of publication was a forbidding place to me. It was made less so initially by the kind counsel of James V. Murfin of Rockville, Maryland; Mark S. Carroll of Bethesda, Maryland; Robert H. Fowler of Harrisburg, Pennsylvania; and Gary Gallagher, then of the Lyndon Baines Johnson Library in Austin, Texas. I am particularly indebted to the latter for introducing my manuscript to the University of North Carolina Press. Ron Maner edited the manuscript there. He did so with patience, tact, and skill. It was a pleasure to work with him and other members of the Press staff.

Since this was a major personal effort, my family could not escape it. My wife, Letitia, worked with me in the course of visits to several libraries and helped me with proofreading and other chores. Both she and my daughter Marion abided with my efforts at home during the long period of preparation. My oldest son, Captain Frederick W. Pfanz, walked over the scene of this action with me on several occasions and favored me with helpful observations based on his own special knowledge of the battle and his professional training.

Gettysburg

THE SECOND DAY

CHAPTER

From the Potomac to Pennsylvania

GENERAL ORDERS, } WAR DEPARTMENT, ADJT. GEN.'S OFFICE
No. 194
Washington, June 27, 1863.

By direction of the President, Maj. Gen. Joseph Hooker is relieved from command of the Army of the Potomac, and Maj. Gen. George G. Meade is appointed to the command of that army, and of the troops temporarily assigned to duty with it.

By order of the Secretary of War:

E. D. TOWNSEND,
Assistant Adjutant-General[1]

Maj. James A. Hardie, an officer from the War Department in Washington, delivered General Order 194 to General Meade in Meade's tent near Frederick, Maryland, before dawn on 28 June 1863. It was an hour of destiny for both Meade and the Army of the Potomac. Four army commanders—Maj. Gens. George B. McClellan, John Pope, Ambrose E. Burnside, and Joseph Hooker—had battled Gen. Robert E. Lee and the Army of Northern Virginia, had been found wanting, and had been relieved of command. Meade had not sought the appointment; it was thrust upon him. Other candidates were allowed to decline or were considered less qualified. Meade protested the appointment to Hardie, but Hardie assured him that his protests had been anticipated and would be denied. Meade then telegraphed his response to the order to the general-in-chief, Maj. Gen. Henry W. Halleck: "As a soldier, I obey it, and to the utmost of my ability will execute it."[2]

As a professional soldier Meade must have found some satisfaction in his new assignment, but he had no cause to rejoice. Few Americans have so unexpectedly received as heavy a burden as the command of the Army of the

Potomac on 28 June 1863. It was an awesome responsibility. The fate of the nation was in Meade's hands and might be decided in a single impending battle that was almost certainly to be fought within hours or days. The Army of the Potomac was near Frederick; Hooker had brought it there shadowing Lee's Army of Northern Virginia as the Confederates crossed the Potomac River and marched north into Maryland and Pennsylvania. General Hooker had fought his magnificent army poorly at Chancellorsville in May, and President Lincoln and General-in-Chief Halleck lost confidence in him. Political considerations and difficulties in selecting a successor had delayed Hooker's removal from command, but the opportunity to relieve him came on 27 June. On that day Hooker protested that he would be unable to comply with instructions to cover both Harpers Ferry and Washington with the forces at his disposal while confronting an army thought to be larger than his own. He asked to be relieved. The president quickly accepted his resignation, and without delay Halleck ordered General Meade to take command.[3]

Meade faced a dilemma. The Army of Northern Virginia had crossed the Potomac without opposition, had taken Carlisle, Pennsylvania, and was threatening Harrisburg. Only the Army of the Potomac could bring it to bay. If the Federal army engaged the Confederate host in battle and defeated it, all might be well; but a defeat of the Army of the Potomac might result in the Confederate seizure of Washington, Baltimore, or even Philadelphia and could conceivably create a political climate that would lead to an independent Confederacy. The situation was critical.

General Meade was a capable, aggressive, and prudent officer. At age forty-seven he was tall, thin, and balding. Whitelaw Reid, the correspondent "Agate," saw him at his headquarters later and described his appearance there as "tall, slender, not ungainly, but certainly not handsome or graceful, thin-faced, with grizzled beard and moustache, a broad and high but retreating forehead, from each corner of which the slightly-curling hair recedes, as if giving premonition of baldness . . . altogether a man who impresses you rather as a thoughtful student than a dashing soldier—so General Meade looks in his tent."[4]

George Gordon Meade was no man on horseback, and though a member of a prominent Philadelphia family, he lacked the charisma associated with public heroes. But he was a thorough professional who would fight, and at Fredericksburg it was his division that almost shattered Stonewall Jackson's line. Col. Philip Regis de Trobriand, a brigade commander in the Third Corps, later wrote that prior to Gettysburg General Meade's "services had not been so brilliant as to eclipse those of his rivals. He was, besides, more reserved than audacious, more modest than presumptuous, on which account he treated his corps commanders rather as friends than as inferiors." Another Third Corps officer wrote at the time of Meade's appointment that he knew little of the general, but that Meade appeared to be an "earnest, patient man." He might have been wrong in his estimate of Meade's capacity for patience, but he went on to observe that he anticipated no great disasters or great victories under Meade's command. Somewhat significantly he observed that Meade was not liked within the Third Corps and especially not by Maj. Gen. David B. Birney, Meade's fellow Philadelphian. After serving as Meade's commander in the last year of the war, Lt. Gen. Ulysses S. Grant described him as a brave, conscientious subordinate but with a temper that could rise beyond his control. Col. Theodore Lyman saw him as a "thin old gentleman, with a hooked nose and a cold blue eye," who, though irascible, was a magnanimous man. Gen. Henry J. Hunt, his chief of artillery, though never his close friend, was pleased to have him as a commander because, in Hunt's opinion, Meade was a gentleman.[5]

Meade's instructions from Halleck were simple enough. Halleck reminded him that "no one ever received a more important command" and that his was the "covering army" of Washington as well as the "army of operation" against the Rebels. He was to maneuver it to cover Washington and Baltimore insofar as circumstances would permit, and should Lee move on either of these cities, he was to give battle.[6]

General Meade responded to Halleck's instructions with a statement of his intentions. He would advance his army toward the Susquehanna River, an apparent Confederate objective, keeping Baltimore and Washington well covered. If he "checked" the enemy from crossing the river or if the Confederates turned toward Baltimore, he would give battle. To his wife he wrote on 30 June that though Confederate cavalry was rampaging in his rear, hoping to cause him to turn back, "I shall not do it—I am going straight at them—and will settle this thing one way or the other."[7]

On the night of 28 June, as Meade settled into his new assignment, a tired man in soiled civilian clothing picked his way through a bivouac area of the Army of Northern Virginia near Chambersburg, Pennsylvania. He searched for the headquarters of Lt. Gen. James Longstreet, commander of the Army of Northern Virginia's First Corps. He was Henry Harrison, a Mississippian and a spy, sent by Longstreet a fortnight before to get information on the Army of the Potomac. Lt. Col. G. Moxley Sorrel of Longstreet's staff received Harrison and took his report. Sorrel hurried him to Longstreet, who talked with the spy and then sent him at once to General Lee. He was not known to General Lee, but Longstreet vouched for him. Harrison had just come from the Army of the Potomac and reported that that mighty host had crossed the Potomac at Edwards Ferry and was concentrated around Frederick, Maryland. Furthermore, it had a new commander, because George G. Meade had replaced Joseph Hooker just that day. This was startling news indeed, but General Lee heard the report with "composure and minuteness."[8]

General Lee had attained the reputation of a great commander. He was fifty-six years old in 1863, a graduate in West Point's class of 1829. In his thirty-two years of military service he spent time constructing fortifications and other engineering works, earned three brevets as an engineering officer on Gen. Winfield Scott's staff in Mexico, and served as superintendent of West Point, lieutenant colonel of the Second Cavalry Regiment, and, briefly, colonel of the First Cavalry Regiment. He had served the Confederacy in western Virginia, in South Carolina and Georgia, and in Richmond on President Davis's staff. He had commanded the Army of Northern Virginia for about a year.[9]

General Lee was 5 feet 10½ inches tall and weighed about 165 pounds. His complexion was florid; his once dark hair and beard were gray. Lee was handsome and distinguished in appearance, a man of kindly bearing and gentle charm. Women sometimes begged for locks of his hair, and one flag-waving Unionist woman in Chambersburg exclaimed as he passed, "Oh, I wish he was ours." He wore a long gray jacket, a black felt hat, and blue trousers that he tucked into his Wellington boots. He was neat in dress and appearance, as befitting an officer and a gentleman, and always looked clean—no easy task, even for a general, on campaign.[10]

General Lee had always been robust and until March 1863 had avoided serious illness. Then he suffered a sore throat that brought on an attack of pericarditis that incapacitated him for several weeks. He recovered, however, in time to outgeneral Hooker at Chancellorsville. If his pericarditis had any lasting effect, it seems not to have been in evidence during the Gettysburg campaign. However, he might have been slowed somewhat by a more common camp ailment[11]—Capt. William W. Blackford, of Maj. Gen. James E. B. Stuart's staff, wrote that when he visited army headquarters on the night of 2 July, he learned that the general was suffering from diarrhea. If so, that disorder could have been a handicap.[12]

If not greatly influenced by physical problems, General Lee was greatly affected by other things. One of these was his optimism based on the previous successes of the Army of Northern Virginia. It caused him to believe that his army was close to invincible, and that conviction engendered overconfidence. As if to balance this optimism, he had a well-founded feeling of anxiety. General Stuart and much of his cavalry were away, out of contact, Lee knew not where, and their absence left him all but blind. Further, though he knew General Longstreet well as an experienced corps commander, General Lee had not worked closely with Lt. Gens. Richard S. Ewell and Ambrose Powell (A. P.) Hill. It remained to be seen whether, as commanders of the army's Second and Third corps, they could replace the fallen Stonewall Jackson.

A spy's report was no way for the commander of the Army of Northern Virginia to learn that the enemy, the Army of the Potomac, was near at hand. This news ought to have been provided by his absent cavalry. General Lee pondered the report's credibility. He could not confirm it, but it was too dangerous to ignore. There was no alternative but to take the information at face value and act on it without delay. Lee sent off a courier to General Ewell, whose corps was moving toward the Susquehanna in the army's van. Ewell was to halt his march to the east and concentrate his corps east of South Mountain in the Gettysburg-Cashtown area. A concentration there would draw the Federals to Lee's army and away from the Cumberland Valley and the Army of Northern Virginia's line of communication and supply back to Virginia. So ended the first phase of the Gettysburg campaign that carried the Army of Northern Virginia to the Susquehanna River and the outskirts of Harrisburg, Pennsylvania's capital.[13]

General Lee had conceived this thrust into the North soon after his victory at Chancellorsville. That brave effort had stopped a Federal movement toward Richmond and enhanced his army's reputation, but it had been costly. Stonewall Jackson had been the most prominent of the Army of Northern Virginia's irreplaceable casualties. Yet, after its defeat the Army of the Potomac remained on Stafford Heights opposite Fredericksburg, where Lee could not get at it, poised for another strike. Something had to be done.

General Lee's first task was to compensate for the loss of Jackson. He sought to do this, in part, by reorganizing his army. Its two corps of eight infantry divisions became three corps of three divisions each (see Appendix). Two divisions, those of Maj. Gens. Robert E. Rodes and Richard H. Anderson, each had five brigades, while the other seven divisions each had four. The brigades were composed of five or so regiments and numbered in the area of 1,500 to 1,700 men apiece. Each division except Anderson's had the direct support of a four-battery battalion of artillery, and each corps had two additional artillery battalions as a corps reserve. Unfortunately, though most batteries had four guns, some batteries often had two or more types of guns, each requiring its own kind of ammunition. General Stuart continued to command the army's cavalry, a division of six brigades.

Dependable, stubborn James Longstreet, who with Jackson had been a corps commander prior to Chancellorsville, continued to command the First Corps. This corps had divisions led by Maj. Gens. John B. Hood, Lafayette McLaws, and George E. Pickett. Much of Jackson's old corps went to General Ewell, an excellent officer, who was reporting back to duty after having lost a leg at Groveton (Second Manassas) less than a year before. Ewell's corps had divisions commanded by Maj. Gens. Robert E. Rodes, Jubal A. Early, and Edward Johnson, and it was Rodes's and Early's divisions that had led the army into Pennsylvania. Lt. Gen. Ambrose Powell Hill, an impetuous, contentious officer, who had won a fine reputation as commander of the Light Division, had the newly created Third Corps. His division commanders were Maj. Gens. Richard H. Anderson, Henry Heth, and William Dorsey Pender. Although both Hill and Ewell had rendered outstanding service as division commanders, neither general had commanded a corps or had worked directly under General Lee. As a result, they were not accustomed to his style of command. In addition, in an army brimming with individualists, each corps commander had a distinct personality, and there were strained relations between Hill and Longstreet. In the reorganization

Gen. Robert E. Lee (National Archives)

Maj. Gen. George G. Meade (National Archives)

Longstreet had retained an advantage: his three division commanders had experience in their assignments. Of the other six division commanders only Rodes, Anderson, and Early had commanded divisions before the reorganization.[14]

In his report made after the campaign, Lee stated that three objectives lay behind it. First, he wished to disrupt Federal operations for the 1863 campaigning season, not only in Virginia but elsewhere as far as the effects of the invasion might be felt. Second, he felt that the Confederacy could gain little if his army remained on the defensive and allowed the Federals to occupy Virginia's farms while they prepared for the next onslaught. Better that the

Army of Northern Virginia should draw the enemy from the Old Dominion and permit its farmers to harvest their crops for the Confederacy. Furthermore, the land beyond the Potomac had been virtually untouched by war, and it teemed with supplies enough to delight any Confederate quartermaster. Lee felt a great need for these supplies in 1863.[15] Third, Lee realized there was a pressing need for a decisive victory. Fredericksburg and Chancellorsville had won only plaudits and time at great cost but obviously had not gained independence and peace. The Army of the Potomac continued to menace Virginia, and satellite forces continued to occupy the lower Shenandoah Valley and western Virginia and nibble away at the Atlantic coastline. Although Longstreet and others urged direct assistance to the armies in Tennessee and Mississippi, General Lee showed little positive interest in such detachments. He would aid the armies elsewhere by winning a decisive victory in the East, where its shock waves might crumble the entire Federal effort.[16]

To this end, on 3 June General Lee began to shift his 75,000-man army from Fredericksburg northwest to Culpeper and around Hooker's right. Ewell's corps led the way, followed by Longstreet's, while Stuart's cavalry, 10,000 strong, guarded the roads and the Rapidan River fords that led to the resting foe. An attack by Federal cavalry supported by infantry surprised Stuart's brigades at Brandy Station on 9 June, but after a confused fight, the Federals were repulsed. This cavalry brawl was the only blemish up to that point on an otherwise masterful move. Ewell's corps crossed into the Shenandoah Valley and on 13–15 June gobbled up the Federal force at Winchester along with its ordnance and supplies. Longstreet's corps edged northeast of the Blue Ridge to face the Army of the Potomac as Ewell made for the Potomac crossings. On 15 June, when it became clear that the Army of the Potomac was moving north from Fredericksburg in response to the Confederate move, Hill's corps left Fredericksburg and moved north behind Longstreet and after Ewell.[17]

Ewell's corps performed well. Following Brig. Gen. Albert G. Jenkins's brigade of cavalry, it began to cross the Potomac at Williamsport, Maryland, and Shepherdstown, Virginia, on 15 June. It entered Maryland, marched north to Hagerstown, and continued on to Chambersburg, Pennsylvania. From Chambersburg Early's division crossed the mountain to Gettysburg, York, and finally Wrightsville on the Susquehanna. In the meantime Rodes's division, followed by Johnson's, continued northeast up the Cumberland Valley to Carlisle. Ewell's march was a grand raid. The rewards for his corps's audacity and celerity were countless horses and cattle, barrels of flour, bushels of grain, and other supplies needed to sustain a nineteenth-century army. On 29 June as he prepared to seize Harrisburg, Ewell received General Lee's fateful summons to rejoin the main army at once in the Gettysburg-Cashtown area. The days of harvest were over; the days of battle were drawing nigh.[18]

As Ewell's men streamed north and east from Chambersburg, Hill's and Longstreet's corps crossed the Potomac at Williamsport and marched to the Chambersburg area. In the meantime, two cavalry brigades covered the gaps in the Blue Ridge and the army's rear, Jenkins's brigade screened the van of Ewell's corps, and Stuart, with his remaining three brigades, rode north and east to pass behind the Army of the Potomac, which was then spread over the Virginia countryside west of Washington. After this was done, Stuart expected to cross the Potomac and take his assigned position on Ewell's right, where he would screen the Confederate advance. But, as is well known, it did not work out that way. The Federal army marched when Stuart's small force was east of it and blocked its direct route to Ewell. Stuart and his three brigades did not rejoin the main army until 2 July, too late to make the reconnaissances needed by General Lee that day and in too poor a condition to give battle.[19]

The men of Longstreet's and Hill's corps must have found the invasion less exciting than did those of Ewell's corps, who led the army into the land of milk and honey. And yet, they wrote and spoke of their experiences in later years with pleasure and nostalgia that reflected the high morale and soldierly pride that made them a dauntless fighting force. In retrospect they were proud of their good behavior but took pleasure in recalling mischief that added a little spice to their recollections. They were in clover. The invasion was something of an outing for them; they were tourists able to indulge themselves as superior beings and righteous conquerors. They believed that their army was invincible and had no concern over the outcome of any scrap to come.

The Potomac River was swollen by the frequent rains that marked the Gettysburg campaign. In spite of a width of about two hundred yards, the river was not an impassable obstacle—though one soldier's memory broadened its width to half a mile. It was raining when a portion of Longstreet's corps crossed it at Williamsport. The men took off their trousers, shoes, and stockings, and maybe their underwear as well, made bundles of them, and fixed the bundles, with their cartridge boxes, to their rifle-muskets, which they carried high over their shoulders.[20] The forders whooped and yelled, their banners dipped and swayed, and bands on the Maryland shore welcomed them with "Maryland, My Maryland."[21] Some, including the Washington Artillery, met carriages of curious young women at the ford and, as Capt. William M. Owen observed, "The sight of thousands of 'Confeds' in the water and in the fields, '*sans culotte*' must have been astounding and novel in the extreme, and something the young ladies would not soon forget. Fifty thousand men without their trousers on can't be passed in review every day of the week."[22]

Once across the river, Longstreet's men had a treat that many recalled and probably enlarged on the rest of their lives. The Confederates had confiscated in Williamsport a large amount of whiskey, a tonic for wet soldiers, and some high-ranking officer, probably Longstreet, authorized each man a gill of it. McLaws remarked that to the credit of his division he had heard of no one's refusing it, and as a result his men were all in a good humor.[23] Hood's men got their share of the ration by passing in line before barrels with the heads knocked out, each man dipping out his own gill. Some portions were larger than others and taken on empty stomachs, and as a result many men got quite drunk. Ranking officers were inclined to be tolerant of those in a drunken condition, but Col. Van Manning of the Third Arkansas Regiment had the Third's drunks heaved into a cold stream. Some officers were as drunk as the most tipsy of their men, and those who were sober were busy keeping the peace. One enlisted man wounded an officer in the face but received no punishment. Some Texans found more whiskey elsewhere and drank it too. When the march continued, many drunks had to sober up on the move, and some who fell by the wayside were dumped into wagons. As Cpl. Joseph B. Polley said, some were in such a state that it was the width of the road rather than its length that bothered them. After they sobered up, some had eyes that looked "like two burnt holes in a blanket." One man remarked that on the day of the crossing Longstreet's men had breakfast in Virginia, dinner in Maryland, supper in Pennsylvania, and slept in a state of intoxication.[24]

The Confederates had marched well back in Virginia, where "that unmerciful driver our beloved General, . . . Hood, simply strikes a trot and is satisfied that the Texas Brigade, at least, will be with him at nightfall."[25] Col. James Arthur Fremantle of Great Britain's Coldstream Guards, an observer, was with the brigades of Brig. Gens. Paul J. Semmes and William Barksdale at the Potomac crossing. He saw them as "well shod and efficiently clothed" until they lost their shoes in the mud, and they marched without straggling. Many carried carpets for blankets and had some Federal knapsacks and accoutrements. Behind each regiment trailed a group of slaves together with some men of the ambulance corps. The latter were distinguished by red badges on their hats and by stretchers that they carried. Fremantle might not have known it, but a field officer and a surgeon marched with the ambulance corps men, checked each man who wished to fall out, and gave those who were disabled permission to do so. And then behind each brigade there was a train of twenty wagons together with a surgeon and a staff officer who rechecked the stragglers and added their signatures to the passes of those they deemed worthy. Fremantle was intrigued by the high spirits and vociferous yelling and cheering of the troops. Perhaps the men of Britain's Guards regiments did not behave that way. Capt. Fitzgerald Ross, a visiting hussar from the Austrian army, echoed Fremantle's observations and remarked further that the roads were crowded and knee-deep in mud. After the Confederates entered Pennsylvania, where less delicacy was required of them, the infantry marched on the sides of the road, trampling paths twenty feet wide in the fields. The correspondent of *The Times* of London described these paths as being as wide as Regent Street.[26]

The Pennsylvania farmers cared little for the Southern soldiers, particularly their tramping over the fields of ripening grain and knee-high corn. Col. E. Porter Alexander stopped at a farmhouse for a drink of water from a pump on the porch. He found the Pennsylvania Dutch farmer in great anguish as he pointed to mud tracked on the porch by thirsty Confederate soldiers and to a broad path on the road edge of his wheatfield. When the gentlemanly Alexander asked the hard-pressed farmer for water, the poor man shouted, "No! Dere ain't no water! De well is done pump dry! And just look at dis porch vere dey been! And see dere vere dey tramples down dat wheat! Mein Gott! Mein Gott! I'se heard of de horrors of war before but I never see what dey was till now!"[27]

Pennsylvanians encountered by Longstreet's and Hill's men had already been visited by Ewell's and had good reason for viewing Confederates with apprehension. In spite of General Lee's orders, there was plenty of private foraging. Fence rails fed cooking fires, and more than commissary food went into Confederate kettles. While bivouacked south of Chambersburg, some Texans got a cooked meal at a farm and, after eating, took the trouble to rob some beehives by pulling them over with ropes. That done, they visited another farm, where they plundered the milk house and the chicken house. There was some justice, though, for the chickens stolen as fryers turned out to be bantams that were inedible for those soldiers with discriminating palates.[28]

The experiences in Maryland and Pennsylvania provided an exhilarating overture to battle that did its part in boosting Confederate morale and confidence. But the overture was drawing to an end. On 26 June the men of the Army of Northern Virginia were cautioned to be on guard for bushwhackers, and those under arrest for noncapital offenses were returned to duty. During the Chambersburg respite Generals Pickett and McLaws received orders to send out strong parties to destroy the railroad north and south of the town. They had to burn the ties and "injure the rails as much as practicable." Things were getting serious—the grand excursion was about over.[29]

The Chambersburg lull ended on 29 June when Hill's corps began its march east over South Mountain toward the Gettysburg-Cashtown area. Maj. Gen. Henry Heth led his division through Cashtown Pass and down the mountain to Cashtown. The division bivouacked there, and the next day, 30 June, Heth sent Brig. Gen. James Johnston Pettigrew and his North Carolina brigade toward Gettysburg eight miles to the east in search of supplies, particularly shoes that he had heard might be there. Pettigrew's men tramped east and saw Union troops in front of the town. They returned later to Cashtown with word of the soldiers they had seen but without definitive information or shoes. In the meantime, General Hill accompanied Pender's division over the mountains, and Anderson's division prepared to join them the next day.[30]

The army's headquarters shifted east from Chambersburg to Greenwood at the west foot of the mountain slope on 30 June, and McLaws's and Hood's divisions also moved to that area. Pickett's division stayed behind at Chambersburg to cover the rear of the army until it could be relieved by Brig. Gen. John D. Imboden's brigade of cavalry that would be coming east from McConnellsburg, Pennsylvania, across Tuscarora Mountain. The march from Chambersburg to Greenwood was a short one. After putting his battalion into bivouac, Colonel Alexander rode over to the army's headquarters, which were nearby. He had been on the headquarters staff earlier in the war and felt welcome there. He found his old friends "unusually careless & jolly." The army was concentrating just beyond the mountain, but there were no signs of early battle and there was no pressure to hurry east. Soon the Army of Northern Virginia would be concentrated; and when it was united, what or who could hope successfully to oppose it?[31]

The answer, as General Lee had learned from the spy Harrison, was the Army of the Potomac—about 95,000 strong, divided into seven corps of infantry and artillery, a corps of cavalry and artillery and a twenty-one-battery artillery reserve. On 28 June, when General Meade took command, the Army of the Potomac was spread in a thirty-mile arc that bulged from the Potomac River northeastly to Middletown and Frederick, Maryland. General Meade knew that his opponents were marching up the Cumberland Valley toward Harrisburg, and in the spirit of his instructions to cover Baltimore and Washington, he advanced his host to meet them. On 29 June the Federal commander concentrated much of his infantry around Frederick, and on the next day he deployed it into a line of separate columns that streamed north from Frederick and east of Catoctin Mountain on roads that led to Pennsylvania. By this time General Meade had learned from his cavalry and civilian sources that Longstreet's and Hill's corps were moving east toward Gettysburg and that Ewell's corps had been in Carlisle and York. On 30 June Brig. Gen. John Buford's cavalry division, screening the army's left, saw Confederates west of Gettysburg, and Brig. Gen. H. Judson Kilpatrick's division clashed with Stuart's force at Hanover. Therefore, Meade had every reason to expect a confrontation near Gettysburg, but the area east of that town could not yet be ignored.[32]

On the night of the thirtieth, then, when A. P. Hill's corps concentrated at Cashtown and Longstreet's corps waited beyond the mountain at Greenwood, the Federal host extended along the Mason-Dixon Line from Catoctin Mountain east about twenty miles to New Windsor, Maryland. Buford and his two brigades at Gettysburg had seen Heth's force approach the town and then fall back to the west. Maj. Gen. John F. Reynolds, commander of the left wing, was forward with the First Corps at Marsh Creek between Gettysburg and Emmitsburg only about five miles south of where Buford had seen Pettigrew's brigade just that day. The other two corps of the left wing, the Third and the Eleventh, were near Emmitsburg, Maryland, only eight miles south of Gettysburg. From Emmitsburg they could guard the army's left or move to the support of the First Corps if need be. The remaining four corps were to the east: the Twelfth just inside Pennsylvania at Littlestown, seven miles from Gettysburg; the Second at Uniontown, Maryland, in a central position; the Fifth to the Second's right at Union Mills, south of Hanover; and the Sixth at Manchester, covering the army's right and Baltimore. General Meade's headquarters were at Taneytown, Maryland, near the center of his line and just south of the Mason-Dixon Line.[33]

The Federal commander, like General Lee, knew that his army's long march was nearly over and a battle was at hand. To be ready for it, he ordered "all empty wagons, surplus baggage, useless animals and impediments of every sort" to the rear at Union Bridge. As it worked out, the trains, including 4,000 wagons, assembled ten miles to the east at Westminster, Maryland, along the pike and railroad tracks leading to Baltimore. Only the ammunition wagons were to accompany the troops.[34] In a circular Meade announced that there were strong indications that the enemy was moving on Gettysburg, "probably in strong force," and that it was his intention to hold the army in place until the situation developed more fully. Corps commanders were to hold their commands in readiness to move, with trains parked and the men supplied with three days' cooked rations in their haversacks and sixty rounds of ammunition in their boxes and on their persons. The corps commanders were also to become familiar with the roads connecting the different corps.[35]

General Meade was concerned about the effect of hard marching on his troops. The Pennsylvania Reserves, fresh from the defenses of Washington, and Lockwood's brigade of garrison troops from Baltimore were not keeping up. He also felt it necessary to send a note to Maj. Gen. Daniel E. Sickles expressing disapproval of the slowness of the Third Corps on 29 June. It had delayed the movements of the units behind it, and its slow twelve-mile march compared poorly with that of the Second Corps, which had marched double that distance. Maj. Gen. George Sykes reported that his Fifth Corps had marched twenty-five miles on 30 June and that its men were footsore and tired.[36]

In preparation for the next day, orders went out for the Eleventh Corps to move to Gettysburg in support of the First Corps, the Third to Emmitsburg, the Second to Taneytown, the Fifth to Hanover, the Twelfth to Two Taverns, and the Sixth to Manchester. These were short, deliberate moves, in keeping with the caution mandatory in the presence of the Army of Northern Virginia. Clearly the bulk of the army was leaning toward Gettysburg and the Union left, but still two corps remained to the right where they could cover the approaches to Baltimore and guard against any threat that might develop on that flank.[37]

General Meade's right arm in planning and directing the army's march had to be his chief of staff. General Hooker's had been Maj. Gen. Daniel Butterfield, an officer who had compiled an impressive record with the Army of the Potomac. Butterfield, age thirty-two, was a New Yorker, the son of John Butterfield, president of the Overland Mail and organizer of the American Express Company, whose stage lines were playing a large role in the opening of the West. The younger Butterfield graduated from Union College at the age of eighteen and was one of the American Express Company's general superintendents when the war began. He had been active in militia affairs, and at the beginning of the war he led the Twelfth New York State Militia Regiment to Washington. Probably because of political influence, he received a commission as lieutenant colonel of the Twelfth U.S. Infantry Regiment, an appointment that scores of more deserving Regular Army officers must have coveted. He also received, more understandably, the rank of brigadier general of volunteers. He commanded a brigade of the Fifth Corps on the Peninsula and a division at Second Manassas, and in November 1862 he became a major general and commander of the Fifth Corps. He commanded that corps at Fredericksburg, but when Hooker took command of the Army of the Potomac, Butterfield became that army's chief of staff. Whatever his military accomplishments might have been, he did two things that assure him a place in America's military history: he is widely credited with having composed "Taps" and designed the corps badges of the Army of the Potomac.[38] But Butterfield was Hooker's man and no friend of General Meade. When General Meade took command of the army, he sought to replace Butterfield with a more congenial officer but could not find a replacement immediately. Therefore, he asked Butterfield to stay on for the time being, and Butterfield graciously consented to do so. Butterfield would do his job well enough, but at a personal cost to Meade that would plague him to his death.

Thus, apart from personal aides, there were no immediate changes in the staff of the Army of the Potomac. Gouverneur K. Warren continued as chief engineer, Jonathan Letterman as medical director, Henry J. Hunt as chief of artillery, Rufus Ingalls as chief quartermaster, Marsena R. Patrick as provost marshal, and Capt. Lemuel B. Norton as chief signal officer. All were capable, and each did his job, but some others on the large staff, as will be seen, did not do so well.

The campaign in Maryland and Pennsylvania was as rare an experience for the men of the Army of the Potomac as it was for those of the Army of Northern Virginia. But while the latter enjoyed the novelty of being tourists in a strange land, the euphoria of being conquerors, and the feeling of their army's invincibility, the Northern soldiers received expressions of public friendship and appreciation. These were rare commodities for the men in blue and must have boosted their patriotism and steeled their commitment to punish the Confederates for violating Northern soil. The men of the Federal Third Corps reveled in the experience of being in a friendly land. On

Saturday, 27 June, the corps passed through Jefferson, Maryland, a place remembered fondly thereafter for many years. A soldier in Clark's battery (Battery B, First New Jersey Light Artillery), which was near the rear of the corps's column as it descended the slope of Catoctin Mountain, thrilled at the view ahead—the long blue column of men winding down the mountain road into a handsome and fruitful land. And when the battery reached the village of Jefferson, a teacher and her students greeted it with "The Battle Cry of Freedom," while bells clanged in greeting from the steeples of nearby churches, reminding the men of home and better times. Maj. Gen. David B. Birney was so pleased with this reception that he halted his division and ordered the band of the 114th Pennsylvania Regiment forward to an intersection where it played to the delight of the citizens as his division passed through the town. Then the bandsmen had to run forward to regain their places in the column.[39]

The Third Corps spent the night near Middletown and on the following day paraded through Frederick on its way to its next bivouac around Woodsboro. The townsfolk offered cool water, while the band enlivened the march with "John Brown's Body." The corps marched through the town with ranks closed and in step, colors uncovered and flying. Its soldiers did not see Barbara Frietchie as far as they knew, but they cheered an old man who waved a flag vigorously from a second story window and with delirious joy shouted, "Still they come! Still they Come!"[40]

It was a "gay and jolly march" to the cannoneers of Capt. James E. Smith's Fourth New York Battery, a triumphal procession amid an appreciative populace. One young lady gave Col. Calvin A. Craig of the 105th Pennsylvania Regiment a small flag and asked him to carry it into the next fight. When Colonel de Trobriand passed a group of citizens, a mother pointed out the colonel to her little girl and probably gave her a gentle shove. The girl scooted into the street to the front of de Trobriand's horse and held a bouquet up to him. As he leaned down to take it, de Trobriand later recalled,

> she said, with a rosy smile: "Good luck to you, general!" I thanked her to the best of my ability. I would have liked to have embraced the little messenger with her happy wishes; but the march could not halt for so small an affair. When she rejoined her family, . . . I turned to kiss my hand to her in adieu. She nodded her head, and, blushing, hid it in her mother's bosom. "Well!" said I, riding on, "that little girl ought to bring me good fortune."

Soon the colonel would need all the help he could get.[41]

But all good things come to an end. Sergeant John C. Shaler, Jr., of Thompson's battery (C & F, First Pennsylvania Light Artillery) of the Artillery Reserve passed through Frederick at dusk, probably after the day's parade of three corps had tired the residents and dulled their curiosity and sentiment. The streets were no longer lined with cheering bystanders, but

Shaler got a thrill, not from throngs of admiring onlookers but from the speed of the battery as it rolled through the cobbled streets, the clopping of the horses' iron-shod hooves, the grinding noise of iron-rimmed wheels upon the paving stones, and the echoes from the brick buildings that lined the streets. These were strange and thrilling sounds that the men of the battery had never heard in Virginia.[42]

Frederick was the largest town on the Union line of march and was a magnet for stragglers. The Fifth Corps reached the vicinity of the town on 27 June and spent the next day there while the other corps passed through. Although soldiers were supposed to stay in their bivouac areas, many went into the town for food, drink, and recreation.[43] Maj. Gen. Henry W. Slocum, whose Twelfth Corps passed through the town on the twenty-ninth, complained to General Meade of stragglers from every corps who were lying beastly drunk in the streets. He urged General Meade to send cavalry into the town to "bring them up." Whitelaw Reid, the war correspondent, who passed through Frederick on the thirtieth, wrote, "Frederick is Pandemonium." The town was full of stragglers, and the saloons were going full blast. There were drunken brawls in the streets, and the stragglers were stealing and making nuisances of themselves. Other stragglers lined the roads north of town and loafed around farmhouses. Whatever their reasons for straggling, they brought no credit to the Army of the Potomac.[44]

General Meade ordered Provost Marshal Patrick to send his cavalry back to take care of the stragglers, and Patrick sent two squadrons back to do so. But Reid complained that some of the cavalrymen got drunk too. Maj. Gen. William H. French's troops from the Harpers Ferry garrison reached Frederick on 30 June and presumably restored order. Be that as it may, it is unlikely that any stragglers found in Frederick on 30 June fought at Gettysburg on 2 July.[45]

The Maryland villages north of Frederick emulated the hospitality given by Jefferson and Middletown. Girls serenaded men of the Third Corps as they passed through Woodsboro and Ladiesburg. In Taneytown "groups of fair damsels bewitchingly posted in conspicuous places" sang patriotic songs, and one sang "When This Cruel War Is Over" very charmingly. In addition, some families opened their houses and served refreshments to officers and enlisted men, and many people visited the Third Corps camps north of the town.[46]

In return for their hospitality the citizens were treated to the music of army bands and soldiers' songs—the 106th Pennsylvania, led by its glee club, sang marching songs as it passed through Maryland's villages. At one stop citizens visited the camp of the Second Pennsylvania Reserves, which was escorting the pontoon train. The pontoons were something of an oddity to the farmers, one of whom amused the men of the Reserves by observing that they could not do much with "gunboats" in the mountains.[47]

The heartwarming reception received in Maryland must have given the Army of the Potomac a great boost in morale and stiffened its will to fight.

Certainly it was recalled with pleasure in later years. But the campaign really was a grueling experience that placed greater physical demands on the Union soldier than on his Confederate counterpart. General Lee had the initiative, and his corps commanders could plan marches according to the capabilities of their soldiers. Hooker and Meade did not have this luxury. They were forced to react to conditions that they could not readily predict with accuracy and could divine only in part after the fact. Thus, to bring the Army of Northern Virginia to bay the soldiers of the Army of the Potomac had to make both long and short marches, often forced. It was hurry up and wait on a grand scale, and it took its toll on the Federal force and its ability to fight. Brig. Gen. Eugene A. Carr's brigade of the Third Corps, for instance, marched twenty-seven miles on 25 June, crossing over the Potomac on the pontoon bridge at Edwards Ferry and hiking up the towpath of the C & O Canal. It trudged 10 more miles on the twenty-sixth, 14 on the twenty-seventh, 17 on the twenty-eighth, 20 on the twenty-ninth, and then only 4 on the thirtieth, as it closed into its Emmitsburg bivouac. That portion of the Third Corps was lucky, however, when compared with the 110th Pennsylvania Regiment of de Trobriand's brigade. After slogging up the towpath and bivouacking, the 110th had to return to Edwards Ferry to guard the trains as they crossed. They worked there a day and a half round the clock, pushing wagons up the muddy slope from the bridge, before they were told to march on to Frederick. At the same time, Brig. Gen. Romeyn B. Ayres's division of the Fifth Corps logged 14 miles on 29 June, 23 on the thirtieth, and 18 on 1 July. These were not pleasant hikes. The roads were either dusty or slippery with mud, depending on the weather; the days were warm and sometimes wet; and there must have been a lot of stopping and going in the course of a day's march.[48]

Maj. Gen. Winfield Scott Hancock was a driver, and the most lasting complaints about the march's severity seem to have come from his Second Corps. Early on the morning of 29 June Hancock notified General Meade that his march had been delayed three hours—a headquarters clerk had received Meade's orders for the day but had neglected to deliver them to anyone in authority. Meade replied that he regretted the delay and suggested that the clerk be punished. Hancock wrote that he had already punished the man, though he did not say how, and that the corps would make up the lost time.[49]

On the twenty-ninth, the day of the hard march, the Second Corps forded a stream. Capt. Benjamin Thompson thought that it was the Monocacy River, but it might have been Linganore Creek or another stream near Frederick. When Willard's brigade reached it, instead of halting so that the men could remove their shoes and stockings or cross dry shod over some logs, its regiments were called to attention and marched through the water at a quick step with rifles at right shoulder shift. Once across, they had to march for several miles in wet shoes before halting to care for their feet. Thompson claimed that nearly every man in his company developed blisters and that he spent the halt in doctoring them and dosing his men with whiskey. Hancock had placed a staff officer at the ford to see that there was no stopping there. The corps was already late and any halt to change shoes and socks could take a considerable time. And yet camp gossip held that the fording was forced because Hancock was in a pique over an order from Meade and Meade's promotion to the command of the army.[50]

Other Second Corps units shared this memorable experience. When Cross's brigade, Caldwell's division, reached the ford, Col. Edward Cross sat on one side of the road and a staff officer on the other to see that the brigade went through the ford without pause. There were complaints, of course, and when Cross heard some, he gave the complainers the flat of his sword, hitting Cpl. George J. Duffy of the 148th Pennsylvania on the neck. It was a little different in Brig. Gen. Alexander S. Webb's brigade of Gibbon's division. When the 106th Pennsylvania, lead regiment of the brigade, reached the stream, it halted so that the men on foot could remove their foot gear. But Webb could have none of this and ordered them forward. Then Webb rode to the center of the stream, jumped from his horse, and stood in the water while his brigade passed through it. But even this gesture was not appreciated fully. An Irishman from the Sixty-ninth Pennsylvania got a laugh when he called to Webb, "Sure it's no wonder ye can stand there when ye are leather up to your waist." Webb ignored the comment but had a captain arrested for walking across the stream on a nearby log. He released him later, however, when a surgeon certified that the captain was disposed toward rheumatism.[51]

When Brig. Gen. William Harrow's brigade reached the ford, Col. Charles H. Morgan of Hancock's staff was there astride his horse. Col. William Colvill, Jr., of the First Minnesota approached at the head of his regiment, and Morgan ordered him to keep his ranks closed up as they passed through the water. Colvill gave the necessary orders, but some members of the First broke ranks anyhow to walk on the logs or planks. The Fifteenth Massachusetts followed the First, and when its men saw what they were in for, some booed and hissed. Morgan was already displeased with Colvill's men, and the catcalls added fuel to the fire. Morgan heaped his displeasure on General Harrow, who then placed Colvill under arrest. Such was discipline in the Second Corps.[52]

It was a difficult march over rolling countryside and on secondary roads of powdered dust and rocks that might trip the weary soldier. Capt. Benjamin Thompson fell out before the day ended and did not rejoin his regiment until he reached its bivouac on the following day. He wrote that only twenty officers and men arrived with the colors at the end of the march. It was about the same in Gen. Samuel M. Zook's brigade—only 27 of the Fifty-seventh New York's 175 men were present at day's end, and its ambulances were full. Months later Hancock testified that the weather had been sultry on 29 June and that his troops had been much exhausted at the end of their march of thirty-two to thirty-four miles. Fortunately, they had no battle to fight when they reached the Uniontown area. The Second Corps did not move on 30 June, and the fact that it was payday probably did much to attract its stragglers and return it to its strength.[53]

But there were pleasant recollections of 29 June, though not necessarily among those who had to walk. Capt. Josiah M. Favill of General Zook's staff recalled that the day was beautiful and hot and that he traveled at the head of the column, alternately riding and walking. There was less dust to breathe there. Being a staff officer, he found it easy to pause at the side of the road for drinks of water and to talk with girls who were watching the troops file by. Even with that, the day was long and boring, and to relieve the monotony Favill suggested that each staff officer, like the Canterbury pilgrims, do something for the amusement of the others. His contribution was to quote from Ovid's *Metamorphoses*. What the others did, he did not say.[54]

Sometime during the day Zook's brigade passed a flock of belligerent geese, and a soldier of the Fifty-seventh New York broke ranks and bayoneted one. Unfortunately for him, General Zook saw the skirmish. The general whipped out his sword and spurred after the fellow, who fled into the ranks of his regiment. The incident probably caused a lot of yelling and comment, and Zook did not press the matter—then. But he did not forget about it. At day's end, when the regiment settled in, he sent for the fellow and his bird, and after an interview the poor soldier left without his prize. The soldier of the Fifty-seventh had fouled out, and Zook dined on goose that night.[55]

By sundown the long march from Virginia was nearly over. The Army of Northern Virginia had made tenuous contact with the Army of the Potomac at Gettysburg. Union cavalry bivouacked near the town, and Hill's infantry was massing at Cashtown to the west. Lee's army seemed invincible to the Confederates, but its new organization was untested in battle. It faced an opponent tired from marching but steeled by a resolve to drive the invader from Union soil. General Lee also faced a new and dangerous commander who had stripped his army for action and was determined to fight. There would be a showdown soon.

CHAPTER

The Army of Northern Virginia, 1 July

Ewell's corps had found Pennsylvania to be a hospitable place, though there had been occasional disappointments. General Early had requisitioned $100,000 from the town of York along with hats, socks, shoes, and three days' rations. York had, on the whole, generously provided clothing and rations, but it had given him only $28,600. Still, Early thought that the burghers of York had done their best to please him, and he was satisfied. All told, Ewell's troops had collected nearly 3,000 head of cattle and 5,000 barrels of flour for the Army of Northern Virginia, not to mention numerous wagonloads of medical, ordnance, and other supplies that would be useful.[1] This was done before Ewell received General Lee's orders to concentrate in the Gettysburg-Cashtown area and the army began to gather there.

On 30 June, in compliance with General Lee's instructions, Rodes's division marched south toward Gettysburg from Carlisle, as Early's trudged west from York. The two concentrated that night near Heidlersburg, a crossroads hamlet about nine miles north of Gettysburg on the road to Harrisburg. While there with Rodes's division, General Ewell learned that Hill's corps was thirteen miles to the west at Cashtown, and he received orders to take his corps to either Cashtown or Gettysburg, as the situation might dictate, on the next day.[2]

Ewell elected to continue west toward Cashtown with his divisions on the next morning, but while on the march he learned that Hill's corps was advancing on Gettysburg. This called for a change in plan, and he turned Rodes's division toward that town by way of the Middletown (Carlisle) Road and Early's toward it over the Heidlersburg (Harrisburg) Road. This done, Ewell sent Maj. G. Campbell Brown, his stepson and assistant adjutant general, to Lee to tell the general of the change in his destination.[3]

As Ewell's two divisions approached his left, General Hill worried about the nature of the Federal force that Pettigrew's brigade had seen near Gettysburg on 30 June and sought to learn more about it. He sent Heth's whole division toward the town at daybreak in a reconnaissance in force. As a precaution, Hill had Pender's division follow Heth's in support. Thus, on the morning of 1 July four Confederate divisions from two corps, nearly 25,000 men, approached an area containing a Union force of unknown strength.[4]

Four other Confederate divisions—Anderson's, Johnson's, McLaws's, and Hood's were also moving or ready to march on 1 July. All had to cross South Mountain through Cashtown Pass. Anderson's division started before sunup in the pleasant early morning hours of a Pennsylvania summer day, ascended the mountain as the temperature climbed, and descended its east slope to Cashtown. From high on the mountain's side the soldiers could see the rolling fields that stretched east to Gettysburg, some gold with ripening wheat and oats and others of varied shades of green. To Francis Lawley, correspondent for *The Times* of London, the landscape was "remarkably English in its general aspect," something like portions of Surrey. It was then that they heard distant cannon fire ahead, and saw the gray puffs of air bursts that marked the battlefield. This overture stirred feelings so strong that they remained distinct in the recollections of some soldiers in spite of all the competing memories of the events of later days. The head of Anderson's column halted at Cashtown and waited for further orders. There Brig. Gen. Cadmus M. Wilcox's soldiers first saw wounded from the battle and Federal prisoners going to the rear.[5]

General Lee heard the sound of distant artillery fire as he and Longstreet followed Anderson's division through Cashtown Pass. Some of their staff officers thought that it signaled "a cavalry affair of minor importance," but the scout Harrison, who rode with Longstreet's entourage, cautioned that there was a "pretty tidy bunch of *blue bellies* in or near Gettysburg." Leaving Longstreet behind, Lee and his staff pressed ahead to Cashtown, where they found the head of Anderson's division at rest awaiting orders. The sounds of battle could be heard clearly there, and the continuous firing convinced Lee that there was a serious fight ahead. The general displayed great anxiety and spoke regretfully of General Stuart's absence. Where could he be? Some of the uncertainty passed when a courier arrived with the news that Hill's corps was engaged. With this news came Hill's request for Anderson to bring his division forward. Anderson summoned the Florida Brigade from the rear, where it had been escorting the corps train; then Anderson's division and General Lee hurried east toward Gettysburg.[6]

When Anderson's division reached the approaches to Gettysburg, Hill ordered Anderson to deploy four of its brigades on Herr Ridge. Pender's division had vacated this high ground a short time before when Hill sent it forward into the attack. Hill directed Anderson also to send a brigade and a battery "a mile or more on the right of the line, in a direction at a right angle with it and facing to the right." This detached brigade was to guard the army's right flank. Anderson appointed Wilcox's Alabama Brigade and Capt. Hugh

M. Ross's battery (Company A of the Sumter Battalion of Georgia Artillery) to the task.[7]

Earlier in the afternoon, when General Lee was in the Cashtown area, Maj. G. Campbell Brown rode up to him with dispatches from Ewell announcing that Ewell's divisions had turned south toward Gettysburg. Brown recalled that, though troops were passing then, the Chambersburg Pike was full of halted wagons that belonged to Hill's train or a hospital train and that all could hear firing to the east. After receiving Ewell's messages, General Lee asked "with a peculiar searching, almost querulous impatience, which I never saw in him before and but twice afterward" whether General Ewell had heard anything of General Stuart. Brown replied that Ewell had not heard anything for three days and that Stuart had not complied with his instructions—probably those requiring him to place his cavalry on Ewell's right. Lee complained that he had seen in Northern papers that Stuart had been near Washington and that all he knew about the Army of the Potomac's location was that a scout (Harrison) had told him that it was marching toward them. Then Lee asked that Ewell send out patrols to his left to try to contact Stuart. Lee had heard reports of firing east toward Hanover Junction and thought that Stuart might have been involved. He then stressed that a general engagement was to be avoided. As soon as their conversation ended, Brown returned to Ewell.[8]

Ewell had one division moving toward Gettysburg over the Chambersburg Pike. Maj. Gen. Edward Johnson's division and the corps train had followed Rodes's division toward Carlisle, but when Rodes turned south toward Gettysburg, Johnson's division and the train were ordered to the concentration point via the Cumberland Valley and Cashtown Pass. On 30 June Johnson's division bivouacked at Scotland, near Greenwood at the west gate of the pass. Then on 1 July, with the remainder of Ewell's corps already beyond the mountain, the division and the corps train were allowed to take the road ahead of Longstreet's corps.[9] Instead of ordering his trains to the rear as General Meade had done, General Lee allowed them to move east of the mountains with their corps. Obviously he did not expect a battle that would limit his army's ability to maneuver as early as 1 July or he would not have given hundreds of wagons precedence over much needed infantry.

General Longstreet's corps, minus Pickett's division, which was still in Chambersburg, had early reveille on 1 July and prepared to take the road. McLaws's and Hood's divisions had marched to Greenwood on 30 June and bivouacked there, while Law's brigade and Capt. William K. Bachman's battery (German Artillery, South Carolina) were detached to New Guilford, about three miles south of Fayetteville, to cover the Confederate flank. After arriving at Greenwood, McLaws's and Hood's men received orders to cook three days' rations as early as practicable on 1 July. Longstreet obviously anticipated busy times ahead.[10]

The men of these divisions awakened early to cook rations and prepare for the day's march. Before the march began, McLaws, whose division would lead Longstreet's corps, received orders to follow Johnson's division. McLaws formed his regiments along the pike ready to go as soon as Johnson's men filed by. When Ewell's train appeared immediately behind Johnson's division, McLaws asked if he should follow the troops or wait for the train to pass. Longstreet told him that he should wait. The train seemed endless; McLaws estimated that it was fourteen miles long. If so, its leading wagons could have been parked near Gettysburg before those in the rear passed beyond McLaws.[11]

McLaws received another order about 10:00 A.M. directing him to wait an hour after the wagons passed before starting in order to give the roads time to clear; Hood would follow him. This was thoughtful advice. McLaws waited, afternoon came, and it was nearly 4:00 P.M. before his division could take the road.[12] McLaws's and Hood's divisions had waited a good ten hours, and in that time a battle had opened, been fought, and was drawing to a close at Gettysburg, less than fifteen miles away.

A few men later mentioned how they spent this tedious day. In Robertson's Texas Brigade there was a "dress parade," probably an inspection, shortly before the march. Late in the afternoon some bored soldiers of the Seventeenth Mississippi mixed up some dough on a rubber blanket and were heating it in a skillet when their drummer beat the "Long Roll." They had to go, and their skillet was too hot to carry, so they left it behind. They were certain that men of the "thieving Eighteenth Mississippi" got their skillet and their meal.[13]

Once started, the march soon became tiresome. The exuberance of conquest gave way to the tedium of road congestion, stop and go, a few steps at a time. Previous hilarity was stifled by the shuffling of feet on a dusty road, soiled plentifully, no doubt, by the excrement of thousands of horses and mules that had recently passed that way. As the infantrymen plodded over the crest of the pass, they heard the thud of distant cannon fire and cheered. Darkness came, but the men of Longstreet's corps trudged on. About ten o'clock Longstreet returned from the front, told McLaws something of the day's events, and directed him to bivouac at Marsh Creek a few miles ahead. The division reached the creek about midnight, and the men fell out to rest. Hood's division came up later. Despite a long and tiring day, Longstreet's divisions had marched only about twelve miles.[14]

When Kershaw's brigade of South Carolinians passed some tents belonging to Hill's corps, a cordial officer invited Lt. Augustus Dickert of the Third South Carolina to pause and have a drink. Dickert would have been churlish to refuse such an invitation, and so he and Lt. John Watts of the Third entered the officer's tent and imbibed. The drink so relaxed Watts that during one of the innumerable halts that followed, he stretched out by the side of the road and fell asleep. For some reason his company went on without him. An ambulance driver spotted Watts later, assumed that he was a battle casualty, and carted him to a hospital. Watts did not catch up with his company until late the next day.[15]

While Longstreet's infantry toiled over the mountain, the battalions of his Artillery Reserve, Alexander's battalion and Maj. Benjamin F. Eshleman's Washington Artillery of New Orleans, bided their time in bivouac, ignorant of the events beyond the mountain. The artillerymen took care of their routine chores but did little more. Alexander wrote a letter to his wife, oblivious to a festering quarrel (discussed in Chapter 8 below) between two of his officers—Capt. Pichegru Woolfolk, Jr., of the Ashland (Virginia) Artillery and George V. Moody of the Madison (Louisiana) Light Artillery. But both the quarrel and routine matters were put aside when news of the battle at Gettysburg trickled in late in the afternoon. At dusk the Artillery Reserve commander, Col. James B. Walton, received orders from Colonel Sorrel to march at 1:00 A.M. The Artillery Reserve rolled out on time. By then the congestion on the road had cleared and a large moon lighted the way. The two battalions reached the Gettysburg area shortly after sunrise, parked beside the road, and the drivers unhitched their teams so that the tired horses could graze. Colonel Walton went on ahead to Seminary Ridge to report to General Longstreet.[16]

Longstreet and his staff had ridden ahead of his corps in the company of General Lee. They passed first through Johnson's division and for a time rode among the men of the Stonewall Brigade. These Virginians had seldom, if ever, seen Longstreet close up, and some asked Colonel Fremantle which of the officers in the party was he. When told, some of the soldiers ran a hundred yards for a close look, an act that Fremantle considered a great tribute to the general.[17]

The Stonewall Brigade's curiosity to see General Longstreet was natural, for if their own revered Jackson had been Lee's right arm, Longstreet had been his left. He was a native South Carolinian who had lived also in Georgia and Alabama. He graduated from West Point in the class of 1842, fifty-second in a class of sixty-two, a suggestion that then, at least, he was an indifferent scholar. Longstreet received a commission in the infantry and, except during the War with Mexico, had an uneventful career. The war gave him a chance to display some of his soldierly attributes. He emerged from it with a wound received at Chapultepec and two brevets, the second to the rank of major. There was little distinction and remuneration for a line officer between wars in those days, and Longstreet, like Hancock, traded the drill field for a desk and ledger. He become a paymaster with the rank of major. This was his status in the Old Army when secession came and he resigned his United States commission.[18]

Longstreet, who in 1861 was the ranking officer from Alabama in the Old Army, became a brigadier general in the Confederate service in June 1861 and commanded a brigade at the battle of Manassas. His role in that battle was minimal, but his presence was impressive—Fitzhugh Lee recalled seeing him there and thinking "there is a man that cannot be stampeded." Longstreet commanded a division on the Peninsula and, in the period before the Army of Northern Virginia was organized into corps, commanded one of its wings. It was his wing that struck the Federal left at Second Manassas, held the Confederate right at Antietam, and defended the Sunken Road at Fredericksburg. Longstreet and much of his corps were absent and campaigning without particular distinction in tidewater Virginia, south of the James River, during the battle of Chancellorsville. They were summoned back soon after that battle, however, and Longstreet continued to be General Lee's senior corps commander.[19]

Longstreet was forty-two years old in the summer of 1863. He was a large man, six feet two inches in height, it is said, "a soldier every inch, and very handsome, tall and well proportioned," with "glint steel-blue, deep and piercing eyes" and sandy hair and beard. He seemed fearless and tireless. He was slightly deaf and naturally taciturn, and after the untimely death from scarlet fever of three of his children in 1862, he became even more withdrawn. Lawley of *The Times* described him during the Gettysburg campaign as belonging to "the class of undemonstrative, unselfish and natural men whose worth is chiefly known to their soldiers." Fremantle, who saw him often in General Lee's company, observed, "It is impossible to please Longstreet more than by praising Lee." This was "Old Pete," General Lee's "Old War Horse," as he rode to Gettysburg. Other facets of his complex character would become apparent there.[20]

When Lee hurried forward at the sound of the firing, Longstreet and his staff followed at a slower pace and were riding among the men of Anderson's division as they approached Gettysburg. Anderson's division had served under Longstreet before the recent reorganization, and they knew one another rather well. As Longstreet passed through the Florida Brigade, one man shouted, "Look out for work now, boys, for here's the old bulldog again." They met casualties coming back, some half naked and with obvious wounds, spectacles that could have had a depressing effect on troops going into a battle. Fremantle observed, however, that Anderson's men paid little attention to the wounded for they had seen a lot of them before. The Englishman saw prisoners too, some of whom were wounded and some of whom were getting along pretty well with their captors. By 4:30 or so, at the time that his own divisions across the mountain were beginning their march, Longstreet and his staff had reached Seminary Ridge. They were there in time to see soldiers of the Union First Corps falling back to Cemetery Hill, pursued part of the way by yelling Confederates.[21]

After a short time Longstreet and his staff found Generals Lee and A. P. Hill. Hill's brigades had not pressed their attack beyond Seminary Ridge. Hill remarked that he had been unwell all day. Longstreet learned some of the details of the day's battle from Lee and Hill. Hill's two divisions, Heth's and Pender's, had met troops from the Army of the Potomac west of town, and together with Rodes's and Early's divisions of Ewell's corps had driven units from the Union First and Eleventh corps from their positions west and north of Gettysburg back through the town to the hill mass south of it.[22]

Longstreet and Lee talked about the enemy, the enemy position, and what was to be done next. Longstreet, as the officer next in rank to General Lee, had a privileged position and deemed it his duty to exercise it. As he wrote to his uncle three weeks later: "I consider it a part of my duty to express my views to the Commanding-General. If he approves and adopts them, it is well; if he does not, it is my duty to adopt his views, and to execute his orders as faithfully as if they were my own."[23] This was a fine philosophy, expressive of a thoroughly professional attitude; it was easy to hold in times of agreement but difficult when views differed and the lives of men hung in the balance. The generals talked, and much, no doubt, was said that was not reported completely and with unfailing accuracy. Col. Armistead H. Long of General Lee's staff was one of those present. Years later Long wrote that Longstreet had advocated turning the Union left to force the enemy from his new position. General Lee, however, objected; he thought such a move impractical.[24]

Longstreet too wrote of his conversation with Lee later. He had urged General Lee to move his army around the Federal left, take a strong position nearby, between the Army of the Potomac and Washington, and await attack. If the Army of the Potomac did not oblige, the Army of Northern Virginia would be in a condition to move "tomorrow night" toward Washington and to a selected position where it could receive battle the "next day." The Federals would then have to attack, and "we shall beat them, as we proposed to do before we left Fredericksburg, and the probabilities are that the fruits of our success will be great." " 'No,' said General Lee, 'the enemy is there, and I am going to attack him there.' " General Longstreet observed then that such a move as he advocated would place the Confederates in control of the roads between the Federal army and Washington and Baltimore, enabling them to carry out what he believed was their original plan—to conduct a campaign that was "offensive in strategy but defensive in tactics." To this Longstreet recalled that Lee replied, "No; they are there in position, and I am going to whip them or they are going to whip me."[25] Then, according to another account related by General Longstreet, Lee supposedly replied, "If the enemy is there to-morrow, we must attack him." To this Longstreet said that he responded: "If he is there, it will be because he is anxious that we should attack him—a good reason in my judgment for not doing so."[26]

Although the precise words of the dialogue will never be known, their meaning is clear. Reports of the conversation must have spread quickly through the upper echelons of the army. Lawley was aware of Longstreet's warning against an attack. He wrote that Longstreet "shook his head gravely" over the advantages of the Federal position and that thoughts of the enemy's position were uppermost in his mind and that of General Lee.[27]

Longstreet's recommendations made a lot of sense in the abstract. Had the Army of Northern Virginia been able to maneuver as he suggested, his prediction could have been realized. But could it? What route could have been taken in making the maneuver? How long would it have taken? Who would have screened the Confederate army's advance and covered its left during the move? What would have been done with the miles of wagons in the army's trains that had been hauled so laboriously over South Mountain and were scattered over the fields north and west of Gettysburg?

And what of the Federals? Where were they? Was it not possible that some of them would be off in the direction of the proposed movement and be able to stop or slow it? Those met that day in battle had fought hard and had roughly handled Heth's, Pender's, and Rodes's divisions; was it likely that General Meade would sit quietly by as the Confederate army slipped around his flank?

These are obvious questions that, along with others, must have been considered as Longstreet pressed his point. With the advantage of hindsight Lawley pondered them for his English readers. He wrote that both generals had considered a turning movement. To move to the right would have exposed their vulnerable and lengthening flank to attack. To settle back and await attack was a possibility, but one that could not be realized quickly because of the trains. The Chambersburg Pike was already clogged with horses, mules, and wagons, and any early withdrawal along it seemed impossible. On the other hand, "Hope reigned triumphant in every Confederate breast." In Lawley's opinion, the course least objectionable "in design" was adopted by General Lee.[28]

Lawley's point was well taken. A shift to the left and away from the valley that sheltered the Confederate line of communications was virtually out of the question. A shift to the right, south from Cashtown toward Fairfield, might have been physically possible over the roads in that area, but it meant moving virtually into the unknown, with the mountain wall on one side and the Union army on the other. Awaiting attack in the area occupied was worthy of consideration, but it had an obvious drawback. It would be tantamount to surrendering the initiative to the enemy, who could restrict or prevent foraging and whose strength would grow as Confederate strength declined. It did not seem to be a practical course of action. In General Lee's words, "A battle had, therefore, become in a measure unavoidable, and the success already gained gave hope of a favorable issue."[29]

It was about this time, between 5:00 and 6:00 P.M. according to Colonel Long's recollections, that General Lee asked him to reconnoiter the enemy's position. Just what sort of reconnaissance Long made is not known, but he reported the seemingly obvious—the Union position was occupied in force. On hearing the colonel's report, Lee turned to Generals Hill and Longstreet and said, "Gentlemen, we will attack the enemy in the morning as early as practicable." He went on to ask them to make necessary preparations, but Longstreet recalled no other orders.[30]

In later years a faction led by Generals Early and Pendleton charged that General Lee had given an order for a sunrise attack, one that Longstreet did not obey. In response to queries made to them by Longstreet about such an order, four of Lee's principal staff officers—Colonel Long, Col. Walter Taylor, Col. Charles Marshall, and Maj. Charles Venable—each wrote Longstreet that he knew nothing of it. Colonel Long, however, believed that General Lee wanted an assault as early as practicable. Longstreet, of course, denied having received an order for a sunrise attack. The testimony of the staff officers and the events of the night of 1 July and morning of 2 July show that the "sunrise order" charges by Early, Pendleton, and others, whatever the motive behind them, were nonsense.[31]

General Lee rode over to the left to talk with General Ewell before dark that evening, perhaps even before Longstreet rode back to the west. He talked with Ewell, Early, and Rodes. From them Lee learned of some of the difficulties associated with an assault from Ewell's front in and east of Gettysburg. Later that evening the one-legged Ewell rode to see General Lee in order to tell him of an opportunity that his corps might have to occupy Culp's Hill. General Lee gave him permission to try.[32]

Although Lee was determined to attack the next day, he seemed undecided still about how the attack should be made. He wondered to Colonel Long if he should attack before Stuart's cavalry arrived. Even if such an attack were successful, the Confederates might not be able to reap the harvest of victory without the cavalry's help. Colonel Long observed that it seemed best not to wait: they did not know when the cavalry would arrive, and the enemy had two or three corps in their front (by that time there were in fact four). Reassured somewhat by the logic of his able military secretary, General Lee returned to his tent to sleep. After the campaign, when it was time to recollect, reflect, and report, Lee summed up his views and his decision to attack.

It had not been intended to fight a general battle at such a distance from our base, unless attacked by the enemy, but, finding ourselves unexpectedly confronted by the Federal Army, it became a matter of difficulty to withdraw through the mountains with our large trains. At the same time, the country was unfavorable for collecting supplies while in the presence of the enemy's main body, as he was enabled to restrain our foraging parties by occupying the passes of the mountains with regular and local troops. A battle thus became, in a measure, unavoidable. Encouraged by the successful issue of the engagement of the first day, and in view of the valuable results that would ensue from the defeat of the army of General Meade, it was thought advisable to renew the attack.[33]

And so General Lee decided to attack on 2 July. The long march, the pleasure and euphoria of being conquerors in a land of plenty, were all but over. The apparently invincible regiments of Hood's, McLaws's, and Anderson's divisions would attack the Federal position on the morrow.

3

The Army of the Potomac,
1 July

George Gordon Meade was in a quandary on the morning of 1 July. His headquarters were at Taneytown, Maryland. Two of his corps had just entered Pennsylvania: the First Corps was in bivouac on Marsh Creek about 5½ miles south of Gettysburg on the Emmitsburg Road, and the Twelfth was at Littlestown. Two brigades of Buford's cavalry division were just north and west of Gettysburg, and Maj. Gen. John F. Reynolds would move the First Corps there that day. Meade's remaining corps were in Maryland, just south of the Mason-Dixon Line, resting in areas from which they could change position without delay if need be. General Meade knew the approximate location of the Army of Northern Virginia but did not know, of course, what General Lee planned for it. It seemed probable that there would be a battle soon, but Meade could not be certain where.[1]

The trusted Reynolds had broad options in his handling of the army's left wing, for it was closest to the enemy and he would have to react quickly to situations as they arose. Reynolds had decided that if the enemy advanced against him in force, the First Corps should fall back to Emmitsburg, unite with the Third and Eleventh corps, and fight there. To this end the Third Corps was to move closer to that village.[2]

Meade asked General Reynolds for his views. His latest information suggested that the enemy would be concentrating either at Chambersburg or somewhere north of Gettysburg on a line between Chambersburg and York. If the enemy concentrated east of Gettysburg, Gettysburg seemed not the place for him to plan to fight. On the other hand, if the Confederates concentrated in front of or west of Gettysburg, Meade wanted Reynolds's opinion about what should be done. He reminded Reynolds that Brig. Gen. Andrew A. Humphreys, a career officer in the topographical engineers, was at Emmitsburg in command of the Second Division, Third Corps, and could give him excellent advice.[3]

The commanding general also had some further thoughts about other contingencies. It was desirable to have a positive plan that all corps commanders could follow in event of an emergency. For that reason his head-quarters issued the "Pipe Creek Circular." Pipe Creek is a small stream that winds to the southwest from the rolling countryside near Union Mills, Maryland, passing south of Taneytown to the Monocacy River about seven miles south of Emmitsburg. The preamble of the circular announced that the object of the Army of the Potomac's movement "in this direction"—that is, north—had been achieved: Harrisburg was relieved and the enemy's movement toward the Susquehanna halted. Therefore, it was not Meade's intention to assume an offensive "until the enemy's movements or position should render such an operation certain of success." In the meantime, if the enemy assumed the offensive and attacked, it was his intention to hold the Confederates in check until his trains could be withdrawn to Westminster. Then the various corps would form a line along Pipe Creek. Although the circular assigned each corps a sector it would defend and designated a route to that sector, it did not define a specific line along Pipe Creek. Further, since the circular was issued on the morning of 1 July, it is likely that General Reynolds did not see it before his death.[4]

Although never implemented, the circular became the subject of much controversy after the battle when it was offered as proof that General Meade never intended to fight at Gettysburg. Chief of Staff Butterfield, who must have drawn up the circular, later said that he believed it would have had a bad effect on the army's morale and discussed it at length with Brig. Gen. Rufus Ingalls, the army's chief quartermaster, and with General Hancock.[5] Hancock's corps was to make a short march on 1 July from Uniontown to Taneytown, and the general had ridden in early that morning to set up his headquarters and call on General Meade. Meade talked with Hancock about his plans to take a position along Pipe Creek. He had not seen much of the terrain there, but he judged from maps that it offered the best position available, and it covered Washington and Baltimore. Some of his engineers were out looking over the ground at that time. Later, at noon, Meade advised Halleck that it was his intention to prepare to receive an assault at Pipe Creek, but that if he was not attacked, he would order an advance by the Army of the Potomac. Obviously, there was still some doubt in Meade's mind about the enemy's intentions and, therefore, about what he should do.[6]

Shortly after noon the situation began to get clearer. Capt. Stephen M. Weld of General Reynolds's staff rode in with news of a Confederate advance on Gettysburg and Reynolds's intention to fight there. "Good!" said Meade, "that is just like Reynolds; he will hold on to the bitter end." Weld's message was followed soon by a dispatch from Buford reporting that A. P. Hill's force was advancing and that Reynolds was within three miles of him.[7] At this time Meade sent General Warren to Gettysburg to examine the field of battle, but ironically the chief engineer took the wrong road and went roundabout by

Lt. Gen. James Longstreet (National Archives)

Lt. Gen. Ambrose P. Hill (National Archives)

Maj. Gen. Winfield S. Hancock (National Archives)

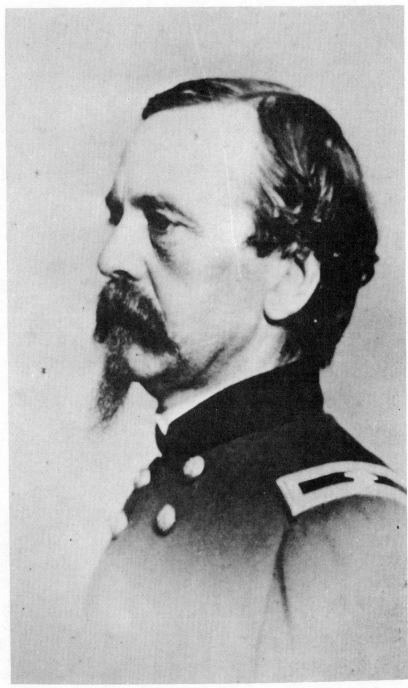

Maj. Gen. Daniel E. Sickles (National Archives)

Maj. Gen. George Sykes (National Archives)

way of Emmitsburg. Then, about 1:00 P.M., came the shocking news that Reynolds had been shot and was seriously wounded or dead. Now, Hancock observed, Meade "felt that the matter was being precipitated very heavily upon him and he felt the responsibility." The fat was in the fire. Meade had to reach a decision soon—he must either implement the Pipe Creek Circular or fight at Gettysburg.[8]

Although the events at Gettysburg and the nature of the town's terrain were critical elements in General Meade's decision and the situation at Gettysburg called for his presence on the field, Meade did not deem it wise just then to leave his headquarters, the nerve center of his army, and go to Gettysburg himself. Most of the Army of the Potomac was still a good march south and east of the new battlefield, and at the time of Reynolds's death Meade was still seriously contemplating a concentration along Pipe Creek. Such a major move would require his presence at his headquarters. Who then should he send in his place? Hancock was close by, and Meade had talked with him at length just that morning. Hancock knew what the various corps of the army were doing, and he knew of Meade's views. Further, he had Meade's confidence, and he had in Brig. Gen. John Gibbon a man who could be trusted with the Second Corps while he was away. At 1:10 P.M. Chief of Staff Butterfield sent a note to Hancock. He wrote that Reynolds had fallen and that Hancock was to turn the Second Corps over to Gibbon and go to Gettysburg. If Reynolds were dead, Hancock was to take command of the left wing. If, then, he considered Gettysburg a better place to fight than Pipe Creek, he was to advise Meade accordingly, and Meade would order the army forward.[9]

Winfield Scott Hancock requires some special notice. He was thirty-eight years old, a Pennsylvanian and a West Pointer of the class of 1844. Like others of his generation, he had served in Mexico, where he had earned brevets for gallantry and was wounded. In the post-Mexico years his attention to detail and meticulousness resulted in his appointment as adjutant of the Sixth Infantry and, in 1855, his promotion to captain and assignment as a quartermaster. He served in Missouri, Florida, Kansas, the "Mormon War," and finally California, where he was stationed when the Civil War began.

Hancock got a late start in Civil War service, but he did not suffer from it. His reputation stood him in good stead, and he received a promotion to brigadier general of volunteers and command of a brigade in September 1861. He commanded brigades of the Fourth and Sixth corps through the Peninsular campaign. He received command of the First Division, Second Corps, at Antietam after Maj. Gen. Israel B. Richardson's fatal wound, was promoted to major general, and led his division at Fredericksburg and Chancellorsville. He took command of the Second Corps on 22 May, shortly before the Gettysburg Campaign opened.[10]

Meade relied heavily on Hancock. Though junior in rank to other corps commanders, he became one of the most influential and active of Meade's generals. General McClellan had termed Hancock's conduct at Williams-burg "superb," and Hancock had built on that reputation. Colonel Lyman described him a bit later as "a tall, soldierly man, with light-brown hair and a military heavy jaw . . . who always wears a clean *white* shirt (where he gets them nobody knows) . . . a very great and vehement talker but always says something worth hearing." General Grant later developed a high opinion of Hancock; he knew of no blunder that he had committed in battle. Grant recalled him as having been "tall, well-formed and . . . young and fresh-looking, he presented an appearance that would attract the attention of an army as he passed. His genial disposition made him friends, and his per-sonal courage and his presence with his command in the thickest of the fight won for him the confidence of troops serving under him. No matter how hard the fight, the 2d corps always felt that their commander was looking after them."[11]

After receiving the order to go forward, Hancock gathered some of his staff and returned to army headquarters without delay. He and General Meade held a hurried conversation. Hancock reminded Meade that he would be junior to other major generals on the field. Meade replied that this was an emergency, that he had explained his views to Hancock and had not done so to the others, and that Hancock could—as Hancock later put it—"better accord with him in my operations than anyone else." They could not be too concerned with rank. With this assurance, Hancock climbed into an ambulance and rattled away.[12]

Hancock bumped along in the ambulance for two or three miles while he studied his maps and the orders that governed the movements of the army. Then he mounted his horse and rode with his staff toward the Federal position at Gettysburg. After traveling about five miles, Hancock's party met an ambulance containing General Reynolds's corpse. There was no longer any doubt that Hancock was in command of the Union force at Gettysburg. Further along they met wagons that he ordered to the rear; and as he continued to ride along, Hancock studied the terrain. Finally, about 3:30 P.M., he arrived on Cemetery Hill and at a milestone in his career.[13]

The scene that met his eye must have dismayed him. The remnants of the First and Eleventh corps were streaming back to Cemetery Hill, and there appeared to be much confusion. Yet the situation was not as bad as it seemed; all was not lost—far from it. Maj. Gen. Oliver O. Howard had left Col. Orland Smith's brigade and Capt. Michael Wiedrich's battery (Battery I, First New York Light Artillery) of the Eleventh Corps on Cemetery Hill to hold it in case of just such an emergency. Although most regiments had suffered heavily enough and there were those that might have fought a lot better, the two corps, though in confusion, were basically intact. Surely there were many who shared the spirit of the Sixth Wisconsin Regiment, which assembled around its colors in the streets of the town to give "hearty cheers for the old Sixth and the good cause." The Federal artillery could still give an account of itself. Of the nine batteries of the two corps that had gone into the battle earlier in the day, only one was unable to continue the fight on Cemetery Hill. The artillery took positions along with Wiedrich's battery on the hill, and soon about forty pieces with ample ammunition dared the Confederates to come on.[14]

Hancock met and spoke with Howard, the then ranking officer on the field. Though Howard did not concede it, Hancock took command of the forces there. The two officers cooperated in the work to be done—Hancock concentrating his efforts west of the Baltimore Pike and Howard east of it. With the help of others they brought order from the seeming chaos and established a line from Culp's Hill to the north end of Cemetery Ridge. Buford's two brigades of cavalry and Capt. John H. Calef's battery (A, Second U.S.) of horse artillery, in the fields between Cemetery and Seminary ridges, covered the weaker Union left. Soon the Federal position became even more secure when Brig. Gen. Alpheus S. Williams's division of the Twelfth Corps occupied Wolf Hill north of the Baltimore Pike and Brig. Gen. John W. Geary's division took possession of the ground near Little Round Top.[15]

Things had quieted down considerably by the time Maj. Gen. Henry W. Slocum's Twelfth Corps arrived, and Hancock turned the command over to him. Hancock had acted that day with what, for him, must have been unaccustomed tact. He had not found it necessary to display his written order until he turned the field over to Slocum. Even then the sight of the order was too much for Howard, though he must have known its content. Howard believed that he had done well that day and that the order disgraced him.[16]

Both Hancock and Howard had sent General Meade reports of the situation at Gettysburg. Howard sent a dispatch, probably his first, at 2:00 P.M. In it he reported Federal troop dispositions just prior to Early's assault and indicated that the forces at Gettysburg were engaged with both Hill's and Ewell's corps. He stated also that he had ordered the Third Corps forward. A second dispatch sent at 5:00 P.M. briefly described the day's battle and reported Hancock's arrival. It reported also that Slocum was near but would not come forward and assume command.[17]

Hancock sent Maj. William G. Mitchell to General Meade with his first report at 4:00 P.M. Mitchell told Meade of the situation on the field and reported that the forces there could hold until night. Capt. Isaac B. Parker carried Hancock's second report at 5:25 P.M. This message described the Federal position as one that could not be taken readily but could be turned. Hancock reported also that Williams's division had arrived on the right, that he had sent the trains to the rear, and that the force at hand could hold the Gettysburg position until dark, when a decision might be made on future courses of action. He thought that the army could pull back or stay, for the ground was not unfavorable for the deployment of good troops. He said that Warren had reached the field and that he, Hancock, would soon turn command of the forces there over to Slocum.[18] He started back to Taneytown about dark. The Third Corps was coming up by then, and Hancock learned that General Meade had ordered the rest of the army to concentrate at the battlefield.[19]

Meade had already obtained some knowledge of the battle's progress from officers back from the field—what officers he did not say. He knew, of course, that the Twelfth Corps was at Two Taverns, close to the field, and by midafternoon that Slocum was moving up. By 4:30 he learned that Howard had ordered up the Third Corps, and at 6:00 P.M. he wrote that the two brigades of the Third Corps left at Emmitsburg could be advanced and that he would order the Sixth Corps forward also if it were required. By this time Meade believed that the army was so concentrated at Gettysburg that a battle there "is now forced on us." But his attitude was aggressive, for he concluded a dispatch to Generals Hancock and Abner Doubleday with the observation, "If we get up all our people, and attack with our whole force to-morrow, we ought to defeat the force the enemy has."[20]

At 6:00 P.M. Meade sent a wire to Halleck to bring him up to date. He reported that the First and Eleventh corps had fought at Gettysburg; that the Third, Twelfth, and Fifth were moving there; and that the Sixth would follow. He stated that he saw no alternative to a general battle there and that he hoped to defeat the corps of Hill and Ewell. By this time, therefore, Meade was personally reconciled to, if not eager about, giving battle at Gettysburg; the Pipe Creek alternative was dead. He had apparently made the decision to fight at Gettysburg sometime between 4:30 and 6:00 P.M.—before the messages from Hancock and Howard would have reached him. Nevertheless, their confirmation of the appropriateness of his decision must have been welcome.[21]

Meade thought that General Slocum, commander of the right wing, had ordered the Fifth Corps to Gettysburg, but at 7:00 P.M., after he had committed the Army of the Potomac to battle there, he sent a dispatch directly to General Sykes to remove all doubt. He ordered Sykes to start his corps for Gettysburg at once if his corps was not already on the way and to contact Slocum under whose orders he had been placed that morning. Later in the day he instructed General Hunt to order up the Artillery Reserve. That was a commitment: in giving such instructions to the Artillery Reserve and the army's ammunition train he passed the point of no return.[22]

At least five dispatches went from army headquarters to Maj. Gen. John Sedgwick, commander of the Sixth Corps, on 1 July, though one possibly did not arrive and two or more were probably carried by the same courier. Brig. Gen. Seth Williams, Meade's adjutant general, sent the first one late in the morning. It told Sedgwick of the situation as it appeared before news of the battle's opening reached army headquarters, and it instructed Sedgwick to have his corps ready to move in any direction at a moment's notice.[23] Maj. James C. Biddle, one of Meade's aides, arrived with this dispatch just as

Sedgwick was sitting down to his midday meal. Sedgwick read the message and observed that he was ready to move at once. He invited the major to eat with him and no doubt queried him about the goings-on at the army's headquarters. On learning that Butterfield was staying on as chief of staff, Sedgwick said that "he regretted to hear it, that he knew Butterfield well, that he was a bad man & he feared Gen'l Meade would regret retaining him." After eating, Biddle headed back to Taneytown and on the way met another aide, Lt. Paul A. Oliver, who told him of the battle, that Reynolds was dead and that he had orders for the Sixth Corps to march to Gettysburg. According to Biddle's recollections, he reached army headquarters between 8:00 and 9:00 P.M., just as Meade was setting out for the battlefield.[24]

Butterfield sent another dispatch at 4:30 P.M. It ordered the Sixth Corps to Taneytown and announced Reynolds's death. Probably a dispatch from Seth Williams accompanied it. The latter directed Maj. Gen. John Newton, commander of the Third Division, Sixth Corps, to come forward and take command of the First Corps. Before these dispatches could have arrived, however, Sedgwick, stimulated by the passing of daylight and rumors of battle, sent his aide, Maj. Thomas W. Hyde, to Meade's headquarters for information and orders. Hyde set out with an orderly at 5:00 P.M., reached Taneytown after dark, and chanced to see Hancock, from whom he learned up-to-date news of the battle. When he reached army headquarters, he told Butterfield that Sedgwick had not received the 4:30 P.M. orders but that he had met Lieutenant Oliver when about halfway there.[25]

Hyde also spoke with Seth Williams and General Meade. Meade, and perhaps Butterfield too, sent Hyde back to Sedgwick with a fistful of yellow papers, copies of previous dispatches that had been sent to Sedgwick. Meade told Hyde that he expected the Sixth Corps to come in on the army's right and hoped that it would be up in time. He offered Hyde an escort back to the Sixth Corps, but Hyde declined the offer and departed at midnight. He did not have an easy return trip; he had been warned to look out for Confederate cavalry and therefore hid in the woods several times out of caution. Finally, he met Newton and Sedgwick somewhere on the road.[26]

Sedgwick had been receiving messages from headquarters even though headquarters had not been hearing from him. Why he did not ride on ahead of his corps as Sickles and Hancock had done he did not say. But officers at army headquarters were anxious about the corps. They had expected Oliver to return, and he did not appear; they expected Sedgwick to ride in, but he did not come. Finally, General Meade could wait no longer and rode north to Gettysburg, leaving instructions with Butterfield to await Sedgwick and give him Meade's views. The wee hours of the morning came and sunrise followed, but Sedgwick did not appear. Butterfield chose to wait no longer, and at 5:30 sent another dispatch to Sedgwick. He was to get in touch with General Meade as soon as possible and heed an enclosed memorandum written the night before as his judgment dictated. That memorandum stated that Meade proposed to attack vigorously on 2 July and that he doubted that the Sixth Corps would be up before the issue was settled. Therefore, Sedgwick was to advance his corps as far as possible, take up a position at some strongpoint, and prepare to cover the army's retreat in the event that it was forced to withdraw. If the Federals were successful, though, he should push his corps forward from that point to the army's aid.[27]

The commanding general set out at 10:00 P.M. for Gettysburg with General Hunt, Capt. George Meade, Capt. Charles Cadwalader, Sgt. William Waters (an orderly), and Capt. William H. Paine, an engineer from General Warren's staff. Paine was the party's guide. He in turn had secured the help of a civilian who was to identify places passed on the way. Paine led the party, which moved fast, and the civilian, who probably was not accustomed to such nocturnal rides, soon fell behind. The Second Corps was using the road, and the general's party had to take to the fields to avoid it. This was fine except that when they rode beneath some trees, a branch brushed Meade's spectacles from his face, and they were lost. Fortunately, he was not hurt, and he had extra glasses. In about an hour the hard-riding group reached Gibbon's headquarters, the headquarters of the Second Corps.[28]

General Meade paused with General Gibbon for about fifteen minutes and ordered him to push the corps forward at daylight. The party then continued its ride and at about 11:30 P.M. clattered up to the gate house of Gettysburg's Evergreen Cemetery on Cemetery Hill. General Meade dismounted stiffly, and probably gladly, and greeted Generals Slocum, Howard, Sickles, and Warren, as well as others who were there. One of them spoke favorably of the Gettysburg position, and General Meade replied that this was just as well, for it was too late for the Army of the Potomac to leave it. He told them that the whole army was moving up and that it would fight there. Then, with Captain Paine and some others, he stepped outside the gatehouse to have a look at the field where the next battle was to be fought.[29]

While General Meade grappled with the problems of command, his Second, Third, and Fifth corps tramped the roads that ultimately led to Gettysburg.[30] The Third began its day by shifting five miles from its bivouac at the hamlet of Bridgeport on the Monocacy west to Emmitsburg where it arrived as the Eleventh Corps marched north from Emmitsburg to Gettysburg. Emmitsburg was the Third Corps's objective for the day, and its divisions prepared to bed down where, if need be, they could readily cover the Federal left or move toward Gettysburg in support of the First and Eleventh corps.[31] Birney's division was along the north-south road to Gettysburg, on the grounds of St. Joseph's College and in the fields north of the village. The three brigades of Humphreys's division moved west of the village along the Waynesboro Pike, where they would be able to deploy and block any turning movement that General Lee might try east of the mountains against the Union left.[32]

The day was warm, cloudy, and humid. Occasional showers made the roads and fields soggy and slippery and the wool uniforms uncomfortable and odorous. But the war went on. As the corps pickets took their posts, Sickles examined the recently arrived Pipe Creek Circular and prepared to implement that portion of it applying to his corps.[33] As he did so, Humphreys and his staff, in response to Meade's earlier instructions to Reynolds, looked for suitable terrain west of Emmitsburg from which to fight.[34] The men made the best of the situation; they foraged and bought food from the "Dutch farmers" whose business sense, if not unalloyed patriotism, they aroused. Some soldiers prepared to bed down for the night by making beds of pine boughs and sheaves of wheat taken from the newly cut fields.[35]

Sometime that morning, perhaps as the Third Corps approached Emmitsburg, Sickles sent Maj. Henry E. Tremain, his senior aide, forward to Reynolds to report the corps's arrival at Emmitsburg. Tremain rode hard and found Reynolds helping with the posting of Wadsworth's division of the First Corps. Tremain delivered Sickles's message and asked for orders. Reynolds replied, "Tell General Sickles I *think* he had better come up."[36] Tremain rode back to Emmitsburg in all haste and found that Sickles had set up his headquarters at an old farm house. Sickles was away but soon returned and received Reynolds's message. He asked Tremain to return to Gettysburg immediately and ordered the corps quartermaster to provide him with a fresh horse. While Tremain waited for his new mount, couriers arrived bearing astounding news.[37]

One message from Gen. Oliver Howard's chief of staff, sent at 1:00 P.M., reported a fight with A. P. Hill's corps and the approach of Ewell's. Another, timed 1:30, from Maj. Charles H. Howard, the general's aide and brother, announced Reynolds's death and requested Sickles's support.[38] Sickles weighed this request against the instructions in the Pipe Creek Circular, and, to his everlasting credit, decided to go to Gettysburg without delay. He sent dispatches announcing his intentions as fast as they could be scribbled. At 3:15 he wrote to Howard that his corps would move up immediately. In two notes to army headquarters he informed General Meade of Howard's messages and of his intention to move up to Gettysburg over two routes. He personally would follow the Emmitsburg Road, the most direct way. But he would leave two brigades at Emmitsburg to guard the army's flank.[39]

Sickles ordered his two divisions to take the road. The First Division, commanded by Maj. Gen. David B. Birney, led the way over the Emmitsburg-Gettysburg Road. Birney had with him the brigades of Brig. Gens. J. H. Hobart Ward and Charles K. Graham, as well as two batteries, Lt. John K. Bucklyn's (E, First Rhode Island Light Artillery) and Capt. A. Judson Clark's (B, First New Jersey Light Artillery). Birney left de Trobriand's brigade at Emmitsburg. In Birney's words, his division reached Gettysburg after "marching with enthusiasm and alacrity over the road, rendered almost impassable by mud and the passage over it of the First and Eleventh Corps through the rain." According to his watch, which seems not to have been synchronized with Sickles's (Sickles's order was timed 3:30 P.M.), he received the order at 2:15 and reached Gettysburg at 5:30.[40]

The march was not an easy one: the weather was hot and sultry, and the road, which was not a turnpike, was in poor condition. Soldiers of Graham's brigade found the road muddy and slippery, and Ward described it as "horrible."[41] An officer of the 124th New York remembered the road's being strewn with blankets and equipment, officers' horses packing the equipment of worn-out men, and, somehow, dust instead of mud. All agreed that it was a hard march, a harder one than suggested by Birney, and many recalled arriving at dusk or later.[42]

Humphreys's division had a longer and more adventurous march than Birney's. The general returned from his reconnaissance to find that Gen. Joseph B. Carr had already started on the way his own and Col. William R. Brewster's brigades and Lt. Francis W. Seeley's battery (K, Fourth U.S.). He left Col. George C. Burling's (Mott's) brigade behind with de Trobriand's to guard the Emmitsburg area. Both were placed under de Trobriand's command.[43] Humphreys caught up with his division a mile north of Emmitsburg and found it guided by Lt. Col. Julius Hayden, the inspector general of the Third Corps, and by a Dr. Anan of Emmitsburg.[44] The division traveled northwest on a country road that angled from the main road taken by Birney. At dusk the column reached Marsh Creek south of Black Horse Tavern on the Fairfield Road, where Wilcox's Confederate brigade waited.[45]

Distant artillery fire could be heard when Humphreys's march began, but it faded with the day. When Carr's brigade crossed the Mason-Dixon Line just north of Emmitsburg, there were "wild huzzas" and a band played "Home Sweet Home" in the best tradition of the campaign. Later a Pennsylvania farm woman approached the men of the Eleventh New Jersey with a bucket. She shouted, "Here's Pennsylvania water for you boys," and the boys answered with three cheers for the Keystone State. They forded Marsh Creek about dark, halted, and fell out along the side of the road.[46]

Humphreys received three pieces of information along the way. A staff officer, Capt. John G. McBlair, brought him a copy of a dispatch from Howard to Sickles that wisely warned Sickles to be on the lookout for enemy on his left as he approached Gettysburg. At about the same time he learned from a civilian who had guided some First Corps units (probably Biddle's brigade) earlier in the day that there were no Union troops west of the Emmitsburg Road. (This was probably wrong technically, for Buford's troops were west of the road, although east of Seminary Ridge.) And then, as the division approached Marsh Creek, an officer appeared with orders for it to go in on the left of Gettysburg when it arrived.[47]

Just short of Marsh Creek, Humphreys's division came to a fork in the road. Should it turn left or right? Lieutenant Colonel Hayden, who was its guide, insisted that it should turn left toward the Fairfield Road. Humphreys must have looked at his map, perhaps by the light of a match, and seen that if he turned to the right the road would take him to the Emmitsburg Road via Pitzer's Schoolhouse and away from the danger that might lurk on his left. He took issue with Hayden, but the colonel, whose job it was to know where Humphreys was to go, insisted that the column take the road to the left. Humphreys yielded with misgivings and ordered that the column close up and move quietly.[48] They marched a short distance, Hayden and perhaps Anan to the front, Humphreys and Carr back near the head of the column. Hayden soon developed some misgivings of his own, and the column halted. Humphreys ordered quiet; he, some of his staff, and Dr. Anan walked cautiously ahead on foot. Some noise had to be expected from so many men and their rattling equipment, but the hearts of many officers and men must have missed a beat when the bugler of Seeley's battery sounded the signal to halt. There are always some who do not get the word; fortunately the call did not carry to the Black Horse Tavern area.[49]

General Humphreys and his party approached the road and tavern stealthily. When they reached the tavern, Humphreys spoke to Mr. Bream, the proprietor (whom he suspected of having Southern sympathies), to Bream's two sons, and to a disabled Union soldier who was home on furlough and happened to be there. From them he learned that there was a Confederate picket post about two hundred yards away. Not wishing to be discovered, the party quietly withdrew.[50]

About the time Humphreys was scouting the Fairfield Road, a straggler from the Seventy-first New York Regiment visited a farmhouse near the line of march and captured a Confederate artillery sergeant there.[51] The sergeant's presence confirmed the information received at the tavern—Humphreys's division was where it did not belong. At the general's order, the column faced about and in "majestic silence" retraced its steps. As General Carr, his staff, and servants made their way through his regiments to reach the new head of the brigade, someone in a mock command whispered loudly: "Officers and niggers to the rear, march!"[52]

In the welcome light of a rising moon (it rose at about 8:09 P.M.) Humphreys's two brigades recrossed Marsh Creek. They followed the road along the creek's west bank, crossed to its east side by a covered bridge near the John Sachs farmyard, went on to ford Willoughby Run, and came to Pitzer's Schoolhouse. There they took the road to the right and ascended the west slope of Seminary Ridge. By this time the moon was shining brightly and the rifles gleamed—"their bright barrels look like a bridge of polished steel as they stretch along the road." At this time Humphreys thought it well to learn where they were. He dismounted at a small house, James Flaharty's perhaps, to question again the captured sergeant and to speak with the occupants of the house.[53]

Here, according to Capt. Adolphus F. Cavada, they encountered another "wolf." The sergeant knew nothing of the Pitzer Schoolhouse area. The man of the house, however, assured Humphreys that the woods one-third of a mile beyond his house were occupied by enemy cavalry. (The man must have been talking about Pitzer's Woods, into which some scouting parties of the enemy's infantry might have probed.) Humphreys responded by having a company of infantry deployed as skirmishers a hundred yards in front of his column and then resumed the march. They went about eight hundred yards to the Emmitsburg Road at the Peach Orchard before they met a cavalry vidette. Instead of being Confederate, this proved to be one of Buford's pickets. The column turned left along the Emmitsburg Road and soon met Lt. Col. Orson H. Hart, the assistant adjutant general of the Third Corps, who guided Humphreys to his division's place on the field. It was midnight then, and the division had had an unnecessarily long and vexing march that sapped strength that might be needed when daylight came. The men took no time for amenities, stretching out in the grass at once to sleep.[54]

Daniel Sickles had acted promptly. Though his divisions had not arrived in time to take part in the afternoon's battle, the threat of their approach would have intimidated the Confederates and stiffened the spines of the Federals at Gettysburg had the fighting continued. General Sickles himself arrived late in the afternoon, shortly after Slocum appeared but long before his Third Corps troops reached the field. General Howard gave him a warm welcome, saying, "Here you are, general, always reliable, always first." Major Tremain joined him soon after. Once greetings and discussions were out of the way, Sickles and Tremain sat down to a meal of pancakes in the cemetery's lodge.[55]

Sickles's prompt decision to march to Gettysburg and to the sound of the guns was thoroughly in keeping with his decisive and flamboyant character. Sickles was a native of New York City, born on 20 October 1825. He ardently pursued the joint career of lawyer and Tammany Hall politician, and he prospered in both endeavors. He served in the state legislature, was corporation counsel of New York City for a brief period, held the post of secretary of the American legation in London for a short time when James Buchanan was minister there, and in 1857 began a two-term stint in Congress. Sickles was a Tammany Hall Democrat in all that the name implies, and in Congress he was generally sympathetic to the efforts of Southern Democrats. However, toward the end of his second term, when the Southern states threatened secession, he vigorously opposed their action and came out foursquare for the Union.[56]

Sickles had trouble in Washington that would have ruined the careers of most prominent men. During his first term in Congress, he and his young wife entertained lavishly in their leased mansion on LaFayette Square opposite the White House. This came to a sudden end early in his second term, on 25 February 1859, when Sickles, who was no paragon of conjugal virtue, publicly shot and killed Philip Barton Key for having an affair with Mrs. Sickles. Sickles was imprisoned, and the whole sordid business was exposed by the press and the publicity attendant to Sickles's trial for murder. Surprisingly, however, Sickles was acquitted on the grounds of temporary insanity, and the decision set a legal precedent. Sickles then scandalized many by not divorcing his wife, although he left her in New York while he completed his term in Congress. His insistence on being in Washington, where he was a social outcast, was typical of the man.[57]

His political career then went into recess. But when war came, he threw his support to Lincoln and the war effort. Sickles had had only a little militia experience, but with initial state approval he raised the Excelsior Brigade. Then, with New York's opposition but with Lincoln's backing, he succeeded in having the brigade mustered into Federal service. In due course, Sickles, as its commander, became a brigadier general. Sickles was a scrapper, adept at functioning within a political environment, and he was diligent in cultivating the friendship of President and Mrs. Lincoln. He commanded the brigade successfully on the Peninsula and in November 1862 became a major general. He commanded the Second Division, Third Corps, at Antietam and Fredericksburg and received command of the Third Corps when Hooker advanced to army command. Sickles performed aggressively at Chancellorsville and led his corps to Gettysburg.[58]

Sickles became a friend of Generals Hooker and Butterfield, participated in their social affairs, and contributed to what some considered the "barroom and brothel" atmosphere at the headquarters of the Army of the Potomac while Hooker was in command. In doing so, he alienated such officers as Reynolds, Meade, and Hunt.[59] In later years General de Trobriand, who probably knew of him in New York before the war and served under him in the Third Corps, wrote of Sickles:

> He was gifted in a high degree with that multiplicity of faculties which has given rise to the saying that a Yankee is ready for everything. . . . He has a quick perception, an energetic will, prompt and supple intelligence, an active temperament. Naturally ambitious, he brings to the service of his ambitions a clear view, a practical judgment and a deep knowledge of political tactics. When he has determined on anything, he prepares the way, assembles his forces, and marches directly to the assault. Obstacles do not discourage him . . . he has many strings in his bow, if one breaks he will replace it by another.
>
> In him, ability does not exclude frankness. He likes, on the contrary, to play with his cards on the table with his friends and against his enemies.[60]

Although a mover and a shaker, Sickles lacked military background and knowledge. Furthermore, he must have found it galling sometimes to work in harness within the military hierarchy. In regard to Sickles's military ability, General Warren observed to the Committee on the Conduct of the War that had Sickles been educated as a soldier, he might have stood very high. As it was, Warren believed that he was not as good a soldier as others, such as Reynolds, Hancock, and Meade, "but he did the best he could, and with the corps he had managed very well. His corps was composed of a little different material from the others." Warren went on to say that he did not think Sickles would be a good man to fight an independent battle, as corps commanders sometimes had to do. For "when you come down to all the details of a battle, General Sickles has not had the same experience which others have had. The knowledge of those details do not make a soldier, but he should be possessed of them as much as he is his own language."[61]

Birney arrived before dark, and Sickles, fortified with pancakes, designated an assembly area for his division and a site for corps headquarters on the lower end of Cemetery Ridge. Once Birney was squared away, Sickles asked Tremain to locate an area for Humphreys's division to occupy when it arrived. This was more easily said than done, for darkness was falling and the young major had to contend with rocks, trees, fences, and other hazards of an unfamiliar landscape.[62] At 9:30 P.M., with Birney's division settled in and Humphreys somewhere on the way, General Sickles took the time to send a dispatch to General Meade. He explained his going to Gettysburg and said that he had left two brigades at Emmitsburg to cover the army's left and rear. But he was worried and wanted to suggest that the left and rear were not sufficiently guarded. He had left that vital area only at the earnest and frequent appeals of Howard and believed that the emergency justified his doing so. Now the question was, should he remain at Gettysburg or should he return to Emmitsburg? Though troubled by the weakness on the left and rear, he closed his dispatch with the encouraging observation, "This is a good battle-field."[63]

While their Third Corps comrades marched to Gettysburg, the officers and men left at Emmitsburg bided their time. Although General Meade had initially approved Sickles's wisdom in leaving them behind, he felt that the situation had changed rapidly, and at 7:30 he had Butterfield send an order to the "Commanding Officer at Emmitsburg" to move his troops to join his corps "with the greatest dispatch." He was to take care that his force did not come into collision with the enemy on the way up and was expected to be there at daylight on the following morning.[64]

Sickles also gave an order concerning the force at Emmitsburg. Sometime on 1 July, presumably in the evening after he reached Gettysburg, General Sickles ordered Gen. Charles K. Graham, commander of Birney's division's First Brigade, to return at once to Emmitsburg and take command of the Third Corps units there. He was to give special attention to the corps's ammunition and headquarters train, which had been left there and, in case of danger, send it to Taneytown. There is no knowing when Graham received the order, but he seems not to have acted on it until morning.[65]

While the Third Corps marched to the sound of the guns, almost in the enemy's presence, the Fifth Corps, under its new commander, Maj. Gen.

George Sykes, trudged northward, apparently unaware that battle had been joined. Sykes had three divisions: Brig. Gen. James Barnes commanded the First Division in place of its assigned commander, Brig. Gen. Charles Griffin; Brig. Gen. Romeyn B. Ayres commanded the Second Division; and Brig. Gen. Samuel W. Crawford, the Third. Barnes's division was rather typical in that it was composed of regiments from several states, but two of Ayres's three brigades were composed wholly of infantry regiments of the Regular Army. Some of them had fought under Sykes at Bull Run two years before and had distinguished themselves by their disciplined behavior on that field.

Crawford's division was unusual too. It was composed wholly of regiments of "Pennsylvania Reserves." Two brigades of Reserves marched to Gettysburg, while one remained in Washington manning its defenses. The Reserves were veteran units—initially fifteen regiments whose men had answered the call for volunteers in 1861 but were in excess of Pennsylvania's quota. The Federal government would not accept them, so Pennsylvania organized and trained them and called them the Pennsylvania Reserves. They had been commanded at the outset of the war by no less than Generals John F. Reynolds, George G. Meade, and Edward O. C. Ord, and they had performed well in the campaigns of 1862. Now Samuel Crawford commanded the lot, and the brigades marching to Gettysburg were under two colonels, William McCandless and Joseph W. Fisher.[66]

Fifth Corps headquarters and Barnes's and Ayres's divisions reached Union Mills, Maryland, on Pipe Creek about ten miles south of Hanover, Pennsylvania, on 30 June. Crawford's division, which had marched twenty-five miles that day, was not quite able to keep up and bivouacked at Frizzelburg a few miles to the southwest.[67] Sykes's men, who had been marching in the rain, were all badly in need of rest. One soldier recalled their being ragged, footsore, and chafed, plodding along in their drawers with handkerchiefs of various colors on their heads. Some were barefoot; some walked along in the remnants of their stockings. The gallant Fifth Corps was not turned out for a dress parade, and its appearance belied the stereotype of the Army of the Potomac as a well uniformed and equipped force. On top of that many men were sickened by the heat.[68]

While at Union Mills on 30 June the corps, like the rest of the United States Army, mustered for pay. Some of its regiments, like the Fourth Michigan, attempted to get needed equipment, including the ordinary regulation caps for men who still wore hats. Even during a campaign there were administrative chores that had to be done.[69]

The corps's objective on 1 July was Hanover, twelve miles to the north of Union Mills and about thirteen miles east of Gettysburg. That morning, in accordance with Ayres's division's procedures, headquarters musicians sounded "The General," and the call ran through the regiments. After leaving its train at Westminster, the corps traveled light. Each regiment had four wagons in column—two for company baggage, one for headquarters, and one for the surgeons. In addition, the officers of each company were allowed a pack mule or horse for their food and mess equipment. In keeping with Meade's circular, an officer and twelve men of each division remained behind with the train as its guard.[70]

The march scheduled for the Fifth Corps on 1 July was relatively short, but the day was hot and the roads were dusty. The dust hung in clouds over the column, irritating eyes, parching throats, and stifling breath as it puffed up from beneath the thousands of pounding and scuffling feet. Although apparently ignorant of the fight at Gettysburg, Crawford's men in particular were concerned about reports of Confederate cavalry nearby. In response Crawford put out flankers, a proper safeguard but one that must have slowed his march.[71] There was some straggling. Pvt. Robert G. Carter of the Twenty-second Massachusetts recalled that what seemed like whole companies fell out. In the 155th Pennsylvania alone, fifty-five men received passes because the surgeon deemed them too incapacitated to keep up.[72]

The march also had some redeeming features, particularly for the soldiers from Pennsylvania. Years later, when they dedicated their Gettysburg memorials and the events of the war assumed a much rosier hue, a speaker of the Second Reserves recalled that 1 July

> was one of the happiest [days] of our lives, and every heart beat warm with the thought we would soon press the soil of our Mother State to whose defense we were marching. The bands and regimental drum corps poured forth their soul-inspiring airs from morning until night, and light was the tread of our feet to their notes. About 3 o'clock we were drawn up to hear a patriotic address from General Crawford, after which we marched on, and as we crossed the line cheer after cheer rang out from the regiments, which rolled over the hills and through the valleys until lost in the far distance.[73]

When the Eighty-third Pennsylvania Regiment of Vincent's brigade approached the Mason-Dixon Line, the enthusiasm of its soldiers knew no bounds. At Col. Strong Vincent's order the color-bearers slipped the covers from their flags, the fifes and drums played "Yankee Doodle," and cheers ran from the regiment down the line of march. State ties were strong, and it was good to be in Pennsylvania, even for men from the opposite corner of the Keystone State.[74]

But not all were Pennsylvanians, fatigue dulls enthusiasm, and the long miles stretched ahead. Some men broke the monotony, as did the Confederates, by breaking limbs from cherry trees and breaking the farmers' hearts. At one point the men of Ayres's division heard band music off in the distance that so pepped them up that the division's bands were ordered to work, and the magic of music seemed to revive the tired men.[75]

The Fifth Corps march through Hanover provided an opportunity for a display of scruffy pomp and circumstance that could not be overlooked. Colonel Vincent ordered up the fifes and drums of the Eighty-third Pennsylvania to play his brigade through the town and ordered the regiments to uncover their flags again. As he sat astride his horse, probably in Hanover's square, and watched the Stars and Stripes float by above his old regiment, Vincent turned to his adjutant, Lt. John M. Clark, and remarked prophetically, "What death more glorious can any man desire than to die on the soil of old Pennsylvania fighting for that flag?" The feeling behind that remark, echoed many times along the blue columns, boded trouble for General Lee.[76]

The Fifth Corps halted for the night on the western outskirts of Hanover, stacked arms, and prepared for a night of rest still oblivious to the battle that day at Gettysburg. Townspeople came to the camps to gawk and perhaps in the hope of finding friends and loved ones. The troops received an issue of sixty rounds of ammunition, boiled their coffee, and charred some newly killed beef. Some of the townsfolk offered food for the troops, but the enlisted men were not allowed to leave camp, and only the officers could go where the food was. One former enlisted man recalled, "Didn't we swear!"[77]

As the men of the Fifth Corps settled in for a night's rest, a horseman rode hard in their direction. Capt. Addison G. Mason of Meade's staff had set out from army headquarters late in the afternoon with messages for Generals Slocum and Sykes. He was to tell them of the battle, Reynolds's death, and Hancock's taking command and to instruct them to move to Gettysburg without delay. Mason rode first to the Baltimore Pike and to Slocum's headquarters at the crossroads hamlet of Two Taverns, four miles southeast of Gettysburg. Slocum was not there when Mason arrived; he had already gone forward. After showing his dispatches to Slocum's assistant adjutant general, Mason hastened on to Gettysburg, and sometime between 5:00 and 6:00 P.M. he saw Slocum near Cemetery Hill. Mason then started off in search of Sykes. He rode back along the pike, probably to Two Taverns, turned northeasterly on a country road that led to Bonnaughtown (Bonneauville), and then turned east toward Hanover. He found Sykes already in camp, but in response to Meade's summons Sykes said that he would make all haste to Gettysburg.[78]

Mason's message ended the evening's rest for the soldiers of the Fifth Corps. Barnes wrote that the men received the order to march with "enthusiasm," but "excitement" might have been a better word.[79] At any rate, Barnes's division got a fast start, in part because its Second and Third brigades vied to be the first through a gap in a wall and the first in the division's line of march. Sweitzer's Second Brigade won the race and led the corps toward Gettysburg, allowing others to eat its dust.[80]

There were those who recalled that a bright moon lighted the way for the Fifth Corps, as it had for others, that night. As the corps passed through McSherrystown and Brushtown and by the neat farms that lined the road, the people cheered them and gave them water and food.[81] By this time the long day's march was taking its toll, and some soldiers were in no mood for gracious gestures. As the residents of McSherrystown called "Godspeed," there were those who shouted back, "Fall in!" and "Take a rifle and defend your own firesides!"[82]

One of the most memorable events of the evening stemmed from a hoax or plain rumor that held that George B. McClellan had returned to the command of the Army of the Potomac. Some said that the news came from civilians who had been to Gettysburg and had seen him there. Others remembered hearing it from a courier who rode along the column. Col. Joseph Hayes of the Eighteenth Massachusetts was so convinced of it that he halted his regiment and announced it formally with the result that "one grand hurrah arose from the ranks, and all through the night the men were in the best possible mood." Regardless of its origin, the effect of the rumor was electric, and there was cheering all along the column. The men of the Fourth Michigan threw their hats into the air—the hats that Jeffords wanted to replace, it is hoped—hollered, and kicked up their heels. Lt. Charles E. Hazlett, whose battery would occupy Little Round Top, told Lt. Benjamin F. Rittenhouse that "if that is true I'll get tight on the strength of it."[83] It was not true, Hazlett stayed sober the rest of his life, but the corps's reaction was a great tribute to McClellan and not exactly a vote of confidence for General Meade, who had been the commander of the Fifth Corps less than a week before.

Sykes did not take his corps all the way into Gettysburg that night. Had he attempted to do so, he would have risked colliding with Confederates already there, and the corps's presence before Meade was able to post it might have caused problems. Instead he halted the head of the column at Bonnaughtown, five miles to the east, and Crawford's division, in the rear, got no farther than McSherrystown, just west of Hanover. The Fifth Corps troops rested along the road until daybreak. At 12:30 A.M. Sykes sent Butterfield and Slocum dispatches reporting the location of his corps and his intention to continue forward at 4:00 A.M.[84]

Hancock's Second Corps approached Gettysburg from the south. It had rested at Uniontown on the 30 June. Stragglers who had fallen behind on the previous day joined it there while the first sergeants and company commanders prepared muster rolls. Some Uniontown people gave a ball; there were some, probably staff officers, who were able to go and stay until the small hours. But most must have been content to rest, receive their pay, and prepare for the work ahead.[85]

Taneytown, just seven miles northwest of Uniontown, was the Second Corps's objective for 1 July. The march to it was a short and not particularly hurried one. The troops had a reveille formation at dawn, received three days rations and sixty rounds of ammunition, and took to the road. Although Meade believed on 30 June that the main body of the enemy was west of

Gettysburg, Hancock was to communicate with Sykes and be ready to support the Fifth Corps in case it met the enemy in the Union Mills area.[86]

Hancock and the van of the corps reached Taneytown before noon, but the length of its column was such that at 9:00 A.M. some of its units had not yet cleared the Uniontown area. Willard's brigade, Hays's division, guarded the corps trains in the rear. Sometime about midmorning, after the train had been on the road for a while, couriers galloped up, and suddenly the ponderous wagons began to turn around and head to the rear. Apparently Hancock had received the Pipe Creek Circular and they were responding to it. The brigade continued its march to Taneytown.[87]

The stay of the Second Corps near Taneytown was a short one. At 12:30 P.M. Meade ordered it to march toward Gettysburg. He feared that if Reynolds fell back ahead of the Confederates by way of Emmitsburg there would be a gap in the army's front. Soon Meade heard of Reynolds's death and sent Hancock forward as his emissary. The corps followed at 1:30 under the command of General Gibbon.[88] The march continued until after dark, when the column reached the area just south of Round Top. Hancock met it there as he journeyed back to Taneytown from the battlefield. He instructed Gibbon to post the corps across the road in such a way that it would block any flanking movement that the Confederates might attempt. So ended the march of the Second Corps on 1 July.[89]

The march itself had been uneventful enough. Dust had enveloped everything, uniforms became dirty brown, and facial features were obliterated. Some men heard firing when they crossed into Pennsylvania, and they met a lot of vehicles traveling away from Gettysburg, getting in their way. Among these was the ambulance carrying Reynolds's body. Officers tried to force this traffic from the road, even at gunpoint. As in other corps, the Pennsylvanians in the Second vented their enthusiasm when they reached their native soil, but by and large the corps simply made a fifteen mile march over a relatively poor road. Although Gibbon and the head of the column reached its halting place at sundown, it was midnight before the rear elements of the corps closed in and were able to rest for the night.[90]

On arriving south of Round Top, the corps posted pickets and erected some defensive works, all in the light of a hazy moon. Those men engaged in the latter job stacked arms and piled up knapsacks; and, after pioneers chopped down trees, the men piled up the wood and the other usable material available. It seems unlikely that the defenses erected were either extensive or strong.[91]

The Second Corps picket line connected with that of the Twelfth Corps on the right and ran west to the Emmitsburg Road.[92] Apparently some of Brig. Gen. John C. Caldwell's regiments had already collapsed in sleep before this line was posted. Maj. John Hancock of Caldwell's staff awakened Maj. St. Clair A. Mulholland, commander of the 116th Pennsylvania Regiment, and ordered him to take four hundred men and establish a picket line beyond the

Emmitsburg Road and at right angles to it. Major Hancock attempted to indicate the place where the line was wanted by drawing a sketch for Mulholland in the light of a flickering candle, but since neither he nor Mulholland was familiar with the area they were talking about, the sketch made little sense. Hancock then gave Mulholland the name of a farmer who lived beyond the road and might be able to help him. About 1:00 A.M. Mulholland led his force to the Emmitsburg Road and the house of the man whose name he had been given. He awakened the poor farmer and found him unwilling to talk at that hour of the night, so unwilling that he attempted to close the conversation by closing his window. The poor rustic was unaware of the persuasiveness of the Army of the Potomac when engaged in its lawful duties. Mulholland reopened the conversation by calling up some of his infantrymen and having them batter the man's door with their rifle butts. The farmer raised his window. He tried to beg off serving as a guide until the major gave him the choice of cooperating or being shot. At this, the farmer hurried down and guided Mulholland's force to the place where the major thought it should be. Soon after dawn Mulholland's pickets were relieved by men of the Third Corps.[93]

Posting pickets in the darkness when the men were already tired was not an easy task. Lt. Josiah A. Favill, General Zook's aide, attempted to awaken some men for this duty but could not do so. Such laxness in Hancock's old division seems hard to fathom, but when Favill complained to General Caldwell about his problem, Caldwell told him to let them sleep. And so fatigue, if not disobedience, was recognized and rewarded.[94]

The day of 1 July had been a momentous one for the Army of the Potomac and the nation. A portion of the army had suffered a resounding defeat at Gettysburg and yet General Meade had decided to continue the battle there rather than retire from Pennsylvania to the security of the planned position along Pipe Creek. He ordered the Army of the Potomac to concentrate at Gettysburg and rode forward to command it there. Because of his aggressive decision, by midnight of 1 July the bulk of the Army of the Potomac, like the Army of Northern Virginia, was at or near Gettysburg and would be prepared to give battle next day.

CHAPTER

4

Meade's Scattered Corps
Assemble, 2 July

In the faint first light of dawn on Thursday, 2 July 1863, Capt. Adolphus F. Cavada of General A. A. Humphreys's staff awakened to the grip of a hand that shook his shoulder. A voice asked, "Cavada, are you awake?" Cavada grunted that he was. The voice went on, "The General wishes you to ascertain the Regiment on picket that is to be relieved by one from our Division." "Who am I to ask?" mumbled Cavada. "I don't know," the voice replied. "What regiment am I to relieve?" asked Cavada. "I don't know," said the voice, and then it spoke no more.[1]

Cavada stood, stretched, and looked around. A light rain or heavy mist had wet the trampled grass around him, and in the dim light he was able to make out the dark forms of his comrades sleeping nearby. Here and there he could see saddle horses cropping grass among the sleeping men. Nearby, beneath two large trees that loomed above him was the soggy, blue division flag that marked the headquarters of the Second Division, Third Corps, its white diamond mostly concealed within its folds. The flag "drooped heavily from its staff—weary, weary, weary!"[2]

As Cavada collected himself, another voice growled from beneath a rubber poncho, "General Birney—find out." With these terse instructions the captain caught his horse, Brickbat, which stood in a briar patch by a nearby rail fence, tightened the cinch, mounted stiffly, and posted through still sleeping regiments toward some distant campfires. After some searching, he found Birney's headquarters and got the information he sought from a staff officer. Then, guided by the two large trees that marked his own headquarters site, Cavada picked his way back toward his starting place. By now the light was stronger, revealing dark masses of distant woods and hills, and the regiments along his route began to stir. Suddenly a bugle blared, and before its notes faded, others sounded the summons to arise, their brazen tones underscored by the rattling and thumping of infantry drums. The Third Corps and its

1

2

3

4

5

6

7

*1. Brig. Gen. John C. Caldwell
(National Archives)
2. Brig. Gen. John Gibbon
(National Archives)
3. Maj. Gen. David B. Birney
(National Archives)
4. Brig. Gen. Andrew A. Humphreys
(National Archives)
5. Brig. Gen. James Barnes* (MOLLUS-MASS/
U.S.A.M.H.I., *Carlisle Barracks, Pa.)*
*6. Brig. Gen. Romeyn B. Ayres
(National Archives)
7. Brig. Gen. Samuel W. Crawford
(National Archives)*

comrades in the Army of the Potomac awakened to this special day in history.[3]

The day dawned with a cover of clouds, stratocumulus clouds it was said. About 4:15 A.M. the sun appeared, rising in a blaze of red, red enough to admonish sailors to take warning of foul weather and to remind soldiers familiar with Napoleon's campaigns of the red sun of Austerlitz. Professor Michael Jacobs of Pennsylvania (Gettysburg) College, who recorded the local weather, noted that the morning was a pleasant one with a temperature of seventy-four degrees at 7:00 A.M., somewhat overcast, with a mild breeze from the south. As days go, it was satisfactory for battle.[4]

Perhaps General Meade looked at the sun, recalled accounts of Austerlitz, and saw an omen in it. But probably not—he was not the type to be concerned with omens, and he had other things on his mind. Certainly, he must have viewed the dawning day with mixed feelings and without the composure ascribed to Napoleon. He needed daylight to post his divisions properly and bring up those not yet on the field. But of course the light would also benefit General Lee and permit him to attack before the Federal force was up and deployed, an eventuality greatly to be feared. For all that the Union generals knew, the Army of Northern Virginia was at hand, and almost all of them believed that it equaled the Army of the Potomac in size, if in fact it was not larger. Time was precious to General Meade; he had none to spend in musing over past campaigns or in rest.[5]

Earlier, after his arrival at the cemetery and announcement of his intention to fight at Gettysburg, Meade had walked from the cemetery gatehouse out on Cemetery Hill among the batteries of the First and the Eleventh corps. He could see but little plainly in the moon's faint light, but Confederate campfires must have been visible across the fields east, north, and west of town. About 2:00 A.M., accompanied by Generals Howard and Hunt and Captain Paine, the engineer, he set out for a look at the Federal position. The party rode westerly across Cemetery Hill by Brig. Gen. Adolph von Stein-wehr's division of the Eleventh Corps, crossed the Taneytown Road, and rode on to Cemetery Ridge. They passed by the temporary positions of Doubleday's and Robinson's battered divisions of the First Corps and south by the bivouac of the Third Corps to the vicinity of Little Round Top. While in the First Corps sector about 3 A.M., they met Brig. Gen. George J. Stannard, who was that night's general field officer, and who must have given them a description of the situation on his front. By the time they had ridden the length of Cemetery Ridge there must have been some light in the east, and they could have gotten a feel for the terrain. No one mentioned the noisy Third Corps awakening. It was, perhaps, too commonplace a thing to notice.[6]

Captain Paine sketched a map of the field as they rode along and, at General Meade's direction, marked the position that each corps was to occupy. From this map he made tracings for the corps commanders so that each would know his corps's place in line. Paine was an expert at this—"he could prop a drawing board on the pommel of his saddle and as he rode along sketch a map of the surrounding terrain that would be accurate enough to go right to the engraver."[7]

After riding to the left, General Meade and his party trotted east toward Culp's Hill. Perhaps it was then that correspondent Whitelaw Reid (Agate) saw them:

> Two or three general officers, with a retinue of staff and orderlies, come galloping by. Foremost is the spare and somewhat stooped form of the Commanding General. He is not cheered, indeed is scarcely recognized. He is an approved corps General, but he has not yet vindicated his right to command the Army of the Potomac. By his side is the calm, honest, manly face of General Oliver O. Howard. An empty coat sleeve is pinned to his shoulder—memento of a hard fought battle before.[8]

At this time the Union line east of the Baltimore Pike probably extended only as far as Wadsworth's division's right, the crest of Culp's Hill, and Wadsworth's line fronted north toward the town. There was a gap in the line between the hill's crest and Rock Creek at the Baltimore Pike. Williams's division of the Twelfth Corps was beyond Wolf Hill east of the creek. This division had come into the Gettysburg area late in the afternoon of 1 July but had left the Baltimore Road east of Rock Creek and moved north toward the Hanover Road along Wolf Hill, the hill mass that rises so prominently east of what became the main battlefield area. Williams's vanguard met Confederate skirmishers as it approached Hanover Road but did not become heavily engaged. On learning that the First and Eleventh corps had fallen back to Culp's Hill, Williams pulled his men back to the Baltimore Pike area, where they spent the night. Williams's division advanced north again next morning and again encountered a Confederate force east of Rock Creek.[9]

Generals Meade and Hunt rode to the right as far as the point where the Baltimore Pike crossed Rock Creek. Somewhere in the Culp's Hill area they met General Slocum. Slocum spoke to them about the gap on Culp's Hill between the right of the First Corps and the temporary left of the Twelfth Corps's line. He feared that the enemy would exploit this gap in an assault that might soon be made. In response, Hunt spoke to Maj. Thomas W. Osborn, chief of artillery of the Eleventh Corps, who posted three batteries where they could cover the gap temporarily. Geary's division would soon provide the permanent plug.[10]

Brig. Gen. John W. Geary's division had reached the field late in the afternoon of 1 July after the Federal retreat to Cemetery Hill and Hancock's arrival there. Hancock ordered Geary to cover the Union left. Slocum placed that division's Second Brigade (Brig. Gen. Thomas W. Kane's) and Lt. David H. Kenzie's battery (K, Fifth U.S.) in corps reserve and posted the First and Third brigades (Col. Charles Candy's and Brig. Gen. George S. Greene's) on the Cemetery Ridge line between Little Round Top and the Third Corps. Greene's brigade was in the front line, but just before dark Geary sent the Fifth Ohio and 147th Pennsylvania regiments of Candy's brigade, under command of Col. John H. Patrick of the Fifth Ohio, forward and to the left to occupy Little Round Top. They took position there—exactly where is not known—sent skirmishers forward, and remained through the night.[11] Early on the morning of 2 July Geary somehow concluded that his brigades had been relieved by the Third Corps and shifted his division to Culp's Hill and to the gap on the right of Wadsworth's division. Later in the morning Williams's division formed on Geary's right and in doing so established a line that ran from Rock Creek north over Culp's Hill to Cemetery Hill.[12]

General Meade's attention seemed to be absorbed by the right of his line. He believed that the Confederates might attack his position there. In turn, he seriously considered making his own assault on that front. He asked Generals Slocum and Warren to examine the terrain on the right preparatory to an attack that the Army of the Potomac might launch there after the Sixth Corps reached the field. The attack, if made, would probably take place east of Rock Creek and involve the Twelfth Corps, the Fifth, which was just coming on the field, and the Sixth, which was marching toward Gettysburg over the Baltimore Pike.[13]

It must have been the Baltimore Pike, together with the known strength of the Confederate force east of Gettysburg, that riveted Meade's attention to his right that morning. Should the Confederate army attack vigorously and in strength before the Army of the Potomac was up and in place and force it back, the Baltimore Pike might have to serve as the Federals' principal line of retreat. Unlike the Taneytown Road and even the Emmitsburg Road, the Baltimore Turnpike was an improved road, and it led directly to the Union trains and supply point at Westminster and to Baltimore beyond. An army needs a reasonably continuous flow of supplies, and most of those for the Army of the Potomac had to come up over that road. And then, of course, the Sixth Corps was coming in by that route.

Critics of General Meade in later months and years, with the advantages of hindsight, disparaged his seeming preoccupation with his right on the morning of 2 July, if not later that day. But his knowledge of the Army of Northern Virginia's early dispositions must have nourished his concern. He must have known that the Confederate right, Hill's corps, was opposite the northern portion of Cemetery Ridge—the later front of the right of his Second Corps. Its left, he knew, was somewhere along the Hanover Road east of Gettysburg, where Williams's division of the Twelfth Corps had found it the evening before. He knew that Hill's and Ewell's corps were already in his front and that Longstreet's must soon arrive if it was not already there. If General Lee placed Longstreet's divisions opposite or beyond Meade's right and attacked before the Sixth Corps was up, the Army of the Potomac would be in a precarious position indeed.

This was not as farfetched as it later seemed. General Lee, as will be related in Chapter 6, visited Ewell's corps that morning to look into the possibility of a demonstration, if not an attack, against the right of the Federal line, the area of Meade's concern. It was midmorning before he determined against it. And it was about the time of Lee's decision, or perhaps a little later, that Slocum and Warren finished their reconnaissance of the Union right and reported to Meade that the terrain there was not suitable for a Federal assault. Now Meade's attention could be directed elsewhere.[14]

There was constant movement within the Federal position throughout the day. The most pronounced early activity occurred, of course, with the posting of the several corps and their divisions. Geary's division was one of the first to move—it shifted from its position in the Little Round Top area to Culp's Hill shortly after daybreak—about 5:00 A.M. Since no mention was made of that movement's disrupting the approach of the Second Corps, the division must have moved across the Taneytown Road before the van of the Second Corps reached the Federal position.[15]

The Second Corps was the first major reinforcement to reach the field on 2 July. Gibbon saw that the corps was stirring at first light. Before they had to march, some men tried to clean some of the night's accumulation of dust off themselves, and officers encouraged those with rations to eat heavily. There was an inspection of arms, and in due course the corps took to the road.[16] The Taneytown Road was narrow and rough and could not carry an abundance of traffic. To make the most efficient use of it, the corps vehicles and artillery used its crown while the infantry walked to the sides.[17] Once the march was under way, Gibbon likely rode on ahead to find out where the corps was to go. He found General Meade in a field northeast of his headquarters site, the widow Lydia Leister's house. This small frame building was beside the Taneytown Road behind Cemetery Hill.[18] Meade instructed Gibbon to place his corps east of the Taneytown Road near Granite Schoolhouse Lane. The Second Corps massed there facing toward the Union right, its back to Cemetery Ridge, and it remained there approximately an hour.[19]

While waiting there the men of the Second Corps heard their colonels or adjutants read General Meade's circular of 30 June. It exhorted the soldiers of the army to strive for victory and authorized corps and other senior commanders to order the deaths of those who failed to do their duty.[20] It was at this time that the men of the Philadelphia Brigade got their first chance to view their new commander, Brig. Gen. Alexander S. Webb, under such formal conditions. Webb, new to his star and enthusiastic, elaborated on the circular. He asked the men of the brigade to do their duty and threatened to shoot anyone caught leaving the line of battle. In turn, he asked the men of the brigade to shoot him if he failed to do his duty; and there were surly fellows, no doubt, who muttered a willingness to oblige him.[21]

The First and Second divisions of Sykes's Fifth Corps trudged wearily into the fields to the east of Gettysburg, beyond Wolf Hill, about 7:00 A.M. They had halted to rest along the Hanover Road sometime in the wee hours of the morning, the corps stretching then from Bonnaughtown to McSherrystown.[22] The corps took to the road again at daybreak and in time turned off the Hanover Road at the E. Deardorff farm on Brinkerhoff Ridge about two miles east of the town. Barnes's and Ayres's divisions massed there on the right of Williams's division, which had returned to that area during the morning from the Baltimore Pike. Brig. Gen. Thomas H. Ruger's brigade was skirmishing with Confederates screening Ewell's left, and some of the Fifth Corps deployed to help out Ruger's people.[23] Capt. Frank C. Gibbs's battery (L, First Ohio Volunteer Light Artillery) dropped trail in a wheat field between the Fifth Corps's main line and skirmish line and was supported by the Eighteenth Massachusetts Regiment of Tilton's brigade.[24] The Ninth Massachusetts Regiment of Sweitzer's brigade, also of Barnes's division, deployed in a skirmish line south of the Deardorff buildings facing north or northwest and remained there the rest of the day.[25] Ayres's division squeezed between the Twelfth Corps and Barnes's division, and both of the Regular brigades became lightly engaged on the skirmish line.[26]

The Fifth Corps's stay east of Wolf Hill turned out to be a short one. Sykes reported that the position on the right was thought to be too extended, and so it was.[27] It was appropriate, perhaps, so long as General Meade contemplated an assault against the Confederate left; but once that plan was abandoned, Meade could not afford to have an infantry corps on Brinkerhoff Ridge so far from the army's main position. Therefore, at about 10:00 A.M. Sykes's First and Second divisions, leaving the Ninth Massachusetts Regiment behind,[28] withdrew south by way of farm roads that led to the Baltimore Pike.[29] On reaching the pike, they turned right toward Gettysburg, crossed Rock Creek, and filed into the fields between the creek and Granite Schoolhouse Lane.[30] The Third Division, Crawford's, brought up the corps's rear. Unlike the First and Second divisions, it did not halt in the fields east of the town; it marched directly to the assembly area west of Rock Creek and at least some of its units stacked arms on the G. Musser farm. There, at noon or shortly thereafter, the men had their first good meal since leaving Frederick.[31]

Williams's division pulled back also. It withdrew to the Baltimore Pike, crossed Rock Creek, and established a line between the lower crest of Culp's Hill and Rock Creek, there forming the right of the Twelfth Corps.[32] Williams's division was reinforced there that morning by Brig. Gen. Henry H. Lockwood's brigade, a new addition to the Twelfth Corps, which had just arrived over the Baltimore Pike.

Lockwood's brigade merits some special attention here because of the role that it was to play later in the day. This brigade had only two regiments, but they were as large as they were inexperienced. One was the First Maryland [Regiment] Potomac Home Brigade, one of four such units of like designation that had been recruited to guard the Potomac Valley, the B & O Railroad, and Federal interests in Maryland. The other was the 150th New York Regiment. It had been raised in Dutchess County, New York, and enlisted at the sheriff's office in Poughkeepsie under a banner bearing the legend, "Come in out of the draft." Organized in 1862, the regiment under Col. John H. Ketcham moved to Baltimore, where it garrisoned that city until June 1863.[33] At that time the two regiments were brigaded under Lockwood and transported to Frederick to join the Twelfth Corps. The brigade moved with the corps, or more properly behind it, for it could not keep up with its hardened comrades, and bivouacked at Littlestown on the night of 1 July. It continued on to Gettysburg on 2 July, and Lockwood reported there to General Williams, the acting corps commander.[34] Lockwood's arrival created a small but vexing problem for Williams. The brigade was intended for Williams's division. But if it were so assigned, Lockwood, who outranked General Ruger but lacked his field experience, would command the division so long as Williams was acting corps commander. To prevent this, the legalistic Twelfth Corps commander adopted the transparent subterfuge of employing Lockwood's force as a separate brigade within the corps, not a part of the division.[35] Although Lockwood's men were short on campaign experience, they were well disciplined and excited about the prospects of a battle. Time would show them to be an asset to the corps.

General Meade's decision to abandon the projected assault from his right and his shift of the Fifth Corps to a reserve position behind the Union center freed the Second Corps for use on Cemetery Ridge.[36] This in turn made Brig. Gen. John C. Robinson's division and Stannard's brigade, both of the First Corps, available for posting on the reverse slope of Cemetery Hill in support of the Eleventh Corps. Robinson's division had fought valiantly and well on 1 July near the Mummasburg Road and had sustained heavy casualties, but Stannard's brigade was composed of five nine-month regiments whose term of enlistment was just about up without their having seen a battle. The Vermonters had been assigned to the First Corps during the campaign but had not overtaken it until after the fighting on 1 July. Then, when Stannard reached Gettysburg and tried to report to Brig. Gen. Thomas A. Rowley, the acting division commander, Rowley was already asleep and his aides refused to disturb him.[37] Two regiments of the brigade were back guarding the train, and someone posted the three at hand on the field near the Copse of Trees.[38]

The night of 1 July had passed quietly for the tired men of the First Corps on Cemetery Ridge. In the morning, when their relief became available, they shifted across the road to their new position in support of the Eleventh Corps.[39] There they received rations and ammunition. Stannard's men got their rations from brigade wagons that Lt. Charles Field, the commissary officer, had brought forward contrary to the order that would have sent them to Westminster.[40]

The new Second Corps front on Cemetery Ridge extended from Cemetery Hill, where it is crossed by the Taneytown Road, south through Ziegler's Grove, by the Copse of Trees, and south along the ridge crest toward the George Weikert house. It is hard to know precisely how far south it reached because the location of the line was temporary. Suffice it to say that Hancock's Second Corps, which on 30 June numbered 927 officers and 11,436 enlisted infantrymen "present for duty equipped," manned a line nearly a mile in length from flank to flank and rendered that portion of the ridge secure.[41]

Brig. Gen. Alexander Hays's Third Division, whose insignia was a blue clover leaf or trefoil (he called his men the Bluebirds), was on the corps right and probably was the first of the Second Corps to form on the ridge. As the division moved to its position, an ambulance carrying a stretcher red with fresh blood passed by Willard's brigade. In the hours before casualties became commonplace, it was a sobering sight for the relatively green men of this brigade, a startling omen of things to come. Hays placed the division's right in Ziegler's Grove, a crescent-shaped area of woods that ran two hundred yards along the crest of the ridge between the Brian (Bryan) buildings and Cemetery Hill. Although the grove was shallow, it must have enhanced the formidable appearance of the north end of the ridge when viewed from the Confederate lines. The grove's twenty feet of elevation and the batteries on Cemetery Hill to its right rear gave it considerable strength, but it had a measure of vulnerability. Unlike the northern slope of the hill, it had few buildings in front of its base to break enemy formations in an assault. Should the Confederates wish to risk the casualties, batteries might be posted between the town and Seminary Ridge that could enfilade it from the north.[42]

Lt. George A. Woodruff's battery (I, First U.S.) of six Napoleons took position along the west front of the grove with its left piece just north of the Brian house. This battery would have stretched across most of the grove's west front. The 108th New York Regiment of Col. Thomas A. Smyth's brigade supported it from a line immediately behind the guns, so close that its line was said to have been between the guns and their limbers. Woodruff protested to no avail that the 108th would be in his way and that his men could take care of their own front. Although some of the men of the 108th helped the battery's cannoneers, the regiment's role in the battle was a passive one. It ought to have been one of the least envied of the regiments at Gettysburg. It could only rest prone in line while the shot and shell attracted by Woodruff's guns and by the position itself whizzed in on it and ricocheted among the trees of the grove. Figuratively at least, the 108th did not fire a shot in anger during the battle, yet it sustained 50 percent casualties.[43] How its men must have sweated, how they must have prayed, how they must have cursed Hays! Most of the remaining regiments of Smyth's brigade were more actively employed. The First Delaware, Fourteenth Connecticut, and Twelfth New Jersey regiments occupied the wall just in front of the ridge line running south from the Brian barn and had skirmishers to the front. The Tenth New York Regiment, only ninety-eight strong, was posted in the division's rear to act as its provost guard.[44]

Hays's two other brigades had other tasks. Col. Samuel S. Carroll's brigade rested in column in the low ground between the Taneytown Road and Ziegler's Grove fronting north rather than west in order to plug the gap between Cemetery Ridge and Cemetery Hill. Its location was testimony to the concern that Meade, Hancock, and others had for the Union center. As the day wore on, the Fourth Ohio Regiment occupied a skirmish line west of Ziegler's Grove, and in the late afternoon the Eighth Ohio had a picket line across the division's front. The Eighth Ohio's commander, Lt. Col. Franklin Sawyer, had orders to place four companies on his advance line, support them with his remaining six companies, and hold the line to his last man. Sawyer obeyed his orders.[45]

In his report of the battle Hancock wrote of sharp skirmishing on the morning of 2 July, particularly in front of Hays's division.[46] Col. George L. Willard's brigade was heavily involved in this action. Willard had four New York regiments: the Thirty-ninth, 111th, 125th, and 126th, reasonably large units whose combined strength exceeded 1,600 officers and men. But they had an unfortunate past and were butts of some derision. Ten months before, when all but the Thirty-ninth were new to the service and so inexperienced that some men scarcely knew how to load and fire their muskets, they had been gobbled up by Stonewall Jackson in the ignominious surrender of the 12,000-man garrison at Harpers Ferry. The Confederates paroled them, and they spent their parole at Camp Douglas, Illinois. When exchanged, the regiments returned to Washington, where they were organized as a brigade under Brig. Gen. Alexander Hays, a West Pointer from the Old Army. Hays commanded and trained them until the Gettysburg campaign, when they were assigned to the Second Corps, and Hays then received command of the Third Division of that corps. Even then the Third Brigade, now commanded by Colonel Willard, still smarted under the stigma of Harpers Ferry and was uneasy in its new assignment.[47]

Perhaps Hays believed that a turn on the skirmish line would be good experience for Willard's brigade. Skirmishing was a perpetual element of the battle scene, so much a matter of course that reports and descriptions of battles usually ignored it. According to the drill manuals men on the skirmish line functioned in groups of four, the habitual interval between men within each group being about five paces. Between these groups the manuals prescribed a space of up to forty yards. Such a line might cover the front of an entire army. Skirmishing had an informal quality about it, but like all activities requiring teamwork and interdependence, it was covered extensively in the manuals and must have been practiced on the drill field. A given section of the skirmish line had a reserve force about 150 paces behind it to support it if the line became hard pressed, to replace its casualties, and to supply it with ammunition when needed. The size of the reserve varied with the size of the line that it was to support and the distance of the line from the main body.[48] When skirmish lines deployed as far in advance as some did at Gettysburg, the reserve might be of company size or larger.

Hays's division occupied a key portion of the line and was in something of a hot spot. Although the moderately rolling terrain between the ridges provided some cover, there were no major barriers separating the Union and Confederate forces on Hays's front. One landmark that dominated the disputed ground was the William Bliss farmyard midway between the rival lines. The Bliss buildings, particularly the fortlike brick barn, proved a magnet that skirmishers could not resist.[49]

On the morning of 2 July most of Willard's brigade rested on the reverse slope of Cemetery Ridge with orders to stay out of sight. It was not a bad place to be then, for the morning was pleasant and they could even hear Union army bands playing in the distance.[50] The Thirty-ninth New York did not share this idyll long, for it was one of the first of Hays's units deployed into the disputed ground near the Bliss buildings. The Thirty-ninth was a peculiar organization that had a more colorful history than most of the units of the brigade. It had begun as a flamboyant organization more typical of a fictional European principality than the republic that it was recruited to serve. When first organized, according to regimental accounts, it had three companies of Germans, three companies of Hungarians, and single companies of Italians, Swiss, French, and Iberians. In keeping with the idealism of the day, it took the name "Garibaldi Guards," and its enlisted men wore belted red shirts when doing duty around their camps. But on parade the men wore a distinctive blue uniform faced in red with gold shoulder knots, black leggings, and broad-brimmed "Garibaldi" hats. The hats were trimmed with green cock feathers, reminiscent perhaps of those worn by the Bersaglieri. The regiment made a colorful display and must have attracted a lot of attention on the day when it paraded down Broadway singing the "Marseillaise."[51]

The Thirty-ninth originated in great part in the fertile mind of its first colonel, Frederick D'Utassy (born Frederick Strasser), from Vienna or elsewhere within Franz Josef's heterogeneous empire. D'Utassy claimed to have been a comrade of Kossuth and had gained entrée into New York society as a language teacher. He led his regiment at Bull Run, Cross Keys, and, finally, Harpers Ferry, where against his protests he was forced to surrender it but not before its rifles were broken and its colors concealed within his personal baggage to save them from capture. That was D'Utassy's peak. Soon after, his free and easy ways led him to trial on an assortment of charges involving peculation, and he was cashiered and sent to Sing Sing prison. But all that was in the past. On 2 July 1863 the Thirty-ninth served without its colonel, its finery, and its vivandières and consisted of a four-company battalion under the steady, less colorful Maj. Hugo Hildebrandt.[52]

Hildebrandt took the Thirty-ninth out to the north, or right, side of the Bliss farmyard.[53] Probably because the entire battalion went forward, Hildebrandt took its colors along. When Colonel Willard noticed this, he saw "the needless peril of their loss" and sent out Lt. Lyndon H. Stevens of his staff to bring the flags back to the main line. This the lieutenant did after an exciting ride during which "he was a fair target for 100 rifles or more."[54] The Thirty-ninth engaged the Confederate skirmishers in their front but not aggressively enough to suit General Hays. He decided to give the Thirty-ninth some close personal attention and asked for an orderly to ride forward with him. One man, identified only as a Corporal Carroll of the Fifth New York Cavalry, was detailed to go. Hays asked Carroll if he was a brave man. Carroll, who, like many Irish soldiers, was deemed quotable, replied, "*Gineral*, if ye's killed and go to hell, it will not be long before I am tapping on the window." Presumably this implied adequate bravery, and Hays and Carroll, followed by two orderlies from the First Ohio Volunteer Cavalry Regiment, rode forward. Hays straightened things out to his satisfaction, and the skirmishing went on.[55]

Hildebrandt and the Thirty-ninth were on the skirmish line for about four hours and suffered twenty-eight casualties. Three companies of the 126th New York under Capt. Charles M. Wheeler were also out that morning and aided in the capture of the Bliss barn.[56] The Bliss buildings then became the province of Smyth's brigade, and the First Delaware Regiment in particular spent most of the day in that area, five hundred yards in front of the main line. The heaviest fighting at the Bliss barn took place late in the day and falls with the action described in Chapter 15.[57]

While the skirmishers on Hays's front popped away, some sharpshooters, either from the First Company of Massachusetts Sharpshooters or the Second Company, Minnesota Sharpshooters (Company L, First Minnesota Volunteer Infantry), provided a diversion for some of the men on the main line. Capt. Benjamin W. Thompson of the 111th New York wrote that after the men of his regiment cleaned their weapons and had been issued their ammunition, they had little to do but lie behind the ridge and wait. (They seemed not to think of entrenching.) Out of curiosity or boredom, some of the officers strolled forward to the crest of the ridge, where they found a sharpshooter behind a stump. He had a special target rifle with a telescopic sight. After some conversation about his work, he suggested that they put their binoculars on a Confederate horseman riding across the fields in the distance. They did so, he took aim and fired, and the rider fell from his horse. Soon after, possibly in response, a shell whistled by the clump of curious officers and fell among the ranks of the 111th New York in their rear. It wounded no one, but it punctured a drum and knocked a knapsack into a bundle of rags.[58]

Capt. Richard S. Thompson of the Twelfth New Jersey Regiment had more to say of these sharpshooters and their work that day. From the Twelfth's position south of Ziegler's Grove he could see a group of sharpshooters armed with target rifles with tripods, who were sniping at Confederates in the Bliss barn seven hundred yards in their front. They had little success for a time, for the Confederates firing from the barn's windows ducked back when they saw smoke from the sharpshooters' rifles and were under cover when the bullets arrived. This prompted a new tactic. The sharpshooters worked in groups of three. All sighted on an opening, one fired, and the other two fired about three seconds later. The targeted Confederate was presumed to take cover when he saw the smoke from the first rifle fired and reappear about the time that the bullets from the other two zipped in. And so the day on Hays's front wore on.[59]

Gibbon's division was on the left of Hays's division and partially separated from it by two Second Corps batteries, each armed with six three-inch Ordnance rifles. The six guns of Capt. William A. Arnold's battery (A, First Rhode Island Light Artillery) nosed over the last seventy yards of a wall that sheltered Hays's first line between the Brian buildings and Arnold's right. Lt. Alonzo H. Cushing's battery (A, Fourth U.S.) was to Arnold's left, between it and the Copse of Trees, and in the rear of the area now called "The Angle."[60] The stone wall in front of Arnold's guns jogged to the west off Cushing's right, ran down the slope of the ridge about eighty yards, and then jogged once more at The Angle and ran south across Cushing's front. The difference in elevation between Cushing's guns and the wall was so slight that the wall section in front of the guns could not be manned by infantry.

Lt. T. Frederick Brown's battery (B, First Rhode Island Light Artillery), with six Napoleons, was to Cushing's left beyond the Copse of Trees at the left of Gibbon's division. Like Cushing's guns, Brown's were back some distance from the fence line that marked the division's front.[61] A total of eighteen pieces of artillery supported Gibbon's line and guarded the Union center.[62]

Brig. Gen. John Gibbon was one of the most prominent officers at Gettysburg, and his importance belied his grade. Gibbon was a native of Philadelphia, but his physician father took the family to North Carolina when Gibbon was quite young. John Gibbon entered West Point a seeming Southerner and graduated in the class of 1847 along with future-Confederates A. P. Hill and Henry Heth. Like many officers of his generation, he served briefly in Mexico and against the Seminoles. While a lieutenant of artillery, Gibbon spent five years at West Point as an instructor in artillery practice. In the course of that assignment he prepared *The Artillerist's Manual*, the standard work on artillery practice and materiel in the Civil War period.

Gibbon left West Point for Utah before the war to command Battery B, Fourth U.S. Artillery. When the war came, though a nominal North Carolinian, he remained loyal to the Union. He led his battery east but left it in the fall of 1861 to become chief of artillery of Maj. Gen. Irvin McDowell's division. The battery served with distinction in the First Corps of the Army of the Potomac. Gibbon became a brigadier general in May 1862 and took command of a brigade of infantry regiments from the Midwest. He whipped it into shape, and it gained the reputation of being one of the best brigades in the Army of the Potomac. It earned the name "Iron Brigade" for its showing at South Mountain and achieved further distinction for its fight along the Hagerstown Road at Antietam and then, without Gibbon, in McPherson's Woods at Gettysburg on 1 July. Gibbon was wounded at Fredericksburg but back with his division in time for Chancellorsville. He was thirty-six years old at Gettysburg and had brown hair, a reddish moustache, and a cropped beard. Col. Theodore Lyman described him as "the most American of Americans, with his sharp nose and up-and-down manner of telling the truth, no matter whom it hurts." He seemed a rock to Lyman: "a tower of strength he is, cool as a steel knife, always, and unmoved by anything and everything." But there was another side to the man, one not cultivated at West Point or with a battery of regulars. On the morning of 3 July, after his adventures of the day before, he wrote to his wife, his "darling Mama," to tell her that he was still well, that God had been good to him, and that she should kiss the children for him and write often.[63]

Gibbon's division formed with Webb's brigade on its right. This brigade had four Pennsylvania regiments, the Sixty-ninth, Seventy-first, Seventy-second, and 106th. Of these only the Sixty-ninth was in the forward line, behind the low wall to the left front of Cushing's battery and in front of the Copse of Trees. Any rounds fired by the Confederates at Cushing's battery would come near it, and any rounds fired back by Cushing's guns, in turn, would pass close to its flank. The position of the Sixty-ninth seemed an unpleasant one to occupy.[64]

The Sixty-ninth Pennsylvania was an Irish regiment. Just before it began active service, it made a special effort to get the numeral "sixty-nine," in admiration of the Sixty-ninth New York State Militia, which had won fame at Bull Run. Being Irish, it carried a green flag with the Pennsylvania arms on one side and Irish symbols—a wolfhound, a sunburst, and a round tower— on the other. Its colonel at Gettysburg was Dennis O'Kane; its strength, 258.[65]

The brigade's other three regiments formed behind the crest of the ridge, probably behind the Copse of Trees and to the left of the caissons of Cushing's battery. Webb had at least four companies on the skirmish line during the day—A and B of the 106th and A and I of the Seventy-second. All four were under the command of Capt. John J. Sperry of the 106th. Sometime late in the morning General Meade rode up to Webb and asked about the strength of the enemy in his front. Webb, new to his job and ambitious, volunteered to find the answer to the question by advancing with his entire brigade. "No, no!" Meade must have hurriedly replied; a brigade was too large a force for such work and might bring on a general engagement, something that he wanted to postpone if possible until the Sixth Corps was up. Instead, then, Webb sent only Company B of the 106th to do the job. The company crossed the Emmitsburg Road and made its way to a field having a triangular area of woods, probably Spangler's Woods, on its south side. There it found the enemy troops from either Perry's Florida brigade or Wright's Georgia brigade, in force. This done, the company fell back to the skirmish line near the Emmitsburg Road.[66]

Alexander S. Webb, age twenty-eight, was a young man of talent and ability, born into a family of distinction. His grandfather had been an officer on George Washington's staff during the Revolutionary War; and his father, James Watson Webb, had been a Regular Army officer when a young man, became an influential New York newspaper owner and editor, and was appointed as minister to Brazil. It is likely that young Webb was at home with men of authority. After graduating from West Point in 1855, he was commissioned in the artillery and served against the Seminoles and as a professor of mathematics at the Military Academy. At the war's outbreak he was at Fort Pickens, but he was able to get back to the Washington area in time to participate in the battle of Bull Run. Subsequently he served on the staff of Hunt's predecessor, Brig. Gen. William F. Barry, and as inspector general of the Fifth Corps. He had a compact build, a bronzed complexion, dark hair and beard (a goatee), and a "handsomely molded head." Col. Charles S. Wainwright, chief of artillery of the First Corps, a friend and social peer of Webb in New York, thought him one of the "most conscientious, hard working and fearless young officers that we have." Before the war ended, Webb became a division commander and chief of staff of the Army of the Potomac and was badly wounded. In later life he became president of the City College of New York. Although he was young, Webb was a good man to command a brigade at the Union center.[67]

Gibbon's Third Brigade was on Webb's left, between it and Brown's battery. Its commander, Col. Norman J. Hall, was a Regular Army officer of great expectations. He was a native of New York who entered West Point from Michigan and graduated with the class of 1859. Hall received a commission in the artillery and was stationed at Fort Moultrie, near Charleston, just before the war began. His presence there resulted in his being detailed to escort Confederate commissioners to Washington for a conference prior to the opening of the conflict, and he was at Fort Sumter when the firing began. Subsequent good work as chief of artillery of Hooker's division and on McClellan's staff during the Peninsular campaign led to the colonelcy of the Seventh Michigan Regiment in July 1862. Although wounded at Antietam, he was able to take command of his brigade when his predecessor as commander, Brig. Gen. Napoleon T. Dana, was wounded, and he commanded it in the assault on Marye's Heights at Fredericksburg and at Chancellorsville. Hall's rapid rise suggests that he was an unusually capable young man and that he might be expected to wear a star or two before the end of the war. But Gettysburg was to be his last battle, and deserved promotions eluded him. Ill health forced his resignation from the volunteer service in 1864, and he died in 1867 at the age of only thirty.[68]

As soon as the First Corps troops vacated his portion of Cemetery Ridge, Hall formed his brigade on Webb's brigade's left, with the Fifty-ninth New York and the Seventh Michigan in the forward line down beside the Sixty-ninth Pennsylvania. The Seventh Regiment was on the left.[69] These were small regiments with less than 350 men combined and, therefore, must have had a front of a little more than one hundred yards. Hall's remaining three regiments, the Nineteenth and Twentieth Massachusetts and the Forty-second New York, formed in column in the rear. The forward regiments stretched behind the remnants of the rail fence that prolonged the wall in front of the Copse of Trees. The men converted it into a rudimentary breastwork by heaping the rails into a long, low pile. Hall's line had thickets in its front that provided it with a measure of concealment but in doing so limited its field of fire.[70]

The regiments in the rear did little to strengthen the position. The Twentieth Massachusetts had one shovel and used it to heap up a mound about a foot high that might have stopped a bullet "if a little weary of flight." Both the Twentieth and Forty-second regiments had skirmishers to the front throughout the day.[71] The Twentieth's colonel was Paul J. Revere, a direct descendant of the famous patriot; and one of its captains was Oliver Wendell Holmes, Jr., who had been wounded at Fredericksburg and had not yet returned to duty. In contrast, the Forty-second New York had been sponsored by Tammany Hall and had been led off to war by its Grand Sachem. But that was long in the past, and at Gettysburg it numbered fewer than two hundred officers and men and was commanded by Col. James E. Mallon.[72]

Gibbon's First Brigade, commanded by Brig. Gen. William Harrow, formed the division reserve. Harrow was the odd man in the division's command structure. At forty he was significantly older than Hall and Webb and somewhat older than Gibbon. Unlike them, he was not a professional soldier, and it can be assumed that he was less "military" than they in deportment and conduct and that he was somewhat mellowed by age. His life bore some similarity to that of President Lincoln, with whom he was acquainted. He was a native of Kentucky and had practiced law in Illinois and Indiana. He entered the army as a captain in the Fourteenth Indiana and rose rapidly to the command of that regiment at Antietam and to the command of the brigade at Fredericksburg and Chancellorsville. Harrow became ill on the march to Gettysburg and was unwell on 2 July but remained with the brigade and assumed command of it, saying that he would not "play safe" during a fight.[73]

Col. George H. Ward of the Fifteenth Massachusetts led Harrow's brigade to the field and at Gibbon's instruction had posted it in a close column of regiments somewhere along the Taneytown Road near the Brown house. The

Nineteenth Maine headed the column, followed in turn by the First Minnesota, the Fifteenth Massachusetts, and the Eighty-second New York. The men rested there, arms stacked, disturbed only by some random shelling, probably directed at one of the batteries on the ridge, that killed one private and wounded a sergeant.[74]

Caldwell's division was on the left of the Second Corps. The division's right must have been somewhere west of the later site of the Pennsylvania State Memorial and the more distant Jacob Hummelbaugh house. Its front extended south along the ridge in the direction of the George Weikert farmyard and Little Round Top. Caldwell's people could look directly west 1,000 yards at the high ground along the Emmitsburg Road that was to figure so largely in the day's events and at the Rogers, Klingle, and Sherfy buildings there. The ridge sloped west from their position about three hundred yards to a swale containing the northern reaches of Plum Run, many rocks, and a thicket. The thicket extended left along the course of the run seven hundred yards to the Trostle farmyard and Trostle's lane. A fence ran parallel to the division's front at a distance of about a hundred yards. The fence could have strengthened the position, but since no one mentioned it, it is likely that it was torn down early on 2 July. Thus, Caldwell's division was on a portion of the ridge that could have provided it with a good defensive position if improved with entrenchments and artillery support.

Maj. Gen. Israel Richardson had commanded this division in the morasses of the Peninsula and in its assaults on Antietam's Bloody Lane, where he fell with a mortal wound. Hancock succeeded him and directed its assault on the Sunken Road at Fredericksburg and commanded it at Chancellorsville. John C. Caldwell, commander of its First Brigade, received command of the division when Hancock took command of the Second Corps.

Caldwell was born in Vermont in 1833, graduated from Amherst, and served as principal of an academy at East Machias, Maine, for five years preceding the onset of the Civil War. His brief biography suggests no special prewar interest or involvement in military matters. But somehow Caldwell made his mark, for in November 1861 he became colonel of the Eleventh Maine Regiment and took it off to the Army of the Potomac and the Peninsular campaign. He must have done well in this campaign, for in April 1862 he became a brigadier general and received command of the First Brigade, First Division, Second Corps. He led it through subsequent battles and by June 1863 had become one of the most experienced brigade commanders in the Army of the Potomac.[75] It was no surprise, then, that Caldwell succeeded Hancock as commander of the First Division, Second Corps. It seems significant, however, that in spite of the fact that Caldwell outranked Gibbon, Meade ordered Gibbon rather than Caldwell to take command of the corps when Hancock left it temporarily to go to Gettysburg.

Unlike the other infantry divisions of the Army of the Potomac, Caldwell's had four brigades, all small. Caldwell formed his division on the ridge in three "columns of regiments by brigades." Hancock must have prescribed the nature of this formation, for it was similar to that of Gibbon's division. Each brigade was a block of regiments, two or more lines in depth, with a close interval of six paces between regiments in line from front to rear. It was not a formation for attack or defense—its depth and compactness would have restricted its firepower and rendered it vulnerable to artillery fire. It seems likely that Caldwell's formation was a temporary one and that the division would be deployed for battle after the situation became more clear.[76]

The remaining battery of the Second Corps was in position on Caldwell's front. This was Battery B, First New York Light Artillery, traditionallly called "Pettit's Battery," after Capt. Rufus D. Pettit, a former commander. Lt. Albert S. Sheldon led the battery to Gettysburg with the Artillery Reserve, and then for some reason, the battery and its four twelve-pounder Parrotts were transferred to the Second Corps and placed under the command of Capt. James McK. Rorty.[77]

It is likely that Caldwell's division formed with Col. John R. Brooke's Fourth Brigade on its right. Col. Patrick Kelly's Second Brigade was in its center, Rorty's Parrotts were next in line, and Cross's First Brigade was on the left. The Third Brigade, Zook's, was directly in Kelly's rear.[78] Cross's brigade had five lines, Kelly's two, Zook's five, and Brooke's probably five also. Caldwell's front was that of three small regiments and a four-gun battery—probably no more than five hundred yards in length from flank to flank.[79]

Of Caldwell's four brigade commanders, General Zook and Colonel Cross have received the greatest attention. Samuel Zook had been a prominent man in civilian life. Born forty-two years earlier, he was reared near Valley Forge, Pennsylvania, and apparently absorbed some of the character of that historic place. He had long been interested in militia affairs, though he seems not to have served in the War with Mexico. He developed a professional interest in telegraphy—and he is said to have made some later discoveries in the new field of applied electricity—that took him to New York in 1848, and in 1861 he was president of the Washington and New York Telegraph Company. As lieutenant colonel of the Sixth New York State Militia, Zook took that regiment into three months of active service. When it was over, he assisted in raising the Fifty-seventh New York, became its colonel, and took it to the Army of the Potomac. He commanded the Third Brigade of the First Division at Fredericksburg as a colonel but afterward became a brigadier general with a date of rank prior to the battle. Although wounded at Fredericksburg, he recovered in time to take part in the battle of Chancellorsville. Zook had the reputation of being a firm disciplinarian, a man without fear, who hated cowardliness and sham. Although good hearted in the eyes of those who knew him well, he had little patience with those who he believed were not doing their duty. He could be blunt and severe.[80]

Unlike Zook, Col. Edward E. Cross was a controversial figure. Cross was born in Lancaster, New Hampshire, in 1832 and went to work in a printing office at an early age. In time he went to Cincinnati, where he worked as a reporter for the *Atlas* and editor for the *Times*. But Cincinnati was too placid for a young man of Cross's temperament, and he left it for the mining business in Arizona. During his brief stay there, he fought a duel, and then in Mexico he fought another—this one with swords, unlike the earlier one, which had been with rifles. He survived them both and in 1861 became an officer in the army of Mexico's liberal party. His service there must have been short, for when the Civil War came, he returned to New Hampshire and became colonel of its Fifth Regiment. He led the Fifth on the Peninsula and in subsequent campaigns, and after Caldwell's promotion, he became commander of the First Brigade. Perhaps it is something of a tribute to Caldwell that he could command a person like Cross.[81]

Cross was an imposing man, erect, tall in the saddle—"like an Indian," but with a full and tawny beard. He saw that his men were well fed and clothed and tried to instill in them a respect for sanitation. He taught them to aim when they fired their rifles, to regard implicit obedience to orders as a cardinal virtue, and to ignore the idea of retreating. All agreed that he was brave and coolheaded in a fight, and one of his men observed that "if all the colonels in the army had been like him we should never have lost a battle." All this was to his credit.[82]

But there was another side to Cross, one that is suggested by his Dickensian surname. He was prone to jump to conclusions and was by nature highly critical—to the extent that his friends believed his outspokenness, especially in regard to politicians and political measures of which he disapproved, retarded his advancement.[83] And there were those who disliked him for himself or because he offended them in achieving his goals. The officers and men of the 148th Pennsylvania Regiment, new to military service and to his brigade, considered him a tyrant. This feeling came to a head on 30 June, when Cross summoned the officers of the 148th to meet Col. H. Boyd McKeen of the veteran Eighty-third Pennsylvania Regiment and announced that McKeen would command them in the upcoming battle. Their own colonel was home recovering from a wound received at Chancellorsville, and Lt. Col. Robert McFarlane commanded in his stead. McKeen was an officer of experience and proven competence, but the strength of his regiment had dwindled to 175. McFarlane, in contrast, was short on experience but was in command of nearly five hundred officers and men. Cross's action was highly logical, but the officers and men of the 148th were insulted by it and never forgave him.[84]

Apart from all of this, at Gettysburg Cross had a presentiment of death and was a troubled man. On 28 June he remarked that the coming battle would be his last and asked Lt. Charles A. Hale of his staff to take care of his belongings after he was killed. He spoke of this to Hale again on the twenty-ninth and became irritated when Hale seemed to make light of his concern.

Yet again on 2 July Cross reminded Hale of his request as the brigade approached the field, but he seemed to forget it in the excitement that followed. Finally, that afternoon, when the artillery was firing and it was apparent that a fight would soon begin, Cross took a new silk handkerchief from his pocket. He folded it and handed it to Hale with the request that Hale tie it around his head. Cross had worn a red bandana around his head in previous battles so Hale was not surprised at the request. But he was appalled when he saw that the handkerchief was not red but black.[85]

Patrick Kelly was the commander of a remnant of a brigade, proud but small. His regiment was the Eighty-eighth New York, the "Faugh a Ballaghs," and he had commanded it since the Peninsular campaign, first as a lieutenant colonel and finally as its colonel. On Gen. Thomas Meagher's departure after Chancellorsville, Kelly succeeded to the command of the Irish Brigade and held it until he was killed near Petersburg in 1864. Kelly never received a star, nor was he given a special biographical sketch of the sort accorded generals in New York's memorial volumes. To his men, though, "he was a father to the brigade, as he was always to his own regiment, a brave, gentle, splendid soldier."[86]

The Irish Brigade, though the smallest in the division, was still one of the best known in the Union army and has remained so. But at Gettysburg it was only a remnant of its former self, a sad reminder of better days and a forceful commentary on a ruinous policy that permitted the recruitment of new units while older and experienced ones were allowed to take their casualties and wither away. The brigade's origins went back to the summer of 1861, when Meagher, one of America's prominent Irish immigrants, and Capt. Robert Nugent of the Regular Army decided to form an Irish brigade. They had been inspired by the return of the Sixty-Ninth New York State Militia from its brief service that had culminated with the battle of Bull Run. Meagher and Nugent had hoped that the proposed brigade's first commander would be Brig. Gen. James Shields, Irish-American hero of the War with Mexico, but Shields was not available. However, Meagher received permission from the State of New York to recruit the brigade and did so.[87]

By autumn 1861 three Irish regiments had been organized—the Sixty-third, Sixty-ninth, and Eighty-eighth New York. Meagher commanded the Eighty-eighth, a unit that had at least four names: the "Connaught Rangers," "Fourth Irish," "Faugh a Ballaghs," and "Mrs. Meagher's Own." In later years Capt. William L. D. O'Grady claimed that a good third of the Eighty-eighth were former British soldiers, veterans of the Crimean War and the Indian Mutiny, and that nearly all of the regiment's officers had been officers or noncomissioned officers in the old Sixty-Ninth New York State Militia.[88] The Sixty-third had less names of record and less of a New York City background than the Eighty-eighth. Two of its companies were from Boston's Irish community, and a third came from Albany. But the Sixty-third was a New York unit by and large, and Irish as well as non-Irish dignitaries presented the regiment with its national colors and a green flag bearing the Irish sunburst.[89]

The Sixty-ninth has been the best known of the three Irish regiments. Although it was not the Sixty-Ninth New York Regiment of Bull Run, it had the same number, many of its officers and men had been with that regiment, and rightly or wrongly the identities of the two seemed to merge. Its new colonel, Robert Nugent, had been a captain of the Thirteenth U.S. Infantry, and its lieutenant colonel, James Kelly, had been a captain in the Tenth U.S. Infantry. Colonel Nugent took his regiment from New York to Washington, where it was joined after a while by the Sixty-third and Eighty-eighth. Nugent commanded all three until March 1862, when Meagher, now a brigadier general, arrived to take command.[90]

The Irish Brigade under Meagher served on the Peninsula and at Antietam. After Antietam two additional Irish regiments, the 116th Pennsylvania and the Twenty-Eighth Massachusetts were assigned to it. The brigade assaulted the Sunken Road position at Fredericksburg and fought on the Federal left at Chancellorsville, accruing casualties as it went along, including 540 at Antietam and 490 at Fredericksburg.[91] After Chancellorsville the green flags waved over only a few survivors of the old regiments. Before the march north, each of the three New York regiments was consolidated into two companies, and their supernumerary officers left the service. Col. Richard Byrnes's Twenty-eighth Massachusetts Regiment had a strength of but 224, and the 116th Pennsylvania became a four-company battalion with a strength of 142.[92] General Meagher left his nominal brigade of scarcely six hundred officers and men in the hands of Colonel Kelly of the Eighty-eighth and went off to other duties.[93]

Like the other corps, the Second had an ambulance train that served it in the field. Lt. Thomas L. Livermore commanded it, and its task was to transport the nonwalking wounded to the corps hospitals in the army's rear. On reaching the field, Livermore sent a dozen ambulances to the rear of each division but parked most of them along the Taneytown Road. This made for a significant number of vehicles there when combined with those of the artillery and the ammunition train that were parked east of the Taneytown Road. Stretcher-bearers went from the ambulances to each brigade to provide direct medical assistance.[94] The ambulances situated, Livermore rode forward to the corps line to get an idea of where he might be needed. Late in the afternoon, when things began to warm up on the left, he rode to Caldwell's front and by Cross's brigade. Cross greeted him in a joking way with the statement, "We shan't want any of your dead carts here today!" A short time later, when the division marched off to the left, Livermore followed to be sure that his bearers were keeping up with their brigades. When satisfied, he left them in charge of the division's ambulance officers and returned to the main line of the corps.[95]

Meade's ace in the hole, the Artillery Reserve, followed the Second Corps to the field. Brig. Gen. Robert O. Tyler, Hunt's principal subordinate, had reached the Second Corps with two of its five brigades on the night of 1 July and moved up with that corps the next morning. When the Second Corps occupied Cemetery Ridge, Tyler parked the nine batteries of the two brigades with him in the fields southeast of the junction of the Taneytown Road and Granite Schoolhouse Lane. About 10:30 A.M. Lt. Colonel Freeman McGilvery joined Tyler with ten more batteries of the remaining three brigades. All told, Tyler had nineteen batteries with 108 pieces at hand to be used to help the corps batteries when they were needed.[96]

Equally important was the supply of ammunition that Tyler's column hauled to the field. Second Lieutenant Cornelius Gillette's wagons carried 23,883 rounds of artillery ammunition to Gettysburg and issued seventy wagonloads of it on the night of 2 July to replace the rounds fired on 1 and 2 July. Altogether the Reserve train issued 19,189 rounds at Gettysburg to the Reserve's batteries and to those of the Second, Third, and Eleventh corps.[97]

The occupation of the Union center by the Second Corps, coupled with the presence of the Third Corps on the left (discussed at length in Chapters 5 and 6) and the massing of the Artillery Reserve and Fifth Corps in the Union rear, made the Army of the Potomac's position seem somewhat secure. At 3:00 P.M. Meade reported to General Halleck that the army was fatigued and that he had delayed attacking in order to allow the Sixth Corps to arrive and to rest the men.[98] Many were able to rest, but a sizable number of men of the Second Corps were on the skirmish line, while others were removing fences that might get in their way, and too few were digging in.[99]

Meanwhile the men of the Fifth Corps in reserve along the Baltimore Pike doctored their sore feet, napped, and bathed in Rock Creek. Since they had arrived after a long march, the roll call would have revealed that there were numerous absentees. Many, like Pvt. Robert G. Carter, had straggled because of blistered feet and, in his case at least, had dallied as well to consume milk and cherry pie given by a farmer's wife.[100] There were also formations at which regimental commanders or adjutants read Meade's circular authorizing the execution of malingerers. At one such formation Col. Patrick H. O'Rorke of the 140th New York, young and new to his command, and Capt. Porter Farley, his adjutant, sat astride their horses in front of the regiment's colors. O'Rorke rode a small brown horse and wore a "soft hat," military cape, and white leather gauntlets. Farley read the circular, and when he finished, O'Rorke made his first and last speech to the 140th. He ended it by saying: "I call on the file closers to do their duty, and if there is a man this day base enough to leave his company, let him die in his tracks. Shoot him down like a dog."[101] Lt. Col. John H. Cain of the 155th Pennsylvania also read the circular and in doing so aroused murmurs of concern. Many men of the 155th had fallen out along the road from exhaustion or other physical problems, and those present feared that they might be punished because of the circular.[102]

There were those who could not or would not rest. The men of Company K, First Pennsylvania Reserves, were excited because they were from Adams County and some were literally in sight of their homes. A few wandered from their assembly area on the L. M. Diehl farm to a hill, probably Culp's Hill or Cemetery Hill, from which they could see their houses in the town, and others who knew nearby farmers went to their homes for food.[103] Officers with horses wandered as far. Some from Fisher's brigade rode to army headquarters to try to find out what was going on and then trotted south along Cemetery Ridge, hurrying back to their regiments as the battle opened.[104]

There were some who rested and even sang. As will be explained in Chapter 10, Brig. Gen. Stephen H. Weed's brigade was held ready to move at Sickles's call and waited for the summons in a loose formation. Weed's headquarters were with the 140th New York, and in a while some of the New Yorkers began to sing. The headquarters party sang "Lorena," "The Virginia Lowlands," "Listen to the Mocking Bird," and "No One to Cherish." Pretty soon the sad lyrics, combined perhaps with tiredness and the afternoon heat, had a depressing and drowsy effect, and the soldiers rested quietly while awaiting their call.[105]

As the Second and Fifth corps whiled away the day awaiting a call to arms, General Meade's strong reserve, the Sixth Corps, trudged to Gettysburg in an endless cloud of dust. A poet wrote:

> In the thickest of the battle,
>   When the cannon's fiery breath,
> Smites many a strong heart, pressing
>   On to victory or to death.
> The foremost in the conflict,
>   The last to say " 'tis o'er,"
> Who know not what it is to yield,
>   You'll find the Old Sixth Corps.[106]

It was not quite that way on 2 July—not yet at any rate. Gen. John Sedgwick, "Uncle John," and his massive corps of about 13,000 officers and men had reached Manchester, Maryland, on the night of 30 June. The corps's march to Manchester had been so rapid that the walking officers and men had joked wryly about wearing out the officers' horses. This haste was in compliance with Meade's orders, no doubt, but some of it might have been stimulated by reports of Confederate cavalry in the area.[107]

In contrast to the preceding day, 1 July was a day of watchful waiting and some rest, a day unique in the recent annals of the corps. Its men rested in a community rife with Unionist sentiment, prosperous, and untouched by the physical ravages of Mars, a virtual Eden to the wearers of the Greek Cross who had campaigned so long in the exhausted Virginia countryside. The presence of so many uniformed visitors in the community awed the residents.

Men, women, and children flocked from miles around to see their brave defenders. It must have been something like a county fair. Of course there were soldiers who took the occasion to drink too much whiskey, but the dissipaters lived to regret their drunkeness. By and large it was a pleasant day.[108]

About 7:30 P.M., as dusk began to cloak the countryside and the men of the corps began to settle in for the night, Lt. Paul A. Oliver of Meade's staff galloped in with a dispatch. He reined up and shouted, "Where is corps headquarters?" to a group of soldiers of the Fifth Wisconsin. He told Sedgwick of the day's events and gave him the order to march his corps to Taneytown at once.[109] Drums and bugles sounded "The General," officers shouted "pack up and fall in!," and the quiet murmur of men at rest swelled to shouts of command, queries, and curses as the corps roused itself, gathered its belongings together, and formed for the march. Some men believed at first that they were going to Westminster to deal with the cavalry they had heard about, but the truth of the matter traveled fast. There were roll calls; and in keeping with the practice of the time, colonels, chaplains, and other officers made speeches of encouragement. Col. James M. McCarter of the Ninety-third Pennsylvania spoke eloquently of "treason's foul foot" that polluted soil dedicated to freedom, of northern mothers whose eyes were gemmed with sparkling tears, who prayed and rededicated their sons to freedom, and even of the spirit of George Washington. He said that should a man fall, the spot would be forever sacred to freedom, and he closed by saying, "Let us go forward then." The Ninety-third and its comrades did, "silently, solemnly and majestically as the ocean tide."[110]

The Third Division, commanded by Brig. Gen. Frank Wheaton in place of John Newton, who had been ordered forward to command the First Corps, was apparently first in the order of march, followed by Brig. Gen. Horatio G. Wright's First Division and the Second Division under Brig. Gen. Albion P. Howe. In accordance with its orders, the corps headed toward Taneytown and marched about seven miles in that direction before the arrival of additional orders changing its destination to Gettysburg and instructing it to come up at all speed.[111]

The corps probably followed country roads toward Taneytown rather than taking the better but less direct route via Westminster. There was no moon early in the evening, and the stars were pale. One farmer, at least, gave some of the men milk from a tub, and they learned from him of the battle that had been fought at Gettysburg. When the destination changed, those who had crossed the Gettysburg-Baltimore Pike had to countermarch to return to it. That manuever, as Longstreet was to experience next day, was more easily ordered than done. Finally, the column turned on to the pike and the hard march began.[112]

It was very long and tiring; the corps shuffled along at route step. When the men quieted down, they could hear sounds of a rural country night quite alien to their condition—the barking of farm dogs, the noises of insects, and even the occasional clanking of cow bells. The moon appeared in time and

That hot, dry, dusty, moonlit night of July 1 presented a scene of weird, almost spectral impressiveness. The roads to the south and southeast of the town flowed with unceasing, unbroken rivers of armed men, marching swiftly, stolidly, silently. Their garments were covered with dust, and their gun barrels gleamed with a fierce brilliance in the bright moonlight. The striking silence of the march, the dust-gray figures, the witchery of the moonbeams, made it seem spectral and awesome. No drum beat, no trumpet blared, no harsh command broke the monotonous stillness of the steady surge forward.[113]

When daylight came, the air was warm, soft, and humid, a promise of heat to come. The marchers, at least those toward the head of the column, halted every few hours to breathe; but the veterans tended to forget these halts in later years. Perhaps they were not worth recalling.[114] As the sun climbed and warmed, the dust welled up from the thousands of foot puffs each second in the powdered road. There was grumbling now and talking. One free spirit in the 119th Pennsylvania must have become increasingly obnoxious by yelling from time to time, "Boys, its rough, but I tell you its regular."[115] When the various Pennsylvania regiments reached the Mason-Dixon Line, a lot of them observed their return home. Some cheered; the drummers of the Ninety-third thumped a quick step, the men took up the cadence, the color guard uncovered the flags, and the men sang "Home Sweet Home."[116]

At Littlestown, nine miles from Gettysburg, signs of the battle began to appear. There were stragglers, of course, and wounded who had been carried there by ambulances and civilians in private rigs. The wounded hoped to be transported by train to Baltimore. In a while, in the distance to the northwest, the men of the Sixth Corps could see smoke and hear the sound of gunfire.[117] General Wright's report mentioned a half hour stop made sometime during the march, probably in the morning after daybreak, so that the men could make coffee. But even this had a sour note for a few. At a break's end some coffee lovers of the 93d Pennsylvania dawdled when told to fall back into ranks. This was not to be tolerated, and their officers gained enmity by walking to the fires and kicking over the pots and their precious contents. Mars will be served.[118]

As Gen. John Buford had thrilled at the sight of the approach of the First Corps about thirty hours before, so others gloried in the Sixth's arrival on the field. The war correspondent Charles Carlton Coffin wrote dramatically, if not accurately:

I was at Meade's headquarters; the roar of battle was louder and grew nearer; Hill was threatening the center; a cloud of dust could be seen down the Baltimore Pike. Had Stuart suddenly gained our rear? There were anxious countenances around the cottage where the flag of the commander-in-chief was flying. Officers gazed with their field glasses. "It is not cavalry, but infantry," said one, "there is the flag, it is the Sixth Corps." We could see the advancing bayonets gleaming in the sun-light. Faces which a moment before were grave became cheerful. It was an inspiring sight.[119]

The arrival of the Sixth Corps must have been no surprise to General Meade; nor should it have been to anyone else at army headquarters. Meade had kept in touch with its progress that day and urged it on.[120] When it drew near, Sedgwick and Lt. Col. Martin T. McMahon, the corps adjutant general, rode ahead for orders while Major Hyde and other staff officers purchased cherry pies from a freckle-faced girl near Rock Creek. Meade was down with Sickles when the Sixth Corps commander arrived so Sedgwick and McMahon rested until the commanding general's return.[121]

As the divisions of the corps reached the Rock Creek area, they filed into the fields then being vacated by the Fifth Corps, which was shifting to the Union left. Water and rest were the corps's first priorities, but the men of one regiment witnessed an interesting thing about this time. A frightened Gettysburgian passed with a wagon loaded with household items. Obviously his house was under fire or had been taken over by one of the armies, and he had small cause for contentment. The men of the 119th Pennsylvania had little empathy for the fellow, but they liked a girl walking beside the wagon, bright-faced and exhibiting courage and resolution—a veritable Joan of Arc. When a shell burst nearby, she exclaimed, "I wish I were a man, I should promptly return and lend my feeble support to the cause of my country." This was almost too much for the soldiers within hearing; they were awed and smitten. One young officer, oblivious to his fatigue, was "impressed beyond restraint." Forgetting that she was the daughter of a fearful father, he declared that if the situation and the girl permitted, he would marry her then and there. But, as it happened, the young people went their separate ways.[122]

Soon after Wheaton's brigade stacked arms, its men were allowed to go to Rock Creek to wash and soak their tired feet. Some of the Fifth Corps was still nearby and some of Sweitzer's Sixty-second Pennsylvania troops had a brief reunion with friends in the 139th Pennsylvania. Minutes later the Sixty-second marched off to its destiny in the Wheatfield.[123]

The arrival of the Sixth Corps in midafternoon meant that all of the infantry of the Army of the Potomac was at hand except for a few units that were guarding the trains. The march of over thirty miles was one of the epic feats of the campaign. In retrospect it can be said that the addition of this large number of fine soldiers to the ranks of the Army of the Potomac at Gettysburg further tipped the scales in its favor and made a victory for General Lee highly improbable.[124]

5

The Third Corps, Morning, 2 July

Capt. George G. Meade, Jr., met his father in the yard of the Widow Leister's house and found the new commanding general in good spirits, his anxiety easing. It was about 9:00 A.M. Both the Second and Fifth corps were at hand and available for action, the Artillery Reserve's batteries and its vital ammunition train were rolling in, and things seemed to be going about as smoothly as they go in large armies. And—best of all—General Lee had not attacked! The general and his novice aide chatted briefly, and, though General Meade was still thinking of launching an assault from his right, he expressed concern about his left. He had ordered General Sickles's Third Corps to relieve Geary's division of the Twelfth Corps and extend the Federal line from the left of the Second Corps to Little Round Top. That seemed plain enough. He left the details of the Third Corps's posting to Sickles, but the morning was getting on and he had heard nothing from the Third Corps. He wondered if all was well.[1]

Therefore, "in his cheery & familiar way" that indicated to his son at least that he was not anxious, he brought their chat to a close by saying, "Now George you just ride down to Sickles" and see if the Third Corps is in position and if General Sickles has anything to report. He also was to tell Sickles where the army's headquarters were located, an indication that insofar as General Meade knew, the headquarters had yet to have any visitors from the Third Corps's staff that morning. Captain Meade posted off on his errand, probably with a feeling of exhilaration and importance. He had recently joined his father's staff, and it was the first time since his arrival that he had been sent upon such a prestigious errand. Truly, this was a lot more exciting than his recent life as a harassed West Point cadet.[2]

Captain Meade trotted down the Taneytown Road, passed the artillery park at Granite Schoolhouse Lane, and probably met batteries of the Artillery Reserve bumping along the road. He found the Third Corps headquarters in tents in an unidentified grove of trees on the west side of the road. It was quiet there; probably most of the staff officers and orderlies were off on errands. He met Capt. George E. Randolph, the young corps chief of artillery, and learned from him that General Sickles was resting in a nearby tent. Captain Meade asked for the information requested by his father; Captain Randolph asked him to wait and entered the general's tent. He emerged from it a few minutes later with the surprising information that the Third Corps was not only not in position but that there was some doubt in General Sickles's mind as to where that position was to be.[3]

Perhaps a higher ranking and more experienced staff officer than young Meade, knowing the army commander's wishes, would have straightened things out on the spot, but the captain did not do so. Captain Meade told Randolph that he would give this report to General Meade and rode hurriedly back to the Leister house no more than a mile away. He found General Meade there talking with several officers and gave him the report. The unwelcome news must have tested the general's cheerfulness. The "Old Snapping Turtle" replied sharply and decisively that the captain was to return to the Third Corps headquarters and tell General Sickles that the Third Corps was to go in on the left of the Second Corps and prolong its line to Geary's position of the night before. This was to be done as rapidly as possible.[4]

When Captain Meade returned to Third Corps headquarters, he found it transformed into a beehive of activity. Its tents were down, and Sickles was mounted with his staff gathered around him. After receiving General Meade's instructions, Sickles replied that his corps would be posted shortly; however, he continued, insofar as he knew, General Geary's division had had no position but was massed. With this observation the general reined his horse away from the staff officer and went on his way. As Captain Meade started his return, Captain Randolph called to him and asked him to relay an invitation to General Hunt to come down and look at the Third Corps's battery positions. Captain Meade rode back to army headquarters.[5]

Probably General Sickles was off to that portion of the front soon to be assigned to Birney's division. Maj. Gen. David Bell Birney was a singular man, whose image, like that of many of his peers, has faded with the passing of time. His father, James G. Birney, was a Kentuckian who had once owned slaves but who became an abolitionist of international reputation. James Birney ran for president twice on the Liberty party ticket and was executive secretary of the American Anti-Slavery Society. At a time when slavery was a burning issue in the Western World, General Birney's father was a very prominent man.[6]

David Birney was born in 1825 in Huntsville, Alabama, where he lived for thirteen years before the family moved to its seat at Danville, Kentucky. He attended Andover Academy and studied law in Cincinnati. He then lived in Michigan until 1848, when he moved to Philadelphia, where he practiced

Meade's headquarters and the Taneytown Road. Stereograph by Alexander Gardner (Library of Congress)

law until the outbreak of the war. Birney belonged to Philadelphia's City Troop, but he had had no real military experience prior to 1861. Through reading and the troop's drills, however, he acquired some knowledge of military matters. When war came, he participated in the organization of a three-month regiment, the Twenty-third Pennsylvania (Birney's Zouaves) and served as its lieutenant colonel. When the Twenty-third reorganized into a three-year regiment, he became its colonel.[7]

Theodore Lyman, who became acquainted with Birney in the post-Gettysburg period, wrote:

> Birney was one who had many enemies, but, in my belief, we had few officers who could command 10,000 men as well as he. He was a pale, Puritanical figure, with a demeanor of unmovable coldness; only he would smile politely when you spoke to him. He was spare in person, with a thin face, light-blue eye, and sandy hair. As a General he took very good care of his Staff and saw they got due promotion. He was a man, too, who looked out for his own interests sharply and knew the mainspring of military advancement. His unpopularity among some persons arose partly from his own promotion, which, however, he de-

*Cemetery Ridge from Little Round Top. Stereograph by Mathew Brady
(Library of Congress)*

served; and partly from his cold covert manner. I always felt safe when
he had the division; it was always well put in and safely handled.[8]

Birney's rise in rank might well have spawned envy, particularly of a man
with pronounced abolitionist antecedents who was cold in personality rather
than comradely. Birney's first star came early for a novice, in February 1862,
and he commanded a brigade in the Peninsular campaign. After Maj. Gen.
Philip Kearny's death at Chantilly in September 1862, he succeeded to the
command of Kearny's division, and his service at Chancellorsville won him a
second star. Although his family credentials might have given him an initial
boost, he proved to be an officer of ability. He was apparently fond of the
trappings of military life. Colonel Wainwright's account of Birney's proces-

sion through Frederick during the march north is something of a comment both on Birney and on others' reactions to him. Birney was then the acting corps commander in Sickles's temporary absence, and he passed through the town at the head of the corps. First came a line or two of mounted orderlies—cavalrymen with drawn sabers—then a band, then General Birney followed by his staff, all in a neat formation, and finally all the Third Corps. Birney's parade gave the officers of the other corps, if not the Third, something to gossip about and elicited the comment from Wainwright that "he certainly means to have all the 'pomp and circumstance of war' he can get. Such feats are not common in this army, and do not take."[9]

Birney's First and Second brigades, under Brig. Gens. Charles K. Graham and J. H. Hobart Ward, straggled into the Gettysburg area on the afternoon and evening of 1 July as described in Chapter 3. They turned right from the Emmitsburg Road at the Wheatfield Road, or perhaps into Trostle's lane, and bedded down in front of Cemetery Ridge, where most spent the night. Graham's brigade stacked arms and dropped packs in the woods south of the George Weikert house, and Ward's brigade and the batteries bivouacked nearby.[10]

Two of Birney's regiments did not share the night's rest. The Sixty-third Pennsylvania of Graham's brigade established a picket line west of the Emmmitsburg Road north of the Wheatfield Road. It erected a breastwork of fence rails somewhere there and remained on picket until late the next afternoon. The Fourth Maine of Ward's brigade had the same duty farther to the right. It stretched behind a fence that paralleled the Emmitsburg Road about 250 yards west of it. The Fourth's line contacted the picket line of the First Corps on its right and touched Buford's cavalry in the Peach Orchard area.[11]

In his report Birney wrote that, in accordance with Sickles's orders, his division relieved Geary's at 7:00 A.M. and formed a line with its left resting "on Sugar Loaf Mountain," a commonly used name for Little Round Top. Its right was on a direct line with the cemetery and connected with Humphreys's division. In short, the line that Birney reported that he established *appears* to have been that desired by General Meade.[12] Later, before the Committee on the Conduct of the War, when the events of 2 July were becoming controversial, Birney changed his story somewhat. He changed the "on" to "at and on" and the time from 7:00 A.M. to 9:00 A.M. Perhaps the change was unintentional and without meaning, or perhaps Birney was attempting to be more precise in his statement to the committee than he had been in his report. On the surface, at least, his later statement might be taken as a more positive declaration of the posting of his left upon the hill rather than at its base. The 9:00 A.M. time suggests that his troops might well have moved on to the hill not as Geary's moved away but as late perhaps as the visit by Captain Meade to Third Corps headquarters. Certainly by midmorning, though, according to both his report and testimony, Birney's division *seemed to be* on the line designated by General Meade.[13]

But was it? Birney's division's deployment that morning was anything but static, and its units were distributed widely within its sector. In retrospect its dispositions seem to have been influenced not only by General Meade's instructions but by Sickles's and Birney's concerns about its position on the army's flank and the perceived need for the Third Corps to protect that flank and to occupy the high ground along the Emmitsburg Road. Early in the morning Birney sent two more regiments to the Emmitsburg Road—the Third Maine of Ward's brigade to the Peach Orchard area to assist the Sixty-third Pennsylvania and the Ninety-ninth Pennsylvania to the area of the Sherfy house, where it deployed at midmorning. At that time, then, of the six line regiments of Ward's brigade, three were out along the Emmitsburg Road, while the three remaining were described only as having been behind a stone wall in woods near the Wheatfield. Probably these regiments were along Plum Run; certainly they were not on Little Round Top.[14]

Graham's brigade spent the night between the George Weikert farmyard on Cemetery Ridge and the three Third Corps batteries parked in the open fields nearby. At daybreak on 2 July, Bucklyn's battery's drivers hitched their six-horse teams to their limbers. As they prepared their breakfasts, an order came for them to limber up and move to the front.[15] Randolph reported that Bucklyn's and Clark's batteries "were placed in position on the line held by General Birney's division, running from near the left of the Second Corps to the base of Signal or Round Top Mountain." Thus, Randolph's description agreed more or less with Birney's about the location of the line occupied. Seeley's battery remained in park and Winslow's and Smith's batteries joined Seeley's when they arrived from Emmitsburg.[16]

Randolph's statement, coupled with those of Birney about the location of Birney's line, reveal, in hindsight at least, that the Third Corps people were interpreting General Meade's instructions quite broadly. Had they taken them more narrowly Birney's division and its guns probably would have occupied ground east of Plum Run and on line with the George Weikert house, the ground occupied later by the Fifth and Sixth corps, and at least the slope of Little Round Top if not its summit. But this was not the line occupied by Captain Randolph's batteries, for aside from Little Round Top itself, which he seems to have eliminated from his consideration, the line east of Plum Run was fronted by woods and offered but limited fields of fire.

As it turned out, Randolph placed Bucklyn's and Clark's batteries in the open fields southwest of the Trostle farmyard, between it and the Peach Orchard and a good five hundred yards in front of the ridge line in the area of the George Weikert house. There they had limited fields of fire west toward the Emmitsburg Road and longer ones south across the Rose farm. These battery positions and those of the infantry that supported them would have been tenable only so long as the enemy did not occupy the high ground in their front, then in the hands of the Third Corps skirmishers and the cavalry. As it was, the position had but little meaning unless it was intended to be a springboard from which to move regiments to support the skirmishers to the front.

Graham's remaining five regiments advanced to the support of Randolph's two batteries and formed behind them in two lines; the Sixty-eighth, 141st, and Fifty-seventh Pennsylvania regiments in the first line and the 105th and 114th in their rear. The batteries might have fired a few rounds off somewhere from this position, but it seems unlikely. The position was a quiet one for Graham's brigade and did not loom large in Third Corps annals.[17] In sum, Graham's brigade's morning position had three characteristics: it was more than five hundred yards in front of the crest of Cemetery Ridge and probably not in the area encompassed by General Meade's instructions; it was dominated by the high ground along the Emmitsburg Road and could be destroyed by Confederate batteries posted there or infantry attacking from that area; and, on the plus side, troops posted there could move quickly to the support of Federal skirmishers along the Emmitsburg Road about five hundred yards to the front in case it was decided to hold that line.

The high ground along the Emmitsburg Road continued to attract attention as the morning passed and skirmishing intensified. Skirmishing increased, it will be seen, because of Anderson's division's occupation of Seminary Ridge off to the right front. In response, the 105th Pennsylvania went forward to the support of the Sixty-third, and the recently arrived Fifth Michigan of de Trobriand's brigade took position there in support of Lt. John H. Calef's (Tidball's) battery.[18]

Calef's battery (A, Second U.S.) was at Gettysburg in support of Gamble's and Devin's cavalry brigades of Buford's division and had been with that division when it opened the battle of 1 July. After the First and Eleventh corps had retreated to Cemetery Hill that afternoon, Buford united the two cavalry brigades in the fields between Cemetery Ridge and Seminary Ridge, from where they could threaten or strike the flank of any Confederate formation that might attempt to assault the Federal position on Cemetery Hill. When evening came and additional Union infantry arrived to extend the Federal line down Cemetery Ridge, the cavalry shifted south to the Peach Orchard area and set up a picket line west along the Wheatfield Road toward Fairfield.[19]

It was said that the cavalry picketed the area all night and that at least two patrols probed to the west. At daylight Capt. Benjamin J. Coffin of the Ninth New York Cavalry led a party from that regiment's Company E to the west. In later years at least, some veterans of the Ninth claimed that this detachment discovered the approach of Longstreet's corps. In the course of this foray Coffin's men captured a black man, said (probably wrongly) to have been a servant of one of Longstreet's officers, who provided them with much valuable information. Later in the morning 1st Sgt. William T. Bradshaw took a half dozen men on patrol west of Pitzer's Schoolhouse. From the high ground beyond Pitzer's Woods, he could see a large force moving into position to the north. It is only logical to assume that these cavalry brigades would have done this sort of thing and more. But the potential results of such endeavors are not reflected in the reports of Maj. Gen. Alfred Pleasonton or Buford or in the various actions and writings of Meade, Sickles, and their people.[20]

At least two squadrons of the Sixth New York Cavalry worked in support of Berdan's Sharpshooters on 2 July. About 10:00 A.M. Col. William Gamble asked Lieutenant Calef to post his battery in support of the troopers. Calef placed his guns "to the right" of the Peach Orchard, near where the brigades had formed their line. The Fifth Michigan Regiment supported the battery. Calef's guns were there for only a short time, but during their stay Sickles and some of his staff rode through their position. In doing this Sickles displayed the disregard of danger expected of a general, for Calef recalled that the Federal sharpshooters were operating in his immediate front. They shot from prone positions using their knapsacks for cover and as rests for their rifles. In firing, they drew return fire into Calef's position.[21]

The sharpshooters belonged to the First U.S. Sharpshooter Regiment. The First and Second regiments of sharpshooters were assigned to Ward's brigade but operated tactically as a demi-brigade under Col. Hiram Berdan, who reported directly to Birney. The two regiments were a collection of particularly expert marksmen, organized and trained to fight as skirmishers and snipers. Berdan had seen a role for such a force at the outset of the war; and, in an era of Zouaves, Highlanders, and other unconventional units, the War Department approved Berdan's suggestion. In 1861 Berdan received permission to recruit his marksmen on a national basis.[22] Berdan's standard of marksmanship was a stiff one. To be eligible for service as a sharpshooter a man had to put ten consecutive shots within a combined distance of fifty inches from the bull's-eye, this at a range of two hundred yards with rest and one hundred yards offhand. Service in the sharpshooters seemed attractive, and in the fall of 1861 Berdan had enough qualified recruits to form two regiments.[23]

Although the regiments were national in concept, the companies that formed them were recruited from single states.[24] Being special units, the sharpshooters wore a distinctive uniform. The coat and cap were dark green, and the cap sported a black plume. The first trousers adopted were light blue, but these were replaced in time by dark green ones, which were worn stuffed into leather leggings. Each man brought his own rifle into the service; but standardization has its merits, and in time the individually supplied rifles were replaced by issued Sharps rifles, caliber .52, with open sights. Most of the sharpshooters carried Sharps rifles at Gettysburg, but companies C and I of the First U.S. Sharpshooters used special target rifles.[25] The First Sharpshooters had rendezvoused at Weehawken, New Jersey, in the fall of 1861 and went from there to Washington for training. The Second joined them in Washington, and both regiments went to the Army of the Potomac in March 1862.[26]

Maj. Homer R. Stoughton deployed his companies of the Second as skirmishers on the left. He guarded a ravine near Little Round Top, presumably the Plum Run Valley, by deploying a company somewhere on the brow of a hill—he did not say where—and another across the ravine itself. In this way, if in no other, the Third Corps might have occupied Little Round Top. Stoughton posted four other companies somehow across the Wheatfield Road, presumably in the Wheatfield area, and held the remaining two in reserve.[27]

Berdan deployed the First Regiment along the Emmitsburg Road. Early in the morning he placed three companies near the Peter Rogers house where they could work with the Fourth Maine and Ninety-ninth Pennsylvania regiments. Col. Elijah Walker of the Fourth had told his superiors that the woods in his front, probably Spangler's Woods, held a sizable enemy force. On two occasions it was suggested that the Fourth drive them out, but Walker balked—his regiment was too small for the job. Walker and Berdan discussed the problem, and both agreed that the woods could be cleared best by a push from the flank rather than head on from the Fourth's position.[28]

Maj. Henry Tremain, Sickles's senior aide, kept a close eye on the skirmish line that morning. Tremain, a prewar law student, had entered the army as a lieutenant in the Seventy-third New York, a regiment of Sickles's own Excelsior Brigade, and became the regiment's adjutant. He came to Sickles's attention and moved from the regiment to the brigade staff as Sickles's aide. The Confederates captured Tremain at Second Bull Run, where he had performed with noted courage, but he was soon exchanged. After his return to Sickles's staff, Tremain's prestige increased with that of his general, and in due course he became a major as befitted the senior aide of a corps commander.[29] Tremain, at age twenty-three, was a self-assured young man, ambitious enough to seek out and gravitate to centers of power and authority and maintain himself there with drive and ability.[30]

Tremain was busy posting troops and checking the skirmish lines early on the morning of 2 July, but sometime not long after Captain Meade's visit to Third Corps headquarters, he made his first of several visits that day to General Meade. As Tremain recalled it, he gave General Meade the approximate locations of the Third Corps picket lines, reminded him that there were no troops on the left of the Third Corps, and told him that Sickles had sent General Graham to bring up the two brigades left at Emmitsburg. Although hindsight suggests that Sickles was worried about his left even then, Meade seemed unimpressed by, if not downright oblivious to, this concern. In Tremain's probably biased opinion, General Meade received his report casually and remarked that cavalry would protect the Third Corps flank.[31]

Maj. Gen. Daniel E. Sickles and staff. Left to right: *Maj. Henry E. Tremain, Lt. Col. Orson H. Hart, General Sickles, Capt. Thomas W. G. Fry, and Capt. Alexander Moore* (MOLLUS-MASS/U.S.A.M.H.I., *Carlisle Barracks, Pa.*)

Time passed. Sickles and Birney became more concerned over what they believed to be the vulnerability and inadequacy of the Third Corps position. Oddly enough, there is no evidence that General Humphreys, the professional soldier and engineer, was asked to take part in the deliberations. In fact, Humphreys testified to the Committee on the Conduct of the War that he did not see General Sickles on the morning of 2 July because he could not leave his division unless sent for. Furthermore, he knew nothing of the ground on the left that he could not see.[32] Perhaps Sickles did not see fit to confer with Humphreys because his attention was riveted to Birney's front and the Third Corps left, or perhaps he did not value Humphreys's opinion as a Regular Army engineer enough to seek it.

After their arrival in the darkness of the early morning hours of 2 July, Humphreys's First and Second brigades massed on the damp west slope of Cemetery Ridge easterly of the Abraham Trostle farmyard. John Bachelder, the contemporary historian, who probably had good information, located their position on his map as being north of the George Weikert buildings. He showed Carr's brigade as having been in column on the right, with the Excelsior Brigade beside it. The two brigades remained in this location much of the morning, doing their chores, improving their formations as stragglers arrived, and removing fences that might impede their movements.[33] Some men napped when their work was done, while others tried to make morning coffee. A majority of them seemed to Captain Cavada to be in good spirits. They could hear shots fired on the skirmish line to the front, and occasionally spent Rebel balls passed overhead or dropped among them. Most balls caused no injury, but a lively one passed through the loose cloth of the pants leg of a sleeping soldier and into his haversack without awakening him. Only after being aroused by the laughter of those around him, seeing the holes, and finding the spent ball among his rations, did the soldier realize how near to death he had been.[34]

In the meantime Sickles worried about his left and the Emmitsburg Road. Not only did the road run along the high ground that concerned him so, but his corps had traveled it to Gettysburg, and his two absent brigades, two batteries, and the corps ammunition train would probably come in that way. In a sense the Emmitsburg Road was as important to the Third Corps as the Baltimore Pike was to General Meade and to the Army of the Potomac as a whole.

At Emmitsburg Colonels de Trobriand and Burling did not receive orders to join their corps at Gettysburg until the early hours of 2 July—Burling said 1:30 A.M.; de Trobriand said 2:00 A.M.[35] At that time the brigades occupied defensive positions on the approaches to the village, some of the Seventeenth Maine, for instance, being posted two miles to the southwest at St. Mary's College.[36] It is no surprise, then, that it was almost daylight before the two brigades could be assembled and formed for their eight-mile march to Gettysburg. Once formed, they set out without delay and without breakfast (some said at 4 A.M.), Burling's brigade in the lead and de Trobriand's bringing up the rear, with Company C, 110th Pennsylvania collecting stragglers. They stopped after a march of about three miles so that the men could make coffee. Thereafter, they halted for a ten minute break each hour.[37]

The march went slowly, too slowly considering the need for troops on Cemetery Ridge. Possibly the march was slowed by the presence in the column of the Third Corps's ammunition wagons—no one said. The company serving as provost guard was delayed by the chore of rounding up the numerous stragglers of the 1 July battle that it met along the way. According to Capt. James C. M. Hamilton, in one field of timothy the heads of stragglers could be seen everywhere, "sticking through the grass like as if they had been tin pins stuck up all over the field. When they saw us, the rear guard, which they seemed to be on the lookout for, they doged down into the grass all at once, as suddenly, as any row of tin pins could be knocked over." Company C attempted to round up the stragglers as it went along, but after a time orders came to forget them and hurry along to Gettysburg.[38] In the meantime General Graham had met the column, and he permitted a rest stop about three miles south of the field. While stopping, they learned, as Graham must already have known, that the enemy was nearby. They pushed ahead and turned off the Emmitsburg Road at the Peach Orchard, where some of them came under long distance fire. At 10:00 A.M. they were ready for work.[39]

By this time General Sickles was worried about his position and General Meade's seeming lack of appreciation for its problems. He decided to go see Meade himself and, guided by Tremain, rode to army headquarters.[40] The conversation between the two generals was not fully reported. Sickles spoke of his concerns, the poor position assigned his corps, the advantages of holding the high ground at the Peach Orchard, and his fear of an assault against his front. In response, according to HISTORICUS, a Sickles partisan, General Meade replied: "O, generals are all apt to look for the attack to be made where they are." HISTORICUS went on to say that Sickles did not stop to consider whether Meade's remark was a jest or a sneer but continued his effort to get General Meade to go over his position with him.[41] Meade declined—other matters required his attention. He explained to Sickles once more the line that he wanted the Third Corps to occupy, and Sickles again made the rather pointless observation that Geary had had no position. The Third Corps commander then asked General Meade if he could post the corps as he saw fit, and Meade was said to reply, "Certainly, within the limits of the the general instructions I have given you; any ground within those limits you choose to occupy, I leave to you."[42]

From Sickles's point of view, he was getting nowhere with the commanding general; and, though General Meade seemed not to know it, he was not being understood by General Sickles. With the flexibility of the lawyer that he was, Daniel Sickles tried a new tack: he asked for the company of General Warren in examining his position area, but Warren was not at hand. General Hunt was Sickles's third choice, and fortunately he had just returned from Culp's Hill and was available. General Meade told Hunt that Sickles was dissatisfied with the area assigned the Third Corps because he could not use his artillery to advantage from it. Would Hunt visit it with General Sickles to see what he had in mind? General Hunt would, of course, and he and Sickles rode off to see Sickles's proposed position along the Emmitsburg Road.[43]

Hunt recalled later that he did not know if General Meade's intentions were defensive or offensive at this time. That certainly suggests a lack of communication between Meade and this key staff officer. Perhaps it is explained by Hunt's absence from headquarters much of the morning and by Meade's change in views as the morning passed, most notably by his having to give up his proposed attack against the Confederate left. Sickles and Hunt, together with Tremain and Capt. Alexander Moore and possibly others, left the headquarters. They rode up to the crest of Cemetery Ridge and then out to the coveted ground along the Emmitsburg Road. Hunt was familiar already with the features of Cemetery Ridge and did not need to reexamine them. Sometime early in the reconnaissance Sickles told of his desire to cover the Emmitsburg Road, and Hunt deduced that Sickles was concerned about its being used safely by his ammunition train.[44]

General Sickles pointed out his proposed position from the high ground near the intersection of the Emmitsburg and Wheatfield roads. Gettysburg was a fruit-growing area in 1863, as it continues to be today. Each farm had its orchard, of course, and some farms, like that of Joseph Sherfy, grew fruit for sale. The battlefield area contained numerous orchards, but one of Sherfy's became *the* Peach Orchard, because of its special importance as a terrain feature and a place of heavy fighting. The Peach Orchard was a rectangular plot in the southeastern corner of the intersection; it measured about 150 yards along its Emmitsburg Road and eastern sides and ran back about 100 yards along its southern boundary and the Wheatfield Road. The high ground along the Emmitsburg Road that so attracted Sickles had its highest point within this Peach Orchard just a few yards east of the Emmitsburg Road.[45]

The ground slopes westerly from the Peach Orchard, beyond the Emmitsburg Road into a broad trough between the Emmitsburg Road and Seminary Ridge. It descends in elevation approximately 20 feet in 250 yards into the bottom of the trough and rises again in about 350 yards to the ridge line, where it is crossed by the Wheatfield Road. The slope southeast from the orchard is steeper, falling about 30 feet into the upper course of the west branch of Plum Run, just 200 yards to the south. The ground rises beyond the draw to a plateau containing the Rose farm's lane. The Peach Orchard's elevation gave guns posted in it a good field of fire both to the west and to the south along the Emmitsburg Road and across that portion of the Rose farm.

The slope to the east from the Peach Orchard and from the high ground north of it is ascended from the east by the Wheatfield Road and is longer and gentler than the western and southern slopes. The ground surface falls about forty feet along the south side of the Wheatfield Road to a low knoll five hundred yards to the east. (General Kershaw called this rise the "stony hill," and, since it has no other name, it will be called that hereafter.) A strip of woods crowned this knoll, beginning about fifty yards south of the road, and covered a much sharper slope into the Wheatfield east of it. These woods extended south to Plum Run, which in that area is about fifty feet lower than the knoll and continues into the larger mass of Rose's Woods.

The slope from the Peach Orchard north along the Emmitsburg Road is so gradual as to be hardly apparent. It slopes down about ten feet into a lower area about three hundred yards away, where Trostle's farm lane (later greatly widened into United States Avenue) joins the road, and rises again to another high point just west of the Daniel Klingle house at Henry Spangler's farm lane. The higher ground is just west of the Emmitsburg Road in this area. It gradually falls off to the northwest and fades into the broad trough between Cemetery and Seminary ridges, while the road descends its eastern slope six hundred yards to a low point south of the Codori buildings. The fields drain into this low area and to the east, helping to create the headwaters of the northern branch of Plum Run. The stretch of the Emmitsburg Road between this drainage area and that forming the west branch of Plum Run at the south base of the Peach Orchard's slope is nearly a mile in length. It was to be the site of the right wing of Sickles's advanced line.

The elevation of the Peach Orchard is about four feet higher than that of another high point near the junction of the road and Spangler's lane. Both are only a few feet higher than Seminary Ridge to the west. However, they are higher than the crest of Cemetery Ridge in the mile between the Copse of Trees and the wooded knolls just north of Little Round Top. Therefore, the height of this mile-long ridge north from the Peach Orchard, when matched with that of the ridge lines to the east and west, gave it a significance and attraction that could not be overlooked.[46]

The course of the road along this mile-long crest was marked by four groups of buildings. The small frame farmhouse that was home to septuagenarian John Wentz, and its outbuildings, were on the east side of the Emmitsburg Road immediately north of the Wheatfield Road and the Peach Orchard. The Sherfy buildings, home of John and Mary Sherfy and their five children, were about two hundred yards north of the Wentz house on the west side of the road. The barn, a moderate-size building, abutted the road, while the two-story brick house stood north of the barn site and back from the road. The Klingle house, a log structure that has since been sheathed with wood siding, still stands on the east side of the road just south of Spangler's farm lane. Its barn is to its left rear. The frame house of day laborer Peter Rogers was on the west side of the road 250 yards north of Klingle's. Each of the farmyards had a nearby orchard that also crowned the crest, and, no doubt, each had its quota of shade trees as well.

General Sickles must have told Hunt of the advantages of this high ground and traced the location of his proposed line upon it. Its right would be back along the Emmitsburg Road near the low ground south of the Codori farm buildings and in front of the left of the Second Corps. From there it would follow the road south along the crest beyond the Wheatfield Road to the south edge of the Peach Orchard. Then the line would angle back almost ninety degrees at the Peach Orchard and follow the high ground above the west branch of Plum Run to Devil's Den. There would be room for gun positions along both roads, and infantry would occupy the wooded areas and the line toward Devil's Den. All told, the proposed line had a front of about 1,500 yards along the Emmitsburg Road and 1,700 yards from the Peach Orchard to Devil's Den.

Hunt viewed the position critically and saw the obvious: the right of the proposed line would not connect with the Second Corps back on Cemetery Ridge, five hundred yards to the rear. Contact could not be made without advancing the Second Corps and placing it in a poor position. The Second

Corps certainly ought not to advance, he thought, unless Spangler's Woods in front of Seminary Ridge were under Federal control. What about those woods?

It was apparent that the Rebels were in Spangler's Woods, for their skirmishers were in front of it. And what of the woods directly ahead, Pitzer's Woods? Of course the cavalry had been beyond it that morning, and a farmer had told them what the cavalrymen also knew and what an infantryman or staff officer could easily have determined by riding or strolling over—that Pitzer's Woods was a narrow strip, about a hundred yards in width, and that there was a broad and open slope between it and Willoughby Run beyond. They had better check out those woods, Hunt observed. This view conformed with local thinking, and Sickles saw that it was done.[47]

General Hunt could see some merit in Sickles's proposed line. He particularly liked the portion of it at the Peach Orchard and along the Emmitsburg Road. This high ground dominates the fields between it and Cemetery Ridge to the east and would be an excellent place for Confederate batteries. Furthermore, because it screened the fields west of it from Federal eyes on Cemetery Ridge, it might prove to be a fine staging area for Confederate troops forming for an assault on the Federal position. Therefore it would be to the enemy's advantage to occupy it, and that in itself would be one reason for the Federals to hold it. The position had certain positive advantages also. As Sickles pointed out, it would provide battery positions the like of which the sector designated for the Third Corps on Cemetery Ridge would not. It also would cover Federal troop movements east of it, and it would provide a launching point in case Meade wanted to attack the Confederate position on Seminary Ridge. If it were in Union hands, the Confederates might think twice about occupying the ridge line just seven hundred yards in its front.[48]

There were definite drawbacks, of course. The Peach Orchard position would be a "salient angle," and if the Confederates occupied the Seminary Ridge line, any troops posted at the orchard might be subjected to both flank and frontal fire. But Henry Hunt was not too concerned about this; he felt that the height of the ridge would provide shelter behind its crest and thereby reduce the dire effects of enfilading fire.[49]

But Hunt mused on; what, he wondered, would it take to hold the proposed line? Certainly it would require the whole Third Corps and probably the Fifth as well. The advanced line would be about double the front that General Meade had asked General Sickles to hold on Cemetery Ridge, not including Little Round Top. Therefore, until the Sixth Corps arrived, Meade could not prudently permit the occupation of the forward line, for if he did, the Army of the Potomac would have no reserve. How did the advanced line compare with the position that the Third Corps had been asked to occupy on Cemetery Ridge? It had its advantages when occupied in strength and would be desirable to hold if General Meade wished to take the offensive from his left. On the other hand, the Cemetery Ridge position that Sickles had been ordered to occupy with the forces at hand was a safe one for the time being. Until the Sixth Corps was up and available, Hunt could not recommend a change. How much of this reasoning Hunt imparted to Sickles and how much Sickles understood of it no one can say. But the sound of cannon fire on Cemetery Hill interrupted their conversation, and Hunt took his leave to see about it. As he turned to go, Sickles asked if he should advance the Third Corps. Hunt shook his head. "Not on my authority," he said. "I will report to General Meade for his instructions." With that Hunt rode away.[50]

Late in the morning, at 10:30 or so (perhaps while General Hunt was still in the area, though he did not mention it), Buford's two brigades of cavalry began to leave their positions in front of the Third Corps. General Pleasonton, commander of the Army of the Potomac's Cavalry Corps, ordered Buford's two brigades back to Westminster to refit and assist in guarding the army's trains. Pleasonton stated that this was done because Buford had been handled so severely the day before, something that the division's casualty reports do not support.[51] The particulars of Buford's departure are obscure at best. HISTORICUS wrote that Sickles was surprised by the cavalry's departure and that he believed its going left the Third Corps's flank exposed. In response to Sickles's protest, General Meade replied that he did not intend to withdraw the cavalry and that part of it would be returned. It never was.[52]

Meade was greatly annoyed when he learned that Pleasonton had not replaced Buford's departed troopers. At his direction General Butterfield sent dispatches at 12:50 and 12:55 telling Pleasonton that when Meade had authorized the departure of Buford's troops, he intended that other cavalry should replace them and that cavalry should continue to patrol the Emmitsburg Road. In response, at 1:45 Pleasonton sent a dispatch to Brig. Gen. David McM. Gregg, commander of the Second Division of the Cavalry Corps, instructing him to provide a regiment for this task as soon as "practicable," but the regiment never appeared. This gave Sickles further cause for alarm and rightly so.[53]

Meanwhile General Hunt, Colonels Walker and Berdan, and perhaps others saw the need for a reconnaissance of Pitzer's Woods on Seminary Ridge. About noon Birney received permission from Sickles to have one made. Birney ordered Colonel Berdan to probe the forbidding woods with a force of sharpshooters supported by the Third Maine Infantry, which at this time was one of the regiments posted in the Peach Orchard area. Birney ordered this movement late in the morning, sometime after Buford's departure.[54]

It was nearly noon, then, when Colonel Berdan and Capt. Joseph C. Briscoe, Birney's aide, led the reconnaissance party forward. Berdan's force consisted of four companies—D, E, F, and I—of the First U.S. Sharpshooter Regiment. The four numbered only about a hundred men and were under the direct command of Lt. Col. Casper Trepp. Col. Moses B. Lakeman's Third Maine Regiment was also small; it had but 14 officers and 196 men at best. The column went south along the Emmitsburg Road, where it would have been in full view of any Confederates on the ridge nearby, to the point where the Emmitsburg Road crosses the ridge just south of the Philip Snyder farmyard. For some reason Berdan halted the column on the Emmitsburg Road in "violation of rules of secret expeditions," and in doing so aroused the ire of Lieutenant Colonel Trepp.[55]

On reaching Biesecker's Woods on the ridge line, Berdan deployed his sharpshooters into a skirmish line across the ridge, with Companies D and E on the left and F and I on the right. Then they walked north. The Third Maine, probably in column, followed in support of the sharpshooters. They found no Confederates south of the Wheatfield Road, but as they passed some buildings near the Wheatfield Road, probably those of Snyder and Warfield, they met a boy who was the bearer of unhappy tidings. Pointing into Pitzer's Woods ahead, he shouted "almost with a sneer," "Look out! there are lots of Rebels in there in rows." The war-wise sharpshooters were skeptical— what would such a smart aleck know about Rebels? The reconnaissance force, with both regiments now deployed as skirmishers, threshed ahead, its progress impeded by rocks and branches, the view to the front limited by trees and undergrowth. Berdan and Briscoe rode up front, the better to see ahead, and after going 600 yards or so glimpsed enemy skirmishers peering from behind trees about 150 yards away. There was a formation behind them. Berdan had made contact with the enemy.[56]

The faces belonged to men of the Tenth or Eleventh Alabama Infantry regiments of Wilcox's brigade, Anderson's division, Hill's corps. Wilcox's brigade had been posted near the Black Horse Tavern the night before to guard the army's right flank and had almost intercepted Humphreys's division as it wandered over the roads west of Gettysburg. When it met Berdan's force, Wilcox's brigade was taking a new position on Anderson's right on Seminary Ridge. Although an approach by the Fairfield Road or on the route attempted by Longstreet's corps later in the day would have been much shorter, the brigade had hiked from its night position above the Black Horse Tavern back to the Chambersburg Pike. It had followed the pike east to the bloodied fields west of the Seminary and then turned south through the fields behind or west of Seminary Ridge. It passed by Hood's and McLaws's divisions, which rested with arms stacked by the line of march, awaiting their orders for the day. Wilcox's men then filed behind the other brigades of Anderson's division that had already taken their places back of the batteries on Seminary Ridge south of the Fairfield Road. Brig. Gens. Carnot Posey's and Mahone's brigades were in the area of McMillan's Woods and south of it. Wright's brigade was just north of Spangler's Woods, and the three Florida regiments of Perry's brigade were in the east edge of Spangler's Woods behind the Spangler farm buildings.

On passing through the fence line that ran west from the south edge of Spangler's Woods, the head of the Alabama column entered an open area of about twenty-five acres defined by trees and high ground that sloped up from Spangler's Woods three hundred yards to Pitzer's Woods. A solid belt of woods bordered the field on the right, while a fence that ran in the direction of the line of march bisected an open area in their front.[57]

Although it was nearly noon, General Anderson's instructions to Wilcox indicate that Anderson knew little or nothing about General Lee's plan for the day's assault. Four of Anderson's five brigades confronted the Federal position on Cemetery Ridge and the Union skirmish line west of the Emmitsburg Road, but Anderson ordered Wilcox to refuse his line, bending it back, fronting southeast and south in the direction of the Peach Orchard and Pitzer's Woods. In doing so it protected the right flank of Anderson's division and the army.[58]

General Anderson had ridden with Wilcox to the brigade's new position before the brigade's arrival and showed him the line that the Alabama regiments were to occupy. Wilcox's right would be in the belt of Pitzer's Woods on the high ground about three hundred yards to the front. There it could overlook the open ground sloping west down to Willoughby Run off the division's right and rear and block any move through Pitzer's Woods against the Confederate flank. From there the line would arc back to the northeast through the open fields, taking advantage of the terrain and fence line, through a swale, and then to a stone wall near the south end of Spangler's Woods. There its left would be about one hundred yards from the right of the Florida Brigade which was in the woods.[59]

Wilcox was wary of the new position—and for good reason. He could see enemy skirmishers in the fields to the east and southeast, and perhaps someone had told him of cavalry that had been there earlier in the day. Therefore, why should not there be Yankees in the woods on the ridge line ahead? The woods ran to Anderson's rear and was a worry for commanders on both sides that morning. Wilcox's brigade approached its new position with caution. Wilcox aligned his right regiments, the Tenth and Eleventh, in the low ground behind the end of Spangler's Woods facing south toward the positions they were to occupy, and held his three other regiments in reserve. Then, skirmishers to the front, the Tenth in the belt of woods on the right, and the Eleventh in the open ground, Wilcox advanced south uphill toward the crest three hundred yards away. The Eleventh swished through a wheat field without meeting any physical obstacles. The Tenth, however, had to make its way through trees and undergrowth over the floor of woods strewn with rocks, some as big as a doghouse, which disrupted its line and slowed its advance. The Eleventh pulled ahead and, as it reached its designated position, began to wheel left, presenting its right flank to that portion of the woods to be occupied by the Tenth. It was at this time that Wilcox's skirmishers spied Union officers on horseback in the woods ahead.[60]

Contact was made. In later years, with some advantages of hindsight, Berdan spoke of the dilemma of the moment. He saw the foe ahead of his line in strength. Should he backtrack quickly and report what he had seen, or should he take the enemy under fire and delay his movements? Because his men believed that they were members of an elite force, it would be unseemly for them to retreat without a fight. Furthermore, Berdan had a strong enough force to make a fight, and he decided to do so. He called Captain Briscoe to him and told Briscoe to ride back and tell Birney what they had seen. Briscoe was to go casually until he was out of the enemy's sight and then ride like hell! The captain reined his horse around and started away; then he turned around and rode back to Berdan simply to say "Goodbye." Amenities concluded, Briscoe disappeared among the trees in the rear. Berdan, still on his gray horse, turned to his line of riflemen and shouted, "Follow me, advance firing."[61]

The sharpshooters advanced at Berdan's command, rifles cracking and smoking, driving the Alabama skirmishers back on their main line three hundred yards to the north. Then, as Berdan reported, he could see three columns of infantry—three of Wilcox's regiments without doubt. The closest was the Eleventh Alabama in the open field opposite his right. It would have been ahead of the Tenth in the woods to its right and somewhat isolated from it and from the other regiments of the brigade in its rear. The sharpshooters fired into the ranks of the Eleventh Alabama, cutting down a mounted officer, probably Maj. Richard J. Fletcher, whom they wrongly believed to be the regiment's commander, and creating great confusion within its ranks. The Eleventh tried to change front to meet the galling fire but had no success. Heeding their instincts for survival, the men hightailed it to the rear and the cover of the line of the Eighth Alabama, which was formed in a lane near the base of the slope at the edge of Spangler's Woods. As the men of the Eleventh approached, those of the Eighth dropped to a prone position to permit the fugitives to pass over them and reform.[62]

The sharpshooters, "mad with success," rushed unwisely into the open ground. Their success was short lived. Col. William H. Forney's Tenth Alabama smote Berdan's sharpshooters with a crashing volley that promptly drove them back to the woods and to the line of the Third Maine.[63] There was brisk firing among the trees, the sharpshooters claiming later that they had fired an average of ninety-five rounds per man with their breech-loading Sharps rifles in the fifteen or twenty minutes of conflict. The Third Maine moved on line with their green-coated comrades, yielding nothing to them in courage and determination. In fact, they fought under a handicap. Colonel Lakeman wrote later that the sharpshooters were able to fire from the cover of trees, while his men had to fill the spaces between them. In spite of the sharpshooters' greater firepower on a man-to-man basis, the solid Tenth Alabama, aided by the Eighth, which came up on its left, pressed Berdan's men hard, and it soon became apparent to Berdan that his force was at a disadvantage. He ordered a retreat, his bugler sounded the call, and the

Union force fell back firing, its withdrawal encouraged by Rebel yells of victory.[64]

Although the action was relatively short, the casualties were respectable even for those days. The Third Maine had forty-eight; the First U.S. Sharpshooters, protected by its trees perhaps, had nineteen. One of the latter was Capt. Charles D. McLean of Company D, who suffered a mortal wound. Some of his men attempted to carry him off in a blanket, but one of them was shot, and McLean told them to go off without him. Pvt. Peter H. Kipp would have obeyed, reluctantly perhaps, but his lieutenant told him to stay with the captain. The Alabamians captured Kipp, of course. His captors attempted to move him to the rear with bayonet pricks until a Confederate lieutenant colonel told the bayonet wielders to allow Kipp to stay with his captain. And so, in effect, the Confederates got three sharpshooters by shooting McLean.[65]

Another sharpshooter, 1st Sgt. Lewis J. Allen of New Hampshire's Company F, an alleged descendant of Ethan Allen, became so engrossed with his shooting that he forgot the duties of his position and allowed his company to fall back without him and a few of his men nearby. When he realized their predicament, they sprinted to the rear. He left the woods to cut across a plowed field toward the Peach Orchard with bullets zipping around him. He reached a house along his way, probably the John Staub house, and collapsed panting in its yard. A woman there gave him sympathy and tried to help him until he told her that he was winded but not wounded. Then her kindness changed to scolding for his making such a fuss, and Allen, his welcome worn and his breath restored, continued his dash for the Peach Orchard and safety.[66]

The Alabamians took up their assigned positions and prepared to guard the Confederate flank while the sharpshooters and Maine men fell back to the Peach Orchard area and took their places in the Federal skirmish line.[67] In later years Colonel Berdan and others were pleased to tell that they had "disconcerted, delayed and annoyed" the enemy. As their enthusiasm waxed with the golden blur of memory, they claimed that they had delayed the Rebel army forty minutes and that the Pitzer's Woods fight had been the turning point of the battle. William F. Fox, compiler of the prestigious *New York at Gettysburg* volumes and in effect New York's official historian of the battle, wrote that Sickles had ordered the reconnaissance "to ascertain the strength and position of the enemy in his front" and that Berdan had acquired that information. Because Sickles seems not to have objected to the statement's being printed, if he knew of it, it can be assumed that he did not take issue with it.[68]

But what did Berdan's reconnaissance really accomplish? The skirmishing of the morning should have left no doubt that there were Confederates in Spangler's Woods, and apparently the cavalry had found Confederates somewhere behind the ridge in strength. Thus the only new information that Berdan's men could have provided was that the Confederates in some force were moving into the north end of Pitzer's Woods. Berdan might have assumed more and told a greater tale, but that is all his expedition uncovered and all he could rightly report. He could have seen nothing of Longstreet's corps, for it was out of his sight. His force might have delayed Wilcox's brigade in occupying its position on Anderson's right, but this was a meaningless achievement, for after Wilcox's brigade reached its assigned place on the field, it had little to do for three hours while awaiting Longstreet's arrival.

It was some time during Berdan's foray that Major Tremain made his third visit to army headquarters. Sickles was becoming increasingly anxious and asked Tremain to do three things. He was to report the arrival of Graham and the two brigades from Emmitsburg, he was to tell General Meade of Berdan's reconnaissance, and he was to see if there were any orders concerning the Emmitsburg Road and its use by the Third Corps trains. (Where were the trains at this late hour?) Tremain dutifully rode off and in due course arrived at the Lydia Leister house. He found army headquarters there to be an informal place and found General Meade alone in the house's kitchen. The general was studying intently a large map of Adams County spread before him on the kitchen table.[69] Tremain stood at the door of the small room for what seemed to him an embarrassingly long time until General Meade acknowledged his presence with a "Well, Sir?"

Tremain spouted his message, and there was a long pause. Unable to abide the silence, Tremain repeated those portions of the message that were of greatest interest to the Third Corps, the nature of the threat that prompted Berdan's reconnaissance and the matter of the Emmitsburg Road—would the cavalry keep it open so that the Third Corps trains might use it? To this General Meade replied only that the cavalry would protect the road and that orders had been issued governing the movements of trains. One wonders if Tremain was overly sensitive or if fatigue and noonday heat might not have made the commanding general drowsy.[70]

Tremain posted back to Third Corps headquarters. In the opinion of the young major it had been an unsatisfactory interview all the way around. He was uncomfortable about General Meade's seeming lack of interest in the messages he conveyed and about the general's apparent lack of appreciation of Third Corps concerns. Sickles, to his way of thinking, had not received much satisfaction from the army's headquarters that morning; and, in retrospect, one must wonder why he did not seek to use the sympathetic offices of his friend Butterfield. Protocol problems would not have deterred either general if it came to that. Possibly Sickles thought that Butterfield could do him no good. In any case, such a course should not have been necessary.

Meade's seeming lack of empathy fed Sickles's growing concern, and Berdan's report brought things to a head. Shortly after noon, therefore, Sickles ordered Birney's division forward again "to change my front to meet the attack," as Birney expressed it in his report. Birney's division occupied the left and center of the forward line that Sickles had shown to General Hunt.[71]

In the weeks after the battle Halleck, Meade, and others, in their disapproval of Sickles's action, attributed it charitably to a misinterpretation of General Meade's orders. Not so, bristled Maj. Gen. Daniel Sickles:

> It was not through any misinterpretation of orders. It was either a good line or a bad one, and, whichever it was, I took it on my own responsibility. . . . I took up that line because it enabled me to hold commanding ground, which, if the enemy had been allowed to take—as they would have taken it if I had not occupied it in force—would have rendered our position on the left untenable; and, in my judgment, would have turned the fortunes of the day hopelessly against us.[72]

There it was. Sickles had made a forthright decision, nothing less, and acted on it. There had seemed to be too little concern at the army's headquarters that morning for the situation on his front, and so Sickles had taken the bit in his teeth and abandoned the position ordered by General Meade for one that he believed to be better. He defended his decision and action afterward—aggressively, if not always credibly and honorably—until his dying day, half a century later. If there was an error, he contended, it was others who had erred, not Daniel Sickles, not the Third Corps.

6

Confederate Preparations, 2 July

Lt. Gen. James Longstreet and his staff awakened early on 2 July, perhaps as early as 3:00 A.M., and breakfasted before daylight. Fitzgerald Ross, a captain of hussars in the Austrian army, thought that he had been aroused by a cannon's roar ("c'est le sanglant appel de Mars"), although it is indeed unlikely that any guns would have been firing then. The headquarters atmosphere must have been tense and hurried, but the hussar found time to wax his moustache before he rode off with General Longstreet and his staff toward a brightening sky in the east and Seminary Ridge.[1]

Longstreet's destination, General Lee's headquarters, was on the west slope of Seminary Ridge in an orchard along the south side of the Chambersburg Pike. If the headquarters there were like the headquarters at Chambersburg, they consisted of a half dozen tents, grazing horses, and a half dozen wagons parked nearby. They would have been marked by a Confederate flag.[2] General Lee was up early, but he must have been at the headquarters site for only brief periods. On the morning of 2 July he spent much time near a log or the trunk of a fallen tree that probably was north of the large seminary dormitory and classroom building. General Hood recalled his being there that morning, pacing back and forth, his coat buttoned up to his throat, sword belt buckled at his waist, and binoculars dangling at his side. Possibly the general was not feeling well, and he might have worn his coat buttoned so tightly not only as a matter of convention but to guard against the morning's dampness as well.[3]

General Lee's vantage point at the seminary provided a view of the center of the enemy's position. The western edge of Gettysburg approached the foot of the ridge about five hundred yards to his front, and some of Rodes's division could probably be seen in the fields and streets ahead. Beyond the town, 1½ miles to the east, he could have seen the Hanover Road crossing over Benner's Hill. He probably could not have seen the men of Early's division, but they were between the far side of the town and Benner's Hill, while Johnson's division was out of sight along the Hanover Road beyond the hill. All three divisions of Ewell's corps fronted the Union position on Cemetery Hill and Culp's Hill, which looked like a single hill mass to the right, or south, of the town. With his field glasses General Lee might have seen Union batteries on Cemetery Hill 1¼ miles to his right front. As the morning progressed, he would have been able to see the arrival of additional batteries and regiments of the Federal Second Corps on the north end of Cemetery Ridge between Ziegler's Grove and the Copse of Trees. Between the ridges he saw skirmish lines of the two armies and possibly some troopers of Buford's cavalry division to the right toward the Peach Orchard area. Pender's division occupied Seminary Ridge for a distance of about 1,200 yards to his right, and Heth's division was out of sight beyond Pender's line. Anderson's division would soon be moving up from the rear to replace Heth's, and Longstreet's divisions were approaching the field.[4]

General Lee's vantage point was a busy place in a low-key way. A few generals and some staff officers and couriers came and went while others waited nearby. Longstreet was there much of the time between daybreak and 11:00 A.M.; A. P. Hill was there part of the morning, and both Hood and McLaws were there for awhile. Colonel Fremantle sat in a nearby tree and watched the Federal position through his spyglass. Some of Lee's staff officers—Brig. Gen. William N. Pendleton, Col. A. Lindsay Long, Maj. Andrew Venable, and Capt. Samuel R. Johnston—had ridden off on early errands but returned over the course of the morning. Col. John L. Black of the First South Carolina Cavalry rode in with a scratched together body of cavalry and Capt. James F. Hart's South Carolina Battery. Black was impressed to see Generals Hill, Longstreet, and Lee in serious conversation. General Lee, to Black, was the best looking man in the universe. Longstreet he saw as "fat and full," and Hill as slender. When the three generals finished their talk, Black reported to General Lee, who introduced Black to Longstreet as one of Lee's former West Point cadets. Lee detailed Black and his troops to the First Corps to guard its flank and rear.[5]

Lee was in a quandary. He did not wish to lose the initiative of 1 July and had expected to resume the attack on the second. But what should be done? His contacts with Ewell and conversations with Longstreet had disturbed him. In an effort to resolve the dilemma of what to do with Ewell's corps, he sent Major Venable over to see Ewell once again to look into the advantages of attacking from his position. Venable rode off. Clearly, General Lee's plans for 2 July had not yet fully matured.[6]

Lee certainly seemed to know little enough about his army's flanks and the particular whereabouts of the Army of the Potomac. But the situation on his right seemed promising. Perhaps as Early, Rodes, and Ewell had said, an attack should be made from that wing. To explore the possibility further, he sent scouting parties off in that direction under Colonel Long, General

Pendleton, and Captain Johnston, his engineer.[7] In his report, General Pendleton stated that the three of them, accompanied by staff personnel and with Col. R. Lindsay Walker, chief of artillery of the Third Corps, rode out to get "some estimate of the ground and the best mode of attack." According to Pendleton, they went to Pender's division's right shortly after sunrise. But the others did not remember this joint effort in quite the same way.[8]

Pendleton's own party included three or four junior officers. Pendleton rode down the ridge a piece, possibly no farther than Spangler's Woods. His staff continued on, perhaps as far as the Wheatfield Road or the Emmitsburg Road, though one officer thought that they had gone somewhat to the rear of the Round Tops. On their return by the "ravine road" along Willoughby Run they captured two Union cavalrymen—stragglers or unwary pickets—who were drinking from the run. They met no other Union troops, oddly enough, and the report they made on their return no doubt contributed to the notion that none were there. Pendleton returned from his ride believing that an attack on the Union left might succeed "should the mountain there offer no insuperable obstacle." They returned by a route that he believed might offer an approach. In sum, Pendleton's effort is an enigma, and its results do seem to have influenced General Lee's planning later in the day.[9]

Colonel Long's primary interest seems to have been in artillery positions. He checked those on Hill's front at sunrise and then those along Ewell's line. In the course of his survey he visited Hill's headquarters, where he found that "everything exhibited signs of preparation for action." Colonel Long met General Lee later at Ewell's headquarters.[10]

Captain Johnston's reconnaissance had the greatest impact. General Lee summoned his engineer about daybreak and asked that he reconnoiter the Union left and report back as soon as possible. At about 4:00 A.M., according to his recollections, the captain set out accompanied by Maj. John J. Clarke, Longstreet's engineer, and a few others. They rode south, probably along the road beside Willoughby Run, crossed the bridge over the run north of Pitzer's Schoolhouse, turned left at the schoolhouse, and ascended the west slope of Seminary Ridge. There, opposite the Peach Orchard in the area later occupied by McLaws's division, they saw no Union troops, an inexplicable thing, for there should have been many to see. They hurried south along the ridge, crossed the Emmitsburg Road, and swung east to the Round Tops and to Little Round Top itself. Even there they saw nothing of the enemy and, seeing nothing, did not tarry. On their return the Confederate officers rode southwesterly down the hill and back to the lower extension of Seminary Ridge. When they approached the Emmitsburg Road, they spied four cavalrymen riding slowly along it. The engineers waited patiently for them to pass and then hurried north by the most direct route to Lee's headquarters. Johnston believed that his scout took about three hours.[11]

After the "usual delay in finding headquarters," Johnston discovered that General Lee had gone from the tent area, where he must have last seen him, to the overlook near the seminary building. He found the general there, sitting on a log talking with Generals Hill and Longstreet. They were looking at a map, and as General Lee talked, he pointed to it. When Lee saw Johnston, he called him over, and the captain stood behind the generals, leaned over their shoulders, and indicated the route that he had just traveled. When he said that he had been to Little Round Top, Lee turned, looked up, and asked, "Did you get there?" Johnston assured him that he had and stepped back when he finished. General Lee talked further with Longstreet and Hill and then told Longstreet that he had better move on.[12] After Longstreet moved away, General Lee invited the captain to sit beside him on the log and the two talked further about the area's topography. When they finished, Lee asked Johnston to join Longstreet for the purpose—Johnston assumed—of aiding him.[13]

Colonel Long's movements that morning seem straightforward enough and raise no major questions. Those of Johnston's and Pendleton's parties invite conjecture on their timing and on routes taken. The greatest mystery, though, is why, on that morning of great Federal activity, the reconnaissance parties met only a half dozen cavalrymen. Certainly there was skirmishing in the fields north of the Peach Orchard, and the orchard was well posted. In addition, there must have been Third Corps stragglers plodding up the Emmitsburg Road throughout the morning and probably other traffic too.[14]

And why did Johnston and Clarke see no Federal troops in the Little Round Top area? Geary's division had started from that area at daybreak and might have cleared it before they arrived. But not the Third Corps; most of its exhausted soldiers had collapsed in the fields north of the hill, but others arrived there throughout the morning. By the time Johnston's party reached the hill, the Third Corps ought to have been stirring, getting ready for the business of the day. If its bivouacs were concealed by the morning mist, its presence ought nonetheless to have been revealed by the noise of animals, guns and wagons, shouting men, and drumming and bugling.

And then there was the Second Corps. It trudged up the Taneytown Road in the several hours after daybreak. The trees on Little Round Top's east slope must have concealed the road and its traffic from Johnston's view, but the road was less than half a mile away, and the noise of a marching corps with no need for concealment might well have been within the ken of vigilant scouts. It must be concluded that when Captain Johnston's reconnaissance party failed to detect Federal units in the area between the Peach Orchard and the Round Tops and on the lower end of Cemetery Ridge, it was somehow the victim of grave misfortune. As a result of this failure, Captain Johnston made an incorrect report to his commanding general that was to have serious consequences later in the day.

While the patrols were out, Hood's division followed its commander toward Gettysburg by way of the Chambersburg Pike and filed into the fields west of Seminary Ridge, where its men stacked arms and fell out to rest.

Maj. Gen. John B. Hood (MOLLUS-MASS/ U.S.A.M.H.I., Carlisle Barracks, Pa.)

Maj. Gen. Richard H. Anderson (National Archives)

Maj. Gen. Lafayette McLaws
(Library of Congress)

McLaws's division followed Hood's, and its van got as close as a hundred yards to General Lee's observation point before it halted. Within a short time, Lee asked McLaws over to converse with him.[15]

General Lee sat on the log, his map beside him, and General Longstreet paced back and forth nearby. Lee pointed to the area on the map where the Wheatfield Road is shown to cross Seminary Ridge and to a line marked perpendicular to the Emmitsburg Road south of the Peach Orchard. He said to McLaws: "General, I wish you to place your division across this road, and I wish you to get there if possible without being seen by the enemy." And then, after a pause, he asked, "Can you get there?" McLaws answered that he knew of nothing that would prevent his doing so, but that he would like to take a party out to look at the road. To this General Lee replied that Captain Johnston had been asked to reconnoiter that ground. McLaws, misunderstanding, thought that Johnston was only then ready to go and said that he would like to join the captain in his reconnaissance. At this point General Longstreet stopped his pacing and said quickly: "No, sir, I do not wish you to leave your division," and tracing with his finger a line perpendicular to that drawn on the map, said, "I wish your division placed so." "No, General," Lee objected, "I wish it placed just the opposite."[16]

That matter settled, McLaws asked permission again to go with Captain Johnston, and Longstreet once more forbade it. It appears that division commanders in both armies had restrictions on their freedom of action. General Lee had no more to say, and Longstreet seemed irritated, so McLaws returned to his division. He wrote that he posted it under some trees a short distance away. Actually those trees must have been along Herr Ridge about 1½ miles west of the seminary, for that was where his division spent the next few hours. Kershaw's brigade, which was in the lead, halted above and east of the Black Horse Tavern in the area occupied by Wilcox's brigade the previous evening. From the head of the column, McLaws and Kershaw could see de Trobriand's and Burling's brigades moving up the Emmitsburg Road toward the Federal position.[17]

In his account of events of the morning McLaws mentioned two efforts of his own to get permission to accompany Captain Johnston on his reconnaissance and a third to have Lt. Thomas J. Moncure, his own engineer, join Johnston. Moncure too was ordered back. If Johnston's expedition began about 4:00 A.M., as Captain Johnston said that it did, McLaws must have misunderstood what Lee said of Johnston or recalled the incident incorrectly. Certainly by the time of McLaws's conversation with Generals Lee and Longstreet, Johnston's reconnaissance was long under way, if in fact it was not over. And what of Major Clarke, Longstreet's engineer, who did accompany Johnston? If already back, he would have talked with Longstreet or could have been expected to provide the information needed by Longstreet's corps. Thus, Longstreet's refusal to have McLaws and Moncure on the expedition could have originated the belief that he was already adequately represented by Clarke.

General Lee had spent much of the early morning with Longstreet and Hill and must have known of the whereabouts of the divisions of their corps. Some were there for him to see. But he must have known comparatively little of General Ewell and his corps, for Major Venable had not yet returned from his visit to Ewell's front. To remedy this deficiency, General Lee set out for his left to see it for himself. Some place his departure at 9:00 A.M., but it could have been earlier. Certainly he would have gone after Captain Johnston's return and after his conversation with McLaws. The general apparently rode east on West Middle Street to Baltimore Street. He turned south on Baltimore Street, passed by the courthouse, and continued to High Street and the Presbyterian Church. He went east on High Street (where he might have had some views of Cemetery Hill) to Stratton Street and from there east somehow to Hanover Street and Ewell's headquarters near Rock Creek just east of the town. When he arrived, Ewell was not there; he had gone out with Major Venable. But Maj. Gen. Isaac R. Trimble was there, and he was probably itching for something to do.[18]

Trimble, age sixty-one, was a scrapper. Although he had not yet fully recovered from a wound received at Groveton almost a year before and had no command, he had returned to the army in order to participate in the Pennsylvania campaign. The two generals exchanged greetings and Lee inquired of a vantage point from which he could get a view of the countryside. Trimble knew of one, the cupola of the almshouse along the Harrisburg Road, though one can wonder if it was the best to fill Lee's needs. The two visited the almshouse and its cupola. Sometime in the course of their conversation, General Lee was said to have remarked to Trimble that "we did not or we could not pursue our advantage of yesterday," a refrain that he voiced several times that day. Feisty Isaac Trimble would have been a sympathetic hearer of any such regrets that General Lee might voice to him.[19]

In the meantime General Ewell and Major Venable were assessing Ewell's opportunities. When he arrived at Ewell's headquarters shortly after sunrise, Venable asked what General Ewell thought of the advantages of an assault from his position. Venable went on to say that General Lee was wondering if Ewell's corps ought to be shifted from opposite the Union right to an area from which it might be used to advantage in an attack on Cemetery Ridge. Ewell had an open mind about this and wished to be cooperative, so they went out for a daylight examination of his front. As Venable recalled it in later years, the errand on which he was sent was not consistent with the concept of a sunrise attack by any part of the army.[20]

When General Lee returned to Ewell's headquarters, the one-legged general persuaded him to permit the Second Corps to stay where it was. He was to cooperate with Longstreet's corps's attack from the right by creating a diversion when he heard the sound of Longstreet's guns. During their talk, Colonel Long, who had finished his tour of artillery positions on Ewell's front, appeared and accompanied General Lee back to Seminary Ridge. Long recalled in later years that the general listened for the sound of Longstreet's attack and was not pleased that it was delayed. Long placed their return at about 9:00 A.M., but perhaps it was a little later.[21]

After his return, General Lee examined a portion of Cemetery Ridge and, according to Colonel Long, became increasingly impatient, "remarking in a tone of uneasiness, 'What *can* detain Longstreet? He ought to be in position now!'" This, Long said, was about 10:00 A.M. What Lee's intentions for Longstreet were at this time were debated vigorously in the postwar period. General Lee's principal staff officers later stated that he wanted to attack early but not at sunrise as Early, Pendleton, and some others had maintained. There were those like Lawley of London's *Times* who wrote of General Lee's impatience and anxiety, and General Hood recalled some of this in later years. As Hood remembered, General Lee declared, "The enemy is here, and if we do not whip him he will whip us." But, as Hood sat and talked with Longstreet, Longstreet remarked: "The General is a little nervous this morning; he wishes me to attack; I do not wish to do so without Pickett. I never like to go into battle with one boot off."[22]

This was an interesting statement from a man who had fought at Antietam with one foot encased in a carpet slipper! But no matter, it reveals a desire on the part of General Lee for an attack, not at sunrise obviously, but as early as practicable consistent with the time required to get proper intelligence on the enemy, develop a plan, and get the troops into position and ready. It reveals also a wish by Longstreet not to attack, at least until Pickett's division was up, which perhaps was tantamount that day to no attack at all. And it suggests a reluctance on General Lee's part, as was his way, to give Longstreet unequivocal orders to get his divisions into position.

Hood suggested no time for the quoted statements of Generals Lee and Longstreet. Lee could have spoken so to Hood quite early in the morning, soon after Hood's arrival on the field, and before his visit to Ewell and to the Confederate left. Longstreet's remark, on the other hand, could have been made either early in the morning or after General Lee's return. Certainly it must have been made after Captain Johnston's return from his reconnaissance and the conversations at the log. Hood's comments, coupled with Colonel Long's, suggest that Lee expected some movement by Longstreet during Lee's visit to the left, even though it seems unlikely that the plan for the day's assault had really matured at that time.

Whatever General Lee's intentions, General Longstreet, his key subordinate, maintained that Lee gave no orders to attack until after his visit to Ewell. Longstreet had been given no orders for an assault on the enemy on 1 July, though he knew of General Lee's inclination to take the offensive and had spoken against it. Longstreet repeated his argument against a direct assault early on the morning of 2 July, but General Lee still would not accept it. They discussed the probable result of such an assault, which implies that they also discussed, in a general way at least, how such an assault would be made and by whom. Then, according to Longstreet, Lee visited Ewell, returned, said "that it would not do to have Ewell open the attack," and announced his decision that Longstreet's corps would make the attack from the right. And then, about 11:00 A.M., he "ordered the movement."[23]

That was it. The order was given, and General Longstreet found himself about to launch an assault minus not only a boot—Pickett's division—but without Law's brigade as well. Law had been left across the mountain at New Guilford but had been called forward late on 1 July, had started out about 3:00 A.M., and was known to be approaching. Longstreet asked General Lee's permission to await the arrival of Law's brigade before moving and apparently received it. Law arrived shortly before noon, occasioning a further delay of about forty minutes, and in a short time Longstreet set his corps in motion.[24]

By this time General Lee must have formulated his plan of attack. This plan was not drawn up on paper by Lee or his staff, nor was it promulgated in any written orders that have survived. Rather it comes to us in fragments from reports and accounts of the battle prepared by officers who could write with assurance of only those portions of the plan that applied to their commands. Significantly, the plan was based on Confederate perceptions of the Federal situation at the time that the plan was imparted and not on the reality of enemy dispositions at the time of the attack.

According to General Lee's reports, his immediate objective was to gain the high ground between Seminary and Cemetery ridges, that along the Emmitsburg Road described above and occupied in force a little later in the day by General Sickles's Third Corps. Hood's and McLaws's divisions were to envelop the enemy left and drive it in; Hill's corps was to threaten the enemy center to prevent enemy reinforcement of his left and then cooperate with and continue Longstreet's effort. Ewell's corps on the left was to "make a simultaneous demonstration" against the Federal right and convert this feint into an all-out attack if warranted.[25]

This was Lee's plan, and he gave specific instructions for its implementation. He explained how he wanted McLaws to attack the Peach Orchard, but we do not know what was prescribed for Hood. Then, after hours passed and the Federal position developed, the orders for Hood and McLaws had to be altered as described in Chapter 8 below. Anderson's orders, however, probably did not change—his division would attack the Union center as McLaws attacked the Peach Orchard.[26]

Anderson's division had a particular role in the plans of the commanding general. Longstreet's corps was to form on its right for the principal assault, and Anderson's division, in turn, was to continue that assault against the Union center. It follows, then, that Longstreet's two divisions could not form for their attack until Anderson's division was essentially in place. The activities of Hill's corps suggest that any delay occasioned by Longstreet's foot-dragging was much less than has sometimes been supposed.

General A. P. Hill's personal activities on the morning are generally unknown. Probably after consultation with General Lee, Hill ordered Anderson's division from its bivouac on Herr Ridge to relieve Heth's battered division occupying the portion of Seminary Ridge between McMillan's Woods and Spangler's Woods. There is no indication in the Confederate reports when Hill ordered this relief and when it began. However, either the order came much after daybreak or the movement proceeded deliberately, if not slowly, for it was nearly noon when Wilcox's brigade approached its position on the right of the division south of Spangler's Woods. Anderson rode ahead with Wilcox to show him the position that the brigade would occupy. The right of Wilcox's line and Anderson's division would rest against "a heavy and thick woods," Pitzer's Woods, at a high point about five hundred yards south of Spangler's Woods. From there, fronting south along the ridge, the line would tail back to Spangler's Woods and terminate about a hundred yards from Perry's brigade, which would occupy the northeastern portion of the woods. In this position Wilcox could protect the army's flank. Whether Wilcox's deployment as guardian of the right was conceived by only Anderson or whether it was ordered by General Lee or General Hill is not known. Obviously it reflected the Confederates' immediate defensive needs rather than the deployment needed for their later assault.[27]

The first serious fighting of the day took place when Wilcox's brigade encountered Berdan's force in Pitzer's Woods. Although this fracas had a rather significant impact on the Army of the Potomac, it had little meaning for the commanders of the Army of Northern Virginia. Wilcox, of course, gave it a prominent review in his report, for he and his brigade were directly involved in it. Anderson, who had a broader view of the day's events, mentioned it as having been only a "sharp skirmish," and the reports of A. P. Hill and General Lee ignored it completely. Its impact on Sickles's thinking and on the Army of the Potomac was unknown to the Confederates. Apart from other things, it was important as an indicator of battle chronology. It provides a positive indication of when the right of Anderson's division went on line and suggests that at that time Anderson was thinking in defensive and not in offensive terms. At noon on 2 July A. P. Hill, like James Longstreet, was not yet prepared to implement General Lee's plan of attack. But this would soon change.[28]

In the early afternoon, shortly after his division was deployed, Anderson learned that Longstreet's corps would occupy the ground to his right, nearly at right angles to that portion of Wilcox's front facing down the ridge, and that from it the First Corps divisions would assault the enemy's left flank and drive him across Anderson's front toward Gettysburg. At the same time, Anderson's division would attack by brigades as soon as Longstreet's assault reached its right. Nothing happened for a while, nothing but "desultory firing between skirmishers." Finally, about three hours after their noon fight, Wilcox's men saw Longstreet's divisions filing south down the Willoughby Run Valley to their right and rear.[29]

Some of Longstreet's delay had resulted from his impractical decision to await the arrival of Law's brigade before moving to the assault position. When the other three brigades of Hood's division had marched to Gettysburg the night before, Law and his brigade had stayed at New Guilford in the Cumberland Valley to cover the army's rear. They had a quiet stay, highlighted for some by the butchering of some Chester White hogs that furnished pork for the day's meal and for their haversacks. Orders came to march on the evening of 1 July, followed by instructions to cook rations and be ready to take the road at 3:00 A.M. The brigade set out on time at a rapid pace, not slowed by other traffic. It passed Thaddeus Stevens's destroyed iron furnace, moved through Cashtown Pass, and continued east to Gettysburg. As it approached the town, its men saw hospitals and relics of the 1 July battle and arrived to find a portion of the division stretched along the Chambersburg Pike. It was a hard march of about twenty-five miles in about eleven hours, "the best marching done in either army to reach the field of Gettysburg," said Longstreet, though there were probably many in the Union Sixth Corps who would not have agreed. It was also the beginning of a very long day.[30]

A short time after Law's arrival, Hood's division left the Chambersburg Pike to take its place in column behind McLaws's division beyond Willoughby Run. There was more waiting there, and the men spent some of their time eating their rations. One of them walked to a "nearby elevation" where he saw Lee and Longstreet and overheard conversation that led him to believe that they would be marching soon.[31]

It was sometime during the morning's marching and waiting that the men of Kershaw's brigade rested by a wall along a road, just where cannot be said. Some dozed; others idled their time away watching a portion of Hill's corps file by. With that august body of troops there was an officer, said perhaps wrongly to have been a general, conspicuous because he was mounted, wore a new uniform with a crimson sash, and had golden curls showing beneath the brim of his hat. Although he might have resembled General Pickett, the officer made such an unusual sight that a soldier from Company D, Third South Carolina, felt obliged to comment. With just the right amount of tact demanded by the occasion he bawled: "Say, Mister, come right down out of that hair." This request caused the officer's temper to flare, and he demanded to know who had spoken so that he might "put a ball in him." The offended dandy got no satisfaction, of course, and being somewhat embarrassed and having important business elsewhere, he reined his horse around and started away. As he passed from the proximity of the Third, an apologetic voice called after him: "Say, Mister, don't get so mad about it, I thought you were some d—n wagonmaster."[32]

Col. John L. Black also had some recollections of this part of the day. On his way in early that morning he had seen Brig. Gen. William Barksdale sitting on a fence at the side of the Chambersburg Pike. Barksdale was feeling unwell. Later, after the 11:00 A.M. order, while Longstreet awaited Law's arrival, Longstreet and Black rode from Seminary Ridge back to Herr Ridge and to the divisions of Longstreet's corps. Black saw the two divisions resting in a column, the regiments with little or no interval between them. Some of the men were busy cleaning their rifles, and others were eating from their haversacks. To Black they seemed "cheerful & bouyant and a more gallant corps never was arrayed for the fatal fray."[33]

Soon Longstreet, Black, and no doubt others of Longstreet's entourage, reached Longstreet's temporary headquarters site somewhere near the Fairfield Road above Black Horse Tavern, apparently near the head of McLaws's column. Here Longstreet asked Black for the service of two trusty subalterns. Black summoned Lts. Fred Horsey and J. Wilson Marshall of the First South Carolina Cavalry. Longstreet directed each of them to take an escort and ride out three or four miles, Horsey down Seminary Ridge and Marshall in an undisclosed direction but probably off to the southwest on the road traveled by Humphreys's division the previous evening. They were to keep an eye open for the enemy and then hurry back to report what, if anything, they had seen. Horsey was back in about an hour and reported seeing no enemy. In the meantime Longstreet had Black post Hart's South Carolina Battery in a spot where it could cover "a road bearing to the right."[34] What road Black did not say.

Black also had another lieutenant check out the Black Horse Tavern. He did so and found some barrels of whiskey, which Black then had destroyed. Soon thereafter, Black mentioned the whiskey to Longstreet. "I suppose," said the general, "you saved some for yourself & me." Shades of Stonewall Jackson! Black, who took some modest satisfaction in being a teetotaler, replied, "Excuse me, General, as I do not drink, I forgot to do so."[35] And with that Black fades from the history of the events of 2 July 1863 as one who did not share a libation with General Longstreet.

In the meantime, Alexander's battalion and the Washington Artillery of New Orleans had arrived and parked along the Chambersburg Pike while Col. James B. Walton, the commander of the Artillery Reserve of Longstreet's corps, rode off for a talk with General Longstreet. When he returned, he told Alexander that Longstreet wished to see him. Alexander rode in to the seminary campus and found his corps commander with General Lee at his observation post. Longstreet, in General Lee's presence, pointed out the enemy's position and said that the Confederates would attack the enemy's left. He told Alexander that he, Alexander, would be the tactical commander of the First Corps's artillery. He advised him to go first and get an idea of the ground and then to bring his own battalion up but to leave the Washington Artillery in park in the rear. He cautioned the young colonel especially to keep his batteries out of view of a signal station whose flags were waving away on Little Round Top. Within ten minutes after his briefing began, Alexander was off to the right to take a look at the ground and see how best to post his guns there.[36]

Edward Porter Alexander merits notice. Born in 1835 in Georgia, he graduated from West Point with its class of 1857 and received a commission in the Engineers. Alexander was a thorough professional, but in the first year of the war he was too young and inexperienced for the command of a brigade and too valuable an officer to be consigned to the obscurity of a regiment. His Confederate service began on the staff of General P. G. T. Beauregard, and it was Alexander who, acting as a signal officer, first spotted the Federal turning movement at Bull Run and alerted his general to the threat to the Confederate left. Alexander was assigned to the artillery in November 1862, when he replaced Stephen D. Lee as commander of his battalion. Because of his ability and because fate, perhaps, gave him a special role in the battles of 2 and 3 July at Gettysburg, Alexander emerged from the campaign a historic figure. He became a general officer in 1864, and his wartime prestige grew with his postwar success as a college professor, an engineer, a businessman, and, especially, an author of lucid and thoughtful accounts of some of his wartime experiences.[37]

Probably at Longstreet's suggestion, Alexander rode first to see General Pendleton, who was at an overlook somewhere near the Fairfield Road. The two officers rode to another observation point closer to the enemy that Pendleton had visited earlier in the day and found that this once-quiet place was now within range of Federal snipers. Pendleton and Alexander did not identify the place, but probably it was the high ground just northeast of Spangler's Woods, the site from which Alexander watched the effects of Confederate fire on the following afternoon. While there, they heard firing to their right and rear, probably Wilcox's noonday fight in Pitzer's Woods.[38]

Alexander continued south into the area just claimed by Wilcox and got the lay of the land there and beyond in the fields to be occupied by Longstreet's corps. Then, in what he thought was just a little more than an hour, he rode north again to find Henry's and Cabell's battalions, which had come to Gettysburg with Hood and McLaws. He gave the two battalion commanders their instructions and then rode west along the Chambersburg Pike to bring up his own battalion. He found its batteries waiting, teams unhitched and grazing near their guns. At his order the buglers sounded "Boots and Saddles," and soon the batteries were rolling out. This gave particular pleasure to some of the men of his battalion who jeered at the cannoneers of the Washington Artillery as they left them behind. Perhaps some would have been glad to have exchanged places with the men from New Orleans before the day was over.[39]

Alexander probably led his batteries over the road that runs from the Chambersburg Pike along Marsh Creek to Black Horse Tavern. The battalion crossed the Fairfield Road to the road leading south beyond it, climbed the hill, and in order to avoid being seen by the Federal signalmen, turned into the fields to bypass the exposed crest. It then returned to the road and followed it along Willoughby Run to Pitzer's Schoolhouse. Somewhere near the schoolhouse, beyond the immediate protection of Wilcox's infantrymen, the battalion pulled off the road and waited for the rest of Longstreet's corps.[40]

Alexander had led his battalion to the Pitzer Schoolhouse area without incident, not a difficult task for a capable officer with a moderate appreciation of terrain. However, it happened that the ordnance sergeant of Taylor's Virginia Battery was Henry Wentz, a native of Gettysburg who had lived in his father's house just north of the Peach Orchard. Sergeant Wentz must have had intimate knowledge of Gettysburg's geography that would have proved useful to both Alexander and Longstreet, and it is likely that Alexander would have been aware of Wentz's Gettysburg connection. What role did Henry Wentz play in the day's events? Did he ride with Alexander on his reconnaissance? Did he help in guiding the battalion to Pitzer's Schoolhouse? Alexander did not say. It seems unlikely that he would have omitted such an interesting bit of information from his postwar accounts had Wentz been with him, and it must be assumed reluctantly that Wentz spent the day with his battery. If so, this ranks as one of the Confederates' most peculiar oversights, and Wentz's role must remain as one of the tantalizing mysteries of Gettysburg.[41]

After reaching the Pitzer's Schoolhouse area, Colonel Alexander waited a while, and then, leaving his battalion under the command of Maj. Frank Huger, he retraced his route toward Black Horse Tavern. He found the head of Longstreet's column, McLaws's division, standing near the crest of the hill that he had avoided a short time before. When it became apparent that the column would be seen if it crossed the crest, McLaws had halted it until he received instructions from Longstreet about what should be done. Alexander spoke to some unidentified officers about his route and pointed out the track made by his battalion when it turned out across the fields. This was to no avail, for no one present would take the responsibility for following his seemingly workable solution and example. They had to await orders from above. So much for Confederate individualism and initiative on that fateful day.[42]

Colonel Alexander had stumbled across one of the most difficult non-combat aspects of the Gettysburg campaign to reconstruct and to understand—Longstreet's approach march to his corps's position on 2 July. The facts of the matter seem to lie forever concealed by a lack of correct information engendered by personal conflicts and the failure of participants simply to report what they had done. The march began after Law's brigade arrived and probably after the fight in Pitzer's Woods; thus, it must not have begun before noon at the earliest. Why it was necessary for Longstreet to hold both

McLaws's and Hood's divisions on Herr Ridge awaiting Law's arrival instead of moving to the assigned positions at once, Longstreet and others did not explain.

Simply stated, the object of the march was to move Hood's and McLaws's divisions from their halting points north of the Fairfield Road south two to four miles behind Seminary Ridge to their positions on Anderson's right. As it turned out, these positions had a front of about 1 ½ miles south from a point in Pitzer's Woods about two miles south of the Fairfield Road. This movement, of course, was more easily ordered than made. The two divisions would each have taken up 1 ½ miles of road space, probably excluding that needed for the artillery, and each had wagons along that might have made them road bound. Although the passing of six score years and the development of new concepts and tactics have sometimes made Civil War procedures and thinking hard to fathom, it does seem apparent that McLaws (who was a competent if not great division commander) felt it necessary to march by roads and lanes rather than follow Alexander's example and cut across fields.[43]

McLaws's division, with Kershaw's brigade at its head, led off. It countermarched a short distance from its waiting area of the morning, cut west by a lane down the slope of Herr Ridge to the road along Marsh Creek about five hundred yards north of Black Horse Tavern, and turned left along the road there toward the tavern. The division crossed the Fairfield Road at the tavern, as Alexander's Battalion had done a short while before. Led by McLaws and Captain Johnston, it passed into the road that ran southeasterly to Pitzer's Schoolhouse. According to a soldier of the Seventeenth Mississippi Regiment of Barksdale's brigade, they moved at a half trot until the head of the column, which was probably marching along at quick time, reached the troublesome hill. Then they halted. The Mississippians apparently broke ranks, since one soldier went into a barn, probably that at Black Horse Tavern, in search of flour.[44]

General McLaws, still at the head of the column, halted when it appeared that his troops could be seen from Little Round Top. He and Captain Johnston, and possibly others, searched for a suitable alternate route out of sight of the signalmen, apparently overlooking or rejecting that used by Alexander's guns, the wheel tracks of which ought to have been obvious to them. McLaws returned to his division after a while, and a veteran remarked in later years that he was "saying things I would not like to teach my grandson . . . to repeat."[45]

When McLaws rode down from the crest, he met Longstreet, who had ridden up from the rear, where he had been with General Lee for a time and with Hood.[46] Longstreet was impatient over the delay and asked the reason for it. In response McLaws asked him to ride back with him to the top of the hill, and when they reached the top, he pointed out how the column would be exposed when crossing its crest. Longstreet looked and complained, "Why,

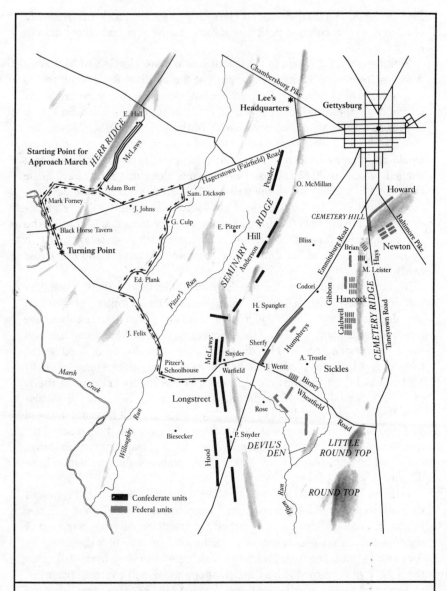

1. Longstreet's march began on Herr Ridge. The head of McLaws's division probably followed the route indicated. Hood's division probably followed McLaws's between the Fairfield Road and Pitzer's Schoolhouse.

2. The approximate positions occupied by the brigades of both armies on the Union left and Confederate right prior to the assault are shown. Much of the Federal Second Corps was formed in masses or columns and not in line.

Map 6-1. Longstreet's Approach March and Troop Positions on Cemetery Ridge and Seminary Ridge at 4:00 P.M.

this won't do. Is there no way to avoid it?" McLaws then told him of a route that he had found in his restricted reconnaissance earlier in the day, but said that it could be taken only after countermarching. Longstreet approved the suggested route. It was about this time, if not a little before, that Hood "in his eagerness for the fray (and he bears the character of always being so)" marched his division into the rear of McLaws's, overlapping it and creating a traffic problem that made the countermarch more difficult. By this time both Longstreet and McLaws were vexed, "both manifesting considerable irritation," as the gentlemanly Kershaw expressed it. Longstreet proposed that Hood's division lead the countermarch as the practical thing to do under the circumstances, but McLaws was in no mood to be generous and did not yield to the suggestion. Longstreet did not press the matter, McLaws's division continued to lead, and the march began once more.[47]

McLaws's division probably returned to Herr Ridge by the lane it had taken from it. In the words of Kershaw, whose brigade still led the division and who made the fullest comment on it, the brigade "moved back to the place where we had rested during the morning [presumably this was on the road to Herr Ridge], and thence by a country road to Willoughby Run, then dry, and down that to the school-house beyond Pitzer's."[48]

McLaws wrote of having made the countermarch with difficulty, "owing to the rough character of the country in places and the fences and ditches we had to cross." This suggests, at least, that the route of the countermarch was not an easy one and that it probably followed a farm lane or a very poor public road. Such a route that could have carried them back to the Herr Ridge road, where they probably had spent the morning, was a farm lane that they probably used in descending Herr Ridge. It left the Marsh Creek road at the Forney farm buildings about five hundred yards north of the Fairfield Road, climbed the ridge, passed through some woods, and entered the Herr Ridge road at the Adam Butt house. A lane ran southeast from the Butt house down to the Fairfield Road, which in turn led east to the road that follows the course of Willoughby Run south to Pitzer's Woods.[49]

McLaws's soldiers found it easier going once they reached the "ravine road" along Willoughby Run. The ground is essentially flat there. Apart from the stream bed itself, there were no natural obstacles. But the road was lined with fences that constricted it enough so that McLaws had to narrow his regiments' company fronts by ordering them to "break files to the rear." This would have stretched the column out and slowed the march, particularly of the rear brigades. Somewhere along the line of march, General Pendleton's aide, Lt. George W. Peterkin, who had been in the area to be occupied early that morning, reported to McLaws in order to guide his division toward its position.[50]

The head of McLaws's division reached the road junction at Pitzer's Schoolhouse without incident and turned left. With Kershaw's brigade still in the lead, the division headed up the west slope of Seminary Ridge toward the crest and the Peach Orchard six hundred yards beyond. About this time, General Longstreet rode up to McLaws and asked, "How are you going in?" McLaws replied, "That will be determined when I can see what is in my front." Longstreet observed, "There is nothing in your front; you will be entirely on the flank of the enemy." That was in accord with what General Lee had said earlier in the day, so McLaws replied, "Then I will continue my march in columns of companies, and after arriving on the flank as far as is necessary will face to the left and march on the enemy." General Longstreet replied, "That suits me," and rode away.[51]

McLaws's division reached the tree line on Seminary Ridge. As soon as his column broke cover in front of the Federal position, "the enemy at once opened on it with numerous artillery," and it was obvious that the Peach Orchard area was occupied by the Federal forces in greater strength than expected. Kershaw sent skirmishers to the front and formed his brigade in line of battle in front of a stone wall that ran along the crest of the ridge. As Kershaw deployed his brigade, McLaws hurried back to hasten his rear brigades forward and ordered up Cabell's battalion so that it could take position on the ridge line and open fire. He hoped that his batteries' fire would relieve the potential pressure on his infantry. It was apparent that his division was not on the flank of the enemy.[52]

Hood's division followed McLaws's. Being far from the front of the column, Hood's men felt the full effects of accordian action—slow moving, starting, and stopping. There were vexatious delays caused in part by concern that the column might be seen from Little Round Top. Longstreet became impatient after a time and, considering it useless to worry any more about concealment, ordered Hood to double McLaws's column and go quickly into position.[53] This made good sense, or so it seems today, but the sophistry used in one of his explanations for it does not. Longstreet stated in one account that, since Captain Johnston was ordered by General Lee to conduct the head of the column—McLaws's division—he, Longstreet, could not interfere with it; but the order did not apply to Hood's division, so he felt free to order Hood forward and did so. In doing this, he broke up the delay.[54]

Neither Longstreet nor Hood said when this happened, but there is no doubt that it did happen. Kershaw, whose brigade formed on the right of McLaws's forward line, reported that while his brigade and the remainder of the division were forming on the ridge, Hood's division was moving in its rear toward the right to gain the enemy's left flank.[55] It seems unlikely that Hood's division was rushed ahead before McLaws's division had reached its position and the location of Hood's left flank was thus defined. But when the order came, the eager Hood sent pioneers forward to level fences in the division's path and clear the way toward the Emmitsburg Road across the Biesecker and Douglas farms. Wisely too, before reaching his position, Hood sent some of his "picked Texas scouts" forward to locate the enemy's flank. Clearly

Hood did not exhibit faith in the reported location of the enemy's left. He was going to find that out for himself.[56]

It was now 4:00 P.M. Anderson's division had been posted for nearly four hours, and Longstreet's two divisions had been marching or marking time in tedious waiting since sunup eleven hours before. The high command of the Army of Northern Virginia had functioned poorly that day. General Lee's plan had matured slowly and, as McLaws discovered when he arrived opposite the Peach Orchard, had been based on faulty intelligence. Hill had not seen to the prompt posting of Anderson's division, and Longstreet's angry dissidence had resulted in further wasted time and delay. But finally the right wing of the Army of Northern Virginia was getting into position for its attack, and the hard and bloody work of the day was about to start.

7

Sickles Takes Up the Forward Line

"I took up that line because it enabled me to hold commanding ground," Maj. Gen. Daniel E. Sickles told the Committee on the Conduct of the War. Had he not done so and had the enemy been allowed to take the commanding ground "as they would have taken it if I had not occupied it in force," he went on to testify, the Federal left would have been untenable. In his judgment, the Confederates would have turned the fortunes of the day "hopelessly against us."[1] And so he marched his Third Corps forward to the high ground above the west branch of Plum Run and along the Emmitsburg Road and deployed it there far outside the position assigned to that corps by General Meade.

Sickles's left was neither at nor on Little Round Top. Instead it rested at Devil's Den, west of Plum Run, five hundred yards to the front of Little Round Top's crest, though not nearly so far from its base. Devil's Den is an extensive rock formation whose massive granite blocks spill like the fruit of a cornucopia from the south end of the low, short ridge (referred to hereinafter as Devil's Den Ridge) that forms the west wall of Plum Run Valley opposite Little Round Top.[2] The granite rocks of Devil's Den are an assortment of huge boulders, slabs, and chunks, some the size of small houses or automobiles, all jumbled together with holes and crevasses between them. This formation extends to the base of Round Top, where it constricts the valley of Plum Run into a gorge. Devil's Den was a wild sort of place, useful at best as a poor site for grazing cattle or as a wood lot and not much more. It covered an area of about ten acres, and no Civil War unit could have attacked through it in formation. Just north and west of its rock spill a knoll rises about seventy feet over Plum Run. This knoll and another one about four hundred yards north of it were key features of Devil's Den Ridge forming the west wall of the Plum Run Valley in front of Little Round Top.

The west wall of Plum Run's valley, like the west face of Little Round Top, had been logged for timber not long before the battle and was essentially bare of trees. This clear cutting extended around the south and west slopes of Devil's Den to include a sloping, rocky field shaped like an equilateral triangle that was enclosed by stone walls each about 150 yards in length. The cleared area gave troops posted above Devil's Den an unobstructed view across the fields 1,000 yards to the west to that portion of Seminary Ridge south of the Emmitsburg Road.[3] Just north of the triangular field and west of the knoll Rose's Woods covered the west slope of the ridge for a distance of about three hundred yards to the south edge of the Wheatfield.

The position assigned to Birney's division on Cemetery Ridge north from Little Round Top had been deemed undesirable not only because it was a little lower than the high ground along the Emmitsburg Road but also because trees on and in front of it made it unsuitable for use by artillery. Good battery positions had to have certain characteristics. Most importantly they had to have fields of fire. At Gettysburg, as elsewhere during the Civil War, field batteries employed what later was called "direct fire." Like riflemen, gunners aimed their pieces directly at their targets. There was practically no lobbing of shot and shell from the protection of hills or woods at unseen targets, for there was no practicable way to control such fire. The guns of a battery had to be up on the firing line ·where the gunners could see their targets and aim directly at them.[4]

Batteries also fired best from ground that was relatively smooth, level, and bare of obstructions. Such surfaces permitted gun crews to work efficiently around their pieces, point the guns, bring up ammunition from the limbers, load, fire, and push the guns back to their proper places after recoil. The guns themselves had no recoil mechanisms and had to be free to roll back sufficiently when fired to take up the shock of recoil. There was an advantage to having guns posted on ground that sloped slightly uphill to the rear, for then gravity might shorten their rollback and cannoneers could more easily push the guns back into battery after firing. It was also advantageous to have gun wheels level to minimize "cant," a sidewise tilt of the axles and barrels that skewed the trajectory and made accuracy more difficult to achieve. Probably the ground surface above Devil's Den did not meet these requirements well.[5]

Battery position also had to be accessible if guns were to be hauled in and out quickly and if limbers were to be parked close enough to supply the guns with ammunition. Because batteries were on or near the infantry line, the guns were vulnerable to assault and had to be readily movable to avoid the possibility of capture. To permit prompt movement and to make ammunition readily available, the noses of the lead pairs of the limbers' six-horse teams were halted and held close behind their guns.[6]

The Peach Orchard area provided good battery positions, as Sickles, Birney, and Captain Randolph readily recognized. This was not so with the left of Sickles's new line. Only one place there offered the most essential requirement—a field of fire. This was the area above the boulders of Devil's

Col. E. Porter Alexander
(National Archives)

Lt. Col. Freeman McGilvery (MOLLUS-
MASS/U.S.A.M.H.I., Carlisle Barracks, Pa.)

Capt. George E. Randolph (MOLLUS-
MASS/U.S.A.M.H.I., Carlisle Barracks, Pa.)

Den and behind the triangular field. At Captain Randolph's direction, Capt. James E. Smith's Fourth New York Battery took position there and symbolically marked the Third Corps's left.

The Fourth New York Battery was a New York City unit and was armed with six ten-pounder Parrott rifles. These guns had cast iron barrels with 2.9-inch bores and wrought iron reinforcing jackets around the breech. Like the three-inch Ordnance rifle, a comparable piece that had a wrought iron barrel without the reinforcing jacket, they were reasonably accurate according to the standards of the day and had ranges in excess of one mile. This distance, of course, was farther than gunners could aim their pieces with any accuracy. Captain Smith saw that the usable space above Devil's Den would not accommodate all six of his guns (the prescribed interval between pieces was fourteen yards), so he placed four there (probably just to the right of where the battery was later marked) and put the other two in the Plum Run Valley to his right and rear. The rear section could sweep the valley as far as the tree-covered slope of Round Top and the rocks of the gorge of Devil's Den. In doing so, the rear guns could give some protection to the flank of the four guns in front. Captain Smith wrote nothing specific about the location of his limbers or of how his crews got ammunition to the four guns above Devil's Den. A sergeant of the 124th New York Regiment noted that each round had to be carried to the guns from the foot of the ridge. This would have been very difficult and slow, and crews might have piled some rounds near their guns—a practice usually forbidden.[7]

Smith's four guns could reach Seminary Ridge and any Confederate guns posted there, but Smith still worried. Any Confederate infantry that could gain the tree-covered slope of Round Top nearby or the rocks of Devil's Den could approach Smith's guns under cover, snipe at his cannoneers, and neutralize his battery.[8]

Birney assigned Ward's brigade to the left of his division's line and to the support of Smith's battery. J. H. Hobart Ward was an old soldier with a rather unusual background. Born in 1823, he left college at the age of eighteen and enlisted in the Seventh U.S. Infantry. He served with that regiment during the War with Mexico, was wounded at Monterrey, and in time became the regiment's sergeant major. He left the Regular Army by 1851 and became New York State's assistant commissary general. He went on to serve as the state's commissary general from 1855 to 1859. When the war came, Ward was in his prime, with military experience in both the field and administrative positions and with obvious political connections. It is no wonder, then, that he was commissioned a colonel and given a regiment, the Thirty-eighth New York Volunteer Infantry. After participating in the Army of the Potomac's early campaigns, he succeeded to the command of the Second Brigade, First Division, Third Corps, in October 1862 and received his star. Ward was an old soldier who could be expected to give a good account of himself.[9]

Initially Ward had five regiments in his brigade's line: the Twentieth Indiana, the Fourth Maine, the Eighty-sixth and 124th New York, and the Ninety-ninth Pennsylvania. His three other units, the Third Maine and the two sharpshooter regiments, as we have seen, were on the skirmish line elsewhere along the Third Corps's front. At about noon, at Birney's order, Ward advanced his brigade from its morning location south of the George Weikert farmyard across the Wheatfield Road to the Wheatfield, where it halted in the yet untrampled wheat. After a pause in the wheat, the brigade shifted to the left and took position on and near Devil's Den Ridge.[10]

Ward posted the 124th New York to the right and rear of Smith's battery. The left of the 124th, therefore, was in the open ground just behind the crest of the ridge, but its right extended beyond a fence to the front side of the ridge and into the east end of Rose's Woods just northwest of the knoll above Devil's Den. Shortly afterward, Ward placed the Fourth Maine to the left of the 124th and behind Smith's four guns, thus extending his infantry line into the upper portion of Devil's Den. The Eighty-sixth New York prolonged the 124th's right north into Rose's Woods, and the Twentieth Indiana and the Ninety-ninth Pennsylvania carried it north to the Wheatfield, though in a short time these two regiments advanced down the slope toward the west branch of Plum Run in support of the skirmish line. Thus, Ward's brigade had a single line, without supports, that extended from Devil's Den northerly along the crest of the ridge, through the east end of Rose's Woods, and up to the south border of the Wheatfield, a distance of about four hundred yards. Except for the Fourth Maine and the left wing of the 124th New York, which faced across the essentially open fields toward Seminary Ridge, Ward's infantrymen overlooked a wooded and rocky slope that ran down about three hundred yards into the west branch of Plum Run.[11]

The Wheatfield was beyond a stone wall that ran at a right angle to Ward's right. The Gettysburg area had scores of wheat and oat fields, all yellow in July with ripening grain, and several of them were on the battlefield. Only one, however, became "the Wheatfield"—that on Rose's farm about midway between Devil's Den and the Peach Orchard. It was about twenty acres in extent and virtually surrounded by woods. Although open, the field contained a few scattered boulders whose presence in the wheat was marked by clumps of bushes and trees. The field was highest along its northern and eastern sides. It drained south and west, and its southwest corner was marshy ground that was part of the valley of the west branch of Plum Run. The run was no more than 120 feet away. A rail fence, which ran back almost perpendicular to the stone wall that bordered the field on the south, separated the Wheatfield proper from the marshy ground into which it drained and from the stony hill and woods along its western side.[12]

The Wheatfield had some of the attributes of a good artillery position, though the fields of fire of any battery posted in it would have been confined practically to the field itself. Nevertheless, Captain Randolph posted Capt. George B. Winslow's Battery D, First New York Light Artillery, on high ground fronting south across the field and roughly parallel to the Wheatfield Road. A space of about a hundred yards separated the right of the battery from the trees on the hill that formed the west boundary of the Wheatfield. Battery D was a veteran unit. It had been organized in western New York by Winslow and Thomas W. Osborn, its first commander. Osborn commanded it through Chancellorsville, and then he became the artillery chief for the Eleventh Corps. The battery had had a unique experience in the summer of 1862 east of Richmond. Osborn rigged one of its pieces, a three-inch Ordnance rifle, to fire at a Confederate balloon and scared the balloonists off with three shots. That was good fun, of course, but there was more serious work elsewhere. The battery particularly distinguished itself at Chancellorsville on 3 May when, according to Winslow, it fired canister at less than a thirty-yard range until it ran out of ammunition and had to retire.[13]

Battery D traded its three-inch Ordnance rifles for Napoleons after the Peninsular campaign. These bronze guns, whose barrels weighed more than 1,200 pounds, had smooth bores that measured 4.62 inches in diameter, and they fired round iron projectiles. The solid shot for a Napoleon weighed twelve pounds, hence the designation "twelve-pounder." It was named for Napoleon III, then Emperor of France, under whose regime this light field gun had been developed. Because of their large, smooth bores, the Napoleons were particularly useful for firing canister and for short range work of the sort characteristic of the wooded theaters of operations of the American Civil War. Therefore Winslow's battery, so armed, was particularly suited to the cramped Wheatfield position. From the gun line in the north portion of the field, Winslow's pieces could cover the Wheatfield without difficulty, for the maximum range in view was no greater than three hundred yards. They could shoot into Rose's Woods in their front, of course, as they did, but hitting a specific object would require a lot of luck, for the gunners could see neither their targets there nor the results of their shooting. Furthermore, the woods on both of the battery's flanks created a potential danger. If not protected, they would permit Confederate infantry to approach the battery and take it under short-range fire.[14]

But that ought not to happen. The woods to the east were behind Ward's line. De Trobriand's brigade occupied the woods to the west, and it in turn was supplemented by Barnes's division of the Fifth Corps. This wooded area warrants special attention too, for it was also a bastion of Birney's line.

Gettysburg area farmers were thrifty people who confined their wood lots to nonarable land. The strip of woods on the west side of the Wheatfield had these characteristics. The high ground at the Peach Orchard slopes downward gradually for five hundred yards to these woods and to a small bare rise that separated them from the Wheatfield Road. The woods were shaped something like a right-hand mitten, palm down. Their fingertip end touched the bare rise by the Wheatfield Road, and their wide cuff was three hundred yards to the south along the open, marshy ground between the southwest corner of the Wheatfield and the Rose farmyard. Their thumb pointed toward the Peach Orchard, and the Wheatfield ran along their east side. Within the woods the ground sloped sharply east and formed an amphitheater facing toward the Wheatfield. The floor of the woods was strewn with boulders and was marshy in its lower areas by the Wheatfield.[15]

Birney assigned his Third Brigade, commanded by Col. Philip Regis de Trobriand, to this wooded area. The brigade had five regiments: the Third and Fifth Michigan, the Seventeenth Maine, the Fortieth New York, and the 110th Pennsylvania, which had but six companies. The brigade had arrived at midmorning from Emmitsburg and rested somewhere within the Third Corps area (even the Bachelder Map does not show where), on the slope of high ground near Little Round Top. Wherever it was, de Trobriand regarded the site as a potentially good position and was reluctant to leave it.[16]

Although de Trobriand believed that the new Third Corps position offered "some great inconveniences and some great dangers," his portion of it was not so bad.[17] His brigade's initial deployment is somewhat hard to figure out. The Fifth Michigan and the 110th Pennsylvania were in line along the south side of the woods on the stony hill overlooking a cleared area by Plum Run. The 110th Pennsylvania was on the right. The Fifth fronted toward the Rose buildings, apparently, and its skirmishers linked up with the skirmish line of the Third Michigan, which connected the Rose farmyard and the Peach Orchard.[18]

The big Fortieth New York, six hundred strong and one of the largest regiments in the Third Corps, was to the rear along the west edge of the woods facing toward the Emmitsburg Road, and the Seventeenth Maine was on its right. The men of both regiments could probably see the skirmish lines of the Michiganders, but the Seventeenth in particular was in support of the Third. Both regiments, as it turned out, would soon leave these positions for others to the left.[19]

Another regiment, the Third Maine, was on the Third Michigan's right. After its adventures in Pitzer's Woods, Birney had ordered it to the south front of the Peach Orchard rather than back to Ward's brigade. The Maine men took a hasty meal from the contents of their haversacks and took position behind a rail fence there. The Third's right touched the Emmitsburg Road, and its left probably connected with that of the Third Michigan's skirmish line.[20]

Charles K. Graham's brigade occupied the Peach Orchard behind the Third Maine and held the Emmitsburg Road as far north as the Trostle farm lane. Graham was thirty-nine years old in 1863. His military career began at seventeen when he entered the navy as a midshipman. Seven years of service with the fleet followed, including duty in the Gulf of Mexico during the Mexican War. After that war, Graham left the navy to study engineering, and in 1857 he went to work as an engineer at the Brooklyn Navy Yard, where he constructed dry docks. A skeletal description of Graham's prewar life suggests that he would have had little in common with Daniel Sickles, and yet they were old friends. Both Graham and his brother Joseph had been associated with Sickles in Tammany Hall affairs. Joseph Graham was a hard-drinking lawyer who gained some notoriety by horse-whipping the newspaper tycoon James Gordon Bennett. It was Sickles who managed to have Charles Graham's predecessor at the Navy Yard fired and Graham given the job in his place, an act of patronage that caused the injured man to make an unsuccessful attack on Sickles.

When the war came, Graham traded the rather arid life of dry dock construction for the glamor of soldiering as practiced by Daniel Sickles and the Excelsior Brigade. He raised the Fifth Excelsior Regiment, or the Seventy-fourth New York as it was designated by the state, and became its colonel. He campaigned on the Peninsula with the Excelsiors and became a brigadier general in 1862. His promotion resulted in an unusual assignment for a New Yorker not of the Old Army, for his new brigade was composed entirely of Pennsylvania regiments. Graham commanded the First Brigade, First Division, Third Corps, at Chancellorsville and led it to Gettysburg.[21]

Although Graham's brigade's occupation of the high ground at the Peach Orchard and north of it along the Emmitsburg Road symbolized Sickles's decision to incorporate this high ground into his position and hold it, the occupation had taken place in a gradual, almost tentative, way. Five infantry regiments plus companies of the First U.S. Sharpshooter Regiment had been there as skirmishers, or in their support, when Buford's cavalrymen pulled out for Westminster. Sickles's decision meant that solid formations of infantry would replace the fluid, flexible cavalry units. More important, the high ground would be protected by the batteries of the Third Corps and the Artillery Reserve.

The infantry of Graham's brigade advanced uphill from their position southwest of the Trostle farmyard early in the afternoon, perhaps at 1:00 P.M., and formed a line east of the Emmitsburg Road between the Trostle lane on the right and Maj. John A. Danks's Sixty-third Pennsylvania Regiment at the Peach Orchard. Company B of the Sixty-third had erected a lunette of fence rails there, one of the few such defenses that the Third Corps seems to have constructed that day. The Sixty-third manned a skirmish line in the fields toward Seminary Ridge, its right resting north of the Wheatfield Road near the Sherfy buildings.[22]

The 105th Pennsylvania, the Wildcat Regiment, recruited from the Scotch-Irish in Western Pennsylvania, was on the right of the line. It had been on the skirmish line near the Sherfy house that morning in support of its comrades of the Sixty-third but had been called back to the brigade's first position near the Trostle buildings, where it was on the right of the support line. When the brigade advanced, the 105th formed northeast of the Sherfy house with its right on Trostle's lane.[23]

The Fifty-seventh Pennsylvania, two hundred strong and still armed with

Austrian rifles, was opposite the Sherfy house, and the 114th Pennsylvania was on its left.[24] The 114th was a Zouave regiment—Collis's Zouaves it was called, after its colonel, Charles H. T. Collis, who had been wounded at Chancellorsville. It was still a large regiment with a strength of 460 at Gettysburg and showy in its red pantaloons, white leggings, and blue jackets. But there were not 460 men on line, for the regiment still had a band and drum corps, not to mention surgeons and sick, all of whom reduced its numbers near the Sherfy house to about 400. It also had a viviandière—Marie Tebe (Mary Tepe), or "French Mary"—who, at one time at least, wore a blue blouse, a yellow bodice, scarlet trousers, and a straw hat with a large feather. French Mary was described as being about five feet tall, robust and strong, educated, and well spoken. She carried a small keg of whiskey for medicinal purposes, and a pistol to protect herself and the keg. In Collis's absence, Lt. Col. Frederick F. Cavada, brother of General Humphreys's aide, commanded the Zouaves.[25]

The Sixty-eighth Pennsylvania, Philadelphia's Scott Legion, was on the 114th's left near the Peach Orchard crossroads and behind the skirmish line of the Sixty-third. Its commander, Col. Andrew H. Tippin, had served in Mexico with the Eleventh U.S. Infantry and was said to have been the first American to scale the Mexican ramparts at Molino del Rey. The Sixty-eighth had captured the flag of the Tenth Virginia at Chancellorsville, where it had been heavily engaged. Now, at Gettysburg with only ten months of service and 383 strong, it manned a key position near the Wentz buildings, initially in support of Clark's battery. Tippin ordered his men to lie down to escape the missiles fired at the batteries near them.[26]

Graham's remaining regiment, the 141st, like the Sixty-eighth, was less than a year old but had taken about 60 percent casualties at Chancellorsville and had a strength of only two hundred. Although deployed initially at the center of the brigade, it was shifted to the left by Graham to support the batteries in the Peach Orchard. There it was to suffer heavily from artillery fire.[27]

In the meantime, after General Hunt's visit with Sickles along the Emmitsburg Road, the artillery chief reported back to army headquarters and then rode on to Cemetery Hill to see why batteries there were firing. He found that the fire meant nothing serious: the batteries were only harassing some Confederate troops seen marching to the Confederate left. Hunt might have cautioned them not to waste ammunition and then rode directly from Cemetery Hill to the Third Corps front, where he found that great changes had taken place in his absence. The infantry had occupied the high ground that had so concerned General Sickles, and he saw Meade conversing with Sickles. Because of Meade's presence there, he assumed that the commanding general had approved Sickles's move, and he went to work with a will to assist Captain Randolph in providing the new position with adequate artillery support.[28]

Hunt found that the Third Corps batteries were pretty well in position and that Randolph was placing additional guns in the Peach Orchard area. Neither Randolph nor others mentioned which batteries were posted first. It seems likely that he would have shown Smith and Winslow where their guns were to go and then given his attention to the Peach Orchard area, where several other batteries could have been employed more effectively.[29]

Although the Third Corps batteries did not take position at the time Graham's brigade went on line, Randolph had three batteries at hand—Bucklyn's, Clark's, and Battery G, First New York Light Artillery, under Capt. Nelson Ames. Ames's battery was from the Artillery Reserve. Randolph probably posted Clark's battery first. Both Clark's and Bucklyn's batteries had been in position that morning with the infantry southwest of the Trostle buildings. Later, at 9:30 according to his report, Clark took his guns forward and to the left and placed them in line on the fold of ground about midway between the Trostle buildings and the Peach Orchard. No one wrote why he did this; probably Birney or someone else of rank perceived a special threat to the skirmish line along the Emmitsburg Road and wanted a battery nearby in case it was needed. (It must have been about this time that Calef's battery was placed in position briefly at the Peach Orchard.)[30] Clark's New Jerseymen remained there until midafternoon, when troops of the Third Maine reported seeing Hood's division filing across the Emmitsburg Road 1,400 yards south of the Peach Orchard. At Sickles's order, Clark's battery rushed forward to the orchard, dropped trail, and shot at the Confederate column. Each gun fired a half-dozen rounds of shell and case shot, slowly and with good effect, making what Randolph believed were excellent shots and driving the Confederate column to cover. Then Clark's men limbered up again and hauled their guns to the left beyond the east edge of the orchard where they would be sheltered by the high ground at the orchard from threats to their right. There, fronting south and the artillery of Longstreet's right, they prepared to continue their afternoon's work.[31]

Clark was attempting to avoid the fire from the Confederate batteries closest to the Emmitsburg Road position, the guns of Cabell's and Alexander's battalions that were going in behind the wall along Seminary Ridge about seven hundred yards west of the Peach Orchard. This was a short range, one ideally suited to Napoleons. Bucklyn's battery had six such guns, and Randolph placed them along the Emmitsburg Road in the 150-yard space between the Wentz buildings and the Sherfy house. The battery's left and center sections were between the Wentz house and the Sherfy barn. For some reason Lt. Benjamin Freeborn's section was farther right beyond the barn in a garden near the Sherfy house. As will be shown, Alexander's guns were already in position when Bucklyn's dropped trail, and they took the Rhode Islanders under fire as soon as they appeared.[32]

Capt. Nelson Ames's battery, recruited initially in Oswego County, New York, reached Gettysburg with the Artillery Reserve on the morning of 2 July.

It had six Napoleons. It first parked east of the Taneytown Road, where its drivers fed and watered their horses. About 11:00 A.M. Ames received orders to report to General Sickles. The battery moved out without delay, but when it reached the Third Corps sector found that there was no immediate need for it. It then parked near the Trostle barn and spent three or four hours there. Ames sent the battery wagon back to the Reserve Artillery park, the cannoneers filled their canteens and the sponge buckets, and Ames explored the ground where there might be fighting.[33]

Randolph ordered the battery to the Peach Orchard about 4:00 P.M., after Graham's regiments had taken their places along the Emmitsburg Road. It was a short but not an easy trip. The battery passed to the left of the barn and probably crossed the lane, entering the field south of it through a gate opposite the farmyard. It then rolled up slope through a corn field and other fields. In spite of the Third Corps's having been there all morning, fences still stood in the battery's way, and it had to halt twice to clear its path. These were dangerous halts within view and range of Cabell's gunners who, fortunately, killed only two horses. When the battery reached the Peach Orchard, the guns went left oblique into battery a few yards south of the Wheatfield Road, all six pieces going into line facing southwest in the direction from which Cabell's fire came. Ames ordered his chiefs of section to fire at will at the guns in their front. He stayed closest to his center and left sections because their lieutenants lacked experience. Since the foliage of the orchard was still relatively undamaged and heavy, he could not see his right section.[34]

As Ames's guns began to boom, the sergeant from the No. 1 piece on the far right burst through the trees. "For God's sake," yelled the sergeant, "come and tell us where to place our guns; we have been running them up and down all over this field, no place is satisfactory to the lieutenant; all my men and Sergeant Hutchinson are tired out." With an oath, Ames hurried through the trees to the right to see what the fuss was all about. He spoke to the lieutenant of the first section, who, among other things, wanted to cut down some trees before his guns opened. Ames was in no mood for delays; the battery was in a perilous spot and had to fire on the enemy batteries before they rained fire upon it. In adamant tones Ames advised the lieutenant to settle down and get busy or else he would take the lieutenant's sword from him and send him to the rear. About this time a shot whizzed by their heads, giving emphasis to Ames's words. Soon the first section opened and the lieutenant calmed down.[35] Not long after Ames's guns opened, General Hunt rode up and asked the captain how long his battery could hold its position. Until the battery ran out of ammunition, the stubborn captain replied. He would get a chance to prove it.[36]

Birney's division was now in place and reinforcements were sent to help it, to try to plug gaps in its long line and to support or replace units already there. Much of this support came from Humphreys's division, which was off Graham's right when the battle opened. Although General Birney had been heavily involved in the actions of the Third Corps on that fateful morning, his fellow division commander had marked time in something of a vacuum. Humphreys could see what was taking place to the north along Cemetery Ridge to his right, for that ground was essentially open, but much of the position of his own corps was screened by trees. He must have seen Graham's brigade's advance to the fields southwest of the Trostle farmyard with great interest and must have regarded the bits of information that he received with concern. Many things were happening that affected his division, yet he remained essentially uninformed and not directly involved.[37]

Humphreys's isolation that morning was most curious in a corps where all of the ranking officers but him were non-Regulars who needed the best advice that they could get on establishing a defensive position. Yet, in this particular area, Humphreys until recently had been something of an amateur too. Andrew Atkinson Humphreys was a native of Philadelphia, born in 1810 into a family of distinction. His grandfather, Josiah Humphreys, had designed some of the navy's great ships including the *Constitution* and *Constellation*. His father, Samuel Humphreys, was in turn the chief constructor of ships for the navy in the years before the War with Mexico, and his mother's father had been an officer in the British army.

Andrew Humphreys turned his back on ships and shipyards and went to West Point, graduating in 1831 in time to serve as a lieutenant of artillery in the Seminole War. This life must have had little attraction for him, for he resigned his commission and went to work for the army as a civilian engineer constructing fortifications on the Delaware River. He was not a civilian long. In 1838 he returned to the army as a lieutenant in the Corps of Topographical Engineers and, like Generals Lee and Meade, became involved with civil works surveys of the Mississippi River and its delta. He also surveyed portions of a railroad right-of-way between the Mississippi and the Pacific. Humphreys won an international reputation for his work as an engineer, but he saw no service with the army in Mexico. Therefore, when the Civil War began, Humphreys had little experience with troops either in garrison or in the field.

Experience came quickly. He joined McClellan's staff as a major in December 1861. In March 1862 he became chief topographical engineer of the Army of the Potomac, and in April of the same year, a brigadier general of volunteers. He commanded the Third Division, Fifth Corps, at Antietam and led it against Marye's Heights at Fredericksburg and at Chancellorsville. He transferred to the command of the Second Division, Third Corps, after Chancellorsville and marched it to Gettysburg. Humphreys became Meade's chief of staff after Gettysburg and ended the war as commander of the Second Corps. On the basis of Humphreys's service after Gettysburg, Assistant Secretary of War Charles A. Dana termed him "the great soldier of the Army of the Potomac."[38]

Unlike Sickles, Humphreys had little charisma and was not a popular

Brig. Gen. Andrew A. Humphreys and staff. Left to right: *Lt. Henry C. Christiancy, Lt. Henry H. Humphreys, General Humphreys, Capt. Carswell McClellan, and an unidentified officer* (MOLLUS-MASS/U.S.A.M.H.I., *Carlisle Barracks, Pa.*)

commander. He was a strict disciplinarian, and his spectacles gained him the nickname "Old Goggle Eyes."[39] He could express himself forcefully. Dana thought him "one of the loudest swearers" he had ever known and ranked him with William T. Sherman as a man of "distinguished and brilliant profanity." But Dana found him also to be a charming man, destitute of vanity. Theodore Lyman, who served under him on Meade's staff, described Humphreys as a nice old gentleman (he was no more than fifty-five) who was boyish, peppy, and extremely neat, "continually washing himself and putting on paper dickeys." In addition, he was fond of conversation with his military family after meals and had knowlege of many things. Fortunately, he developed a fondness for field service and regarded the military profession as a "godlike occupation." Like George Washington and Robert E. Lee, he had a personal fondness for battle and observed once that war was a "very bad thing in the sequel, but before and during a battle it is a fine thing!"[40]

Humphreys must have felt some relief, then, when, about 11:00 A.M., Sickles asked him to send a regiment to the skirmish line. He referred the request to Brig. Gen. Joseph B. Carr, commander of his First Brigade, and Carr sent the First Massachusetts to the Emmitsburg Road to relieve the Fourth Maine of Ward's brigade. The Fourth returned to Ward and was posted beyond Smith's battery at Devil's Den.[41]

The morning passed into afternoon. Graham's brigade had been west of Plum Run and southwest of the Trostle farmyard much of the morning, and Sickles ordered Humphreys to post his division on Graham's right. Humphreys was to extend Graham's line northward and connect with the left of Caldwell's division of the Second Corps. These were the orders, but it was not quite that simple. Caldwell's division was back on the crest of Cemetery Ridge to the right of where Humphreys had been massed all morning. Caldwell had no orders to advance, and if Humphreys's division did so, Caldwell's left would be in Humphreys's rear. Humphreys reminded Sickles of this, but Sickles ordered him forward anyhow.[42]

And so it could be said that at 1:00 P.M. Humphreys's division occupied its first position of the day. Carr's brigade and the Seventy-first New York Regiment of the Excelsior Brigade formed its first line. The Seventy-first was on the left near Trostle's lane and briefly near Graham's right regiment, the 105th Pennsylvania. The line of Carr's brigade ran north from there more or less parallel to and three hundred yards east of the Emmitsburg Road to a point about five hundred yards in front of Caldwell's left. Brewster's brigade was in "a line of battalions in mass" two hundred yards behind the first line, and the Third Brigade massed two hundred yards in the rear of the center of the Second. Although there was a gap of about five hundred yards between Humphreys's first line and Caldwell's division back on the ridge, it did not concern Humphreys at that time. He thought that his position there was only temporary and, if worse came to worse, the offset could be covered by fire from the ridge and plugged by the two rear brigades.[43]

Humphreys made additional changes. He ordered another of Brewster's regiments, the Seventy-third New York, forward to the Klingle house on the road in front of Carr's center. Humphreys told Brewster that the Seventy-third was to hold its position "at all hazards"—an interesting challenge for a regiment posted, not as skirmishers, two to three hundred yards in front of its division's main line.[44]

The Klingle house was the home of Daniel Klingle, a shoemaker and farmer; it was and is a small structure. It was said that it already housed some wounded Confederates, victims of the previous day's battle, although if that was so, one may wonder how they ended up so far from the battlefield. About midafternoon some officers, probably from either the First Massachusetts or the Seventy-third New York, urged Klingle to leave. Klingle's first response was, "If I must die, I will die at home," but the officers insisted that the Klingle family take refuge in the cellar or leave and offered a detail of soldiers to help them move out.[45]

Soldiers scoffed at the Gettysburg civilians and the concern that some exhibited for their personal welfare, but it could not have been easy for them to face with equanimity the probable destruction of their hard-earned property. Probably Klingle weighed the threat to his family against the loss of its belongings and soon elected to take the family east to a friend's house somewhere near Rock Creek. As they trudged east, a mounted officer rode by them and snatched the hat from Klingle's head, an act more often associated with Confederates in Pennsylvania than with the defenders of the Union. Apparently the hat was a valued possession, not readily surrendered. Klingle siezed the bridle of the officer's horse and held it until the officer paid him for the hat. The Klingles reached the Round Top area and stopped there while Klingle returned to the house for some clothing that had been left behind. He met his neighbor, Joseph Sherfy, near Trostle's Woods. Sherfy told him that there was fighting around his house. Klingle then returned to his family, and on his way found a soldier's hat in a pool of muddy water. He rinsed the hat off and carried it with him. As he neared Little Round Top an officer accosted him and asked him to accompany him to the top of the hill. There he identified some terrain features for the officer, who was possibly a signalman. While they were there, artillery fire opened on Seminary Ridge, and Klingle left the hill. He and his family went on to Rock Creek.[46]

Shortly after Humphreys's division advanced, Humphreys received an order from Sickles to send his Third Brigade to the left as a reserve for Birney and make it subject to Birney's orders. The brigade's assigned commander was Gershom Mott, who had been wounded at Chancellorsville and had not yet returned to duty; Col. George C. Burling of the Sixth New Jersey commanded in Mott's absence. The brigade had four New Jersey regiments—the Fifth, Sixth, Seventh, and Eighth—together with the Second New Hampshire and 115th Pennsylvania regiments. Captain Cavada guided the brigade to Trostle's Woods, where it was close to Birney's division in the Wheatfield and the Peach Orchard. A stone wall along the west edge of the woods and low ground there provided some cover, but the brigade would not be there long to enjoy it.[47]

It was time for another contact between the Third Corps and army headquarters. As Major Tremain recounted it (unfortunately, his version is the only one available), he told General Meade of the results of Berdan's excursion into Pitzer's Woods. What, if anything, was said about the Third Corps advance Tremain did not relate, but there was some conversation about the need for more artillery on the Third Corps line. At the Cemetery Ridge position there had been no space for extra batteries, but many were needed in the new position. Without seeming to appreciate the necessity for the additional batteries, Meade made them available from the Artillery Reserve. It was in this interview, according to Tremain, that General Meade dismissed his report of Sickles's fears with the offhand remark that generals were always expecting attacks on their own fronts. The commanding general's seeming lack of cordiality and empathy for General Sickles's concerns, as Tremain saw it, left Tremain feeling "frosted," and he rode back to Third Corps headquarters with the report of his latest interview.[48]

After talking with Sickles, Tremain rode up to the Peach Orchard. He found General Graham there with Clark's, if not Ames's, guns. McLaws's division had obviously arrived on Seminary Ridge, for the balls fired by its skirmishers zipped into the orchard area so plentifully that the officers with horses had dismounted and were moving about on foot. Graham took Tremain to the edge of the trees where he could see Hood's brigades crossing the Emmitsburg Road to the south. The fears of the Third Corps commander finally were being realized, and the specter of a spurious Chancellorsville loomed large. Tremain hurried back down the orchard's east slope, mounted, and galloped back to corps headquarters.[49]

Sickles listened to Tremain's report of what he had seen and sent him once more to see General Meade. Meade's response to Tremain's report was to ask that Sickles come to army headquarters. But to Tremain the request did not seem imperative, and he reported it so to Sickles. Sickles decided that other matters were more pressing at the time and did not go to headquarters. Soon thereafter an aide arrived from General Meade with a second invitation. Sickles asked to be excused, stating that the enemy was in great force on his front and he was preparing to meet an attack. In a short while a second messenger rode up with a peremptory order for Sickles to attend a meeting with the commanding general. There could be no more refusals. Sickles turned his corps over to Birney and galloped off with Tremain toward the Widow Leister's house. As they rode away, they could hear the sounds of gunfire on Birney's front.[50]

Meade had announced the meeting by means of a circular to all corps commanders, but the purpose of the meeting was not indicated. In his later, battling years Sickles stated that the probable purpose of the meeting was to discuss and decide whether or not the Army of the Potomac should withdraw from Gettysburg.[51] But that seems patent nonsense spawned by Sickles's militant self-interest. Probably it was called for the purpose of exchanging information and making certain that all corps commanders understood the army's situation and its commander's intentions. General Meade had just sent a dispatch to General-in-Chief Halleck telling him of conditions at Gettysburg, and it is likely that Meade wished to express his views to the corps commanders and get their reactions to them. To Halleck, Meade wrote that his army was concentrated and that the Sixth Corps was arriving, fatigued from its long march. He said that the Army of the Potomac had awaited the attack that day, for it was in a strong defensive position. In turn, he was not yet determined to attack until the enemy's position was more fully developed, and he wished to wait until the Sixth Corps was up and rested. He was expecting a battle, however, and had ordered his trains to the rear. If his army was not attacked and he could get positive information on the enemy that would justify his attacking, he would do so. On the other hand, if such an attack would prove hazardous or if he found that the enemy was moving to get between the Army of the Potomac and Washington, he would fall back on his supplies to Westminster. In closing, he said that he felt his responsibility and would act with caution.[52]

It was a cautious statement, yet it indicated a desire to fall back only if the enemy was found to be attempting to get between the Army of the Potomac and Washington or if, after probing, it appeared overly hazardous to attack. When such probing would be completed and a decision made, General Meade did not say. Certainly it would have been after the entire army was up and rested and not in the hours immediately ahead, as Sickles later stated.

The corps commanders gathered and had a discussion. Sometime in the course of the brief gathering before Sickles arrived, General Warren reported that the Third Corps was not in position. He had heard this and had sent an officer out to investigate. This was a surprise to General Meade, but it need not have been if there had been communication between Sickles and army headquarters and if General Meade's own staff had been doing its job. After hearing this news clearly—for the first time it seems—Meade turned to George Sykes and ordered him to take the Fifth Corps from its place in reserve to the left and hold the left "at all hazards." He would meet Sykes on the left and help him post his corps.[53]

It was at this time, as the meeting was breaking up with unexpected urgency, that Sickles, Tremain, Captain Moore, and probably some orderlies as well, thundered up to the Leister house in a figurative cloud of dust. Artillery fire could be heard back on the Third Corps front, and General Meade was in a decisive, if not a snapping, mood. There was no time for pleasantries. Captain Paine recalled, "I never saw General Meade so angry if I may so call it. He ordered General Sickles to retire his line to the position he had been instructed to take. This was done in a few sharp words." His temper cooled, Meade then told Sickles not to dismount—there was firing on his front, and he was needed there. He would join Sickles at the Third Corps position. With this the Third Corps officers reined their horses around, applied their spurs, and galloped away.[54]

In later years, when the sound of gunfire was but a memory, replaced by thundering oratory, and when Meade and Sykes were dead, Daniel Sickles fought the continuing battle of Gettysburg with a long and mighty oration. In it he related many things, and among them he said that he received no orders on his troop dispositions after sunup on 2 July and that the meeting he missed had been called to determine whether or not the army should leave Gettysburg. Fortunately, the battle opened, ending what Sickles implied was a budding retreat.[55] Sickles spoke rot on both accounts. Nevertheless, it is apparent that communications between the two headquarters left much to be desired and that there was grist enough for Sickles's mill.

It was the contention of Sickles and his partisans that the activities of the Third Corps were an open book, that they had tried to tell General Meade of their concerns, and that they had been ignored and their concerns dismissed. Sickles stated that Generals Hunt and Warren and Col. Edmund Schriver, the inspector general of the Army of the Potomac, had all visited the left and not one of them had given him any orders respecting his position. In addition,

Schriver had reported his position of the late morning. Sickles also alluded to messages carried to army headquarters by his aides—Tremain and Moore. If army headquarters personnel were ignorant of the situation on the Third Corps front, it was their responsibility, not his.[56]

The Third Corps commander blustered in an effort to mitigate his own blunder but had a good point. At 11:00 A.M. General Meade had ordered his staff, Schriver included, to gather information on the various corps and their positions, and presumably Schriver, who had particular responsibility for liaison with the Third Corps, had done so.[57] What Schriver reported and to whom we do not know. As indicated in Chapter 5, after Captain Meade's morning visit, the Third Corps took positions that seemingly were not in accord with the commanding general's instructions and intent, yet they seem not to have been questioned by anyone with authority at army headquarters or even by Hancock, whose corps they affected directly and who should have been greatly interested in them. Hunt must have seen Birney's position in front of Trostle's Woods at the time of his late morning visit, and Hancock must have been aware of the advance of Humphreys's division just after noon. Yet until Warren's comment at the 3:00 P.M. meeting, no interest was evidenced or questions asked, as far as we know, about the position of the Third Corps. Tremain's communications, even if much less candid than he implied in later years, ought to have raised some questions, but they seem not to have done so.

Without doubt, General Meade's mind, initially at least, was not on his left, and his vaunted staff served him poorly with respect to the Third Corps's activities. In later years Captain Meade wrote that people wondered why the general himself had not gone the short distance from his headquarters to the Third Corps front and settled things to his satisfaction. To this good question Captain Meade replied that until 3:00 P.M., presumably the time of the afternoon meeting, General Meade believed that the Third Corps was in position. He had not heard otherwise and knew nothing of Longstreet's movements.[58] Clearly, either the commanding general was less than truthful about his knowledge of what was taking place, which was not at all in accord with his character, he was functioning poorly—perhaps out of fatigue—or he was poorly served.

General Meade's lack of concern for his left must have resulted in part from information provided by his signalmen. Those few messages of which copies are extant, if they are typical, must have diverted his attention from that flank. At 11:55 Lt. Aaron B. Jerome signaled that the woods in his front, Pitzer's Woods, were full of Rebels and that Federal skirmishers were retreating before them. Undoubtedly this referred to Berdan's foray and should have given credence to the report of this action given to Meade by Tremain.[59]

But there were no additional messages reporting crises on the left that are known to us, even from the vexatious station on Little Round Top. To the contrary, at 1:30 P.M. Capt. James S. Hall signaled Butterfield from there that he saw a heavy column of infantry, 10,000 strong, moving from the Federal "extreme left" toward the right. The meaning of this message is vague today and must have been so to Butterfield, for at 2:00 P.M. Hall signaled clarification—the column was passing Dr. Hall's house toward Herr Tavern on the Chambersburg Pike, and a train of ambulances was following it. The Hall house on Herr Ridge was visible from Little Round Top, as were other segments of the road on Herr Ridge. Captain Hall had no way of knowing it, but he probably saw a portion of Longstreet's corps, perhaps Hood's division, countermarching in the course of its approach march. He had no way of knowing that when it disappeared from his sight, it would change direction and head toward the Union left.[60]

As a result, Meade reported to Halleck at 3:00 P.M. that the enemy was moving on both of his flanks but that it was "difficult to tell exactly his movements."[61] Each commander was thus in a quandary about the intent of the other on 2 July, and neither was served as well by his subordinates as he ought to have been.

The meeting broke up as Sickles and his staff galloped away and General Meade prepared to follow him. His favorite mount, "Old Baldy," was not at hand. Not wishing to wait until he was brought up, General Meade accepted the loan of General Pleasonton's horse. The animal was unaccustomed to Meade's style of riding and his handling of the curb bit. This minor matter led to a situation that will be mentioned below.[62]

General Warren rode along with General Meade. As they passed over Cemetery Ridge, Warren pointed south toward the Round Tops and said, "Here is where the line should be." Meade replied that it was too late to place it there, and Warren, with Meade's permission or direction, left the commanding general's party to ride on to Little Round Top.[63]

Meade started his ride to the left with a small party, but it grew as aides and staff officers left behind in his hurried departure caught up with him. It is hard to know who was with him. The entourage grew to include Meade's senior aide, Major Biddle, Maj. Benjamin C. Ludlow, Captains Mason, Meade, and Cadwalader, Lt. Paul Oliver, and Capt. James Starr, commander of the escort companies of the Sixth Pennsylvania Cavalry at army headquarters. Starr acted as an aide when his other duties permitted. In all, orderlies included, it must have been a sizable group. In later years Oliver admitted that the general would have been better off had he been essentially alone.[64] After the party left Cemetery Ridge, it passed through the area posted by Humphreys's division to the accompaniment of cheers from some of its soldiers. It was probably the first time that these men of the Third Corps had seen their new commander.[65]

General Meade found General Sickles and his staff by the Wheatfield Road at the Peach Orchard. Sickles was seeing to some changes in the Third Corps line, possibly the placing of additional batteries and regiments in the

Peach Orchard area. The two mounted generals and their staffs must have made an attractive target for any Confederate gunners who could see them.[66]

Some present claimed to recall some of the key portions of the generals' conversation. According to HISTORICUS, Meade asked, "Are you not too much extended, general? Can you hold this front?" "Yes," replied Sickles, "until more troops are brought up; the enemy are attacking in force, and I shall need support." Meade then expressed some doubt—"his mind was still wavering"—about the extent of the ground to be occupied by the Third Corps, and Sickles was said to have observed, "General, I have received no orders. I have made these dispositions to the best of my judgment. Of course, I shall be happy to modify them according to your views." "No," said Meade, "I will send you the Fifth Corps, and you may send for support from the Second Corps." "I shall need more artillery," added Sickles. "Send to the Artillery Reserve for all you want," replied Meade; "I will direct General Hunt to send you all you ask for." And then, wrote HISTORICUS, the conversation was ended by a heavy shower of shells. General Meade rode off, and General Sickles heard no more from him that day.[67]

HISTORICUS was Daniel Sickles's alter ego, his partisan, if indeed he was not the general himself. But Sickles could speak for himself and did so before the Committee on the Conduct of the War. General Meade, said Sickles, examined his dispositions and the situation and remarked:

> that my line was too extended, and expressed his doubts as to my being able to hold so extended a line, in which I coincided in the main—that is to say, I replied that I could not, with one corps, hold so extended a line against the rebel army; but that, if supported, the line could be held; and, in my judgment, it was a strong line, and the best one. I stated, however, that if he disapproved of it it was not yet too late to take any position he might indicate. He said "No;" that it would be better to hold that line, and he would send up the 5th corps to support me. I expressed my belief in my ability to hold that line until supports could arrive. He said he would send up the 5th corps on my left, and that on my right I could look to General Hancock for support of my right flank. I added that I should want considerable artillery; that the enemy were developing a strong force of artillery. He authorized me to send to General Hunt ... for as much artillery as I wanted. I then assured him of my entire confidence in my ability to hold the position; which I did.[68]

Major Biddle, Meade's aide, whose perspective was somewhat different, gave an account that was similar in the main but with a significantly different emphasis. In it the commanding general spoke not as one who recognized that the Third Corps commander had taken the best position possible and merited all of the support that could be given him. Instead, he spoke as one who believed that the Third Corps commander had made an unwise move, that it was too late to undo what had been done, and that they would have to make the best of the situation. Biddle recalled that General Meade asked General Sickles why he had not connected with the Second Corps left as he had been ordered to do. To this Sickles answered that he had advanced his corps to possess the high ground between Hancock's left and the enemy. General Meade then replied, "General Sickles, this is neutral ground, our guns command it as well as the enemy's. The very reason you cannot hold it applies to them." Sickles then asked if he should move his troops back. Meade pondered a moment and replied, "You cannot hold this position, but the enemy will not let you get away without a fight, & it may as well begin now as at any time." The two generals then parted.[69]

In one of these two accounts, General Sickles's points are made, and he is offered the help that he needs—a virtual blank check. In the other he is chided by General Meade but is promised support. Both accounts were concerned with the propriety of the move, but neither was concerned with other subjects that might have been discussed or with the later ordering of Humphreys's division to the Little Round Top area.

The end of the talk and of this series of events was not without some drama. The large gathering of mounted men did draw Confederate fire, and one round spooked the horse that General Meade was riding. The horse plunged and bolted, carrying on his back the man who bore the fate of the Union.[70] One can wonder what might have happened that day had Meade been thrown and hurt.

It was when Sickles received Meade's reluctant approval to hold his corps on its advanced line that he ordered Humphreys's division (less Burling's brigade, which had been sent to Birney) to the Emmitsburg Road. Humphreys started his two brigades forward, and the two brigades moved as one, Carr's advancing in line and Brewster's Excelsiors in "battalions in mass." They had only a short distance to go, 250 to 300 yards perhaps, and the movement ought not to have been difficult. While they were moving, an officer of Meade's staff, said to have been Major Ludlow, rode up with a message from General Meade. After Meade's conversation with Sickles, apparently, Meade had received a request from Warren for troops to occupy Little Round Top. Heavy firing indicated that there was an emergency there, and without hesitation Meade sent Ludlow to General Humphreys with orders to take his division to the important hill.[71]

Humphreys sent his aides galloping off immediately with instructions for his brigades to march by the left flank. By chance, perhaps, the brigades changed direction "with a simultaneousness of a single regiment." Amid shells coming in from beyond the Peach Orchard, Humphreys's two brigades marched away from the Emmitsburg Road toward the Wheatfield and the Round Tops beyond.[72]

But what about the Emmitsburg Road? Humphreys told Ludlow to hurry to Meade at once with a message: in turning from the road he would leave a large gap between Graham's right and the left of the Second Corps back on Cemetery Ridge. Ludlow spurred away, and Humphreys galloped to the head of his division's column to show it where to go. This done, and quickly, he started for Meade to talk with him personally, but soon he met the returning staff officer. Ludlow shouted that the order was cancelled, the Fifth Corps was going to the hill, and Humphreys should return his division to the road. Soon after, one of Sickles's officers galloped up with the same order. Humphreys did not delay. He gave the necessary commands, and the brigades turned, retraced their steps, and took their places on the new line.[73]

This march and countermarch did not take long. Humphreys remembered it afterwards as "done with the precision of a careful exercise," but it was more than that. Unlike Birney's advance, it took place in full view of the Second Corps and others and became symbolic of the advance of the whole Third Corps. In the words of Glenn Tucker a century later, Humphreys's advance showed that "Old Dan Sickles was going to the war."[74] Maj. St. Clair A. Mulholland of the 116th Pennsylvania watched it from Caldwell's division's line and described it effusively in later years:

> Soon the long lines of the Third Corps are seen advancing, and how splendidly they march. It looks like a dress parade, a review. On, on they go, out toward the peach orchard, but not a shot fired. A little while longer and someone calls out "there," and points to where a puff of smoke is seen arising against the dark green of the woods beyond the Emmitsburg pike. Another and another until the whole face of the forest is enveloped, and the dread sound of artillery comes loud and quick, shells are seen bursting in all directions along the lines. The bright colors of the regiments are conspicuous marks, and the shells burst around them in great numbers.[75]

William F. Fox wrote of this for New York's official account:

> The sun shone brightly on their waving colors, and flashed in scintillating rays from their burnished arms, as with well-aligned ranks and even steps they moved proudly across the field. Away to the right, along Cemetery Ridge, the soldiers of the Second Corps, leaving their coffee and their cards, crowded to the front, where they gazed with soldierly pride and quickened pulse on the stirring scene. Conspicuous among the moving columns of this division was the old Excelsior Brigade, each one of its five regiments carrying the blue flag of New York. . . . They marched with no other music than the rattle of the rifles on the picket line; they were inspired only with the determination to acquit themselves worthy of the State motto, which the brigade had adopted as its name.[76]

Chaplain Joseph Twichell, who was nearby, wrote soon after the battle that the bugles sounded and "with a firm step with colors flying the bravest men in the army marched into the open field. It was a splendid sight."[77] And so it must have been, for it remained vivid in men's memories long after less splendid sights seen that day were all but forgotten.

Carr's brigade halted just east of the road. The Twenty-sixth Pennsylvania was on the brigade right about three hundred yards south of the Codori barn and above the low ground just south of the barn. It had a strength of 365 on a front of about one hundred yards.[78]

The Eleventh Massachusetts was next in line, near the Rogers house, a small white frame building on the west side of the road, the home of Peter and Susan Rogers and Josephine Miller, an unmarried woman of about twenty-three. The Rogers buildings might have provided some protection for those behind them, but more likely they offered a bull's-eye for Confederate gunners who wanted to fire at Union infantry in that area and needed a specific target to aim at. The men of the Eleventh had a special vista from their position and could see troops preparing for battle in all directions. There were Confederates in their front and as far to their right front as they could see. Their own brigade stretched to their right and left, and the Second Corps was on the ridge in their rear. A herd of a dozen or so cows grazed nearby, providing a scene in contrast to the martial display, and a flock of pigeons fluttered in the trees of the Rogers farmyard, disturbed by the gunfire and the commotion below them. Some of the men purchased chickens from the family, and Josephine Miller baked bread for some of them.[79]

Humphreys placed Lt. Francis W. Seeley's Battery K, Fourth Artillery, in the space between the Rogers and Klingle buildings. Seeley's six Napoleons exchanged fire with Patterson's collection of smoothbore pieces eight hundred yards in their front.[80] Carr's remaining three regiments, the Sixteenth Massachusetts, Twelfth New Hampshire, and Eleventh New Jersey went on line to the left of the Eleventh Massachusetts. The Sixteenth was on the right of the Klingle buildings and to Seeley's left rear. General Carr detached one hundred men from the Sixteenth and posted them in the house area itself. They relieved the Seventy-third New York, sent there to hold at all hazards, and some men occupied the house. They turned the Klingle residence into a fort by preparing to fire from its windows and through holes poked in the chinking between its logs. The Sixteenth's line ran 20 or so yards behind the road so that the troops in the main line were sheltered by the crest in their front. All but the artillerymen and the officers who believed that they had to demonstrate their bravery hugged the ground and waited for things to warm up.[81]

Carr's First Massachusetts Regiment was on the skirmish line beyond the road, where it had been much of the day. Its right was forward of the midway point between the Rogers and Klingle buildings, essentially in front of the brigade right, and its left was at Spangler's lane. Activity on the First's front picked up at noon, and Lt. Col. Clark B. Baldwin, the regiment's commander, became concerned. Carr's response to his request for orders was only that the First should hold on as long as possible. Baldwin translated this to his company commanders by saying that in case of attack they should push their companies forward to the skirmish line and fight there. If forced to fall back, they should do so in good order. Baldwin made sure that his order was understood by riding along his line and repeating it to each company commander. A short time later, from Baldwin's perspective, Carr moved the whole brigade forward to his support.[82]

The name of Brig. Gen. Joseph B. Carr, commander of the brigade, was not a household word in 1863, but he had earned his assignment. He was born in Albany of Irish parents in 1828 and later moved to Troy. He became a tobacco merchant by trade but at one time worked as a dancing master. Carr had been unusually active in militia affairs and in time became colonel of the Twentieth New York State Militia Regiment. When war came, he recruited the Second New York Regiment, became its colonel, took it to the field, and led it at Big Bethel. He commanded the Third Brigade of Hooker's division on the Peninsula, received a promotion to brigadier general, and was then given command of the First Brigade, Second Division, Third Corps, which he led at Fredericksburg, Chancellorsville, and Gettysburg. In eulogizing Carr after his death, someone observed that "a profane or objectionable word was never heard from his lips." If so, Carr had the patience of a saint. In later years a veteran of the Sixteenth Massachusetts complained about the cruelty of generals and wrote that one, presumably Carr, had taught dancing in "schools of low character," though he did not say how he knew this to be so. But once this became known, the men of the brigade razzed him, surreptitiously of course, shouting, "right and left" and "promenade the bar" as he rode by them. Such things can be trying on difficult days.[83]

Although Carr's brigade formed as a unit, the Excelsior Brigade did not. The Seventy-third Regiment had been at the Klingle house but was relieved there by Carr's men and then formed briefly on the left of the support line before going off to Graham's aid.[84] Probably because Carr's brigade could not cover all of the front assigned to Humphreys's division, the general extended its line by simply bringing Brewster's regiments forward where needed. The Seventy-second took position on Humphreys's left by Trostle's lane and Graham's right, and the Seventy-first was between it and Carr's left regiment, the Eleventh New Jersey. The Seventy-fourth went to the support of the right of Carr's line and formed in the rear of the Twenty-sixth Pennsylvania, while the remaining two regiments, the Seventieth and the 120th, remained in the rear as the division's reserve.[85] The Third Corps line occupied a mile of front along the Emmitsburg Road from the Peach Orchard almost to the Codori barn.

General Sickles's Third Corps now held the high ground that had worried him so and that he had coveted increasingly as the hours passed. The new corps front measured 1½ miles from flank to flank, about double the width of that prescribed for it on Cemetery Ridge. With less than 10,000 infantrymen, the corps was too small for such a line. Its flanks were in the air, and there was

a large space between Graham's brigade at the Peach Orchard and de Trobriand's on the west side of the Wheatfield. There were soft spots along its
front; there was virtually no reserve strength within the corps; and the enemy
was beginning his assault. But Sickles had been promised support from the
Fifth and Second corps and from the Artillery Reserve. Would this support
arrive soon enough to help the Third Corps hold its new line and hurl back
the Confederate assault? A very short time would tell.

CHAPTER

Longstreet's Corps Opens
the Attack

MCLAWS'S DIVISION GOES ON LINE

Lafayette McLaws probably had suffered much vexation during his twenty years of soldiering, but hardly any of it could have rivaled the exasperation that he experienced at Gettysburg on 2 July 1863. McLaws had been born in Augusta, Georgia, forty-two years earlier and at the age of twenty-one had graduated from West Point with its class of 1842. This was an accomplished class, as it turned out, for it included not only Longstreet and Richard H. Anderson, whose division was formed to the left of McLaws's division, but also five generals who had come to Gettysburg with the Army of the Potomac. They were John F. Reynolds, Abner Doubleday, and John Newton, all of whom commanded the First Corps, plus George Sykes and Seth Williams.

Like most of the West Pointers of his time, McLaws served as an infantry subaltern in Mexico and in the West. He became a captain in 1851. In March 1861, still a captain, McLaws resigned from the Old Army and returned to Georgia, where he entered the Confederate service as a major. He became lieutenant colonel of the Tenth Georgia Infantry in June 1861 and then advanced quickly in grade, so that by May 1862 he was a major general in command of a division in the Army of Northern Virginia. Lafayette McLaws was not without ability, but his star began to dim, and his performance at Antietam and Chancellorsville gained him a reputation for being insufficiently aggressive. When General Lee reorganized the Army of Northern Virginia in May 1863 and created two new corps commanders for it, he passed over McLaws, who was a senior major general, in favor of A. P. Hill and Richard S. Ewell.[1]

Douglas Southall Freeman described McLaws as a "square and solid" man, a description that seems to apply to both his character and appearance, for photographs present him as a bearlike fellow with much curly hair and a full beard. McLaws demonstrated some mastery of profanity, but he was a sensitive, literate man who shared some of his military experiences in candid letters to his wife. After the war he wrote of his experiences in articles published in the *Southern Historical Society Papers*.[2]

McLaws must have been embarrassed and angered by being placed in the middle when Longstreet disagreed with General Lee over his division's prospective position early that morning. He was thoroughly vexed by the events associated with the division's march from the Black Horse Tavern area to its assigned place on Seminary Ridge. McLaws had reached that area with the division's van after midafternoon, and a quick glance told him that he was on the horns of a dilemma not of his making: his instructions did not fit the conditions in his front. The enemy was on the high ground ahead but not merely in the strength of two regiments and a battery; rather, the enemy's strength seemed greater than his own, and the blue line ran considerably beyond his right. Someone had erred, and changes were in order. McLaws ordered the deployment of Kershaw's and Barksdale's brigades and galloped to the rear to hurry along his remaining two brigades and his artillery.[3]

McLaws's instructions as given by General Lee and possibly refined by General Longstreet were simple enough as he understood them. His division would arrive on the enemy's flank, which presumably would be to his division's left front as it approached Seminary Ridge and the Emmitsburg Road beyond. He would march by the enemy's flank to the east and beyond it in columns of companies, halt, face left, and attack; simple enough if that flank was where it was supposed to be and the enemy behaved himself. Unfortunately, unlike at Chancellorsville, there were no thickets to conceal his division's deployment east of Seminary Ridge, and the enemy would not be greatly surprised.[4]

General Longstreet had talked with McLaws as his division approached the ridge, and he had also talked with General Kershaw. Longstreet had told Kershaw that his brigade was to strike the Federal force in the Peach Orchard area, turn its left, and then form in line to the east along the Wheatfield Road with its left near the Emmitsburg Road. Barksdale would probably form his brigade on Kershaw's left, though nothing was said about this. It seemed easy enough, so Kershaw's brigade, at the head of McLaws's division, filed up the west slope of Seminary Ridge in accordance with Longstreet's orders. Capt. Basil C. Manly's North Carolina Battery bumped along beside the South Carolina infantry, and the rest of Cabell's battalion followed somewhere to the rear.[5]

After marching up the slope the half mile from Pitzer's Schoolhouse, the head of Kershaw's column debouched from the fringe of trees that ran along the crest of the ridge into the open in plain view of the Federal forces in the Peach Orchard area. Kershaw realized that his brigade could not proceed farther according to its orders and, probably with McLaws's approval, he turned it to the right into the field east of the ridge crest and the wall that ran along it. To cover his deployment he sent skirmishers forward on the double quick to engage the Third Corps skirmishers in his front. That done, Kershaw took a closer look at the enemy position.[6]

The sight astonished him. The Federal line to his right front appeared to extend all the way to Little Round Top, where he could see signalmen waving their flags. In addition, the Federal force in the Peach Orchard area was well supported by artillery, and the line continued to the left, north along the Emmitsburg Road as far as he could see. It was readily apparent that, if he was successful in following his orders and somehow was able to clear the Federals from the Peach Orchard, he would leave enemy troops to his right and rear. But perhaps that was academic. Fences in his front would hamper his brigade's movements, and the enemy position seemed almost impregnable. Without hesitation and with a decisiveness displayed all too rarely by Confederate generals so far that day, Kershaw ordered his Carolinians to the cover of the stone wall in the brigade's rear and reported the state of things to Lafayette McLaws.[7]

At forty-one, Kershaw was about the same age as McLaws and Longstreet. He was a good man to have in a situation requiring quick and rational decisions. McLaws had great faith in him and described him as "a very cool, judicious and gallant gentleman." Kershaw was a lawyer by profession—a standard schooling for Confederate brigade commanders, it would seem—but he had seen military service with the Palmetto Regiment in Scott's army during the Mexican War. This experience, combined with his civilian prominence and reputation, secured the colonelcy of the Second South Carolina for him, and he was present with it at Fort Sumter and First Manassas. Kershaw became a brigadier general in February 1862. Douglas Southall Freeman wrote that Kershaw "had been distinguished in almost every battle he had shared. Pious, intelligent, a clear blond of high bred, clean-cut features, he had the bearing of command and a clear voice that seemed to inspire courage when it was raised in battle."[8]

As Kershaw's Carolinians took their places behind the wall, Manly's battery went into position in front of their left center. It had been intended that when Kershaw's brigade filed to the enemy's flank, this battery would take position on Seminary Ridge to the left of the road and rake the enemy line from there. But that was no longer in the cards. Instead Manly's sections obliqued to the right and went in on Kershaw's front about seven hundred yards from its target area in the Peach Orchard. This placed the battery directly opposite the flank of Ames's battery, but that juxtaposition would soon change.[9]

Whether in response to Kershaw's message or simply to have a better look at the situation in his division's front, McLaws returned to the ridge line, dismounted, and walked forward to some trees from which he could see the Federal position. The sight overwhelmed him as it had Kershaw. This was a situation not contemplated by General Lee when the attack plan was made and not envisioned by General Longstreet when they had talked a short time before. If McLaws had sworn mighty oaths when forced to countermarch a few hours earlier that day, he must have strained his vocabulary after studying the Federal position along the Emmitsburg Road.[10]

McLaws deployed his division into two lines. Barksdale's brigade formed on Kershaw's left north of the Wheatfield Road. It extended along the east edge of Pitzer's Woods on a front of over four hundred yards. The remaining two brigades formed in a support line. Brig. Gen. Paul Semmes's brigade was behind Kershaw's in and north of Biesecker's Woods, and Brig. Gen. William T. Wofford's was behind Barksdale's and probably along the west edge of Pitzer's Woods. There was an interval of about 150 yards between the forward and support lines, and McLaws instructed the brigade commanders to maintain that interval during their advance.[11] The stone wall gave the two forward brigades some shelter, and the reverse slope of the ridge, a "gentle declivity," gave cover to all four. The trees of Pitzer's Woods shaded Barksdale's brigade and probably Wofford's as well, and those of Biesecker's Woods covered the regiments of Kershaw's right. Cabell's battalion—the batteries of Manly and Capts. Edward S. McCarthy, Henry H. Carlton, and John C. Fraser—took position in front of Kershaw's right wing, but Kershaw placed one regiment, the Fifteenth South Carolina, in a detached position to Cabell's right near the Snyder farmyard.[12] As McLaws's division formed, Hood's passed along its rear to take position on McLaws's right.[13]

McLaws reported the strong Federal position in his front to General Longstreet, and the barking of dueling cannons there must have underscored his report. The situation had changed. At best McLaws could not order an assault until Cabell's guns had tried to neutralize the Federal batteries at the Peach Orchard. But as McLaws prepared for his attack, Maj. Osmund Latrobe of Longstreet's staff—"a very gallant man and ardent Confederate," as Major Moses described him—rode up. He asked McLaws why the attack had not begun, "as there was no one in my front but a regiment of infantry and a battery of artillery," to quote McLaws's aggrieved account.[14] McLaws replied that he would attack as soon as his division was formed, but that the enemy was in great force in his front, with numerous artillery pieces, and that the enemy line extended far to his right. Latrobe took this reply, left, and soon returned to repeat the order.[15] McLaws replied once more that the enemy was strong in his front and that his assault required careful preparation or it would fail. He added that "the opposite artillery was numerous, and it was necessary to break its force by the fire of our artillery." As soon as the artillery opened—all of it must not have done so by this time—and his men were up, he would advance. In the meantime, perhaps, General Longstreet would come forward and see for himself.[16]

Latrobe rode off again but soon returned. This time he delivered a peremptory order from Longstreet to attack, and somehow McLaws understood that General Lee was with Longstreet and joined in the order. McLaws told Major Latrobe that his division would advance in five minutes.[17] But before the five minutes were up, a courier dashed up with orders for Mc-Laws's division not to go forward until Hood's was in position. McLaws must have been exasperated but relieved. He sent a staff officer to General Hood to act as a liaison between the two division commanders and probably told Kershaw and Barksdale to delay their advance until Hood's attack commenced. Soon after, General Longstreet himself appeared.[18]

In *The Gettysburg Campaign*, Edwin B. Coddington writes that *if* General Longstreet had planned that Hood's division would attack first, as it did, Longstreet's orders for McLaws to attack the Federal position in the Peach Orchard are "inexplicable."[19] So they are, and none of the commanders involved attempted to explain them. Therefore, it may be assumed that McLaws's division was intended to attack first and that a late change was made in the details of the plan of attack.

As related, General Lee gave the orders for the assault and indicated to McLaws the specific position that his division was to occupy before the attack began. According to McLaws, this position was perpendicular to the Emmitsburg Road, on the Federal left, and parallel to the enemy's line. This was the position that Longstreet and McLaws wished the division to occupy when it approached Seminary Ridge. McLaws thought that his division was to open the attack, and that it had led Longstreet's corps in the march to the Confederate right for this reason. Longstreet apparently had confirmed this assignment when, after the confusion and countermarch on Herr Ridge, he permitted McLaws's division, at McLaws's request, to continue to lead the column, although Hood's division might more easily have done so.[20] Hood's orders, in turn, were to place his division astride the Emmitsburg Road and attack.[21] These orders apparently did not come directly from General Lee, and we cannot know if they were the only orders that Hood received or just the last.

Obviously there was a last minute change in the details of the attack plan, for after insisting that McLaws's division advance immediately, Longstreet suddenly changed his mind and ordered it to await the attack by Hood's division. We may presume that this came about when General Longstreet, and probably General Lee, learned that the Federal position was not as envisioned earlier in the day and that the Federal line extended far to the southeast of the Peach Orchard. Of this, Longstreet wrote only that as his corps deployed, he examined the Federal position and that "General Lee at the same time gave orders for the attack to be made by my right—following up the direction of the Emmitsburg road toward the Cemetery Ridge, holding Hood's left as well as could be toward the Emmitsburg road, McLaws to follow the movements of Hood, attacking at the Peach Orchard ... with a part of R. H. Anderson's division following the movements of McLaws to guard his left flank."[22] And so, *if Longstreet's statement was correct*, as it probably was, General Lee himself approved the change in the attack plan if, indeed, he did not make the modification himself.

Such a change in plan would do much to explain another "inexplicable" detail. The orders for McLaws and Kershaw do not jibe well with those received by Hood as part of the same plan. Had both divisions formed across the Emmitsburg Road in the manner intended and McLaws's division opened the attack with Hood following in support or echelon, the operation would have been rational. Had Hood's division opened the attack with such deployment, however, it would simply have collided with McLaws's division to no purpose. The change in plans, however, nullified McLaws's intended deployment in favor of that taken as a matter of expediency. Though Hood's advance did not follow the Emmitsburg Road as ordered, the commanders of the leading brigades of both divisions continued to be influenced by the original instructions to attack up the Emmitsburg Road.

Soon after McLaws received the orders to await Hood's attack, General Longstreet appeared. It was a tense time. Things were not going well, and tempers were short. According to McLaws's recollections, Longstreet greeted him by pointing to the gap in the fringe of trees on the crest where the Wheatfield Road passed over it and asking, "Why is not a battery placed here?" McLaws, who probably was not greatly intimidated by his old classmate, replied, "General, if a battery is placed there it will draw the enemy's artillery right among my lines formed for the charge and will of itself be in the way of my charge, and tend to demoralize my men." Longstreet's response was to order him to call up a battery and place it there, and that ended the conversation. McLaws did as instructed, and as he had predicted, the battery drew fire at once.[23] The incoming rounds, probably twelve-pound shot from Bucklyn's battery, ricocheted among the trees, knocking off limbs, and the shells did the same; but the shells also exploded, killing and wounding some men and "producing a natural feeling of uneasiness among them." McLaws mounted and rode among his restive men, urging them to lie down and seeking to calm them. In McLaws estimation all of this took place within a period of fifteen or twenty minutes.[24]

In later years, after Longstreet's conduct that day had become controversial, Lt. Col. G. Moxley Sorrel remarked in his memoirs that Longstreet was unwilling to fight according to General Lee's plan. According to Sorrel, "There was apparent apathy in his movements. They lacked the fire and point of his usual bearing on the battlefield," and Longstreet "failed to conceal some anger."[25] Lafayette McLaws expressed even less charitable views of his chief in a private letter to his wife. Five days after the battle McLaws still seethed. He stated that Longstreet was to blame for not reconnoitering the ground and for persisting in ordering the assault after his errors were discovered. He went on to write that "during the engagement he was very excited giving contradictory orders to everyone, and was exceedingly overbearing. I consider him a humbug—a man of small capacity, very obstinate, not at all chivalrous, exceedingly conceited, and totally selfish."[26]

It was likely that any battery ordered up because of Longstreet's demand belonged to Alexander's battalion, though such records as exist indicate that none of its guns was placed in the road itself. Alexander was either not aware of the exchange between the two generals or saw fit not to comment on it. He wrote simply that to help Cabell he ran up his battalion, temporarily commanded by Maj. Frank Huger. Sixteen of his twenty-six guns went on line about five hundred yards from the Peach Orchard and opened on the Federal batteries there.[27]

The guns (Alexander wrote that there were eighteen rather than sixteen) belonged to four of Alexander's batteries. The four Napoleons of Capt. Osmond B. Taylor's Virginia Battery went in just south of the Wheatfield Road, and Capt. William W. Parker's Virginia Battery with three three-inch Ordnance rifles and one ten-pounder Parrott dropped trail on Taylor's immediate right. In effect these two batteries filled the gap between Carlton's section of howitzers, on the left of Cabell's line, and the Wheatfield Road. Capt. George V. Moody's battery (Louisiana Madison Light Artillery), which had four twenty-four-pounder field howitzers, large-bored (5.82 inches) bronze guns, took position about forty-five yards north of the road. The fourth battery, South Carolina's Brooks Artillery, four twelve-pounder field howitzers under Lt. S. Capers Gilbert, took position on Moody's left with its left piece about 160 yards north of the road. Moody's and Gilbert's howitzers were in front of Barksdale's right wing, while Taylor's and Parker's guns stood beyond Kershaw's left.[28]

Parker's battery suffered one of the first casualties of the afternoon's battle. As the battery jolted along from Pitzer's Schoolhouse toward its position on the ridge, Pvt. John A. Hightower somehow fell to the ground from his seat on a limber, and the heavy wheel of a gun or caisson crushed his right thigh. Fortunately, Hightower survived the war.[29]

In addition to the four batteries mentioned above, Alexander's battalion also had the Bedford (Virginia) Artillery, a battery of four three-inch rifles commanded by Capt. Tyler C. Jordan, and the Ashland (Virginia) Artillery, which had two twenty-pounder Parrotts and two Napoleons under Capt. Pichegru Woolfolk, Jr. Perhaps Alexander saw no appropriate place for them on the ridge and wanted a reserve; whatever the reason, he left them in the rear at the onset of the fight. In spite of not being engaged, Woolfolk had added to Alexander's problems in a unique way.[30]

As mentioned in Chapter 2, on 1 July Captains Woolfolk and Moody had quarreled because the battery of one had taken the other's place in the march column when it did not take the road quickly enough. Precedence in the column made for less dust and an easier march, and no battery commander could surrender it without protest. For some reason neither Alexander nor Major Huger became sufficiently involved to solve the problem, the quarrel got out of hand, and Moody challenged Woolfolk to a duel. This was to have taken place on the morning of 2 July and was to be no effete affair with small-bore dueling pistols from a plush-lined box—the captains elected to use infantry rifles at ten paces! But the duel had to be postponed because the battalion was too busy that morning to give them time for it. While the battalion waited near Pitzer's Schoolhouse for the infantry that afternoon, Woolfolk showed Alexander the letters that had passed between the two hotheads, but Alexander took no action at that time. Nor did he ever have to, for the captains never saw one another after that day. Woolfolk was wounded, and before he returned to duty, Moody was captured in Tennessee and held prisoner for the duration of the war. Evidently their tempers were cooled by time or distance, for neither died at the other's hand. Moody returned to his law practice in Port Gibson, Mississippi, where a man he had prosecuted shot him at his desk. Woolfolk's death was equally untimely and even more unusual—a ceiling in a chamber of Virginia's capitol fell, crushing him beneath it.[31]

But that was later. On the afternoon of 2 July 1863 both were ready for calamity. Alexander's battalion drew Federal fire among the Georgia and Mississippi infantry in Pitzer's Woods. Barksdale's men had dropped their bedrolls in regimental heaps in the woods, and guards were placed over them. Some men went back to Willoughby Run to fill canteens, and a few picked cherries until Federal fire discouraged them. One of the first shots fired at Alexander's guns exploded in the ranks of the Twenty-first Mississippi, where it took the legs off one soldier and killed another outright.[32]

The men in the woods had to be alert to avoid falling branches. Pvt. Elijah H. Sutton, Company K, Twenty-fourth Georgia, must have been wide awake, because he saw a most unusual thing. A solid shot, a twelve-pound ball from Bucklyn's battery, struck a young hickory tree whose diameter was not much greater than that of the ball. The ball smashed through the tree, causing it to split open and then snap shut. The ball lost a lot of its momentum in passing through the tree, hit the ground, "jumped several times, and then whirled like a top for several seconds." Then the ball took another jump of several feet, rolled a few feet more, and finally stopped. Those who went to look at it found that it was too hot to handle.[33]

General Barksdale, "the fiery impetuous Mississippian," as McLaws described him, became impatient. He had no wish for his men to lie still and take a pounding when the offending batteries in his front seemingly might be had for the taking. Two or three times he approached McLaws pleading, "General, let me go; General, let me charge!"; but McLaws, who was awaiting the order to advance, could only tell him to be patient.[34]

It is likely that Kershaw was able by nature to accept things more calmly than Barksdale. This was just as well, for his brigade's task would be more complicated than Barksdale's and would require special planning. The ground in Barksdale's front simply sloped gently into a broad trough midway between the lines and uphill again to the high ground along the Emmitsburg Road six to seven hundred yards away. It was different on Kershaw's front. The Peach Orchard, which appeared to be held in strength, was somewhat left of the brigade's zone, and there was no high ground directly ahead. But south of the Peach Orchard and almost two hundred yards beyond the Emmitsburg Road, Kershaw could see the massive fieldstone Rose barn and beyond it to the right the stone Rose house. There was a morass behind the barn. This low area was backed by higher ground—the stony hill. The morass, which was an upper segment of the west branch of Plum Run, drained eastward into the northwest corner of Rose's Woods. Through the gap beyond the buildings, and between the stony hill and woods, ran a lane that connected Rose's farmyard with the Wheatfield. Kershaw did not know it at the time, but de Trobriand's brigade of the Third Corps was on and near the stony hill. Tilton's and Sweitzer's brigades of the Fifth Corps would soon also take position there. Kershaw could see batteries in and around the Peach Orchard and skirmishers in front of the orchard and at the Rose farmyard. It must have been apparent to him that any troops moving toward the stony hill and the Rose buildings would have to present their flank to the Federal batteries at the Peach Orchard.[35]

As Kershaw studied the ground in his brigade's front, he received instructions for his advance both "in sundry messages" from Generals Longstreet and McLaws and "in part by personal communication with them." How many cooks were preparing Kershaw's broth? As Kershaw came to understand it, his brigade would go forward as soon as Hood was well engaged, swing left toward the Peach Orchard, and at the same time connect with Hood's left. Hood's division would be sweeping against the Federal line in a direction about perpendicular to his own. Barksdale's brigade on his left would advance with Kershaw's brigade and conform to its movements; Semmes's brigade would follow Kershaw's brigade, and Wofford's would support Barksdale's. This was the plan as Kershaw remembered it. Later, about 4:00 P.M., Kershaw learned that Cabell's battalion would fire a signal to start his brigade. It would pause in its shooting and then signal the advance by firing three shots in rapid succession. Kershaw, in turn, told his regimental commanders that when they heard the signal, their men were to scramble over the wall in their front and form in line of battle.[36]

After reviewing his instructions and fitting them to the terrain that he could see ahead of him, Kershaw soon made some decisions. He would direct the brigade's center toward the stony hill and strike it. As his brigade did this, its left would then "attack the orchard on its left rear." If his center was directed toward the hill, his right should encompass the Rose farm buildings. Barksdale, of course, would strike the orchard's front and in doing so would take much pressure off the South Carolinians' left. These decisions made, all that McLaws's people had to do was complete their preparations and await Hood's assault and the boom of the starting guns.[37]

HOOD'S DIVISION TAKES POSITION

It was about 4:00 P.M. Maj. Gen. John Bell Hood's four brigades had reached their line of departure, to use the terminology of later wars, on Seminary Ridge at the Emmitsburg Road about 2¾ miles south of the Seminary and 2 miles southwesterly of Cemetery Hill. The officers and men of the division, particularly those of Law's brigade, were hot, thirsty, and tired. Being seasoned veterans, they must have suffered no illusions about what was in store for them. Their approach march was over and, in spite of efforts to conceal it, the enemy knew their location. Federal batteries in the Peach Orchard area and on Devil's Den welcomed them with a hail of hot iron.

Hood's division, like McLaws's, deployed in two lines—two brigades in the first line and two in their support about two hundred yards in their rear. Law's brigade of five Alabama regiments was the right brigade of the forward line, and Brig. Gen. Jerome B. Robertson's Texas Brigade was on the left. Both stood in the prescribed two ranks, which were backed by a third partial rank of file closers, noncommissioned officers and lieutenants placed where they could superintend the riflemen at their work.[38]

The commanders of these two brigades were quite dissimilar. Brig. Gen. Evander McIvor Law was born in South Carolina in 1836 and was a graduate of The Citadel. He taught at Kings Mountain Military Academy at Yorkville, South Carolina, and in 1860 moved to Tuskegee, Alabama, where he taught school and studied law. His stay in Tuskegee must have been brief, for in January 1861 he took command of a company of state troops and served with them as a part of the state's garrison in Pensacola, Florida, which was threatened by the continued Federal occupation of Fort Pickens. After the war began, he became lieutenant colonel of the Fourth Alabama Regiment. The Fourth's colonel fell at First Manassas, and Law was wounded in that battle but not severely enough to keep him from taking command of the regiment and becoming its colonel in November. He led the Fourth at Seven Pines and commanded Whiting's brigade at Gaines's Mill, Malvern Hill, Second Manassas, and Antietam. He became a brigadier general in October 1862. In a eulogy of later years someone described him as "one of the handsomest of men, as straight as an arrow, with jet black beard and dashing appearance. The grace of his manner was flawless." Col. William C. Oates of the Fifteenth Alabama, who knew Law well but would not have been greatly concerned with his manners, termed him a "brave man and a good fighter." But Oates complained that Law was "negligent" in writing reports of his brigade's operations, thereby failing to get credit for the brigade when credit was due.[39]

Brig. Gen. Jerome B. Robertson, who appears in his photograph as a stern, bearded man, was of a different mold. Robertson was born in Kentucky in 1815 and was a generation older than Law. He became an orphan at twelve and was apprenticed, but he secured his independence at eighteen and somehow managed to study medicine at Transylvania University. It must have been a short course of study, for, intrigued by the war for independence in Texas, he went there in 1835. He missed the Battle of San Jacinto, to his regret, but became a captain in the Texas army. After becoming a civilian in 1837, he practiced medicine in Washington, Texas, but was able to take the time to fight Indians and serve in the state legislature. After the secession of Texas, Robertson entered military service again as a middle-aged captain in the Fifth Texas; he became its lieutenant colonel in December 1861 and its colonel in June 1862. He led the Fifth in the fighting east of Richmond and was wounded at Second Manassas. He tried to stay with the army during its invasion of Maryland but was too weak to fight at Antietam. Nevertheless, in November 1862 he became a brigadier and took command of the Texas Brigade. Robertson later shared a unique distinction with General Lee: before the war's end both were fathers of Confederate generals.[40]

Law's brigade, composed of the Fourth, Fifteenth, Forty-fourth, Forty-seventh, and Forty-eighth Alabama regiments and about 1,500 strong, formed for its attack behind the crest of Seminary Ridge but east of the Emmitsburg Road. It was on the army's right "at or near an old hedgerow." The Forty-fourth and Forty-eighth regiments were on the right of its line, the Fifteenth in the center, and the Forty-seventh and Fourth on its left. Three companies of the Forty-seventh were detached to guard its right flank and likely served on its skirmish line. The brigade's center, probably the front of the Fifteenth Alabama, was said to have been about fifty yards west of the present site of the brigade tablet. This tablet was placed on Seminary Ridge about five hundred yards south of the Emmitsburg Road.[41]

The Texas Brigade, 1,100 strong, was on the immediate left of Law's brigade. Its Fifth Texas Regiment connected with the Fourth Alabama on its right, the Fourth and First Texas regiments were in its center, and the Third Arkansas was on the brigade's left. The brigade front was astride the Emmitsburg Road in the woods at the head of the M. Bushman farm lane. Colonel Manning, commander of the Third Arkansas, recalled that the road was two hundred yards to his front, and it must have crossed the ridge an equal distance to the right. Manning's line must have been in Biesecker's Woods off the right of the Fifteenth South Carolina of Kershaw's brigade and southwest of the Philip Snyder house. But like many others who wrote reports of the battle, Robertson said nothing of buildings on his part of the battlefield.[42]

The brigades of Brig. Gens. Henry L. Benning and George T. ("Tige")

Anderson formed Hood's division's support line. Thus it happened, by coincidence no doubt, that on 2 July the half of Longstreet's force that was Georgian, four of his eight brigades, was in the support line. Benning's brigade, about 1,400 strong, had four Georgia regiments—the Second, Seventeenth, Twentieth, and Fifteenth, formed in that order from right to left. In his account of the battle, Colonel Oates located Benning's brigade behind Law's left wing and the right wing of the Texas Brigade rather than directly behind Law; and Benning's imprecise report seems to support Oates's recollection. If so positioned, the brigade must have formed westerly of the Emmitsburg Road with its right about two hundred yards north of the A. Currens house, well behind the crest of the ridge and out of sight of the ground over which it was soon to attack.[43]

Anderson's brigade was somewhere on Benning's left, probably in rough extension of Benning's line. It had but four of its five regiments in line: the Fifty-ninth was on the right, the Eleventh and Eighth in the center, and the Ninth on its left. The other regiment, Col. William W. White's Seventh Georgia, was sent off to the right "to watch the movements of the enemy's cavalry," which, we know today, would have still been far beyond the Seventh's range of vision. Probably the Seventh took a position from which it could guard the road as well as have surveillance over the countryside to the left and right. Anderson did not see fit to report his brigade's position with any precision except to say that it was on the left of the division and behind Robertson. The brigade numbered about 1,800 officers and men all told, but with the Seventh Regiment detached, only about 1,400 would have been in line.[44]

Maj. Mathis W. Henry's battalion of artillery was in direct support of Hood's division. Like Hood, Henry was a Kentuckian and a graduate of West Point (class of 1861). He served briefly as a second lieutenant in the Third U.S. Cavalry but left it for Confederate service and was on Stuart's staff for a short time. He took command of a battery of horse artillery in August 1862. In February 1863 he became a major and was given command of the battalion serving with Hood's division.[45]

Henry's battalion had four batteries, but there was only room for two on Hood's front that afternoon. Henry placed the six pieces of Capt. James Reilly's battery (Rowan Artillery of North Carolina) on the ridge crest in front of Hood's right wing, where the ground was open and provided a clear shot toward Devil's Den and the Round Tops. Capt. Alexander C. Latham's battery, the Branch (North Carolina) Artillery, with five pieces, was in front of the Texas Brigade in the area of the Bushman farm lane. Latham's guns could fire on Devil's Den and Little Round Top but, unlike Reilly's, could also fire up the Emmitsburg Road toward the Peach Orchard and the Rose buildings. Unfortunately for Latham's men, numerous Federal guns in the Peach Orchard area could also fire at them. Latham's battery had three Napoleons, a twelve-pounder field howitzer, and a six-pounder bronze gun;

Reilly's was armed with two Napoleons, two ten-pounder Parrotts, and two three-inch Ordnance rifles.[46]

As soon as they were in position, the two batteries, at Hood's direction, opened on the Federals in an attempt to locate their line. The Federal batteries—Smith's at Devil's Den and Clark's, plus perhaps Ames's and others, at the Peach Orchard—returned their fire. The Confederate batteries ceased fire when the infantry advanced through their positions but reopened as soon as the gray lines were downhill below their lines of fire. Sad to say, no one recorded the deeds of these batteries in a meaningful way, and they are now obscure. In the course of the firing on 2 July one of Reilly's three-inch Ordnance rifles burst, and two of Latham's light guns, the howitzer and the six-pounder, were disabled. The casualties of these batteries for the entire battle were three men killed and six wounded.[47]

The division's commander, John B. Hood, like Jerome Robertson, was a Kentuckian by birth and a Texan by adoption. Hood was born in 1831 at Owingsville, Kentucky, the son of a physician of means. He graduated from West Point in its class of 1853 and was a veteran of service in the Old Army. This service included a stint in Texas with the Second U.S. Cavalry Regiment, commanded for a time by Robert E. Lee, who was something of a mentor for young Hood. By the time of Gettysburg, Hood was thirty-two years old, an experienced commander, but young enough to be vigorous. A bachelor still, he was tall and wiry and had a particularly grave face, partially covered by a neat and tawny beard. This combination contributed to his being an admired figure in a romantic era. More important, the record he had made and the reputation he had gained as commander of the Texas Brigade and as a division commander made him both a valuable general officer and a celebrity who transcended most of his peers.[48] The battle at hand promised him further laurels. As fate decreed, his division would open it and in great measure probably determine its outcome. If Hood's division succeeded in its mission, the battle could and probably would be won by the Army of Northern Virginia. But if it did not succeed, the battle likely would not be a Confederate victory. Hindsight tells us that the key to the division's success or failure was John Bell Hood.

Hood was aggressive, but he was also prudent. His division's position was on the right flank of the Army of Northern Virginia, but the enemy's position in his front had not been developed. Therefore, as the division approached its position area, Hood sent a party of Texas scouts to reconnoiter his right in order to determine the location of the enemy's left—the same sort of task that had been entrusted about eleven hours before to Captain Johnston and Major Clarke. The scouts, who probably were all enlisted men, including Sgt. Charles Kingsley, Pvt. Wilson J. Barbee, Pvt. John M. Pinckney, and possibly Pvt. James H. Dearing of the First Texas Regiment, rode ahead to do their division commander's will.[49]

At about the same time, General Law sent six of his men on a similar errand, to see how far the Federal line extended up Round Top. He told them to move as fast as possible, go to the summit of the hill by making a swing to the right, and feel down its slope until they saw the Federal flank. As soon as they gained the information needed they were to send a runner back to him. Having received their orders, the Alabama scouts set off at a trot, whether on horseback or on foot Law did not say.[50]

When their brigades reached their positions, Law and Robertson deployed skirmishers to their front. Law's brigade also sent out details to fetch water, for its men had marched far that July day and needed it sorely. Water would not have been readily available close by: Plum Run in their front was covered by the enemy, Marsh Creek was about a mile in their rear, and there were few wells much closer. Some of the men who were sent returned with water taken from a green pond, and twenty-two men of the Fifteenth Alabama did not return at all. In the meantime the pioneer detail of the Fourth Alabama, Law's left regiment, cleared a space in front of the Fifth Texas for some of Latham's guns. The falling trees attracted the attention of enemy gunners who fired at the work party and, incidentally, at the Fifth Texas as well.[51]

The men in Hood's forward line spent a difficult hour on Seminary Ridge while the division deployed and prepared for its attack. The strain of waiting alone would have been enough for some, but it was intensified by incoming artillery fire directed at the batteries of Cabell's and Henry's battalions and fully shared by the infantrymen in their rear. Much of this fire fell on the Texas Brigade. Pvt. John C. West of the Fourth Texas recalled the terror of the pounding, when "the infernal machines came tearing and whirring through the ranks with a most demoralizing tendency."[52] Before the men of the Fourth settled in, a solid shot hit fifty feet short of their line, bounded over it, and sprinkled the men with dirt. Another whistled over their heads, and a third decapitated one soldier and cut another in two, splattering his blood on the men around him. Still another shell wounded fifteen men of the Fourth before the attack began.[53]

Pvt. Richard Childers of the First Texas was a man of mixed luck that afternoon. An incoming round or a large shell fragment struck his haversack. The bag, which was suspended from his shoulder, was filled with Pennsylvania biscuits, and the missile sent them flying, scattering them over the company area. Childers himself was not hit or knocked down, but he fell in a faint; and when he came to, he was paralyzed, unable to move a muscle, and had to be carried away on a litter. Poor Childers. It is sad to report that there were Texans so unfeeling as to suggest that the loss of the biscuits alone was responsible for his shock. It is sadder to relate, in a more serious vein, that Lt. Col. Phillip A. Work, the commander of the First Texas, reported that Childers was one of the two men in the regiment who did not prove himself a hero at Gettysburg.[54]

Captain Barziza, commander of Company C, Fourth Texas, wrote with feeling about this shelling, an experience the like of which was to be shared by many men in both armies that afternoon. According to Barziza:

> The enemy's shells screamed and bursted around us, inflicting considerable damage. It is very trying upon men to remain still and in ranks under a severe cannonading. One has time to reflect upon the danger, and there being no wild excitement as in a charge, he is more reminded of the utter helplessness of his present condition. The men are all flat on the ground, keeping their places in ranks, and as a shell is heard, generally try to sink themselves into the earth. Nearly every face is overspread with a serious, thoughtful air; and what thoughts, vivid and burning, come trooping up from the inner chambers of memory, the soldier can only realize.[55]

A hundred yards or so to the left the Third Arkansas lay in line among the trees of Biesecker's Woods. A round shot killed the captain of Company H, severed its orderly sergeant's arm, took off another sergeant's head, mangled a corporal's leg, and then bounded off among the trees. Every time a projectile passed close by, a jittery private jumped up, ran a few steps, and dropped to the ground. Throughout all the terror Colonel Manning paced back and forth, keeping the Third Arkansas under his watchful eye and seeing that it stayed in place.[56]

While they waited, Lt. Mat Beasley of the Fourth Texas learned that he was to command Company I in the assault. It was a frightening sort of honor, for the company had a deserved reputation for losing officers in battle and Beasley's future seemed limited. But the men of the company were supportive. They gathered around the lieutenant to congratulate him, saying: "Good-bye, you are gone now," and "I am sorry for you but can't help you any." It was a hard time for Mat Beasley, but as things turned out, he was said to be the only company commander ever to survive a fight with that company.[57]

While the officers and men in the regiments awaited their orders, there were important things happening nearby. Soon after Law's scouting party departed, Law and some others spotted several men moving in the distance off their right toward the Emmitsburg Road. Law sent a detail to investigate, and the men proved to be Union soldiers, probably of the Third Corps, headed toward their onetime rear. Law learned from them that there were lightly guarded wagons behind the Round Tops and that the Union officers there anticipated no danger. He learned also that a road off to his right led to that area.[58]

Law rode off to report this new information to General Hood and on his way met messengers from his scouts. They told him that there were no Federals on Round Top and confirmed the intelligence gained from the prisoners. This was important news. Law was convinced that his "true *point d'appui*," his pivot point, was Round Top. From this anchor the Confederate right could extend off toward the Taneytown and Baltimore roads and sweep against the Federal left and rear.[59]

Law found Hood "where his line had been formed," probably to the front of the Texas Brigade. He gave Hood the new information and his revised views about the attack. According to Law, Hood agreed with him. Hood said, however, that they had positive orders to attack as soon as the division was in position. Law, according to his recollections, then formally protested the assault as it was planned for four reasons. The reasons were, in his words:

1. That the great natural strength of the enemy's position in our front rendered the result of a direct assault extremely uncertain.

2. That, even if successful, the victory would be purchased at too great a sacrifice of life, and our troops would be in no condition to improve it.

3. That a front attack was unnecessary,—the occupation of Round Top during the night by moving upon it from the south, and the extension of our right wing from that point across the enemy's left and rear, being not only practicable, but easy.

4. That such a movement would compel a change of front on the part of the enemy, the abandonment of his strong position on the heights, and force him to attack us in position.[60]

This seemed like good Longstreet doctrine, of course, but whether Law knew it then or not we do not know. After hearing Law's comments, Hood asked him to repeat them before Capt. James Hamilton of his staff. Hamilton listened to Law's recitation and at Hood's direction rode off to pass the comments on to Longstreet. He returned in about ten minutes, accompanied by one of Longstreet's staff officers, who told Hood in Law's hearing: "General Longstreet orders that you begin the attack at once." With that, Hood turned to Law and asked: "You hear the order?" Law did, and he rode off to open the assault.[61]

That is what took place as Law recalled it. Hood had his own recollections, which, as written, did not mention Law's participation in the search for alternatives to the ordered plan of attack, though that does not necessarily mean that he did not participate. Hood recalled that his scouts returned with the report that the Federal left rested on Round Top, that the country to the right was open, and that Hood's division could move through "an open woodland pasture" around Round Top and strike the enemy in the flank and rear. In addition, there were wagons behind the hill that would be Hood's for the taking.[62]

The alternate movement appealed to Hood. It promised to be less costly for his division than that ordered and more fruitful. He sought a change in orders. He remembered making three requests (perhaps one included that described by Law) and "Old Pete" Longstreet, in the tradition of his New Testament namesake, gave him three denials. Three times General Longstreet replied, in effect: "Gen'l Lee's orders are to attack up the Emmitts-burg Road."[63] Lieutenant Colonel Sorrel, Longstreet's adjutant general, wrote that Hood had begged him to look into the situation and "implore Longstreet to make the attack another way." Sorrel delivered Hood's message and was told that the attack must be made as directed.[64]

Maj. John W. Fairfax of Longstreet's staff was one of the actors in this drama. Fairfax, scion of Virginia's noble Fairfax family, resembled his chief in appearance and was sometimes mistaken for him. Major Moses, who knew him well, wrote that Fairfax was "fond of his bottle, his Bible and his bath; always in front when danger pressed, but a fine looking fellow very much given to show."[65] Fairfax brought Hood an order to attack but listened to the Texan's arguments and suggested that Hood delay until he could speak with Longstreet about the alternate opportunity. In response Hood, who stood by the mounted Fairfax as they talked, slapped the major on the knee and said, "I agree with you—bring General Longstreet to see for himself."[66] Fairfax returned to General Longstreet and told him what he had seen and heard. Longstreet answered, "It is General Lee's order, the time is up—attack at once!" Fairfax hurried back to Hood, gave him the message, and waited for the attack to begin.[67]

It seems there were many messengers galloping back and forth between Hood and Longstreet that afternoon while minutes passed and opportunity slipped by, but, in sum, there were only three or four. We cannot be certain of their order, but the last one, according to Hood's recollection, if not Law's, was Maj. William H. ("Harry") Sellers. Hood selected Sellers as his final emissary because he knew that Longstreet had a special regard for him as an officer of courage and ability. Hood instructed Sellers, "Go as fast as your horse can carry you and explain all this to General Longstreet, and ask him to permit me to move by the right flank, so as to be able to envelop that knob."[68]

Sellers galloped off and soon returned with Longstreet's denial, arriving about the same time that Fairfax delivered his version of it. That cinched it. Hood had protested his orders and his protests and recommendations had been denied. He issued orders for the attack. As he did so, Longstreet rode up to talk with him and probably to see that there were no more delays. Hood pleaded with him personally, and the corps commander replied, "We must obey the orders of General Lee." With that Hood reined his horse around and trotted toward the center of his old brigade.[69]

General Longstreet paused for a while. It had already been a long and trying day for him, and it was far from over. It must have been about this time that Captain Barziza saw him behind some batteries "sitting on his horse like an iron man with his spyglass to his eye, coolly watching the effect of our shots. Limbs of trees fell and crashed around him, yet he sat as unmoved as a statue."[70]

In later years, when verbal volleys replaced cannon fire and Early, Pen-dleton, and others attacked him for his performance at Gettysburg, Longstreet became irate and defensive and, like others, saw the events of the day somewhat distorted by passion and improved by hindsight. In justifying his denials of Hood's requests for changes in orders, he insisted that a move to the right—the sort of thing advocated by General Hood—had been discussed with General Lee and that orders had been given for his corps to attack up the Emmitsburg Road. Had General Lee been at hand, wrote Longstreet (Lee probably would not have been far away if he had personally ordered a change in the attack plan a short time before), the messengers from Hood could have been referred to him, but to have sent them "five miles" to propose a move that had been rejected would have been "contumacious." As far as General Hood was concerned, Longstreet said that he had been ordered to bear down on the enemy's left after some artillery practice but that he was not prompt. Therefore, the order to attack had to be repeated "before he would strike down."[71]

If facts are known well or are well fabricated, hindsight can be nearly infallible. As years passed, other solutions to the problems of Gettysburg were voiced with authority, as they sometimes are even today. Certainly the movement advocated by Generals Hood and Law was an inviting alternative from their personal point of view. After all, they faced the prospect of an attack over rough ground under enemy fire against a position that looked to be very strong. The prospect was neither pleasant nor promising. But it was already late in the afternoon, and Hood's men were tired from their day's exertions; how much more time and effort would it have taken to swing around to Round Top's rear? Presumably any such turning movement would have followed the lane or country road about 1,000 yards south of Round Top that connected the Taneytown Road and the Emmitsburg Road. We know nothing of its condition; probably it was no worse than portions of the others followed earlier in the day, but following it would have entailed an additional march of about two miles, and this would have increased the day's exertions by a significant degree.

And what of the assault? If such a movement were made that afternoon, would there be a sufficient amount of daylight left for fighting? And if the assault were delayed until the following morning, would the Federal left still be ripe for the plucking? The Confederate generals had every reason to believe that it would not; knowing of the arrival of the Sixth Corps that afternoon, even as they considered the movement, we can be rather certain that an attack made east of Round Top on 3 July would have proven difficult for the attackers.

How would a change in plan have affected McLaws's division? Its center was a mere seven hundred yards from the Federal position at the Peach Orchard, and its skirmishers and the batteries along its line were already engaged. Would it remain where it was and, in effect, become the Confederate right, as Hood slipped off in a detached Jackson-like move? Or would it stretch its line to the right in an attempt to maintain contact with Hood's left until it became too thin to stretch more and hope for help? Perhaps help might come from Pickett's division, which was not yet on the field, or from Ewell's corps, which already had its mission. And if McLaws's division remained and attacked from where it was, what troops would deal with the Federals still to be seen beyond its right flank (troops that Hood's brigades were to have smashed in the assault that they did not wish to make)? Clearly any change in Hood's orders would require changes in orders for units all along the line, changes that would require the rest of the afternoon to conceive, transmit, and implement.

And what of the Army of the Potomac of which the Confederates knew so little that summer afternoon? The Confederates were in contact with skirmish lines that stretched in front of Little Round Top and along the Emmitsburg Road. Could they reasonably presume that any move to the right might not be detected by them, by lookouts on Little Round Top, or by unknown infantry or cavalry that might be met in the fields to the right? And if the movement were discovered, could they by any stretch of the imagination assume that the Federals would not strike hard against their weakened center on Seminary Ridge or at some other vulnerable point on their attenuated line? These questions would require favorable answers if the Confederate plan was changed. But it was not changed, not greatly at any rate. The attack would be made as ordered.

HOOD'S DIVISION OPENS THE ASSAULT

Maj. Gen. John B. Hood rode along the front of his division and halted in a familiar location—in front of the Texas Brigade. He sat his horse quietly, hat in hand, and when his thoughts were arranged, he made a brief speech, as Civil War generals often did. No one recorded all that he said. His words probably did not carry far—the Texans nearest him might have heard them but not the other troops, not those from Alabama, Georgia, and Arkansas. But the speech was made, and in closing it the warrior Hood stood "majestically" in his stirrups and shouted in stentorian tones, "Fix bayonets, my brave Texans; forward and take those heights!" In echo, Lt. Col. Phillip A. Work of the First Texas pointed to his regiment's Texas flag and shouted, "Follow the Lone Star Flag to the top of the mountain!"[72]

Subordinate commanders repeated Hood's commands, and the troops reacted to them. A private in the Fifth Texas stepped from his place in the ranks of Company A to its front in order to lead a prayer. This was unsolicited by the company commander, and the private was ordered back into line. Moments later, as if in reaction to the officer's order, a shell whistled in and killed three men.[73] There was bustling everywhere, and during it all Capt. Thomas J. Goree of Longstreet's staff rode down the line and, like a cheerleader, gestured toward Little Round Top and yelled for the Texans to take it. "We'll do it!" some shouted back. Then the Texas Brigade's line lurched forward.[74]

On Law's front, where Hood could neither be seen nor heard, Reilly's battery paused in its firing and the Alabamians prepared to step out. Capt. Leigh R. Terrell, Law's adjutant, cantered to the front of the brigade's line and bellowed: "Attention! Shoulder—Arms. Right Shoulder Shift—[Arms]. Guide Center. Forward. March!" Regimental commanders repeated the commands, and the brigade gave Rebel yells and stepped out.[75]

The Alabamians' fatigue must have yielded temporarily to apprehension and excitement. The men of the brigade scuffled quickly through the trees, up the slight slope to the crest of the ridge, and by the guns of Reilly's battery. Ahead the Alabamians could see a long, descending slope, rather steep at first, that ran three hundred or so yards down to the M. Bushman farm buildings to the left front and ahead to a lane lined by stone walls that ran from the Bushman barnyard south across their front to Bushman's Woods. They could also see the John Slyder farmyard about seven hundred yards away, a "low roofed cottage" with barns and a picket fence. Across their line of march, between the walled lane and the Slyder buildings, was a fence that probably sheltered skirmishers from the Second U.S. Sharpshooter Regiment, who, if visible, must have appeared as small and distant figures. The Round Tops and Devil's Den rose beyond the Slyder buildings. Devil's Den resembled a small volcano because of the smoke that belched from the guns of Smith's battery in position there.[76]

Five companies of skirmishers, a tenth of the brigade's strength, preceded Law's line. They were from the Forty-seventh and Forty-eighth regiments, and Colonel Oates believed later that those of each regiment operated separately without a good understanding of the brigade's task. Oates stated that Law had not told his regimental commanders of "what was intended to be done" before the advance began. If this was so, the captains on the skirmish line were not likely to know.[77]

The Alabamians started off at a quickstep, a walking pace. In the excitement some junior officers left their places in the line of file-closers and ran ahead to cheer on their companies from the front. Perhaps this was a brave thing to do. Motivated by this, the downhill slope, and the hope of avoiding the cannon fire that swept the crest of the ridge, the men in the Alabama line broke into a double-quick. But the distance to the Federal position was too long to cover at a trot, much too long for a charge that would only tire the attackers and disorder their lines. Captain Terrell rode to the front again to slow the Alabamians' pace and to urge them to emulate the Fifth Texas Regiment on their left, which was advancing in a disciplined, orderly way.[78]

The terrain crossed by Law's brigade was anything but a parade ground. The walls along the lane, the cross fences, rocks, bushes, trees, plowed ground, and marshy hummocky ground near Plum Run all complicated

Law's advance and made it difficult for the brigade to maintain its formation. The accounts of the advance fail to mention the Bushman buildings, and it is likely that Law's men passed to the right of them. At the same time, it is likely that Law's right regiments, the Forty-fourth and Forty-eighth, brushed the woods and rocks of Bushman's Woods. These must have slowed the advance and made it hard for the right regiments to keep pace.[79]

Smith's battery and Federal skirmishers harassed Law's line. The battery, in particular, was a deadly nuisance. It had to be silenced. Rather than swinging his entire brigade to the left as, presumably, had been intended by the Confederate plan, Law allowed his center regiments to continue straight ahead toward Round Top. He addressed the threat from the battery by withdrawing the Forty-fourth and Forty-eighth regiments from his right, where they were meeting difficult terrain and few Federals, and sending them to the left.[80]

This shift took place in the fields just west of Plum Run. The two regiments halted and probably filed north in columns behind the brigade's left wing toward Devil's Den. Once he had started them on their way, Law rode to Colonel Oates, whose regiment, the Fifteenth, had been in the center of the brigade line but was now on its right. In order to secure the brigade right from threats from Round Top, Law ordered Oates to push ahead to the base of the hill and then swing left, hugging the hill as the Fifteenth swung north parallel to Plum Run. When he reached the Union left, Oates was to "do all the damage [he] could." In the meantime, Lt. Col. Michael J. Bulger and the Forty-seventh Alabama would hold to the Fifteenth's left. If the Fifteenth and Forty-seventh became separated from the rest of the brigade, Bulger would act under Oates's orders.[81]

Oates's and Bulger's regiments pressed directly ahead toward Plum Run and Round Top. The fire of the Federal sharpshooters posted behind a wall in the woods above Plum Run intensified as the Confederates approached. Lt. Col. Isaac B. Feagin of the Fifteenth caught a bullet in the knee that caused him to lose his leg. Two privates were killed and another wounded. But the sharpshooters had no taste for stand-up fighting with solid lines of battle and drifted back, some north toward Devil's Den and others directly up Round Top's slope. The movements of the latter proved critical, for Oates believed that he could not wheel his regiment left as ordered and leave such a force in his rear. Therefore, instead of swinging north toward Devil's Den and Little Round Top, the Fifteenth and Forty-seventh regiments pressed straight ahead after the illusive riflemen. In doing this Oates temporarily removed nearly half of the brigade's strength from its attacking line.[82]

And what of Law's skirmishers? Hindsight suggests that they might have dealt quite adequately with the sharpshooters, but that was less apparent on 2 July 1863. Operating as two separate battalions, they passed to the right around Round Top and ended their movement on its northern slope. They

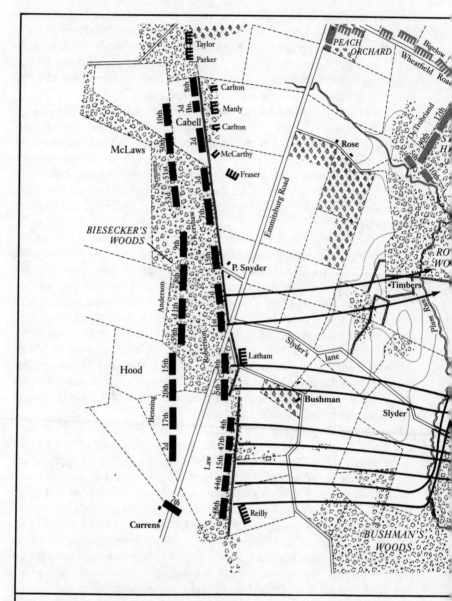

1. Birney's division forms on the high ground north from Devil's Den. The exact position of its skirmish line is not known.

2. Hood's and McLaws's divisions form on Seminary Ridge.

3. Law's brigade advances toward the Third Corps's left flank between the crest of Round Top and Devil's Den. The Forty-fourth and Forty-eighth Alabama regiments shift from Law's right to the left as they near Plum Run.

Map 8-1. Confrontation on the Federal Left: Hood's Division Advances

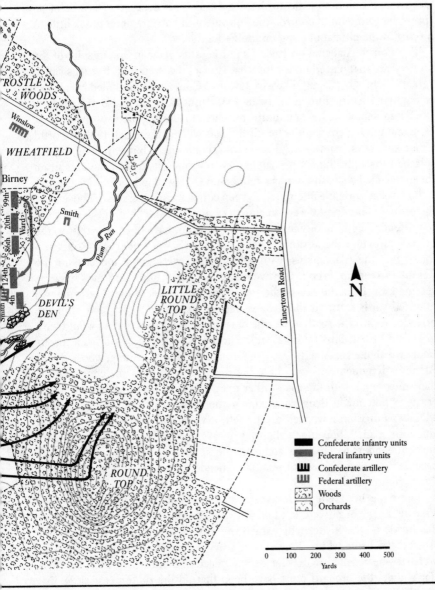

ROSTLE'S WOODS

Winslow

WHEATFIELD

Birney

Ward

99th

20th

86th

124th

4th

Smith

Smith

DEVIL'S DEN

Plum Run

LITTLE ROUND TOP

Taneytown Road

N

ROUND TOP

Confederate infantry units
Federal infantry units
Confederate artillery
Federal artillery
Woods
Orchards

0   100   200   300   400   500
Yards

4. The First Texas and Third Arkansas head for Smith's battery and Ward's brigade north of Devil's Den. The Fourth and Fifth Texas regiments hold to Law's original left and make for Round Top.

5. Benning's brigade, in the support line, advances toward Devil's Den. Anderson's brigade advances later toward Rose's Woods.

6. The Fourth Maine, on Ward's left, shifts further left to block Plum Run's valley. The Ninety-ninth Pennsylvania shifts to the Fourth's initial position.

met no opposition and did no hard fighting; and because of a lack of an appropriate amount of control, the equivalent of half a regiment took little or no part in the crucial fighting on the Federal left.[83]

The Fourth Alabama on Bulger's left kept its place in line in spite of the artillery fire that played on it with what Lt. Col. Lawrence H. Scruggs called "great effect." Ord. Sgt. J. Darwin Taylor of Company I was killed by a bullet or fragment that hit him in the head. Pvt. Rufus B. Franks, also of Company I, who somehow had a new uniform, cheered the regiment on by yelling, "Come on, boys; come on! The Fifth Texas will get there before the Fourth! Come on, boys; come on!" Franks never got there himself. The Fourth splashed through Plum Run, halted, and reformed its line for an assault on the green-clad sharpshooters waiting behind the wall in its front.[84]

Robertson's brigade attempted to keep contact with Law's left. Those were the orders. The Texans were to support Law's left *and* hold to the Emmitsburg Road. The difficulty in doing this might not have been apparent to the brigadiers before the advance began, but once it was underway, Robertson found that the Alabamians, with a head start, were going too fast for the Texans to keep up, even if they went at a quickstep, and that Law's line was veering away from the axis of the road. Therefore, before they had gone two hundred yards some of the Texans had to break into a trot, and after the brigade crossed the road, it became obvious to Robertson that he would have to violate instructions by breaking contact either with Law's brigade on its right or with the road on its left. Both he and Colonel Manning, whose Third Arkansas Regiment was to hold to the road, came to the same conclusion— they must break with the road rather than with Law. To do otherwise would create a potentially dangerous gap in the division's front. Besides, when McLaws's division advanced on the left, it would take care of any problem along the road.[85] The attack plan was unraveling quickly, and the Confederate commanders had to make some on-the-spot decisions. The guidance of a capable division commander was badly needed. Hood would be able to set things right if anyone could.

Where was he? General Hood remained with Robertson for a few minutes after the attack began and left him at two unidentified fences, perhaps those that bordered the Slyder lane, which the Texans would have met after they crossed the Emmitsburg Road. After leaving Robertson, Hood rode to an orchard—he recalled its having been a peach orchard. If it was in his division's zone, the orchard must have been that on the ridge's east slope just west of the Bushman barn. There Hood would have been in the center of his division; from there he could have watched the progress of his forward brigades and seen his support brigades as they emerged from the tree line at the top of the ridge. While he was in the orchard area, a shell exploded above his head, and one of its fragments tore into his left arm. Hood reeled in the saddle from the shock of the blow until a member of his staff caught and steadied him, and comrades lowered him to the ground. Soon stretcher-bearers carried him from the field. In later years Hood recalled that as he was carried away, he experienced "deep distress of mind and heart at the thought of the inevitable fate of my brave fellow-soldiers, who formed one of the grandest divisions of that world-renown army. . . ."[86]

Lt. Frederick M. Colston, ordnance officer of Alexander's battalion, saw Hood a short while later. The wounded general was suffering from his wound and from shock and was no longer a majestic figure. He sat in an ambulance near Pitzer's Schoolhouse, his arm wrapped in bloody bandages. A shell, probably fired by a gun at the Peach Orchard at Parker's or Taylor's battery, whistled in and struck the roof of an ambulance not far from the general's head. Hood glanced up and then took no further interest in it. The day's assault had hardly begun and the Army of Northern Virginia's key division commander was already out of the fight.[87]

Evander Law succeeded Hood to the division's command. The activities of division commanders at Gettysburg are poorly recorded, and those of Law are no exception. How soon he learned of Hood's wounding and of his new responsibilities is not known, and it is equally hard to determine when and how he exercised his new command. Oates, for instance, did not learn that Law had taken command of the division until he reached the top of Round Top. Certainly Law appointed no one to the acting command of the brigade in his stead that afternoon—a peculiar and unfortunate omission on his part. Robertson learned that Law was in command of the division only after his his brigade was fully engaged and he sent back to Hood for reinforcements. Learning then that Hood was no longer on the field, he sent his requests to Longstreet and to Tige Anderson but not to Law. Evidence of Law's work as a division commander is scanty, almost too sparse to support a judgment about it. And yet extant information suggests that his control of the division as a whole that afternoon was not very active and strong.[88]

Once the decision was made to break with the Emmitsburg Road, the First Texas and Third Arkansas regiments on the brigade's left hurried forward under Robertson's watchful eye in an effort to get on line with the troops to their right. Manning reported that the Third Regiment went at a brisk gait for 1,000 yards, part of the way at a double-quick. The Third was exposed to artillery fire much of the way, some of it from the Peach Orchard area and some from Smith's battery on Devil's Den, and to scattered rifle fire from enemy skirmishers. The Texas Brigade's path was reasonably free of obstacles for the first four hundred yards after it crossed the Emmitsburg Road; then it was interrupted by two clumps of woods south of the site of the William Timbers house, and beyond there, by the steep slope down into the rocky valley of the west branch of Plum Run. At about this point in the advance, as Robertson attempted to close right on Law's line and to his own brigade's right wing, the two left regiments received fire from Ward's troops in the woods to his left. The Confederate skirmish line in that area, composed in part of Company I of the First Texas, drove in the Federal skirmish line in their front and advanced toward Rose's Woods and the base of Devil's Den Ridge. By this time Robertson was becoming painfully aware that McLaws's division had not advanced on his left as it was expected to do, and he sent back for reinforcements. He became aware also that the gap between his brigade's wings had grown. Finding that he could not erase the gap by closing his left wing upon his right, he sent a staff officer to order the right wing to shift left. The officer could not find the Fourth and Fifth Texas regiments. Not long afterward, however, Robertson's aide, Lt. John G. Scott, reported that the right wing's two regiments were fighting in the center of Law's line and could not be removed. Robertson must have sworn and then asked that Law look out for them. He then gave his full attention to the efforts of the Third Arkansas and the First Texas.[89]

The gap between Robertson's right and left wings closed before the enemy was able to exploit it. After Law took the Forty-fourth and Forty-eighth Alabama regiments from the right of his brigade line, they filed left behind the left wing of the brigade and then behind the Fourth and Fifth Texas regiments, which must have been closed tightly on Law's line. As the Forty-fourth and the Forty-eighth neared Devil's Den and Smith's battery, the Forty-fourth deployed to assault the Devil's Den position, as will be related in Chapter 9, and the Forty-eighth moved up to its right. Hood's division now had an essentially unbroken line across the slope of Round Top and in front of Devil's Den.[90]

As Law's and Robertson's brigades advanced, Benning's and Anderson's Georgia brigades were to follow in their support. The division's formation and Law's comments in an article written after the war suggest this at any rate, but it did not seem to work out in quite that way. Benning's brigade formed the right of the support line. Henry Lewis Benning, its commander, was born in Columbus, Georgia, in 1814 and, like Robertson, belonged to the Army of Northern Virginia's older generation. Benning had carved out a very successful law career in Georgia and had sat as a justice on the Georgia Supreme Court. Politically he had been a Douglas Democrat, but at the time of the Secession Convention he took a prosecession stance. He entered the Confederate service as colonel of the Seventeenth Georgia in 1861; fought at Second Manassas, Sharpsburg, and Fredericksburg; and became a brigadier general in January 1863. His portrait shows him to have been a bearded, solid-looking, older man; a biographer described him as having been "six feet tall, of noble presence and bearing." His nickname was "Old Rock."[91]

Before the assault began, Hood told Benning that the division would assault the Union left and that his brigade would follow Law's at an interval of four hundred yards. It does not seem likely that Benning was able to study the field over which his brigade was to advance with any care, either alone or in the company of Hood or Law. Apparently he was not invited to any such briefing, and he believed that his place was with his brigade before its attack. At any rate, his report suggests that he was genuinely impressed with the nature of the Federal position when, during his advance, he saw it for the first time.[92]

Federal shells fell around the brigade before it passed over the ridge and into the view of Federal gunners. Benning did not report whence they came. Probably they were from the batteries in the Peach Orchard area, for Smith's gunners must have been concentrating at this time on the forward brigades far down the slope to Benning's front. When his brigade passed through the trees at the top of the ridge, he could see a segment of the first line about four hundred yards ahead. This seemed to be as ordered. He followed it, halting twice to preserve the interval prescribed. His Georgians received some attention from Federal batteries as they crossed the fields; but better targets ought to have been available for them, and their fire should not have been too troublesome. Benning heard from neither Hood nor Law in the course of his brigade's advance, so he followed the first line, waiting for an opportunity to pitch in. It was not long in coming. The line that his brigade had been following needed help, and Benning was there to give it. It was only later that he learned that the line that he had followed so carefully was the left wing of Robertson's brigade and not Law's. Law's had been concealed from him by trees and smoke, and no one from the division staff appeared to give him instruction or advice. But fortune smiled—Benning's brigade was in a right place at a right time.[93]

If Benning's brigade was following Robertson's, what was Anderson's doing all the while? These Georgians awaited their turn to advance near Biesecker's Woods, somewhat behind the right guns of Cabell's battalion. Some of the missiles fired at Cabell's guns, therefore, passed near or into Anderson's ranks, creating, in his words, "a very unpleasant condition."[94] One hit Pvt. Jackson B. Giles, Jr., of the Ninth Georgia, one of Tige Anderson's couriers. Giles had just dismounted and was going to lie down to escape the fire, but he was too late—a projectile struck him in the left leg above the knee, tore off the leg, and sent the poor fellow rolling for ten or fifteen feet. Capt. George Hillyer, who had known him in school, ran over to him. Giles gave Hillyer a message for his parents: "Tell them I died for my country," he said. Giles died in a hospital the next day.[95]

Tige Anderson considered his brigade to be the division's reserve rather than only a support for the Texas Brigade. But soon after he had heard Benning's brigade advance with a yell, Anderson received Robertson's request to come to the aid of the Texas Brigade. Hood had just been wounded, and Anderson had heard nothing from Law. Therefore, he took it upon himself to march his brigade in the direction indicated by Robertson's messenger.[96]

Anderson's Georgians passed through the trees of Biesecker's Woods, on through the orchard and farmyard of the Snyder farm, and across the Emmitsburg Road north of Slyder's lane. They double-quicked across three hundred yards of open ground east of the road in plain view of the Federal batteries about 1,000 yards to their left. The batteries pounded the Georgians, particularly the Ninth Regiment on the brigade's left, and a shell fragment killed Lt. Col. John C. Mounger. The brigade soon gained some shelter from the trees of Rose's orchards and from the cover of Rose's Woods. Finally it descended into the Plum Run Valley on Robertson's left and transgressed on the domain of the Federal infantry. The officers and men of the brigade, particularly those of the Ninth Georgia, could not understand why McLaws's division had not gone forward with them and distracted the gunners near the Peach Orchard. Clearly, either they did not understand the grand plan, or someone had blundered.[97]

The Confederate assault was finally under way. It began about 4:30 P.M., twelve hours after daybreak and Longstreet's arrival on Seminary Ridge. So far, 2 July had been a day characterized by indecision, vexation, and delay, a fatiguing day that must have dulled the fighting edge of the officers and men of the veteran Confederate regiments. But there were about three hours of daylight left—enough time to start the Army of the Potomac from the field, if not to exploit a success. The Army of Northern Virginia had triumphed over adversity before; with a little luck it might do so again.

Devil's Den

The assault of Hood's division came as no surprise to the officers and men of Birney's division. They had taken their forward positions because Generals Sickles and Birney feared that there might be such an attack. Third Corps troops had seen Robertson's and Law's brigades crossing the Emmitsburg Road to the ridge line opposite their left, and Third Corps batteries had fired at them from the Peach Orchard area. This fire had swelled into a full-scale artillery duel between Longstreet's batteries and the Federal batteries near the Peach Orchard and Devil's Den.

Gen. Henry Hunt assisted Captain Randolph in posting the Third Corps and Artillery Reserve batteries in the Peach Orchard area, and, when he did not hear Capt. James E. Smith's guns firing from Devil's Den, Hunt rode there to see why. He dismounted somewhere north of Devil's Den in the battery's rear, tied his horse to a tree, and puffed his way to the top of the ridge. He found that Smith had just gotten his guns to that hard-to-reach position. Smith pointed out to Hunt "the advancing lines of the enemy," probably Hood's skirmishers at this time, and his guns began exchanging fire with Latham's and Reilly's batteries. In Hunt's words, "Many guns were immediately turned on him, relieving so far the rest of the line." Hunt sized up the situation, told Smith that he would probably lose his battery, and went off to seek infantry support for it. By this time Confederate projectiles fired at Smith's guns were whistling into the Plum Run Valley in the New Yorkers' rear. They killed a cow and scared the rest of a herd of cattle pasturing there, causing them to stampede back and forth in terror. Hunt had to pass by them to reach his horse. The frenzied cattle frightened the general more than the Confederate shells, but he got by them safely, secured his horse, and rode away.[1]

Smith's four guns above Devil's Den became a target for Reilly's battery and probably Latham's too, in addition to being an objective of a portion of Hood's infantry in its assault. The four ten-pounder Parrotts sat near the nose of the ridge to the right of the rocks in plain view of the Confederates and had a field of fire that embraced the zone of Hood's attack. But they were vulnerable. Their muzzles could not be depressed enough to enable them to fire down into the rocks of Devil's Den and Plum Run gorge to their left and rear. Perhaps this made little difference in the long run, for most of the Confederates who reached the shelter of Devil's Den's boulders would have been impossible for the battery alone to rout. Smith anticipated this deficiency by placing his two remaining Parrotts in the Plum Run Valley 150 yards behind the others. Though they might cover the valley and the gorge from there, they could not do much damage to the Confederate infantry in Devil's Den itself. Captain Smith sought more reliable protection by asking that the Fourth Maine Regiment, posted on the ridge to his left and rear, be sent into the woods at the base of Round Top. Instead General Ward ordered Col. Elijah Walker to deploy his regiment in a blocking position across the valley, facing the gorge and Devil's Den. On taking this new position, a move that he was reluctant to make, Walker sent three officers and seventy men, probably Company F, south into Devil's Den as skirmishers and another party of skirmishers under Capt. Edwin Libby to the left front into the trees on Round Top's northwest slope.[2]

Smith's battery dueled with the Confederate batteries on Seminary Ridge for perhaps a half hour, though Smith later recalled it as an hour and a half. If such a duel can be routine, this must have been, for it occasioned little special comment in later years. To avoid the incoming shells, Col. A. Van Horne Ellis of the 124th New York, on Smith's right, moved his regiment's left wing away from Smith's guns and into Rose's Woods. The cannoneers, of course, could not leave their pieces.[3] When Law's, Robertson's, and Benning's brigades advanced into the battery's field of fire, the gunners aimed and fired as fast as they were able. They used case shot on the Confederate lines when they were in the open and shell when they were in the trees. Smith watched his sections carefully, giving them instructions in clear, distinct tones that could be heard above the tumult by the men of the 124th. Though Smith's fire might have rendered invaluable service by wounding General Hood (if it did), it did little to slow the advance of Hood's brigades. If the charging lines were to be stopped, it would have to be at close range by canister and musketry.[4]

Hood's two forward brigades approached the Federal position between the main branch of Plum Run and the stony hill in what essentially was a single curved line that measured about 1,000 yards from flank to flank. It extended across Round Top's west front and bent westward along Plum Run's west branch well into Rose's Woods. Although the entire Federal position was attacked when Hood's brigades were committed, the opening fight took place in essentially two areas—first near Devil's Den and then at Little Round Top.

Ward's brigade and Smith's battery met the attack near Devil's Den. When it came, the Fourth Maine was on the brigade left, deployed across Plum Run behind Devil's Den, facing the gorge and the lower slope of Round Top. Next in line, on the high ground above the Den, were Smith's four guns. The

124th New York stood on Smith's right, its left in the right rear of Smith's battery and its right stretching north into the eastern edge of Rose's Woods. Beyond a narrow gap, the Eighty-sixth New York continued the line to the north. Lt. Col. Benjamin L. Higgins, its commander, reported specifically that all but the Eighty-sixth's left company were in the woods; this suggests that the Eighty-sixth's front must have been offset somewhat from that of the 124th. Col. John Wheeler's Twentieth Indiana was on the Eighty-sixth's right, and the Ninety-ninth Pennsylvania was beyond it at the right of the brigade. Both the Twentieth and Ninety-ninth provided strong support to the sharpshooters' skirmish line, and it is likely that both had sizable forces down near Plum Run's west branch. It is probable too that the Ninety-ninth's 339 officers and men fronted south covering the gap across the front of the Wheatfield between Ward's men on Devil's Den Ridge and de Trobriand's near the stony hill.[5]

General Ward wrote that the enemy's first two lines approached "in columns *en masse,*" a formation giving an appearance of depth. Perhaps he saw the columns of the Forty-fourth and Forty-eighth Alabama regiments as they shifted from Law's right toward Devil's Den ahead of Benning's brigade. The Federal skirmishers sniped away and fell back grudgingly before the advancing enemy, but some, like those in Devil's Den, held their ground until pressed exceedingly hard. Ward instructed his regiments on the right, which were in the woods, not to fire until they could see the enemy plainly and those on the left in the open to hold their fire until the Rebels were within two hundred yards. The Confederates, initially the First Texas and Third Arkansas regiments, came on yelling and shouting. When they closed to the prescribed ranges, Ward's regiments opened fire and brought them to a temporary halt.[6]

The First Texas and Third Arkansas regiments, on the left of Hood's division and under General Robertson's watchful eye, advanced to the west branch of Plum Run near the Timbers house and Rose's Woods. As they fronted to the northeast, a gap on their right that must have been well over a hundred yards across separated them from the right of Hood's forward line. The Third Arkansas and the left of the First Texas entered the southern portion of Rose's Woods. The right of the First Texas fronted the stone wall at the base of the triangular field and the open slope beyond the wall that led up to Smith's battery and the left of the 124th New York above Devil's Den.[7]

Two terrain features in this area require some special attention—Rose's Woods and the triangular plot on the slope between the woods and Devil's Den.[8] The woods extended over a trapezoidal forty-acre tract that covered the valley of the west branch of Plum Run between the Wheatfield on the north and Devil's Den. Its east boundary was a fence that ran near the brow of the slope into the valley of the main branch of Plum Run west of Little Round Top. West from this fence the woods covered a slope that descended westerly, dropping 50 feet in 300 yards to the west branch of Plum Run;

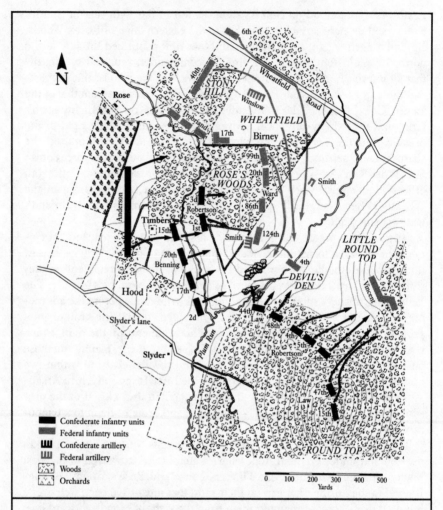

1. *Law's brigade and the Fourth and Fifth Texas regiments cross Plum Run to the slope of Round Top. The Forty-fourth and Forty-eighth Alabama regiments wheel north along Plum Run.*

2. *The First Texas and Third Arkansas open the heavy fighting by attacking Ward's brigade and Smith's battery above Devil's Den.*

3. *The Third Arkansas receives flank fire from the Seventeenth Maine, posted at the wall between the Wheatfield and Rose's Woods.*

4. *The Fourth Maine blocks the advance of the Forty-fourth and Forty-eighth Alabama along Plum Run.*

5. *Benning's brigade advances against Ward's brigade and Smith's battery. The First Texas and Fifteenth Georgia attack Smith's battery.*

6. *The Fourth Maine and Ninety-ninth Pennsylvania counterattack into Smith's position.*

7. *The Fortieth New York blocks Plum Run.*

8. *Benning's and Robertson's brigades attack and dislodge the Federal line.*

9. *The Sixth New Jersey covers Plum Run as Ward's line withdraws.*

Map 9-1. The Action at Devil's Den

beyond the branch it climbed a steep slope that rose 50 feet in 150 yards to reach the east edge of a plateau that ran west across the Emmitsburg Road to Seminary Ridge.

The triangular open plot abutted the eastern third of the south boundary of Rose's Woods, It was an equilateral triangle of about three acres in area bounded by stone walls five hundred feet on a side. The walls faced the north to Rose's Woods, and to the southwest and the southeast. The north wall extended almost directly west from the knoll above Devil's Den, the sector of the 124th New York, and downhill to a point near the marshy floor of the west branch of Plum Run about one hundred yards east of the branch itself. There it connected with the triangle's southwest wall. The southwest wall in turn parallelled the run at a distance of about seventy-five to one hundred yards. When it was in good condition, the wall ran over and between the large granite blocks that are so numerous in the lower end of the plot. The third wall, that on the southeast face of the triangle, climbed up the nose of Devil's Den Ridge, about a hundred yards from the massive rocks of Devil's Den, and angled across the ground occupied by Smith's battery. Beyond its junction with the triangle's north wall, the line of the wall's extension was the fence that formed the east boundary of Rose's Woods. The triangular plot was a curious place. It enclosed a slope that was essentially bare of trees at the time of the battle, but it was too rocky to have been cultivated or to have been a good pasture. Yet some farmer had taken great trouble to erect the walls that formed it. We can only speculate over its intended use; perhaps it was a pen for cattle or hogs.

These two features figured prominently in the battle on this part of the field and had some military significance. The woods restricted the use of Federal batteries in the defense of this portion of the Third Corps line and was both an obstruction and cover for the Confederates in their movements south of the Wheatfield. The walls of the triangle had defensive potential, for the force that held a wall controlled the ground beyond it. The southwest wall provided shelter for the Confederates forming for attacks on the Union line at the crest above it. The north wall gave the Confederates an advantage in their control of the south portion of Rose's Woods. Thus, these two walls were prizes to be safeguarded or sought, and as General Ward wrote of the southwest wall, "for the space of one and a half hours did we advance and retire, both parties endeavoring to gain posession of the stone wall."[9]

The Third Arkansas on Robertson's left was the first of Hood's regiments that was heavily engaged. It met skirmishers in the woodlot southwest of the Timbers house and routed them. Then it came under heavier fire from the skirmishers screening Ward's right wing, who were posted along the south edge of Rose's Woods near the Timbers house. Because the higher ground the Third had taken near the Timbers house dominated the woods beyond, the Third drove this advanced Federal line back into the woods "with but little loss." The Third pushed into the woods, sloshed through the soft ground along Plum Run, and climbed uphill for about 150 yards. Here it received heavy fire from its left and halted. Colonel Manning attempted to change the Third Arkansas's front to meet this threat, but the noise of battle drowned out his commands. He then went to the left wing and pulled it back. This done, the Third was better able to deal with the firing from its flank and to advance again. Ward's men stubbornly retired before it, until it reached a rock outcrop about midway into the woods.[10]

The Third Arkansas and the left of the First Texas, as suggested above, met a force that included companies of sharpshooters together with the Twentieth Indiana, Eighty-sixth New York, and Ninety-ninth Pennsylvania regiments. Thus, about three good Federal regiments were arrayed to oppose an attacking force then at a strength of about half their number. The Federal line counterattacked against the Third Arkansas and forced it back fifty or seventy-five yards to the base of the hill. There Colonel Manning, with the aid of Company G, First Texas, which had fronted to the left to guard the First's flank, was able to reform his line and prepare for another attack.[11]

At some time in the course of the Third's efforts here a Pvt. John B. Adams of Company F suffered a painful wound in the leg or groin. Adams's screams could be heard above the noise of battle, but he got little sympathy from some of his comrades, particularly from Pvt. Hiram G. Smith, who remarked, "Listen to old Adams, he's squalling like a hit coon!"[12]

Colonel Manning's preparations resulted in the Third's line being extended to double its original length. Manning hoped that its broadened front would place its left beyond reach of the enemy and its opened interval would enable its line to move more easily through the trees without sacrificing too much firepower. This done, the Third advanced again. It probably went easily at first, for Company G of the First Texas cleared the opposition from in front of the Third Arkansas Regiment's right at the cost of the life of the commander, Lt. Benjamin A. Campbell.[13] There were also changes in the Federal formation that might have given the Third some early help.

Gen. George Sykes of the Union Fifth Corps had quickly surveyed the Federal position before the fighting opened and became concerned about the vulnerability of Ward's left at Devil's Den. He offered to occupy a segment of the Third Corps position in the Wheatfield area with Fifth Corps units so that Birney could extend his line farther left into Devil's Den.[14] No reference to this offer was made in Third Corps reports, but it probably prompted Ward to pull the Ninety-ninth Pennsylvania from its place on the right of Ward's brigade and shift it to Devil's Den. With the Ninety-ninth's departure, Colonel Wheeler of the Twentieth Indiana tried to fill the gap left by the Ninety-ninth with two companies under Capt. Charles A. Bell. In the meantime, the rest of the Twentieth and the Eighty-sixth New York prepared to do battle from the crest of the ridge.[15]

There were numerous casualties. In twenty-five minutes the Twentieth Indiana lost 146 of its 268 men. A bullet struck Colonel Wheeler in the temple as he rode behind his line and killed him instantly. Lt. Col. William C. L. Taylor took command, and he too was wounded. Capt. Erasmus C. Gilbreath then took over the Twentieth and tried to exercise his new responsibility from the back of Colonel Taylor's horse. The horse, however, was skittish, and Gilbreath had to dismount and command afoot. He sent word of Wheeler's death to General Ward and asked for more ammunition. Soon Lt. Alfred M. Raphall, Ward's aide, galloped up with word that there was no more ammunition. The Twentieth was to hold until it fired its last cartridge and then fall back. No sooner had Raphall delivered his message than a bullet hit him in the arm. Gilbreath gave him help to get to the hospital.[16]

In the meantime Colonel de Trobriand's brigade waited in its position on the stony hill. At Birney's request, de Trobriand sent the Seventeenth Maine Regiment south to the wall that separated the Wheatfield from Rose's Woods. Its experiences there fall later in this account (see Chapter 11). It suffices to say now that after taking position at the wall, the men of the Seventeenth fired at a shadowy gray line advancing through the woods across their front at a range of about seventy-five yards. It was a respectable range, especially in the smoky woods, but after taking the line under fire, the Maine men had the satisfaction of seeing the Rebel line halt. The Rebels were the Third Arkansas, of course, and in Colonel Manning's words, the Seventeenth's flank fire gave the Third "some annoyance." The Third took cover behind the rock outcrop that it had reached before and waited. Help was on the way.[17]

As the Third Arkansas maneuvered among the trees the First Texas tried to push ahead on its right. It met stiff fire. When Company F reached the brow of the slope overlooking the valley of the west branch of Plum Run, a ball knocked the rifle from the hands of Pvt. A. C. ("Cubb") Sims. Sims picked up another. It soon jammed, and he replaced it with a third. Then a cannon ball hit an oak tree in the company's front, and the men of the company scattered to avoid being struck by the falling tree. When the First's line reached the valley, it halted and fired, the first rank probably kneeling behind the wall of the triangular field and the second firing from a standing position.[18] Most of the First's line faced into Rose's Woods, but Company I on the right, under Lt. John H. Wootters, and some volunteers who joined them faced the triangular field from behind its southwest wall and confronted Smith's battery at the top of the ridge.[19]

The Forty-fourth and Forty-eighth Alabama regiments gave Robertson's regiments their first help. Law had ordered them from the right of his brigade's line toward Devil's Den. When they reached the area of Plum's Run fork, they formed a line, with the Forty-fourth in the brush near the main branch of the stream and the Forty-eighth on the right in the woods on Round Top's slope. It was at this time that Law ordered Col. William F. Perry to take Smith's battery. In order to do this the regiment had to wheel to the left about forty-five degrees so that the left of the Forty-fourth could advance upslope between the triangular plot's southeast wall and Devil's Den toward the battery's left while the right wing worked its way through the boulders toward the Plum Run gorge. The Forty-fourth and Forty-eighth advanced.[20]

Colonel Perry maneuvered the Forty-fourth under the fire of skirmishers and perhaps some artillery fire as well. The Forty-eighth, concealed by trees, would have been untroubled by musketry at this time but found its path "a very rough and rugged road—the worst cliffs of rocks there could have been traveled over." The two Alabama regiments must have moved slowly. When the Forty-fourth came to within about fifty yards of Devil's Den, it met a spattering of shots followed at once by a deadly volley. Although the premature shots warned the men of the Forty-fourth to take cover, the volley dealt them a heavy blow. The Forty-fourth replied at once but temporarily halted its advance.[21]

The volley came from the seventy skirmishers of the Fourth Maine and some sharpshooters who had joined them among the rocks. The Yankees had their hands full and must have confined their attention to the Forty-fourth to the exclusion of other Confederate regiments nearby. In the meantime the men of the Fourth Maine's line behind the gorge were heartened to see a brigade of Federal infantry file across the east slope of Little Round Top not more than three hundred yards to their left. The new arrivals threw a line of skirmishers into the trees on Round Top's slope to the Fourth's left front. This was Vincent's brigade, Barnes's division, Fifth Corps. Colonel Walker could have known nothing of the special circumstances that brought Vincent's men to the hill. However, he rightfully assumed that its skirmishers would take care of Round Top's wooded slopes. At the same time, he wrongfully presumed that Vincent's brigade or additional reinforcements would close the gap between the Fourth's left and the troops upon the hill. After Vincent's arrival, Walker ordered Captain Libby's skirmishers back to the main line.[22]

The enemy was not long in coming. Skirmishers from the ubiquitous Second U.S. Sharpshooter Regiment dashed back from Round Top's slope with the news that the Confederate infantry was right behind them and would flank the Fourth. Hardly had the warning been given when heavy musketry broke out on Vincent's front, and a few shots zipped around the Fourth. Walker thought that he saw Vincent's brigade fall back, but likely he saw only the brigade's skirmishers hurrying to the shelter of the main line. Then a column of infantry, probably the Forty-eighth Alabama, appeared in the woods to the left. The Fourth's officers refused the regiment's left, and it gave the Rebels a half dozen volleys before they returned the greeting.[23] Colonel Sheffield of the Forty-eighth reported that his men exchanged fire at a range of only twenty paces, that the enemy's fire was severe, and that his men held until his left was driven back. It is likely that the Forty-eighth's left was in the open rocky area east of Plum Run and Devil's Den that was later called the "Slaughter Pen." The Forty-eighth's right, however, was able to hold its place, and finally the Fourth Maine fell back a short way and formed another line.[24]

The Fourth Maine's position was in the open, and the Forty-eighth Alabama continued to rake it with "a biting musketry fire." It was written that the Fourth was "placed at great disadvantage and suffered large loss."[25] Whether or not the Fourth Maine would be able to continue to guard the valley floor depended greatly on what happened at Devil's Den itself. Confederate occupation of the high ground above the Den would make Federal occupation of the adjacent valley impossible and give the Confederates access to the slope of Little Round Top beyond the right of Vincent's brigade's short line. And Confederates on this high ground above Devil's Den would, of course, flank Ward's line and make its position untenable. Once the Confederates occupied this area in force, the position of the Third Corps's left wing would be unhinged, and the stability of the line along the Emmitsburg Road would even be shaken. So far the forces at Devil's Den, though threatened, had not been in extreme peril. That would change with the arrival of the Forty-fourth and Forty-eighth Alabama regiments and the approach of Hood's support line. When Hood's division was fully engaged, the gaps in its line would close, and its strength would exceed that of the Federal forces in its immediate front.

The 124th New York Volunteer Infantry Regiment held the center of Ward's position. Though small, it was a relatively new organization. It had been recruited in the summer of 1862 in Orange County, New York, a rural area along the New Jersey border. Its three field officers had seen previous service. One, Lt. Col. Francis M. Cummins, was a veteran of the War with Mexico. Although the 124th had joined the Army of the Potomac in the fall of 1862, it saw no heavy fighting until Chancellorsville, where it took 40 percent casualties and had shown that it could fight. It was during a lull at Chancellorsville that its Colonel Ellis gave the men a pep talk in which he referred to them as his "Orange Blossoms"—a name that stuck—and admonished them, "Let the little girls of old Orange hear a good report of this day's work."[26]

The Orange Blossoms deployed above Devil's Den with only 18 officers and 220 men present for duty, hardly enough to form a line seventy yards in length from flank to flank. Ellis posted the regiment with its color company (Company C) and center just east of the junction of the triangular plot's northern and southeastern walls, near the place where the regiment's memorial stands today. Its Company A deployed as skirmishers, not down front but in the gap between the 124th and the Eighty-sixth New York on its right. Smith's four guns were on the regiment's left.[27]

The 124th, like the rest of the Third Corps, still had a lot to learn about war. It rested as the early hours of the afternoon rushed by and made no effort to erect breastworks or otherwise strengthen its position. When the artillery exchange brought shells its way, Ellis shifted its left away from Smith's battery for a while, and some of the men sought shelter behind rocks. But no more than that was done. Later when the firing stopped, the men on the left above the open triangular plot saw Confederate infantry striding in their direction. Capt. William Silliman of the color company remembered Hood's division as coming in long solid lines and in overwhelming numbers. As the men of the 124th saw it, the First Texas marched up to Plum Run at the base of the ridge and paused.[28]

Smith's four guns fired as rapidly as they could at the approaching line— first shell and then canister. One shell hit the stone wall at the base of the triangle in front of the Texas line. It sent rock splinters flying in all directions and scattered the Texans nearby. A Texan recalled that it was "no time for shining shoes."[29]

Apart, perhaps, from Lieutenant Colonel Work, the best-remembered Texan in the fight was Pvt. Wilson J. Barbee. Barbee was one of Hood's couriers and was one of those who had reconnoitered the Round Top area for him before the assault that afternoon. Sometime after the Texans reached Plum Run, Barbee rode up behind the First's line. When his sorrel was shot from under him, he hit the ground running. Barbee climbed up on a huge boulder that sheltered some wounded Texans and gave him a view. From there he fired rifles that were loaded and passed up to him by wounded Texans, firing about twenty-five times in all. Barbee attracted attention, of course. A ball hit him in the right leg and knocked him from his perch. That should have been enough to satisfy him, but it was not, and he climbed back upon the rock again. Another bullet struck him in the leg, and he fell a second time. He again crawled up on the boulder, and a third ball hit him in the body and rolled him to the ground once more. There he lay cursing because no one would lift him back onto the rock a fourth time.[30]

In the eyes of their foe, the First Texas advanced twice against the Third Corps line. The first assault began with a rush accompanied by a "fierce, charging yell," answered by a "fiercer crash of riflery" from the 124th New York. This initial charge must have been a short one that ended almost as quickly as it had begun. Thereafter, the Texas line pressed ahead slowly a few feet at a time, buffeted by a hail of lead. Smith's guns could only do so much. When they used up their case shot, Smith shouted, "Give them shell! give them solid shot! Damn them, give them anything!" "Anything" must have been canister, but though the cannoneers fired fast without sponging, it must have had only limited effect. Canister loads for ten-pounder Parrotts and three-inch rifles were small doses at best, but small or large they would have done little damage to alert troops below their line of fire who had some shelter behind rocks.[31]

The 124th fired from its position on the crest. Colonel Ellis stood behind the color company where he could see his line and the field in its front. In those days when human emotions had their play, ranking officers thought it their duty to demonstrate their bravery and leadership and to indulge in the dramatic in front of their men rather than before photographers and the press. Ellis probably stood much as he is depicted by his statue on the 124th's memorial, his arms folded, surveying the scene with an interested calm. Others were not so poised as he. Maj. James Cromwell ran over to Ellis from his position behind the regiment's left wing and asked Ellis to order a charge. Ellis shook his head no and sent him back to his post. There was more firing, yelling, and advancing until the butternut line was only a few yards from the Orange Blossoms' front—in fact, in later years some Texans believed that they got so close that their muzzle flashes singed the New Yorkers' uniforms. But the Orange Men held them off. Again Cromwell ran over to Ellis, this time with the adjutant, Lt. Henry P. Ramsdell. Ellis sent Cromwell back to his post a second time, but soon after sent someone for the field officers' horses. In a few minutes the orderlies led them forward.[32]

When Captain Silliman saw the horses, he walked back and protested the field officers' mounting amid such an inferno. To this Ellis replied simply: "The men must see us to-day."[33] Ellis and Cromwell mounted, rode to their posts behind the line, and waited. Cromwell was opposite the triangle and Ellis not far away, both only as visible as the smoke clouds permitted them to be. Cromwell sat his iron-gray horse, sword in hand and eyes on Ellis. Ellis finally nodded; Cromwell waved his sword above his head, touched his spurs to his gray, and shouted "Charge!"[34] Cromwell's horse lunged forward to the front of the 124th's line and picked its way down the rocky slope. The 124th followed at the double-quick, bayonets fixed and leveled. When the blue line entered their field of fire, Smith's guns fell silent. Ellis watched the charge for a few moments and then spurred after his regiment's line.[35]

As the New Yorkers recalled it, their onslaught broke the Texans' line, and the Texans fell backward down the slope. The New Yorkers followed them to within a hundred feet of the triangle's southwest wall at the base of the ridge. It was heady stuff. Cromwell waved his sword and shouted in triumph. But the shouts were hardly given when the Confederates fired a searing blast that caught the New Yorkers in the open and dropped one-quarter of them in their tracks.[36] All was pandemonium—"Roaring cannon, crashing rifles, screeching shots, bursting shells, hissing bullets, cheers, shouts, shrieks and groans." Cromwell shouted again and loomed like a specter through the clouds of smoke, waving his sword and urging on his men. But then his sword arm dropped, and his body reeled backward and slipped from the saddle, a bullet through the chest.[37] In later years Texans recalled the officer on the gray horse. Some of them had thought him too brave to kill and shouted for their comrades to shoot the horse and capture the man. But Cromwell and the horse went down, a dreadful thing, for "such courage belongs not to any one army or country, but to mankind."[38]

There was more to come. Seeing Cromwell fall, Ellis shouted, "My God! My God, men! Your major's down; save him! save him." The 124th surged

Brig. Gen. Jerome B. Robertson (MOLLUS-MASS/U.S.A.M.H.I., Carlisle Barracks, Pa.)

Brig. Gen. Henry L. Benning (Library of Congress)

Brig. Gen. J. H. Hobart Ward (National Archives)

Col. A. Van Horne Ellis (MOLLUS-MASS/U.S.A.M.H.I., Carlisle Barracks, Pa.)

Slaughter Pen. Photograph by Timothy H. O'Sullivan (National Archives)

At Devil's Den. Painting by F. D. Briscoe (National Archives)

forward again. As some recalled it, they smashed another Texas line and found a third one not far behind it. But this third line was no rallied remnant of the First Texas; it was Benning's brigade, fresh and ready to fight. The Georgians opened on the New Yorkers and began to reap their harvest.[39]

Colonel Ellis remained in the saddle. Like Cromwell, he rode above the turmoil on the ground, appearing and fading in the smoke:

> We see his proud form rise in his stirrups; his long sharp sword is extended upward, a half-uttered order escapes his lips, when suddenly his trusty blade falls point downward, his chin drops on his breast, and his body with a weave pitches forward, head foremost among the rocks; at which his wounded beast rears and with a mad plunge dashes away, staggering blindly through the ranks of the foe, who is now giving ground again, firing wildly as he goes.[40]

But the 124th had done all it could, and the tide began to run toward the crest again. "Old Rock" Benning was on hand, probably a bit to the left of where Ellis fell, striding back and forth shouting, "Give them h-ll, boys— give them h-ll," vigorously and without hyphens. The boys did just that. Benning's left regiment, the Fifteenth Georgia, pressed into the zone of the First Texas, much to the displeasure of Colonel Work, who did not want the Georgians disrupting his line. He thought that it would have been better had Benning's brigade come in on the left of the Third Arkansas. The First Texas could not or would not let the Georgians take its place, and so for a while there was confusion as Lieutenant Colonel Work and Col. Dudley M. Du-Bose tried to sort things out. It proved nigh to impossible to do under the circumstances, and so they melded their forces together and fought the rest of the evening more or less as one unit.[41]

From his post behind his brigade's line, Benning had perceived that the Confederate force was weak in front of Devil's Den. At Law's instruction, perhaps, or with his concurrence, Benning directed his four regiments toward the gap between the First Texas and the Forty-fourth Alabama. Thus it was that the Fifteenth Georgia shared a front with the First Texas, the Twentieth Georgia was in front of Smith's battery, the Seventeenth made for the boulders on Smith's left, and the Second Georgia advanced on the nose of Devil's Den and into the gorge. There the Second Georgia shared the zone of the Forty-fourth Alabama, which was attacking the Den from the south.[42]

Even as the 124th charged, it was plain to Lieutenant Colonel Cummins that it was only buying time and that, unless help came, the 124th would be forced back. Not wanting to lose the guns of Smith's battery, Cummins went over to them and tried to get them started to the rear. As he walked there, a Confederate shell hit a gun and knocked it against him, crippling him. This hit damaged the piece beyond immediate use, and Smith had it pulled to the rear without delay.[43]

Smith's cannoneers returned to their three pieces after the 124th's withdrawal cleared their front. By this time, Smith's worse fears were being realized. Confederate infantrymen sniped at his cannoneers from the shelter of the Devil's Den rocks. The artillerymen could do little to protect themselves and fire their guns. Cannon fire would have been ineffective against the snipers even if the muzzles of the big guns could have been depressed enough to bring the snipers under fire.

One man who fought back was Pvt. Michael Broderick, an infantryman of the Eleventh Massachusetts Regiment, who had been detailed to Smith's battery, where he had been put to work as a driver of a pair in the battery wagon's team. Broderick had become restive at his place in the rear, walked up to the guns, picked up a rifle, and started a duel with one of the Confederate snipers. He took cover behind a rock and fired at the Rebel who was behind another rock farther down the slope. To tempt his enemy to break cover, Broderick dodged to and from the shelter of his boulder and in doing so caught Captain Smith's eye. The captain began to scold Broderick for leaving his team, but Broderick maintained that there were enough men with the horses and begged to be allowed to stay. Smith apparently consented, for Broderick "again commenced to dance, first on one side of the rock and then on the other, challenging his man to come out and face him; then he would dodge behind the rock to avoid . . . the privilege of stopping a bullet; then he would jump out again, shouting, 'Come on, now, if you dare, bad luck to you.'" After that, Smith's attention turned elsewhere, and he forgot about Broderick until that night, when a roll call revealed that the Irishman was among the missing—but not for long. He had been captured, but in the darkness of the night had somehow impersonated a Confederate guard, escaped, and walked back to the battery.[44]

Smith's position at Devil's Den became very precarious. Unless the Confederate infantry was driven back, his guns could not be fired. The desperate captain ran over to the 124th to ask for help to serve his pieces and returned again with tears in his eyes saying, "For God's sake, men, don't let them take my guns away from me!" But the 124th had its hands full, and as Capt. Charles H. Weygant of Company A, who was now in command, tried to reform the regiment's line, its smaller numbers made for a shorter line whose left no longer reached the battery. Instead of trying to haul his three guns away, however (for it would have been a difficult, dangerous, and time-consuming thing to do), Smith decided to man them as long as possible. This might not be long, and so he ordered his three crews to be sure to carry off their firing tools—their sponge and rammer staffs, sponge buckets, friction primers, and sights—when they fell back.[45]

There was a short lull on the 124th's front, but both sides kept up a brisk fire. When rifles became fouled or too hot to handle, they were discarded in favor of others that were lying nearby. Sgt. J. Harvey Hanford, already wounded four times, lay behind a rock shooting downslope toward a gap in the lower wall that sheltered the Confederates as they reformed. About this time, someone brought news that the Fifth Corps was nearby but that the Regulars were boiling coffee instead of coming forward. This report was untrue, but it could not have helped the morale of the battered men of the Third Corps.[46]

Captain Weygant walked the line of the 124th to check its condition and found only about a hundred men in place. The ranking man in Company G was now a corporal, and the body of the company's commander, Capt. Isaac Nichols, could be seen far downslope, wedged between two rocks. Beside it lay the bodies of two unidentified brave men who had tried to bring the captain out. Nearby, as the smoke that clouded the hill thinned, the men on the crest could see a bloody hand and arm waving feebly to them. They belonged to Cpl. James Scott of Company B. Scott had been wounded in the wrist, but disregarding the wound, he had followed Cromwell in the charge. A ball struck him in the chest and passed through his body, causing him to fall unconscious. While he lay senseless on the exposed hill slope, a shell fragment hit him in the shoulder, and still another bullet entered his left side, breaking some ribs before emerging near his groin.[47]

Lt. Milnor Brown of Company I was among the dead. Poor Brown had joined the 124th only a week before and was resented as a newcomer and an interloper. But he had behaved well and had earned a little grudging respect, which he had no time to build on or enjoy. And so he died among people who were his comrades but not yet his friends. Weygant saw also the bodies of Ellis and Cromwell lying on a rock in the rear of the regiment's line. Ellis's brains protruded from a hole in his head, and a gold locket gleamed on Cromwell's chest. Weygant ordered Moses Ross, the headquarters bugler, to take the bodies to the rear and send them back to Orange County.[48]

The mounting strength of the enemy in his brigade's front and the obvious need to plug the gap between Devil's Den and Little Round Top prompted action from General Ward. As indicated above, he summoned the Ninety-ninth Pennsylvania from the right of his brigade's line in order to place it above Devil's Den. He asked also for reinforcements from the reserve. Only two sources of reinforcements were readily available from within the Third Corps—de Trobriand's brigade and Burling's brigade. Captain Briscoe, Birney's aide, secured the Fortieth New York from de Trobriand and led it across the Wheatfield, in front of Winslow's guns, through Smith's caissons, and into the Plum Run Valley. Birney asked Burling also to send Ward his largest remaining regiment, the Sixth New Jersey—Burling's own regiment, temporarily under the command of Lt. Col. Stephen R. Gilkyson. Oddly enough, no one supplied Gilkyson with a guide, and he marched the Sixth to the sound of Smith's guns.[49]

As Robertson's and then Benning's men pressed Ward's line above Devil's Den, the Forty-fourth and Forty-eighth Alabama regiments renewed their attacks—the Forty-eighth against the left of the Fourth Maine and the Forty-fourth against the skirmishers in the rocks of Devil's Den and Smith's battery above them. Detecting a softening in the resistance in his front, Colonel Perry of the Forty-fourth stepped over his prostrate line, shouted "Forward!," and led its right wing toward the rocks. Two Yankee skirmishers surrendered to him personally at the edge of the rock formation, while the line passed him and scrambled through the crevasses in search of other soldiers posted there. At the same time, Maj. George W. Cary and the Forty-fourth's left wing climbed the slope toward Smith's guns. The Forty-fourth occupied Devil's Den and claimed the capture of forty or so men found among its rocks, but Perry did not claim the capture of Smith's guns. Others would do that.[50]

Colonel Walker of the Fourth Maine reacted to this assault without delay. Warned by skirmishers, no doubt, he pulled the Fourth back, away from the Forty-eighth, which was blasting it from the woods, and away from the threat to his right flank now posed by the oncoming Forty-fourth. Realizing that if the Confederates took the high ground above Devil's Den, they could enfilade his line and unhinge Ward's position, he resolved to secure it. He quickly reformed his line, ordered his men to fix bayonets, and led them in a charge to the right oblique up the steep slope and into the area where Smith's guns sat silent, abandoned by their crews. Twenty-two years later Walker savored this moment, writing "I shall never forget the 'click' that was made by the fixing of bayonets, it was as one."[51]

By this time, Colonel Perry's men were fatigued, and Perry himself was prostrated by his exertions. Major Cary walked up to Perry carrying several surrendered swords as tokens of the Forty-fourth's success but with the bad news that both Confederate and Federal cannon were firing into the Devil's Den area. As emphasis to his comment, a shell identified by Perry as spherical case struck near Perry's head. Such experiences are convincing: Perry ordered his men back from the dangerous crest to the shelter of the slope.[52]

Major Cary went off to do as Colonel Perry directed but returned soon in great haste with the news that the enemy, probably the Fourth Maine, was moving in their direction in sufficient strength to envelop them. Perry stood to see what he could of the situation. As they discussed their predicament, a line of infantry pushed up from their rear in gallant style. Someone called, "There is Benning; we are all right now." As Benning's regiments pressed forward, a furious battle flared.[53]

Benning's left center regiment, the Twentieth Georgia, obeyed its order to charge Smith's guns and the Fourth Maine "with promptness and alacrity," and the Seventeenth went into Devil's Den past the Forty-Fourth Alabama "gallantly and with impetuosity." On the right the Second Georgia moved in splendid order. Before the attack Lt. Col. William T. Harris, its commander, had called some of his friends together to tell them that he would be killed and to bid them goodbye. He led their advance that day, riding about twenty yards ahead of the regiment's line instead of in its rear. When the Second Georgia neared the enemy's position, his horse was shot, and he vaulted to the ground several feet ahead of the fallen animal. He led the regiment on foot from there until it crossed Plum Run and entered the gorge. Harris fell there, still about twenty yards ahead of the Second's line. By this time, going was difficult, but the Second moved ahead with "dauntless courage."[54]

Over to the left in front of the line of the battered 124th New York, the Fifteenth Georgia advanced to the stone wall that paralleled Plum Run. It fell in line with the First Texas there and joined in its firing at the Federals on the heights ahead. Benning was not with the Fifteenth, and Colonel DuBose could not then see the regiments to his right. When the sound of rifle fire swelled there, he assumed that their attack had begun. He ordered his men over the wall immediately, and up the slope they went.[55]

As the Georgians attacked, "the whole line was alive with burning powder," recalled an officer of the Fourth Maine.[56] Anderson's brigade arrived on Benning's left and freed the Third Arkansas from flank fire. The First Texas and the Fifteenth Georgia together worked their way east toward Ward's line. After they reached the crest and drove off the Federal line, they continued to press forward north along the crest of the ridge through the east end of Rose's Woods for what DuBose believed was at least a quarter of a mile. Early in this advance there was some brief competition between the color-bearers of the two regiments. Color Sergeant George A. Branard of the First Texas planted his flag far to the front of the advancing line. The color sergeant of the Fifteenth Georgia placed his flag beside Branard's. At this, Branard went farther forward, almost up to the Federal line, and "there he planted the adored standard of the Texans, adorned with the Lone Star, shining far off to friend and foe with the effulgence of its glory." Then a shell burst near Branard and his shining flag, splintering its staff, and blinding Branard in one eye. A provoked Branard attempted to charge the nearby Federal line with his broken flagstaff, but Texans with cooler heads caught him and hustled him to the rear.[57]

The intermingled regiments captured more than 140 prisoners, according to DuBose's recollection, but they soon found themselves so far north on the ridge line that they were in danger of being cut off by Federal troops in the Wheatfield. DuBose then called off his drive, and most of the Confederates fell back toward Devil's Den, Lieutenant Colonel Work leaving a small party of the First Texas behind to cover the rear.[58]

The regiments on Ward's right had had enough, and troops from the Second and Fifth corps were coming up to relieve them. General Ward ordered the 124th and Eighty-sixth New York regiments and the Twentieth Indiana back before the advancing Confederate line. When Captain Weygant received his orders, he put Captain Silliman in charge of the regiment and went off to the right to make sure that all of his own company was collected from their skirmish line. When Weygant caught up with the rest of the Orange Blossoms, he found them in the rear gathered around General Ward, who was praising them for their good work.[59]

Just to the right, meanwhile, a portion of the First Texas and the Twentieth Georgia clambered toward Smith's guns. The black Parrotts stood silent, almost as symbolic as those that mark Smith's position on the battlefield today. The Texans claimed to be the first to reach the guns. Pvt. John C. Stinson climbed upon one and "shouted victory." Capt. George T. Todd and Pvt. E. P. Derrick took shelter behind a large rock in the course of the attack. A bullet hit Derrick in the head and splattered Todd's face with his brains. Cpl. William A. Duvall fell as he touched one of the trophy guns, and Rick Curtis tried to turn one on the enemy without success. As Pvt. James M. Polk and another man reached the guns, minié balls zipped over their heads and did not harm them. But then a shell burst in front of them. One of its fragments made a hole in Polk's comrade's chest large enough to put an arm through. The wounded man blanched and tried to walk, but he was dead within five minutes.[60]

The batteries that fired into Devil's Den cannot be identified with any certainty. Winslow's battery in the Wheatfield might have fired that way for a brief period as will be described in Chapter 11. Hazlett's guns might have been in position on Little Round Top early enough to fire down into this area, and certainly Reilly's and Latham's batteries could have reached it. But it seems strange that there would have been any intentional fire into the area at all after the Confederates began their direct assault on Smith's battery and on the infantry posted in and around Devil's Den. Given the lack of visibility, the ranges and accuracy of the guns, and the short distances between the Union and Confederate lines, none of the guns of either side could have been fired with any assurance that their rounds would hit enemy soldiers instead of their own. And yet shells whistled in.

After the Confederates captured Smith's three guns, Pvt. John W. Lokey of the Twentieth Georgia saw Third Corps soldiers at the crest of the ridge to the left and rear of the guns. He and others near him fired several shots at them. Then they realized that they were needlessly exposed and fell back a few yards. The new position was a poor one, so they shifted to the right and again started up the hill. The bodies of the dead and wounded were plentiful around them. One body was that of Col. John A. Jones, Lokey's regimental commander. The corpse of Colonel Jones, an "excellent officer and devoted patriot," was sprawled upon its back; half of its head had been carried away by a shell fragment. Lokey's thoughts on seeing his colonel's body remained his own, but he began to fire his Enfield once more. Soon a bullet struck him in the thigh. This ended his fighting for that day, and he turned and limped down the slope. After going a short way, he met a sergeant of the Fourth Maine who was a prisoner and was serving no useful purpose. Lokey called the sergeant to him, and at Lokey's request the sergeant helped him to the rear. After a while a provost guard took charge of the Maine sergeant, who, as he and Lokey parted, observed, "If you and I had this matter to settle, we would soon settle it, wouldn't we?"[61]

The counterattack of the Fourth Maine made for fighting at close quarters at Devil's Den. Colonel Walker's horse went down, and Walker suffered a wound in the foot. The colonel remained on the line, though, so close to the enemy that a Confederate grasped his sword and wrenched it from his hand. After a five-minute melee, the Ninety-ninth dashed into position on the Fourth Maine's left, facing the rocks and crevasses of Devil's Den. Maj. John W. Moore got the Ninety-ninth into an adequate line and shouted, "Up and Charge!" With the shout "Pennsylvania and our homes!" the Ninety-ninth swept the Georgians and Alabamians from the nose of the ridge.[62]

The ridge above Devil's Den was in Federal hands again, but not for long. Lt. Col. James D. Waddell of the Twentieth Georgia believed that his regiment's assault was over in fifteen minutes, but Colonel Walker and Major Moore implied that their regiments held the ground for a much longer time than that. They claimed that they fell back only because the right of Ward's line had already done so, and that the Devil's Den position was then no longer important in the scheme of things. To Moore it was a fierce conflict, and one of its saddest moments came when the Ninety-ninth left the ridge. Cpl. James Casey lagged behind to damage abandoned rifles so that they could not be used by the enemy. While doing so, he found one that was loaded. Turning to Major Moore, who was shouting to him to hurry along, Casey said that he would take one more shot. He fired, and as he did so, was hit himself. Major Moore and Sgt. Robert Graham tried to carry Casey off, but the Confederates were close at hand and Casey urged them to leave him behind and save themselves. Casey's body was never identified among those recovered, though the men of the Ninety-ninth thought that it ought to have been recognizable because Casey's uniform was adorned with a Kearny Cross.[63]

Colonel Walker was unable to walk from the ridge and had to be carried by two soldiers who wrested him from the foe. Both the Fourth Maine and the Ninety-ninth Pennsylvania had lost more than a third of their men in a very short time. Walker recalled with some pride that thirty-two minié balls and two shell fragments had pierced the Fourth's colors and that a shell fragment had broken the colors' staff. On the other hand, Lieutenant Colonel Waddell reported that the Twentieth Georgia's flag was marked by eighty-seven holes, thirty-eight of which were made by minié balls, the others by fragments.[64] If Waddell's report is correct, Smith's battery must have done some good shooting.

As the Fourth Maine and Ninety-ninth Pennsylvania regiments struggled at Devil's Den and Vincent's brigade received its onslaught on Little Round Top, two regiments and a section of artillery fought a doomed action in the Plum Run Valley behind Devil's Den. The Fortieth New York, nearly six hundred officers and men strong and under Col. Thomas W. Egan, was the first of the reinforcements to arrive there. It deployed in line across the valley about where the Fourth Maine had been, with its right west of Plum Run near the rear of the Devil's Den rock formation.[65]

The Fortieth New York had begun its service as a unique New York unit, for its ten companies included four from Massachusetts and two from Pennsylvania. It was a product of the patriotism of 1861, when more men volunteered for service than could be accommodated by the Federal government. It was uniformed and equipped by New York's Union Defense Committee rather than by the national government. It had another distinction too. It bore the designation, "Mozart Regiment," not because its men were particularly musical but because it had been sponsored by the Mozart Hall Committee, an element of the Democratic Party in New York City. One wonders what the composer would have made of it. By the time of Gettysburg, the regiment had two years of service behind it, service not reflected in its large size. Its size resulted not from a lack of casualties but as a result of accretions of men from other regiments that had become depleted and too small to continue as separate units. First the Fortieth was consolidated with the Eighty-seventh New York, and then on 29 May it was enlarged by contingents of men from the Thirty-seventh, Thirty-eighth, Fifty-first, and 101st New York regiments. Thus, it was of diverse origins and not a homogeneous unit.[66]

Captain Briscoe guided the Fortieth to the Plum Run Valley and showed Egan where his line should be; then Egan prepared to take his regiment in. It must have been a tense time. The Fourth Maine had just charged from the valley floor to the high ground above Devil's Den. Probably Colonel Egan could see something of the Forty-eighth Alabama, which was firing from the woods by the Slaughter Pen, the Second Georgia in line across the valley in front of the gorge, and the Seventeenth Georgia on its left, all threatening to exploit the gap between Vincent's brigade on Little Round Top and the left of Ward's line at Devil's Den. It must have been about this time that Colonel Egan met Captain Smith, whose forward guns were threatened by the enemy. Smith begged Egan to save his battery, but the Fortieth New York had more important things to try to do.[67]

Egan formed the Fortieth New York in line. He did not say precisely where, but it is likely that it was at or near the draw between the knolls, east of the midpoint along the east boundary of Rose's Woods. He ordered the Fortieth to charge, and with a shout it double-quicked "with great alacrity" down Plum Run Valley and into the threatened gap.[68] The Second and Seventeenth Georgia regiments were there to greet it, waiting in the open area north of the gorge and in the Slaughter Pen.[69] They probably had halted there briefly to reform under the plunging fire from the right of Vincent's brigade and the cannon fire of Smith's battery's rear section up the valley in their front. The scene in front of the Georgians must have been terrible to see. Little Round Top to their right smoked from the fire of Vincent's brigade and Hazlett's and Gibbs's guns; there was fighting on Devil's Den to their immediate left; and Ayres's division of the Fifth Corps was crossing the valley four hundred or so yards in their front. But the long line of the Fortieth New York, which was bearing down on them, must have been their most immediate concern.

The Georgians recoiled before the New Yorkers' onslaught, falling back a short distance to a more defensible area in the rocks by Devil's Den and under the covering fire of the Forty-eighth Alabama in the woods. There they repulsed several pushes by the Fortieth to dislodge them (Col. Wesley C. Hodges of the Seventeenth Georgia wrote that there were seven). It must have been a short but vicious fight, ended prematurely by the withdrawal of the Federal forces on Devil's Den and the subsequent threat to the Mozart Regiment's right and rear.[70]

It can be assumed that when he was not seeking help, Captain Smith stayed with his two forward sections on Devil's Den, leaving his rear section to the care of the lieutenant who was its chief. Just before the Fourth Maine's counterattack, Smith abandoned the three forward guns and went to the two guns and caissons in the rear.[71] From the accounts available it is difficult to reconstruct the work of this rear section with any certainty. Smith reported that it fired "obliquely through the gully," and this must have been so.[72] It would not have fired until it had a target in the gorge area or on Round Top's slope nearby. By the time that target appeared, the Fourth Maine would have been in the valley masking any target near the gorge. Therefore, any firing done while the Fourth Maine was in the valley would have been at targets off the Fourth Maine's left—the Forty-eighth Alabama or the Fourth Texas as it attacked Vincent's brigade on Little Round Top. But when the Fourth Maine charged from the valley floor, this rear section doubtless came into its own. The Second and Seventeenth Georgia would have appeared in its front at a range of about three hundred yards; and when they appeared, the section must have opened with a vengeance. Benning wrote of the terrible fire of the two pieces that swept the gorge, a fire whose fearfulness must have been magnified when the iron bolts cracked against the granite boulders around the Georgians and ricocheted away.[73]

At about this time an officer on Little Round Top saw Smith's two Parrotts firing into a mass of Confederates near Devil's Den. The Forty-fourth New York had been firing into this mass, but the Confederates seemed to pay no heed to the minié balls; their concern was with the two cannon on the valley floor, and they seemed to fall in scores from those cannons' fire. After a little sustained firing, the area around the guns was so shrouded by smoke that the gunners could not see their targets. After each volley, the officer on the hill saw an artillery officer run to the front of the guns beyond the smoke, stop and size up the target, and then dash back before they fired again.[74]

The usefulness of Smith's rear section virtually ended with the arrival of the Fortieth New York and the Sixth New Jersey regiments. Smith recalled their arrival as one event and wrote that they went down the valley floor "fighting like tigers."[75] Smith's description better suited the action of the Fortieth New York than that of the Sixth New Jersey. At Birney's order Burling had sent the Sixth to the left without a guide—perhaps none was available. Lieutenant Colonel Gilkyson led the Sixth through a strip of woods at the southeast corner of the Wheatfield and halted it at the fence on the knoll beyond. From this vantage point the Sixth could look down the Plum Run Valley toward Devil's Den and see Confederates there. The Sixth opened fire, but the range was close to four hundred yards and the fire ineffective. Gilkyson got his bearings and noted the position of the Union line in his front, probably that of the Fortieth New York, then heavily engaged and falling back. He ordered the Sixth New Jersey forward two hundred yards into the valley, passing in front of Smith's two guns and halting in a strong position among some man-high boulders near the west side of the valley floor. Here the Sixth's right rested against the valley's west wall, and its left extended into the marshy ground just west of Plum Run. From this position Gilkyson could aid the Fortieth with oblique fire to the left across the valley and, after the Fortieth fell back up the slope to its right, by direct fire toward the gorge. Gilkyson believed that the Sixth held its position two hours. If so (and it seems much too long a time), it would have been helpful in the defense of Little Round Top's west slope and would have protected the flanks of the Fifth Corps brigades crossing the valley to the Wheatfield.[76]

Covered by the Sixth New Jersey's fire, the Fortieth New York fell back from Devil's Den in the direction whence it had come and returned to the shelter of Rose's Woods. It rallied north of Devil's Den but was driven back farther from there by the Fifteenth Georgia and perhaps by the First Texas, and it fell back to the Wheatfield, which was still in Federal hands. From there, like the other regiments of Birney's division, it left the field for a bivouac in the Union rear.[77]

Captain Smith removed his rear section from Plum Run Valley up to the Wheatfield, near the flank of Winslow's battery. Winslow was limbering up to withdraw. Smith got some of the remnants of his battery in order, loaded his wounded on his limbers and caissons, and began a sad procession to the Union rear near the Baltimore Pike. Most of the battery was saved, though it had lost three guns and had had two men killed, ten wounded, and at least one missing. Smith's horse had been shot, and the tired captain borrowed that of Lt. Thomas Goodman so that he might hurry to the head of his column. As he rode along, someone pointed to his bloody boot and exclaimed, "Captain, you're shot!" Smith looked down, saw the blood, and for the first time felt pain and blood inside his boot. He dismounted carefully, and, coached by Smith's warnings to act with care, one of his batterymen pulled the boot from his leg. There was no wound! The blood had come from the horse and was father to the imagined pain. Feeling foolish but relieved, James Smith rode on to prepare his battery for more fighting.[78]

Captain Smith brooded about the loss of his three guns, for a loss of guns often meant a loss of honor in those days, and honor was a precious thing. In losing the guns his battery had achieved some dubious distinction, for the Army of the Potomac lost only six permanently in the entire battle. In his report and in his writing in later years, Smith seemed to feel compelled to explain and justify the Parrotts' loss. Smith maintained that he could have withdrawn the guns on three occasions without censure, for their infantry support had fallen back leaving them without its protection. To have fallen back, however, would have been difficult and time-consuming and might have demoralized the infantry. So he had held them in position and their crews had fought them as long as they were able to do so.[79]

Smith received no official censure. Captain Randolph termed the guns' loss "one of those very unpleasant, but yet unavoidable, results that sometimes attend the efforts of the most meritorious officers," and General Hunt was kinder still. Hunt, after all, had predicted their loss early in the fight.[80] And yet we can wonder. Smith's battery had fewer casualties than the other Third Corps batteries that day and fewer even than all the batteries of the Artillery Reserve on the Third Corps line except that of Captain Ames. More blood might have expiated some of the stigma, real or presumed, of the Parrotts' loss and might even have saved another gun or two. It is hard to say; but apart from its symbolism and impact on Smith's honor, the loss of the guns, in itself, was not a serious thing.

The Confederate assault on Devil's Den, "one of the wildest, fiercest struggles of the war" in the eyes of James Bradfield of the First Texas, was over; and the Confederates were victorious there.[81] Hood's division had outflanked and outgunned Sickles's advanced line at Devil's Den before it could be reinforced enough to make its position tenable. The hard fighting in Devil's Den, together with the sinister character of the spot, gave it a hallowed place in America's history that might even exceed its actual significance. What meaning the Confederate success there would have would depend in great measure on battles that were raging in other places nearby in the waning hours of that summer evening.

10

Little Round Top

"Warren! I hear a little peppering going on in the direction of the little hill off yonder," spoke General Meade. "I wish that you would ride over and if anything serious is going on . . . attend to it." Lt. Washington A. Roebling, Warren's aide and the future builder of the Brooklyn Bridge, said that he recalled this request verbatim fifty years after the event. In accordance with the commanding general's wish, Warren rode to the "little hill" and thereby rode to prominence and a small place in history.[1]

General Meade probably made this request as the generals and their staffs rode south along Cemetery Ridge to the Third Corps's position, and they could see the Round Tops looming above the Third Corps left. The two generals parted, and as General Meade rode to see General Sickles near the Peach Orchard, Warren continued south along Cemetery Ridge to the rocky hill whose name he would not yet have known.

Gouverneur K. Warren's background equipped him well for his service that day. He was born in 1830 in Cold Spring, New York, across the Hudson River from West Point. After graduating from the Military Academy in its class of 1850, he became a lieutenant of topographical engineers and had a variety of assignments that included working with Andrew A. Humphreys on the Mississippi River Survey and with surveying parties on the Great Plains and in the Black Hills. In 1859 he returned to West Point to teach engineering and was there when the war began. He entered the volunteer service in May 1861 as lieutenant colonel of the Fifth New York Regiment (Duryee Zouaves) and fought with that regiment at Big Bethel. He received command of the Fifth in August 1861 and drilled it to perfection while it served in the garrison of Baltimore.

The Fifth New York went to the Peninsula with Sykes's division, Fifth Corps, and became a part of the Army of the Potomac. Warren received command of the division's Third Brigade and commanded it through the battle of Fredericksburg. He became a brigadier general in September 1862 and the chief topographical engineer of the Army of the Potomac in February

Brig. Gen. Gouverneur K. Warren
(National Archives)

Col. Strong Vincent (MOLLUS-MASS/
U.S.A.M.H.I., *Carlisle Barracks, Pa.)*

Brig. Gen. Evander M. Law (MOLLUS-
MASS/U.S.A.M.H.I., *Carlisle Barracks, Pa.*)

1863. Hooker appointed Warren chief engineer of the Army of the Potomac at the outset of the Gettysburg campaign, and General Meade continued him in that position.[2]

Warren took leave while the Army of the Potomac marched north in the early stages of the campaign. He arrived in Baltimore on the morning of 17 June, married Emily Forbes Chase, and hurried back to army headquarters that afternoon. Ten days or so later, when General Meade took command of the Army, he asked the bridegroom to act temporarily as his chief of staff in place of General Butterfield, but Warren declined. He urged General Meade to continue Butterfield in his post because of that general's particular knowledge of the state of things within the army. It was as chief engineer, then, that Warren reached Gettysburg on 1 July in time to assist Hancock and Howard in establishing the Federal position on Cemetery Hill. He went back to Taneytown that evening but returned on 2 July early enough to make a reconnaissance of the Confederate left. Warren was a well-grounded professional engineer with a wealth of experience both as a regimental and brigade commander. Meade's almost casual request that Warren go to Little Round Top was one of the most important acts of their joint careers.[3]

Warren must have reached Little Round Top about the time that General Meade met General Sickles near the Peach Orchard. The Third Corps had long since taken position at Devil's Den and the Peach Orchard, but the Fifth Corps had not yet arrived to shore up the army's left. Warren needed but a glance to appreciate the hill's importance:

> His well-trained eye is quick to see,
> That this small hill, once gained by Lee,
> > The field is lost.

He found it occupied by only a signal station. He saw that the height was "the key of the whole position," and so it was.[4] It might have been used to advantage by a few artillery pieces, as many have since said, but its real significance was in its being the potential anchor of the Union left. So long as Little Round Top was in Union hands, the left of Cemetery Ridge was likely to be secure. But should the Confederates take it, they would have access to the Union rear and be able to pry the Federal army from its position. Once the Confederates held the hill, artillery or not, the Cemetery Ridge line would have to be abandoned. It was as simple as that.

Warren must have known little or nothing of Birney's division's position when he reached the hill and nothing of Confederate deployment in his front. He probably sought information on them from the signalmen there, who were intelligent fellows. He could have seen some of the left of Sickles's line at Devil's Den in his front and could have learned that it ended there. He could have seen plainly the tree line that marked the crest of Seminary Ridge and concluded that it might screen Confederate formations and movements behind it. Therefore, he requested that Smith's battery fire a shot into the trees on the ridge line where Hood's division must have been. Smith did so, and, as Warren later described the situation,

> As the shot went whistling through the air the sound of it reached the enemy's troops and caused every one to look in the direction of it. This motion revealed to me the glistening of gun-barrels and bayonets of the enemy's line of battle, already formed and far outflanking the position of any of our troops; so that the line of his advance from his right to Little Round Top was unopposed. I have been particular in telling this, as the discovery was intensely thrilling to my feelings, and almost appalling.[5]

The presence of Confederate troops south of the Emmitsburg Road was a surprise to Warren, but, as discussed above, it was surely known to Sickles, Birney, and many others of the Third Corps, particularly those near the Peach Orchard. By the time that Warren reached the hilltop, the batteries at the Peach Orchard should have been trading shots with Cabell's if not Henry's guns. Warren was not the first to discover that Hood's and McLaws's divisions were opposite Sickles's front—that was already known to many others if not to him. What Warren did discover, perhaps, was the extent of the Confederate line south of the Emmitsburg Road, that Little Round Top was not manned, that the Confederates might seize it, and that Sickles's line might be flanked. "With the *promptitude* which was his distinguishing characteristic," Warren sent for troops to occupy the hill.[6]

An officer, probably Capt. Chauncey B. Reese, carried Warren's request for troops to General Meade. Warren wanted a division, and General Meade took measures to give him one. As indicated in Chapter 7, he ordered Humphreys's division, which had not yet taken position along the Emmitsburg Road, to man the hill; but as Humphreys's brigades began to move toward it, Meade learned that the Fifth Corps was coming up and cancelled the order.[7]

Warren also sent Lt. Ranald S. Mackenzie for a brigade of the Third Corps. After all, that corps was near at hand and should be able to respond quickly. Mackenzie rode down the hill and carried the request to General Sickles. Sickles refused him, saying that his whole command was needed to defend its front. Possibly at Sickles's suggestion, Mackenzie hurried to General Sykes, who assented to his request. Mackenzie then rode back to Warren while Sykes ordered General Barnes to post troops on the hill.[8]

Time has not been especially kind to George Sykes's memory, and he has joined the ranks of nearly forgotten generals. Sykes was born in Dover, Delaware, in 1822 and graduated from West Point in its stellar class of 1842. Like a number of his contemporaries, Sykes served against the Seminoles and in the War with Mexico, where he won a brevet captaincy at Cerro Gordo. He achieved the rank of major before the Civil War began, and in that rank performed the service at Bull Run for which he is probably best remembered. It was Major Sykes and his battalion of Regulars who showed the volunteer soldiers of both armies how soldiers ought to behave in battle; when others around them were losing their heads and order, Sykes's Regulars behaved with discipline and courage and covered the retreat of some of the Federal forces from the field.

Sykes went on to higher commands in the Army of the Potomac, but the Regular infantry of that army stayed within his command. He commanded the Second Division, Fifth Corps, in the campaigns of 1862 and at Chancellorsville and thus was well qualified by seniority and experience to take command of the corps when George Meade left it to command the army. Sykes was a thorough professional and was deemed a likable man. Confederate General Daniel H. Hill, with whom he roomed at West Point, described him as "a man admired by all for his honor, courage, and frankness, and peculiarly endeared to me by his social qualities." Colonel Lyman saw him as a "mild, steady man, and very polite," and a Fifth Corps soldier regarded him as "a man who had always proved to be a brave and efficient officer."[9]

Not much has survived in the way of specific information on Sykes's activities between 10:00 A.M. and 3:00 P.M. It is likely that he talked with Slocum, the commander of the army's right wing, tried to become acquainted with the general nature of the Federal position, and took care of the myriad duties relating to his corps. Capt. William Jay, his senior aide, recalled in later years that, as Sykes's agent, he was busy the better part of the morning riding between corps headquarters on Powers Hill and the corps ordnance train several miles in the rear. The day was hot and wearing on both Jay and his horse.[10]

Sometime in the early afternoon (no one recorded when) General Meade instructed Sykes to make a brigade available to the Third Corps if Sickles asked for it. Sykes designated Weed's brigade for this detail and sent Lt. Col. Frederick T. Locke and Capt. John W. Williams of his staff to see where the brigade might be used. But no call for it came until midafternoon.[11]

Meade summoned Sykes and his brother corps commanders to a meeting a little before 3:00 P.M. Sykes left his staff and his corps flag on Powers Hill and rode to army headquarters with only his junior aide, Lt. George T. Ingham, and an orderly. After the meeting, as the generals began to disperse, Meade called Sykes to him and conversed with him briefly in low tones. The tenor of the conversation, as Sykes recorded later in his report, was that he was to throw the whole Fifth Corps in on the left and hold it "at all hazards." This, as Sykes saw it, negated the earlier request that he provide Sickles with a brigade. It also meant to him that he was not to parcel out his units to other corps but that he was to fight the Fifth Corps as a whole.[12]

His conversation with Meade ended, Sykes told Ingham that he was to carry instructions for Captain Jay to lead the corps forward toward the Little Round Top area. He was also to tell the corps staff and the corps headquarters escort to wait at Powers Hill until Sykes's return. Then Ingham was to ride southeast on the Baltimore Pike until he met the Sixth Corps. He was to tell the commander of the leading division of the corps to come up to Gettysburg immediately. This done, he was to return to Sykes. Ingham probably had only a short ride, for the van of the Sixth Corps was then not far away.[13]

Sykes set off to the left with but a single orderly to select positions for his divisions. He probably did not ride to Little Round Top, for he made no later claim of having done so. He must have ridden to the Devil's Den area, however, for he saw the gap there between Smith's battery and the Fourth Maine and noted mentally that it ought to be filled. He rode then across the Wheatfield and found Birney and Ward in a woods to the "right" of the Wheatfield—whether it was the woods on the stony hill or Trostle's Woods we cannot know. He spoke to Birney of the gap at Devil's Den and promised to deploy some of his own troops in the stony hill area if Birney would shift troops left to fill it. It was about this time that Captain Jay and Capt. John Williams, the corps adjutant general, appeared. They had become impatient at Sykes's failure to return to Powers Hill and had ridden out to find him. Sykes sent Jay off to bring up Barnes's division.[14]

After seeing General Sickles, Mackenzie found Sykes and asked him for a division. Barnes's troops, with Vincent's brigade in the lead, had approached the battlefield by way of Granite Schoolhouse Lane and crossed the Taney-town Road; Vincent's brigade had halted to await orders near the George Weikert house on Cemetery Ridge. Colonel Vincent was on horseback at the head of his brigade, and Pvt. Oliver W. Norton, the brigade standard-bearer, waited beside him. At this point, accounts vary. General Barnes reported that he directed Vincent to Little Round Top, while Norton related a more dramatic story.[15]

According to Norton, Sykes and Barnes were not together when Warren's request for troops reached Sykes, so Sykes sent an aide (it must have been Jay or Williams) to Barnes with his instructions. As the aide approached Vincent and Norton, Vincent, "with eyes ablaze," trotted forward to meet him and called out:

"Captain, what are your orders?"
The Captain replied, "Where is General Barnes?"
Vincent said, "What are your orders? Give me your orders."
"General Sykes told me to direct General Barnes to send one of his brigades to occupy that hill yonder," shouted the captain.
Vincent said, "I will take the responsibility of taking my brigade there."

With that promise Vincent rode back to the brigade. He asked Col. James C. Rice of the Forty-fourth New York to lead the brigade to the hill as rapidly as possible. Then, trailed by Norton and the brigade flag, a white pennant bordered in red and bearing a blue maltese cross, Vincent galloped off toward the threatened hill.[16]

Colonel Strong Vincent's name reflected the man. He was just twenty-six years old, of medium stature, and "well formed." Although quiet and considerate of others and of a cheerful disposition—a gentleman by nature—Vincent was a strict disciplinarian. Beyond that he was a fine horseman, which in that day was an asset for a military man. He had learned the iron molder's trade at his father's foundry in Erie, Pennsylvania, but had not found it to his liking and left it to attend Trinity College and Harvard. He graduated from Harvard in 1859 and read law in Erie until the outbreak of the war.[17]

When war came, Vincent, who had no military experience, became the adjutant of a three-month regiment, an assignment for which reading law might have conditioned him. When the three months were over and that experience was under his sword belt, Vincent became the lieutenant colonel of the newly organized Eighty-third Pennsylvania Regiment that was recruited from counties in the northwestern corner of the state.[18]

The Eighty-third joined the Third Brigade, First Division, Fifth Corps, on the Peninsula and served with that brigade through Gettysburg and afterward. Vincent took charge of the Eighty-third after its colonel had fallen at Gaines's Mill and received formal command of it after Chancellorsville to "the cheers that broke through the solemn decorum of dress parade." It was his privilege to lead it to his native state.[19]

Because Vincent judged that the northwest slope of Little Round Top was too difficult for their horses to climb readily, Vincent and Norton rode around to the hill's east slope and climbed it at an angle toward the crest at the southern end. After passing about three hundred yards across the slope, they came to a rise created by a spur, later called Vincent's Spur, that extends from the body of the hill about one hundred yards to the southeast at an elevation about twenty feet lower than the south end of the crest itself. The spur has the effect of doubling the width of the south face of the hill, that slope fronting the Confederate assault. After Vincent and Norton reached the juncture of the spur and the main hill, they rode over it to the hill's south nose and to a broad shelf about fifteen feet below the south end of the crest. As Vincent explored the area on foot, a shell whistled in and struck nearby. Vincent yelled, "Down with that flag, Norton! D–n it, go behind the rocks with it!" Norton made haste to obey. Vincent followed him to the shelter of some boulders, gave him the reins of his horse, and continued the reconnaissance on foot.[20]

Viewed from the west, Little Round Top can be described simplistically as having three elevations. The long north slope rises gradually about forty feet above the Wheatfield Road to a rock-faced shelf on which the monuments of the 146th New York and the 155th Pennsylvania regiments stand today. This shelf, in turn, is at the base of another bluff of boulders that rises at the north end of the hill's crest. The signal station was established at the top of this bluff, and later Warren's statue was erected there. From this north end of the crest the surface rises gently over a distance of fifty yards to a knob near the

Little Round Top from Devil's Den. Photograph by Timothy H. O'Sullivan
(Library of Congress)

center of the hill that forms its highest point. This knob, about 150 feet above the valley floor in front of it, contains today the monuments of Hazlett's battery and the Ninety-first Pennsylvania Regiment. It masks the south portion of the crest from the signal station area and in 1863 screened events that took place there from General Warren's view. From the knoll the crest's surface declines gently one hundred yards to the south, where it ends in an abrupt slope and, to the front, another bouldered bluff. The south end of the crest is topped today by the massive memorial of the Forty-fourth New York Regiment.[21] At the base of the rock ledge, ten or fifteen feet below the crest and in front of the castlelike New York memorial, is another shelf, something of a counterpart of that at the north end of the hill. The shelf, in all probability, was that first visited by Vincent and became the site of the right of his brigade's line.

Vincent saw that the slope to the right of the shelf fronted west toward the rear of the Third Corps position at Devil's Den. Therefore it seemed safe from attack. The south slope of the hill, that to the left of the shelf, in contrast, faced the saddle between Little Round Top and the long, tree-covered northwest slope of Round Top. Little Round Top's spur, further to the left, was opposite Round Top's north slope and crest. The saddle between

Little Round Top from the northwest. Photograph by Timothy H. O'Sullivan (National Archives)

the hills was covered with trees that would conceal any force with stamina enough to advance over the larger hill. Apart from a few sharpshooters, there were no Third Corps troops on Round Top—thus it was a dangerous area that Vincent's brigade would have to watch. The south slope of Little Round Top and the spur were essentially bare of trees, but they were studded with boulders large and small. Although the boulders were strewn across the slope, Vincent's quick eye saw that some of them were ranked in vague rows that divided the hillside into two or three terraces that were obvious in some places but in others were interrupted and indistinct. These vague terraces and the shelf would provide positions for his regiments when they arrived.

The end of the spur, to the left and rear of the hill, was the portion of Little Round Top closest to Round Top, and it dominated the saddle between the two hills. Because it rested behind the line of Little Round Top's crest, it stood in the path of any turning movement that the Confederates might make over Round Top against the Union left. In addition, the Taneytown Road was only five hundred yards away. The spur tip, then, was the obvious place for the left of Vincent's brigade, for if his brigade did not occupy it, attackers could outflank any line that he might post on the hill. From the spur Vincent would string his line west around the hill as far as it would reach, hopefully far enough to cover the gap between the hillside position and the Third Corps left in the valley below, far enough to face the forbidding woods on Round Top's northwest slope.

As Colonel Vincent scrambled across the south slope of Little Round Top, Colonel Rice approached it with the Third Brigade. The men of the brigade double-quicked a short way east along the Wheatfield Road and swung right on to the hill's east slope toward their brigade commander. As the brigade passed along Little Round Top's reverse slope, some Confederate shells crashed through nearby trees. No doubt the Confederate gunners had fired these rounds at the Union signal men on the hill's crest. It is likely that the brigade's line-of-march was well below the crest at this point, for General Warren, who was near the signal station, was unaware of the brigade's presence.[22]

The brigade column, which must have extended a quarter of a mile from front to rear, probably halted with its head near the reverse slope of the spur and its rear near the Wheatfield Road while the regimental commanders went forward to learn where their positions would be. Col. Joshua L. Chamberlain of the Twentieth Maine wrote in later years that his regiment was first in line. If so, it probably was followed by the Eighty-third Pennsylvania, the Sixteenth Michigan, and the Forty-fourth New York in that order. Vincent took Chamberlain to the tip of the spur, probably to a point amid the rocks beneath the large boulder on which the monument of the Twentieth Maine rests today. This would be the Twentieth's left. Vincent emphasized the importance of the Twentieth's position by saying, "You understand! hold this ground at all costs!" At Chamberlain's order the Twentieth crossed over the spur and took its position, and the remaining three regiments prepared to come on line in turn.[23]

The line occupied by Vincent's regiments cannot be defined with certainty. The Twentieth Maine's original left was probably below the site of its memorial. The Maine line extended right along the spur, probably behind an irregular line of boulders. It continued west across the present avenue's right-of-way, where all vestiges of the wartime slope have been removed, to the main hill and the left flank of the Eighty-third Pennsylvania, the next regiment in line.[24]

The Eighty-third Pennsylvania's memorial is about two-thirds of the way down Little Round Top's slope, and its line is presumably indicated by flank markers in its front. This line, like that of the Twentieth Maine, was near the base of the slope almost at the saddle's floor. It had the advantage of a few boulders that might have provided some cover, but they would not have provided enough cover to render it impregnable.

Vincent showed his regimental commanders their regiments' positions. He and Colonel Rice of the Forty-fourth New York walked to the shelf at the right of the line. Vincent said to Rice: "Form your regiment here, Colonel, with the right against this rock." Rice replied, "In every battle in which we have been engaged the Eighty-third and Forty-fourth have fought side by side. I wish it might be so to-day." To this, Vincent responded: "All right, let the Sixteenth pass you." And so it was that the Twentieth and the Sixteenth regiments occupied Vincent's flanks while the Eighty-third and Forty-fourth, "Butterfield's Twins," stood side by side in the brigade center.[25]

Vincent placed the right regiment of the brigade, the Sixteenth Michigan, on the shelf that first had caught his eye. The front of the shelf rested on massive boulders that raised it high above the slope below, making it almost impregnable to frontal attack. It was protected on the left by a jumble of boulders, but on the right the shelf merged into the slope of the hill, making it vulnerable to any force able to attack up the hill's west face. From its aerie the Sixteenth had a commanding view of the incline in its front toward Devil's Den except for a dead space in front of the smaller shelf halfway down the slope between the Sixteenth and the saddle.[26]

The Forty-fourth New York connected the Sixteenth and the Eighty-third. Because Colonel Rice made a special point of its association with the Eighty-third, it seems likely that the left of the Forty-fourth was far down the slope near the right of the Eighty-third. One man of the Forty-fourth recalled that its line was a third of the way down the hillside, but it must have angled from low down the slope on its left up the hill among the plentiful boulders to connect with the Sixteenth at the shelf. Thus, Vincent's line must have slanted from the shelf (which was fifteen or so feet lower than the south crest) diagonally across the south slope of the hill to the point of the spur near the hill's juncture with the top of the saddle.[27]

When the brigade arrived, Vincent sent Capt. Eugene A. Nash of his staff and a mounted orderly forward to Round Top to seek out the enemy. As Nash rode forward, he could see a Rebel line advancing in the open field toward Devil's Den, but trees shielded from view any movements of that sort across the slope of Round Top. Nash and the orderly made their way up the hill to a spot that provided some view, and there Nash dismounted, gave his reins to the orderly, and climbed upon a large rock. As he swept the slope ahead of him with his field glasses, he heard shots, and bullets thudded against the rock. The Confederates had found Nash, and they were almost upon him.[28]

As soon as Vincent's regiments reached their positions, each deployed a company of skirmishers to the front. Colonel Chamberlain sent Capt. Walter G. Morrill and Company B out to screen the Twentieth's front and left. Morrill and his men were climbing Round Top's north slope when firing broke out to the company's right and rear. Morrill shifted his line left to avoid any Confederates that might have gotten in his rear and then pulled his company back to the saddle. Instead of rejoining the main line there, he placed his company behind a stone wall that crossed the saddle on the hill's east slope about 150 yards to the left of the main line, put out some men to guard his left flank, and prepared to fight. Soon a sergeant and a dozen men from the Second U.S. Sharpshooter Regiment joined Company B, and they waited there together.[29]

Two companies of the Sixteenth Michigan, Company A and Brady's Independent Company of Sharpshooters, went out to the brigade's right front to close part of the gap between Vincent's right and the Fourth Maine Regiment in the valley below. This detail left only about 150 men in the regiment's line. Companies also went forward from the Eighty-third and Forty-fourth, but there is no extant evidence that a single officer commanded the brigade skirmish line. Perhaps such coordination was taken for granted when preparing reports, or perhaps there was none.[30]

Capt. Lucius S. Larrabee and his Company B went out for the Forty-fourth New York Regiment. Larrabee was a symbol of the Forty-fourth's origins. He was a New Yorker who was living in Chicago just prior to the war and, while there, became one of Elmer Ellsworth's United States Zouave Cadets. Ellsworth and his cadets became rather well known as they traveled over the country exhibiting their exotic and colorful Zouave uniforms and their flashy and lively Zouave drill. When war came, the well-drilled Larrabee got a commission in the Eleventh New York Regiment, Ellsworth's Fire Zouaves, and fought at Bull Run. Ellsworth was shot in Alexandria and became one of the North's first martyrs. In Ellsworth's honor the State of New York authorized the organization of a three-year regiment—the "People's Ellsworth Regiment," or Forty-fourth New York Volunteer Infantry—in the fall of 1861. It was conceived as a select body of unmarried men between the ages of eighteen and thirty, and each man was at least five feet eight inches tall. The Forty-fourth was recruited statewide, one man from each town or ward in the state, and each man had to contribute twenty dollars to the regimental fund for the privilege of joining. Many of the Forty-fourth's officers, like Larrabee, had come to it from the Fire Zouaves. After a year, the Forty-fourth's declining strength was augmented by the addition of two new companies. One, designated Company E, was enlisted from the State Normal School at Albany and ought to have given the Forty-fourth a certain scholarly tone.[31]

After reaching the field that day, Larrabee had a premonition. He told two of his fellow captains that he would be killed the next time that the regiment came under fire, and he placed his watch and some other valuables in the keeping of the regiment's quartermaster. Larrabee's foreboding was taking him out on a limb, for though the regiment had had considerable service and many casualties, no officer had yet been killed in action. When his company left for the skirmish line and Capt. William R. Bourne of Company K wished him good luck, Larrabee replied, "Good bye, Billy, I shall never see you again." Larrabee took his company to the front about two hundred yards, probably to the first rise of ground south of the saddle. There it met a line of Texas infantry, exchanged shots, and Larrabee ordered the company back. As it withdrew, a Confederate shot Larrabee through the body. His premonition was fulfilled.[32]

The skirmishers on the right of Vincent's line had met the Fourth and Fifth Texas regiments and probably the Fourth Alabama on the Texans' right. These hardy Confederates on the right of Robertson's line had passed near the Bushman and Slyder farmyards and, as the First Texas and Third Arkansas veered left toward Devil's Den, had continued straight ahead toward Round Top. Like the Fifteenth and Forty-seventh Alabama, they had splashed through Plum Run, wheeled left into the woods on Round Top's slope, and found the sharpshooters waiting there behind a stone wall. Members of each of the three regiments recalled reaching Round Top somewhat differently. To the Fourth Texas on the left the stone fence was the place from which the sharpshooters had killed Lt. Joe C. Smith and where both Col. John C. G. Key and Lt. Col. Benjamin F. Carter were wounded. Apparently the sharpshooters were picking their targets with some care. To the right the sharpshooters fell back before the Fifth Texas; the Fifth gained the west side of the wall, paused until its slower men caught up, and at Colonel Powell's command, "Forward!," jumped it, met no opposition, and angled left across the wooded shoulder of the hill. On the right the Fourth Alabama, Law's left regiment, double-quicked across the space between Plum Run and the fence, halted before the fence, fixed bayonets, and piled over it. When it became apparent that the sharpshooters had drifted away, the Fourth Alabama halted, dressed its line, probably returned its bayonets to their scabbards and, with the Fourth and Fifth Texas, swung left over the shoulder of Round Top easterly of Devil's Den and made for Little Round Top.[33]

The march between the fence or wall above Plum Run and the saddle between the hills was a short one of four hundred yards or so, but it was rendered difficult by the heat, trees, underbrush and "large boulders, from the size of a wash pot to that of a wagon bed."[34] Because farmers probably ran cattle in the woods and harvested its fallen trees for firewood, it can be assumed that the woods floor was more open then than it became after it was included within the park and those activities were stopped. But even then the terrain would have been difficult and would have fragmented the Texans' line. The roar of battle at Devil's Den just to the left must have added to the moment, but it is likely that the Texans met no serious opposition until they encountered the skirmishers of Vincent's brigade.

When the Fourth Texas passed to the east of Devil's Den, the men on its left could see Smith's battery above and could also see something of the fighting there. At this time the Texas formation must have been loosened by the obstacles in its path enough that the file-closers were not as attentive as they might have been. Under these circumstances, one soldier, Cpl. Miles V. Smith of Company D, was tempted to stop and snipe at the cannoneers. He settled himself among some boulders that gave him cover, and while his regiment pressed ahead toward Little Round Top, he remained there and

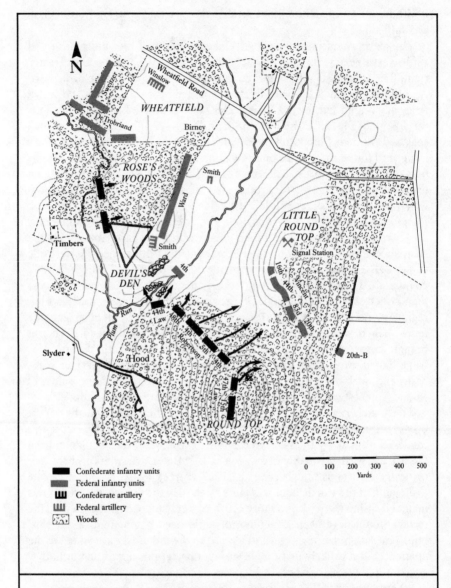

1. Vincent's Brigade forms in an ascending line on Little Round Top's southwest slope.

2. The Fourth Alabama and the Fourth and Fifth Texas regiments advance from the northwest slope of Round Top against Vincent's line. The Fifteenth and Forty-seventh Alabama climb to Round Top's summit and then start down toward Vincent's left.

3. The Fourth Maine on the right of Ward's line blocks the Confederates' access to the west slope of Little Round Top.

4. The Confederates attack Vincent's line twice and are repulsed.

Map 10-1. Little Round Top: The Opening Assault

fired at the cannoneers. He saw men of the First Texas and Twentieth Georgia capture the battery, though he credited the capture to the Fifth Texas, and then he witnessed Federal efforts to retake the high ground at the battery. At this time, when his own regiment was heavily engaged on Little Round Top, Smith claimed that he collected "forty or fifty Rebs scattered around there," and they fired into the Federal flank. When the fighting ended there, he and his fellow stragglers went off to find their units. He found the Fourth Texas halfway up the slope of Little Round Top, but by that time the fighting there was over.[35]

As the Texas regiments crossed Round Top's slope, the right of Hood's division's line was having troubles of its own. Both regiments there, the Fifteenth Alabama and Lieutenant Colonel Bulger's Forty-seventh Alabama, were operating under Colonel Oates. General Law had told Oates to wheel left after crossing Plum Run, but conditions persuaded Oates to do otherwise. After the sharpshooters fell back from the fence, those in front of Oates went directly up the hill. Oates decided that he could not wheel left and leave them on his flank or in his rear, so instead he decided to disregard Law's instructions and directed his regiment to wheel right toward the top of the hill. The Forty-seventh, in turn, held to the Fifteenth's left.[36] Thus, three of Hood's regiments swung directly toward Little Round Top while the two on the right of the line continued straight ahead uphill toward the summit of Round Top.

The fire of the retreating sharpshooters did little real damage to the Alabama line. At some point on Round Top's slope the skirmish line of the green-clad riflemen split; and those on Oates's left slipped northerly around the hill while others sidled south beyond Oates's right. Since the latter threatened Oates's flank and rear, he ordered Capt. Francis K. Shaaff's Company A to leave the regiment's line and deal with them.[37]

The main body of the Fifteenth climbed to the summit of the conical hill; the Forty-seventh moved beside it lower down the slope. When the Fifteenth reached the crest, both units halted. The Alabamians were exhausted from their long day's ordeal. The march from New Guilford, the approach march, and then the assault were bad enough, but to cap it off the twenty-two men sent with their comrades' canteens for water had not yet returned, and many of the men on Round Top must have had parched throats. It was small wonder, then, that the Alabamians needed a rest when they reached the top of the hill.[38]

It was during this halt that Captain Terrell of Law's staff rode to the summit by way of a path that Oates said was on the hill's southeast slope. Terrell told Oates of Hood's being wounded and Law's having taken command of the division. He reminded Oates that there were no Confederates on his right, asked why his regiments had halted, and told him that Hood's orders were for them to press on, turn the Union left, and capture Little Round Top without delay.[39] Oates protested. His position there would be difficult to assault and, as he later recalled, "within half an hour I could convert it into a Gibraltar that I could hold against ten times the number of men that I had, hence in my judgment it should be held and occupied by artillery as soon as possible, as it was higher than the other mountain and would command the entire field."[40] But why? The battle was already raging below, the division was attacking, not defending. His regiments were needed on the firing line, not in a defensive position on Round Top that had no value in the situation at hand. In addition, infantry officers have sometimes proved themselves to be poor judges of artillery positions and capabilities, and Oates's judgment in this might have been lacking.

Colonel Oates demands special notice, for like Colonel Joshua Chamberlain of the Twentieth Maine, he will always figure prominently in any narrative of the events of 2 July 1863 at the Round Tops. Oates was born in Pike County, Alabama, and was twenty-nine years old at Gettysburg. His early years were marked by poverty mixed with a brawling sort of adventure as he passed through his late teens into his early twenties. At sixteen, following a thrashing from his father, he ran away from home for several months. After returning home, he taught school for a brief period. When he had a fight that he ended by hitting his opponent in the head with a mattock, he fled the area again, this time one step ahead of the law. His subsequent wandering took him through the Gulf states and eventually to Texas. In his travel he supported himself by working as a laborer, particularly as a painter. He claimed to have had some good luck at gambling with cards and some mixed fortune in escapades involving young women that also created problems for him. In time he returned to Alabama, where he settled down, became a schoolteacher in Henry County, a part-time student, and a reader of law. He passed the bar in 1858 and for the next three years displayed his pugnacity in the courtroom.[41]

Oates's military service began in the summer of 1861, when he became the captain of the Henry Pioneers, a rather typical sort of early Confederate company. The Henry Pioneers became Company G, Fifteenth Alabama Infantry Regiment, and went off to Virginia. They wintered in Manassas, then campaigned with Jackson in the Valley, and joined up with the Army of Northern Virginia in June 1862 in front of Richmond. Oates and the Fifteenth participated in the various battles of that army in 1862 except that Oates became ill and had to miss Antietam. When he returned to duty, he found himself a candidate for the command of the regiment; he received the command along with a colonelcy in May 1863. It was a new and rather inexperienced regimental commander who led the Fifteenth north to Gettysburg. One of Oates's comrades described him as having been "regarded by many as too aggressive and ambitious but he usually was well to the front and did not require his men to charge where he was unwilling to share the common danger."[42] His conduct at Gettysburg seemed to bear out some but not all of this description. It was not aggressive to want to halt in the course of an attack and construct a citadel on Round Top. Perhaps Oates's fatigue, his concern for the condition of his tired men, and an excessive caution growing out of increased responsibility temporarily blunted his natural combativeness.

Terrell insisted that Oates get his command moving, and Oates had to do so. Reluctantly the colonel brought his tired men to their feet, and they shuffled down the hill far enough to clear a bluff on the hill's east side. Then they faced right and stumbled down the hill's north slope without meeting any opposition, their descent stimulated, no doubt, by the roar of musketry both at Devil's Den and at Little Round Top.[43] As his line approached the saddle, Oates spied a collection of Federal wagons through the trees, wagons parked behind the Round Tops and only a short distance away. He again pulled Shaaff's company from the Fifteenth's line and sent it to capture the tempting wagons. As the main line continued its descent of the hill, Shaaff's company slipped off to the right and soon became separated from it. Wagons were highly prized, and these attracted Oates as others had attracted J. E. B. Stuart only a few days before. Stuart captured the wagons that he coveted, but Oates did not. Morrill's men may have blocked Shaaff's way. Shaaff and his company did not return to the regiment until the fight was over.[44]

When the Fourth Alabama and the Fourth and Fifth Texas regiments emerged from the woods into the saddle between the Round Tops, they must have been staggered by the sight in front of them. Little Round Top's steep and rocky slope loomed directly in their front. The blue-clad skirmishers, whom they had just driven from the woods, were scrambling up the hill to join a line of troops—Vincent's brigade, 1,000 strong—that slanted across the face of the hill in their front. Probably those on the left of the line could see the signalmen in the distance, and soon they would see artillery pieces arriving singly on the top of the hill. For now, the blue line was half concealed by rocks and bushes on the slope, but the commotion in its ranks and its bright-barreled rifles must have made it obvious enough.

The Rebel regiments paused, dressed their lines, and advanced. No one bothered to record if anyone other than Law as division commander exercised command of all three; probably no one did. Colonel Powell of the Fifth Texas might have assumed control of the two Texas regiments, for he was the ranking officer on that portion of the Texas Brigade's line, but he wrote nothing later about having done so. The Butternut line approached Vincent's men, trying to maintain its formation as it moved along, but that was very hard to do. Powell wrote that the "ascent was so difficult as to forbid the use of arms." The larger granite boulders blocked their way on the left and forced the Texans to file through the gaps between them. When the firing opened, someone (probably Powell) yelled for Maj. Jefferson C. Rogers on the left of the line to swing his wing left. Rogers bellowed back, "I'll do it, Colonel, by

Col. William C. Oates (reproduced from   *Col. Joshua L. Chamberlain*
William C. Oates, The War between the   *(National Archives)*
Union and the Confederacy *[New York:*
Neale Publishing Company, 1905])

Jingo!" For some reason it became very quiet in the instant of Rogers's reply and the words "by Jingo" sounded loudly, clearly, and ludicrously over the Fifth's part of the field.[45]

On the left the Fourth Texas went in yelling and whooping in the Texas way, but such noise does not move boulders. As he saw the Texans contending with the rocks, John West thought of the line, "Round the rude rock the ragged rascal ran."[46] But this was no game. A ledge of boulders, probably that by the lower terrace, stopped the advance. The men of the Fifth Texas took shelter around them, fought individually, and fired with some accuracy in the opinion of Lt. Col. King Bryan. At this time Bryan left his position behind the regiment's right and went in search of Colonel Powell to get his instructions. He did not see Powell at first but found him wounded and prostrate behind the center of the Fifth's line. As he approached Powell, a ball struck Bryan in the left arm. In spite of his own wound, he examined Powell closely enough to find a hole in Powell's coat where the bullet had left his body. By this time Bryan's arm was bleeding so badly that it demanded his full attention, and he turned the Fifth over to Major Rogers and left the field.[47]

The Fifth was still firing when Major Rogers took command. Perhaps he was the field officer who walked behind the color company and admonished its men to aim well. In doing so, he and those with him drew fire on themselves and the men nearby. Such exhibitions of bravery are not always appreciated by those forced to share the risk. Pvt. William A. Fletcher called, "Cousins, move on; you are drawing the fire our way." An order came then from "some unknown source" to fall back. Rogers looked to his flanks and saw that the Fourth Alabama and the Fourth Texas had gone. He then moved his men back to the shoulder of Round Top above Devil's Den, where they reformed.[48]

The two Texas regiments, and possibly the Fourth Alabama, paused briefly while they prepared for another try. Then they were again ordered forward and advanced a second time with coolness and determination over ground now strewn with the bodies of those killed or severely injured in the first assault. The terrain had not become more favorable, the Federal fire was no less severe, and again they fell back, some in spite of officers' attempts to hold them on the fatal hill. As they turned, a Federal ball took off the big toe of a lieutenant of the Fourth Texas. This hurt considerably, and the lieutenant hopped and "squealed" and, to the unsympathetic Fletcher, made more of a racket than he had ever heard from a wounded man.[49]

The separate assaults described by veterans of the Fourth and Fifth Texas are not reflected in the short report of the Fourth Alabama Regiment, and there is no contemporary account that describes the extent of the cooperation between the Alabamians and the Texans on their left.[50] Tree cover and the configuration of Vincent's line would have permitted the Alabamians to move close to the Federal line with some concealment and might have allowed the Fourth Alabama to maintain continuous contact with it. In addition, the rough surface of the saddle in the Fourth's zone would have made movement across it difficult.

It is likely too that there was little coordination between the two Alabama regiments on the right under Oates and the Fourth Alabama and the Texans. The left three regiments were probably engaged before Oates's men started down the hill, and no one assumed direct command of the whole line.[51] When the Fifteenth and Forty-seventh Alabama regiments reached the saddle, they saw the Federal line on an irregular "ledge" of rocks parallel to the Forty-seventh's seven companies and the Fifteenth's left but bending back somewhat from the Fifteenth's right. Vincent's line welcomed Oates's command with what Oates characterized as "the most destructive fire I ever saw." Oates's line halted but it held.[52]

The Alabama regiments which struck Little Round Top had been proven in battle. One incident that took place on Little Round Top indicates one reason why they fought so well. Company K of the Fifteenth had a belligerent private, John Nelson, who enjoyed brawling in camp but who disappeared at the first opportunity when the bullets began to fly. At Gettysburg, Capt. William Bethune asked 1st Sgt. Patrick O'Connor to "hold Nelson to the work." O'Connor did so literally. He kept an eye on the brawler and collared him when he saw him starting for the rear. O'Connor held the frightened fellow in the ranks until a bullet struck and killed him. With that, O'Connor released him and let him topple to the ground. As he fell, O'Connor observed, "Now I guess you will not run away."[53]

From the view of Vincent's men, the Confederate assaults, including Oates's when it came, struck first at the center of Vincent's line—the fronts of the Forty-fourth New York and the Eighty-third Pennsylvania—spread right from there to the front of the Sixteenth Michigan, and later, when Oates appeared, continued to the front of the Twentieth Maine.[54] The task of Vincent's center regiments was straightforward enough—to shoot down the Confederates in their front while taking what cover they could to protect themselves. But even this had its complications. An "overgrown uncouth" young soldier of the Eighty-third Pennsylvania stood up each time he fired in such a way that he over exposed himself to Confederate fire. Overexposure was sometimes an officer's privilege and duty rather than an enlisted man's, and one officer told the young fellow to get down. This so incensed him that he stood up, gestured in defiance, called upon God as his witness, and exclaimed: "I am on the soil of old Pennsylvany now, and if they get me down they'll have to shoot me down."[55] Perhaps they did.

During a lull in the fight, Pvt. Philip Grine of Company H of the Eighty-third went forward down the slope and carried back a wounded Confederate soldier, who was then taken by others to a hospital. Soon after, Grine went out again and brought in a second wounded Confederate. Later he was too tired to bring a third in by himself, and so he asked for help. Others of the Eighty-third started forward with him, but the Rebels commenced firing, and the others returned to their places in the Eighty-third's ranks. Grine went on alone and was shot. After the fighting was over, the Pennsylvanians found Grine and the Confederate that he was trying to save. Both were dead.[56]

Colonel Vincent must have directed his brigade's fight from the hillside behind it. He was far from idle, and his staff was on the go. Captain Nash, who had been driven from Round Top, was sent to the left to watch for threats against that flank; Capt. John M. Clark went back for additional ammunition; and Capt. Amos M. Judson was sent in search of reinforcements.[57] Over on the right Lt. Col. Norval E. Welch of the Sixteenth Michigan directed his small regiment from a rock near his colors, a dangerous place, for bullets hit the flag several times.[58] On the left the Twentieth Maine fired initially to the right oblique into the ranks of the Fourth Alabama until Oates's men appeared in its front. In the course of this early fighting, before casualties became numerous, Sgt. Charles Steele of Company A, Twentieth Maine, took a bullet in the chest. Steele staggered over to his company commander. "My God, Sergeant Steele!" said the captain in horror and disbelief as he looked at the bleeding sergeant. "I am going, Captain," gasped the sergeant, and then he fell, "weltering in his blood."[59]

Vincent had occupied the south slope of the hill in answer to Warren's request to Sykes. But Warren was unaware of Vincent's arrival there, for the brigade had passed behind the hill where he could not see it from the signal station area at the north end of the crest.[60] As he waited, minié balls zipped around him, an indication that the Confederates had already worked their way into the Devil's Den–Slaughter Pen area and were threatening Vincent's right. The balls flew so thickly and the danger seemed so great that the signal officer began to close his station, but at Warren's request the signalmen stayed on and continued to wave their flags.[61]

Insofar as General Warren knew, Lt. Charles E. Hazlett's battery (D, Fifth U.S.) was the first unit to reach the threatened hill.[62] When the Fifth Corps moved from the rear to the support of the Union left, Capt. Augustus P. Martin, commander of the Fifth Corps's artillery brigade, ordered three batteries—Hazlett's, Walcott's, and Watson's—to follow Joseph Barnes's division; and Gibbs's and Almont Barnes's batteries were to follow Ayres's division. Hazlett's battery would lead. According to Martin, Hazlett hesitated over the assignment and said that he wished that another battery would take the lead. He had recently received some bad news from home and had had a premonition that it would be his last battle. Martin did not accept his protest. He had a special regard for Hazlett's abilities and wanted him at his right hand.[63]

When the head of Hazlett's battery reached Trostle's Woods, Martin and Hazlett rode ahead to the area of the stony hill, where Tilton's and Sweitzer's brigades would take position. It was at this time, no doubt, that Martin saw General Sykes and asked him for orders. Sykes had none to give him, but told the captain that he would hold him responsible for the corps artillery doing its work. With that expression of confidence the two young officers looked for positions on the front of Barnes's division and found none that suited them. It was then that they appreciated Little Round Top's relationship to the Wheatfield area. Martin ordered Hazlett to place his battery there; Hazlett, in turn, ordered Lt. Benjamin F. Rittenhouse to bring the battery along while he and Martin rode ahead to reconnoiter the position on the hill. As they did so, Martin asked Capt. Paul Nason of his staff to bring up Walcott's and Watson's batteries so that they might be posted on Hazlett's right.[64]

Martin and Hazlett rode to Little Round Top and up its north slope. They met General Warren on the crest. The officers examined the surface of the crest with a critical eye and saw that it was narrow from front to rear, almost inaccessible to artillery pieces, and that its rough, rocky surface would make bringing in and working the guns difficult. Furthermore, cannon placed there would not be able to depress their muzzles enough to protect themselves against a frontal attack. Warren believed that it was "no place for efficient artillery fire." "Never mind that," said Hazlett, "the sound of my guns will be encouraging to our troops and disheartening to the others, and my battery's of no use if this hill is lost."[65] The responsibility was Captain Martin's, and he decided that the crest of the hill ought to be occupied in spite of its disadvantages. Let the guns come up!

Hazlett's men covered themselves with glory that day. Simply getting their guns to the crest was a feat in itself, one of the exciting vignettes of the battle. The gun teams started up the back side of the hill at a trot—spurs and whips "vigorously" applied by the drivers. They could not maintain that pace long, and as they neared the crest must have been moving slowly and deliberately at best. In fact, all but one of the guns were forced to halt behind the crest. The left piece of the First Section, the battery's No. 2 gun, went into position first, the No. 1 piece next. Both had been unlimbered behind the crest and had been lifted, pushed, and pulled into position by cannoneers and infantrymen borrowed for the work. Even General Warren was said to have lent a hand.[66] Thanks to the expertise of the driver of the wheel pair of the team of the third piece, Pvt. Quinlan Sullivan, it reached the crest by horse power alone. The drivers of this gun's team all must have done exceptional work, the sort that could be done only by capable men in unusually stimulating circumstances.[67] Warren, who had known the battery since Bull Run, remained while the first pieces were put in on the hill. In later years, he wrote of Hazlett: "There he sat on his horse on the summit of the hill, with whole-souled animation encouraging our men, and pointing with his sword toward the enemy amidst a storm of bullets—a figure of intense admiration to me, even in that desperate scene. . . . There stood the impersonation of valor and heroic beauty. No nobler man fought or fell that day than he.[68]

No one knows just where Hazlett posted his guns. When the fourth piece was in place and its No. 1 cannoneer was dipping the sponge preparatory to firing its first shot, a bullet hit the sponge bucket, and its water gushed out. The cannoneer "paused, turned to the front, grit his teeth, said 'damn.'" He then sponged and rammed, and, as the first shot was fired, said "Take that, damn you!"[69]

Hazlett's men had their work cut out for them. Limbers and caissons had to be parked on the steep east slope of the hill. There was no place to park them on the crest even if the cannoneers and drivers had been able to take them there. This meant that the ammunition had to be carried to the guns from somewhere down the hill. Hazlett ordered the lead and swing pair drivers, when the limbers were parked, to work with the gun crews and take the places of those who were killed or wounded. The drivers from the teams hitched to the battery wagon and forge were to carry water to the hill in camp kettles for drinking and sponging. Lieutenant Rittenhouse wrote that four guns went into position "in less time than it takes me to tell it," that a fifth piece went in a few minutes afterward, and that "a little later" the sixth piece was "fairly lifted into position by the cannoneers and the infantry." Each opened fire as soon as it was ready.[70]

It was a long shot with a rifle from Devil's Den to the crest of Little Round Top, but targets on the hill were becoming plentiful, and sooner or later some bullets fired in that direction would find a mark. Warren was lucky that afternoon, for one simply grazed his throat and drew blood but did not cause enough damage to force him to leave the field.[71] By then he had been on the hill long enough: he could see infantry crossing the north base of the hill on the Wheatfield Road and realized that more infantry was needed on the crest. He mounted his gray horse, and with Lieutenant Roebling he headed down the north slope of the hill.[72]

When Warren reached the Wheatfield Road near the foot of the hill, the Second Division, Fifth Corps, was passing there. It had made a hurried march from Rock Creek, some of it at a double-quick, for there was no time to waste.[73] On the way it passed a Third Corps hospital whose surgeons were standing by with their hands in their pockets waiting for patients. Nearer the battlefield the division met wounded on their way to see the waiting surgeons and an ammunition wagon from which men were taking boxes of cartridges for their regiments up on the firing line. All the while, the company officers, as was their pleasure, contributed to the scene by running alongside the column shouting, "Close up," "Keep your places," "Steady," and later, perhaps, "Load as you go." At one point an unnamed battery came up from the rear at a full gallop, and the infantry ranks had to open to let it pass.[74]

The Third Brigade, once Warren's, now Weed's, led Ayres's division to the field. Sykes had designated the brigade as support for the Third Corps earlier in the day, and its men had virtually rested in ranks while awaiting Sickles's summons. Weed, not realizing that this assignment had been cancelled, had ridden on ahead of the brigade in the company of Capt. Edgar Warren of his staff and Capt. Alexander Moore of Sickles's staff. He wanted to see Sickles and get his orders. Capt. Azor S. Marvin, Jr., of Weed's staff, guided the brigade, and Col. Patrick O'Rorke of the 140th New York, who had commanded the brigade at Chancellorsville, probably commanded in Weed's temporary absence.[75]

Paddy O'Rorke was a native of Ireland but had lived in Rochester, New York, from childhood. He gave up an apprenticeship as a stonecutter and at the age of twenty-one entered West Point. He graduated at the head of his class in 1861. Commissioned in the engineers, he served as a staff officer until the fall of 1862, when he took command of Rochester's 140th New York Regiment. All agreed that the new colonel was a man of great promise, and one person penned the well-intended compliment, "He was a man of noble character, and had nothing of the wild Irishman about him."[76]

As the 140th began its crossing of Little Round Top's slope, O'Rorke and his staff heard shouting and looked up the hill to their left. They saw General Warren and Lieutenant Roebling riding toward them. Warren shouted excitedly as he approached and, according to Capt. Joseph Leeper, said, "Paddy, give me a regiment." O'Rorke answered that Weed had gone on ahead and expected the brigade to follow him. Warren replied, "Never mind that, bring your regiment up here and I will take the responsibility." O'Rorke knew

Col. Patrick H. O'Rorke (MOLLUS-MASS/
U.S.A.M.H.I., Carlisle Barracks, Pa.)   *Brig. Gen. Stephen H. Weed (MOLLUS-*
MASS/U.S.A.M.H.I., Carlisle Barracks, Pa.)

Warren well and hesitated no further. He turned the 140th from the road and, guided by the impatient Roebling, led it up the hill.[77] After sending the 140th New York to the hill, Warren spoke to General Sykes, who had ridden back from the position of Barnes's division to see to the posting of the remainder of his corps. Warren then rode north to report to General Meade.[78]

Meanwhile, General Weed met with General Sickles near the Trostle farmyard, but what passed between them cannot be known with any certainty. Weed left no clue. Captain Warren implied that Sickles gave Weed an assignment, since he, Warren, was sent back to guide the brigade to an area that he did not identify. HISTORICUS wrote nothing about it, but in later years, when Sickles's comments on his part in the battle were sometimes less than accurate, the general said that he had told Weed to report to General Warren, who had asked for troops to defend Little Round Top.[79]

Captain Warren returned to the brigade and began to lead it toward its assigned position. They had gone but a short distance when a Fifth Corps officer galloped up to the captain and asked him where he was taking the brigade. Warren explained that he was taking it to Weed and Sickles. At this, the officer asked to be taken at once to General Weed instead. Captain Warren and the officer hurried off and found Weed still at the Third Corps headquarters near the Trostle barn. The staff officer told the two generals that Sykes could not spare Weed's brigade. Weed then mounted and rode back to the brigade.[80]

All of the brigade except the 140th New York had passed Little Round Top and probably had turned right into the open and low ground along the northeastern side of Trostle's Woods that lay between the Wheatfield Road and the Trostle farmyard. There it halted, some of it by a battery thought to have been Watson's, but more likely Walcott's. While it waited there, stray rounds fell among its ranks, but fortunately it did not have to wait long. At Sykes's summons it retraced its steps to Little Round Top.[81]

In his report, which he wrote about four weeks after the battle, a smarting, testy Sykes stated that after posting Barnes's two brigades at the stony hill, he rode back toward the Taneytown Road to bring up the remainder of his corps. He found Weed's brigade moving away from Little Round Top, "where it had been stationed, and where its presence was vital." He wrote that he dispatched a staff officer to Weed at once to ask why his brigade had left the place assigned it. Weed's reply was that he had led his brigade away "by order of General Sickles." Sykes then ordered the brigade to return.[82]

In preparing his report Sykes overlooked the fact that he had not assigned Weed a position. He had not seen Ayres or Weed since his visit to Meade at 3:00 P.M. It seems likely that these two officers had not known that Sykes's instructions for Weed to support Sickles had been terminated by Meade's order for the Fifth Corps to take position on the left. The Third Corps command was feverishly seeking all of the aid that it could find and did purloin batteries intended for use elsewhere that would better have been left alone. Nevertheless, it seems idle to presume that officers of the caliber of Weed and Ayres would have permitted a Third Corps officer to commandeer a brigade in those tense times unless they believed that Sykes would have had no objection to the action.

By the time that Weed's brigade turned back toward Little Round Top, Hood's division had smashed Birney's line, taken Devil's Den, and opened an attack against Vincent's left and right. The Fourth and Fifth Texas had assaulted Vincent's line twice without success. Now, with the help of the Forty-eighth Alabama Regiment on their left and Oates's force on their right, they attacked a third time over the rough terrain that had twice impeded their efforts. It was now or never. With the approach of evening—and an abundance of battle smoke—darkness was falling on the field.[83]

Both lines were nearly used up. Vincent's men had taken heavy casualties and were running low on ammunition. On the other side the Texans were reaching the end of their rope, discipline was breaking down, and some of the Fifth Texas advanced only a short distance before they turned around and returned to the cover of Round Top's woods. But with the help of the Forty-eighth Alabama and perhaps others on the left, the Texas line pressed ahead, and suddenly success seemed within their grasp. The right of Vincent's line was crumbling; the colors there were going back.[84]

Indeed this was the case, although the seeming retreat was not due entirely to Confederate effort. Someone had blundered. An officer, improbably thought by some to have been Sykes or Weed, shouted that the Sixteenth Michigan's line should fall back closer to the top of the hill. Perhaps the officer who shouted intended that the right of the Sixteenth's line should be refused to better meet the assault that threatened the right flank of the brigade. But the order, if it was an order, only created confusion. Lt. William Kydd, by an "unwarrantable assumption of authority," ordered the Sixteenth's colors back. Lieutenant Colonel Welch maintained later that only the color guard retired; but forty-five men, a third of those of the Sixteenth present for duty, left the line during or after the fight for one reason or another and did not return until the following morning.[85]

Probably at Vincent's order, the Forty-fourth New York tried to relieve the pressure on the Sixteenth by firing to the right against some of its attackers. Vincent himself hurried to that end of the line, and "throwing himself into the breach he rallied his men." It was a hot spot, and Vincent fell with a mortal wound. He died for the old flag on Pennsylvania soil five days later. Colonel Rice of the Forty-fourth New York stepped into the brigade's command.[86]

Other help for Vincent's brigade and the Sixteenth Michigan was on the way. O'Rorke's 140th New York rushed at an angle up the east slope of Little Round Top in a column of fours. O'Rorke, Lt. Porter Farley, the regiment's adjutant, and Washington Roebling led them on horseback. Their approach must have been slowed by some of Hazlett's guns that were crossing their line of march. When O'Rorke and Farley reached the crest, they found that its surface was too rough to ride over easily, so they dismounted and turned their horses over to the 140th's sergeant major.[87]

The arrival of the 140th New York on Little Round Top must have been a dramatic thing. The regiment had received new Zouave uniforms on 3 June, and the men were "jaunty but tattered" in baggy blue trousers, red jackets, and fezzes. The air around them was sulfurous with smoke; it was rent by the wild whooping of the attacking Confederates and the shouts of the defenders, all underscored by the crash and rattle of musketry and the bark of the one or two of Hazlett's Parrotts that were in position and firing. Company A led the regiment, and Company G was behind it. The instinct of the men was to halt and fire, but O'Rorke ordered them forward. Once the line reached the crest, it might have moved to the area above the right of Vincent's line, faced right, and fronted toward the enemy; but that would have taken time, and the file-closers would have been in front and in the way. Instead, O'Rorke simply drew his sword and yelled, "Down this way, boys!," and the 140th trailed after him. The column scrambled down the hill in considerable disorder until those at its head were abreast of the Sixteenth's right and forty or so feet from the Confederates panting up the slope in their front. Here the head of the column halted and loaded while the rear companies strung into a ragged line

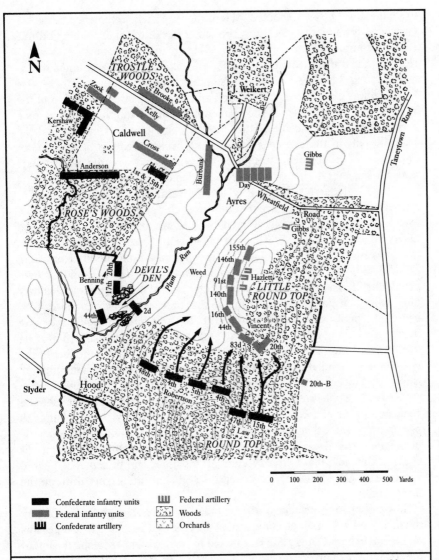

1. The Fourth Alabama and the Fourth and Fifth Texas have attacked Vincent's line twice and been repulsed.

2. Benning's and Robertson's brigades have driven Ward's line from its position on Devil's Den.

3. The Confederates occupy the Devil's Den area and secure access to the southwest slope of Little Round Top.

4. Law's and Robertson's brigades attack Vincent a third time. The Fifteenth Alabama threatens Vincent's left flank, and the Forty-eighth Alabama and Fourth Texas climb the hill in an attempt to work around Vincent's right.

5. The Twentieth Maine holds the left flank. The timely arrival of the 140th New York and Weed's brigade secures Vincent's right and the hill.

Map 10-2. Little Round Top: The Final Assault

to their right. O'Rorke shouted, "Here they are men, commence firing!" A Confederate about forty feet away spotted O'Rorke and shot at him; O'Rorke fell with a minié ball through his neck. Many men from Companies A and G returned the fire immediately, and after the battle the curious counted seventeen holes in the brave Confederate's body.[88]

There was a lively exchange of fire, and the companies on the left of the 140th's line, those closest to the Sixteenth Michigan and to the enemy, took particularly heavy casualties. But O'Rorke's five hundred men tipped the scales heavily in the defenders' favor. The firing lasted but a few minutes until some of the Confederates raised their hands in surrender, while others risked being shot in the back as they bounded down the slope.[89]

As the Confederates struggled against the 140th New York and the right of Vincent's line, there was action elsewhere along that line. Colonel Rice exercised his new command about as well as any colonel could have done under the circumstances.[90] Rice was called "Old Crazy," according to Norton, because "he is brave enough, but in a fight too excitable to do anything right." But he seemed to be doing some things right. He first told his own people that he was leaving them to take command of the brigade and that they must hold their position. He did this so that they would realize that Lt. Col. Freeman Connor was in command and so that no confusion would arise. He then passed along the line to tell the other regimental commanders that he was in command of the brigade and was determined to hold the line to the last. Some responded by telling him that they were almost out of ammunition. Although Vincent had already sent Captain Clark for ammunition, Rice pressed into service some officers and men in the rear who seemed not to be "engaged in the action." He made them pledge that they "would deliver in person every order that I should send by them" and sent four off for ammunition. Some arrived soon after, and it was distributed promptly. Probably it was at about this time that Oliver Norton left his horse and brigade flag behind some rocks, got a musket, and joined his regiment, the Eighty-third on the firing line.[91]

The troops in the center of the brigade line were strongly posted among the rocks and held their position against the renewed assault. The danger was on the left, where Oates's line threatened to outflank and envelope the left of the Twentieth Maine and get into Vincent's rear even as other Alabamians and Texans assailed the center and the right. Colonel Oates's description of this portion of the battle corresponds vaguely at best with those given by men toward the left of the Confederate line. Perhaps it was at the time of the pullback of the left regiments from their second assault that the Fourth Alabama allegedly fell back, exposing the left of the Forty-seventh Alabama, which apparently was still under the command of Oates.[92] According to Oates, the Eighty-third Pennsylvania, and possibly the Forty-fourth New York, raked the Forty-seventh Alabama with fire, wounded Lieutenant Colonel Bulger, and disconcerted the men of Bulger's seven companies. It had not been a good day for the Forty-seventh: its colonel had not advanced with the regiment, and now Bulger was down. Major James M. Campbell took command of it and attempted to rally it without great success.[93]

At this time Oates attempted to advance the Fifteenth and swing it left against the left flank of the Federals. He hoped to drive them from their ledge, relieve the Forty-seventh, enfilade the whole Federal line, and drive it from the hill. It was a big order, but it seemed possible. In response to Oates's commands, the Fifteenth advanced about halfway to the enemy's position. There it met a fire so destructive that the Alabama line "wavered like a man trying to walk into a strong wind" and then began to fall back. Oates ordered the Fifteenth forward again and forced his way to the front of the line, where he shouted, "Forward men, to the ledge!" The regiment responded to his leadership and, in Oates's opinion, forced the Federals back uphill to another ledge. The Maine men then counterattacked in turn and charged the Alabamians five times by the Southern count, closing so near that Oates's men had to resort to their bayonets.[94]

The fighting was hot and close, and Oates lost many brave men. When the colonel ordered his troops forward, the noise was so great that Capt. James H. Ellison, commander of Company C, could not hear him. Ellison looked at Oates and cupped his hand to his ear, and Oates shouted again. Ellison ordered his company forward, a bullet passed through his head, and he fell on his side. As Oates watched in horror, Ellison turned on his back, raised his arms, shuddered, and became still. Instead of advancing, the men of Ellison's company gathered around their fallen leader. Oates could not have that and ordered Lt. LeGrand L. Guerry to get the company back in line and move it forward. Company C returned to its work.[95]

As the Fifteenth pressed slowly up the slope, Pvt. William R. Holloway of Company G, Oates's old company, stepped up on a rock beside Oates and said, "Colonel I can't see them." Oates told him to stoop beneath the smoke and look. He did so and then took deliberate aim and fired. As he lowered his rifle, a bullet struck him in the head. Oates caught him as he toppled and lowered him to the ground. Then he picked up Holloway's rifle and fired it a few times in revenge before he returned to the duties of a colonel.[96]

The commander of Company G, Capt. Henry C. Brainard, fell while leading his company at a portion of the Federal line posted on the rock ledge near where Oates was standing. His last words were remembered as "O God, that I could see my mother!"[97] Lt. John A. Oates succeeded to Brainard's command, but he soon fell, struck by several balls. John Oates had been sick that day and was able to reach the field only because the colonel, his brother, secured a horse for him to ride. Just before the advance, the colonel saw him lying on the ground behind his company and told him not to go forward with it. John Oates received this suggestion with indignation, saying: "Brother, I will not do it. If I were to remain here people would say that I did it through cowardice; no, sir, I am an officer and will never disgrace the uniform I wear; I shall go through, unless I am killed, which I think is quite likely."[98]

Oates's effort to extend his line to the right so as to strike Vincent's left did not go unnoticed. Acting Major Ellis Spear, whose post was behind and probably above the left wing of the Twentieth Maine, saw movement that indicated this and told Chamberlain what he thought was happening. Colonel Chamberlain climbed upon a rock for a better view and from it saw a large body of Confederates passing along the saddle toward his left.[99]

The Twentieth was already heavily engaged, and Vincent's brigade had no reserve. Chamberlain had to guard the brigade left with the Twentieth Maine alone. Without giving the officers and men on the firing line the reason for doing so, Chamberlain ordered the regiment to extend its front "by taking intervals by the left flank." At the same time he refused the regiment's left wing so that it was nearly at a right angle with its right. In order to effect the extension, the Twentieth's nine companies stretched to a single rank. In later years Chamberlain described his new line as a horseshoe, though in the late stages of the fight at least, it was closer to the shape of a hairpin. The men of the Twentieth did not yet know of the special threat that faced them, but Chamberlain was pleased to see that the regiment's training was paying off. In his opinion they kept up their fire so effectively during the movement that the enemy had no reason to believe that the thinned line was giving him an advantage.[100]

It should be noted that, unlike the other regiments of the brigade, the Twentieth Maine had neither seen extensive field service nor gained a particularly outstanding reputation. It had been mustered into Federal service in August 1862 and rushed to Washington, where its members learned the basics of soldiering. Adelbert Ames, a brigade commander in the Eleventh Corps at Gettysburg, was its first colonel, and Chamberlain its lieutenant colonel. The regiment had fought at Fredericksburg but had received smallpox vaccinations just before the battle of Chancellorsville, and while the rest of the army fought, it was in quarantine guarding a telegraph line somewhere in the rear. Although it had seen only limited service and had added men from the disbanded Second Maine to its rolls, the Twentieth Maine had but 28 officers and 358 men present for duty on Little Round Top.[101]

Only minutes after the Twentieth's line was lengthened and refused, the Confederates struck Vincent's line, particularly its new left wing, "with an impetuosity which betrayed the anticipation of an easy triumph." The Alabamians came on with yells and a crash of musketry again and again, sometimes coming as close as ten paces. (This must have been the assault described by Colonel Oates.) The opposing lines seesawed up and down the slope, both firing rapidly and well. Chamberlain wrote of being attacked by four lines, but it might have been the same line returning. Who could be certain in the confusion and darkness created by the dusk and the smoke that burned eyes and throats alike? The fighting became hand to hand in places, and squads of the enemy forced their way into the Union position here and there, so that the fallen found themselves lying alternately behind the Union and the Confederate lines. In the words of Chamberlain, "The edge of the fight rolled backward and forward like a wave." When the Alabamians fell back toward the base of the slope to reform their lines, the Maine men tried to bring their wounded within their position and salvage their precious ammunition. They tried also to erect small breastworks of wood and stone, none of which became more than eighteen inches high.[102]

At one time Chamberlain feared greatly that the Twentieth Maine's colors would be lost. Its center companies were riddled badly, the color guard cut down. But then, when the pall of gray smoke parted for a moment, there stood Color Sergeant Andrew J. Tozier on the boulder where the regimental memorial stands today. Tozier stood seemingly alone above the tumult around him; he had planted the butt of the flagstaff at his feet and held it erect in the hollow of his shoulder while he fired a rifle. Seeing his peril, Colonel Chamberlain told his brother, Lt. Thomas D. Chamberlain, the regiment's adjutant, to take some men and give Tozier some help. In order to ensure that the job would get done, the colonel gave the same instructions to Sgt. Ruel Thomas, a staff orderly. At the same time, he asked for help from the Eighty-third Pennsylvania; but the Eighty-third's hands were full, and its commander could not spare a man.[103]

In this melee Colonel Oates fired his pistol at Yankees only a few feet in front of him. Once when Oates was within ten feet of the Fifteenth Alabama's flag, a Maine man tried to grab it. Color-bearer John G. Archibald saw the grasping Yankee in time to step back and allow Sgt. Pat O'Connor to jab his bayonet into the brave fellow's head.[104]

While the Twentieth defended its position, there was fighting all along the brigade front. As Chamberlain's fight boiled to a climax, he could hear a great roar of musketry up the slope to his right rear and feared that the crest behind him had been taken. Likely the roar signaled the arrival of the 140th New York and the repulse of the attack against the brigade right, but Chamberlain had no way of knowing that. He did know one thing—the Eighty-third was stoutly holding its position on the Twentieth's right, and he had no fears for the security of that flank.[105]

About this time, Capt. DeBernie Waddell, Oates's adjutant, asked the colonel if he might take forty or fifty men to the right of the line and advance them from there to some rocks from which they might enfilade Chamberlain's line. It was a lot of men to spare, but Oates gave him permission to do this. Waddell did it, but to no avail.[106] Also about this time, Chamberlain realized that his regiment might not be able to stand up against another heavy assault. A third of the Twentieth was down, and its line was stretched into a single rank without a reserve. The men of the Twentieth had gleaned all of the ammunition that they could find from the slope, and some had even exchanged their Enfields for better rifles apparently dropped by the Alabamians. But things still looked grim. Officers complained with some exaggeration that their companies were nearly annihilated, that their ammunition was almost gone, and that some of their men were beginning to "face to the rear." In the meantime the Alabamians had retired to the saddle as if to reform for another charge.[107]

Oates also believed that his regiment was running out of steam. He received reports of Federal infantry on his right and sent Sgt. Maj. Robert C. Norris to the Fourth Alabama to get some help. Norris returned shortly with the report that the Fourth was not to be seen and with the highly unlikely intelligence that the enemy was swarming in the woods south of Little Round Top. Capts. Frank Park of Company I and Blanton A. Hill of Company D reported that the enemy was closing in on their right rear, and Oates asked Park to find out how many there were. Park left and returned in a short while to say that there were two hundred of them behind a stone fence. Park pointed them out to Oates—yes, here they were, just about two hundred yards away (he must have spotted Morrill's men). The captain suggested a retreat, and Oates began to consider it. He looked around. Bullets seemed to be flying in from several directions. The hillside was a shambles, with blood spattered on the rocks and bodies scattered around. Oates said, "Return to your companies; we will sell out as dearly as possible.[108]

Hill said nothing, but Park saluted, smiled, and simply said, "All right, sir"; then the two walked off. Oates reflected a bit more, saw that there seemed to be little hope for success, and decided to get the Alabamians off the hill. He sent Sergeant Major Norris along the line to tell the company commanders that they should not try to fall back in good order; rather at the signal each man should run back in the direction whence they had come and halt and reform on the summit of Round Top.[109]

Chamberlain, who was equally concerned, chose an opposite course. His regiment could not fall back, and it could no longer hold its position; therefore, it seemed to him that the Twentieth Maine would have to strike before it was struck if it were to survive. At his command the men would fix bayonets, and the left wing would open the counterattack by wheeling right down and across the slope of the hill. When the left wing was on line with the right, the right too would go forward, and they would sweep the Confederates from their front or be destroyed in the attempt.[110]

As Chamberlain prepared for the assault, Lt. Homer Melcher of the color company, Company F, came to him and asked permission to try to recover some wounded men from the slope in front of his company—an indication that the regiment had fallen back from an earlier line. The men of Company F thought it a shame to leave them on the dangerous slope between the lines and would try to rescue them if they could get covering fire. To Melcher's request Chamberlain replied, "Yes, sir. Take your place with your company. I am about to order a 'right wheel forward' of the whole regiment."[111]

His preparations made, the colonel walked to his place behind the color company, behind the apex of the Twentieth's line. By this time the enemy had begun to move—the Federals thought that they were beginning another charge. Oates denied this, so perhaps they were preparing to cover their withdrawal. Chamberlain shouted, "Bayonet!" and the command "ran like fire along the line, from man to man, and rose into a shout, with which they sprang forward upon the enemy, now not 30 yards away." The left wing of the Twentieth Maine, bayonets fixed and leveled, charged down the hill and, under the watchful eye of Major Spear, wheeled right, sweeping the disordered Confederates before it. When the left wing came abreast of the right, the whole line pivoted forward on the Twentieth's right companies "like a reaper cutting down the disconcerted foe." So great seemed the confusion among some of the Confederates that one officer offered his sword to Chamberlain with one hand and fired his pistol at his head with the other.[112]

Colonel Oates recalled it somewhat differently. Said Oates, "I ordered a retreat." The Fifteenth was not driven back in other words; it was ordered back. But the result was about the same, for "when the signal was given we ran like a herd of wild cattle." Oates ran right along with the rest, and Pvt. John Keels ran beside him. Keels had a bullet hole in his windpipe, and as he ran his heavy breathing sprayed blood on the colonel.[113] Captain Morrill's force entered the fight in a very violent way when the retreat began. It raked the retreating Alabamians with fire; and then, with a shout, it charged the Confederate flank, adding to the disorder and doing such a job that Oates believed that two regiments assaulted his flank.[114]

The men of the Twentieth drove the Confederates across the saddle and a short way up the slope of Round Top, where the Maine soldiers became disordered and lost their momentum. Chamberlain halted this advance on Richmond, reformed the regiment, and posted it again in its original position. When Chamberlain counted noses he found only about 200 of the 386 officers and men with whom he had started the battle. Strangely enough, only six of the officers had been wounded, two mortally. Chamberlain had two wounds. Only two men of the color guard remained unhurt, while all of the other noncommissioned officers of the color company were killed or wounded. Six corporals and two sergeants of Company A on the left of the color company were also casualties, testimony to the lethal character of the fighting at the apex of the Twentieth's line.[115] The Twentieth Maine claimed the capture of about four hundred Confederates, mostly from the Fifteenth and Forty-seventh Alabama regiments, though there were men from the Fourth Alabama and the Fifth Texas in their bag as well. This seems to have been an excessive claim, one that Oates disputed in later years as a gross but honest exaggeration. (The reported casualties for Law's brigade were 496.) Oates believed that most of the Fifteenth's losses due to capture, eighty-four men, were from the party taken to the right by Captain Waddell. They had not fallen back quickly enough, and only Waddell was able to escape. Pvt.

William C. Jones had another explanation. He and seven others were behind a large rock when they received the order to retreat. He and another man obeyed the order, and the other man was shot. The remaining six believed it too dangerous to leave the shelter of the rock and became prisoners. Colonel Oates was so fatigued by heat and exertion that he fainted while climbing Round Top and might have been captured had not two soldiers carried him to the rear. The Fifteenth finally reformed in front of Round Top.[116]

Lieutenant Colonel Bulger of the Forty-seventh Alabama was one of those captured. In later years Oates wrote that a captain of the Forty-fourth New York found the fifty-seven-year-old officer sitting with his back against a tree, sword in hand and blood running from a hole in his chest. The captain asked for his sword in surrender, but the feisty colonel refused to give it to an officer of lower rank. The captain sent for Colonel Rice, to whom Bulger surrendered, and Rice arranged for medical care for Bulger that probably saved his life.[117] When Colonel Chamberlain read this story, he denied it. He claimed that Bulger had fallen in front of the right of the Twentieth Maine and that it was he and not Colonel Rice who had arranged for Bulger's care. Chamberlain was probably correct in this, for Bulger ought to have been in front of either the Twentieth Maine or the Eighty-third Pennsylvania and not the Forty-fourth New York.[118]

The third and final assault of the Texans died against the front of the Forty-fourth New York, the Sixteenth Michigan, and the the newly arrived 140th New York. Company K of the Fifth Texas worked its way to within about twenty yards of the Union line and could go no farther. It was a dangerous place to be, for the bullets whizzed around them so thickly that it seemed "a man could hold out a hat and catch it full." Two twin brothers from Company C who were inseparable got into K Company's line. A bullet hit one, and his brother caught him and lowered him gently to the earth. Before he could rise, the second boy was also shot, and the two remained together on Little Round Top. Capt. Robert W. Hubert called for Company K to stand fast, but it was a futile thing to do, for at the time there were only three officers and eight enlisted men there to obey him.[119]

Valerius C. Giles of the Fifth Texas fired his rifle so often that its barrel became fouled and the ramrod stuck in it. Giles finished ramming by pounding the ramrod's head against a boulder. This done, he yelled "look out!" and pulled the trigger. The gun roared and flew from his grasp, striking another Texan in the ear. There were loud curses heard above the noise of battle. It was then that Giles became aware that there were rifles strewn all over the slope and that a cleaner one might be had for picking it up.[120]

But darkness was at hand, and the Texans' attack had been repulsed; they had done all they could, and they knew it. Friendly artillery shells with fuses cut too short burst above them and encouraged disorder along the Texas line. There was a lot of shouting, private soldiers gave commands as loudly as officers, and no one paid attention to either.[121] Finally, at someone's order the Texas regiments pulled back and reformed on Round Top's shoulder southeast of Devil's Den. Colonel Powell of the Fifth Texas was so badly wounded that he was left behind. The noise of battle faded into a quiet that prompted Powell to raise his head to see what was happening. He saw, as a symbol of the end of the fight, a sergeant from his regiment simply walk down the slope, stop and leisurely pick up a ramrod that was leaning against a rock, and then continue into the cover of the woods. Many minutes passed before Union soldiers came down the hill in search of wounded. By then it was almost dark.[122]

But the Forty-fourth New York took a number of prisoners when the fighting ended. First Sergeant Consider A. Willet of Company E, the Normal School company, saw numerous Confederates stranded on the hillside in their front. He arranged covering fire, if needed, and took a half dozen men forward with him to bring them in. All told, the Forty-fourth claimed to have picked up ninety prisoners that evening.[123] John W. Stevens of the Fifth Texas was probably one of them. He fired at the blue line from the shelter of a rock. Though many Texans fell around him, he had little personal fear of being hit by enemy fire—it was the fire of Confederates in his rear that worried him. When he saw Texans fall back, he was certain that they would return, so he waited for them in the shelter of his rock. Suddenly a sword blade slapped him across the back, and an order came like a thunderclap for him to throw down his gun and behave himself. He looked around in surprise to see blue uniforms everywhere. He was a prisoner of war.[124]

Colonel Rice claimed the capture of more than 500 Confederates for Vincent's brigade that evening and more than 1,000 stands of arms, a worthy haul even if exaggerated. One of the Forty-fourth New York's prisoners stood before Captain Nathaniel Husted and begged not to be shot. As he did so a bullet that might have been intended for Husted struck the poor fellow in the back. The 44th sent its prisoners to the rear and settled itself back into the position that had served it so well.[125]

Though they had fallen back, the Texans were still not far away. They probably reformed on the rise above Devil's Den where they had formed for their attacks. Things were quieter there, but a counterattack was still possible. There was initial confusion in the ranks. Private Giles recalled that after a while the men of the Fifth Texas were lying down, taking advantage of the available cover, and that only Major Rogers and another officer were standing. Major Rogers, as the regiment's new commander, thought that it was incumbent upon him to say something. He climbed upon a log and launched into a "Fourth of July" speech to which few listened. As he spoke, a courier from General Law rode up, saluted, and said, "General Law presents his compliments, and says hold this place at all hazards." Major Rogers glared at the rider from his perch on the log and shouted in reply, "Compliments, hell!

Who wants any compliments in such a damned place as this? Go back and ask General Law if he expects me to hold the world in check with the Fifth Texas Regiment!"[126]

While Vincent's brigade and the 140th New York received and repelled the last assault by Hood's division, the remainder of Weed's brigade hurried to the hill. No one said so, but it is likely that Weed rode ahead and left his three remaining regiments to follow at their slower pace. Theirs was not an orderly arrival. The men scrambled up the hill as best they could, and some of Hazlett's guns and caissons interfered with their approach. Some men left the ranks to help the cannoneers, though they and their rifles probably were needed on the crest just then more than their help was needed with the cannons.[127] There was confusion on the summit: the barking of the guns in position, the zip and whine of Confederate minié balls, the explosion of Confederate shells, the crash of musketry to the left, and the disorder associated with the movement all contributed. Weed took measures to straighten things out. He saw to the posting of the regiments' colors and had the colonels align their men on them. Most occupied lines near the crest, but some were sent down the slope as skirmishers.[128]

There were differences of opinion in later years about the fighting that the latecomers were able to do. Some recalled that the enemy swarmed in their front when they reached the crest and that there was close fighting. Others recalled a half-hour lull, and perhaps both recollections contained some truth. It was possible that remnants of Hood's division were still on the hill when the troops following the 140th New York arrived and that cannon fire intended for Hazlett's battery and rifle fire from Devil's Den fell among their ranks. It seems unlikely, however, that Weed's last three regiments assisted materially in the repulse of the left of Hood's line. The 140th New York would have been more than capable of taking care of the job that needed to be done.[129]

The brigade settled in among the rocks and prepared for action. Though Hood's men had been beaten back, it is likely that McLaws's troops were still attacking across the Wheatfield area in their front. The Ninety-first Pennsylvania went into position on the right of the 140th New York near the high point of the hill, and the 146th New York and the 155th Pennsylvania continued their line northward along the crest and the upper north slope. As soon as they deployed, Weed's men strengthened their position by piling up rock walls along their front.[130]

In the meantime, Capt. Frank C. Gibbs's Battery L, First Ohio Light Artillery, was taking position to Hazlett's right on the north slope of the hill. Lt. Herbert F. Guthrie's section went in south of the Wheatfield Road, while the remaining two sections took position to the right of the road, where they could better cover the Plum Run Valley. The ground occupied by Gibbs's guns was so rough that they had to be unlimbered and shoved in by hand.[131]

Two other Fifth Corps batteries entered the area. One, Capt. Almont

Barnes's battery (C, First New York Light Artillery), followed Ayres's division to the field and was guided only by Captain Martin's admonition to "follow the Regulars and don't let Sickles get you." On his own initiative Barnes placed his four three-inch rifles to the right of Gibbs's battery. It was a poor position with practically no field of fire to the front, though the battery could fire obliquely down Plum Run Valley if the occasion warranted. Barnes's battery played little or no active part in the battle of 2 July and suffered no casualties.[132]

Martin's orders to his battery commanders to be wary of Sickles were not entirely idle ones. Sickles's staff did shanghai Watson's and Walcott's batteries. Watson's adventures will be discussed in Chapter 13. Captain Martin left his former command—the Third Massachusetts Battery, now under Lt. Aaron F. Walcott—somewhere behind Barnes's division on the stony hill with instructions to stay there until he ordered it elsewhere. But a Third Corps officer discovered it and told Walcott, who was commanding the battery for the first time and possibly was impressionable, that he had the authority to commandeer the service of any battery that he could find no matter to whom it belonged. Walcott believed him. As a result, his six Napoleons ended up on a slight rise on the north side of the Wheatfield Road just east of Plum Run. Because of the boulders there and a stone fence that bordered the lane to the J. Weikert house, Walcott had a hard time putting his guns into position. How he used them there we shall see in Chapter 16.[133]

While his batteries took position on the ridge line below, Captain Martin was on Little Round Top with Sykes, Weed, and others, watching the course of the battle in the fields below. Had they been there long enough, they would have seen the Confederate expulsion of the Third Corps left from Devil's Den, the sweep of Caldwell's division across the Wheatfield, and the occupation of the Plum Run Valley in their front by Ayres's division. They would have been aware of the Confederates' last efforts to shatter Vincent's line on the south slope of the hill nearby and would have witnessed their withdrawal to the shelter of the trees on Round Top's southwest slope. Thanks to the misfortune and mismanagement that plagued the Confederates' brave effort, Warren's good fortune, and the tenacity of Vincent, O'Rorke, and others of the Fifth Corps, Little Round Top and the Union left seemed secure. But there was still fighting in the darkening Wheatfield area below and in the fields far to their right. It was an awesome spectacle that so impressed Weed that he remarked to his old subordinate: "Martin I would rather die on this spot than see those rascals gain one inch of ground." He provided for the contingency of his death by having Capt. Edgar Warren tell Col. Kenner Garrard of the 146th New York that Garrard would take command of the brigade in the event that he was shot.[134]

After talking with Weed, Martin walked to another part of the crest to talk with General Sykes. From his vantage point Sykes could see that Caldwell's division might soon need support on its left, and he sent Lt. George T.

Ingham to General Ayres with instructions to advance his division into Rose's Woods. Before he reached Sykes, Martin glanced back in the direction whence he had come and saw Weed fall forward.[135] Weed fell near Lieutenant Rittenhouse's section of Hazlett's battery. A corporal called Rittenhouse's attention to Weed's fall, and Rittenhouse hurried to him. He discovered that Weed had been shot and was paralyzed from the shoulders down. Rittenhouse bent over the fallen Weed, who said, "I am cut in two, I want to see Hazlett."[136]

Rittenhouse sent for Hazlett, who rode over, dismounted, kneeled at Weed's side, and spoke with him. Rittenhouse overheard Weed say something about the payment of some small debts; then, possibly because he had something confidential to say, he pulled Hazlett closer to him. There was a thud, and Hazlett slumped forward, a bullet through his head.[137] Cannoneers of his battery carried Hazlett to the aid station a few yards to the rear. Rittenhouse tried to speak with his battery commander, but Hazlett did not reply. Rittenhouse ordered the battery bugler to take Hazlett to the hospital and stay with him as long as he lived. Rittenhouse then returned to the guns. At about the same time, Capt. Edgar Warren walked to the north end of the crest to find Colonel Garrard and tell him that he was in command of the brigade.[138]

They carried Weed also to the aid station behind the crest, where surgeons might attend him. Lt. William H. Crennell of the 140th New York, who acted as Weed's aide that day, tried to comfort the general by saying, "General, I hope that you are not so very badly hurt." To this Weed replied, "I'm as dead a man as Julius Caesar."[139]

The Opening Attacks
in the Wheatfield

Col. Philippe Regis Denis de Kerenden de Trobriand must have seemed somewhat out of place among the officers of the Army of the Potomac. He was an exotic, unique in the army of the American republic even among the cosmopolites from the better families of Boston, New York, and Philadelphia. There were some Europeans of note in the Eleventh Corps, of course, but a Carl Schurz or an Adolph von Steinwehr was not exactly a de Trobriand. The aristocratic, cultured Frenchman must have seemed like someone from the retinue of the Duc de Chartres and the Comte de Paris who had tarried behind for some serious work when those titled visitors to the Army of the Potomac returned to France. But appearances can be somewhat deceiving.

Colonel de Trobriand was an aristocrat to be sure. He had been born in a château near Tours, France, in 1816, a younger son of a genuine baron of ancient lineage who was a general in the army of France. Young de Trobriand was not slated to inherit his father's barony or inclined to carve out a career in the French army; instead he studied in Paris and at the Universities of Tours and Poitiers. Although a lawyer by training, he turned his talents to poetry and prose and published a novel in 1840. He fought duels as a young man; and if he was bested in any of them, he obviously suffered no mortal wound. De Trobriand visited the United States in 1841, hobnobbed with the social elite of New York City, and wooed and won an heiress with the plain American name of Mary Jones. The young couple lived in Europe for a time but then returned permanently to New York City, where de Trobriand, fittingly, kept himself occupied by writing and editing for French language publications. This period in de Trobriand's life ended in 1861 when he became a citizen of the United States and the colonel of the Fifty-fifth New York Volunteer Infantry Regiment, the LaFayette Guard.

Colonel de Trobriand commanded the Fifty-fifth in the Army of the Potomac's campaigns through Fredericksburg. Then the depleted regiment was merged with the Thirty-eighth New York. He commanded the Thirty-eighth at Chancellorsville, and when the Third Corps was reorganized, he received command of the Third Brigade of its First (Birney's) Division. He led this brigade to Gettysburg and to the Wheatfield.[1] As previously indicated, de Trobriand's brigade occupied the stony hill area on the west side of the Wheatfield, midway between Ward's brigade at Devil's Den and Graham's at the Peach Orchard. One of his regiments, the Third Michigan, was on the corps skirmish line between Rose's farmyard and the Emmitsburg Road and probably was not under his direct control. Another, the Fifth Michigan, manned the skirmish line near Rose's farmyard. The 110th Pennsylvania was in position near the base of the stony hill, fronting the ravine of the west branch of Plum Run and Rose's Woods; and the remaining two regiments, the Fortieth New York and the Seventeenth Maine, were in reserve in the rear, close to the Wheatfield Road. The brigade's position was a strong point on a weakly manned line that Birney and his staff worked feverishly to strengthen.

Birney cannibalized Burling's brigade to meet his needs, parceling its regiments out to various places along the division's front. The unfortunate Burling labored to dispatch his regiments to their assigned positions until only two remained under his direct command; then someone—Birney, Sickles, or a staff officer—commandeered one of these. It was the Eighth New Jersey, 170 strong, and it was led to the southwest corner of the Wheatfield and posted behind the stone wall there. Soon after, it shifted to the right, into the gap between Rose's Woods and the stony hill. Under Col. John Ramsey's direction the men of the Eighth tried to strengthen their position by piling up a breastwork of fence rails. Although the Eighth New Jersey was in de Trobriand's sector, there is no reason to believe that the French colonel was given or assumed command over it, and certainly it did not operate under Burling's control. When Burling discovered that the Eighth had been taken from him and that he had only the 115th Pennsylvania still at hand, he told its commander, Maj. John P. Dunne, to report to General Birney. Burling and his staff then reported back to General Humphreys for instructions.[2]

Colonel de Trobriand could not watch the early progress of Hood's assault from his brigade's position because Rose's Woods obscured his view. But his ear was attuned to the sounds of battle, and he was able to gauge Hood's progress by the noise that accompanied it. The cracking of skirmishers' rifles, the distant shouts, and Rebel yell's marked Hood's advance. Later the crash of musketry and the rapid barking of Smith's Parrotts, Union cheers, and Rebel yells told him that Hood's men were grappling with Ward's brigade in the woods to his left front. Then, at Birney's order, he sent the Seventeenth Maine Regiment to the stone wall between the Wheatfield and Rose's Woods and the Fortieth New York to the main branch of Plum Run. The Seventeenth, as stated in Chapter 9, helped Ward's regiments repel the left of

Hood's first line and settled in to await additional assaults that were sure to come.[3]

When de Trobriand ordered the Seventeenth and Fortieth regiments from his support line to the firing line, he bared the right of his brigade's position to assault from the west. Perhaps this concerned him, but any concern that he felt was not reflected in his later writings. Without doubt he had some assurance from Birney that his brigade's right would be covered, for Sykes had agreed with Birney that the Fifth Corps would occupy the stony hill so that Birney could increase his strength at Devil's Den. Still, in retrospect de Trobriand seemed little concerned about his possible vulnerability in that quarter.

Sykes placed two brigades of his First Division there. This division's commander, Brig. Gen. Charles Griffin, had been wounded at Chancellorsville, and Brig. Gen. James Barnes, commander of the division's First Brigade, led it to Gettysburg. Barnes's division was the first Fifth Corps division to reach the Union left. Vincent's brigade went to Little Round Top while its First and Second brigades marched to the stony hill. The two brigades did not arrive in the blink of an eye, though it was written that the First Brigade under Col. William S. Tilton of the Twenty-second Massachusetts moved quickly and that Col. Jacob B. Sweitzer put his Second Brigade in position promptly. Tilton's brigade had only 654 officers and men in its four regiments; Sweitzer's, 1,010 in its three. In their combined strength they were about the size of a single average brigade at Gettysburg.[4] It is likely that they approached in a column of fours that must have measured about six to seven hundred yards from front to rear. Therefore, it would have taken about ten minutes for them to pass a given point and much longer for them to form lines in the places designated by General Sykes. Much could have happened on the Third Corps front in the time that it took them to occupy the hill.[5]

Sometime in the course of Sweitzer's brigade's approach there was a halt, and some of the men of the Fourth Michigan Regiment received permission to fill their canteens. The only water nearby was in a ditch, but it had to do. Pvt. James Houghton got his by pushing the scum on the water to the side. Then he slapped the bared surface with the flat of his hand to drive the insects and wigglers away and filled the canteen with water free of flora and fauna. This done, he hurried back to his place in the ranks.[6]

The division's temporary commander, Brig. Gen. James Barnes, was from Massachusetts, distinguished in appearance and in civilian accomplishment. He was sixty-one years old and had been a West Point classmate of Robert E. Lee. Certainly he was one of the older generation of officers on the battlefield. After about seven years of active service as an artillery lieutenant, he resigned his commission and embarked on a career in railroading. He became superintendent of the Western Railroad in 1839 and had his offices in his hometown, Boston. He lived there, comfortably no doubt, until the war began and he went into active sevice again as colonel of the Eighteenth Massachusetts Regiment. He and the Eighteenth joined the Fifth Corps. Barnes commanded the First Brigade of its First Division at Antietam, became a brigadier general, and commanded the brigade at Fredericksburg and Chancellorsville. In this time Barnes "secured the esteem and confidence of his subordinates and the admiration and regard of his soldiers."[7]

Col. Jacob Sweitzer's brigade arrived first, and Sykes told Sweitzer where he should place its right. Jacob Bowman Sweitzer's name was not a household word in 1863. He had entered service as major of the Sixty-second Pennsylvania Regiment and became its colonel in June 1862. He commanded the Second Brigade for the first time at Fredericksburg and continued to command it after Gettysburg until he left the service in the summer of 1864—all without getting a star. He did receive a brevet as brigadier general on 13 March 1865 in belated recogniton of his war service, but by that time he was again practicing law. He was an attorney and court official in Pittsburgh until his death in 1888. A year later, at Gettysburg, the veterans of his old regiment spoke of him with affection and termed him the "brave and ever faithful colonel of the regiment."[8]

Sweitzer's brigade had but three regiments with it—the Sixty-second Pennsylvania, the Fourth Michigan, and the Thirty-second Massachusetts. The Fourth Michigan took position on the brigade right in the north end of the woods and fronted west toward the Peach Orchard. The Sixty-second was next in line, and the Thirty-second was on the left in the low, open, and exposed ground at the south end of the hill, probably to the right of the Eighth New Jersey and 110th Pennsylvania and possibly even in their fields of fire. Sweitzer saw that the Thirty-second's position would not do. He directed the commander of the Thirty-second, Col. George L. Prescott, to move the Thirty-second back up the slope on line with Tilton's brigade. In its new position it was refused from the brigade's line and fronted across the Plum Run ravine toward Rose's Woods.[9]

The First Brigade, Barnes's, commanded temporarily by Col. William S. Tilton of the Twenty-second Massachusetts, went in on an angle to Sweitzer's on its left front. Tilton's left regiment, the Twenty-second, was on the nose of the hill, its southwest slope, and the brigade extended westerly down the hill's west slope toward Plum Run's course east of the Rose barn. Col. Ira C. Abbott's First Michigan Regiment continued the line from the Twenty-second down into the thumb of trees that protruded west from those on the hill, and the 118th Pennsylvania Regiment, the Corn Exchange Regiment, was on the right. Instead of allowing the 118th's right to tail away into the low ground near the stream, Lt. Col. James Gwyn refused it, pulled it back, so that its right wing faced west toward the Rose barn. Tilton's remaining regiment, the Eighteenth Massachusetts, which had only 120 men, occupied a second line behind the brigade's left center and near the crest of the hill. For reasons not explained, it stood in a double line, four ranks deep. It is both interesting and confusing to note that initially the two brigades were connected by their respective left flanks.[10]

It is hard to determine when Barnes's two brigades took their places on the hill. Was it before the Seventeenth Maine shifted over to the stone wall? Was it after the Seventeenth went to the wall but before Anderson's brigade attacked? Or was it during the lull between Anderson's first and second assaults? Colonel de Trobriand, who should have been aware of developments on his right, claimed to know nothing of their presence until during or after Anderson's second assault, when the Federal situation became precarious. On the other hand, Colonel Egan of the Fortieth New York reported that Fifth Corps units had relieved the Fortieth on the stony hill so that they could go to Ward's left in the Plum Run Valley. The Fortieth departed, according to de Trobriand, "soon after" the Seventeenth went over to the wall.[11] General Barnes, however, insisted that his two brigades were in place before the engagement commenced on his front. Tilton reported that the Confederates attacked almost immediately after his line was formed, and Sweitzer wrote that his brigade had not been in position long before the assault struck Tilton's front and that of the Thirty-second Massachusetts.[12] This testimony together with some homely incidents mentioned below suggest that the Fifth Corps troops were on the stony hill prior to the assault of Anderson's brigade.

Certainly if Barnes's two brigades were in position at the time of Anderson's first assault, they took little or no active part in repelling it. That fell to the Eighth New Jersey and later perhaps the 115th Pennsylvania regiments of Burling's brigade and to de Trobriand's four regiments. The Seventeenth Maine on de Trobriand's left stood behind the stone wall, a barrier a little less than three feet high, and looked down a slope that ran through Rose's Woods to Plum Run. The Seventeenth's left extended midway along the wall to a boulder close enough to Ward's right so that the Twentieth Indiana, whose line was at nearly right angles to the Seventeenth's, and the Seventeenth could cover the gap between them with a heavy cross fire. The right of the Seventeenth, in contrast, stood in the marshy ground beyond the rivulet and a rail fence that marked the southwest corner of the Wheatfield. Companies K and C were there. Company C's right rested near a heavy clump of alders that partially closed the gap between the stony hill and Rose's Woods. Its men knew that there were Union troops beyond the alders but could not see them. They assumed that they belonged to either the 110th Pennsylvania or the Fifth Michigan Regiment, for they did not know that the Eighth New Jersey and 115th Pennsylvania, as such, were even in the area.[13]

After the Seventeenth Maine helped Ward's brigade drive back the Third Arkansas and the First Texas, Brig. Gen. George T. ("Tige") Anderson stormed briefly onto the scene. Anderson was a native of Covington, Georgia, who was thirty-nine years old. After attending Emory College, he served a year as a lieutenant during the Mexican War with a Georgia cavalry com-

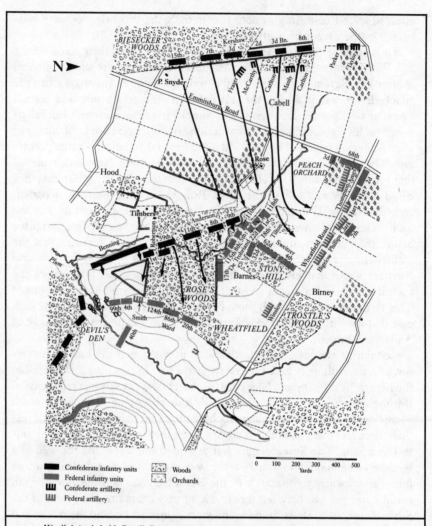

N►

1. Ward's brigade holds Devil's Den against the opening assaults of Robertson and Benning.

2. De Trobriand's brigade plus the 115th Pennsylvania and Eighth New Jersey regiments hold the wall along the south side of the Wheatfield and the south slope of the stony hill. Tilton's and Sweitzer's brigades occupy the stony hill.

3. Anderson's brigade advances through Rose's Woods to attack Ward's right and de Trobriand. Benning and Robertson attack Ward's left.

4. The Eighth New Jersey and 115th Pennsylvania withdraw. Anderson is repelled.

5. Anderson reforms and attacks again with Kershaw on his left. Kershaw strikes the stony hill from the west.

6. Tilton's and Sweitzer's brigades fall back to Trostle's Woods.

7. De Trobriand's and Ward's brigades retire beyond the Wheatfield. De Trobriand fights a delaying action from the north end of the Wheatfield.

8. The Confederates occupy Rose's Woods, Devil's Den, and the stony hill.

Map 11-1. The Wheatfield: The Opening Attack

pany. Following that he secured a commission in the Regular Army and was a captain in the Second U.S. Cavalry Regiment when he resigned his commission in 1858. Anderson became colonel of the Eleventh Georgia Regiment in 1861, and as a colonel he led his brigade in the Seven Days battles and in the Maryland Campaign. He became a brigadier general in November 1862, was transferred from David R. Jones's division to Hood's, and fought with it at Fredericksburg.[14]

Anderson's brigade advanced to Robertson's relief at about the time that Hood was wounded. It passed east north of the Timbers buildings as it advanced, swept Federal skirmishers from its front though not its flank, stampeded some cattle, and entered Rose's Woods. It scuffled and slid into Plum Run's ravine and pushed uphill toward the Federal line. Anderson's right regiment, the Fifty-ninth Georgia, joined the line of the Third Arkansas. The Eleventh and Eighth prolonged the brigade line northwesterly through the woods, and the Ninth Georgia, on the left, approached the ravine area near the stony hill. The men of the Ninth advanced more slowly than their comrades on their right. Artillery fire harassed them until they gained the cover of the woods, and skirmishers from the Third and Fifth Michigan regiments picked away at their left. A staff officer, Lt. William A. Tennille, approached Capt. George Hillyer on the left. Tennille told Hillyer that all the field officers were down and that he was now commander of the regiment. Tennille also told Hillyer that Anderson wanted him to refuse his left three companies. Hillyer tried to pivot them by shouting the necessary commands, but they could not hear him. He had to turn them by gesturing to each commander.[15]

The regiments along de Trobriand's line braced themselves for Anderson's blow. The men of the 110th Pennsylvania, who stood in the open ground at the base of the stony hill, heard a Rebel yell from the high ground in the woods beyond Plum Run. Then "a flock of cattle and hogs," flushed by the Confederate line, stampeded by them, and soon they saw a line of Rebel legs high on the slope above the stream. The Georgians descended the slope and, under fire, pushed to the cover of Plum Run's bank. By this time, the 110th, the Fifth Michigan, and probably the 115th Pennsylvania and Eighth New Jersey, were heavily engaged with the Georgians in their front. To the left the riflemen of the Seventeenth Maine opened on the Georgians in Rose's Woods at a range of seventy-five yards. Their fire slowed Anderson's brigade's assault but certainly did not halt it.[16]

It must have been about this time that some men on the right of the Seventeenth Maine saw a small force, led by an officer on a gray horse, marching through the Wheatfield toward their right. A shell exploded near it and unhorsed the officer. The formation scattered a bit but reformed and continued toward the Seventeenth's right. The men of the Seventeenth did not know the unit's identity, but likely it was Burling's last and smallest regiment, the 115th Pennsylvania, commanded by Maj. John P. Dunne. The

Brig. Gen. Joseph B. Kershaw (MOLLUS-
MASS/U.S.A.M.H.I., Carlisle Barracks, Pa.)

Brig. Gen. George T. Anderson
(National Archives)

Col. Jacob B. Sweitzer (MOLLUS-MASS/
U.S.A.M.H.I., Carlisle Barracks, Pa.)

Col. William S. Tilton
(National Archives)

Col. P. Regis de Trobriand
(National Archives)

unhorsed officer could have been Dunne, but more likely it was a staff officer, for Dunne was able to lead his men to the wall west of the alders, where he posted them between the bushes and the Eighth New Jersey. There the 115th opened on the Eighth Georgia Regiment in its front.[17]

The Georgians pressed closer, some in open order, taking advantage of the cover offered by the trees and rocks. The six Napoleons of Winslow's battery, posted on the crest of the rise three hundred yards to the Seventeenth's rear, hurled their iron balls over the Seventeenth's line "in a quartering direction." Before the infantry fight began, General Hunt, strangely enough, had ordered Winslow to fire at the base of a smoke column in the distance thought to mark the position of some of Longstreet's guns. Winslow complied by firing a few solid shot at the smoke, but he could not assess the damage done, and he decided that the target was beyond his battery's range. Actually it was not, but there were better marks not far away.[18]

When Robertson's brigade struck Ward's line, General Birney rode up to the battery and ordered Winslow to fire solid shot toward the sound of the Confederate musketry. Winslow's gunners pointed the muzzles of their pieces high enough so that the balls would clear the Federal line in their immediate front and fired away. There was a slight chance that the fire could have been effective so long as it avoided the Federal lines and was on target, for Winslow's guns were so positioned that they could practically have enfiladed Robertson's and Benning's lines. Once the fighting opened on the front of the Seventeenth Maine, though, Winslow's battery had an even better opportunity. The gunners still could not see their targets, a major drawback, but they had a better idea of where they were and had a better chance of wreaking havoc upon them. They simply fired over the Maine line and into the trees of Rose's Woods. Captain Randolph believed that this fire was very effective, "as such use of solid shot always is when troops are engaged in woods, the moral effect being at least equal to the physical. . . ."[19]

The crash of musketry, the roar of Napoleons, and the cracking of splintered trees "made a fearful din." But in spite of all the noise, the men on the right of the Seventeenth's line could hear the zip of bullets flying by them from their rear. Lt. Edward Moore, commander of Company C, asked Lt. George Verrill to go back and see who was doing the shooting. Verrill did so and found a small force behind them that seemed to be at fault. He urged it to come forward to the Seventeenth's right, but he could not persuade it to do so. Instead, it withdrew.[20]

Verrill noticed also that the Georgians were taking advantage of the cover afforded by the banks of Plum Run to sidle left toward the Federal position beyond the alders. Then there seemed to be a movement among the Federal troops posted there. The men of the Seventeenth did not know it at the time, but Burling's two regiments were pulling back to avoid being flanked. The Eighth New Jersey's flag got caught in the branches of a tree. The regiment stayed with the flag until the color bearer freed it but paid for the short delay in casualties, including Col. John Ramsey, who was wounded. Both the Eighth New Jersey and the 115th Pennsylvania pulled back into the Wheatfield behind de Trobriand's line. When the 115th reached Winslow's guns, the captain begged Major Dunne to stay and give the battery infantry support. Dunne assented, and the 115th knelt in line to the battery's right, between it and the woods on the stony hill.[21]

When Burling's two regiments fell back, they exposed the right flank of the Seventeenth Maine to enemy attack. Verrill believed that the fighting had been going on from thirty to forty minutes by that time. Lieutenant Moore then sent Verrill on a second errand—to tell the Seventeenth's field officers of the new threat. Probably it had not yet developed sufficiently so that it was apparent to them. Verrill jogged over to the center, where he found Maj. George W. West near the color company. Major West told Verrill that the right should be refused and that it should be done without haste and confusion. Lt. Charles W. Roberts, the adjutant, soon appeared on the right with orders for the Seventeenth's three right companies—H, K, and C—to pull back behind the remnants of the rail fence that ran back perpendicular to the wall and the regiment's front and separated the Wheatfield from the soggy ground by the stony hill. Lt. Col. Charles B. Merrill appeared then, and under his supervision the three companies swung back while firing, so that the Seventeenth now fronted in two directions. Seven companies faced over the wall into the woods and three toward their right into the alders, now about fifty yards away, and toward the gap at the base of the nose of the stony hill.[22]

The noise was now terrible, the fighting fierce. General Anderson's old regiment, the Eleventh Georgia, opened a galling fire on the blue line across the wall, causing it to recoil, and the Georgians surged forward and placed their battle flag upon the wall. But the Seventeenth's line was resilient, not brittle, and its soldiers considered the presence of the Georgia flag upon the wall an affront. The Maine men rallied and pushed for the flaunted flag and thrust those that carried and guarded it back from the wall into Rose's Woods. They captured one Georgian, a brave fellow who, in the brief lull that followed, they exhibited along the Maine line as something of an honored guest and praised as a "gallant prisoner" and "model soldier."[23]

In the meantime the Eighth Georgia and part of the Ninth were trying their luck against the Seventeenth's right and against de Trobriand's regiments on the south slope of the stony hill. As the Georgians pushed against the Fifth Michigan and the 110th Pennsylvania, which were strongly posted on the slope above them, the Seventeenth's refused companies raked their flank. Then, when the Georgians pushed toward the Seventeenth, they received flank fire from the two regiments on the slope. It was a hellish place to be, and the Georgians could not push ahead until McLaws came to their help on the left.[24]

Tige Anderson saw readily enough that his brigade was in trouble. Its left could not advance without help on the left. The Fifty-ninth Georgia on the right had lost its momentum quickly and attributed its failure to exhaustion. Its men, like others no doubt, had double-quicked four hundred yards in the heat of a July day to reach the enemy, and they needed some time to recover. Anderson rode to the Eleventh Georgia's rear and ordered Col. Francis H. Little to break off the assault. Little was wounded soon thereafter and Lt. Col. William Luffman took charge. The Georgians under Luffman would have to fall back to the far edge of the woods where it was relatively quiet, reform, and try again.[25]

After pulling his brigade back, Anderson went to the left to find Colonel De Saussure's Fifteenth South Carolina Regiment in order to get its cooperation in the next assault. Anderson wrote nothing of the arrangements made, but they apparently satisfied him, and he returned to his brigade. His staff was dispersed on errands, and he walked alone toward the right of his line to oversee its preparations for the next attack. As he passed a large boulder, a minié ball struck his right thigh. Tige Anderson was wounded and out of the fight. The command of the brigade now fell to Lieutenant Colonel Luffman of the Eleventh Georgia.[26]

After an hour of fighting, there was a lull. By this time Barnes's two brigades, his own under Tilton and Sweitzer's, certainly occupied the stony hill and were prepared to do battle. The Twenty-second Massachusetts had skirmishers out, probably near the Rose house. There was firing then, for back in the line of the Twenty-second Massachusetts, the Yankees could hear the "melancholy ring" of the Rose farm's bell as bullets struck it. Lt. Edwin C. Bennett, who had charge of the stretcher-bearers and ambulances serving Tilton's brigade, placed his stretchers four paces behind the brigade line, where the bearers would wait until they had wounded to carry away.[27]

A few yards to the left Cpl. Oscar W. West of the Thirty-second Massachusetts collected some canteens and asked his captain if he could go down to Plum Run and fill them. The captain said no, for if he permitted West to do so and he was killed, the captain would be blamed. West persisted and, perhaps in the tradition of New England democracy, the captain permitted West to take his request to the colonel. The colonel heard West out and remarked that there was going to be a battle. To this West replied with some logic that that was why he wanted the water. This clinched it, and the colonel allowed West to go. West went down to the run and filled the canteens, an indication that as yet there were probably no battle casualties lying in that part of Plum Run and that the water was being polluted only by the usual runoff of Rose's farmyard, which did not count.[28]

De Trobriand and others might have found no fault with the stony hill position, but Barnes and Tilton had qualms about it. Apart from the Third Michigan, which was deployed as skirmishers, there was no infantry between the hill and the Peach Orchard three hundred yards to the right. The batteries that covered this gap were along the road about three hundred yards to the rear, but artillery without infantry support was vulnerable. There was some insurance in Sweitzer's two regiments, which partially connected Tilton's position with the batteries, but they did not fill the gap. Barnes called Sykes's attention to the problem as he saw it but apparently got little satisfaction. Once Tilton and Sweitzer were posted, Sykes rode off to see to the posting of the remainder of his corps.[29] In light of later happenings it is somewhat ironic that Barnes and the Third Corps generals in his area had similar concerns.

In the lull after Anderson's first assault an unsuccessful effort was made to supply the Third Corps regiments with ammunition; the Seventeenth Maine's valiant prisoner was sent to the rear; and the wounded were helped from the firing line. It was probably at this time that General Birney asked de Trobriand for another regiment. The colonel told the aide to tell Birney that his brigade's hands were full and that it would need reinforcements in fifteen minutes. He observed later that his brigade fought a superior force, and if the Confederates had charged with bayonets, his men would have been swept from the field. But instead the Confederates contented themselves with firing, and the Federals' better position enabled them to hold on.[30]

Another test was coming. According to Kershaw's recollections, about an hour had passed since his brigade had arrived on Seminary Ridge. It was time for McLaws's division to give Hood's some active support. An order to cease fire traveled down the line of Cabell's battalion and perhaps Alexander's as well. The cannoneers sponged their pieces, loaded, and waited impatiently while Federal shells whistled and exploded around them. Then one battery commander in Cabell's battalion (no one mentioned which one) ordered a salvo from three of his guns. At his command, the guns fired in measured succession: 1 - 2 - 3. There was a pause to give the salvo emphasis as a signal, and the Confederate batteries returned to their firing.[31] No one recorded who decided when it was time for McLaws to advance and the signal for it. General Law, needing support on his left, had spoken to Kershaw and probably to others. Kershaw waited for orders from McLaws, and McLaws awaited "General Longstreet's will." Longstreet was nearby, and it is reasonable to assume that he determined when McLaws's division should attack and that he or a member of his staff, with Alexander's help, contrived the signal for it.[32]

At the salvo signal, Kershaw's men stepped over the wall in their front, formed ranks, and awaited the command to go forward. Col. John W. Henagan's Eighth South Carolina was on the left of the brigade line near the Warfield house; the Third South Carolina Battalion, commanded by Lt. Col. William G. Rice, was on its right, and Col. John D. Kennedy's Second South Carolina was next in line. These three units constituted Kershaw's left wing. The Third South Carolina Regiment under Maj. Robert C. Maffett and Col. D. Wyatt Aiken's Seventh Regiment stood in order to the right. The Fifteenth South Carolina waited alone beyond Cabell's guns near the Snyder house. All told, there must have been about 1,800 men in line. All regimental officers were on foot, and at Kershaw's command the brigade advanced "with great steadiness and precision, followed by Semmes with equal promptness." A line of skirmishers commanded by Maj. William Wallace of the Second South Carolina screened the brigade front.[33]

Although the Federal force opposite Kershaw seemed much stronger than it had been earlier in the day and although some plans had changed, Kershaw's orders remained essentially the same. His brigade was still to cross the Emmitsburg Road, which angled two to six hundred yards in its front, wheel left into a line parallel to the Wheatfield Road, and advance along with Hood's division against the Federal left. To do this, Kershaw intended to direct the center of the brigade toward the stony hill to the left and rear of the Rose barn, which was Barnes's division's position, and to swing his left against the Peach Orchard's left and rear.[34]

The Second South Carolina, near Kershaw's center, moved toward the entrance of Rose's lane. Pvt. John Coxe of the Second saw cannons being loaded at the Peach Orchard and officers on horses dashing about, but the Federal batteries held their fire for a time. Kershaw's men became a tempting target for Ames's battery in the Orchard and for the skirmishers of the Third Michigan and Sixty-eighth Pennsylvania regiments as the Carolinians crossed the clover fields toward the road "with the precision of a brigade drill." Fortunately, Alexander's and Cabell's guns were able to divert some of the Federal batteries' attention from them.[35]

In spite of Federal harassment, the left wing of the brigade reached the Emmitsburg Road, climbed its fences, and crossed it; then they moved "majestically" across the fields to the left of the lane, with the "steadiness of troops on parade." From a twentieth-century perspective, it is often considered foolish to have advanced so under fire, but, within the context of that time, it was rightly considered to be a sign of soldierly skill and courage. When the line neared the Rose barn, the units of the left wing halted briefly, probably formed up, and then wheeled left toward the batteries ranged against them east of the Peach Orchard.[36]

Confederate surgeon Simon Baruch, father of Bernard Baruch, the statesman and financier, was new to battle and curious to see his brigade in action before he went to work on its wounded. He watched the charge of Kershaw's left wing, as he later recounted, "upon a battery supported by infantry in the Peach Orchard while sitting some distance in the rear at the first aid station. The storm of shot and shell that cut down 400 of our men passed over me in uncomfortable proximity, so that when orders came to proceed to the field hospital I lost no time in departing." Pvt. John Coxe and Lt. Alexander McNeil both recalled the terrible fire of the Federal batteries against the Second's line after it wheeled toward Bigelow's and Phillips's batteries. In recollection Coxe sighed, "O the awful deathly surging sounds of those little black balls as they flew by us, through us, between our legs, and over us!" Capt. Robert C. Pulliam was one of those killed by this hail of pellets.[37]

Two sections of Ames's and Thompson's batteries and Hart's, Clark's, Phillips's, and Bigelow's batteries—a total of thirty guns—fired at the South Carolina line, at the line of Semmes's brigade that followed in its support, or at the guns of Cabell's battalion. The artillery story belongs particularly to the action at the Peach Orchard and will be dealt with in Chapter 13. The artillery fire, it can be said for now, had great effect but did not halt the advancing lines. Sgt. William T. Shumate of the Second Regiment saw comrades fall on either side of him and felt his face "fanned time and again by the deadly missiles," but the veteran Carolinian line of which he was a part trudged on without firing a shot. Major Maffett of the Third Regiment found the fire that reached south of Rose's lane galling, and Pvt. James B. Suddath of the Seventh believed that sixty cannons were pouring deadly missiles into the Seventh and that his life "was not worth a straw." But the Seventh marched steadily east toward the Rose farmyard, not even halting to return the fire of the enemy skirmishers in its front.[38]

After the brigade's left wing wheeled toward the batteries, Kershaw ordered the Third South Carolina to slip gradually to the left so that it could go between the Rose house and barn while the Seventh passed to the right of the house. These massive buildings and their smaller outbuildings were obstacles in the brigade's path.[39] Somewhere near the Rose buildings, a regiment, probably the Third, flushed a rabbit. The animal wanted nothing to do with the South Carolinians and bounded off in haste toward the Union line. As it scooted away, one of the Carolinians called, "Go it, old fellow; and I would be glad to go with you, if I hadn't a reputation to sustain!"[40]

As he passed the Rose buildings, Kershaw personally experienced the impact of the canister that whooshed against his regiments. In later years he recalled it well, particularly "the clatter of grape" against the buildings' stone walls.[41] After the Third and Seventh regiments cleared the farmyard, they descended into marshy ground along Plum Run in front of the gap between the stony hill and Rose's Woods. Although the pressure on them eased a bit, the regiments crowded together. To straighten them out Kershaw called to Colonel Aiken to move the Seventh's line to the right until the lines were untangled. Aiken did so, and once it was done, the Third and Seventh were ready to attack Barnes's position on the hill.[42]

But Kershaw's shouts to Aiken created a complication that proved tragic and costly. This took place as the left wing regiments approached the line of batteries in an attack that was "magnificently conducted." The South Carolinians pushed close, so close that some of them thought they could see bewildered expressions on the faces of the cannoneers as they struggled between their desires to do their duty and to be elsewhere. Success seemed at hand for the Carolinians when some unauthorized person, who probably had heard Kershaw's orders to Aiken and construed them wrongly, shouted a command that turned the well-disciplined infantry toward the right flank and away from the guns. Before the error could be recognized and corrected, the Federal gun crews began pounding the Confederates with a vengeance and "for a time destroyed their usefulness." Kershaw lamented that "hundreds of the bravest and best men of Carolina fell, victims of this fatal blunder."[43]

Two officers were among the casualties associated with this maneuver. Both were men of tested courage and patriotism, but they reacted differently to their situations. A canister ball hit the foot of one and gave him a painful wound. He asked Sergeant Shumate to cut off his boot, and Shumate did so. The officer looked quickly at his bleeding foot and then at the thundering guns in their front. Without further hesitation he "turned his back to the foe and made the best time on record until he reached a place of safety."[44] The other officer, Capt. William Z. Leitner of the Second South Carolina, was badly wounded. When his men attempted to move him he said, "Men I am ruined but never give up the battle. I was shot down at the head of my company, and I would to God that I was there yet." Leitner refused to be taken from the field, but when his friend Dr. Thomas W. Salmond learned of the captain's injury, he got his horse and rode to the field. In spite of the battle around him, Salmond was able to lift Leitner onto the horse and bring the wounded captain off.[45]

After the debacle in front of the Federal batteries, Kershaw's left wing regrouped. About a third of the men of the wing's three regiments were down. All three units reformed as quickly as possible, and in a short time the Third Battalion and Eighth Regiment were ready to join with Barksdale in a belated attack on the Peach Orchard. The Second Regiment, under twenty-three-year-old Col. John D. Kennedy, collected in the woods on the left of the Third Regiment, in the swale that drains the area east of the Peach Orchard into the thumb of trees west of the stony hill. From there the Second engaged the batteries along the road in its front.[46]

As Kershaw's and Anderson's brigades approached, Barnes's two brigades waited for them anxiously on the stony hill. The Confederate attack was no surprise, for it had been well announced by skirmish fire and the rapid booming of Federal cannons to their right. Sgt. Maj. Walter Carter of the Twenty-second Massachusetts dashed forward to order in the regiment's skirmishers, and soon they could be seen running back before the advancing foe. Lt. Col. Thomas Sherwin, Jr., ordered the Twenty-second to fix bayonets, and a metallic rattle ran along the Twenty-second's line. Many men placed percussion caps and cartridges on the ground in front of them where they could reach them quickly, a suggestion that perhaps the Twenty-second was preparing to meet the assault while lying under cover if possible.[47]

On the Twenty-second's right the men of the 118th Pennsylvania were lying down, nervously awaiting the clash. Suddenly a rabbit, quite possibly the one flushed by the Third South Carolina, approached the 118th's front.

In its haste the careless hare jumped onto the neck of one of the prone Pennsylvanians, an unnerving experience for both man and beast. The rabbit scooted on, but the Philadelphian jumped up shouting, "Oh! I'm shot! I'm a dead man! Shot clean through the neck!" The men around him laughed, and tension eased within the 118th's ranks.[48]

The Confederates were not too far behind the rabbit. In the distance they were an indistinct, dirty gray line, dimly visible through the dust and smoke, sectioned off by battle flags. The Confederates yelled as they advanced "in good style moving rapidly." As the line got close the defenders could see that it was composed of begrimed, dirty-looking fellows in all sorts of garb, but the Confederates loaded and fired with great deliberation, an awesome sign of seasoned soldiers. The Federals opened fire, all perhaps but the First Michigan. Colonel Abbott kept his regiment prone while the Confederate balls zipped through the trees above it. Then, when the Confederate line was well within range, he ordered the Wolverines to stand and fire. In his view, they created "a dreadful confusion" in the Confederate ranks. The Carolinians recoiled perhaps but then came on again. The Michigan men stood like rocks but fell like sheep before the slaughter. Abbott was wounded and went to the rear.[49]

Tilton's men fired all along the brigade line. Those in the 118th, once the battle was joined, stood erect, fired, stepped back a pace to load, and stepped forward again to fire. One man, a mule driver, was particularly conspicuous. He stood to the front, shooting and shouting, "Give them hell, boys!" But while all of this was happening, Lt. Col. James Gwyn noticed with concern that Carolinians were working around the 118th's exposed right flank.[50] On the other end of Tilton's line the cheering, yelling, and firing were deafening. Bullets clipped leaves and twigs that rained down on the troops, and the air became foul with a heavy smoke. Pvt. Charles Phillips of the Twenty-second Massachusetts was one of the first men hit. Pvt. Robert G. Carter, who stood beside him, heard "a thud, a sickening, dull cracking sound," and saw Phillips collapse, "his face streaming blood which filled his eyes and nose and gurgled in his mouth." Phillips's head struck Carter's foot. Carter paused in his firing, knelt, and rolled his comrade over on his back. Then Carter stood and shot some more.[51]

Anderson's brigade advanced on Kershaw's right against the fronts of Sweitzer and de Trobriand and possibly Tilton's left. The Georgians attacked with spirit, but later recorded virtually nothing of what they did. Corporal West of the Thirty-second Massachusetts had hurriedly filled his canteens in Plum Run and returned to his company. The Georgians reached the stream where he had been by the time he returned to his place in ranks, and the Georgians and Yankees traded fire. Not long after the attack began, and before the enemy appeared on his brigade's front, Sweitzer ordered the Sixty-second Pennsylvania and Fourth Michigan to change front to the left so that they might support the Thirty-second Massachusetts and Tilton's left.

When the shift was completed, Sweitzer's brigade stood in a column with the Fourth and Sixty-second behind the Thirty-second Massachusetts and above it on the slope.[52]

Smoke filled the ravine in front of the Thirty-second, hiding the Confederates there. Lt. James E. Marsh, who stood near Corporal West in the Thirty-second's line, pointed to a flag that stood out above the smoke. Marsh said that there was a crowd around it, but the smoke was too thick for the men of the Thirty-second to see it; however, they could see jets of flame spurting from the muzzles of Confederate rifles, and aimed just beneath them.[53]

Not long after the attack began, General Barnes sent word to Sweitzer, saying that when his brigade retired it should fall back through the woods. Perhaps these instructions were meant only to be precautionary, but Sweitzer relayed them down to his regimental commanders. Colonel Prescott of the Thirty-second, which was fully engaged, assumed that he had received an order to retreat then and there and became highly incensed. "I don't want to retire," complained Prescott. "I am not ready to retire; I can hold this place." Sweitzer calmed Prescott down, and the Thirty-second continued to fight awhile.[54]

Anderson's regiments struck de Trobriand's a second time. The Seventeenth Maine, supported by Winslow's battery's overhead fire, held manfully to the wall, but it was the fighting on their right that gained attention in later years. The greatest threat was at the angle in the Seventeenth's line and beyond, against the color company and against those on its right. The coaching there was, "Aim low, boys! make every shot tell!" They easily spotted Confederates coming through the alders and shot them down. For a time, the men of the Seventeenth Maine there were "hilarious," but this euphoria gave way to sobriety soon enough. The Confederate strength seemed to increase while the Seventeenth's numbers and ammunition supply dwindled.[55] It was not a promising situation.

De Trobriand saw trouble ahead and looked for assistance. His aide, Lt. Edwin B. Houghton, told him of some Fifth Corps troops that were lying to his rear. De Trobriand went back to find them, and to his consternation he saw them starting for the rear. He galloped toward them and asked an officer, probably of Sweitzer's brigade, why they were falling back. The officer told him that they had been ordered back but that he did not know why.[56]

Kershaw's advance was the reason why. Kershaw maneuvered his Third and Seventh regiments to strike the stony hill as Anderson pushed east again through Rose's Woods. Kershaw reported simply that the two regiments occupied the hill, but it was not quite as simple as that. The Third South Carolina caught artillery fire from the left and rifle fire from the front, and four of the color guard fell. Someone called, "Lower the colors, down with the flag." In reply Color Sergeant William Lamb stepped to the front, where all could see him, and shouted, "This flag never goes down until I am down!"[57] Kershaw's line neared the hill and, to the general's surprise, the force defending it seemed to melt away. The Third and Seventh took over the vacated ground.[58]

Barnes and Tilton, if not Sweitzer, were probably intimidated before Kershaw pushed his attack home. Barnes had called Sykes's attention to what he conceived to be the gap between the stony hill and the Peach Orchard, then had watched it with anxiety, and had even issued a precautionary order for withdrawal. It seems in retrospect that caution had gone beyond prudence to pessimism. Tilton, as Barnes's accustomed subordinate, shared his concerns and must have watched Kershaw's left wing advance toward the batteries in the gap with alarm. No matter that the batteries, with luck, had repulsed the attack—the Confederates had threatened Barnes's right and might do so again.[59] If this is so, one can wonder why Barnes permitted Sweitzer to pivot his Sixty-second and Fourth regiments from their positions fronting the Peach Orchard and the gap toward the more immediate but less serious threat from Rose's Woods. These two regiments became at best only lightly engaged there and probably were not really needed; yet Barnes did permit the redeployment and did not return the regiments to their original position.

The attack against the hill by the Third and Seventh regiments and the presence of the Second South Carolina in the low ground off Tilton's right, poised perhaps to drive toward the Wheatfield Road in Tilton's rear, posed too great a threat to be ignored. Barnes ordered Tilton "to change his front to the right." Tilton's brigade shifted far right, north through the woods, across the Wheatfield Road, and to the wall along the west edge of Trostle's Woods. Barnes told Sweitzer of Tilton's change and directed the Second Brigade to fall back in good order to the Wheatfield Road at the south edge of Trostle's Woods. Not only did this leave a gap in the Federal line at the stony hill; the shift itself was courting trouble. Maj. James C. Biddle of Meade's staff, who happened to be present, feared that the retiring brigades might go too far and implored them to make a stand. But the movement itself went well enough. Barnes claimed that the withdrawal was deliberate and orderly. Colonel Gwyn of the 118th Pennsylvania, whose flank was most vulnerable, commanded, "Change front to the rear on 10th Company, battalion about face, by company right half wheel, march!" The 118th knew what to do and obeyed. Obviously it was not being hard pressed at this time. The Corn Exchange Regiment wound up on the right of the brigade's first line and retired firing as it went toward its new position on the edge of Trostle's Woods.[60]

On being ordered to move, Colonel Sherwin of the Twenty-second Massachusetts commanded, "Change front to the rear by the right flank," but his command was lost in the noise. The order was then relayed from company to company and the men of the Twenty-second collected their ammunition and started back. Two soldiers carried Pvt. John Morrison, who had been shot in the abdomen. Morrison had great pain and alternately pleaded to be put down and then, fearing capture, to be carried off. He had had a presentiment of death during the march north and it had depressed him. He had been a farmhand and expressed the longing "to swing that scythe once more." Morrison died in a Twelfth Corps hospital.[61] It was hard for Sweitzer to obey the command to fall back, for his line had not been directly threatened by anything that it could not handle. The Second Brigade retreated in good order to the north side of the Wheatfield Road.[62]

Barnes congratulated his two small brigades. In his opinion they had carried off a difficult movement well under fire. The congratulations went, of course, to Colonel Tilton among others. Tilton's Gettysburg image is not that of one of the great commanders. He had been a merchant in Boston and at the age of thirty-three had joined the Twenty-second Massachusetts in September 1861 as its adjutant. He had been wounded and captured at Gaines's Mill and had been held prisoner for about a month. Tilton became colonel of the Twenty-second in October 1862. In the recollections of the 118th Pennsylvania, Tilton, as a brigade commander, was said to be an officer of eminent courage and superior attainments, who at Gettysburg was seen in all the heaviest fighting and "conceived and personally conducted the delicate manoeuver which relieved the brigade of the imminent peril of its first position."[63]

But there was personal trouble ahead for Barnes and Tilton. Barnes's division was on the stony hill to fight and to hold it, but, for reasons that he thought good, Barnes had ordered the two brigades to Trostle's Woods seemingly without the permission of a higher ranking officer. This left Barnes and his command open to insinuations and accusations, if not outright charges, of unsoldierly conduct. In his report de Trobriand wrote that he would have tried to break the enemy's line had not the two Fifth Corps "regiments" sent to his support fallen back without engaging the enemy (not so, of course), leaving his brigade in danger of being surrounded. Birney reported the simple truth—that Barnes had withdrawn his force and formed it three hundred yards in the rear.[64] All well and good, perhaps, but there were also manifestations of less charitable feelings.

Birney spoke to Sykes and Sedgwick at the Council of War that night and quoted Sykes as having said that Sweitzer "had reported the same thing." Barnes became aware that there was such talk and quizzed Sykes and Sedgwick about it. Sedgwick replied to him, in April 1864, that he recalled having talked with Sykes and Birney that night but could not remember what was said. Sweitzer denied talking with Sykes about it until the army reached Williamsport on the Potomac more than a week later. He said then that he had fallen back because he was ordered to do so.[65]

What had been army gossip only perhaps, reached the public on 18 March 1864, when HISTORICUS wrote an account of the battle from the perspective of Sickles, and probably Birney as well. It included many errors and much that was controversial, and of Barnes it said:

The columns of Longstreet charged with reckless fury upon our [Third Corps] troops; but they were met with a valor and stern fortitude that defied their utmost efforts. An alarming incident, however, occurred. Barnes' division, of the Fifth Corps, suddenly gave way; and Sickles, seeing this, put a battery in position to check the enemy if he broke through this gap on our front, and General Birney was sent to order Barnes back into line. "No," he said; "impossible. It is too hot. My men cannot stand it."[66]

Barnes reacted vehemently to this statement, called it "pure invention," and wrote that there was not a particle of truth in it. He had never received orders from Sickles or Birney; there were no orders to advance.[67] Tilton was less restrained in a letter that he wrote to Barnes. He called HISTORICUS's account a slander with the object of foisting Sickles on the public as an injured but capable soldier and termed HISTORICUS's statement that Barnes's division broke "diabolical." Tilton claimed, without apparent foundation, that Barnes's two brigades had not budged until the troops on the right and left were routed.[68]

HISTORICUS criticized the withdrawal that Barnes believed had gone so well. He wrote that "Barnes' disordered troops" impeded the advance of Zook's brigade and that Barnes ordered his men to lie down so that Zook's could march over them. These were fighting words in the context in which they were presented and will be discussed in some detail in Chapter 12 in connection with Zook's advance. In making such a statement, HISTORICUS did more than question Barnes's fortitude and judgment, he slurred the conduct of the officers and men of the Fifth Corps.[69]

After their withdrawal to Trostle's Woods, Barnes's two brigades were still on the field. They still had fighting to do, and some of their regiments would acquit themselves nobly. Barnes was present too and wounded in the left thigh. Somehow, though, all that happened to him after he pulled his troops from the stony hill seems anticlimactic. Though it does not seem so now, his presence must have been deemed important at the time. The division's appointed commander, Brig. Gen. Charles Griffin reached the field on 3 July but elected not to resume command of the division until 4 July. Whether he knew of the blame to be heaped on Barnes, we cannot say. Certainly he would have talked with Sykes and must have been aware of the division's performance on 2 July. It was written that he declined to replace Barnes as the acting division commander in spite of the latter's leg wound until the battle was over, saying, "To you, General Barnes, belongs the honor of the field; you began the battle with the division, and shall fight it to the end." The chronicler of the 118th Pennsylvania wrote of Barnes at Gettysburg that he "rode valiantly amid the thickest of the fray, encouraging, persuading, directing with that same courageous judgment which had ever been his distinguishing characteristic." But physical courage and command ability can be two different things, and Barnes's career with the Army of the Potomac was all but over. After recovering from his wound, he did not return to his brigade and the Fifth Corps. Instead he performed administrative duties in Washington until the war was over. Then he returned to Boston and railroading until his death in 1869.[70]

After de Trobriand saw Barnes's brigades falling back north through the trees on the stony hill, he returned to the hill's south slope where the 110th Pennsylvania and the Fifth Michigan still held their ground. De Trobriand arrived at the Fifth's position in time to see its color-bearer reel back, gasping that he had been shot in the throat. De Trobriand pulled him to his feet and found that he was not wounded. Instead he had been bruised and staggered when a minié ball hit the leather sling at his neck. Colonel Pulford came up brandishing a piece of his revolver. A bullet had hit and smashed it, giving Pulford only a scratch on the hand. By this time both regiments had taken significant casualties: the Fifth, whose bravery had been "unflinching," had lost half its number.[71]

The firing increased to the left on the other side of the Wheatfield, and Capt. Israel C. Smith of de Trobriand's staff rode over to see what was happening there. A ball hit Smith's horse in the shoulder and passed through it into Smith's leg. The horse reared up in pain and shock and turned on its hind legs as if ready to fall. Smith calmed it down and rode back to de Trobriand, where, as de Trobriand recalled, he "saluted me with perfect coolness, expressed to me the regret he felt in not being able to be of further service to me, and went off without hurrying."[72] Capt. Benjamin M. Piatt, de Trobriand's adjutant, rode up about this time also. He had been over to the left and had lost his horse, but was riding one that belonged to a wounded officer. Piatt's boot had been shot away, and he had been wounded slightly. De Trobriand learned that the Federal situation was bad on the left and feared that his brigade was in danger of being surrounded.[73]

Barnes had gone back, Ward's brigade had been driven from its position in fragments, and de Trobriand's brigade had to give ground too. The Fifth and 110th regiments fell back through the woods on the stony hill as Barnes's troops had done. The Seventeenth Maine kept pace with them in the Wheatfield, and the brigade united near the Wheatfield Road.[74] At this point there are some conflicting stories that seem beyond resolution. Some of the Seventeenth's accounts hold that the regiment remained at its position at the wall until Winslow's battery left the Wheatfield. They imply that the Seventeenth stayed there deliberately to cover the battery's departure.[75] This makes some sense and might have been at least partially true. However, Pvt. John Haley wrote that the Seventeenth Maine retired toward the battery and that although the battery was shelling the Rebels and the Seventeenth was firing at them, they could not hold them.[76]

Captain Winslow's report amplifies Haley's observation. While the Seventeenth was along the wall in his front, Winslow's guns fired solid shot low over its line. But when the Seventeenth fell back, possibly to the base of the rise on which the guns were posted, the guns could have fired over the Seventeenth's line only so long as it was sufficiently below them. Winslow's guns switched to shell and case shot and fired at about a one-degree elevation with fuses cut to 1 or 1½ seconds.[77]

By that time, Confederate bullets were flying thickly around the battery, clipping heads from the stalks of the standing wheat and thudding occasionally into men or horses. The battery's fire, together with that of the 115th Pennsylvania and possibly others, held Anderson's Georgians behind the stone wall and under the cover of Rose's Woods. Soon Lt. Albert N. Ames, chief of Winslow's left section, told him that the enemy was on that flank about sixty yards away. Winslow rode over to see for himself and found a deteriorating situation there. The woods along the east side of the field contained a line of troops, perhaps one of Ward's regiments or the Fortieth New York. The line fronted away from his guns at a right angle to his gun line, and the enemy was pressing it back. As Winslow watched, the regiment retreated across his battery's front, and he was discouraged also to see a portion of Smith's battery file past his left. Winslow ordered Lieutenant Ames to swing his guns to the left and open with canister. The captain then rode to General Birney, who was in the northwest corner of the Wheatfield, to tell him what he had done. Birney approved of Winslow's action, and the fight went on. Soon one of Birney's staff officers rode up and relayed Birney's advice to "be careful and not get cut off" and to find a withdrawal route for the battery to use if necessary.[78]

The enemy on the left, probably troops from the Fifteenth Georgia and the First Texas regiments, which had pushed north along the ridge above Devil's Den after driving Ward's brigade from its front, opened on Winslow's battery's left. It was at close range; Winslow thought about twenty-five yards, but that seems too close. Winslow ordered his left section to pull back a short distance to the left and rear where it could drop trail and continue the fight. Before it did so, Kershaw's men opened on the right section from the cover of the woods on the stony hill. This fire was at close range, a hundred yards or less. It cut down men and horses, including Winslow's own mount, and convinced Winslow that it was time for him to order the battery away if it was to be saved. Winslow mounted his orderly's horse, rode to the left section, and sent it away. The center section followed, and the last gun to start off was the No. 1 piece of Lt. Thomas H. Crego's section on the right.[79] Crego's section had been protected by the 115th Pennsylvania, which had charged the Rebel line twice before it ran out of ammunition and left the field. When the 115th reached the shelter of Trostle's Woods, Burling, who was collecting his men as they returned, greeted Colonel Dunne with the interesting remark, "I thought you were captured as you staid so long after the 8th N.J."[80]

The Confederate riflemen shot ten of Winslow's horses, probably most of

Company C, 110th Pennsylvania Volunteer Infantry Regiment (National Archives)

them from the right section, and enough from one gun's team to immobilize it. The artillerymen were able to get the gun off by hooking it to a caisson's limber. They got the caisson away by hitching it to two horses belonging to Smith's battery that they had found harnessed but without drivers. Winslow closed his report by remarking, "All of my pieces could not have been brought off had my men been less brave." Ten men were wounded and eight missing at the end of the day.[81] Captain Randolph praised Winslow and his men both for the way that they had worked in a poor position and for their handsome withdrawal. It was merited praise, but Winslow had regrets. As he rode back through Trostle's Woods with his last piece, he saw a brigade of Federal infantry that was about to advance. Had he known that such help was so near, he might have tried to hold on a little longer. It was too late then. He reported to General Sickles and was told to collect his battery and await orders.[82]

When Winslow's battery pulled away, Anderson's Georgians stepped over the stone wall, and their skirmish line entered the field of trampled wheat. Kershaw's men, the Third and Seventh South Carolina regiments, were working their way north through the woods on the stony hill at the same time. It was a critical period for the Army of the Potomac. McLaws's division had finally advanced: Kershaw's brigade had joined forces with Anderson's brigade on Hood's left, and the two brigades had driven Tilton's and Sweitzer's brigades from the stony hill and de Trobriand's from the Wheatfield. This success, coupled with the eviction of Ward's brigade from its position at

Kershaw attacks Winslow's battery in the Wheatfield. Sketch by Alfred R. Waud
(Library of Congress)

Devil's Den, meant that the whole left wing of Sickles's line had been smashed and that its right wing along the Emmitsburg Road was in jeopardy. Caldwell's and Ayres's divisions were on their way to the Wheatfield front, but would they arrive in time? If so, the Union position there might be restored and the rear of the line along the Emmitsburg Road covered. If not, and the Confederates drove north of the Wheatfield Road, the Emmitsburg Road position would have to be abandoned.

Birney must have known that Caldwell's division was on the way and thought it necessary to buy a little time. He saw the Seventeenth Maine standing in line in the Wheatfield, catching its breath and waiting for ammunition. The men of the Seventeenth had taken sixty rounds apiece into the fight and had fired at least forty of them; more ammunition would be needed if the regiment was to fight long again.[83]

Birney rode up to Lieutenant Colonel Merrill of the Seventeenth and, with a word of explanation, ordered the regiment forward to buy a little time. To their credit, the men from Maine responded with a cheer "in the good old-fashioned Union style" and followed General Birney and the ever-present Captain Briscoe back into the Wheatfield. The Georgians scampered back to the shelter of the stone wall when they saw the blue line advancing on them. Birney halted the Seventeenth midway across the field, probably at the brow of the slope, near where Winslow's guns had been. From that high ground, the Seventeenth, like Winslow's battery, could cover the field to its front and yet not be under the very muzzles of the Georgians in the woods behind the stone wall.[84]

Birney rode to the rear again to get help for the Seventeenth Maine. He ordered the Fifth Michigan back into the Wheatfield, and Colonel Pulford posted it on the right of the Seventeenth close to the stony hill.[85] The Confederates in the woods to their right and behind the wall to their front raked the the two regiments with fire. The Georgians did not advance then, but the South Carolinians did, and there was some close fighting on the Michigan end of the line. There were numerous casualties. A ball hit Lieutenant Roberts in the leg, and he bled profusely. Lieutenant Colonel Merrill made a tourniquet for him with a strap cut from his sword belt, and then he ordered four men to carry Roberts off in a rubber blanket. This was understandable compassion, but it took from the firing line four men who were needed badly there. Lieutenant Verrill received a leg wound also, but he walked to the rear. As he limped away, he saw troops with red patches, Caldwell's division, approaching the Wheatfield.[86]

After a very short time, the able men ran low on ammunition and scavenged the pouches of the fallen for more. Lieutenant Colonel Merrill told the soldiers of the Seventeenth Maine that they would hold their ground with bayonets if necessary, but it was not. Caldwell's division came up from the rear and, as de Trobriand wrote sarcastically, *"They* did not lie down behind us." It had been a hard fight. The Fifth Michigan's casualties exceeded 40 percent, and the Seventeenth Maine's 35 percent, including seven of the ten men in the color guard. Many other regiments at Gettysburg had higher casualty rates, but few accomplished more. In his report Birney observed that de Trobriand deserved his heartiest thanks for the skillful disposition of his command and the gallant holding of his position until relieved. He observed also that de Trobriand was one of the oldest officers in the volunteer service in the grade of colonel, that he had been distinguished in nearly every engagement of the Army of the Potomac, and that he deserved the promotion to the grade of brigadier general for which he had been recommended. De Trobriand received his star a half year later in January 1864.[87]

CHAPTER

12

The Confederates Seize the Wheatfield

Maj. Gen. Winfield S. Hancock and Brig. Gen. John Gibbon met at about 4:00 P.M. near Cushing's battery at the right of Gibbon's division's line and discussed the events of the day.[1] More than six hours had passed since the Second Corps had deployed on Cemetery Ridge, and there had been only some skirmishing and intermittent cannonading. Hancock had just come up from General Meade's meeting with his corps commanders, where he must have learned that the Sixth Corps was arriving and that there was activity brewing on the Third Corps front. Now Gibbon and Hancock gazed off to the left with interest if not concern.

There was a sudden stir in the fields to the left of the Second Corps, though at that distance not much that was happening was discernible to the naked eye. Lines of troops were marching west toward the Emmitsburg Road, where until then only skirmishers had been. The two generals and their staff officers raised their field glasses and through them must have seen Humphreys's division, Third Corps, advancing with great precision. What did it mean? Hancock had not been told of such a deployment on his left, but he admired the spectacle. He turned to Gibbon and to others close at hand and observed, "Gentlemen, that is a splendid advance. But, those troops will be coming back again very soon."[2]

Then Hancock cantered down the ridge to the left about eight hundred yards to Caldwell's division. The view of the Third Corps's activities was much better from there, and that division would likely be the first of Hancock's troops to be affected by changes on the Third Corps front. Soon afterward, someone, most certainly Hancock, ordered Caldwell's division to march to the support of the Third Corps. Caldwell moved his troops out at once, first to the left and then forward. His left brigade, the first away, marched the farthest because the time needed to get the whole division moving must have enabled it to travel a considerable distance before the brigade on the right took up the march. No one recorded where the division went, and perhaps the movement was of little importance. What is important is that after it had gone a significant way, perhaps half a mile if Colonel Kelly was correct, "a column of the Fifth Corps appeared," and the regiments of the division retraced their steps to their places on the ridge. The Fifth Corps column must have been Barnes's division, which moved from an assembly area near the Baltimore Pike to the stony hill by way of Granite Schoolhouse Lane and passed near Caldwell's position on Cemetery Ridge. Hancock wrote nothing of this aborted movement in his report and in his accounts of the battle, yet such a movement was in keeping with the understanding that the division, when sent to the aid of the Third Corps, would return after being relieved by the Fifth.[3]

After Caldwell's division returned, Hancock watched the activity near the Emmitsburg Road from a vantage point near the center of the division's line. Caldwell and his staff were with him, as were a number of field officers including Colonels Kelly and Byrnes and Major Mulholland of the Irish Brigade. It was a natural gathering, for Hancock had been their division commander from Antietam through Chancellorsville, and they knew him well. The division's officers must have been quite curious about what was going on around them and about Hancock's views on it. Hancock watched awhile, kneeling and leaning on his sword. Then, turning to the officers around him, he smiled and repeated the observation made to Gibbon, "Wait a moment, you will soon see them tumbling back."[4] Soon an aide from army headquarters galloped up with a request for Hancock to send a division to the left to assist not Sickles but Sykes![5] The left was beyond the woods, out of Hancock's view, and he could have known little of what was happening there. Nevertheless, orders were orders. He turned to Caldwell and said quietly, "Caldwell, you get your division ready."[6]

Caldwell did so. He sent aides for instructions from Sykes and ordered his brigade commanders to prepare to march. His regiments formed again behind their stacked rifles, took arms, and awaited the order to move.[7] Now the noise of battle off to the left was heard. It grew loud, the deadly character of the battle obvious. This movement would not be recalled. Feeling a special sense of foreboding perhaps, the Reverend Father William Corby proposed to give the Irish Brigade a general absolution. Colonel Kelly or his adjutant called the brigade to attention and commanded it to "Order Arms." Father Corby stepped up on a boulder about three feet high, explained what he was about to do, and ended his remarks with the observation that the "Catholic church refuses Christian burial to the soldier who turns his back upon the foe or deserts his flag." The men of the brigade knelt, each man on his right knee, head uncovered, hat in left hand, rifle in right, and head bowed, while Chaplain Corby, raised his right hand and pronounced the Latin words of absolution. The occasion was solemn and impressive, its drama enhanced by the roar of battle to the south, which "rose and swelled and re-echoed through the woods, making music more sublime than ever sounded through cathedral aisles."[8]

The men of the First Brigade, Cross's, were on the division's left flank, that closest to the fighting. They waited in ranks, concerned about the meaning of the noise and smoke of battle that was spreading on their left. Hancock rode up to the brigade's front and to his old subordinate, Colonel Cross. Hancock, "in his measured suave manner," greeted Cross and remarked, "Colonel Cross, this day will bring you a star." Colonel Cross, looking up at Hancock, shook his head gravely and replied, "No General, this is my last battle." When Hancock rode away, Cross gazed pensively south toward the Wheatfield, the place of noise and smoke.[9] Cross's reverie ended when Lt. William P. Wilson, of Caldwell's staff, rode up with an important message. Cross lifted the bridle reins over his horse's head, swung into the saddle, and called to his staff, "Mount, Gentlemen." Soon Cross's brigade led the way south to the Wheatfield. Cross was riding at its head, straight as an arrow and tall in the saddle, taking note of everything of significance that came within his view.[10]

In the meantime, Caldwell's aide, Lt. Daniel K. Cross, looked for General Sykes and did not find him. But Caldwell's four brigades marched south. Instead of taking the time necessary to file off by regiment with the right of each one in its lead, the whole division moved at one time. The brigade commanders simply faced their brigades to the left and moved them off in four brigade blocks—or chunks, as one soldier called them. Cross's brigade led, followed by Kelly's, Zook's, and Brooke's. They headed southwesterly down the front slope of the ridge and through the open fields in the general direction of the Trostle buildings. Somewhere near the farmyard they splashed through the upper reaches of Plum Run and saw Anna Etheridge, a Third Corps nurse, ride by. They were out of sight of the Confederate batteries, but shot and shell fired at targets in the Peach Orchard area whizzed around them and ploughed the earth nearby.[11]

As the men of Zook's brigade saw the Irish march away, a soldier of the 140th Pennsylvania called, "Tighten your belts, boys, our turn next." At this time, Lt. Alexander M. Wilson, who was lying on the ground by his place in the file-closers' rank of the 140th, sick and weak with dysentery, told Sgt. John R. Paxton that the sergeant must help him into the fight. Wilson had been the company's first sergeant, was recently commissioned, and was particularly sensitive about his image and reputation. He told Paxton that if he did not go in with the regiment, "the boys might think I funked." Soon the brigade moved off, and Sergeant Paxton, who must have had enough problems of his own, helped the sick lieutenant along.[12]

While the division was moving south, a Third Corps aide rode up to General Zook and asked for his brigade's assistance. Caldwell had gone on ahead and could not be readily consulted, so General Zook galloped off with the aide to see General Sickles, who was nearby at the Trostle farmyard. In a short time Zook came galloping back, jumping his horse over walls and fences in his haste. By this time the First and Second brigades were some distance ahead. Zook's brigade marched off to the right, halted in the western portion of Trostle's Woods, which was a short distance from the line of march, deployed in two lines, and advanced.[13] There would be complaints about the Third Corps impressing units of other corps that day, but none was issued in this instance. Perhaps Zook's deployment in Caldwell's zone did not incur the Second Corps's displeasure. We cannot now know.

After passing the Trostle house, Caldwell's column reached the eastern half of Trostle's Woods, the long triangular grove between the Trostle lane and the Wheatfield Road. Cross's brigade entered that portion of the woods adjoining the east end of the Wheatfield, its four regiments tramping in columns side by side (the 148th Pennsylvania regiment was in two columns). The brigade halted behind the fence along the road and deployed in an unconventional manner. First the right column, the Sixty-first New York, which had been in the forward line on Cemetery Ridge, filed to the right and moved far enough along the fence and road so that the three remaining regiments could do the same in their turn. After this was done, the brigade was in a three-ranked column strung along the fence facing west, its rear at the east end of the woods near Plum Run. Cross then faced them left so that the four regiments fronted toward the Wheatfield.[14]

This or a very similar movement was undertaken in turn by the brigades of Cross, Kelly, and Brooke as they reached the fence.[15] Many recalled the movement in later years because, in a day when linear formations were essential to controlled movement and firepower, it resulted in an awkward formation that placed the right of a regiment on the left and its rank of file-closers in front rather than in the rear. The resulting lines of battle were backward—noncommissioned officers and lieutenants were in the front in the way of the riflemen, the colors were in the rear rather than in the front, and the guides on the left rather than the right. In the case of the 148th Pennsylvania, which had been in two lines because of its size, the colors were in the rear rank on the right of the regiment's line rather than in the center of the front rank. It was a topsy-turvy situation. In the words of a veteran of the Sixty-first New York, "To have fronted would have presented our *backs* to the Rebels, and that was not the side we had been accustomed to present to them." Officers made attempts to rectify matters in an expedient way by passing file-closers to the rear, but that was the best that could be done in the time available.[16]

At about the time that Cross was unreeling his brigade into line, two officers galloped up. One was one of Caldwell's aides, probably Lieutenant Wilson, the other an officer of Sykes's staff. The latter rode a skittish horse that plunged and kicked every time a cannon shot crashed through the nearby trees, demanding that he be given plenty of room. One rider, probably Sykes's man, shouted, "The enemy is breaking in directly on your right—

strike him quick." As soon as he had a line, Cross ordered his brigade across the road and into the golden wheat.[17]

The Fifth New Hampshire on the brigade left moved south with its left flank near the stone wall that runs north from Devil's Den above the Plum Run Valley. The 148th Pennsylvania advanced on its right. The Fifth and the left wing of the 148th, probably five hundred men all told, entered the woods on the east side of the Wheatfield. The right wing of the 148th, the Eighty-first Pennsylvania, and the Sixty-first New York were in the Wheatfield itself. They advanced in a good line in spite of the handicap of their formation. Some men noticed puffs of smoke from Confederate rifles ahead of them and how the wheat heads flew when clipped by minié balls. Fortunately the Confederates fired high, at least those in the woods did so, and not many of the Fifth were hit. Cross and his staff and the ranking officers of the regiments followed the brigade line on horseback, Cross shouting and gesturing with his sword. When the brigade reached a point about midway across the field, where its monuments stand today, the officers on horseback dismounted and turned their horses over to orderlies. Riding through trees and commanding troops in battle are not necessarily compatible activities.[18]

The brigade's advance to this point had been so rapid that it had captured some Confederate skirmishers. Cross placed them in the care of Lt. Charles A. Hale. With the help of a sergeant and two privates from the 140th, Hale collected the prisoners at a sassafras clump by a rock outcrop northwest of the site occupied later by the 148th's monument. The prisoners were not pleased to be captured. One officer snapped his sword blade off at the hilt to prevent Hale's taking it and scornfully hurled the pieces at Hale's feet.[19]

The brigade stood on a slight rise in the waist-high wheat and returned the Rebel fire. The Confederates were getting the range of Cross's line, and men fell here and there. Capt. Willard Keech of the Sixty-first New York noticed that one of his lieutenants in the line of file-closers, which apparently was now in the rear, was bending his head to keep it behind the heads of those in front of him. Keech walked over to him and amid the noise of gunfire shouted, "Stand up! What are you crouching for?" "I'm not crouching," replied the lieutenant. "Yes, you are!" Keech shouted back, hitting the lieutenant across his humped-up back with his sword and commanding, "Stand up like a man!"[20] Keech's treatment must have effected something of a cure, for Lt. Col. K. Oscar Broady, in his report for that day, wrote that officers and men behaved with utmost coolness and valor and that all were worthy of praise.[21]

The file-closers had an important function. From their places in the rear they could see and direct the men with rifles in the front ranks and make sure that they kept to their places in line. Lt. Charles A. Fuller of the Sixty-first observed that it was the tendency of men on the firing line to work from good lines into clumps. This happened because the more steady or more daring soldiers, when firing, tended to move to the front, while the less steady or

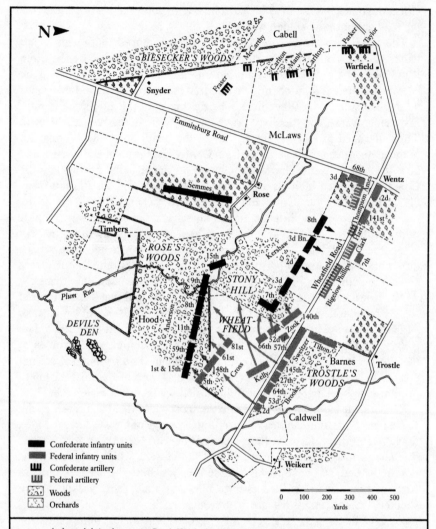

N▶

1. *Anderson's brigade occupies Rose's Woods, Kershaw the stony hill, and the First Texas and Fifteenth Georgia the east edge of Rose's Woods.*

2. *Caldwell's brigades form successively in Trostle's Woods and advance into the Wheatfield. Cross's brigade advances across the east half of the Wheatfield. It strikes the First Texas and the Fifteenth Alabama and the right wing of Anderson's brigade.*

3. *Zook's brigade advances from Trostle's Woods against Kershaw's position on the north end of the stony hill. Kelly strikes the south end of the stony hill. Kershaw's Third and Seventh South Carolina regiments fall back to the Rose farmyard.*

4. *Brooke's brigade drives Anderson's brigade from Rose's Woods.*

5. *Anderson and Kershaw rally. Supported by Semmes's and Wofford's brigades, they reform for a counterattack against Caldwell.*

6. *Sweitzer's brigade is sent to Caldwell's support. Caldwell's brigades are driven from the field.*

Map 12-1. The Wheatfield: Caldwell Sweeps the Field

daring crowded in behind them. The resulting clusters cut down on a unit's ability to deliver fire, handicapped its control and movement, and increased its vulnerability.[22]

Cross was behind the right wing during the first leg of the advance. After the halt, he wanted to get his brigade moving again. First, though, he had to see what was happening on that part of his line in the trees to his left. Turning to his staff, he said, "Boys:—instruct the commanders to be ready to charge when the order is given; wait here for the command, or, if you hear the bugles of the Fifth New Hampshire on the left, move forward on the run."[23] Cross walked into the woods to the rear of the line of the Fifth New Hampshire, where its memorial now stands. A rifle cracked from a large boulder about forty-five yards to the front. The shot was accurate, and Cross fell with a minié ball in his abdomen. Lt. Col. Charles E. Hapgood, commander of the Fifth, saw the flash and smoke and ordered Sgt. Charles Phelps of Company I to shoot the man who fired the shot. Phelps watched the rock, saw the sniper, and brought him down.[24]

Colonel Cross had been a controversial officer and was particularly disliked by the officers and men of the 148th Pennsylvania Regiment, who considered him a tyrant. Others, for some reason, thought him hypocritical but a good officer nevertheless, who took care of his men whether they wanted him to or not, and insisted on implicit obedience to orders. If this is so, he might have given the 148th plenty to growl about until they became accustomed to his ways—which they never did. Unlike Vincent, Cross did not get a deathbed star. They carried him to a field hospital and tried to make him comfortable on a bed of sheaves of wheat. When the death presaged by his black scarf neared, he said, "I did hope I should see peace restored to our distressed country. I think the boys will miss me. Say goodbye to all."[25]

Col. H. Boyd McKeen of the Eighty-first Pennsylvania took command of Cross's brigade and the attack went on. The Confederates were in the brigade's front in force. Anderson's brigade now occupied the stone wall so jealously guarded by the Seventeenth Maine just a short time before. Some of its men rested their rifles upon the wall. To a Pennsylvania soldier facing them, the bright barrels "glittered like a looking glass." Colonel Work's First Texas and DuBoses's Fifteenth Georgia regiments were in the woods to Anderson's right in front of the Fifth New Hampshire. After they drove Ward's men from Devil's Den Ridge, these two fine units pushed north along the ridge, captured numerous prisoners, and finally were able to fire at Winslow's battery from a distance. As Cross's men approached, the First Texas and Fifteenth Georgia waited for them on a high point to the right of the Wheatfield whence they could fire not only ahead but into the Wheatfield itself.[26]

The Fifth New Hampshire engaged the Fifteenth Georgia and the First Texas in the woods; the Sixty-first and Eighty-first regiments on the right fought with Anderson's men behind the wall. The 148th Pennsylvania, which now had three companies in the Wheatfield and seven in the woods, struck hard at Anderson's right behind the wall. While the three companies in the field and the Sixty-first and Eighty-first regiments threatened Anderson's line from the front, the seven companies on the left worked around Anderson's right flank and forced it to fall back through Rose's Woods, probably to the outcrop that had sheltered it and the Third Arkansas earlier in the battle. At the same time, the First Texas and the Fifteenth Georgia fell back to the stone wall at the north face of the walled triangle west of Devil's Den.[27]

After driving the Georgians from the wall between the woods and the Wheatfield, some of the men of the 148th dropped prone in the woods south of it and fired away. In the days of muzzle-loaders this was not the usual position taken by attacking infantrymen, but the smoke was so thick amid the trees that they could see better prone than standing. One young soldier of the 148th, a boy known for his piety and tender conscience, loaded and fired his rifle into the air at an angle of forty-five degrees that promised no harm at all to any Confederates. What in thunder was he up to, someone asked, and the boy replied that he was firing in this way in order to "scare 'em."[28]

Earlier in the day two men of Company F of the 148th had fussed over the ownership of a tin cup. Capt. Martin Dolan, their commander, an officer "who was very cool and unconcerned under fire," could not resolve the problem then. As luck would have it, the wall area taken over by the company was strewn with cups, probably the remains of an interrupted attempt of some Third Corps soldiers to have some coffee. Seeing them, Dolan shouted loudly over the din of battle, "Here, any of you fellows that hasn't a tin cup come and get one and don't be fightin' about them hereafter."[29] An army does travel on its stomach.

The 148th captured some Confederates in its front. One of them had a pistol that he concealed until he was passed to the rear. Then he whipped it out and shot a sergeant. It was his final act of defiance. Sgt. Ezra B. Walter bashed him in the head with his rifle butt, and an officer struck him with his sword. Walter saved his regiment's colors later that day and was nearly hit by a fragment from a shell that burst over his head and knocked a band from his rifle.[30]

Although the Irish Brigade followed Cross, Zook's special assignment from Sickles to occupy the area vacated by Barnes's brigades on the stony hill enabled Zook's troops to move at a double-quick to the area near the northwest corner of the Wheatfield. They deployed there before the Irish were able to form on Cross's right. Zook formed his regiments into two lines—the Sixty-sixth and Fifty-second New York and the 140th Pennsylvania from left to right in the first line and the Fifty-seventh in support in their rear.[31] Sergeant Paxton again tried to persuade the sick Lieutenant Wilson that he had come far enough, but Wilson was adamant. Like Ellis near Devil's Den and John Oates on Little Round Top, Wilson insisted that "the boys must see me in it with them."[32]

Trostle's Woods was a nightmare sort of place as Zook's regiments formed in it for their attack. Musketry roared in their front and cannon thundered along the road to their right. Bullets and shells shot at targets to their front and right flew into the woods, smashing into trees and knocking off their branches. There were shouted commands and grumbled curses and occasional cries of wounded men. Complicating it all to a degree we cannot really know were the troops of Barnes's division, who were falling back from the stony hill. Tilton's line collected along the wall on the west side of the woods and Sweitzer's along the road near where Zook's men were trying to form. Barnes denied that his brigades interfered with Zook's advance, and this might well have been so. Nevertheless, it seems likely that at least some of Sweitzer's men must have been in Zook's front. Robert Carter of the Twenty-second Massachusetts Regiment of Tilton's brigade admitted becoming entangled with Caldwell's formation. HISTORICUS, who might well not have been there, wrote: "When they [Zook's brigade] reached the ground, Barnes's disordered troops impeded the advance of the brigade. 'If you can't get out of the way,' cried Zook, 'lie down, and I will march over you.' Barnes ordered his men to lie down, and the chivalric Zook and his splendid brigade, under the personal direction of General Birney, did march over them and right into the breach."[33]

Zook had no opportunity to write of this, and no mention of such obstruction was made in the brigade's reports. Lt. William S. Shallenberger, adjutant of the 140th Pennsylvania, at the dedication of his regiment's memorial in 1889, spoke of passing "over the prostrate forms of troops exhausted whom we are expected to relieve." In 1913 Maj. Thomas B. Rogers of the 140th wrote that they had picked their way gingerly over Fifth Corps men who said, "Don't mind us, step anywhere; step on us," for they were glad to have Zook's men between them and the enemy. It is likely that Zook's brigade did pass over men from Barnes's division, but that action in itself was of no particular significance. It happened elsewhere on the field as a matter of course when one line relieved another. Any stigma involved resulted from something beyond the act itself.[34]

In the brief interval between the time when the 140th Pennsylvania formed its line and when the brigade went forward, Col. Richard P. Roberts, "a brave man but no tactician," took the opportunity to give the men of the 140th a pep talk. Among other things, he said: "Men of the 140th! Recollect that you are now defending your own soil and are fighting to drive the invader from your own homes and firesides. I shall therefore expect you to conduct yourselves as if in the presence of your wives, your sisters, and your sweethearts, and not disgrace the flag you bear or the name of Pennsylvanians."[35] The regiment answered its colonel with a cheer, for Roberts meant what he said and they knew it. He had been on sick leave in Washington, D.C., when the campaign began. Learning of the march north, Roberts traveled up the Chesapeake and Ohio Canal along the Potomac to meet the regiment at the crossing point at

Col. Edward E. Cross (Library of Congress)

Brig. Gen. Samuel K. Zook
(National Archives)

Col. Patrick Kelly (MOLLUS-MASS/
U.S.A.M.H.I., Carlisle Barracks, Pa.)

Col. John R. Brooke (MOLLUS-MASS/
U.S.A.M.H.I., Carlisle Barracks, Pa.)

Edwards Ferry. Roberts was a forty-three-year-old widower, and he had at home a small daughter whose future worried him. Before the 140th marched down from Cemetery Ridge, he asked Lieutenant Shallenberger to befriend her in case he should be killed.[36]

Roberts's 140th Pennsylvania had 589 officers and men at Gettysburg, though a smaller number than that must have been in its line of battle. Nevertheless, it was one of the largest regiments on the field. The Sixty-sixth and Fifty-second New York regiments on its left had but 134 and 176 officers and men respectively available for duty and the Fifty-seventh New York in the support line numbered but 179. The 140th, therefore, was larger than all the other regiments of the brigade combined. Perhaps for that reason, Zook placed it on the right and instructed his other regiments to guide on it.[37]

At Zook's command the brigade crossed the Wheatfield Road into the Wheatfield and on to the stony hill. Zook rode in front and on to the hill, trailed by an aide, Lt. Charles H. H. Broom, and an orderly. His other aide, Lt. Josiah M. Favill, rode with the Fifty-seventh New York in the support line. The tumult was deafening. No command could be heard. As always, smoke shrouded the field, limiting the visibility of those fighting there.[38] Mounted officers were natural targets: they shared air space with a lot of bullets fired too high to hit foot soldiers, and, of course, they tended to be important people and filled rifle sights in a tempting way. Thus it was that Zook had no sooner led his brigade beyond the road than Capt. Jonathan F. McCullough of Company A of the 140th touched Lt. James J. Purman with the flat of his sword blade and shouted, "There goes poor Zook." Purman looked ahead and saw Zook reeling in the saddle. He had been hit in the abdomen by a minié ball.[39] With Zook's fall, the advance slowed to a halt. From his place in the rear Favill saw Zook, Broom, and the mounted orderly, who had been sharing Zook's peril if not his distinction, ride off to the left. Broom and the orderly supported the general in the saddle as they left the field. Favill hastened to them. Zook grasped his hand and said: "It's all up with me, Favill."[40]

They placed Zook in an ambulance. A surgeon examined his wound and pronounced it mortal. The ambulance carried Zook to a house on the Baltimore Pike that was crowded with wounded, where attendants tried to make him comfortable for the night. On the next day he moved to another house inhabited by several women. The women made the general some chicken soup, which he tried, and he sipped a little whiskey. He declined to see a chaplain. During the day he expressed some wishes and inquired about the battle's progress. Pickett had been repulsed, and Favill told him "that the bands had been ordered to the front, flags were flying and the enemy were in retreat." "Then I am satisfied," said Zook, "and am ready to die."[41]

After speaking with Zook and before leaving the field, Favill sought Col. Orlando H. Morris of the Sixty-sixth New York to tell him that he was to take command of the brigade, but he could not find him. (Morris had been wounded also.) Favill stated that he then asked Lt. Col. John Fraser of the 140th to take over. Fraser asked Favill to stay with him on the field, for he had no experienced staff, but Favill declined, believing that his duty was with Zook. Col. John R. Brooke, commander of the Fourth Brigade, appeared then and, according to Favill, took command of the whole line.[42] In effect, Zook's fall left the brigade leaderless. In spite of Favill's neat recollections, it is not at all clear who, if anyone, really exercised command of the brigade in Zook's stead.[43]

Favill might well have confused Fraser in his recollections with Lt. Col. Charles G. Freudenberg of the Fifty-second New York. The Fifty-second was at the left center of the forward line, and Freudenberg would have been in a position to be aware of Zook's demise. In addition, Freudenberg stated plainly in later years that he had taken command of the brigade after Zook's fall. At this time the brigade was trading shots with Kershaw's men on the stony hill a hundred or so yards away. Like de Trobriand's brigade a short time before, Zook's men were at a disadvantage, for they were in the open while their enemy had some cover. Freudenberg said that he ordered the brigade to cease fire and, placing himself at the head of his regiment, ordered it forward. The brigade advanced, but not behind Freudenberg. He fell almost immediately with three wounds.[44]

The Irish Brigade had started to the Wheatfield ahead of Zook's brigade, but the latter was already forty yards into the Wheatfield when the Irish Brigade began its advance across it.[45] Although small, this demi-brigade spanned much of the interval between Cross's right and the stony hill. It made an inspiring picture as it stepped lively through the the trodden wheat, its green flags and the Stars and Stripes making splashes of color above the line, its burnished arms at right shoulder shift. The Irish still carried .69 caliber muskets and buck and ball in their cartridge pouches. Their entry on the scene inspired a bard who wrote:

> Here, on the field of Gettysburg, where treason's banner flew,
> Where rushed in wrath the Southern Gray to smite the Northern Blue,
> Where'er that Blue, by valor nerved, in serried ranks was seen,
> There flashed between it and the foe the daring Irish Green![46]

General Kershaw and the South Carolinians on the stony hill saw the lines of battle—the brigades of Zook and Kelly—headed in their direction. After his Third and Seventh South Carolina regiments had driven Tilton's and Sweitzer's brigades from the hill, Kershaw had directed the left wing of the Third against Bigelow's and Phillips's batteries. The batteries were posted on the Wheatfield Road just west of the stony hill. The Third's right wing was in the woods on the hill along with the Seventh, and both regiments must have fronted north, for Barnes's brigades had fallen back in that direction, the enemy was there, and Anderson's brigade was to the right facing the Wheatfield itself. But the Federal brigades advancing across the field threatened the

South Carolinians' right, and Kershaw pulled the right wing of the Seventh back to face them. Giving Lt. Col. Elbert Bland of the Seventh responsibility for that wing's conduct, Kershaw hastened back to see General Paul Semmes, whose brigade was about fifty yards to his right and rear. He hoped that Semmes's brigade and his own Fifteenth South Carolina Regiment, now separated from his main line by Semmes's brigade, would come up on his right in the ravine area and close the gap between his right and Anderson's left.[47]

Kershaw conversed with Semmes, and the latter began to shift his Georgia brigade right to uncover the forward line east of the Rose buildings before going on. Believing that Semmes would carry out his wishes, Kershaw continued his ride south to the Fifteenth South Carolina. That regiment had been advancing with its colonel, William D. De Saussure, walking in front of it, sword drawn, leading it on its way. But at Kershaw's arrival, De Saussure fell with a mortal wound, and Maj. William M. Gist took command of the Fifteenth in his place.[48]

Kershaw gave Gist some instructions and hurried back to the stony hill. He arrived just in time to see the Federals halt about two hundred yards away, fire a volley, and assault the Seventh South Carolina's position. In Kershaw's opinion, "They were handsomely received and entertained by this veteran regiment, which long kept them at bay in its front."[49]

Once Zook's brigade renewed its attack, it went forward with alacrity. Whether it was Lieutenant Colonel Freudenberg, Colonel Roberts, or even Colonel Brooke who got it moving we do not know. Capt. William Scherrer, who succeeded to the command of the Fifty-second New York, wrote that his Germans went at the double-quick but in good order. Maj. Peter Nelson, who had a lively imagination, recalled that the Sixty-sixth New York advanced undaunted "through wheat-fields, woods, over rail fences 10 feet high, stone walls, ditches, deep ravines, rocks, and all sorts of obstructions, every one of which had served as cover for the enemy, and from which a murderous fire was poured upon us as we advanced." Viewing the terrain more calmly, it is obvious that most of the obstructions remembered by Nelson were not really there; the Sixty-sixth crossed the hundred yards or so of space at the double-quick and without firing. At the end of its dash, at the west side of the Wheatfield, the Sixty-first clashed with the Carolinians at close range, and "here fell many noble men."[50]

Lieutenant Colonel Fraser of the 140th Pennsylvania on the right of Zook's brigade line wrote of a more deliberate advance. On being ordered forward, he recalled, the 140th "opened a brisk fire, which it kept up with great firmness and coolness, steadily driving the enemy before it until we reached the crest of a small hill." Fraser's account suggests that the right wing of the 140th fronted directly south across the road toward the stony hill and the trees upon it, which were only two hundred or so feet from Trostle's Woods. The six companies on the right of the 140th went onto the bald portion of the hill, while the left four companies, together with the Fifty-second and Sixty-sixth New York regiments, entered the Wheatfield and, to assail Kershaw's men on the hill, "gradually made a considerable wheel to the right." The left of Zook's line was covered and aided greatly, without doubt, by the Irish Brigade, which was advancing to its left and rear.[51]

The woods were a fearsome place to approach. While the right of the 140th had an open gentle slope on its right and faced downslope through the woods, the left of the 140th and the rest of the brigade pushed from the Wheatfield into a tree-covered amphitheater, studded with large rocks, that extended about seventy yards into the trees and then sloped up a distance of twenty feet to the woods' west edge. The tree canopy confined the smoke, which became so dense that it half concealed the rocks and trees. Through the dense pall of smoke the men of the 140th suddenly saw a blaze of light to their left front that revealed a line of troops firing at the enemy before them. It was the Irish Brigade coming up, and it was apparent that the adjoining flanks of the brigades were overlapping. Colonel Roberts tried to remedy this by shifting the 140th to the right in order to make room for the Irish. When the 140th shifted, its right protruded about fifty yards into the open oat field west of the hill toward the Peach Orchard and the field of fire of Bigelow's battery.[52]

Things were not much better for the three companies of the 140th now that they were in the open than they had been in the trees. The smoke was still dense, so thick and dark that the left of the Third South Carolina in their front appeared as an indistinct line behind a continual flickering row of lights made by the muzzle flashes of the Third's rifles. The 140th fired at will. Colonel Roberts reminded the men of the 140th that they were Pennsylvanians and that they should fire low. They must have needed little reminder that they faced the enemy, for the Second and Third South Carolina regiments were firing at them, and probably Confederate batteries were shooting at them too. Colonel Roberts fell, a Pennsylvanian to the end, and his daughter Emma became an orphan.[53] Among the most lamented of the 140th's casualties here was Capt. David Acheson, a prominent young man from Washington, Pennsylvania, and from Washington and Jefferson College, for whom life had held great promise. He suffered a breast wound while on the firing line, and was hit a second time as he was carried from the field. Another bullet struck poor, sick Alex Wilson in the forehead, but he at least had the satisfaction of dying with his men—he had not funked. Sgt. John F. Wilson of Company G was shot in both arms and walked from the field with them dangling helplessly at his sides.[54]

Lieutenant Colonel Fraser, now in command of the 140th, pulled its right back so that it faced the fire that was coming from the direction of the Peach Orchard. It was then that he saw a great danger. Many men on the 140th's left seemed to be streaming to the rear, and an orderly Confederate line seemed to be threatening the brigade's right.[55]

As Zook's men assaulted the northern half of the stony hill, the Irish Brigade moved up on Zook's left against the southern half, where de Trobriand's, Tilton's, and Sweitzer's brigades had fought only a short while before. The men with the green flags met only scant opposition at first, for Kershaw's regiments were giving their attention to Zook. But as the Irish line neared the trees, perhaps as Kershaw returned to the hill, the South Carolinians gave them a volley. Fortunately it was high and did little damage. The Irish pushed on until they were within twenty yards of the tree line. At this point someone spotted a Confederate line among the trees and shouted, "There they are!" With that, the Irish line halted and opened fire, each man firing at will.[56]

The Irish Brigade's histories give Gettysburg short shrift because most of its veterans served earlier in the war and were not there. An exception, though, are the writings of Major Mulholland of the 116th Pennsylvania Regiment, who recalled the battle for the brigade with more pride than objectivity. In Mulholland's recollections the Irish Brigade assault against the stony hill was readily made, its alignment well preserved. The Confederates, some behind boulders, held the higher ground in the western half of the woods, far enough up the slope so that their feet were about level with the attacking Irishmen's heads. The Confederates sheltered by the rocks had a peculiar disadvantage, for they had to stand high above them in order to fire down the slope. This created a tendency for them to fire high and made those who were firing good targets for the Irish Brigade's buck and ball. The Irish were able to work their way so close to the Seventh South Carolina's position that the officers were able to use their pistols, and one man shot a Confederate just six feet in front of his rifle's muzzle.[57]

The lines blazed away at one another at close range for several minutes; then Colonel Kelly ordered a charge. The Irish cheered, and the green flags ascended the slope, went on to the crest, and continued into the Carolinians' position. All was confusion there—Zook's men pressed from the right, formations mingled, and the opposing lines stood but a few yards apart. Then the firing stopped, or so it was recalled, and there was a comparative silence in that limited area as soldiers in butternut and in blue stared at one another in bewilderment and awe. The hiatus offered an opportunity. According to his own account, rendered before a friendly and noncritical audience, Major Mulholland, quick of mind and tongue, stepped up on a boulder and bellowed, "Confederate troops lay down your arms and go to the rear!"[58] In recalling the incident, Mulholland reflected with pleasure, "This ended a scene that was becoming embarrassing. The order was promptly obeyed and a large number of what I think were men of Kershaw's Brigade became our prisoners." As the Irish looked around, they saw a shambles, dead men shot in the upper portions of their bodies by buck and ball. Behind one rock lay five bodies, mute testimony to the tenacity of the Confederate defenders.[59]

Mulholland's account was colorful and probably lost nothing in the telling.

On his side, Kershaw recalled that the Seventh Regiment, which the Irish Brigade must have outnumbered, received their Celtic guests along with Zook's Germans and entertained them handsomely. He said nothing about seeing Mulholland's performance, but he worried about a hundred-yard gap at the Plum Run ravine on his right, which existed even though one of Semmes's regiments had taken a position nearby. The Federals pushed their way into the gap and forced the Seventh's right wing back toward its left wing, which faced northerly toward Zook's line. Kershaw tried to shift the Second South Carolina over from the left so that it could help the Seventh, but he could not do so in time. The Irish pressed hard, and finally the Seventh could hold no longer. "These men were brave veterans who had fought from Bull Run to Gettysburg," wrote Kershaw, "and knew the strength of their position, and held it as long as it was tenable." The time had come to fall back, and Kershaw ordered Col. D. Wyatt Aiken to retreat across Plum Run's marsh and form behind a wall near Rose's farmyard.[60]

The Seventh's withdrawal left only the Third South Carolina and a portion of Semmes's Fiftieth Georgia on the hill. Their plight was desperate. Zook's men assailed them from the east, southeast, and north. They threatened envelopment on the left and right. To protect his right, Major Maffett held his left in place opposite the right of the 140th Pennsylvania and allowed his right to come back slowly in order to present a front toward what had been the brigade right. Soon the right wing of the Third, like that of the Seventh, was almost doubled back on its left, and the enemy was but thirty yards away. Maffett believed that he had held his attackers off for an hour, with some help from the Fiftieth Georgia, being subjected all the while to rifle and artillery fire. Probably it was not nearly so long a time, but it seemed so. It is hard to understand how a Federal battery could properly have fired on the Third when visibility was so poor and the Federal infantry so close. And yet shot and shell were flying in unlikely places that day, and Maffett's men probably received their share of them.[61]

Kershaw knew of Maffett's fate but was unable to help the Third Regiment. His staff was still off to the left, and one can only wonder what its members were doing away from the brigade commander all this while.[62] The Fifteenth had not arrived from the rear, and Kershaw did not know precisely where it was. Catastrophe loomed over the Third. Therefore, Kershaw ordered it to fall back and join the Seventh near Rose's farmyard. As Kershaw followed it from the woods, he saw one of the grand sights of that day's battle—Wofford's brigade was "coming in in splendid style."[63]

The regiments of Kershaw's left wing joined in Wofford's drive as those Georgians came abreast of their positions. John Coxe of the Second South Carolina, which was just west of the stony hill, heard the artillery fire and musketry along the Wheatfield Road die away. Then there was a Rebel yell and a crash of musketry to his left. An officer yelled, "That's help for us! Spring up the bluff, boys!" and they did. Soon an officer, whom Coxe

Brig. Gen. Paul J. Semmes (Gettysburg National Military Park)

Brig. Gen. William T. Wofford (Library of Congress)

The Wheatfield. Painting by F. D. Briscoe (National Archives)

believed to be Wofford, rode up and asked the Second to join his right in the chase. They gave a yell, and Wofford waved his hat and rode off to the left. The Second then wheeled right toward the stony hill and the Wheatfield beyond.[64]

While Wofford's Georgians were bearing down on Zook's line on the stony hill and Barnes's position in the west end of Trostle's Woods, much was happening elsewhere in the Wheatfield area. In order of arrival, the Fourth Brigade of Caldwell's division, Brooke's, followed the Irish Brigade to the Wheatfield. Brooke's brigade was Caldwell's reserve, his ace in the hole. Like the other brigades of the division, it had marched south from its position near the midpoint of Cemetery Ridge, but when it arrived at the Wheatfield Road, there was no place for it in the restricted confines of the Wheatfield. Thus, for a few minutes Caldwell had the luxury of holding it in reserve.[65]

John Rutter Brooke, a native of Montgomery County, Pennsylvania, had been twenty-five years old for just eleven days. He had entered the army in April 1861 as a captain in the Fourth Pennsylvania Regiment, a three-months unit that had returned home after Bull Run, where it had seen no fighting. This inconspicuous service provided a springboard for the young captain, who soon became the colonel of the new Fifty-third Pennsylvania Regiment. The Fifty-third received its colors from Governor Curtin in November 1861, and Brooke took the regiment south to the Army of the Potomac. The Fifty-third's history was that of the Third Brigade, First Division, Second Corps, from the Peninsular Campaign through the battle of Fredericksburg. Then it was placed in the newly organized Fourth Brigade, with which it fought at Chancellorsville. Brooke commanded the Third Brigade at Antietam and was given command of the newly organized Fourth Brigade, which he led to Gettysburg.[66]

Brooke had five nominal regiments in his brigade of about 850 officers and men. In its reversed formation the 145th Pennsylvania was on the right and the Twenty-seventh Connecticut was next in line, followed to the left by the Sixty-fourth New York, the Fifty-third Pennsylvania, and the Second Delaware.[67] Tension must have been high in the brigade's ranks as it awaited the order to go in. Its men could see the Wheatfield action in front of them, and bullets and shells came in their direction. So dangerous was the wait that the 145th, if not the rest of the brigade, was ordered to lie down. Brooke took the wait as an opportunity to give a pep talk. He said in part, "Boys—remember the enemy has invaded our own soil. The eyes of the world . . . [are] upon us and we are expected to stand up bravely to our duty."[68]

It is hard to say how long the brigade waited. Caldwell reported that he did not send it forward until Cross's men ran out of ammunition, but Brooke wrote that it was only a short time.[69] At the time of Brooke's advance, Cross's Fifth New Hampshire would have been in the woods east of the Wheatfield, and the 148th Pennsylvania would have been astride the stone wall in the southeast corner of the Wheatfield and in the adjoining portion of Rose's

Woods. Cross's two right regiments were in the Wheatfield, a third of the way across it, about where their monuments stand today. Kelly's and Zook's brigades were pushing toward the stony hill.

Perhaps it was during this wait that Brooke took on responsibilities that might have been better exercised by Caldwell. As stated above, Captain Favill, Zook's aide, wrote that after Zook's fall Brooke came up and took command of the whole line. But neither Caldwell nor Brooke wrote anything of this in his report except that Brooke stated after his advance that he ordered a part of Zook's brigade, which was on his right, to his brigade's support. The reports of Kelly's and Zook's brigades say nothing of it.[70]

Brooke, however, later claimed taking on additional responsibility on two occasions. In 1885 he wrote Francis A. Walker that Zook's regiments had gone forward under his command, and in 1886 he wrote Walker again that it was Colonel Freudenberg who told him that Zook was dead. Brooke wrote also that Zook's regimental commanders had reported to him after Zook's fall. It is probable that these assertions were the basis of Walker's statement in his *History of the Second Corps* that Brooke had command of the entire line. That claim was also made by the Fifty-third's adjutant at the time of the dedication of that regiment's memorial.[71]

The truth of all this might never be known. Ambitious officers abhor a vacuum in command, and Brooke's career suggests that he was ambitious. If Brooke did exercise the broad authority he later claimed, it must have been for only a brief period after Freudenberg was shot. His doing so was important only in that it might have improved coordination in these last stages of the attack and might have reflected adversely on Caldwell's performance as a division commander.

Brooke's brigade's assault began on Caldwell's orders for it to relieve Cross's brigade. Brooke's five small regiments swept across the Wheatfield, through or over Cross's right regiments and to a point beyond the center of the field.[72] They moved briskly after their colors, met sharp fire halfway across the field, and, as they recalled it, swept all before them. Probably it was not quite so easy as that. They advanced without hindrance beyond Cross's line; then they halted and exchanged fire with the Rebels in their front, probably behind the west half of the stone wall. Lt. Col. Henry C. Merwin of the Twenty-seventh and Col. Hiram Brown of the 145th fell at this time.[73]

Brooke's and Tige Anderson's brigades exchanged fire for a few minutes, and then Brooke gave the command, "Fix Bayonets." Brooke's brigade, probably aided by the 148th Pennsylvania on its left and Kelly's and Zook's brigades on its right, pressed forward and swept Anderson's men from the north half of Rose's Woods, forced them across Plum Run's ravine, and pushed them from the western edge of Rose's Woods. The Confederates attempted to rally on the high ground west of the ravine, but the Federals sent them packing. Here the Twenty-seventh captured some prisoners, including two officers.[74]

It was a gallant charge, one of the few during the battle made by troops of the Army of the Potomac, and it required some leadership. At one point Brooke restored momentum by seizing the colors of the Fifty-third Pennsylvania and leading the way with them. By the time that the brigade reached the west edge of Rose's Woods, its advance faltered. Both color-bearers of the Sixty-fourth New York were shot, and their flags passed into the hands of others. Brooke's men must have needed to catch their breath, and resistance had stiffened, possibly with the arrival of Semmes's brigade in their front.[75] But at this time the colors of Union regiments waved over a north-south line from Trostle's Woods, across the stony hill, to near the west front of Rose's Woods. The Wheatfield was again in Federal hands, and except for the Confederate's presence at Devil's Den, Sickles's position had been recovered.

Colonels Work of the First Texas and Du Bose of the Fifteenth Georgia viewed Brooke's sweep with alarm. From these regiments' position at the little knoll about three hundred yards north of Devil's Den and east of the corner of the Wheatfield, they enfiladed Caldwell's regiments, firing into the 148th Pennsylvania and the left regiments of Brooke's line. Brooke's charge had not struck them, but it had driven away the support on their left and threatened them with isolation and destruction. Therefore, the colonels decided to abandon the advanced position for the greater safety of their main line. Du Bose ordered the Fifteenth back to the stone wall of the triangular field near Devil's Den, and Work followed suit. In doing so, Work ordered Capt. Henry E. Moss of Company D to stay behind with the colors of the First Texas and make a show of strength until the bulk of the two regiments was safely to the rear.[76]

It did not happen as Work intended. Many soldiers of the First Texas refused to fall back and leave their colors behind and remained with Moss's company on the knoll. As it turned out, this rear guard was able to handle all of the attention it received and held its place until the Confederate tide flowed once more. That portion of the First Texas that fell back, the Fifteenth Georgia, and other units at the triangular field continued their fight at long range by raking Brooke's left and providing support for Anderson's right.[77]

Brooke's advanced position in the western end of Rose's Woods had strength so long as it was attacked only from the front—the direction of the Emmitsburg Road. Brooke's brigade was particularly vulnerable to attacks on its left as soon as Anderson's troops could rally and, with help from Semmes's brigade, give Brooke's line the attention it deserved. Semmes's brigade had come up "handsomely" at Kershaw's request, but Semmes fell with a wound in the thigh at some unidentified place. Someone applied a tourniquet, and Paul Semmes was carried from the field with a mortal wound.[78]

The meager accounts of the action on Brooke's brigade front are almost entirely from Federal sources. They hold that Brooke's line was in the form of a crescent with the center bulging toward the front. For a time, at least,

Brooke directed his brigade standing on a boulder behind its left center. As Brooke recalled it, the enemy in his front had come from the area of Biesecker's Woods as the Fifteenth South Carolina and Semmes's brigade had done. Soon after striking Brooke's brigade in the front, a body of Confederates with a flag tried to turn its left. Brooke met this threat by refusing the line of the Second Delaware, which dealt with it for a short time.[79]

The fight was savage, the firing heavy. The Confederates, who undoubtedly took advantage of a stone wall about two hundred yards in Brooke's front and a closer fence line at the edge of the woods, poured a withering fire on the hitherto triumphant little brigade. Brooke's troops had one thing in their favor—the cover provided by the shoulder of the ravine. The Twenty-seventh's colors were on top of it in the enemy's view, but its riflemen loaded beneath the brow and when ready stepped up to shoot.[80]

It was only a short fight, probably not much longer than fifteen minutes, and coordinated loosely, no doubt, with the fighting on the stony hill. By this time the fighting on Vincent's front on Little Round Top must have been drawing to a close, the troops of Anderson's brigade were tightening their belts for another assault, Kershaw was trying to reform his brigade at the Rose farmyard, and Barksdale's brigade was attacking the Third Corps positions along the Emmitsburg Road.

Things were not going well for Brooke and his brigade now. The brigade received a cross fire from the Devil's Den area and from the low ground south of the stony hill. Both of Brooke's aides were wounded, and Brooke himself had been wounded in the ankle badly enough that he could not walk without help. He sent an appeal to Caldwell for help to secure his flanks and succor his own line, which was down to its last five rounds of ammunition.[81]

In the meantime Caldwell was seeking help for his four hard-pressed brigades. Lt. William P. Wilson of his staff sought help from Barnes, and Caldwell himself went to Sweitzer and Barnes to get support from Sweitzer's brigade (see below). After receiving the promise of that aid, he galloped across the Wheatfield to speak with General Ayres, whose division was approaching from the east. Suffice it to say here that the help readily available would not enable Caldwell to hold the ground gained. The tough resistance and aggressiveness of Hood's and McLaws's divisions had all but doomed the First Division of the Second Corps.[82]

When it became obvious that his position was no longer tenable and help was not at hand, Colonel Brooke ordered his brigade back. Regimental reports say little of its withdrawal, but Brooke wrote that the brigade went back slowly, and firing, and that it brought off most of its wounded. Capt. Henry Fuller, commander of Company F of the Sixty-fourth New York Regiment, fell with a leg wound as that unit started back. Private George Whipple and another soldier helped him along until another ball hit Fuller in the back and passed through his body. They laid the captain down beside Plum Run; and as Whipple tried to comfort him, Fuller looked up and said,

"George keep up good courage." Then Fuller died. The next words Whipple heard were those of a Georgian who demanded that he surrender and told him, "Go to the rear you d—d Yankee son of a b—h." Brooke himself could not walk alone by this time and left the field with a burly soldier supporting him under each arm.[83]

If Brooke was able to bring off his wounded it was because other brigades were keeping the Confederates busy. Some help came from the stony hill, where Zook's and Kelly's regiments were still vying with Kershaw's right and Semmes's left. Most of Semmes's brigade was fighting Brooke, but the Fiftieth Georgia was in the rear of Kershaw's right. While the Fiftieth awaited orders to advance, its lieutenant colonel, Francis Kearse, who was commanding that day, addressed each company individually, telling the men that they must fight and win. Kearse was killed by the artillery fire that pounded the Fiftieth during its advance. The Fiftieth, then commanded by Capt. Peter McGlashan, followed the South Carolinians to the stony hill and fell back with their repulse. As they rallied in Rose's lane, Lt. William Pendleton, and likely others too, drank water from Plum Run that was already tinged with blood. This done, Pendleton challenged his company, "Let's show we can fight in Pennsylvania as well as in Virginia." There followed then what McGlashan called "the hottest and sternest struggle of the war." It was hand-to-hand fighting with clubbed rifles and bayonets. Although McGlashan thought that they were engaged for an hour, it must have been for a much shorter time. Finally the Federals in their front—it must have been the Irish Brigade—retreated beyond the woods and the fighting ended there.[84]

Major Mulholland had the most to say about the last minutes of the Irish Brigade on the stony hill. During a lull sometime before the end, perhaps after the Seventh had fallen back and before the Fiftieth Georgia became closely engaged, the Irish regiments reformed their lines and made ready for the next onslaught. Mulholland walked down the slope in his front to a spot occupied earlier by the 110th Pennsylvania. He saw the bodies of its dead above the ravine. One in particular caught his eye. It was that of young man, and it was lying on a large rock in a relaxed way with its face to the sun. The major looked more closely and discovered a small hole in its forehead from which blood slowly oozed and trickled to the gray rock that pillowed the boy's head.[85]

From the 116th's position the major could see across to the Peach Orchard, and he saw a line of infantry moving down toward Trostle's Woods and the 116th's rear. The major hurried over to Colonel Kelly and told him what he had seen. Kelly thought that they must be Federal troops but permitted Mulholland to go see for himself.[86] Then, according to the major, whose accounts are sometimes hard to believe, he saw one of Zook's regiments standing idly to the right and rear and presumed to make it useful by taking it on his reconnaissance. Turning the 116th over to his next in rank, Mulholland went over to the idle regiment. He learned that it had lost its field officers and persuaded whoever was in charge to escort him to a point from which he could identify the suspect line. They had to go only about fifty yards before they were able to see that the troops were Confederates and up to no good. Mulholland and his escort beat a hasty retreat to the hill, where the regiment halted to the Irish right and rear.[87]

Another of the Irish Brigade's bards later wrote a poem applicable to the Wheatfield and the stony hill. He cautioned:

> O comrades, step with reverent tread
> Tow'rd this historic mound;
> The soil once wet with brave men's blood
> Is always holy ground.
> Here five-and-twenty years ago
> An Irish phalanx stood,
> And here they swelled the battle-tide
> With generous Celtic blood.[88]

The approach of the line from the Peach Orchard—Wofford's brigade, no doubt—plus the pressure on Brooke's front, was a signal to the regiments on the stony hill that they must leave that bloody, hallowed ground with a certain haste. Colonel Kelly ordered his regiments to fall back firing, a laudable but difficult thing to do. He had no alternative. One of Kelly's staff officers brought Kelly's order to Mulholland. When the major received it, he believed that the 116th was nearly surrounded and that if his men were to get back, they must go as individuals. He pointed the direction in which they should go and sent them off. In the meantime the color-bearers rolled up the once flaunted flags. When this was done, Mulholland, the flags, and about thirty members of the 116th ran back through the Wheatfield. Although they drew fire from the left and right, most made it to the shelter of the Union line on Cemetery Ridge.[89]

There was comparable confusion in Zook's brigade. Lt. Col. Fraser of the 140th Pennsylvania saw a line of infantry bearing toward his regiment's right and rear. Perhaps at this time the 140th's right still fronted south toward Kershaw's men, near the Rose buildings and the Second South Carolina, which was even closer to it. Fraser had not yet learned of Zook's fall and sought orders or advice from Zook or his staff. When he learned that none were available, Fraser decided that the 140th must fall back. This it did, pausing occasionally to exchange fire with its attackers.[90] Meanwhile, the imaginative Major Nelson was trying to bring order to the Sixty-sixth New York's line, which had mixed with others. When he saw the 140th retire, he recalled his orders to conform with the movements of the unit on his right. Nelson then ordered the Sixty-sixth to fall back too.[91]

The officers reporting for the Fifty-second and Fifty-seventh New York regiments both claimed that their units were ordered to fall back. The Fifty-seventh, which apparently had remained in the brigade support line, was about to wheel right to face the attackers when the forward line gave way, some of its men falling back through the Fifty-seventh's ranks in disorder. Like Fraser of the 140th, Lt. Col. Alford B. Chapman of the Fifty-seventh halted his troops several times, but the two regiments seemed not to be working together, and they delayed the enemy little if at all.[92]

Lt. Col. Charles H. Morgan, chief of staff for the Second Corps, rode into the Wheatfield area in time to see Caldwell's division falling back in seeming disorder. It must have come as a rude shock to see the First Division, Second Corps, which had charged close to the Sunken Road at Fredericksburg, in such a state.[93] Morgan recalled seeing many things. There was Col. Orlando H. Morris of the Sixty-sixth New York, Zook's brigade, walking briskly to the rear, his unbuttoned coat displaying a shirt stained with the blood of a chest wound. He met Brooke limping through the woods looking for his brigade. He saw officers making unsuccessful attempts to reform units of the division and spoke with officers who complained that Caldwell had put the division in badly. To add salt to the wound, Sykes told Hancock later that evening that Caldwell's division had done poorly. It had been an unfortunate afternoon for Hancock's old command.[94]

When Caldwell sought help for his division, he rode to Sweitzer's brigade, the three regiments of which were in Trostle's Woods along the Wheatfield Road. Caldwell approached Sweitzer and told him that his division was driving the enemy "like h-ll" in the woods in front of the Wheatfield but that he needed the support of another brigade. Would Sweitzer help him out?[95] In response Sweitzer referred him to General Barnes, who was nearby, and remarked that he would obey Barnes's orders in the matter with pleasure. Caldwell trotted over to see Barnes, and soon Barnes rode to see Sweitzer. Barnes asked Sweitzer if he would take his brigade forward. Sweitzer replied that he would do so if Barnes wished it, and Barnes said that he did. Sweitzer called his brigade of about 1,000 men to attention; Barnes rode out front and made a few patriotic remarks, to which the brigade responded with a cheer. Amenities over, Sweitzer launched his gallant 1,000 into the maelstrom of the Wheatfield.[96]

At this time there was a lull on the stony hill, as narrated above. Wofford's brigade was approaching the arena, and Brooke's brigade must have been firing its last rounds in Rose's Woods beyond Plum Run. Sweitzer's brigade stepped out in grand style, crossed the road, and entered the Wheatfield. Col. Harrison Jeffords's Fourth Michigan Regiment was on the right, and its right flank was close to the west end of the field. Sweitzer's Sixty-second Pennsylvania, under Lt. Col. James C. Hull, was in the center, and Col. George L. Prescott's Thirty-second Massachusetts Regiment was on the left—the same order in which they had formed on the stony hill earlier in the afternoon. Their line must have extended about three hundred yards from flank to flank and most of the way across the field. The brigade's zone embraced the positions of the regiments of Cross's right wing, and these units considered Sweitzer's brigade to be their relief.[97] As the right of the brigade approached the south end of the field and the stone wall there, Sweitzer saw a bad omen that he did not understand and appreciate at the time: two or three regiments were leaving the stony hill. Sweitzer assumed that the departing regiments were falling back after having been relieved. Sweitzer continued his brigade's unobstructed march to the stone wall, the position occupied an hour or so before by the Seventeenth Maine. This time, instead of being on the hill, the right of the Fourth Michigan occupied the marshy ground by the rail fence, and the Sixty-second and Thirty-second regiments carried the line east along the north side of the wall.[98]

Sweitzer and the Fourth Michigan heard shooting on the stony hill as they passed behind it, but they did not consider it a cause for alarm. When they reached the wall, it became apparent that bullets were coming at them from the direction of the hill. Sweitzer thought first that it was friendly fire, that units on the hill were shooting over their heads toward Rebels in the woods beyond the wall and that some of the rounds were falling short.[99] Sweitzer did not realize that this fire came from Kershaw's left wing. This wing, advancing on Wofford's right, had occupied the hill as Anderson's and Semmes's brigades and the Fifteenth South Carolina pressed into Rose's Woods.[100]

It soon became apparent to Sweitzer that his own brigade was the target. The bearer of the brigade pennant, Pvt. Edward Martin, who, like Sweitzer, was on horseback, remarked, "Colonel, I'll be —— if I don't think we are faced the wrong way; the rebs are up there in the woods behind us, on the right." At about the same time some of the men of the Fourth Michigan, who were nearest the woods on the hill, heard the rattling of canteens and the heavy tread of rebel infantry only fifty yards in their rear.[101] Sweitzer also received alarms from the Fourth Michigan and the Sixty-second Pennsylvania. He quickly emulated Colonel Merrill of the Seventeenth Maine and refused the brigade's right, not just three companies as Merrill had done, but the entire Fourth Michigan. Colonel Jeffords somehow pivoted the Fourth's left forward and its right back from the marsh, thus forming a line facing west toward the woods on the stony hill.[102]

Lieutenant Colonel Hull of the Sixty-second voiced further alarm. The fire from his right was more troublesome than that from his front. Sweitzer thereupon gave permission to Hull to change front to the right also.[103] Now two regiments of Sweitzer's brigade fronted west. But how? Were they in a single line? If so, the Fourth would have had to shift right to give the Sixty-second an open field of fire, or the Sixty-second would have had to advance to the Fourth's right, leaving a large gap between these two regiments and the Thirty-second Massachusetts off to the left. No one said exactly how the regiments were positioned, so we do not know, but all were heavily engaged.

The Thirty-second was something of a stepchild in this fight. Posted on

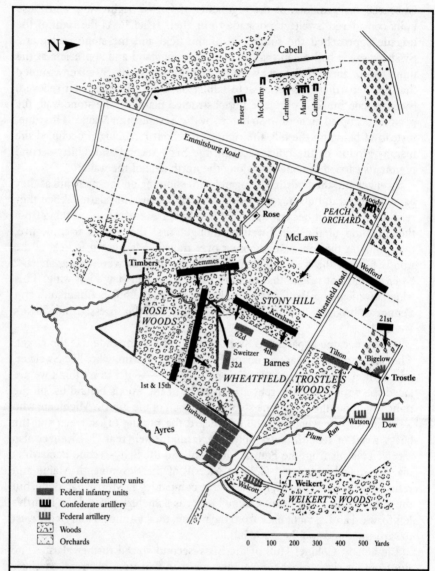

1. Sweitzer's brigade, Barnes's division, sent to Caldwell's support in the Wheatfield, is attacked both from the stony hill and from Rose's Woods. Sweitzer retreats from the Wheatfield.

2. Ayres's division has formed east of the Wheatfield in support of Caldwell. As Sweitzer is struck, Burbank's brigade of Ayres's division wheels left into the Wheatfield preparatory to an advance into Rose's Woods. Anderson's brigade strikes its left, while Kershaw's and Wofford's brigades hit its right. Ayres's two brigades retreat across Plum Run and rally north of Little Round Top.

3. Wofford drives Barnes's division from Trostle's Woods.

4. No Federal units remain west of Plum Run on this part of the field.

Map 12-2. The Confederates Seize the Wheatfield

the left at the east end of the wall and near the woods where the 148th Pennsylvania had been, it was farthest from the flanking fire that bothered the rest of the brigade and from Sweitzer's thoughts. (Sweitzer did not mention it in his report of this portion of the battle.) Yet it was posted so that it met the attack of Anderson's brigade head-on and received fire from the First Texas in the woods to its left. When the Thirty-second advanced, Colonel Prescott deployed its Company H to guard the regiment's left flank. This company laid down in the wheat, and Confederate bullets clipped wheat heads off above it. Cpl. Oscar West found the time to admire the quality of Mr. Rose's wheat and collected some to send home for seed. Since the Rebels were firing at the Thirty-second, he had to be careful while doing so. Unfortunately the company moved before he could get the wheat into his haversack.[104]

Colonel Prescott was wounded early in the fight and left the field, turning the regiment over to Lt. Col. Luther Stephenson. In later years none of these Yankees could recall having seen Colonel Sweitzer on the Thirty-second's front during the fight, though he might have been there, and Stephenson received no orders from him during this stage of the battle. The officers and men of the Thirty-second believed that the regiment was fighting on its own.[105]

When he was forced to change the fronts of the Fourth Michigan and Sixty-second Pennsylvania, Colonel Sweitzer became alarmed over his brigade's situation and sent his aide, Lt. John A. M. Seitz, back to General Barnes to tell him of the brigade's plight. Seitz galloped to Trostle's Woods, where he had last seen Barnes, but could not find him. In the meantime, Barnes had seen the Confederates moving against Sweitzer's flank and sent an orderly to Sweitzer with orders to get the brigade out. For some reason Sweitzer did not get the message and another was not sent. The feeling at Barnes's headquarters at this time was expressed by Lt. Charles H. Ross, Barnes's aide, who said, "There goes the Second Brigade, we may as well bid it goodbye."[106]

Not finding Barnes, Lieutenant Seitz headed back to his brigade. The Confederates on the hill shot at him as he galloped by and killed his horse, and Seitz had to finish his trip on foot. Seitz reported to Sweitzer that he could not find Barnes, that the brigade was nearly surrounded, and that it was in a "bad snap."[107] Sweitzer could not have been surprised. The Confederates had already emerged from the cover of the trees on the hill, and there was fighting at close quarters. For some reason the color-bearer of the Fourth Michigan dropped the national flag. It was a new flag, and Jeffords, when appointed colonel, had "pledged himself in decisive terms to be its special defender and guardian." At the time of a visit by Senator Zachariah Chandler and Governor Austin Blair of Michigan shortly before the campaign began, Jeffords showed them the new colors and with the ardor of youth "repeated his determination to be its especial guardian and defender."[108]

Jeffords meant every word of his pledge. When he saw his beloved flag lying in the wheat, he shouted to his brother and to Lt. Michael Vreeland to help him recover it. The three dashed for it; the colonel and a Rebel soldier grabbed for it at the same time. There was swearing and tugging until Jeffords's brother struck the soldier in the neck with his sword and laid him low. Other Confederates attacked the knot of officers, which drew other men of the Fourth to the spot, and there was a melee. The brother took a ball in the chest, and Maj. Jairus Hall killed the man who shot him. A Confederate shot Vreeland in the chest and right arm and another clouted him in the head with a clubbed musket. Both of these officers survived. The colonel did not. A Confederate ran him through with a bayonet, inflicting a mortal wound. Soldiers of the Fourth carried Jeffords and their flag from the field. Jeffords died soon, but his last words were not of the flag; they were simply, "Mother, mother, mother!"[109]

The Confederates shot Sweitzer's horse and put a bullet through the colonel's hat. It was a tight situation; people were excited. Sweitzer lost his temper and with it some good will in Massachusetts. As the Thirty-second was falling back in accordance with a message delivered by Seitz, Sweitzer went up to Lieutenant Colonel Stephenson and "demanded with an oath" to know why the Thirty-second was retreating. He accused it of running away, and Stephenson "indignantly resented the charge." Then Stephenson ordered the Thirty-second to face about and fire. It was a proper but futile thing to do, for the regiment merely drew increased fire its way on front and flank. A ball hit Stephenson in the face but did not kill him. According to Corporal West, every man was then ordered to get out as best he could. West took to his heels, and remembered that the "bullets were singing a 'double quick march' all around me."[110]

The three regiments of Sweitzer's brigade crossed a stone fence at the end of the Wheatfield and rallied behind a battery, probably Barnes's or Walcott's. The Ninth Massachusetts Regiment, which had been detached beyond Wolf's Hill, rejoined the brigade there. The brigade had had an eventful day. In later years it shared the stigma of having left the stony hill position prematurely and then the distinction of having been a forlorn hope. Jeffords's attempt to save his flag became one of the remembered vignettes of the Wheatfield battle and brought notice to the Fourth Michigan, but little accrued to the brigade as a whole: it became only one of the near-anonymous units that fought in the confused battle of the Wheatfield on that bloody day.[111]

Tige Anderson's Georgia Brigade carried the burden of the assault against the south side of the Wheatfield. Unfortunately, there is a paucity of Confederate accounts of its hard fight. The brigade made three attacks. The first was made with Benning's and Robertson's brigades against the lines of Ward and de Trobriand and was repulsed. Then it attacked along with Kershaw's brigade on its left and dislodged de Trobriand from the wall, but it was, in turn, hurled back by Caldwell's division's counterattack and driven from Rose's Woods by Brooke's brigade. And then, with Wofford's, Semmes's, and Kershaw's brigades, it advanced for the third time, routed Brooke's regiments, and confronted Sweitzer's brigade in the Wheatfield.[112]

Capt. George Hillyer, the Ninth Georgia's third commander that afternoon, called the Ninth's three refused companies back to their places in the regiment's line and, after Brooke's troops were repelled, occupied Plum Run at the northwest corner of Rose's Woods. Some of Semmes's men were in the stream bed to the Ninth's left, and the water flowing in it was already tinted with blood. The smoke was heavy in the area, but it lifted at intervals and gave the men of the Ninth something of a view. At such times they fired diagonally to the right across the front of the the Eighth and Eleventh Georgia regiments. Then Hillyer saw a fresh Federal line coming toward them across the Wheatfield. It must have been Sweitzer's brigade, though Hillyer did not know its identity. The closest color-bearer, probably that of the Fourth Michigan, and his color guard strode proudly about six feet in front of the blue line; Hillyer thought him to be a handsome fellow and saw that the flag was new.

When the Federal line approached to within about forty yards of the waiting Georgians, the line halted; the color-bearer flaunted his flag and stepped back into the front rank. The Federals then brought their rifles down from right shoulder shift and fired. The men of the Ninth had the cover of the run's banks, and the sheet of lead dispatched by the Federals' volley passed over their heads. Hillyer commanded the Ninth to return the fire. The Georgians rested their rifles on the lip of the stream's bank and blazed away. The firing was rapid, and soon the smoke became so heavy that they could see only the legs and feet of the men in the Federal line. In a short time even that view disappeared. When the fire slackened and the smoke lifted a little, Hillyer walked forward carefully, fully expecting to find the dead color-bearer and his flag, but both were gone. If the Federal line was that of the Fourth Michigan Regiment, it seems likely that it moved away from Hillyer's immediate front when Sweitzer ordered it to change front to face Kershaw's and Wofford's men who were assailing it from the stony hill. Anderson's men then advanced with Kershaw and Wofford across the Wheatfield toward new foes near its eastern edge.[113]

After the scattering of Caldwell's division and Sweitzer's brigade, only one substantial force remained near the Wheatfield to oppose the Confederate onslaught. This was the two Regular brigades of Ayres's division, Fifth Corps. Unlike most of the volunteer regiments on the field, some of the Regular regiments had a prewar existence and tradition. Half of them—the Second, Third, Fourth, Sixth, and Seventh U.S. Infantry regiments—had been in existence since the War of 1812, and the Second and Third regiments had fought with Sykes at Bull Run. Since the Peninsular campaign, the history of the two Regular brigades had been that of Sykes's division, Fifth Corps. In an army of many hard-fighting units, they set a standard of soldierly quality for others to emulate. With Meade's elevation to army command and Sykes's to that of the corps, the Regular brigades lost their close association with Sykes. Brig. Gen. Romeyn B. Ayres received command of Sykes's old division.

Ayres was born in New York State on 20 December 1825 and graduated from West Point in 1847 with John Gibbon and A. P. Hill. He entered the Third Artillery, served in Mexico, and thereafter had routine assignments. Ayres became a captain in the Fifth Artillery at the outset of the war and commanded its Battery E at Bull Run. Subsequently he served as chief of artillery of Sumner's division, Fourth Corps, on the Peninsula and chief of artillery of the Sixth Corps. He became a brigadier general to date from 29 November 1862 and received command of the First Brigade of Sykes's division. When Sykes was promoted, Ayres took his place. Ayres was a competent professional, tall and distinguished in appearance, who received six brevets during the war but little public attention and adulation. He had his ups and downs in command levels because of reorganizations, but as a brigadier general commanded the Second Division, Fifth Corps, at Appomattox. After the war, Ayres served as a lieutenant colonel in the Twenty-eighth and Nineteenth U.S. Infantry regiments and colonel of the Second Artillery. He died in 1888.[114]

Ayres's division, like Barnes's, had rested along the Baltimore Pike behind the Union center until midafternoon when General Meade ordered the Fifth Corps to the Union left. It moved there after Barnes's division, but instead of following Barnes's approach by Granite Schoolhouse Lane, it took country roads to the left that led to the Taneytown Road near the Wheatfield Road's junction behind Little Round Top.

Weed's brigade led the division to the Union left. Its movements have already been described in connection with the action on Little Round Top. The two Regular brigades deployed first at the foot of the north slope of Little Round Top and to Weed's right. The Second Brigade, commanded by Col. Sidney Burbank, had eighty officers and "less than 900 muskets" in its five regiments. It formed the first line, its left near Gibbs's Ohio Battery. From there it extended north two hundred yards across an open field to a wooded area east of the main branch of Plum Run—the low ground shunned by the Third Corps and occupied later by the Sixth. The Seventeenth Infantry Regiment was on its left, the Second on its right, and the Seventh, Tenth, and Eleventh somewhere in line between them.[115] Day's brigade was in Burbank's rear and in its support, its five Regular infantry regiments—the Third, Fourth, Sixth, Twelfth, and Fourteenth—probably formed in a column of regiments rather than in line. After taking this position north of Little Round Top, the Regular brigades received orders to shift left to occupy the area on Little Round Top said to have been vacated by Weed's brigade, but the return of Weed's brigade to the hill made that shift unnecessary.[116]

The Regulars' stay north of Little Round Top was a short one. When Hood's division drove Ward's brigade from Devil's Den and Caldwell's division marched down Plum Run's valley to the Wheatfield area, Sykes ordered Ayres's two Regular brigades into the Wheatfield to Caldwell's division's left.[117]

Burbank's brigade advanced southwesterly toward Rose's Woods where Ward's line had been. The five small regiments descended into Plum Run's valley, wheeled left about forty-five degrees, and headed toward their objective. It was a tense time. One excited lieutenant of the Seventeenth kept leaving his place in line and running alongside his company, shouting, "Give 'em hell, Men! Give 'em hell!" The company commander told him twice to get back to his place and keep quiet, but the fellow was too excited to be long repressed. When the line reached a marshy area along Plum Run, which in places was ankle-deep in mud, the lieutenant began to run and shout again, swinging his sword around his head. This time, though, his scabbard got between his legs and tripped him so that he pitched headlong into the mire. The mud bath calmed him down.[118]

Another incident occured during the Regulars' advance that showed that they were not automatons. A somewhat disliked officer of the Fourteenth Infantry had been a shoemaker in civilian life, and this was known to the men. (The vast majority of the junior officers in the Regulars at this time were not West Pointers.) To taunt him, after "Taps," when all was quiet in camp and darkness concealed the participants, someone would begin a chorus of shouts by chanting "W-A-X! W-A-X!" The offenders, of course, were not apprehended. That was in quieter times; but as the Fourteenth started down into the Plum Run Valley someone broke the tension in its ranks by shouting "W-A-X!"[119]

When Burbank's Regulars crossed Plum Run, some Confederates over by Devil's Den began to fire into their flank. Burbank tried to counter this by posting a company of the Seventeenth Infantry off to the left to confront it. The brigade continued on without firing, out of the marsh and up the slope of the knoll that dominated the valley just east of the Wheatfield. Someone commanded double-quick and the men in line cheered—or "shrieked," as Capt. Dudley H. Chase described it—as Burbank's line charged toward the stone wall east of the Wheatfield and about a hundred yards west of the knoll's crest. Burbank halted the brigade there and ordered it to take shelter behind the wall. It could go no farther just then for Caldwell's division was advancing through the field across its front.[120]

Day's brigade halted in Burbank's rear. We cannot know with certainty what sort of formation it had then or just where it was. Capt. Levi C. Bootes of the Sixth Infantry reported that it had one line, Capt. Thomas S. Dunn of the Twelfth wrote that there were three, and Lt. William H. Powell, who wrote the Fifth Corps's history, reported that the brigade was in a column of battalions. Because the brigade was in support and subjected to sniping from the left, Colonel Day permitted its men to lie down.[121]

Ayres rode to the front of Burbank's line and through the strip of trees in front of the wall so that he could see the Wheatfield and the action in it. Caldwell, seeking support for his division—particularly Brooke's left—found him there and the two generals talked. Lieutenant Powell, who was Ayres's aide, interrupted their conversation. Aides, after all, cannot be shy. He said to Caldwell, "General, you had better look out, the line in front is giving way." Caldwell, anxious and probably unaccustomed to such remarks about his division from strange lieutenants, retorted sharply: "That's not so, sir; those are my troops being relieved." The generals continued to talk, and Powell's concern increased. In a moment he spoke again, this time directing his remarks to Ayres's more sympathetic ear: "General Ayres, you will have to look out for your command. I don't care what any one says, those troops in front are running away." The generals scanned the field more intently; and then, without a word, Caldwell spurred his horse and rode off to the right along the wall.[122]

Lieutenant John H. Page, Third Infantry, arrived on the scene at about this time. The Third was in Day's column not far away, and Page had walked forward to see what was going on. In the Wheatfield, about four hundred yards away as he estimated it, he saw troops coming back "with their colors drooped." Seeing Ayres and a cluster of officers a short distance away, he ran over to alert them to what he had seen. On approaching, he heard Ayres say, "Those regiments are being driven back." In reply someone observed that they were probably just retiring to a new position. To this Ayres responded: "A regiment does not shut up like a jack-knife and hide its colors without it is retreating." Hearing this, Page then hurried back to his company.[123]

After posting Barnes's brigades on the stony hill at the beginning of the fight, Sykes cantered back to the Taneytown Road to see to the remainder of his corps. Ayres's division was just arriving there. Sykes gave his aide, Lieutenant Jay, instructions about the posting of Burbank's and Day's brigades and sent another officer off to retrieve Weed's, which had gone to the assistance of the Third Corps.[124]

A little later Lt. George Ingham found Sykes on a rock on the slope of Little Round Top watching the events taking place in the fields below through his field glasses. Sykes chided Ingham for what he perceived as tardiness, which Ingham explained, and asked that his cavalry escort (Companies D and H, Seventeenth Pennsylvania Volunteer Cavalry), which Ingham had brought forward, be placed behind a nearby rise. Sykes spoke then with General Warren, who was bleeding from a slight neck wound and was leaving the hill. When Warren had gone, Sykes and Ingham, and perhaps others, rode further up the back side of the hill, left their horses under the cover of a ledge, and climbed up to the crest at Hazlett's gun position. As they

Col. Sidney Burbank (MOLLUS-MASS/ U.S.A.M.H.I., *Carlisle Barracks, Pa.*)

Col. Hannibal Day (National Archives)

neared it, someone warned them to beware of certain places that were subjected to Confederate fire. They did this, and Sykes spent several minutes gazing into the cauldron below. Then, turning to Ingham, he asked him to have Ayres push his column a little farther into the woods.[125]

Ingham dashed away, jumped from a ledge down the rear slope of the hill where the horses were tied, and stooped there to tighten a loose spur strap. As he worked at it, another young officer flew by his head and startled him. In response to Ingham's shouted comments on the carelessness of some fellows, the jumper yelled back, "Weed's shot and I'm after a surgeon." That was bad news certainly, but there was nothing that Ingham could do about it. He got onto his horse and rode down the hill to order Ayres forward.[126]

Events moved faster than Ingham, and he did not deliver his message. After Caldwell's abrupt departure, Ayres decided that his brigades should sweep the woods in their front and gave orders for it to be done. In response, Burbank's brigade advanced, wheeling left from its north-south line behind the wall. Its left would cross the wall, hold to it, and pass through the strip of woods, while the right of the brigade swung on a wider arc into the Wheat-field in the brigade's front. When this was done the brigade would be in an east-west line, with its right behind the stone wall along the south side of the Wheatfield; its left would be in the woods where the Fifth New Hampshire and the 148th Pennsylvania regiments had been. Such a line would confront the Confederates at Devil's Den and cover Caldwell's division's left. As Burbank's men crossed the wall, they met a regiment in the woods, possibly the Fifth New Hampshire Regiment, which had held on in the woods until the Regulars relieved it.[127]

The men of the Second Infantry on the right of Burbank's line jumped over the wall on command, passed through the fringe of trees, and wheeled into the trodden wheat. When about halfway through their pivot and well into the open field, they saw Confederates on their right bearing down on their right flank and threatening their rear. Maj. Arthur Lee halted the Second then and there and ordered it to commence firing. The Confederates re-turned their greeting, and both sides blazed away, the Federals firing "rap-idly," the Southerners "sharply," wounding Major Lee and others. Additional Confederate regiments appeared in the smoke and threatened Burbank's flank and rear. Ayres ordered the Regulars back to the wall and then back still more, so that their left would rest on the north slope of Little Round Top and at Weed's brigade's right.[128]

The withdrawal here as elsewhere that day was easier ordered than made. The noise was so loud that some men of the brigade did not hear the orders to fall back, and the Wheatfield was now swarming with Georgians and South Carolinians inspired by the stimulating smell of victory. They had destroyed Caldwell's and Sweitzer's lines, and now they were bent on the destruction of Ayres's two small brigades. To Major Lee, now wounded, there seemed to be three lines of Confederate infantry, one higher than the others, and all were firing on his regiment. The colors made a good target, of course, and one ball cut the flagstaff of the Second U.S. Infantry, causing the flag to drop over into the bearer's hands.[129]

The Second fell back along with Burbank's other regiments, first to the welcome shelter of the strip of woods and then to the stone wall. The wall must have seemed a snug place for a while, as hard to leave as a warm bed on a cold morning, but there could be no stopping there. Wofford's "reckless fellows" were pouring over it to their right and might soon get to their rear and cut them off; so the Regulars retreated some more, down the slope and through the marsh along Plum Run. By this time they were catching bullets from three directions, "a perfect storm of shot and shell," though there could have been few if any artillery rounds falling there. To Capt. David P. Hancock of the Seventh Infantry it was "frightful" and to Maj. De Lancey Floyd-Jones of the Eleventh it was "most deadly," but the Regulars went back in good order.[130]

Before their retreat, the men of Day's brigade had been sheltered by the valley's west slope and exposed only to long range sniping from the left. On returning to the Third Regiment, Lieutenant Page learned that the brigade would soon be falling back, as soon as Burbank's brigade came back out of the trees to the front. While the brigade waited, Colonel Day rode up with a newly filled pipe of tobacco and asked Page for a light. Page dug out a match, struck it, and raised it toward the mounted colonel. Day bent over for it, and as he did so, a bullet zipped between the two officers and thudded into the neck of Day's horse, giving the animal a fatal wound.[131]

Day's brigade waited impatiently as the Confederates—Wofford's or Kershaw's men—appeared on their right, toward the Wheatfield Road, and opened fire on them. Finally, when Burbank's men came back across the wall, Day's were able to start for the rear. They fell back with a measure of order. The Twelfth regiment moved at quick-time and then at the double-quick until it reached a stone wall, probably near the Wheatfield Road near the base of Little Round Top. Capt. Thomas S. Dunn halted it there and ordered the left wing to face around and fire. This done, the Twelfth went on to its old position on the ridge line.[132]

As Day's men sloshed through Plum Run, Lieutenant Page saw artillery officers waving their hats to hurry them along. Such urging was probably less necessary than it was natural, but it was apparent that Gibbs's battery was impatient to fire and wanted Ayres's men out of its way. The Regulars attempted to double-quick, but it was hard to do in the sloppy marsh. Capt. Henry W. Freedley, commander of the Third U.S. Infantry, took a bullet in the leg and fell against Page, sending him sprawling in the mire. Page staggered to his feet, wiped his eyes, and saw that the artillerymen were motioning for them to lie down. They dived for cover behind a boulder and huddled there while the Buckeyes' Napoleons belched canister over them at the Confederates in their rear.[133]

The Regulars had spent less than an hour in the Wheatfield area and had had little opportunity to display their fighting skills there. But, in the words of Lt. Col. William F. Fox, New York's official historian of the battle:

> they moved off the field in admirable style, with well-aligned ranks, facing about at times to deliver their fire and check pursuit. Recrossing Plum Run Valley, under a storm of bullets that told fearfully on their ranks, they returned to their original position. In this action the regulars sustained severe losses, but gave ample evidence of the fighting qualities, discipline, and steadiness under fire which made them the pattern and admiration of the entire army.[134]

Burbank's brigade sustained 447 casualties in the battle, a comparatively small number until it is recalled that it was a small brigade. Half of its officers were killed or wounded, and nearly half of its enlisted men were casualties. Day's brigade, which had spent its time essentially in reserve and in retreat, had 382 casualties.[135]

Ayres's two brigades were the last away. After their retreat, there were no Federal units west of Plum Run and south of the Wheatfield Road—or south of Trostle's lane, for that matter. Seven brigades from Hood's and McLaws's divisions had encountered ten brigades from the Second, Third, and Fifth corps and had shattered them. Now, led by Wofford's brigade, the bloodied regiments of Longstreet's corps yelled their way through the darkening Wheatfield area in pursuit of the fleeing remnants of regiments that were falling back to and beyond the ground that Sickles's corps had vacated six hours before. Longstreet's men could relish the distinct taste of victory in the acrid powder smoke.

CHAPTER

13

McLaws Strikes the Peach Orchard

Stephen D. Lee called the battle of Antietam "Artillery Hell," but E. P. Alexander, who succeeded him in the command of his artillery battalion, thought that the fighting at Gettysburg's Peach Orchard was worse. Alexander compared the battalion's losses in the two battles and wrote of the Gettysburg ordeal, "I don't think there was ever in our war a hotter, harder, sharper artillery afternoon than this."[1]

Artillery dominated the action in the Peach Orchard area that day. Alexander's and Cabell's battalions on the Confederate side dueled with nine batteries of the Federal Third Corps and the Artillery Reserve and pounded the infantry around them. The artillery action was the bitter fruit of General Sickles's intention to man and hold the Peach Orchard and the high ground to the north along the Emmitsburg Road and of General Lee's design to smash the Federal left by an attack up the axis of that road. The battle fought, as we have seen, was not the battle planned.

To review, it was the task of McLaws's division to advance from Seminary Ridge, take the high ground along the Emmitsburg Road in and around the Peach Orchard, and, with Hood's division, roll up the Federal left. To do this, the division's four brigades formed in two lines on Seminary Ridge astride the Wheatfield Road opposite the Peach Orchard. Cabell's battalion, the division's integral artillery support, formed along the ridge in front of the division's right with the line of its right batteries curving almost perpendicular to the ridge, so that its guns could assail the Peach Orchard area from the west and from the southwest. Cabell's fire would be augmented by that of four batteries of Alexander's battalion. Alexander's guns stood in front of the center of McLaws's line, astride the Wheatfield Road and opposite the Peach Orchard and Sherfy's farmyard. Only six to seven hundred yards separated these guns from those of the enemy, and Cabell's ranges were but a little greater.[2]

McLaws's attack did not go quite as planned. The failure of Hood's division to drive the Federal forces from the Wheatfield area required that the right wing of Kershaw's brigade and all of Semmes's brigade take part in the fighting there rather than drive north along the axis of the Emmitsburg Road. The responsibility of the assault against the Peach Orchard area and the high ground north of it fell principally, then, to Kershaw's left wing and to Barksdale's brigade, supported by Wofford's.

When the Army of the Potomac's Third Corps advanced to the high ground along the Emmitsburg Road, General Birney assigned his First Brigade, Graham's, to a five hundred-yard front along the Emmitsburg Road between the south edge of the Peach Orchard and Trostle's lane. The 105th, Fifty-seventh, 114th, Sixty-eighth, and 141st Pennsylvania regiments took position there between the Wheatfield Road and the lane, while the Sixty-third Pennsylvania skirmished in the fields west of the Peach Orchard. This left a five hundred-yard gap south of the Wheatfield Road between the Emmitsburg Road and the stony hill. Birney covered the gap by deploying the Third Michigan and Third Maine regiments in front of it as skirmishers. Fortunately, Ames's and Clark's batteries at the Peach Orchard added strength to that face of the salient, while Bucklyn's battery confronted the Confederates from its position at Sherfy's barn. Therefore, when the artillery fire began, Birney had approximately 2,000 infantry and three batteries to man a line that ought to have been defended by 3,000 rifles backed by a strong reserve. He sought further assistance and obtained three additional regiments of infantry from Humphreys's division and four batteries from the Artillery Reserve.[3]

Two of the regiments came from the Third Brigade, Second Division, commanded at Gettysburg by Colonel George C. Burling. General Birney first halted this brigade in Trostle's Woods, where it had some shelter and was near the center of his overstretched line. When Hood attacked and the firing spread along the south face of the Third Corps position, Birney ordered Burling's command to a high point in a rye field just west of the woods, where it might support Graham's line and, if need be, block the gap between the Peach Orchard and the stony hill. Here the brigade stood in view of some of Cabell's gunners, and Confederate shells fell around it. One hit the staff of the Second New Hampshire's colors, broke it into three pieces, and wounded several members of the color guard. Burling deemed such exposure unnecessary when the enemy infantry was not threatening. After consulting with his regimental commanders, he moved the brigade a hundred yards back toward the woods to a depression that gave it some shelter from Cabell's fire.[4]

Hardly had Burling's men begun to appreciate their cover when Capt. John S. Poland of Sickles's staff rode up and "in an excited manner" demanded to know by whose authority Burling had shifted his brigade. Burling replied that he had done it by his own authority, and Poland ordered him to return the brigade to the exposed position. Before he could do so, one of Birney's aides galloped up and ordered it to a spot behind the threatened stony hill.[5] Things were warming up, and Burling soon received other orders. The first was to send his two largest regiments to General Graham; he dispatched the Second New Hampshire and the Seventh New Jersey west up the slope to that front. Additional requests came for other regiments, and soon Burling's brigade was scattered along the Third Corps line.[6]

Col. Louis R. Francine's Seventh New Jersey Regiment formed to the left rear of Clark's battery where it could support the battery and watch the gap to the left. There it endured a long wait under artillery fire.[7] The Second New Hampshire's 24 officers and 330 men double-quicked in a column of fours up the hill behind the right of Clark's battery. Its colonel, Edward Bailey, had been a post office clerk in Manchester when the regiment was formed in August 1861 and became its colonel in April 1863 at the age of twenty-one. Bailey led the Second up to the Peach Orchard, where he deployed its left wing behind Ames's battery, which was dueling then with Cabell's batteries. Bailey posted the Second's right wing initially so that it faced the Emmitsburg Road near the Wentz house; and Company B deployed as skirmishers. After things settled down a little, Bailey had his company commanders call their rolls and found that only eight men were absent. They had been felled by the heat when the Second double-quicked up the slope. When it became apparent that the regiment's right wing was overly exposed to the fire of Cabell's batteries, Bailey formed nine of the Second's companies back along the Wheatfield Road so that the main line of the Second faced south, its right in the garden at the Wentz house. There it was sheltered somewhat from Alexander's guns by the house and slope, and it fronted toward the guns of Cabell's battalion that fired up the Emmitsburg Road.[8]

Manly's battery of Cabell's battalion, which was posted in an oblong clump of trees on the crest of the ridge about seven hundred yards west of the Peach Orchard, was probably the first Confederate battery to fire on the orchard area. Its two Napoleons and two three-inch rifles fired from the partial cover of the trees, and its limbers and caissons had the shelter of the trees and the reverse slope of the ridge. Therefore, in spite of its nearness to the Federal position, Manly's battery had only eleven casualties in its two days of battle and lost only twenty horses. Manly reported proudly that all of his men had acted splendidly but gave one particular mention. This was Pvt. Henry E. Thain, whose job was to prepare fuses at a limber. One fuse ignited accidently. To prevent an explosion near the limbers, Thain carried the shell away and pulled the burning fuse from it with his bare hands. Manly believed that this courageous act saved many lives.[9]

One section of Capt. Henry H. Carlton's battery, Georgia's Troup Artillery, two ten-pounder Parrotts, went into position on Manly's right. The battery's other section of twelve-pounder howitzers took position on Manly's left. They dueled with batteries in the Peach Orchard area. One man wrote that he never saw guns served better—it was the most rapid fire that he had seen, and the earth around them vibrated. As the duel went on, Carlton's men worked like beavers and were covered with dust and smoke. The battery fired until dark, and its casualties were light.[10]

Capt. Edward S. McCarthy's First Richmond Howitzers and Capt. John C. Fraser's Pulaski Artillery continued Cabell's line to the right. Although McCarthy had two three-inch rifles and two Napoleons, he used only the rifles on the afternoon of 2 July and fired only two hundred rounds from them. Captain McCarthy described the fire his battery received as the most severe experienced during the war and credited Lt. Robert M. Anderson's courageous example for the good work done by his gun crews. The battery had seven casualties, enough considering that only two gun crews were regularly exposed to the enemy's fire.[11]

Captain Fraser's battery took greater punishment than the other batteries of Cabell's battalion. The battery was probably posted between Biesecker's Woods and the Emmitsburg Road and fronted toward the Peach Orchard.[12] It opened on the batteries near the Peach Orchard and shot rapidly at first but soon settled into a slower less nervous pace, pausing occasionally to allow the smoke that blurred its targets to blow away.[13]

Lt. William J. Furlong described the fire of Fraser's battery as having been slow and deliberate and wrote that the enemy "replied with spirit, their fire being incessant, severe, and well directed." After an hour of shooting, a Federal shell burst in Fraser's position, mortally wounding Fraser and wounding or killing three enlisted men.[14] Furlong took command, but by this time the battery's casualties forced him to combine his four gun crews into two and continue at half strength. Fortunately for these Georgians, the Federal fire slackened, except for one gun that continued to snipe away at them. Furlong gave it the battery's full attention, and in a while he believed that his efforts silenced it.[15]

Although Cabell's four battery commanders reported having dueled only with Federal batteries on the Wheatfield Road line, Cabell wrote that they received some fire from guns on Little Round Top. He ordered two guns to "play upon" them, and they did so after the infantry advance with what he believed was great effect.[16] It was Clark's New Jersey Battery that first dueled with Cabell's guns. It had opened initially on Hood's infantry from the Peach Orchard, but in a short time it pulled back to safer ground out of sight of Manly's gunners. Its new position was near the northeast corner of the Peach Orchard, north of the road, and it fired from there while Ames's battery trotted into the orchard. Someone recalled that Sickles, Birney, and Hunt were all nearby when Clark's battery took its second position and that Sickles admonished the captain, "Hold this position while you have a shot in your limbers or a man to work your guns."[17]

Clark's six ten-pounders fired slowly with shell at ranges up to 1,400 yards. This range indicates that it shot at Latham's battery early in the fight and at the Texas infantrymen near it. Clark controlled the firing carefully at first, moving from gun to gun to check his crews and caution them to take deliberate aim. After he was satisfied that they would do well on their own, he permitted them to fire at will. The firing went on for about thirty minutes, when an explosion in the target area led the Jerseymen to believe that they had hit a limber chest. In celebration of this tangible sign of their accurate shooting, one man climbed upon a gun and cheered. The nearby infantrymen, who had had enough Confederate fire for the day, cheered with him.[18]

There was space, three hundred yards of it, for more batteries along the Wheatfield Road line. About 3:30 a courier rode into the Artillery Reserve's park with Captain Randolph's request for batteries. In response, General Tyler sent Lt. Col. Freeman McGilvery forward with Bigelow's Ninth Massachusetts Battery and Phillips's Fifth Massachusetts Battery, both from his First Volunteer Brigade.[19] Bugler Charles W. Reed of the Ninth Battery blew "Assembly," the cannoneers removed grain sacks and other impedimenta not needed at the battery position from the guns, limbers, and caissons, and in a few minutes the gun sections were heading west at a trot toward the Trostle farmyard.[20] By this time the air whistled with missiles fired above targets in the Peach Orchard area. The battery halted near the Trostle barn. From there Reed, who was an artist, was able to sketch Sickles at his headquarters beneath a tree a few yards away. During the halt Lieutenants Richard S. Milton and Christopher Erickson asked permission from Captain Bigelow to ride forward and see what was happening. Bigelow assented and, turning to Lt. Alexander Whitaker, remarked, "They will see enough before night."[21]

McGilvery and Bigelow then rode forward, and McGilvery showed the captain where his battery should be. Bigelow led his Napoleons forward. They filed into Trostle's lane and passed through a narrow gate opposite the farmyard into an orchard beside the west end of Trostle's Woods. When the third section cleared the gate, Bigelow shouted, "Forward into line, left oblique, trot!" The first section headed south beyond the orchard into a rye field, and the rear guns fanned left to take their position on line. By this time, the first section had traveled the three hundred yards to the Wheatfield Road. There the line halted with the right guns in the field on the north side of the road and the left in the road itself. A quick glance sufficed to determine that there was a problem. A rise in the ground just south of the road blocked the left section's field of fire. Rather than move beyond the road to the crest of the rise, Lieutenant Whitaker led the section's fifth and sixth pieces across the rear of Bigelow's other four and posted them on the right of the gun line. As formed then, Bigelow's guns were probably just north of the road.[22]

Batteries were vulnerable when going into position because they were targets that could not defend themselves. It was so with Bigelow's battery. Before it had a chance to open, one of Cabell's batteries, undoubtedly Manly's, assailed it with spherical case, killing one man and wounding others, including Lieutenant Erickson. Erickson took a shrapnel ball or small shell

The Ninth Massachusetts Battery going into position. Sketch by Charles W. Reed (MOLLUS-MASS/U.S.A.M.H.I., Carlisle Barracks, Pa.)

fragment in the chest, and it probably reached a lung. Bigelow sent him to the rear. The Boston Norwegian rode back toward Trostle's farm but returned in a while and told Bigelow that he was ready to resume command of the first section. Bigelow was glad to have him back and probably assumed that he was well enough to do his job. Erickson rode up to the gun line, borrowed a canteen from a cannoneer, and drank most of the water in it.[23]

The Ninth Massachusetts Battery went to work and, in the opinion of Bigelow, temporarily silenced some enemy guns. The smoke from its guns gave the battery some cover, but it blinded the gunners. Bigelow saw that one gunner, Augustus Hessie, was dropping to the ground after each shot. He deemed this rather cowardly and improper conduct while firing and went over to Whitaker's section to see about it. As he got closer he could see that Hessie was dropping down beneath the smoke just to see the effects of his shots.[24]

Bigelow believed that his battery had caused the Confederates to slacken their fire, but other batteries were coming up and taking their share of it. Capt. Charles A. Phillips's Fifth Massachusetts Battery was probably the next to arrive and went in on Bigelow's right, between Bigelow's and Clark's batteries.[25] It had followed the Ninth Battery out of the artillery park after a lapse of several minutes and headed for the Third Corps line at a jingling trot. As the Fifth Battery neared the scene of fighting, its men found the air filled with smoke, but they could see snatches of action here and there where the smoke was thin. An unidentified officer tried to persuade Phillips to take his battery to the Little Round Top area, but Phillips stayed on the route to Trostle's farm. On reaching the Trostle farmyard, Phillips's battery turned south through the gate into the orchard and headed for the gap on Bigelow's right with limbers bouncing and crewmen holding to the seats for dear life.[26]

Haste made waste—two men of the crew of the first piece lost their seats and plunged to the ground. One of them, Cpl. John Egan, a gunner, broke his arm in two places, and both men were lucky that nothing worse happened. As the battery approached the road, it went left into line and over a rail fence so that the first piece was in the road on Bigelow's right, and the remaining five guns went on line to its right just behind the road.[27]

Cabell's guns, which already had the range to Bigelow's position, were able to zero in on Phillips's pieces as soon as they arrived. One of the first rounds that whistled in killed two horses in the first piece's team. The drivers scrambled to remove the harness from the dead horses and replaced a wheel horse with the bugler's mount. Phillips hurriedly sent to the rear for more horses to replace those killed at the guns.[28] Phillips's gunners gave special attention to the smoking woods that concealed Cabell's guns, and they fired on those which they were able to see. After a time, Phillips's men, like Bigelow's, thought that they had silenced the Confederate batteries in their front, but they were not nearly as successful as they had supposed.[29]

Confederate shells fired at Ames's and Bucklyn's batteries enfiladed Phillips's and Bigelow's batteries from the right. Most came from Alexander's battalion, whose guns were only six hundred or so yards away from the Federal pieces and at the same elevation. It is no wonder, then, that any rounds fired a little high or any that ricocheted from the ground at the Peach Orchard created problems for the batteries and troops in the orchard's rear.[30] Alexander's four batteries sat astride the Wheatfield Road. Capt. William W. Parker's battery with four three-inch rifles was on the right of the line, and Capt. Osmond B. Taylor's Virginia Battery with four Napoleons was on Parker's left between Parker's guns and the Wheatfield Road. These two batteries, together with Manly's and with Carlton's section of howitzers, were directly opposite the Peach Orchard and closest to the Federal batteries there.[31]

Capt. George V. Moody's Madison (Louisiana) Light Artillery and South Carolina's Brooks Artillery (Rhett's battery), commanded by Lt. S. Capers Gilbert, were on the ridge line north of the road. Each battery had four howitzers—Moody's were twenty-four-pounders, Gilbert's the smaller twelve-pounders. Both types were quite capable of reaching the Federal line in their front. They were behind the stone wall that bordered the east side of Pitzer's Woods and occupied fronts from 50 to 165 yards north of the Wheatfield Road. The gap between the wings of the battalion permitted the batteries to fire by the Warfield and Snyder buildings.[32]

Captain Taylor's orders were to dislodge the Union batteries in his front. In his words, "I opened upon the batteries with my four Napoleons, firing canister and spherical case until our infantry . . . began their charge." Taylor's choice of ammunition seems strange, for solid shot was usually preferred for counterbattery fire. Taylor's battery's casualties turned out to be comparatively heavy while it occupied this position. One of its best gunners, Cpl.

William Ray, was hit while sighting his piece. After being hit, he straightened up, walked a few steps, and fell dead without a word.[33]

Parker's battery's three-inch rifles had a higher muzzle velocity and potentially greater accuracy than Taylor's Napoleons and were better suited to knocking out enemy guns. But no one boasted of any triumph of this sort. Rather the Virginians found the Federal shrapnel rattling through the trees nearby to be frightening. When a scared cannoneer started to flee, Captain Parker swung his sword around the fellow's head and kept him at his post. At the same time, another cannoneer, a recruit, performed so well under fire that Parker wrote a letter to the boy's father extolling his courage.[34]

Moody's battery's cannoneers had their own special problems during the artillery exchange. The wall in front of the howitzers gave them some protection, but the reverse slope behind the wall allowed the heavy twenty-four-pounders to roll back excessively in recoil. Pushing them back up the slope took a lot of effort, and in a little while the howitzer crews became quite tired. After a half hour, Moody asked permission to get help from Barksdale's men who were lying nearby, and eight Mississippi infantrymen offered their services. By that night, five of them were either dead or seriously wounded.[35]

When his battalion took its position, Colonel Alexander had expected a "short, sharp & decisive" fight, but it was not working out that way. Gilbert's battery, like Moody's, confronted not only Ames's right section at the Peach Orchard but a section of Thompson's battery and Bucklyn's whole battery at the Sherfy buildings. It was also within range of Seeley's and Turnbull's batteries near the Klingle house. It is not too surprising, then, that this South Carolina battery had exceptionally heavy casualties—forty men out of seventy-five were killed or wounded and two of its howitzers were dismounted. A newly arrived lieutenant was with it that day, a cavalryman who had no experience with a field battery. Because he knew too little of his duties to be helpful, Alexander told him to look on until he got the hang of things. That afternoon during the heavy firing Alexander was amused when he saw the ex-cavalryman standing apprehensively behind a sapling at the battery position, watching helplessly while the Federals knocked his new unit to pieces. The lieutenant remained with the battery during the battle but went back to the cavalry after it was over.[36]

Alexander received a slight wound while walking near Gilbert's guns. A shell fragment ripped through his pants leg and underdrawers and skinned a knee. It was a close call. The colonel summed up this portion of the afternoon by observing that the Federal batteries in his front were "in their usual full force and good practice." Annoyed by the failure of his guns to dislodge them and by their commendable obstinacy, he sent back for Woolfolk's and Jordan's batteries. But the situation changed before they arrived.[37]

Bucklyn's Battery E, First Rhode Island Light Artillery, was a worthy adversary of Alexander's batteries that day. It had one section under Lt. Benjamin Freeborn between the Sherfy house and barn, and its remaining two sections were south of the barn. These left sections caught a cross fire from Cabell's guns down the Emmitsburg Road and from Alexander's in their front. Freeborn's section, on the other hand, was harassed by skirmishers who fired on it from the shelter of the Staub barn until the section ousted them with a few shots that must have wrecked the barn. Regrettably, Lieutenant Bucklyn fell wounded at the end of the duel and made no report; Lt. Benjamin Freeborn, his successor, made too brief a statement to explain adequately the battery's many casualties.[38]

When Confederate batteries opened from his right and rear, Captain Ames shifted his battery's right section to confront them. The battery's Peach Orchard position was a hot one, and the peach trees and noise made it difficult for Ames to watch and command his three sections. Lt. Samuel McClellan, chief of his first section, wanted to fire canister instead of shot, as Ames had ordered, at Alexander's gun crews. He thought that even at a range of six hundred yards the shotgun approach would be more effective against gun crews than shot would be against the guns themselves. Captain Ames told McClellan plainly that he wanted shot fired to knock out the enemy's guns. That matter settled, Sgt. Jesse Burdick, chief of the first piece, fired at a Confederate gun, and the round fell short. He raised the muzzle a little, and the second one whizzed over the target. He then lowered the muzzle a bit, and the third hit the enemy piece and dismounted it. That was exceptional shooting. In the meantime, Sgt. James Hutchinson's second piece hit the wheel of another gun. In spite of its nervous start, Ames's first section did well that day, for even as close as six hundred yards cannons make very small targets. In the meantime Ames's center and left sections boomed away at Cabell's guns and, in Ames's words, "for a short time I had as sharp an artillery fight as I ever witnessed."[39]

Bucklyn's and Ames's batteries had help from a section of Thompson's battery late in their duel with Alexander's guns. Capt. James Thompson had a battery of three-inch Ordnance rifles that represented a temporary and not altogether happy union between two Pittsburgh batteries—Thompson's Battery C and Capt. Robert B. Hampton's Battery F of the Independent Pennsylvania Light Artillery. Both units had commendable records and had sustained such casualties, including Captain Hampton, in previous battles that it was impractical for them to continue to operate separately. Therefore, at the outset of the campaign they were combined temporarily under the command of Captain Thompson and remained so until the spring of 1864.[40]

Thompson's battery had been in position along the Baltimore Pike until 4:30 or 5:00 P.M., when it received orders to go to the Union left and report to Colonel McGilvery. When the battery reached him, McGilvery placed two sections in the Peach Orchard on Ames's left and the other north of the Sherfy barn.[41] Thompson's report raises a question about what batteries were actually in the Peach Orchard itself. Thompson recollected that his battery relieved Ames's, but other accounts hold that Watson's battery (I,

Fifth U.S.) replaced Ames's battery, and General Hunt reported the unlikely fact that Thompson's guns replaced Hart's Fifteenth New York Battery. Probably Thompson replaced neither Ames's guns nor Hart's, but squeezed his four guns into the east half of the orchard between the two New York batteries.[42]

Capt. Patrick Hart's Fifteenth New York Battery arrived on the Wheatfield Road line after Phillips's battery but before Thompson's. Unlike the other batteries on the line, the Fifteenth New York had only four guns, Napoleons, and correspondingly few men, sixty-eight. It had been recruited as an adjunct of the Irish Brigade, but that was a year and a half before Gettysburg, and the "exigencies of the service" had terminated the association.[43]

The Fifteenth New York Battery saw little fighting prior to Gettysburg, and Patrick Hart did not receive command of it until February 1863. Hart, in his late thirties, was older than most of the battery commanders. He had served as a private in the artillery in the Mexican War and had "much distinguished" himself at Chapultepec. He served in the army and in the Marine Corps between the wars, most of the time in the grade of sergeant. He was regarded by some as odd and could be irritating. After the war, Capt. John N. Craig, who had been on Hunt's staff, wrote of Hart that "it was exactly his way to be riding about in the manner most likely to attract the attention of anyone swelling for someone to swear at."[44]

When Hart's battery arrived at the Trostle farmyard that afternoon, Hart halted it and, with McGilvery and Capt. Nathaniel Irish of McGilvery's staff, rode ahead to look for a place for his guns. When Hart led his battery to the area selected for it, General Hunt appeared and assigned it to a spot between the left of the Peach Orchard and to the right of Clark's battery. In Hart's recollection, Hunt admonished him, "It will be a gold chain or a wooden leg for you. Sacrifice everything before you give up that position."[45]

By the time McLaws's infantry attacked, the three batteries in the Peach Orchard area had been increased to seven. A virtually solid line of forty Federal guns extended south from the Sherfy house to the Peach Orchard and east from there along the Wheatfield Road to Trostle's Woods and the stony hill. The Federal line confronted eight Confederate batteries exclusive of Henry's battalion. Alexander recalled having fifty-nine guns in action, but thirty is more like it, not counting those in Woolfolk's and Jordan's batteries. Fortunately, most of the Confederate batteries had some cover, particularly for their limbers and caissons, and had the advantage of converging fire.[46]

The savage artillery duel lasted more than an hour and was particularly hard on the infantrymen posted near the guns. The skirmishers suffered little from it, for they were poor targets and the shot and shell arced over their heads. Furthermore, as one soldier explained, the excitement and activity of being on an active skirmish line could be so intense that it fully occupied the mind, leaving little time for worrying about personal dangers.[47]

It was different for the infantrymen near the Peach Orchard and along the Emmitsburg Road by the Sherfy house. They suffered heavily, particularly if they were close to one of the Federal batteries that was a target of the fire. They could not seek safety elsewhere, for the position was theirs to hold. Yet they could not relieve their terror and tension by fighting back. They could only wait, try to control their fear, and hope and pray that the pounding would soon end.[48]

The Second New Hampshire near the Peach Orchard had no cover and caught shells from both Cabell's and Alexander's guns. The air around the Second seemed alive with whistling canister and bursting shells. Some of the projectiles that fell short ricocheted toward the Second, bounding and skimming the ground, causing casualties and great fear. One hot fragment hit the cartridge box of Sgt. James House and set off his cartridges, but he was able to yank the box off quickly and got only a severe wound. Another struck the box of Cpl. Thomas Bignall and drove some of the cartridges into his body. There they popped away like firecrackers in Bignall's "quivering form." A fragment hit Pvt. John Barber in the head, knocked him out, and blinded him. Barber finally reached a hospital, where surgeons trephined his skull. A canister ball hit Lt. Col. James W. Carr's sword with a ringing sound, broke its blade into three pieces, and drove the pieces against his groin. To this Carr remarked, "Well, better a sword out than a leg, anyhow."[49]

Although the 114th Pennsylvania, posted north of the Peach Orchard, was subjected to heavy crossfire, it had relatively few men killed or wounded. Its men had no cover, and while "every conceivable kind of missile" flew through the air around them, they could only lie on the ground, each man wondering whether he would be struck and whether, if he was, he would be killed outright or wounded. The fire lasted for over an hour, and when the time for action came some, perhaps only a few, men were rendered helpless by shock. One man in the 141st Pennsylvania was in such shock that when the regiment was ordered to stand and prepare to advance, he could only raise himself to his hands and knees and bob his head as Confederate shells flew by.[50]

It was a relief for the infantry, therefore, when the Confederate fire slackened so that Kershaw's and Semmes's brigades could advance. The South Carolinians and Georgians moved off with great steadiness and precision, though their advance was obstructed by some standing fences and the fire of batteries in the Peach Orchard area. Kershaw described his left wing, the Second and Eighth South Carolina regiments and the Third Battalion, as "moving majestically" across the slope between the Peach Orchard and the Rose farm lane before they wheeled left against the rear of the Orchard and the batteries posted there.[51]

The Federal artillerymen who witnessed the assault and fired at the advancing lines did not know the identities of their targets. Colonel McGilvery recalled that two bodies of infantry crossed his battalion's front. One passed through a grain field 850 yards away beyond Rose's farm, where the fighting

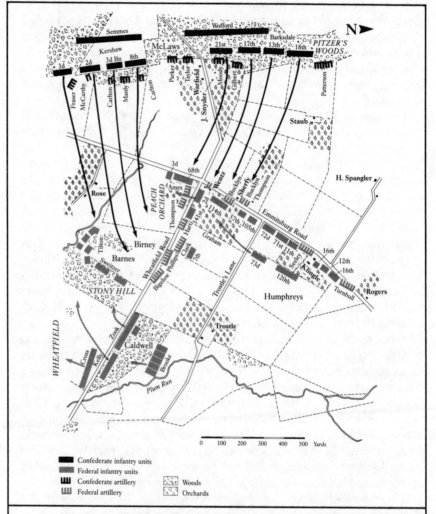

1. *After a heavy artillery exchange, Kershaw's brigade advances. While its right wing assails Federal positions on the stony hill its left wing crosses the Emmitsburg Road, passes the Peach Orchard, and wheels left against the Federal batteries along the Wheatfield Road.*

2. *After a short delay Barksdale's brigade advances on Kershaw's left. Barksdale strikes Graham's brigade's position between the Peach Orchard and Sherfy's barn.*

3. *The Seventy-third New York shifts left to the support of the 114th Pennsylvania.*

4. *Barksdale breaks Graham's line at the Wentz buildings. The Twenty-first Mississippi, supported by Wofford, drives the Federals from the Peach Orchard. The Twenty-first, with the support of Kershaw's left wing, then drives the batteries from their positions along the Wheatfield Road.*

5. *Barksdale's three left regiments wheel left and drive Graham's regiments from their positions near the Sherfy buildings.*

6. *This breakthrough exposes both the flanks of Humphreys's division along the Emmitsburg Road to the north and the Federals in the Wheatfield area.*

Map 13-1. The Peach Orchard

was already in progress. This must have been Tige Anderson's brigade, which the artillery pounded well. McGilvery saw the cannon fire drive some men back into Biesecker's Woods, though most continued on their way.[52]

Another column appeared later. The range to it was about 750 yards, and it presented a "slight left flank" to McGilvery's batteries. His guns assailed it with various types of ammunition and wreaked havoc upon it. The formation moved at the double-quick to the Rose buildings about five hundred yards in front of Bigelow's battery, the guns of which raked it with solid shot and canister. The artillerymen saw some men retreat and others take shelter among the stone farm buildings. This must have been Kershaw's right wing, for, as mentioned in Chapter 11, Kershaw well remembered the clatter of canister balls against the stone walls.[53]

Ames's battery in the Peach Orchard must have been the first to open on Kershaw's and Semmes's brigades. Because his battery's ammunition was nearly gone by then, Ames had all of his spherical case carried to his left section, Lt. James B. Hazelton's, which would shoot at the advancing infantry, while the center and right sections continued their counterbattery fire with shot. After Hazelton's section fired all of its case, the lieutenant ordered his men to take cover until the Confederate infantry approached within canister range. Battery G would then defend its position with the "unwelcome messenger—grape and canister."[54]

Kershaw's left wing crossed in front of the batteries with its left passing along the base of the slope. It was three hundred yards from Clark's battery and was in partial defilade. When the Confederate line swung toward the batteries, Clark's guns assailed it with canister, blasting holes in the Carolinian ranks and knocking down a stand of colors. As the Confederate line pressed nearer, Clark paced back and forth behind his guns, inspiring confidence. Sgt. William H. Clairville, the chief of piece, exuded calm as he notched the stick on which he recorded the number of rounds that "Old Betsy," the first piece, fired. As his gun crew loaded and fired, Clairville chanted to his gunner, Cpl. Elias H. Timm, and the crew, "This is the stuff to feed them; feed it to their bellies, Timm; mow them down, Timm."[55]

Hart's and Clark's batteries and Thompson's two left sections, thundered at the infantry in their front, Hart's Napoleons giving them both case and canister. It was probably during this firing that a Confederate shell exploded near one of the caissons of Clark's first section, killing a swing horse and wounding horses of the other pairs. A fragment disemboweled the near wheel horse. In its pain and fright the whole team started to bolt and went fifty feet before the gutted animal fell and broke the limber pole. The drivers managed to replace the pole and horses and returned the caisson to its place. Another shell passed between the barrel and a wheel of Clairville's piece, grazed the axle, and exploded. The force of its explosion threw the trail to the side, injuring two cannoneers and tossing Corporal Timm and cannoneer William Riley into the air. Timm regained his senses about twenty feet from the gun and called to Riley, asking if he were hurt. Riley, a skinny fellow, had a sizable chunk of flesh torn from a buttock, and complained, "By Jiminey, I didn't think they could touch me without taking a limb, and now, d— 'em, they have taken half the meat that I did have." Sergeant Clairville got two drivers to replace the two injured men, while Riley stood by in a daze. The chief of section, Lt. Robert Sims, saw Riley standing idly while others labored, and he yelled, "Riley, why the bloody h—l don't you roll that gun by hand to the front?" In answer, Riley turned his backside to the lieutenant and yelled back, "Lieutenant, if your hip was shot off like that, what the bloody h—l would you do?" And with that Riley limped back from the gun line.[56]

To add insult to Riley's injury, a shell fragment punched a hole in the first piece's sponge bucket, and its water ran out. The crew had to find a replacement bucket and fill it with precious water from their canteens. This irritated them. As the No. 2 cannoneer rammed the next round, he growled, "Take that for Riley," and the first piece fired on.[57] The guns became hot, some men were wounded, and all who served Clark's Parrotts became soaked with sweat and black with the grime of powder smoke. When the advancing line was within two hundred yards of the Parrott's muzzles and the Carolinians obeyed the mistaken command and moved to the right (as described in Chapter 11) Clark's men gloried in the notion that their servings of canister had driven the Carolinians from their front.[58]

Phillips's and Bigelow's batteries got in their licks. In Phillips's opinion the Confederate line moved in pretty fair order in spite of the pounding given it.[59] Bigelow thought at first that the Carolinians might be Union troops coming back and would not let the Ninth Battery fire at them. Then one of the red battle flags unfurled enough to display a cross instead of stars and stripes, and Bigelow's Napoleons opened on it at a range of four hundred yards. The artillery fire did not stop the Confederate formation. It came as close as two hundred yards to Bigelow's guns before its men took shelter in the trees and in the low ground down toward the Rose buildings. This probably was the Second South Carolina Regiment. McGilvery was nearby pointing out targets to the battery commanders. One was a man on horseback who seemed to be trying to organize an attack. One of Bigelow's shells struck beneath the horse and brought down both horse and rider.[60]

Kershaw's attack and threat to the right of Barnes's two brigades caused Barnes to order the brigades from the stony hill. Tilton's brigade, only six hundred strong, fell back to the stone wall along the west edge of Trostle's Woods 150 yards from the left and rear of Bigelow's battery.[61] It was fitting that a brigade with two Massachusetts regiments should stand by two of that state's batteries, and Tilton halted where the brigade could do so. Pandemonium reigned. Bigelow's and Phillips's twelve Napoleons thundered away, belching clouds of gray smoke with each shot. Shells whistled into the area, horsemen dashed about, and there was always shouting—except at the batteries, where the well-drilled crews ought to have worked with precision and with a minimum of such noise. General Barnes and Colonel Tilton, as well as their staffs, all on horseback, were out near Bigelow's position, a dangerous place to be. Barnes was wounded, and Tilton's horse was killed. Tilton's new position promised to be no haven of rest. Even as his men took their places behind the wall, they could see Confederates coming through the Peach Orchard six hundred yards to their front.[62]

As Kershaw's brigade regrouped, Ames's battery prepared to withdraw. Its ammunition was almost gone, and another battery, Lt. Malbone F. Watson's Battery I, Fifth U.S. Artillery, waited to take its place. Watson's battery had come on the field with Barnes's division and had been gobbled up by someone on Sickles's staff. How Watson's guns happened to be there did not concern Ames, who ordered his own guns out by section from the right and instructed them to cover their withdrawal by firing as rapidly as possible.[63]

Just before the battery pulled away a shell fragment mangled one of Pvt. John Krouse's feet. Krouse, a No. 1 cannoneer, had sponged just before the shell exploded. When the smoke cleared, he stood ready for the No. 2 to place a shell and its charge in the gun's muzzle. Instead of loading, the No. 2 looked at Krouse in astonishment, probably expecting him to collapse and someone to take his place. At this Krouse shouted, "D— you, what are you waiting for; put your charge in; I am going to have one more shot at them leg or no leg." The startled No. 2 obliged, and Krouse rammed the shell home." Just then Ames came up. Said the captain, "Well, John, they have wounded you at last?" Krouse replied, "Yes, the d— fools have shot my foot off, that was the best they could do." Ames offered Krouse a swig of whiskey, and Krouse gratefully accepted. Krouse drank so thirstily that when he returned the flask, Ames felt relieved that the cannoneer had not swallowed it as well as all that it contained.[64]

Battery G rolled slowly back through the fields to the gate to Trostle's lane carrying the battery's wounded on its caissons. Ames rode from the orchard with the last section like a captain leaving a sinking ship. Watson's battery of four three-inch Ordnance rifles took Battery G's place.[65] Watson's battery's stay was a short one that added no glory to its reputation. Kershaw's left pressed toward the Peach Orchard. The Third Maine fell back from its skirmish line through the gun positions and went into line on the right of the Second New Hampshire. When the Maine men were out of the way, Watson's guns opened on the Confederates in their front. It was not long before Colonel Bailey of the Second New Hampshire thought that he saw one of Watson's men trying to spike a gun, and in his report he accused the battery of inefficiency. The attempted spiking, if that was what it was, suggested to Bailey that the Confederates were getting close. He asked General Graham's permission to advance through the Peach Orchard to save the guns, and Graham gave it.[66]

The men of the Second struggled to their feet, relieved that the nerve-racking ordeal of quiet waiting under artillery fire was over. The regiment formed a hasty, imperfect line without Company B and at the command "Forward, guide center!" headed through the Peach Orchard. As Watson's guns belched a last volley of canister at the Carolinians, the Second crowded between the limbers and guns, reformed, and emerged at the orchard's southwest corner, its right extending to the Emmitsburg Road. The Second opened fire on the South Carolinians in its front, the Second Battalion and the Eighth Regiment. The South Carolinians' attack stalled, and they fell back to the bottom of the slope 150 or so yards from the orchard's edge. Bailey then shifted the Second's line to the rear of some fence rails that were piled along the side of the orchard where a fence had been.[67]

At the same time, the 141st Pennsylvania fired a murderous volley at the attacking Carolinians from its position along the shoulder of the Wheatfield Road. At General Graham's order it advanced with the Third Maine on its right and the Third Michigan on its left. The three regiments crossed to the south edge of the orchard and went in on the left of the Second New Hampshire. Kershaw's left regiments were now moving east across the Federal front. Mess pans, which hung on haversacks suspended over their left hips, glinted in the late afternoon light. The Federals harried them with oblique fire from the left, aiming at the mess pans, which made convenient bull's-eyes.[68]

There was a lull of a few minutes. The Sixty-eighth Pennsylvania shifted from a position near Clark's battery to the west side of the Peach Orchard— the Second New Hampshire's right and rear. Colonel Bailey sent some men back to help the cannoneers get their guns away while the rest settled in to await the next assault. It came soon. The Confederate cannoneers worked their guns with vigor, showering a hail of metal on the Orchard that made the trees that were still standing sway as if in a storm. Heralded by the increased fire, a line of infantry emerged from Pitzer's Woods and headed for the Emmitsburg Road.[69]

It was Barksdale's brigade—the Thirteenth, Seventeenth, Eighteenth, and Twenty-first Mississippi regiments—the valiant defenders of the Rappahannock crossing at Fredericksburg. Brig. Gen. William Barksdale stood out in an army of colorful leaders. He was forty-one years old, about the same age as Kershaw, and trained in law, but there the obvious similarities between the two generals ended. Barksdale had been a newspaper editor, a noncommissioned officer in the Mexican War, and a politician. As a congressman, he had walked the national stage in the 1850s, and he was an ardent states' rights Democrat and fire-eater. When secession and war came, Barksdale became the colonel of the Thirteenth Mississippi Regiment. He led his regiment at Manassas, commanded a brigade on the Peninsula, and received a general's wreath around his stars in August 1862. Barksdale was a large, rather heavy man, with a light complexion and thin, light hair. He was not a graceful horseman, as Confederate heroes ought to have been, but his impetuous bearing compensated somewhat for that deficiency.[70]

The Peach Orchard. Painting by F. D. Briscoe (National Archives)

Birney's division awaits Kershaw's attack near the Peach Orchard. (The Rose barn is on the left; the Peach Orchard on the right.) Sketch by Edwin Forbes (Library of Congress)

Barksdale chafed while awaiting the order to attack. Shot and shell fired at Moody's and Gilbert's batteries crashed through the trees of Pitzer's Woods and fell among his men, rounds fired from batteries that seemed to be his for the taking. It was an ordeal. Barksdale's requests to McLaws for permission to attack had gained him nothing, and so when Longstreet appeared along the Mississippians' line, Barksdale confronted him, saying, "I wish you would let me go in, General; I would take that battery in five minutes." "Wait a little," replied Longstreet, "we are all going in presently."[71]

While Longstreet was on Barksdale's front, he spoke also to Capt. Gwen R. Cherry of Company C, Seventeenth Mississippi Regiment, whose company was on the skirmish line, and asked him to send two unarmed men forward to an unidentified house that had a paled fence around its yard.[72] They were to knock the palings from the fence. Cherry told Company C's orderly sergeant to send out such a detail. It looked like a job with a limited future, and the sergeant got no volunteers. Those whom he told to go would not obey him. On learning of this, Cherry announced, "I *will* make the detail." He called out, "Jim Duke and Woods Mears, they will go." When Duke heard this, he commented to Mears, "We will be killed." Pvts. James W. Duke and Woodson B. Mears left their rifles with the company and dashed forward to the house. They knocked the boards from the offending fence and returned to the company unscathed in spite of a Federal skirmish line that was only about fifty yards away and artillery that was posted at the Sherfy house. Perhaps the Federals considered it to their advantage to have the fence torn down and were pleased enough to avoid the danger of doing it themselves.[73]

During the trying waiting period Barksdale called his regimental commanders together and gave them their orders. Only he, and probably his staff, would go forward on horseback; the other officers would advance on foot. This, apparently, was the practice throughout the corps that day. The regimental officers, therefore, would send their horses to the rear. Barksdale no doubt said some other things, and then, pointing to high ground along the Emmitsburg Road, he concluded, "The line before you must be broken—to do so let every officer and man animate his comrades by his personal presence in the front line."[74]

Kershaw's and Semmes's brigades to Barksdale's right had already advanced. After advancing three hundred or so yards toward the Emmitsburg Road, Kershaw heard drums beating "Assembly." Barksdale was to assault the Peach Orchard from the west, but his brigade was not starting soon enough to cover Kershaw's flank. As a result, the Federal batteries and the infantry in the Peach Orchard were able to rake Kershaw's lines severely, and Kershaw's brigade had reached the stony hill and was being repulsed before Barksdale's brigade came up on its left.[75]

This delay, which was so injurious to Kershaw's brigade, seems not to have become an issue after the battle or in the postwar disputes that sullied the reputations of some Confederate leaders. Perhaps, if some believed that Barksdale's regiments were not as ready to advance as they might have been, there was a reluctance to criticize him, and Kershaw himself seems to have been the sort not to waste his time in complaints. McLaws did not mention the tardy drumbeat, but he did indicate that Barksdale's and Wofford's brigades had gotten mixed up with Alexander's batteries somehow and "were temporarily delayed in extricating themselves therefrom." In particular, this involved one of Wofford's regiments that did not get free to join the brigade until it had gone a hundred yards.[76]

General McLaws sent his aide, Capt. G. B. Lamar, Jr., to General Barksdale with orders to advance. Here we may wonder why the signal fired by Cabell's battalion for Kershaw's advance did not apply also to Barksdale? Perhaps McLaws sent Lamar to Barksdale after it was apparent that his brigade was delayed; no one said. But when Lamar reached Barksdale with the orders to go forward, the news made the general's face "radiant with joy."[77] Barksdale ordered his four regiments over the wall. (Had they gone beyond the wall too soon they would have masked Moody's and Gilbert's batteries and exposed themselves to Federal fire unnecessarily.) The general passed around the right of his line, rode across the fronts of the Twenty-first and Seventeenth regiments, and halted in front of his old regiment, the Thirteenth. In the meantime, Kershaw's and Semmes's brigades were advancing. Once the Mississippians were beyond the wall, the regimental commanders called their regiments to attention. It was written of Col. Benjamin G. Humphreys that although he was "noted for excelling in the soundfulness of the word of command, never before did Colonel Humphreys shout 'Attention' with such imperative insistence."[78]

"From his chafing charger," a horse that mirrored its rider, Barksdale addressed his men, reminding them that each man was expected to do his duty.[79] That done, he shouted, "Attention, Mississippians! Battalions, Forward!" And then, wrote Colonel Humphreys, "Fourteen hundred rifles were grasped with firm hands, and as the line officers repeated the command 'Forward, March' the men sprang forward and fourteen hundred voices raised the famous 'Rebel yell' which told the next brigade (Wilcox's Alabamians) that the Mississippians were in motion."[80] Captain Lamar said that he never saw anything to equal the Mississippians' heroism and dash. Barksdale rode in front, leading the way, hat off, his wispy hair shining so that it reminded Lamar of "the white plume of Navarre."[81] When the line reached a fence, the barrier disappeared like magic. The Mississippians met and destroyed with a crashing volley what they deemed to be a Federal line, though it was probably the support for a skirmish line. This done, they continued on, loading and firing as they advanced. They passed over a rail fence and confronted a second line. This one was supported by infantry, particularly red-legged Zouaves. This was Graham's main line. In Confederate recollections, they swept the enemy before them like chaff before the wind.[82]

Although the Federal position at the Peach Orchard was stronger than the Confederates first believed, it had great deficiencies. That portion of Graham's line fronting west along the Emmitsburg Road was bolstered by eight guns—Bucklyn's battery and a section of Thompson's battery. This amount of artillery was nothing to be sneezed at, but after the long pounding that Bucklyn's battery received, it had lost a lot of its sting. The Federal infantry line was thin. The Sixty-third Pennsylvania Regiment, which had screened the Peach Orchard on the skirmish line, had been sent to the rear after it had run out of ammunition. This seems to have been a wasteful thing to do, for its casualties were low and it must have had a lot of fight left in it.[83] This left four Pennsylvania regiments that had been shaken by the artillery fire to cover the broad front. The Peach Orchard–Emmitsburg Road line had some natural strength, but Graham's brigade, like others that day, had done little to improve it with entrenchments or even piles of rails that could have been collected from nearby fences.[84]

The Confederates focused attention on Bucklyn's battery because it had given them a lot of trouble and, so long as it was firing, would give them more. Alexander's guns pounded it with shot and shell, and Confederate skirmishers drilled its men and horses with minié balls. The battery's four officers displayed coolness and daring, and 1st Sgt. Charles Winslow commanded its center section so well that there were those who believed that he would have been rewarded with a commission had he not been disabled in the fight.[85]

Cannoneer William Phinney was a fatalist. When told to take cover during a lull in the firing, he refused to do so on the dubious ground that he was as safe in one place as another. As the Confederate missiles zipped around him, Phinney stood by his piece, arms folded, rocking back and forth on his feet awaiting his fate. Phinney had close calls but came through unscathed. About the same time some kind of missile decapitated Pvt. Ernest Simpson. Simpson was the battery clerk and need not have been with the guns that day. But Simpson's parents had disapproved of his intended bride, and he had no wish to live. A missile from one of Alexander's guns relieved his misery.[86]

Lieutenant Bucklyn believed that Kershaw's attack had drawn his infantry support to the left and away from his battery except for two companies of sharpshooters.[87] This was not quite so. The 114th Pennsylvania remained in its position east of the road and in the battery's rear throughout the shelling. Barksdale's line approached to a distance of about forty yards from the battery's front and fired a volley at it. As it did so, the infantry on the battery's left seemed to give way. Bucklyn then moved the battery's sixth piece back from its position on the Emmitsburg Road. The artillery fire on the battery seemed to increase, and it appeared to be time for the battery to pull out. Captain Randolph, who though wounded was still in the saddle, rode back to the 114th and spoke with Capt. Edward R. Bowen. Said Randolph, "If you want to save my battery, move forward. I cannot find the general [Graham]. I give the order on my own responsibility." Bowen took the order and led the 114th through the guns and across the road toward the advancing Mississippi line. As the 114th move to its front, the Rhode Islanders limbered up and began to pull away.[88]

Battery E sustained heavier casualties that day than any other battery on the Third Corps line; twenty-eight officers and men were killed or wounded, and one man was missing. The Confederate fire killed or wounded forty of its horses, nearly a third of its complement, and for a lack of horses, the battery had to leave one of its caissons behind. Sgt. Arthur Hargreaves, chief of the third piece, lost all but two horses out of the twelve in his two teams. His piece was unable to keep up with the battery in its withdrawal, but Hargreaves was able to get his gun to safety using one sound horse and some wounded animals. Lieutenant Bucklyn had three horses shot as he rode around his battery's position and received a chest wound from a shrapnel ball as the battery started away. Six months later Bucklyn was back on duty, but he continued to be bitter about the battle along the Emmitsburg Road. He wrote at year's end, "My battery is torn and shattered and my brave boys have gone never to return. Curse the Rebs."[89]

When Barksdale's line approached the Emmitsburg Road between the Sherfy buildings and the Peach Orchard, the Fifty-seventh and 105th Pennsylvania regiments crossed the road into the farmyard and the fields to the Confederates' left. Probably they did so to cover the right of the 114th Regiment and to give added support to the gun sections near the Sherfy house. The Fifty-seventh joined its skirmishers in the house and farmyard and the 105th went into line on the brow of the rise to the Fifty-seventh's right. Some of the men of the Fifty-seventh occupied the Sherfy house and its outbuildings and fired from them at the advancing line, which was very near.[90]

By the time of Barksdale's advance, it was obvious that Graham's line was weak, probably too weak to hold its position along the road. At Graham's request and with Sickles's concurrence, Major Tremain galloped off to see General Humphreys, whose two brigades were not yet engaged, and asked him for a regiment. With Humphreys's permission Tremain borrowed the Seventy-third New York (also called the Fourth Excelsior and the Second Fire Zouaves), which conveniently awaited action at the left of Humphreys's support line. Tremain led the Seventy-third south toward the Sherfy buildings and halted it on the rise in the ground in the rear of its fellow Zouaves of the 114th Pennsylvania Regiment, who were already blazing away at Barksdale's nearby line. The men of the Seventy-third were panting from their hurried march, but there was a clicking of hammers being cocked that indicated that they were ready for action. The yelling Mississippians emerged from the smoke in their front and greeted the New Yorkers with a volley. The men of the Seventy-third could not reply because the 114th line still masked their front.[91]

Brig. Gen. Charles K. Graham
(National Archives)

Brig. Gen. William Barksdale
(Library of Congress)

Col. Benjamin G. Humphreys
(Library of Congress)

Col. Henry J. Madill (MOLLUS-MASS/
U.S.A.M.H.I., Carlisle Barracks, Pa.)

Col. Edward L. Bailey (MOLLUS-MASS/
U.S.A.M.H.I., Carlisle Barracks, Pa.)

The right regiment of Barksdale's brigade, the Twenty-first Mississippi, bore down on the orchard itself and the Federals posted there. The Sixty-eighth Pennsylvania, over 350 strong, must have been comparable in size to the Twenty-first Mississippi and with some help from the Second New Hampshire ought to have handled the Twenty-first easily. But the Sixty-eighth did not do so. The right of the Second, which was fronting south, turned and poured an oblique fire in the direction of the Twenty-first, but it cannot have been too damaging. Colonel Tippin of the Sixty-eighth told his companies to hold their fire until the Mississippians reached a certain point and then to blast away. The Sixty-eighth did this and brought the Twenty-first to a stand at a fence, probably that bordering the Wheatfield Road, until the Seventeenth Mississippi supported the Twenty-first on its left and threatened the Sixty-eighth's flank. Both regiments then continued their advance against the Union line.[92]

Colonel Alexander had become annoyed by the obstinacy of the Federal batteries, for what had promised to be a short and successful Confederate artillery preparation had grown very long. Therefore, just before Barksdale's brigade went forward, Alexander sent to the rear for Jordan's and Woolfolk's batteries, which he had left in reserve. He placed them under the temporary command of Maj. James Dearing whose own artillery battalion was back with Pickett's division but who had come forward to see the fight. The two batteries came up the road at a trot about the time of the infantry's advance.[93]

From the Peach Orchard area Pvt. Wyman W. Holden of Company B, Second New Hampshire, saw two Confederate batteries charge from the tree line on Seminary Ridge. One followed the road toward his company and then turned left into a field and dropped trail. Holden adjusted the sight on his Sharps rifle and fired at a cannoneer. Others fired at the battery also. The battery replied with canister, which—if indeed this was the case—indicated that at that time there was no Confederate infantry between it and the Wentz buildings. After the battery's second volley, there was so much smoke around it that the men of Company B were able to fire only at its muzzle flashes rather than at individual cannoneers.[94]

It seems likely that the batteries seen by Private Holden were Woolfolk's and Jordan's. From positions east of the Warfield and Snyder houses they could have fired toward the Federals along the Emmitsburg Road near the Sherfy buildings before Barksdale advanced. More important, as Barksdale's brigade closed on the Sherfy farmyard area, the batteries could have fired to its left and enfiladed Humphreys's line along the Emmitsburg Road. This could have been done until Wilcox's brigade charged into their fields of fire.

Holden and others of the detached companies near the Wentz buildings probably deployed in an open formation rather than in a compact line, and in reality did not fill the gap in the Third Corps line. Some of the men of Holden's company took shelter behind a chimney, but Holden stayed in the open and fired as fast as he could at that portion of Barksdale's line that was bearing down on him.[95] He could see a cannon nearby, which he identified as Ames's right piece, manned then by only two artillerymen in their shirt sleeves, but soon it pulled away. The nearby Wentz barn was riddled. Splinters from it littered the ground and finally caught fire. In contrast, the Wentz house off to the left and nearer the Wheatfield Road seemed virtually unharmed.[96] The Confederate lines, particularly their battle flags, made good targets. But they were formidable, and as they drew near, the detached companies fell back. Some of the wounded of Company B took shelter in the cellar of the Wentz house, where the Mississippians captured them.[97]

Barksdale's 1,400 Mississipians advanced in a tightly closed, compact line. The Twenty-first Regiment on the right of the brigade line guided for the Peach Orchard, while the Eighteenth on the left made for the Sherfy barn.[98] The 350-yard section of the Union line toward which Barksdale directed his brigade, therefore, was that manned by the Sixty-eighth and 114th Pennsylvania regiments until they were reinforced by the Seventy-third New York. The Pennsylvanians had half the strength of the Mississippians and were too few to cover the alloted space without leaving a soft spot, particularly when they were assaulted by a hard-charging brigade like Barksdale's. Since the Sixty-eighth was pinned to the Peach Orchard and the 114th to the Sherfy buildings, the weakest spot had to be between them at the road intersection and the Wentz farmyard.[99]

Wofford's brigade supported Barksdale's, but instead of moving in its rear, it veered to the right, as discussed above, and swept east astride the Wheatfield Road.[100] This fine brigade of Georgians was composed of the Sixteenth, Eighteenth, and Twenty-fourth regiments and the infantry of Cobb's Legion and Phillips Legion. The brigade had gained a niche in American military history when, under Brig. Gen. Thomas R. R. Cobb, it had slaughtered troops of the Army of the Potomac's Second Corps in front of the Sunken Road at Fredericksburg. After Cobb's death, William T. Wofford, colonel of the Eighteenth Georgia, had succeeded to its command. Wofford, like McLaws's other brigadiers, had been a lawyer before the war. He was born in Georgia in 1824, had been a captain during the Mexican War, and, like Barksdale, had been active in politics. He served in the state legislature and as a delegate to Georgia's secession convention but had opposed secession. When war came, Wofford became commander of the Eighteenth Georgia Infantry. Prior to Fredericksburg he had served with it in Hood's brigade. Wofford did not become one of the luminaries of the Army of Northern Virginia but served it well until he was transferred south to aid in Georgia's defense in 1865. Wofford's distinguishing features were a military bearing and a bald head. McLaws characterized him as being "very ambitious of military fame and one of the most daring of men." B. G. Humphreys remarked that "we all know that he was but too prone to go forward . . . even into disaster."[101]

At least half of Wofford's line must have been deployed south of the

Wheatfield Road, and its right moved through Taylor's and Parker's batteries. Wofford himself rode by Parker's battery, hat in hand and bald head glistening through the smoke in the late afternoon sun. The men of the battery stopped firing as the infantry passed through and gave the Georgians "a thousand cheers from full and admiring hearts." When he spotted Wofford, Captain Parker was so enthused that he saluted him with his sword and shouted, "Hurrah for you of the bald head!" The cannoneers took his cue and repeated the shout. Wofford's response to this peculiar salutation was not recorded.[102] But Parker had been truly inspired. In recording his recollections weeks later, he wrote of Wofford's advance and commented, "Oh he was a grand sight, and my heart is full now while I write of it. . . . Long may Gen. Wofford live to lead his men to victory!"[103]

Sometime early in the advance, perhaps after the brigade crossed the ridge, or even when it was in the Peach Orchard area, General Longstreet rode to the front of the Georgians' line to lead it on. Although McLaws believed Longstreet to have been disconcerted and annoyed because the battle plan was not working out, the corps commander's conduct before his Georgians was "gallant and inspiring." In response some of the Georgians cheered, but the dour Longstreet cut the cheering short with the admonition, "Cheer less, men, and fight more."[104] It was not a gracious reply, but it was good advice.

Wofford's brigade took little active part in the smashing of the Federal position at the Peach Orchard, for Barksdale's took care of that. Wofford's brigade's impact was on morale. It was a fresh, disciplined body of men that intimidated the battered and disorganized Federals in the Peach Orchard, in the stony hill area, in Trostle's Woods, and in the Wheatfield. Its appearance gave new life and hope to Kershaw's and Semmes's men on its right, and its advance carried them in its wake. Sometime in the course of its sweep the brigade flushed a rabbit that probably had been cowed by the events of the day. The creature fled from the awesome Georgians toward the Federal position. As it did so, "Wofford's men, reckless fellows as they were, raised a shout, and about fifty shots were fired at the rabbit." But the rabbit got away.[105]

The Confederate shelling, the onset of Barksdale's brigade, and the sight of Wofford's line marching grandly in Barksdale's rear discouraged the Federal regiments in the Peach Orchard. The Sixty-eighth Pennsylvania's colors fell, but a corporal caught them and waved them defiantly. The Sixty-eighth's lieutenant colonel and major both fell, along with numerous others in its ranks. The yelling Mississippians were crossing the Emmitsburg Road to its right and threatening to enfilade it and take it in the rear. It is no surprise, then, that Colonel Tippin thought that the Sixty-eighth's roadside position was untenable and ordered it to fall back to the rear of the batteries east of the Orchard. The regiment withdrew to the center of the Peach Orchard.[106]

The Sixty-eighth's withdrawal symbolized, if it did not signal, the demise of the Peach Orchard position. Once that keystone began to crumble, the salient was doomed. The Wheatfield Road line became untenable because an enemy force at the Peach Orchard could enfilade and flank it; the Emmitsburg Road line could not be held because an enemy force at the Peach Orchard could assail its left and reach its rear. Whether at Graham's orders or at their own volition, the Third Maine and Third Michigan regiments pulled back from their position facing Kershaw and changed front to the west. This left the Second New Hampshire and the 141st Pennsylvania on the original line fronting south with flanks open, facing Kershaw's men in their front, and with Barksdale's and Wofford's men threatening their right. Thus, the two Federal regiments had no option but to fall back and change front to the west.[107]

Colonel Bailey's Second New Hampshire faced about and fell back to the slightly higher ground midway through the orchard, about faced again, and prepared to deliver a volley at short range.[108] The nearby 141st Pennsylvania, with 180 men in its ranks, stood alone. Col. Henry J. Madill held them in this position for a short time and then backed off to the Wheatfield Road and the remnants of a board fence, where he formed a new line near the Sixty-eighth.[109]

The batteries had already started away. Just as no one wrote of the arrival of Watson's battery, no one described its departure. Thompson's four guns in the east side of the Orchard must have gone next, for they too could no longer fire with Union infantry in their front. Thompson's guns pulled back about three hundred yards to a point near the right of Clark's battery, where they unlimbered fronting south and prepared to open again.[110] Hart's battery had exhausted all of its ammunition but a few solid shot by this time, and it limbered up also and headed for the rear. In later years Hart fumed about running out of ammunition. He maintained that he had sent back for two of his caissons that he had left in the rear. At first they had been moved and could not be found. A second messenger found them, but before they reached Hart they were ordered back. Why he had not kept them with the gun sections he did not say. Hart believed that his reputation was at stake, for no one had ever seen his battery leave the field because of an ammunition shortage. Hart thought that McGilvery was the culprit: the men left with his caissons said that it was McGilvery who had ordered them from the field. This was a great grievance for Hart in the long postwar years.[111]

Barksdale's center regiments, the Thirteenth and Seventeenth, pressed over the Emmitsburg Road north of the Wheatfield Road to the Wentz farm. The Seventeenth Mississippi overran the Wentz buildings and supported the Twenty-first's attack against the Peach Orchard by clearing the Federals from the ground north of the Wheatfield Road. The Seventeenth and Thirteenth pivoted left on the Eighteenth Mississippi at the Sherfy barn and drove along the east side of the Emmitsburg Road against the left of the 114th Pennsylvania and Seventy-third New York regiments. The 114th gave way to the right and retreated up the Emmitsburg Road past the Sherfy house into the rear of the Fifty-seventh and 105th regiments, which still clung to their positions. Sometime early in the 114th's withdrawal, Captain Bowen saw its commander, Lt. Col. Frederick F. Cavada, sitting exhausted by an outbuilding. Bowen begged Cavada to fall back with the regiment, but Cavada could not. Since the Confederates were pressing them hard, Bowen left Cavada behind to become a prisoner of war. The 114th cut from the road into the fields that stretched east back to Cemetery Ridge. Bowen, now in command of the 114th, employed a tactic that served the regiment well. He sent the colors some distance to the rear and then ordered the Zouaves to fall back to them. The 114th repeated this simple manuever several times in its retreat to Cemetery Ridge.[112]

The Zouaves of the Seventy-third New York witnessed the Confederate assault from their thin line a hundred yards in the rear of the 114th's. It was a spectacle. There were the yelling, smoke-stained Confederates; mounted officers and couriers dashing about; Zouaves in their exotic uniforms fleeing, fighting, and dying; whistling shells; and zipping minié balls. The Sherfy barn in their front was full of holes, and a shell hit a rail pile and sent the rails flying like toothpicks. The noise was so loud that it drowned out officers' shouted commands even at a distance of only twenty paces.[113]

As soon as the 114th cleared its front, the Seventy-third poured a volley into the incoming Mississippians, dropping many of them among the fallen of the 114th. Both sides blazed away at short range, polluting the air with noise, lead, and acrid smoke. The Seventy-third's color sergeant fell; the next man to hold the flag was struck in the arm by a minié ball; and then a third man grasped the staff and held the banner high. Maj. Michael W. Burns rode behind the Seventy-third's line, conspicuous on his gray horse. Capt. Frank E. Moran of Company H was told that the regiment was about to charge, and the men cheered the news, but no charge was made. It was too late. The Mississippians were already among the Wentz buildings on their left, and the Federal troops in the Peach Orchard were falling back.[114]

When it became apparent that the Seventy-third was flanked on the left, a courier brought an order to Major Burns to take the Seventy-third back toward Humphreys's division, which, as yet, had not been attacked by infantry. As the Seventy-third started off, an artillery officer, probably from Thompson's battery, rode up to Captain Moran and begged him to help save a couple of guns whose horses had been shot. Moran got permission from Major Burns to do so. Moran and his company started for the guns, guided by the artillery officer, and apparently recovered one piece. A shell burst close to them and knocked Moran unconscious. When he regained his senses, a Rebel officer was trying to pull him from beneath a dead horse, and the Thirteenth Mississippi Regiment went charging by them, "firing and shrieking like Indians."[115]

The Sherfy barn was an easy point for Barksdale's left regiment, the

Eighteenth Mississippi, to guide on, and the regiment moved around it. As it did so, Maj. George B. Gerald asked some of its men to follow him, went to a barn door, and yanked it open. The barn was filled with smoke but was not large. In a couple of minutes Gerald's party rounded up all of the Union troops inside of it. In the meantime, beset by such diversions, Barksdale was trying to keep his brigade moving by shouting, "Forward, men, forward!" and probably some things that were more profane. He did not wish to give the disordered enemy a chance to rally.[116]

The Fifty-seventh and 105th Pennsylvania regiments to Barksdale's left were the Mississippians' next victims. This meant, of course, that instead of continuing his thrust to the east toward the Trostle farmyard with the entire brigade, Barksdale wheeled the Thirteenth, Seventeenth, and Eighteenth regiments left more or less up the Emmitsburg Road. The two Pennsylvania regiments now in its path had fired on the Mississippians' left as soon as it came within a reasonable range. Barksdale's men did not return the fire until they reached a rail fence that was about one hundred yards in front of the Pennsylvanians' position. They exchanged fire, but then, as the Confederates pressed closer, Capt. Alanson H. Nelson said to Col. Peter Sides, "It looks as though we will soon have to move out of here, or be captured." The colonel looked to the left and right and replied, "Yes, I think we will go now."

As their conversation suggests, the Fifty-seventh was not being stampeded. In fact, it had delayed too long. A number of the Fifty-seventh's men were scattered through the Sherfy buildings and could not be rounded up quickly. That portion of the regiment at hand would start back at once, while Captain Nelson tried to retrieve its scattered lambs.[117] Nelson turned his company over to a lieutenant and ran first to the more distant outbuildings and then back to the house. By this time the noise was so great that he could not call to the men about to be captured. Calling was not enough; he had to get each man's attention by shaking him by the shoulder, and this took time. While going from room to room in the house, he looked from a window and saw the Confederate line only fifty feet away. That was too close. Without further ado Nelson sprinted from the building toward the retreating Fifty-seventh, trailed by demands for his surrender and passed by the minié balls that missed him. In a few minutes Colonel Sides was wounded, the major was captured, and Nelson was in charge of what was left of his regiment.[118]

The 105th Pennsylvania on the brigade right was the last of Graham's regiments to leave the forward line. As the Confederates approached, it formed across the road in a futile effort to stop them, but the Mississippi line extended far enough east of the road and beyond the 105th's left to envelop it. The regiment retreated a distance and then rallied. Then, at what was said (probably wrongly) to have been an order from Sickles himself, the 105th counterattacked and pushed the Rebels in its front back to the Sherfy farmyard. This was but a very small and temporary victory. Soon the 105th, like its sister regiments, was heading back toward Cemetery Ridge. In the estimation of Col. Calvin A. Craig, the 105th had rallied eight or ten times after the brigade disintegrated—"the boys fought like demons. Their battle cry was 'Pennsylvania.'" About half of them became casualties that afternoon.[119]

As the remainder of Barksdale's brigade struck Graham's center and right north of the Wheatfield Road, the Twenty-first Mississippi pushed into the Peach Orchard and a Federal line that was forming there. The Second New Hampshire had swung back from its position along the south edge of the orchard and gave the Twenty-first a volley at close range. But the movement through the littered orchard and the pressure from the Twenty-first created disorder in the Second's ranks. This prompted Bailey to move the Second to a position behind the crest within the orchard and reform there. Having a little time, he ordered the regiment to dress on its colors. There was the usual shuffling and muttering, and soon the Second had a line. In keeping with the regiment's informal surroundings, Capt. Henry Metcalf of Company H called to Bailey, "How does that line suit you, Colonel?" Bailey replied, "Excellent! excellent!" With that approval, Metcalf turned to Cpl. William H. Piper and remarked, "A good line, that, Henry," and fell dead with a bullet in his head.[120]

Captain Metcalf's fall signaled the opening of another round, but this time the Second New Hampshire was not alone. Its good line formed the lead of a V-shaped echeloned formation with the Third Maine to its left rear and the Sixty-eighth Pennsylvania twenty paces to its right rear and ready to move forward. It is likely that the 141st Pennsylvania and the Seventh New Jersey were nearby, somewhat to the right and rear beyond the road.[121] It was at this time, perhaps, that Colonel Tippin of the Sixty-eighth met General Graham and received orders to take on the Seventeenth Mississippi, which was off the Sixty-eighth's right flank. Then Graham was wounded. The general turned his brigade over to Tippin, what there was of it, and started to the rear. That was the last that Tippin saw of him.[122]

The new line stemmed the Confederate flood no better than had the old. The Mississippians smashed the Sixty-eighth and sent it reeling back. The Second New Hampshire swapped fire with the Twenty-first Mississippi until the Second's line had gaping holes. Then, fearing envelopment by Wofford's line and capture, Bailey ordered the Second to break off the fight and pull back toward Cemetery Ridge. The location of the Second's last line is unmarked today, but it was obvious to all those who visited the Peach Orchard immediately after the battle. Each company's dead marked its place in line. The Second New Hampshire, once 354 strong, had 21 of its 24 officers and 136 of its 330 enlisted men killed or wounded in the Peach Orchard that day; the Sixty-eighth's casualties numbered 152.[123]

The retreat of the Sixty-eighth Pennsylvania left the 141st alone somewhere just north of the Peach Orchard and the Wheatfield Road. Capt. John F. Clark asked Colonel Madill if it was not time to leave. Madill replied stubbornly, "I have no order to get out." Then, looking at his short line, he said, "If I had my old regiment back again, I could whip all of them."[124] But the old regiment was gone. A formation appeared on the 141st's right, but the Pennsylvanians could not see it clearly through the smoke. Some men fired at it, but Maj. Israel P. Spalding ordered them to stop because he thought that it might be Union troops. It was not, and it repaid Spalding's caution with well-fired volleys that chopped the 141st's line into pieces. Confederate balls hit twenty-seven men in the first volley, and soon all of the men in the color guard were dead or wounded. The color corporal refused to give over the Stars and Stripes until a fourth wound rendered him incapable of carrying it. A ball shattered Major Spalding's femur, and only three of the regiment's nine officers emerged unscathed. Madill thought that the 141st had delayed the Confederate advance about twenty minutes. Colonel Madill, whose horse had been killed, carried the colors and led twenty men from the Peach Orchard area. They left Major Spalding sitting with his back against a tree and did not see him alive again.[125] As Madill and the remnant of the 141st trudged to the rear, they met General Sickles. Sickles said, "Colonel! for God's sake can't you hold on?" Looking at his corps commander with tear-filled eyes, Madill replied simply, "Where are my men?"[126]

This must have been one of Sickles's last conversations on the field. Sickles, the wounded Captain Randolph, and perhaps some orderlies and clerks of the headquarters staff started for the east side of the Trostle barn to avoid some of the Confederate shot and shell that were falling in the area. Sickles must have been preoccupied with the fate of his corps. He had disregarded Meade's orders because he had considered the Cemetery Ridge position to be a poor one and had advanced the Third Corps to what he deemed to be a better one. And now his line was crumbling. Hood's division had driven Ward's and de Trobriand's brigades from Devil's Den and the Wheatfield and the Fifth Corps brigades from the stony hill; the Wheatfield area remained in Federal hands only through the exertions of Caldwell's division of the Second Corps. To make matters worse even the troops of Graham's brigade were being driven from the Peach Orchard, the salient of his line. With its capture by the Confederates, the corps's right wing, Humphreys's division, would also have to fall back, and the Wheatfield would be untenable. He had sown good intentions and reaped a bitter harvest.

What Sickles would have done in an attempt to salvage the situation we cannot know. A round shot struck him in the right knee. It was a freak wounding, for the shot flicked the rider so lightly that it did not spook or hurt his horse, which already had one wound, and the animal remained under control. Somehow or other Sickles was able to dismount without further injury and those present made makeshift dressings for his wound with hand-kerchiefs until additional aid appeared.[127] Pvt. William H. Bullard, a musician from the Seventieth New York, who was serving as a stretcher-bearer, soon came on the scene. Bullard made a tourniquet from a saddle strap and stopped the general's bleeding. By then Sickles had grown pale with shock and loss of blood, and Bullard gave him a drink from a canteen. They placed him on a stretcher and waited for an ambulance to come. The general remained conscious throughout the ordeal, alert enough to appreciate his helplessness and show understandable apprehension. He asked to be placed behind a large boulder and expressed concern about being captured. He repeatedly urged those around him not to let him be taken prisoner.[128]

Major Tremain wrote that he returned to headquarters at about this time and found his chief lying propped against the barn (or was it a boulder near the barn?) and a soldier applying a tourniquet. The general told Tremain to tell Birney of his condition and that Birney was now in command of the Third Corps. Sickles then took a small flask of brandy from his pocket and took a sip. General Birney rode up as Tremain was starting off to find him, and Tremain began to relay Sickles's message. But Sickles saw Birney and with a voice that belied his condition shouted, "General Birney, you will take command, sir."[129] Birney and Sickles talked briefly, and Birney rode off to attend to his duties. Sickles asked Bullard for a cigar. Bullard took a case from the general's pocket, took a cigar from it, bit off an end, lighted it and gave it to him. Sickles took it and puffed away.[130] Sickles's condition soon attracted attention. In order to present a brave and calming front, Sickles raised himself on the stretcher so that passers-by could see that he was alive if not well and asked them to stand firm.[131]

An ambulance rattled up in a short while. They put the general into it, and Tremain joined him. One cannot help but reflect that though Tremain was of some use to Sickles at this time, Birney and the Third Corps might have needed him much more. As they bumped along, Tremain feared that the ambulance might be hit by an artillery round, but it was not. Tremain tried to fortify Sickles with sips of brandy from the flask as often as he would take them. Somewhere along the way they met Father Joseph B. O'Hagan, the chaplain of the Seventy-fourth New York, who joined the general in prayer. The ambulance reached the Third Corps hospital about dusk. Chaplain Joseph H. Twichell of the Seventy-first New York met it there and helped lift Sickles out. Sickles went under the care of the Third Corps surgeon, Dr. Thomas Sim. Twichell, who administered chloroform to Sickles, wrote that the general's bearing and words were of the "noblest character." "If I die, let me die on the field," said Sickles, and "God bless our noble cause."[132]

Sim amputated at once, cutting the leg off just above the knee. It was a dramatic scene worthy of a fine artist's skill. Sickles lay on a makeshift operating table surrounded by the surgeon and his assistants, their anxious faces glowing dimly in the light from candles held in the sockets of bayonets. Some aides were probably standing close by, and there was still the sputter of distant firing on Culp's Hill and Cemetery Hill.[133] The operation went well. Sickles remained at the field hospital that night while his aides and at least one orderly cared for him. Someone there, possibly Dr. Sim, took care of Sickles's special souvenir of the battle, his amputated leg.[134]

The 141st Pennsylvania Regiment had come to Gettysburg with 209 officers and men, and 149 became casualties in the Peach Orchard action; the Second New Hampshire suffered 193 casualties. Graham's brigade's casualties numbered 740. Confederate casualties for the Peach Orchard alone cannot be ascertained and, though not as heavy, were great enough. Company D, Twenty-first Mississippi, lost half of its men. Lt. James Ramsaur of the Seventeenth was wounded in both his hand and mouth. He could not shout orders but pushed his men on by waving his hat with his wounded hand and brandishing his sword with the other.[135]

Pvt. Archibald Duke of the Seventeenth fell in front of the Emmitsburg Road with a leg wound. He had had a presentiment of trouble and had asked his brother, J. W. (James) Duke, the fence-buster, to write home when the battle was over. J. W. found Archibald after the fight, and the wounded man exclaimed, "Thank God! My prayers are answered. I have asked Him to take me in place of you as I am prepared and you are not." Gangrene set in, and Archibald Duke died.[136]

After the fighting had passed on to the east, Capt. Francis E. Moran of the Seventy-third New York, who had been partially blinded and wounded in the ankle, limped into the Sherfy yard. Here on the ground that had seemed so vital to the Union a short while before, he washed his powder-stained and bleeding face and bandaged up his eye, perhaps with a handkerchief obtained from a Confederate officer in exchange for a sword belt. He saw dead men from both armies lying thickly around the splintered Sherfy barn. It was a sad sight that inspired sober thought. Most of all Moran was affected by the presence there of numerous dead and wounded horses from Bucklyn's and Thompson's batteries and from other units as well. "The poor horses had fared badly," Moran wrote, "and as we passed scores of these ungazetted heroes stood upon their maimed limbs regarding us with a silent look of reproach that was almost human in expression."[137] Humans had made the Peach Orchard salient a particular kind of hell.

14

From the Peach Orchard
to Cemetery Ridge

Colonel Alexander saw McLaws's division sweeping victoriously to the east beyond the Emmitsburg Road. He saw enemy batteries hurrying from the Peach Orchard, the Federal infantry abandoning the high ground along the road in confusion. He was not surprised—a Confederate victory was inevitable—"Providence was indeed 'taking the proper view.'" The battle had been fought, all the rest was anticlimax. All that the Confederates needed to do now was to exploit their success and bring the war to an end.[1]

The artillery would continue to do its part with pleasure. Woolfolk's and Jordan's batteries were already going forward with the infantry, and the rest must follow. Alexander ordered the remaining four batteries of his own battalion to limber up and advance. It was easier ordered than done. They were crippled by casualties in men and horses and fatigued from two hours of tension and firing. Alexander rode among them urging haste and telling them that the war would end that afternoon.[2]

The batteries moved out as they were able, the slower sections following the faster when they could. The battalion's advance was piecemeal. There was "a general race and scramble to get there first," but even with all of the chaos, Alexander deemed the advance a splendid sight—there was, he declared, "no more inspiriting moment during the war" than the seven-hundred-yard charge of his six batteries at Gettysburg. More than twenty guns, and their caissons, like the chariots of the ancients, rolled down the east slope of Seminary Ridge, horses at the gallop, and then up the slope to the Emmitsburg Road. Some cannoneers rode the limbers, and others ran alongside, trying to keep up. To their commander, "they were in great spirits, cheering & straining every nerve, to get forward in the least possible time."[3] A fence in the way of Jordan's and Woolfolk's guns threatened to delay their rush. Maj. James Dearing galloped over to some prisoners nearby, gestured with his sword, and roared, "God damn you, pull down those fences," and the fences "literally flew into the air."[4] As Taylor's battery hurried forward, Cpl. Joseph T. V. Lantz, an excellent gunner, fell beneath the wheels of his piece. Lantz had both legs broken and probably received some internal injuries as well. Some of his crew stopped to help him, but the dying gunner declined their assistance heroically, saying, "You can do me no good; I am killed; follow your piece."[5]

When the guns reached the Emmitsburg Road, one battery turned north onto it, and it was rolling well when its commander ordered it to a sudden halt. Limbers had no brakes, and quick stops were not easily made. This one must have required a lot of reining in, whoaing, and bumping as limbers and horses pushed into the pairs in their front. The battery commander had spotted wounded men lying in the road, Zouaves of the 114th Pennsylvania and probably some of Barksdale's men as well, and had no wish to run over them. He had some of them carried into Wentz's cellar and given water. The battery then continued on, the captain promising that he would return to help the wounded when he caught their compatriots who were still able to fight.[6]

Those portions of Alexander's batteries that advanced took position on the forward slope of the high ground east of the road. Only Moody's twenty-four-pounder howitzers occupied the Peach Orchard itself. Probably its guns were just east of the orchard's highest point, its left piece near the road, and one may wonder how it maneuvered and functioned in an area so thickly strewn with debris and the Third Corps's dead and wounded. Taylor's battery was on the left of Alexander's new line at a point about 150 yards north of the Wheatfield Road and 150 yards east of the Emmitsburg Road. The other batteries were more or less on line between Moody and Taylor. As soon as they were able to do so, the excited cannoneers opened fire on the numerous targets in the fields ahead. Alexander then left them in the care of Major Huger and rode back to bring Cabell's batteries forward. It was a futile effort. They had lost numerous horses and could not get organized enough to advance before darkness set in.[7]

When Alexander reached the high ground east of the Emmitsburg Road and looked around, he was disappointed in what he saw. Contrary to his expectations, the Federal line at the Peach Orchard had not been the true main line: "That loomed up near 1,000 yards beyond us, a ridge giving good cover behind it & endless fine positions for batteries. And batteries in abundance were showing up & troops too seemed to be marching & fighting everywhere—There was plenty to shoot at. One could take his choice & here my guns stood & fired until it was too dark to see anything more, & both sides were glad to stop & rest."[8] Alexander's different perspective permitted him to see what Sickles and Birney had not seen in the strength of the Cemetery Ridge position, and he saw to his sorrow that the afternoon's battle would not end the war. There were still plenty of targets, and "a spirited duel now ensued with their new line."[9] One of Longstreet's couriers who was searching for Alexander found the noise so great and the smoke so heavy that he became disoriented and a cannoneer had to guide him to the colonel. Accurate Federal fire, probably from McGilvery's guns beyond the Trostle buildings, wounded five of Parker's men, two of Taylor's, and perhaps others. But darkness soon enveloped the field and obscured its visible horrors. The darkness also accentuated the flashes from the muzzles of rifles and cannons, from bursting shell and the trails of lighted fuses of shells in flight. The area then took on a festive appearance of a sort. One impressionable young cannoneer of Parker's battery viewed the scene with wonder and, forgetting the tragedy of the day, exclaimed to his battery commander, "Oh! Captain, this is beautiful!"[10]

When Barksdale's three left regiments—the Thirteenth, Seventeenth, and Eighteenth Mississippi, wheeled left up the axis of the Emmitsburg Road, Col. Benjamin G. Humphreys's Twenty-first Mississippi broke with them. Humphreys saw Federal batteries and infantry in his front. If he wheeled left with the brigade line, he would leave a dangerous enemy force in his rear. They might have been left to Wofford, perhaps, but if McLaws had arranged for Wofford to deal with them, Humphreys knew nothing of it. Therefore, the Twenty-first Mississippi plowed straight ahead after Graham's left regiments and the batteries along the Wheatfield Road.[11]

Humphreys was quite capable of independent thought and action and might have coveted it. At fifty-four, he was substantially older than most regimental and brigade commanders. He had been a lawyer; he had also been a Whig and had opposed secession. Forty years earlier he had attended West Point but had been dismissed in 1826 for taking part in Christmas "pranks." Humphreys would soon become a general and after the war would be a governor of Mississippi,[12] but that was in the future; there were Federal batteries just ahead for him to deal with in the present.

With the departure of Thompson's and Hart's batteries, Clark's was closest to the advancing Mississippians. Its sections began to limber up when the Confederates appeared on the high ground in the Peach Orchard to its right. It was certainly time to go because the battery had used up its canister on Kershaw's formations and could no longer protect itself against a line of charging infantry. As the teams wheeled their limbers around so that the crews could hook up the guns, the Rebels shot the lead horses of one team. There was a delay while the drivers cut them free, and this enabled the Twenty-first Mississippi to get within haling distance. One of them shouted, "Halt, you Yankee sons of——; we want those guns!" In answer Cpl. Samuel Ennis shouted back, "Go to h—l! We want to use them yet awhile." Some men of the Sixty-eighth Pennsylvania on the road nearby slowed the Twenty-first with a volley, and the battery pulled away. As it did so, one of Alexander's batteries opened on it from the high ground along the Emmitsburg Road. This fire wounded some cannoneers and all of the horses hitched to the caisson of the fourth piece and four of the horses of the team of the third piece's caisson. Clark's battery had to leave the caisson of its fourth piece in enemy hands.[13]

The battle was just about over for Clark's battery. Its guns and caissons trundled to the rear past the Seventh New Jersey Regiment, which had taken up a delaying position about two hundred yards in the battery's rear and then filed into Trostle's lane, moving on to the artillery park beyond the Taneytown Road. The battery had fired 1,300 rounds, and Sergeant Clairville had cut 241 notches for "Old Betsy" in his tally stick. The holes in the copper sleeves in the Parrotts' vents had worn from .2 inch to half an inch in diameter. Twenty men of the battery had fallen, and twenty-two of its horses had been killed or abandoned.[14]

The four pieces of Thompson's battery, which had fallen back from the Peach Orchard and had stopped at the right of Clark's battery, had a more difficult time of it. The Confederates shot down all of the horses of a caisson's team and all those of a gun team as well. Thompson's men abandoned the caisson with little ado, for there was little stigma attached to that; but they freed the gun's limber from its dead horses and tried to move the piece off by hand. Some infantrymen were helping them, but when the Confederates came close, the infantrymen, who had no personal stake in the gun's loss, disappeared. Thompson's men felt compelled to leave it.[15] Thompson's battery nearly lost a second gun here also. The Confederates shot the horses and drivers of its lead and swing pairs and badly wounded one horse of the wheel pair. Thompson and the remaining driver, Pvt. Casper R. Carlisle, freed the gun from the dead horses, and Carlisle pulled it to safety with the crippled wheel pair. In his report Thompson recommended that Carlisle be given a medal, and he later received the Medal of Honor.[16]

When Captain Phillips saw Hart's battery pull away, he knew that there was special danger on the right that he could not see. To be ready for it, he ordered Lt. Frederick Lull, whose section was on the right of his line, to reverse the section's limbers and be ready to move back to a rise about three hundred yards to the battery's rear. The chiefs of piece made ready also by uncoiling their prolonges from the hooks on the trails and stringing them out so that they would be available for instant use. About this time, Lieutenant Colonel McGilvery ordered both Bigelow and Phillips to take their batteries to the rear. In McGilvery's opinion both captains were displaying great coolness.[17]

Phillips ordered Lull's section to withdraw at once. By this time the Confederate infantry could be seen advancing through the Peach Orchard, but they seemed to be in disorder. For some reason Lull's two guns did not halt at the covering position but went on to the gate to the lane. There both they and Phillips's center section had to halt to allow batteries already in the lane to pass.[18]

Before Phillips's remaining section, the first, under Lt. Henry D. Scott, was able to pull away, skirmishers from Kershaw's brigade worked their way across the Wheatfield Road and into the front of Trostle's Woods. (Where was Tilton's brigade?) From there they sniped at Phillips's and Bigelow's batteries. A minié ball hit a sergeant in the chest, penetrated his jacket near the buttons, and followed the jacket's lining around to the back, where it exited. Another ball ricocheted off the barrel of one of the Napoleons when a sergeant was sighting along its side and tore through the top of his hat. It was hard for the gun crews to work under such circumstances and time for them to pull out.[19]

Lieutenant Scott and a crewman on the No. 2 piece hooked that gun to its limber to move it off in spite of the lead and swing pairs' drivers having been shot. The No. 1 piece, closest to Trostle's Woods, had more difficult problems. In response to Phillips's order for it to retire by prolonge and firing, its crew had toggled the rope to the trail and stretched it back ready to be hooked up. When the limber swung around, Cpl. Benjamin Graham, the gunner, hooked the prolonge into the limber's pintle and shouted, "Drive on!" It did not move. Graham stepped to the side to see what was wrong and saw that in the few seconds it had taken him to hook up, the Confederates had shot down the five remaining horses of the piece's team.[20]

On seeing the predicament of the No. 1 gun, Captain Phillips told Graham to break the sponge staff and to abandon the piece if necessary. Graham replied that the crew would stay with the gun, and they grabbed the prolonge and started to pull it away. What battery commander could have asked for greater devotion? Phillips dismounted and joined the crew, pulling the rope with one hand and holding his horse's reins with the other. The captain and the crew pushed and pulled their near ton of wood and metal over plowed ground and turf about halfway to the Trostle farmyard. Phillips left his crew there, mounted, and rode off toward the gate. He found the caisson's limber there and sent it back for the gun. They saved the No. 1 piece, but it was useless temporarily, for Confederate balls had knocked out half the spokes on one wheel and there was a shell fragment embedded in its hub. McGilvery wondered how they had gotten the gun off at all, for they were virtually surrounded and fired at from all sides.[21]

The two guns had been Lieutenant Scott's special responsibility. He had started the second piece on its way and was helping with the first when a minié ball smashed his cheek bones and the roof of his mouth and knocked him unconscious. When he came to, the Rebels were close at hand, but Orderly Sergeant Otis B. Smith was there with a horse. In spite of the danger to himself, Smith led the horse bearing Scott from the field.[22]

When Captain Phillips reached the heavily used gateway into Trostle's lane, he learned that Captain Hart had taken two of the Fifth Battery's guns off with his own battery. This irritated Phillips considerably, but he had no time for fussing about it then. McGilvery ordered him to place his three

Captain Phillips bringing off a gun by prolonge. (The Trostle barn is on the right.) Sketch by Charles W. Reed (Library of Congress)

remaining and usable guns along with others on a shelf just east of Plum Run and to prepare for more action.[23]

Bigelow's Ninth Massachusetts Battery was the last to leave its position on the Wheatfield Road line. By the time that McGilvery had dismissed it with a "limber up and get out," the men of the Twenty-first Mississippi, and perhaps some of Kershaw's men, were passing east from the Peach Orchard against the battery and the last Federal formations in the Wheatfield. Kershaw's men, probably from the Second South Carolina, assailed Bigelow's battery from the front and left; Alexander's guns had opened on it from the Emmitsburg Road; and the Twenty-first Mississippi swept toward it from the Peach Orchard. McGilvery's terse order came almost too late.[24]

Bigelow feared that if his guns stopped firing to limber up, the Confederate infantry would be on them like a pack of wolves, shoot the drivers, and capture the immobile guns. To prevent this Bigelow ordered the guns to retire by prolonge. He wrote that the guns' recoil propelled their withdrawal and that the prolonges were used to steer them in the proper direction. And yet the limbers had to be there also to supply ammunition and to move the guns between shots.[25]

The Confederates shot the near wheel horse on Bigelow's sixth piece soon after the battery began its rearward trek. The driver, Pvt. Eleasar Cole, cut out the fallen animal, and the limber started off again with Cole wrestling with the pole and trying to control the off horse. By the time the sixth piece crossed the field, the open lid on the limber chest, which partially shielded Cole, had thirteen bullet holes in it. Cole apparently had none in him.[26]

Kershaw's skirmishers shot the minié balls that hit the limber chest as they dogged Bigelow's retreat toward the Trostle buildings. Bigelow's guns fired canister at the South Carolinians in their front and spherical case at the Mississippians coming down on their right.[27] Bigelow believed that he had no infantry support when his battery withdrew toward the Trostle farmyard. This was essentially so. And yet there was infantry around. The Eighth Alabama exchanged fire with a regiment posted briefly near the Trostle barn, and the Twenty-first Mississippi's advance was slowed by regiments falling back from the Peach Orchard and by Tilton's brigade, which was in Trostle's Woods to Bigelow's left and rear. Cpl. James J. Donnelly, orderly for the commander of the 118th Pennsylvania Regiment, which was on the right of Tilton's brigade and nearest to the Trostle buildings, fired a carbine at the advancing Confederates until he used up his ammunition. At a lieutenant's suggestion he then jumped over the wall from the woods into a grain field west of it to get a rifle and cartridge box from a dead soldier lying there. It was said that Donnelly shot the color-bearer of the Twenty-first Mississippi before Tilton's line pulled back from the wall and that the 118th Pennsylvania's losses were greater in this position than in any other that it occupied that day. Such support would have been helpful to both Bigelow's and Phillips's batteries as they left the Wheatfield Road.[28]

When Bigelow's sections neared the gate in the wall, they should have been concealed from the approaching Mississippians by a rise in the ground about one hundred yards west of the fence corner and the gate. By this time the jam of batteries at the gate and along the lane had cleared, and the Ninth Massachusetts Battery ought to have been able to pass through it without impediment on its way to Cemetery Ridge. Bigelow ordered that his guns limber up, and they were busy at that when Colonel McGilvery reappeared. In concise and emphatic tones that prompted understanding and obedience from the hard-pressed captain, McGilvery stated that there was no infantry on the ridge in the rear, that the Ninth Battery must cover the withdrawal from where it was, and that it must sacrifice itself if need be until McGilvery could find some batteries to form a new line of artillery. As McGilvery reported it, Bigelow was "to hold his position as long as possible at all hazards," an expression often used that afternoon.[29]

Bigelow had no time to waste. He ordered his three sections to prepare for action and to pile their ammunition near the guns so that they could fire as rapidly as possible. They occupied the fence corner across the lane from the Trostle farmyard, and faced from it in a quarter circle. The left section, Whitaker's, was on the right by Trostle's lane. Both of its pieces fronted

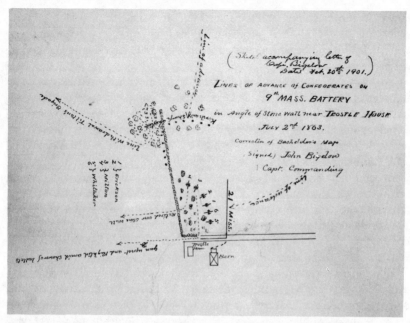

Lines of the Confederate advance on Bigelow's battery. Map drawn by John Bigelow (Gettysburg National Military Park)

generally west, parallel to the lane, and had a field of fire of about a hundred yards to the top of the rise ahead of them. Erickson's section in the center also fired west and had a field of fire to the top of the rise. Milton's section was on the left by the wall that ran along the west front of Trostle's Woods. Its pieces fronted south and southwest and also had a field of fire of about a hundred yards. The battery's caissons unloaded and hurried to the rear, but the limbers and their teams remained with the guns and were also crowded into the corner. The battery must have made a splendid target, protected only by the rise of ground in its front and the smoke that was bound to settle around the guns. The smoke would limit the visibility of the artillerymen and their attackers alike.[30]

Bigelow could see little or nothing of the Mississippians when the battery dropped trail in the fence corner. He knew where they ought to be, however, and attempted first to strike them by firing shot aimed so that the balls would hit the rising slope a short distance in front of the four right guns, ricochet over the top of the rise, and drop, hopefully, into the Confederate ranks beyond. This must have been a desperate stopgap measure at best and required more luck for success than Bigelow's battery was having that afternoon. Bigelow then ordered his four right guns to load with double canister and to wait. When the Mississippi line appeared breast high over the crest, Bigelow commanded the four guns to open, and they fired as rapidly as they could. In the meantime, Milton's section, which had been belching occasional rounds of canister at skirmishers in its front, moved farther to the rear with each shot and became cramped against the wall. Bigelow told Milton to get his section away if he could.[31]

That was easier said than done. Milton's third piece limbered up, passed to the rear of Erickson's and Whitaker's sections, and proceeded out the gate into the lane. It upset there, blocking the gate until the cannoneers were able to right it and move it off. The fourth piece went over the wall on the battery's left, a difficult thing made possible only by the desperation of the occasion. The cannoneers took some stones from the wall before the attempt was made, and then Bigelow asked them to remove some more, so that the other sections might also go that way. As Bigelow and Bugler Reed sat on their horses by the cannoneers who were trying to open the gap, six Confederates fired at them. Reed pulled his horse back sharply on its haunches in time to avoid being hit, but two bullets hit Bigelow and his horse. Reed then heard a Confederate officer order his men to cease fire.[32]

Humphreys's Mississippians pressed Bigelow's battery from the front and extended their line beyond the lane to its right. Bigelow recalled that "the enemy crowded to the very muzzles of Lieut. Erickson's and Whitaker's sections, but were blown away by the canister. . . . Sergeant after sergt. was struck down, horses were plunging and laying all around, bullets now came in on all sides for the enemy had turned my flanks. The air was dark with smoke. . . . The enemy were yelling like demons, yet my men kept up a rapid fire, with their guns each time loaded to the muzzle."[33] Bigelow claimed that no Confederates got into his battery from the front, only by the flanks. The men of the Twenty-first pressed down Trostle's lane and into the farmyard and got behind the battery's limbers. A color-bearer climbed up on one and waved his battle flag while more deadly men attempted to fire from the limbers at the cannoneers working the guns. The Rebels shot all of the horses in the team of Whitaker's fifth piece, condemning it to capture. Sgt. Charles Dodge, chief of the second piece, fired his last round of shot and someone shot him. The devoted, courageous Erickson was shot five times and fell dead from his horse. The animal bolted into the enemy lines.[34]

When Bigelow saw Federal batteries going into position three hundred or so yards in his rear, he ordered the remnants of his battery to fall back. Whitaker's fifth piece had no horses to pull it, and it had to be abandoned. His sixth piece, which the crew was able to limber up somehow, upset at the gate and had to be left behind. Lieutenant Whitaker, who was mounted and must have been a conspicuous target, was shot in the knee, but he stayed in the saddle and trotted from the shambles. Both of Erickson's guns were overrun and lost. In the final tally it is surprising that only eight officers and men of the battery were killed, eighteen wounded, and two missing. Forty-five horses fell, some near Trostle's farmyard, where they were photographed

Milton's section, Ninth Massachusetts Battery, going over the wall. Sketch by Charles W. Reed (MOLLUS-MASS/U.S.A.M.H.I., Carlisle Barracks, Pa.)

after the battle. Bigelow reported proudly that the battery had fired three tons of ammunition, including ninety-two rounds of canister.[35]

The men of the Twenty-first Mississippi pressed among the Massachusetts guns as their crews reluctantly abandoned them. Lt. George C. Kempton mounted one, waved his sword, and exulted, "Colonel, I claim this gun for Company I." Lt. William P. McNeily took possession of another in the name of Company E. The men of the Twenty-first were in tall cotton on a Pennsylvania Dutchman's farm—the capture of four Napoleons and a brigadier general was a good day's work, and there seemed to be more booty ahead just for the taking.[36]

After he was shot, Captain Bigelow rode to the rear about a hundred feet and slumped from his horse. Bugler Reed, who was still with him, secured the help of Pvt. John H. Kelly, Bigelow's orderly, and the two prepared to help the captain get back on his horse. About this time Lieutenant Whitaker rode up and offered Bigelow a swig from his flask. Taking more than one swig, Bigelow "took them in small swallows (all that I took in the service)," and returned the flask to Whitaker. With help from the stimulant, Kelly and Reed got him back into his saddle. In the meantime the Confederate infantry was only a few yards away. The three horsemen continued their ride, but Whitaker could go faster than Bigelow and Reed, and he was soon out of sight.[37]

Reed led Bigelow's horse at a walk, avoiding capture and death by the grace of God and momentary confusion in the Confederate ranks. They rode directly into the field of fire of Lt. Edwin B. Dow's Sixth Maine Battery, which had just come up to help Colonel McGilvery plug the great gap in the Federal line. The battery's four Napoleons were loaded and ready to fire. An officer of the battery galloped forward and told Reed and Bigelow to hurry. Bigelow replied that they could not hurry, and that the battery should go ahead and shoot. It did so. The right section fired canister, and the left fired shell, which would have been of less danger to the riders. Reed did not flinch as the projectiles swished by. He guided the two horses with one hand and supported Bigelow with the other, and the two passed between Dow's guns to safety. Reed's conduct greatly impressed both Bigelow and Dow. Thirty years later Reed received a Medal of Honor in recognition of his bravery that day.[38]

Dow's four Napoleons were a key component in the line of guns that McGilvery was trying to assemble on the high ground in front of Cemetery Ridge. The guns would be about three hundred yards east of the Trostle house, halfway between Trostle's and the crest of the ridge north of the George Weikert farmyard. General Hunt had noticed this shelf during his late morning visit to Sickles's front, but because it was dominated both by the high ground at the Peach Orchard 900 yards to the west and by Cemetery Ridge 350 yards or so to the east, he did not believe it a suitable place for the Third Corps line. And yet it was there and later was useful, and so in retrospect he called it "The Plum Run Line."[39]

McGilvery put his line together from guns that he was able to intercept as they passed back from the Peach Orchard area, and unfortunately, it is likely that he met only those that got away last and were in the poorest condition. The line formed was not a stable one, and we shall never know what batteries were in it at a given time. McGilvery reported that it included Watson's battery, three guns of Phillips's battery, two of Thompson's, a volunteer battery whose identity he did not know and which escapes us today, and Battery B, First New York Light Artillery, which was then commanded by Lt. Albert S. Sheldon. These batteries were joined by Dow's, which, being fresh, became the nucleus of the line. As the line was first formed, Watson's four three-inch rifles were on the left and Dow's four Napoleons were next in line, followed by Phillips's and Thompson's guns. If Battery B, First New York Light Artillery, was really there as McGilvery wrote, its service was recounted so vaguely as to give it little credence. The unknown battery's position, if it had one, was not recorded. McGilvery's guns faced two principal foes—the Twenty-first Mississippi Regiment and Alexander's guns near the Emmitsburg Road.[40]

While McGilvery tried to form his line of guns, Colonel Humphreys tried to reform the Twenty-first Mississippi and get it moving again. He wanted to shift it left so that it could join the rest of the brigade, but before he could do so, he saw a battery unlimbering in his front beyond Plum Run and preparing to open fire. Wofford's brigade was somewhere to the Twenty-first's right, and Humphreys could not leave the battery there to rake the Georgians' flank. Therefore, instead of shifting north to rejoin the brigade line, he directed the Twenty-first to charge the threatening battery.[41]

The battery was Watson's, just back from the Peach Orchard. It opened on the Twenty-first, first with shell and then canister. Its efforts were to no avail. Young Malbone Watson, two years out of West Point, suffered a knee wound early in this action. There were twenty-one other casualties, and half of the battery's horses were shot. The battery seemed to fall apart. In the words of Lt. Charles C. MacConnell, who succeeded Watson and made the battery's report, the conduct of its men was generally "unexceptional." The battery was "abandoned." Watson's leg was amputated.[42] The men of the Twenty-first tried to turn their captured guns on their former owners but could not do so. The gun crews had carried off their tools and friction primers, and the guns could not be loaded, aimed, and fired.[43]

The Twenty-first had to reform again. As it did so, Colonel Humphreys took stock of the situation. He saw no organized troops on the ridge ahead, but some Federal formations were moving south along the ridge in his direction. The rest of Barksdale's brigade was three hundred or so yards to the left and fighting. Humphreys wanted to join it, but the approaching Federal columns would not permit the Twenty-first to do so. There was a crisis at hand.[44]

While the Twenty-first Mississippi spun off Barksdale's brigade's pivot toward the Trostle farmyard, the left three regiments advanced north along the axis of the Emmitsburg Road. The left regiment, the Eighteenth Mississippi, must have been on and to the left of the road until the brigade passed the Sherfy buildings, because it was essential that the Fifty-seventh Pennsylvania and others be driven from the cover of the buildings. This would have permitted the Thirteenth and Seventeenth regiments to advance east of the road on a front two hundred yards wide. The front was broad enough to deal with any Federal units that attempted to reform there. It was broad enough also, as the Mississippians neared Trostle's lane, to endanger the left of Humphreys's division's line and render that division's position insecure.[45]

Barksdale's advance along the road dovetailed with an order from General Birney, now commanding the Third Corps, for General Andrew A. Humphreys to pull back his division's left. Birney was trying to replace the smashed salient at the Peach Orchard with a line that would run between Humphreys's position and the Round Tops. It was a futile thing to do, but only hindsight tells us that. Except for Barksdale's brigade, the Confederates were no longer attacking on a north-south axis, but instead were moving from west to east. And, though Barksdale's brigade provided ample threat to the remnant of the Third Corps line along the Emmitsburg Road, that line was threatened also on its front and right.[46]

Humphreys tried to comply with Birney's order. The Eleventh New Jersey, Carr's brigade's left regiment, changed front from its position on the left of the Klingle house along the Emmitsburg Road and swung back behind the house to form a line perpendicular to the road and facing Barksdale. Although the reports of the Seventy-first and Seventy-second New York regiments say nothing of it, we can be sure that they also pulled back from their position along the road north of Trostle's lane to positions parallel with the lane and fronting toward Barksdale. It is likely also that the 120th New York, which was on the left of the division's support line, also changed front at this time. This refused line on Humphreys's left should have provided a rallying point for those of Graham's men who came that way and were still inclined to fight and for the Seventy-third New York, which had been posted there before being sent to Graham's aid.[47]

Soon after the Eleventh New Jersey's pivot, its men saw a Confederate horseman, a conspicuous figure mounted on a gray horse and wearing a red fez. They could not have known the identity of the officer, but someone with authority thought him important enough to kill. Lt. Ira W. Corey of Company H was told to shoot him down. Since the range was great, Corey ordered the entire company to fire at him. They found the rider later with five bullets in his body and wrongly believed that he was General Barksdale.[48]

The Mississippians smashed the lines of the Seventy-first, Seventy-second, and possibly the Seventy-third New York regiments without great difficulty. Capt. Thomas Rafferty of the Seventy-first admitted some temporary confusion but wrote nothing more about it. Probably these Excelsiors performed poorly and had no wish to remember this important phase of the battle. Captain Cavada of Humphreys's staff wrote of enfilading fire that dealt destruction, of Mississippians attacking "like devils incarnate," and of portions of Graham's men fleeing toward Humphreys's division, broken and in disorder. Cavada stated that the Seventy-first and Seventy-second became infected by the contagion and broke also, in spite of staff officers' efforts to rally them, and "for a moment the route was complete."[49]

Capt. Carswell McClellan carried the order from Humphreys to the left regiments to form a new line and stayed to see them execute it. Then he returned to Humphreys. McClellan and Humphreys saw Graham's men falling back and saw the left of their own division's line begin to break. Humphreys ordered McClellan back to the left and told him to get the men there back into line and keep them there. Accompanied by a single orderly, McClellan rode rapidly back to the left. On the way he saw General Birney riding in the opposite direction. When he reached the faltering regiments, he found a general stampede imminent, caused, he thought, by Birney's having called to some of the regiments to fall back. McClellan cancelled Birney's instructions and told the Excelsiors to face around and charge, and his unnamed orderly led them. This done, the troops who had fallen back behaved well. It is appropriate to note that McClellan had an interesting idea about troop behavior. He believed that if men were formed close to the enemy, they could not run and would have to fight.[50]

One regiment did not melt away. As Barksdale's line approached, the 120th New York of the Excelsior Brigade waited for it, prone in Humphreys's support line. When the regiments in its front gave way, the men of the 120th stood and, with the help of some stragglers who had joined them, brought the

Mississippians to a halt a few rods in their front. Col. William R. Brewster, the brigade commander, who had been forward with the first line and had been unhorsed, fell in with their file-closers. General Humphreys and the commander of the 120th New York, Lt. Col. Cornelius D. Westbrook, rode back and forth behind their line. Westbrook was angry. He could see Carr's brigade along the road to the 120th's right rear. It seemed to be doing nothing while the 120th was being shot apart. He complained to Humphreys and to Brewster. Neither took the time to tell him that Carr's regiments had, or soon would have, all that they could do to hold off the brigades of Anderson's division, which were approaching their front.[51]

There were those who thought that the 120th stood its ground for an hour. This seems impossible—certainly it was not opposing Barksdale's line for that long. It must have given ground grudgingly as Carr's brigade gave ground, until both became a single command facing Wilcox's brigade. Unlike the old Excelsior regiments, the Seventy-first and Seventy-second in particular, the men of the 120th New York pointed with great pride to their performance in this fight and the 203 casualties sustained.[52]

As Wilcox's brigade approached from the west and Barksdale's brigade from the south, the Third Corps line must have given way to the northeast. To avoid a collision, as Barksdale's line approached Wilcox's zone, Wilcox's brigade veered slightly left. After crossing Trostle's lane, Barksdale's swung right to the east and Cemetery Ridge northeast of Trostle's farmyard.[53]

Barksdale's drive had been a great success, and it became even more glorious in the golden glow of memory. It was recalled as "forward" and "onward" all of the way. No one managed an orderly account of it—no one mentioned its being slowed by the resistance of the 120th New York and Humphreys's left or its caroming from Humphreys's flank to the east. All of the Mississippians were caught up in the movement, the shouting, the euphoria of success, and the shattering of the blue formations that could not stand against them. Barksdale tried to keep up the momentum, tried to keep the bluecoats on the run. But there also were second, more sober, thoughts: Colonels Holder and Griffin of the Seventeenth and Eighteenth regiments saw that the brigade's line was becoming ragged and urged their fire-eating brigadier to pause and reform. "No," was his answer. "Crowd them—we have them on the run. Move your regiments." Perhaps it was at this time that Barksdale held his sword high, pointed to the front, and shouted, "Brave Mississippians, one more charge and the day is ours."[54]

"Will nothing stop them?" wrote Colonel Humphreys rhetorically in later years. And then he replied, "Yes *death* will do it and has already done it!"[55] To death he might have added fatigue, disordered lines, diminished firepower, and a dangerous enemy brought to bay and reinforced. One soldier, Pvt. Joseph C. Lloyd of Company C, Thirteenth Mississippi, yelled and panted his way through a wheat field, probably the south end of the large field between the Rogers house and Plum Run, until the Thirteenth neared Plum

Run's swale. Suddenly something whacked him in the arm, jarring him as though a fence rail that he had been holding at one end had struck the ground hard with the other. He had been shot, and the blow halted him in his tracks. A comrade helped him make a sling for his arm and then went on, leaving him to care for himself.[56]

Lloyd caught his breath as the battle swirled ahead of him. Then he started for the safety of the rear. He went but a short distance when he found General Barksdale lying on the ground, alone, wounded, and resigned to his fate. Where was his staff? Perhaps some were urging the brigade forward, perhaps one had gone for help—no one said. Private Lloyd gave the general a drink from his canteen, and Barksdale drank until Lloyd saw water seeping from a hole in the general's chest. And then, at Barksdale's insistence, Lloyd continued on to the rear, leaving the general for stretcher-bearers who would soon be coming to carry him to a hospital.[57]

Barksdale's fall and Plum Run's swale marked the end of the Mississippians' grand effort. It had come far, its charge was one of the grandest of the war. But the brigade was in disorder, its strength sapped by the loss of many men in its mile-long advance. Cemetery Ridge was still ahead, and there was a heavy line of blue-uniformed infantry rising "as if from the earth and . . . moving down upon them."[58] It was twilight, Barksdale's regiments had no support troops to push its attack home, and the battle was taking a new turn.

15

Anderson's Division Attacks

WILCOX'S AND PERRY'S BRIGADES
STRIKE HUMPHREYS'S DIVISION

The men of the Eleventh Alabama Infantry Regiment "sweated, sweltered and swore"—and with reason. A short time earlier in the day the regiment had taken a score of casualties and tumbled back in confusion when suddenly assailed by Berdan's Sharpshooters near Pitzer's Woods. After the Tenth Alabama, aided somewhat by the Eighth, had driven the sharpshooters away and earned the glory of the action, the Eleventh took position behind a fence in an open field, where the sun roasted it mercilessly. The sun's rays were not as deadly as bullets, of course, but it was obvious to all that there could be shooting aplenty before the afternoon was over.[1]

The Eleventh Alabama had advanced with Anderson's division that morning to relieve Heth's battered division on Seminary Ridge. The division completed this movement soon after noon when Wilcox's brigade drove Berdan's reconnaissance party from the woods and took its place on the right of Anderson's division's line. When formed, Anderson's five brigades stretched a mile along the ridge, south from McMillan's Woods on the left to the center of Pitzer's Woods. Pender's division, also of Hill's corps, occupied the ridge line to Anderson's left, but Anderson's right was in the air. At that time, Wilcox's brigade was on the division's, the corps's, and the Army of Northern Virginia's right flank. In order to protect that flank, General Anderson posted the brigade's right at an angle to the remainder of his line. Wilcox's right regiment, the Tenth Alabama, deployed in Pitzer's Woods fronting south across the ridge where Berdan's force had been. From this high ground the Tenth could guard against any further Federal attempts to gain the Confederate flank by approaching it through the woods, and it could watch the broad Willoughby Run Valley on the right through which a Federal force might approach the Confederate rear.

Wilcox's line curved northeasterly from Pitzer's Woods to the south end of

Spangler's Woods. Its center fronted toward the high ground along the Emmitsburg Road at the Sherfy and Klingle buildings, and its left rested in the low ground behind Henry Spangler's farm buildings. Brig. Gen. Edward A. Perry's Florida Brigade, commanded at Gettysburg by Col. David Lang of the Eighth Florida Regiment, occupied Spangler's Woods. Wright's, Posey's, and Mahone's brigades occupied the ridge crest between Spangler's Woods and McMillan's Woods half a mile north.[2]

The division's commander, Maj. Gen. Richard H. Anderson, was a South Carolinian, born in 1821, and a graduate of West Point in its class of 1842 along with his comrades Longstreet and McLaws. Anderson served in the Old Army in the Mexican War and in the West, becoming a captain in the Second Dragoons before he resigned in March 1861 to enter the Confederate service. He became the colonel of the First South Carolina Regiment and in July 1861 was made a brigadier general. He took command of a South Carolina brigade in Virginia in February 1862 and from that time on was associated with that theater of operations. Douglas Southall Freeman described him as being "tall, strong, and of fine background . . . never . . . disposed to quibble over authority or to indulge in any sort of boastfulness."[3] Anderson had a reputation for kindness, amiableness, and unselfishness, fine traits under any circumstance, but especially welcome in an army having its share of contentious generals. Anderson became a major general in July 1862 and was wounded at Antietam. When the Gettysburg campaign began, he enjoyed the reputation of having performed in an exceptionally competent way against Hooker's left at Chancellorsville and was marked for future promotion.[4]

Until the Army of Northern Virginia's reorganization, Anderson had served under General Longstreet and not under Ambrose Powell Hill. Hill was a Virginian, thirty-seven years of age, who had graduated from West Point in the class of 1847 along with Henry Heth and John Gibbon, whose division was opposite Hill's corps on Cemetery Ridge. Hill served as an artillery subaltern in Mexico and against the Seminoles but capped his prewar career in the Office of the U.S. Coast Survey. He entered the Confederate service as colonel of the Thirteenth Virginia Infantry Regiment and gained favorable attention at Romney. His rise was rapid. He became a brigadier general in February 1862, fought at Williamsburg, and was promoted to major general. He commanded the "Light Division" with distinction during the Peninsular campaign. Hill's toleration of a newspaper article that claimed too much for him and for his division at Frayser's Farm at the expense of others brought on a quarrel with General Longstreet that intensified nearly to the point of a duel. It was then that General Lee transferred the proud and prickly general and his Light Division to Stonewall Jackson's command in time for Second Manassas and the Antietam campaign. Hill got along no better with Jackson, who, on 4 September 1862, placed him under arrest because he and his division were not observing prescribed march procedures. Although Jackson soon restored Hill to duty, the offended Hill clamored for a court-martial and vindication until Jackson's death. Then, in recognition of his potential ability rather than his amiableness, Hill received the grade of lieutenant general and command of the newly created Third Corps.[5]

Hill led the Third Corps to Gettysburg, where it brought on the battle. Heth's and Pender's divisions had fought well on 1 July; and though Hill was a victorious commander, he was rather ill, and his conduct on that day is something of an enigma. Perhaps because of illness or because he was overshadowed by the proximity of General Lee, Hill does not emerge as having been a great general that day. But A. P. Hill, a new corps commander who until 1 July had not worked closely with Lee and who had strained personal relations with Longstreet, was to participate in Longstreet's attack. It may have been significant too that this proud general was to carry out his role through Richard Anderson, an officer of much different temperament, accustomed to the ways of command of the blunt and rugged Longstreet rather than the enigmatic Hill.

The artillery of Hill's corps was available to support Anderson's assault, though the brief reports of Col. R. Lindsay Walker and the officers reporting for Hill's battalions say precious little of its work. Prior to Longstreet's assault, Walker received a note from Hill telling him that Longstreet would soon attack and that he and his battery commanders were to watch the movement of Longstreet's corps and aid it as much as possible. Walker's adjutant, Lt. William W. Chamberlaine, showed the letter to each battalion commander.[6] Of the day's operations, Walker, Alexander's counterpart for all practical purposes, wrote only that the battalions of Pegram, McIntosh, and Lane, and the rifled pieces of Garnett's battalion, were in position south of the Fairfield Road that afternoon and that they fired at intervals "enfilading the enemy's guns when they were attempting to be concentrated, and also diverting their attention from the infantry of the First Corps." This is an interesting statement, for it makes no mention of Anderson's division's assault on 2 July or the artillery support given it.[7]

Garnett's and McIntosh's battalions were the farthest away from the scene of that day's action. The guns of both were in position on Anderson's division's left between the McMillan house and the Fairfield Road. Garnett's batteries had nine rifled pieces under the immediate command of Maj. Charles Richardson that went into position on the morning of 2 July just north of the McMillan buildings and remained there throughout the day. They were essentially quiet until the battle opened on the right and then fired until nearly sunset.[8]

Only three of McIntosh's batteries were on the firing line. Capt. William B. Hurt's Hardaway (Alabama) Artillery was in Schultz's Woods just south of the Fairfield Road. Capt. Marmaduke Johnson's Virginia Battery and the Second Rockbridge Artillery, commanded by Lt. Samuel Wallace, were on

Hurt's right. Like Garnett's rifled guns, McIntosh's were relatively quiet until the late afternoon when they fired to attract the attention of the Federal batteries. Neither McIntosh's nor Garnett's reports described their batteries' targets. It is likely, however, that they fired at the batteries on Cemetery Hill and at troops on Cemetery Ridge north of Ziegler's Grove, for Union regiments posted there took a pounding late in the afternoon.[9]

Maj. William J. Pegram's battalion was in position on the ridge line in front of McMillan's Woods between the McMillan house and the present North Carolina Memorial. It had four batteries: Crenshaw's Artillery of Richmond, Capt. Edward A. Marye's Fredericksburg Artillery, Capt. Joseph McGraw's Purcell Artillery, and Lt. William E. Zimmerman's Pee Dee Artillery.[10] Marye's battery was on the right, and Crenshaw's, Zimmerman's, and McGraw's were east of the woods to the left in that order. Pegram's battalion's contributions to the day's events must have been highly important, yet Capt. Ervin B. Brunson, who made the battalion's report, stated only that the battalion "opened upon the enemy at intervals, enfilading their batteries whenever they opened upon the batteries on our right."[11]

The Sumter Battalion, three Georgia batteries commanded at Gettysburg by Maj. John Lane, was on the right of the corps line. Its three batteries were identified as "companies" in the old manner and each had only a letter designation and not a name. Company A was commanded by Capt. Hugh M. Ross, B by George M. Patterson, and C by John T. Wingfield. Early in the morning Colonel Walker asked Major Lane to attach Patterson's battery of two Napoleons and four twelve-pounder howitzers to Wilcox's brigade and for good measure to add another howitzer from Ross's battery. Since these smoothbore pieces were effective at lesser ranges than the rifled guns, it is likely that Walker intended them for use against the Federals along the Emmitsburg Road rather than the doubly distant troops on Cemetery Ridge. Lane placed the remainder of his guns—Wingfield's five Navy Parrotts, Ross's three ten-pounders, and one three-inch Navy Parrott and a Napoleon—further left in Posey's portion of the line.[12]

It is likely that Ross's and Wingfield's batteries went into position about the time the infantry did, but Patterson's did not. Wilcox's part of the line did not provide good potential battery positions, and that occupied by Patterson's guns later in the day was on the east side of Pitzer's Woods to Wilcox's right, where that brigade could not readily have supported it. Therefore, Patterson probably did not post his seven guns until McLaws's division occupied Pitzer's Woods and the enemy opened on Alexander's guns on McLaws's front.[13]

Hill's report gives no clue to the time of day when he learned that Longstreet's corps would be taking position on Anderson's right. Since Hill visited army headquarters during the morning of 2 July, it is likely that he was almost as aware of General Lee's thinking as was Longstreet. He must have known of Lee's order for Longstreet to attack the Federal left at the Peach Orchard when or soon after it was issued—even before Wilcox's brigade had taken its position on Anderson's right and deployed to protect the flank of the army. But if he did, he communicated it poorly to Anderson, for that division commander learned that Longstreet's corps would occupy the ridge line to his right shortly after the division was in position. That was as much as two hours after Longstreet received his orders. Anderson also learned that Longstreet's line was to be nearly at right angles with his own. Why Wilcox's brigade was not realigned to conform to the new situation Anderson did not say. Hill also advised Anderson that Longstreet would assault the enemy left and that he was to advance his brigades as soon as Longstreet's action reached his front.[14]

General Lee, who reached Wilcox's front about the same time that McLaws's division took its position on Seminary Ridge, personally reiterated the order already given. He directed Wilcox's Brigade to advance and strike the enemy's flank. Wilcox pointed out where he thought that the flank ought to be—about six to eight hundred yards in front of McLaws's division's left—and replied to General Lee that it could be done. Wilcox wrote later that he had already determined how he would do this: he would move his brigade off to the left to uncover McLaws's advance and then move by the right flank. There was no other practical way that his brigade could enter the battle.[15] General Lee apparently said nothing of a need to realign Wilcox's brigade during the waiting period prior to the assault.

Many details of the deployment of Wilcox's brigade are lacking, and others are contradictory. Col. William H. Forney's Tenth Alabama Regiment was on the brigade right in Pitzer's Woods somewhere near the present location of the U.S. Sharpshooters' memorials.[16] That seems plain enough. According to Lt. Col. Hilary A. Herbert, the Eighth Alabama was east of the wall that edged the woods and to the Tenth's left, or perhaps its left rear, and like the Tenth, it faced south perpendicular to the line of Barksdale's brigade. To Herbert's way of thinking, his regiment was on the brigade left. This would have been so, assuming that the Eighth and Tenth regiments were considered to be in the brigade's front line and its orientation was south rather than east.[17] Bachelder's map for 2 July 1863 depicts the Ninth Alabama as having been along the wall that extends south perpendicular from the south edge of Spangler's Woods, with its left near the woods. This seems a logical position that would have connected Wilcox's left to the Florida Brigade, which was in the woods, though at some distance from Wilcox's flank. Probably then the Eleventh and Fourteenth regiments formed from the right in that order somewhere between the Ninth and Tenth. Since the Eleventh was near a fence and in the sun, it could have been in the open field to the left and rear of the Eighth. The Fourteenth would likely have been along the high ground and fence line to the right of the Ninth.[18]

Wilcox's men were not bothered greatly by artillery fire while they waited in this position. They were probably concealed from those Federal batteries

Brig. Gen. Cadmus M. Wilcox
(National Archives)

Col. David Lang (Valentine Museum, Richmond, Va.)

Brig. Gen. Joseph B. Carr (National Archives)

Col. William R. Brewster (National Archives)

Col. George C. Burling (MOLLUS-MASS/ U.S.A.M.H.I., Carlisle Barracks, Pa.)

that might have fired on them, and there were no Confederate batteries in their area to draw Federal fire. However, some of Wilcox's men were actively skirmishing. The skirmishers of the Eighth Regiment kept up the usual brisk fire, undoubtedly with skirmishers of the Sixty-third Pennsylvania at first and then those of the Fifth New Jersey Regiment somewhere near the Staub house. The Ninth Regiment's Company D was on the skirmish line with its right at the Henry Spangler barn and its left north of there and in contact with the line of the Florida Brigade. The Ninth Alabama's skirmishers exchanged shots with the First Massachusetts Regiment's skirmishers and with U.S. Sharpshooters. The barn provided some cover and a place for a lookout for a time, but it became much less useful after the Federal batteries shelled it.[19]

In the meantime, Perry's (Lang's) Florida Brigade, only seven hundred strong and with skirmishers in its front, occupied the northern half of the fence that separated Spangler's Woods from the open fields to the east. At 5:00 P.M. Colonel Lang learned from General Anderson that Longstreet was engaged and that his brigade was to "advance with General Wilcox, holding all the ground the enemy yielded."[20]

Humphreys's division and Seeley's battery were along the Emmitsburg Road opposite Wilcox's and Lang's fronts and prepared to do battle with them. Cabell's batteries and Latham's battery, Henry's battalion, were dueling with Federal batteries in Devil's Den and the Peach Orchard when Humphreys's division deployed, and some of their rounds fell among his men. Humphreys realized the need for another battery on his front and sent Lt. Henry C. Christiancy to the rear to find one. Meanwhile, he and Capt. Carswell McClellan searched for a better position for Seeley's battery than that to the right of the Klingle house and selected one just to the left of it. Seeley moved his battery there at once and opened on Confederate guns eight hundred yards away. Seeley's target undoubtedly was Patterson's collection of two Napoleons and five twelve-pounder howitzers, which had just gone into position off the right of Wilcox's brigade.[21]

Lieutenant Christiancy was fortunate in his search for a second battery. When the afternoon's firing had first opened, General Tyler of the Artillery Reserve sent four batteries from Capt. Dunbar R. Ransom's First Regular Brigade up to the rear of the Second Corps line so that they would be near the firing line if needed. Christiancy contacted Ransom there, and Ransom responded to Humphreys's call by leading Lt. John G. Turnbull's battery (F & K, Third U.S. Artillery) forward at a gallop. Like Seeley's, Turnbull's battery had six Napoleons, and it fitted handily into the position north of the Klingle house just vacated by Seeley's guns. As Turnbull's pieces were dropping trail and preparing for action, Captain Ransom rode to the front to make sure that there were no Union troops there that might be hurt by Turnbull's fire. He made a conspicuous target, one that the Confederates could not ignore, and a skirmisher put a bullet through his thigh. As soon as the wounded Ransom was brought in, Turnbull's guns opened, probably on Patterson's seven pieces in his front.[22]

After finding a suitable position for Seeley's battery, General Humphreys sent Captain McClellan to Sickles's headquarters. The captain found the headquarters beneath a large tree near Trostle's barn. The Third Corps adjutant and a clerk sat on the ground taking care of some paperwork while Sickles and a couple of officers were on horseback about fifty yards away. It was no place to concentrate on clerical matters, for shot and shell fell frequently in the area.[23] McClellan asked Sickles for orders, particularly for orders to advance. Sickles's only order for Humphreys then was to hold his division in its position. Humphreys was sorry to hear this, for he believed that there was "always a great deal in the spirit of advancing," and he wanted to go forward.[24] But the Third Corps had advanced enough that day and was hard put to man the line it had.

In a little while the Fifth New Jersey Regiment of Burling's brigade arrived back on Humphreys's front. The Fifth was to relieve the Fifty-third Pennsylvania Regiment, which was in support of the line of sharpshooters that screened Graham's brigade and Humphreys's left wing. This relief took place shortly before McLaws's advance.[25] Soon after McLaws's attack began, Major Tremain approached Humphreys in search of a regiment to bolster Graham's line. At this time Col. William J. Sewell of the Fifth New Jersey Regiment also advised Humphreys that the Confederate infantry was driving in his pickets. Things were warming up. Humphreys was reluctant to send another regiment to Graham, and Captain McClellan argued against doing so, but the demand was so urgent that Humphreys sent the Seventy-third New York with Tremain, with the results already described in Chapter 13. This done, he sent Lieutenant Christiancy back to ask General Hancock to lend a brigade to his division's support.[26]

Some of the artillery fire that had so troubled Graham's brigade had reached Humphreys's line but had done only minimal harm. This fire intensified when McLaws's division advanced. As Captain Cavada, who happened to be near Seeley's battery, remembered it, "The air was soon full of flying shot, shell and canister—and a groan here and there attested their effect. For more than a quarter of an hour the roar of musketry [off to the left no doubt] and the crashing, pounding noise of guns and bursting shells was deafening. Our own immediate line suffered severely from the enemy's guns enfilading us."[27] One or two of the headquarters orderlies fell. Humphreys, in the manner of a proper nineteenth-century general, moved among the troops who were lying down during the iron storm and gave special attention to the batteries that were returning the Confederate fire. He walked among the guns, giving directions to their crews, wholly intent upon his work and oblivious to "the murderous missiles that were felling the very gunners around him." Afterward Humphreys wrote his wife that the fire was hotter than at Fredericksburg and for a time was "positively terrific" but that it had little effect.[28]

The soldiers experienced it in many ways. Those on the right of the line near the Rogers house, which provided the gunners with a handy target to shoot at, saw shot bouncing over the ground. One shattered an outdoor oven, perhaps the one in which Josephine Miller had baked bread earlier that day. At the Klingle house between Turnbull's and Seeley's batteries, a soldier was up in a cherry tree when the intense fire began. A solid shot clipped off the limb on which he stood, and though he went up like a squirrel, he came down more "like a dead possum." In honor of the occasion he rhymed:

> I heard something snap, and felt something "*drap-*"
> Make no queries;
> For th' next thing I knew I had got all through
> Picking cherries.[29]

Back in the support line the men of the 120th New York were lying down. Capt. Abram L. Lockwood, who was probably lying prone, warned Lt. Edward H. Ketcham, who was standing, not to expose himself needlessly. Ketcham flouted the advice and proclaimed that "a dead man is better than a living coward." Some young men outgrow such bravado, but not Ketcham—a shell killed him instantly and left the burden of the battle on those whom he thought to be less brave. Nearby a shot whipped off the haversack of Capt. Lansing Hollister of Company D, and as he spoke to those around him while recovering his composure, a ball killed him.[30]

The men of the Eleventh New Jersey near the Klingle house found the fire nerve-racking. But to their colonel, Robert McAllister, it was "perfectly magnificent!" as missiles clipped off the branches of the apple trees around him and fell among the guns of Seeley's battery. McAllister thought the artillery duel grand beyond description, and it so excited him that he had to stand and watch it.[31]

Chaplain Joseph Twichell of the Seventy-first New York Regiment was with other noncombatants somewhat to the rear of his regiment's line when the shelling began. When a shell from the left hit nearby, he and some others dashed to the shelter of the Trostle barn. But even there it was not safe. Two shells almost hit his packhorse, which was tied to a nearby tree, and a fragment killed two chickens. The chickens probably did not go to waste.[32]

Twichell could not have been of much use to the men in the regiment's line—each would have to pray for himself. Cpl. Silas Auchmoedy of the 120th New York made some comments on religion and soldiers under fire shortly after the battle, which were probably influenced by it. He wrote to his father:

As Man cannot call the next minute his own those who have the Conso-lation of Religion can stand up & say not my will but thine O Lord be done. A Sinful Man has that fear which no sinner can shake off. That is why troops don't like to lay under a fire of artillery. They have to lay down & lay there til ordered to raise up. If a man gets killed along side of you let him lay. Use him for a breastwork. Then you have to advance before you can get in an engagement. After you are fairly to work all fear leaves you. You see no danger.[33]

It is interesting to speculate on the source of the shells that for a brief time excited Colonel McAllister and were so troublesome to others. Patterson's collection of seven Napoleons and howitzers was only eight hundred or so yards away, and they fired 170 rounds that afternoon, not really very many for seven pieces. Seeley's and Turnbull's batteries opposite Patterson's position had his seven pieces outgunned. Seeley's men believed that they had silenced Patterson's guns after pounding them for about fifteen minutes with shot and case.[34]

But the shelling that proved so troublesome in the brief period prior to the infantry attack came not from Hill's guns ahead and on the right, although they probably contributed to it, but from the left. Captain Cavada wrote that it came from a battery of "heavy guns skillfully planted" to enfilade their line. Humphreys reported that it came from the left and front. Lt. Benjamin Freeborn of Seeley's battery wrote of fire from the left and front.[35] Whose guns were they? Cabell's guns could have enfiladed Humphreys's line from their positions, but most of the gunners could not have sighted on it, and they would have been fully occupied with other targets. The pieces of Alexander's right batteries can be ruled out for the same reason. Moody's and Gilbert's batteries had dueled with Seeley's and Turnbull's, particularly after the guns in the Peach Orchard had ceased firing. Yet, by the time Humphreys's line was so severely shelled, Gilbert's battery had become a wreck and probably was doing the Federals little harm. This leaves two candidates—Jordan's battery, with its four three-inch rifles and Woolfolk's, with its four twenty-pounder Parrotts, which were "heavy guns" in the context of the battle.

Confederate sources are silent on this matter, but two Federal statements suggest that one or both of those batteries raked Humphreys's line. Colonel Sewell of the Fifth New Jersey, whose left was driven in by Barksdale, reported that a battery took position where the Fifth's left had been. This was probably near a fence about 250 yards west of the Sherfy barn. As related in Chapter 13, Private Holden of Company B, Second New Hampshire Regi-ment, when firing near the Wentz house, saw a Confederate battery approach over the Wheatfield Road, wheel left, and unlimber in an open field. He fired at it at an estimated range of four hundred yards. Both sources, therefore, seem to agree that a battery was in position north of the Wheatfield Road about 250 yards west of the Sherfy barn. From this area it could have enfiladed Humphreys's line at a range of about six hundred yards, and it could have done deadly work for a brief time.[36]

Cadmus Marcellus Wilcox had explained his battle plan to his officers during their long wait, and now the time had come to execute it. Wilcox was a thoroughly professional soldier. There were only a half dozen West Point graduates in command of Confederate infantry brigades at Gettysburg, and he was one of them. Wilcox was not pleased to be in this exclusive group. He was thirty-nine years old and had been a classmate of both Stonewall Jackson and George Pickett, and the careers of those officers, in different ways, must have suggested to the Alabamian that his promotion to a higher grade was overdue. After graduating from the academy in 1846, he had shown special bravery at Chapultepec, where he won a brevet, and his subsequent service in the Old Army had not been routine. It included five years as an instructor in tactics at West Point and two years of study in Europe. Beyond this he had attested to his literacy and his professionalism by preparing a manual, *Rifle and Infantry Tactics*, and translating an Austrian manual on infantry tactics. Wilcox ended his Federal career as a captain in the Seventh Infantry in June 1861. He then entered Confederate service as colonel of the Ninth Alabama and became a brigadier general in October 1861. He commanded his brigade in subsequent battles of the Army of Northern Virginia except at Second Manassas, where he commanded a division, and at Antietam, which he apparently missed. He had distinguished himself particularly at Salem Church. Lee termed him a highly capable officer, and Douglas Southall Freeman wrote that "in all the Army's battles he had been dependable and by every campfire he had been the gentleman." Wilcox was not only reliable, devout, and a gentleman, he was "precise and insistent on precision." Perhaps this attribute was responsible for his nickname, "Old Billy Fixin."[37]

Wilcox's advance required some special preparations. Because of the way the brigade was deployed, its regiments could not march from their positions directly at the foe. Had they done so, they would have trespassed into the zone of McLaws's division. Therefore, when the advance began, the first thing the brigade had to do was file four hundred yards to the left to the low ground between Spangler's Woods and the Spangler farmyard. This would place it on the right of the Florida Brigade. In the words of Wilcox, "This was done as rapidly as the nature of the ground with its opposing obstacles (stone and plank fences) would admit. Having gained 400 or 500 yards to the left by this flank movement, my command faced by the right flank, and advanced."[38]

Or did it? Lieutenant Colonel Herbert wrote and spoke otherwise, and his contention, though surprising because it is not supported by Wilcox's report, is so convincing that it cannot be ignored. According to Herbert, at the order to move, the Eighth simply marched in a column of fours by the left flank to the east until the regiment crossed over the rise near the Staub farmyard. There it broke cover and attracted the fire of the Union skirmish line. To meet this fire Herbert deployed the Eighth into line and advanced east toward the Emmitsburg Road. In the meantime, the Ninth, Fourteenth, and Eleventh regiments, which were behind the wall that runs along the rise but to the north of the Eighth Regiment, apparently were not bothered by the Federal fire enough to take notice of it. And so, after moving forward far enough to clear the southeast corner of Spangler's Woods, they filed left to the jumping-off point. The Tenth Alabama, in turn, probably moved directly from its position in Pitzer's Woods to the right of the Eleventh Regiment, leaving a gap of about two hundred yards between the right of the Tenth and Herbert's Eighth. Herbert wrote that the two-hundred-yard gap, "strange to say, so completely escaped our attention at the time in the excitement of battle, that it was not known to the writer [Herbert] until it came to his attention some thirty years afterward." Also strange to say, it seems not to have come to the attention of Wilcox or the members of his staff either, or else they elected not to close the gap and did not mention it—which would be a surprising omission.[39]

When deployed, the Tenth Alabama on the right of Wilcox's main line was about a hundred yards north of the Staub house, and the line ran north beyond the Spangler buildings, so that when it advanced, it would go forward astride Spangler's lane. As Wilcox rode along the line giving orders to charge, cheer after cheer filled the air. Spirits were never better—on the surface at least. Lt. Edmund D. Patterson of the Ninth Alabama looked ahead at what seemed like a solid mass of Union soldiers in the regiment's front and felt more like praying than cheering. He asked that God in that hour assist him to do his whole duty to his country.[40]

As soon as Wilcox's four regiments formed east of Spangler's Woods, they advanced uphill toward the Emmitsburg Road. The fire from Seeley's and Turnbull's guns was terrible. A round of spherical case burst above Wilcox and his staff, who were mounted and must have been a conspicuous target. A fragment cut one of Wilcox's bridle reins, and his horse became skittish and unruly. Worse, the round killed Pvt. John C. J. Ridgway of the Eleventh Alabama, who was serving as a staff courier.[41] The Florida Brigade advanced on Wilcox's left. It moved into "a murderous fire of grape, canister, and musketry." In Colonel Lang's opinion the Florida regiments suffered terribly but advanced nobly and uphill at a double-quick.[42]

Colonel Sewell of the Fifth New Jersey, from his regiment's position behind a fence two hundred yards southwest of Humphreys's left, saw the sharpshooters on the skirmish line fall back and Barksdale's brigade come into view to his left front. He sent word of the Confederate advance to General Humphreys. Barksdale struck the Fifth New Jersey's left and drove it in. Although his regiment was enfiladed, Sewell tried to hold his ground in the hope that Humphreys would send aid.[43]

But Graham needed help badly, and things were heating up for Humphreys too. Seeley's and Turnbull's batteries fired as fast as they could. Hum-

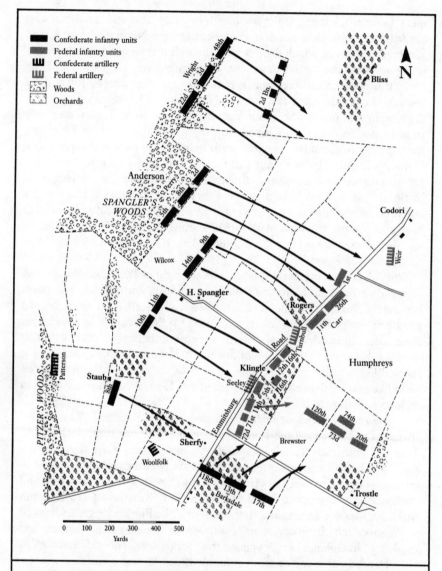

1. *After smashing Graham's line near the Sherfy buildings, Barksdale drives north against Humphreys's division's left and smashes its two left regiments.*

2. *Humphreys retires Seeley's and Turnbull's batteries and refuses the remains of his left wing to meet Barksdale.*

3. *At Barksdale's advance, Wilcox's brigade shifts left and forms behind the Spangler farmyard. It then advances east against Humphreys's position along the Emmitsburg Road.*

4. *Perry's brigade advances on Wilcox's left.*

5. *Humphreys's division retreats to Cemetery Ridge.*

Map 15-1. Barksdale's, Wilcox's, and Perry's Brigades Attack Humphreys's Position along the Emmitsburg Road

phreys wrote that his artillery "smashed into them fearfully," but the artillery fire was not enough. Humphreys thought that when the Confederate infantry closed, his line might have more firepower if he replaced the batteries with infantry formations. He thought also that he might advance his left to Sewell's support and strike the enemy, presumably Barksdale's left and not Wilcox's brigade, which apparently had not yet advanced, but he did not do so. Orders came down that changed the complexion of Humphreys's part of the battle. There would be no advance, and Sewell would get no help in his forward position.[44]

Humphreys learned that Sickles had been wounded and that Birney commanded the corps. Birney's first order to Humphreys, as Humphreys recalled, was "to throw back my left, and form a line oblique to and in rear of the one I then held, and [I] was informed that the First Division would complete the line to the Round Top ridge."[45] Humphreys could see no reason for pulling back his left at the time he received the order, so it could have come before Barksdale smashed through the line at the Peach Orchard. At the time he issued the order Birney could have been concerned about a breakthrough at Devil's Den or at the stony hill.[46] Nevertheless, as we have seen, Humphreys took measures to pull back his left, the three Excelsior Brigade regiments posted there, together with the Eleventh New Jersey, Carr's left regiment. But he did so with misgivings, for he knew that his troops could suffer heavily if they were attacked while the movement was in progress.[47]

Humphreys had no choice but to obey, though he later called the attempt to set up a new line "bosh." While the maneuver was going on, Barksdale smashed through Graham's line at the Peach Orchard, and the Federal troops who were to have continued the line beyond Humphreys's left retreated beyond the proposed location of the new line back toward Cemetery Ridge. Barksdale's brigade, as we have seen, then moved against Humphreys's left and Wilcox's brigade and the Florida Brigade assaulted his division's front. There would be no second line for the Third Corps west of Cemetery Ridge that afternoon.[48]

Captain Cavada watched the battle beyond the Sherfy buildings with special interest because his brother Fred commanded the 114th Pennsylvania there. He saw confused fighting and heard its terrible pounding and crashing. A southerly breeze wafted heavy, sulfurous smoke clouds in his direction and sometimes hid the action from his view. And then—but not so separately in reality as in Cavada's memory—Humphreys's skirmishers "began a lively popping, the first drops of the thundershower that was to break upon us." About this time, an aide from Birney rode up with the news that the enemy was gathering on Humphreys's front. Since the division was prepared to meet the attack, Humphreys's staff waited quietly on their horses, moving only occasionally to avoid shot and shell seen coming in their direction.[49]

On the skirmish line to the right of the Fifth New Jersey and north of

Spangler's lane, the men of the First Massachusetts Regiment had been skirmishing most of the day and experiencing some tense moments as Anderson's division deployed beyond the tree line in their front. At one time, one company became a little "tremulous," and its commander, Lt. James Doherty, steadied it by putting it through the manual of arms.[50] Then they saw the Confederate skirmishers push forward, followed by three heavy lines of infantry, possibly the three regiments of Perry's brigade. In keeping with instructions received earlier in the day, Lt. Col. Clark B. Baldwin ordered his companies forward to bolster the skirmish line. The First Massachusetts opened on the enemy skirmishers and drove them back on their main line. Baldwin knew of Humphreys's orders to swing back the division's left and was told to hold his position as long as possible while this was done.[51]

The Fifth New Jersey, threatened by Barksdale on its left and by Wilcox's brigade in its front, fell back toward Seeley's battery, for which it somehow felt a special responsibility. The First Massachusetts gave ground grudgingly too. Carr had ordered Colonel Baldwin to reform his men behind the main line along the Emmitsburg Road, but before he was able to do that a staff officer rode up and ordered the First to form instead in front of the Twenty-sixth Pennsylvania at the right of the line. Baldwin was incredulous, but the officer insisted that those were the orders. The First complied and fell back to the rear of the broad crest north of the Rogers house to await the enemy's onslaught.[52]

When Wilcox reached the worm fence that had sheltered the Union skirmishers, he dismounted and climbed upon the fence for an undisturbed look to the front. He could see the heads and rifle barrels of Humphreys's soldiers directly ahead along the Emmitsburg Road near the Klingle house. As he looked, a shell struck the fence close by him and exploded ten feet beyond. It knocked down a section of the fence and jarred the general. Its burst sent Wilcox's remaining courier, Pvt. James W. Brundridge of the Ninth Alabama, flying head over heels. Wilcox thought that the poor fellow was torn to pieces, but he was only badly bruised and was in fact fit for duty again in several weeks. Wilcox hurried over to Colonel Forney, whose Tenth Alabama was on his right (Herbert's Eighth Alabama excepted) and who could not see the Federal line. He gave Forney some instructions and told him that his regiment would strike the Federal position after an advance of eighty yards.[53]

After the skirmishers fell back and the Confederate lines disappeared from sight beneath the brow of the slope, Seeley's and Turnbull's guns fell silent. There was a flurry of Confederate cannon fire, but it also ceased. Then there was a "diabolical cheer and yells" from the oncoming Rebels that was echoed by shouts of "here they come" from the Union line. Cavada's horse, Brickbat, was wounded in the leg at this time, and he whirled around in a frantic way.[54]

As the men of the Eleventh Massachusetts over to the right awaited the onslaught, a snake wriggled near their line. Even under those trying circumstances someone took the time to kill it. A hail of Confederate bullets ripped into the Rogers house and scared a kitten there so much that it scooted from the building and took refuge on a soldier's shoulder. Before the Eleventh Regiment opened on the approaching foe, it made a right half wheel under fire. The author of the Eleventh's history, who had no respect for General Carr and his staff, wrote that when the Rebels fired at them, a "block head" general (presumably Carr) ordered them to hold their fire because he was too far back to see that the people firing at them were not Union troops. He also accused the general of having sent the brigade flag to the rear as the bullets began to fly, an act that he said would have demoralized the men had they not been veterans.[55]

The Twelfth New Hampshire Regiment, in support of Seeley's battery, moved to the front of the Klingle house just before the assault began. Its men could hear, and possibly see, some of the action on their left and worried about the Confederates getting behind them. Shells fired at Seeley's guns sometimes ploughed through their ranks, causing casualties. Then the infantry of the gentle and punctilious Wilcox hove into view "with screeches and yells, mingled with the volleys of musketry." The men of the Granite State were as solid as the rock for which their state was named and did not panic. They stood awhile and gave as good as they got.[56]

Seeley's and Turnbull's batteries shared the infantry's trauma. Under Humphreys's direction they had given the men from Florida and Alabama servings of shell and case until the approaching line gained the cover afforded by the slope in their front. When the Confederates reappeared, they welcomed them with canister. As Seeley walked among his guns, a rifle ball hit him in the chest, wounding him severely. Lt. Robert James took charge of the battery.[57]

Humphreys himself ordered Turnbull's battery to the rear. Turnbull's cannoneers fixed prolonges and retired, their Napoleons belching canister. The Rebels shot so many of Turnbull's horses that the infantry had to help move some of the guns. In the four-hundred-yard retreat back to Plum Run at the foot of the slope, Turnbull's battery lost nine men killed and fourteen wounded, together with forty-five horses killed. When it reached the swale at the base of the slope, it could go no farther. At Humphreys's order, Turnbull abandoned four pieces there to be reclaimed later if fate would be so kind.[58] Seeley's battery had better fortune. It lost only nine horses killed outright, though another sixteen of the nineteen wounded animals had to be shot. Therefore, it was able to pull back under its own horsepower to the right and rear, where it dropped trail again and prepared for more action.[59]

When Humphreys refused his left in response to Birney's order to form a new line, the Eleventh New Jersey on Carr's brigade's left pulled back to a new position to the left and rear of the Klingle buildings. There the regiment lay down. Colonel McAllister ordered its men to fire volleys by rank, rear rank first, so as to hold the enemy in check after the first fire. Capt. LeGrand Benedict of Carr's staff rode up at about this time and, pointing to some men near the Klingle house (possibly soldiers of the Fifth New Jersey back from the skirmish line), cautioned the soldiers of the Eleventh not to fire on them. The men near the house were staying there as if no enemy were near.[60]

It was not long before the Eleventh New Jersey Regiment saw Wilcox's brigade on its right and Barksdale's in its front. Maj. Philip J. Kearny, kinsman of his namesake general, was excited by the Confederate threat and exclaimed, "I tell you we are going to have a fight!" A Confederate minié ball struck Kearny in the knee, and he spun like a top before falling to the ground ten feet to the rear. It was a mortal wound. Colonel McAllister commanded the Eleventh to fire. Lt. John Schoonover, the adjutant, had Kearny carried to the rear and walked over to the colonel to tell him that the major was hit. He learned then that the colonel was also down. McAllister had been struck by a minié ball in the left thigh, and a spent shell "undermined" and injured his left foot. Capt. Luther Martin, the second of five commanders of the Eleventh that day, took charge.[61]

There seemed to be less of a threat to the right of Humphreys's line. The First Massachusetts reformed to the right and slightly forward of the Twenty-sixth Pennsylvania, and the Seventy-fourth New York was in the Twenty-sixth's support. Then the Seventy-fourth advanced to the right of the Twenty-sixth, where Lt. Col. Thomas Holt had its men pile fence rails into breastworks. They did this with an alacrity never before witnessed.[62] But the Seventy-fourth had had the luxury of the rail pile's cover for only a few minutes when an order came for it to change front and move left to the rear of the Seventy-third. The Seventy-third had just returned from Graham's front and probably was facing Barksdale on the left. At first the Seventy-third masked the Seventy-fourth, and it could fire only to the left oblique. When the forward line gave way, the Seventy-fourth had a clear field of fire until it was forced to retreat.[63]

At the time the Seventy-fourth shifted left, the positions of the First Massachusetts and Twenty-sixth Pennsylvania on the right seemed temporarily secure. It was a false security soon dispelled, for a Rebel force, Perry's Florida Brigade, appeared suddenly over the rise from out of the smoke and fired into the exposed right flank of Carr's brigade. The two right regiments tried to wheel to face the Floridians and soon thereafter began a grudging retreat to Cemetery Ridge.[64]

Not long after Humphreys acted on Birney's instructions to swing back the left and form a new line, he received a second order directing him to withdraw his division all the way to Cemetery Ridge. Birney did not comment on his reason for having Humphreys do this, but it seems apparent that Birney believed that the situation in the Wheatfield–Devil's Den area had deteriorated so that the advanced line no longer could be held. Humphreys, who knew only the situation on his own front and was still hopeful about it, was irate. He thought his division capable of fighting it out on the Emmitsburg Road line and of avoiding, in the process, the casualties it was sure to sustain in the retreat. In later years he wrote that the Confederates had attacked simultaneously—or almost so—on his right, left, and front, possibly because his left had been swung back.[65] He maintained, however, that he did not retire because of a loss of artillery or because his line was broken. He pulled back his division because he was ordered to do so.[66] Needless to say, Carr fully agreed with him. The order to retreat had been given to Carr by Birney in person, but Humphreys received it through an aide.[67]

Humphreys was technically right, perhaps, but he could not have held his position without secure flanks, and he no longer had them. Two days after the fight, when its heat still affected him, he complained to his wife that "they" had taken away his reserve brigade, that a part of his second line had to occupy the front, and that some of it went to other commands. He complained too that after the enemy had defeated others (Graham's brigade, no doubt) who, he implied, had not fought as well as they might have, the enemy turned their attention to his division. He summed up his complaint by writing, "Had my division been left intact I should have driven the enemy back but the ruinous *habit* (it doesn't deserve the name of system) of putting troops into position and then drawing off its reserves & second line to help others who if [not] similarly dispossessed would need no such help is disgusting."[68]

Being ordered to fall back and doing so without being wiped out were two different things. General Carr sent a staff officer to Capt. John F. Langley, commander of the Twelfth New Hampshire Regiment, with the orders to retreat. The Twelfth was along the road just north of Klingle's house. The officer asked Langley if he could depend on his men. "Yes," said Langley, "if I can make them understand the order." The noise was so great then that Langley feared he could not be heard. The staff officer replied, "Then shout it in the ears of every company commander, and let them watch the motion of your sword as the signal for its execution." Langley did as suggested. It took time to shout commands in the ears of ten company commanders when the regiment was in line and fighting, and there was no guarantee that Langley would not be shot while giving the commands or that the company commanders would not be killed before they could be carried out. But, on Langley's signal, the Twelfth pulled back. It did so with steadiness and some precision even though half of its men fell during the movement.[69]

The deadly fire mortally wounded Sgt. Luther H. Parker, bearer of the Twelfth's state flag, and killed Sgt. William J. Howe, who carried the national flag. Cpl. John R. Davis took Howe's flag, but Sergeant Howe's dead hand clasped the cloth of the flag so tightly that a twelve-by-fifteen-inch swatch tore loose and stayed within his hand. Pvt. Albert W. Bacheler saw the remnant in Howe's hand and could not leave it behind. As the regiment moved off, he tarried until he could pry Howe's fingers open one by one and save the fragment from Confederate capture.[70]

Humphreys's division's half-mile retreat was recorded no better than its fight along the Emmitsburg Road. The withdrawal began, no doubt, on the left where Barksdale's brigade hit Humphreys's flank and sent the Excelsior regiments back in some disorder. One Excelsior Brigade officer wrote:

> The men understood the matter as well as their officers. They knew that the position could not now be held, and they seemed to have simultaneously made up their minds that they were going back to a position they could hold; and back they did go, but fighting, not disorderly. They would fire at the enemy, walk to the rear, loading as they went, take deliberate aim and fire again, and so on, but slowly and deliberately, and so deliberately that the enemy kept at a respectful distance. . . . They had deliberately made up their minds that they were going back to the old line, not as though they were forced to go, but were going there to reform; that was all. They went back to the old line and halted there.[71]

These were words written or spoken long after the fact, which, though containing truth, were intended to please the middle-aged veterans who years before had felt the pressure and had gone to the rear. Men may agree that it is time to fall back, but they are unlikely to do so in an orderly manner amid such chaos as existed on that field unless the command structure functions. In addition, as a technical thing, they had had no old line where they were going—they really had had no line on any part of Cemetery Ridge, let alone in the area previously occupied by Caldwell's division of the Second Corps.

But there was truth in the comment. There was no rout. Most of the Third Corps units did go back slowly, sustained by regiments and officers who still had a lot of fight left in them. Capt. Thomas Rafferty, leading his horse, walked off with Colonel Brewster, whose horse had been killed. Brewster had been with the 120th New York during its valiant stand, but that was over. As the two officers went along, seeming like men out for a stroll, a private from Rafferty's company in the Seventy-first approached them carrying a handsome bridle covered with blood and gave it to Colonel Brewster. He had taken it from Brewster's dead horse. This was not the act of a man in disorderly flight, though the danger in the area was so great that the poor soldier was killed less than two minutes later.[72]

Carr's brigade, or the division's right, likely went back in better order than the regiments that had to deal with Barksdale's Mississippians. All reports tell of its retiring in good order, rallying, and turning to fire. The Eleventh New Jersey was on the left of Carr's line and also had to deal with Barksdale's assault. Two of its color-bearers fell, and Cpl. Thomas Johnson of Company I carried the flag. Lt. John Schoonover, its adjutant and its third commander in that brief time, saw that the regiment was wavering and sought to stiffen it. He posted Corporal Johnson and the color guard twenty feet in front of the regiment's line where all could see them and be inspired. Schoonover told Johnson to stay there until he was ordered back. The battle went on; in its confusion the regiment gave ground, and Schoonover temporarily forgot Johnson and his color guard. Suddenly Schoonover remembered them and returned to them. He found that Johnson and the color guard had not moved, but were standing like statues at their post with lead and iron flying through the air around them. They did New Jersey proud that day.[73]

The Eleventh fell back slowly, keeping up a continual fire but receiving shots in turn that decimated its ranks. Soon its line was hampered by wounded men, its own and others swept up as it backed across the field, and it began to lose cohesion. When it neared a line of caissons standing off to the left, Schoonover too was shot. He became faint and lost control, and the Eleventh, without captains and field officers to steady it, gave up the fight and headed for the rear. There Capt. William H. Lloyd, who had been wounded, met and rallied the regiment. Sixty percent of the Eleventh New Jersey's men were casualties that afternoon.[74]

Humphreys himself did much to hold his division together. When Captain McClellan rode in from the left to tell him of Birney's order to fall back, he found Humphreys supervising the pullout from horseback on the Emmitsburg Road between Carr's line and the enemy. It was no place for a division commander to be, but Humphreys could see what the brigade was doing from there, and its people, in turn, could see and be motivated by him.[75] The fire was hot. Suddenly Humphreys's horse, which was bleeding already from seven wounds, was hit by a shell. It jumped and pitched headlong to the ground. Humphreys vaulted from the saddle. One of his staff, whose horse was limping along on three legs, tried to help the general. They were able to remove his holster from his saddle but not his saddlebags, which contained papers that he did not wish to lose. The officer offered Humphreys his horse, but the general preferred to rely on his two legs rather than the horse's three. About this time, Pvt. James F. Dimond, Sixth U.S. Cavalry, one of Humphreys's orderlies, rode upon the scene. He had been wounded in the right arm, but his horse was uninjured. Dimond dismounted and offered his horse to the general. Humphreys accepted it, mounted, and rode away. Dimond was not seen again.[76]

One of Humphreys's aides, Capt. William H. Chester, was hit in the abdomen. He reeled in the saddle, and the general grabbed him to keep him from falling. Lt. Henry H. Humphreys, the general's son and aide, took Chester from the general and started with him toward the rear. They met the sergeant in charge of the staff orderlies, and Humphreys placed Chester in his care. Riding was too painful for the wounded man, so with a soldier's help, the sergeant lifted Chester from his horse and the two carried Chester between them, the sergeant also leading the horse by its bridle reins. They had not gone far when a shot tore away part of the horse's head and the lower portion of the sergeant's body. The unwounded man abandoned Chester and fled to the rear, leaving Chester on the ground beside the mutilated bodies of the brave sergeant and the horse.[77]

Humphreys reported later that he had obeyed Birney's order to fall back to Cemetery Ridge by "retiring very slowly, continuing the contest with the enemy, whose fire of artillery and infantry was destructive in the extreme."[78] The men of the 120th New York claimed that Humphreys fell back with them, but he must have been elsewhere as well. They remembered him as riding alone in the confusion of the battle and the retreat and by his presence proclaiming that theirs was the vital point.[79] Lt. Jesse B. Young, the division's provost martial, recollected Humphreys as "without a superior on the field of battle—full of fire, and yet in absolute equipoise," parrying blows and pulling his regiments back. General Carr, who shared Humphreys's burden, if not his accolades, commented on the general's "conspicuous courage and remarkable coolness."[80]

Humphreys did more than just inspire—he led. Like Hancock, he was a master of the Old Army's profanity and could use it like a whip or club. And he was something of a martinet as well. To his wife he wrote, "Twenty times did I [bring] my men to a halt & face about, myself & Harry and others of my staff forcing the men to it." In later years a soldier wrote that he and his cohorts did not like him before the battle but swore by him afterward, "for he showed himself a hero and leader." Later Humphreys had some second thoughts about what he had done that afternoon and reproached himself for not letting his troops fall back quickly and avoid some casualties. But it was too late to change things then, and he consoled himself with the belief that the situation demanded that they fight their way back to Cemetery Ridge.[81]

Wilcox's and Perry's brigades pressed ahead against a line softened by Barksdale's assault against its left and by Birney's order for it to fall back. Colonel Forney of the Tenth Alabama on Wilcox's right still had Seeley's battery in his front as the Tenth approached the road, and he found its fire "fearful." A fragment wounded Forney, but it did not stop him. Although Seeley's guns slowed the Confederate advance, the Alabamians replied in good measure. Seeley displaced to the rear, and soon the road and its high ground was in Confederate hands.[82]

The Alabamians took some prisoners at the Emmitsburg Road, and some of them came under the care of Pvt. Pat Martin of the Tenth Alabama. Martin was young and small in stature. Until a few days before, he had been deemed too small to soldier in the regiment's line and so was assigned as the driver of a headquarters wagon. Then Wilcox saw him with a pilfered Pennsylvania chicken and reasoned that if he was old enough to steal chickens, he was old enough to fight. The general reprimanded the private and sent him back to the Tenth Regiment for duty that would require him to hold a gun instead of reins. Wilcox next met him at the Emmitsburg Road, where Martin was herding along a flock of prisoners. When Martin saw Wilcox, he halted his charges under a fearful fire, saluted the general, and in tones of anger and triumph said, "Here are your chickens, Sir."[83]

The Eighth Alabama off to the right crossed the Emmitsburg Road at

Trostle's lane. It could have met no opposition there for Barksdale's brigade must have driven the Federal regiments from that area. The Eighth advanced east with Trostle's lane on its left and the Twenty-first Mississippi two hundred yards to its right on a converging course. When the Eighth reached a point about 130 yards west of Trostle's house, at the fence that bordered the west side of Trostle's orchard, it exchanged fire with a line of infantry drawn up on the south side of Trostle's lane opposite the barn. It is likely that Bigelow's battery had not yet taken position in the corner ahead, for Herbert saw two guns pass through the gap into the lane. The Federal infantry moved off and the Eighth Regiment, probably pressed by the Twenty-first Mississippi on its right and animated by the desire to close on its own brigade, wheeled left across the lane's two worm fences. Color Sergeant L. P. Ragsdale led the movement by marching in slow time with the Eighth's flag held aloft. The regiment turned behind him and crossed the fences. The fences broke up its formation, of course, and it reformed near Trostle's barn. There it fronted north toward the Tenth Alabama, beyond Barksdale's line. Herbert now saw some guns about a hundred yards in his front and prepared to charge them.[84]

The guns wheeled about and fired some canister at the Eighth, and some infantry fired also. As soon as Herbert got the Eighth's line reasonably reformed, it charged the battery and "swept like a hurricane over cannon and caissons." Herbert did not identify the battery to which the guns belonged, for he probably did not know its identity; nor did he state what kind of guns they were. Probably they were Turnbull's guns, but we shall never know for sure. But he did remember one thing. A young fellow who was the driver of a lead pair of a caisson team whipped and spurred his horses as the Alabamians approached in an effort to get away. He did this without realizing that the swing and wheel horses behind him were down and that he could not move. The Alabamians came up behind him, and Herbert was close enough to touch him with his sword when dust puffed from the boy's jacket beneath his shoulder blade: a minié ball had struck and killed him. To Herbert the boy's death became an indelible and horrible memory.[85]

The Ninth Alabama, on Wilcox's left, struck the road at the Rogers house in the sector guarded by the Eleventh Massachusetts Regiment. When the Federals fell back, the Alabamians moved in among the few buildings there, some taking temporary shelter behind the house and a chimney corner. The house drew fire from Federal artillery. Pvt. James McC. Scott saw this danger and backed away from the bull's-eye just before a ball struck the chimney and sent bricks and soldiers flying in all directions. Scott received a wound in the neck and fell in the road. Another soldier gave him a "deep draught" from a bottle of camphor found in the Rogers house, and the next day Scott was back under arms.[86]

Colonel Lang and his Floridians went forward at a double-quick part of the way, probably to close on Wilcox's left and to shorten the time spent in front of the Federal batteries. According to Lang, they suffered terribly but nobly from fire that could have come from Turnbull's battery, from Seeley's in its second position, or from Weir's battery south of Codori's barn. It was the Floridians who flanked the right of Carr's brigade and did much to make the Emmitsburg Road line untenable. Humphreys believed that the attacks on his division's right and left were nearly simultaneous.[87]

Wilcox's brigade, apart from the Eighth Alabama Regiment, had struck that portion of Humphreys's line between Seeley's battery and the Klingle house on its right and the Rogers house on the left. Perry's small brigade swept through the trough between the Rogers house and Codori's barn. After crossing the Emmitsburg Road, as noted above, Wilcox found that his and Barksdale's lines "impinged." To avoid their overlapping, Wilcox veered slightly to the left. After crossing the road, Wilcox's regiments came under fire from two batteries spaced widely apart on Cemetery Ridge. To strike them both, he sent the Ninth Alabama against that on the left and the Tenth, Eleventh, and Fourteenth regiments against the one on the right. The identity of the left battery is uncertain, but the right was probably Battery C, Fourth Artillery, six Napoleons commanded by Lt. Evan Thomas. Wilcox deployed his three right regiments with the Eleventh in front and the Fourteenth and Tenth in echelon on its flanks.[88]

By this time, surely, the lines of both Wilcox's and Perry's brigades had become disordered. Barksdale had pressed his brigade forward without halting to reform, while the Alabamians and Floridians had double-quicked for some distance, split to pass buildings, and fought with Humphreys's line. Their ranks must have thinned as they advanced. Regrouping was in order, but not quite yet, not while they had momentum and the enemy was on the run. All three brigades were headed for the gap in the Union line on Cemetery Ridge where Caldwell's division had been and for the left of Gibbon's division—straight for that portion of the ridge that was the responsibility of the left wing of Hancock's Second Corps.[89]

In order to support the Third Corps's right flank, which was in the air south of the Codori barn, General Gibbon had ordered two regiments from Harrow's brigade to take position along the Emmitsburg Road. He did this before the assault began. At Harrow's direction, the Eighty-second New York and the Fifteenth Massachusetts regiments advanced to the road at the right (north) of the Codori house and prepared a defensive position there by piling up a barricade of fence rails behind the road. Col. George Ward's Fifteenth Massachusetts Regiment was on the right, while Lt. Col. James Huston's Eighty-second New York (or Second Militia, as its members preferred that it be called) went into line on the left by the Codori house. Huston sent two companies into the Codori farmyard with orders to burn the buildings there if necessary.[90] A little later Gibbon ordered Brown's Rhode Island Battery to a small rise to the right and rear of the Fifteenth Massachusetts and midway between the Codori house and the Copse of Trees. The battery fronted to the northwest there and covered Ward's and Huston's flanks in measure, but it was poorly posted to deal with any threat against its left. Capt. John G. Hazard, commander of the Second Corps's artillery, was said to have been apprehensive about the battery's location, and Hancock supposedly disliked it; but they accepted Gibbon's decision, and Brown's guns remained down front.[91]

Two batteries from Ransom's Regular brigade of the Artillery Reserve stayed on the Second Corps front. As stated above, the six Napoleons of Thomas's battery were on the ridge line beyond Gibbon's left where Caldwell's division's right had been (near what is now the site of the Pennsylvania State Memorial). The First Minnesota Regiment of Harrow's brigade went down to its left to support Thomas's guns. The First Minnesota had only seven companies present and was hardly a substitute for Caldwell's whole division.[92]

At Hancock's instructions, a second battery, Lt. Gulian V. Weir's battery (C, Fifth U.S. Artillery), went forward to a slight swell of ground just south of the Codori barn. From this forward position Weir's six Napoleons could cover the trough between Humphreys's right and the barn, but they were very vulnerable to attacking infantry. The first advice that Weir received there was to watch his front because the troops on his left were falling back. Gibbon also told him to fire shot to the left at a four-degree elevation in the hope that the solid iron balls would rake the lines of Wilcox's and Perry's brigades as they pressed Carr's line back from the Emmitsburg Road.[93]

General Hancock sent the Nineteenth Maine Regiment of Harrow's brigade forward to give Weir's battery close support. As the Nineteenth advanced under Hancock's watchful eye, a battery (was it Seeley's, Weir's, or another?) ran through its ranks. This was too much for Hancock, who "always swore at everybody, above all on the battlefield."[94] Col. Francis Heath of the Nineteenth commented, "General Hancock spoke in a good deal of passion to the officer in command of the Bttry saying if I commanded this Regt. I'd be God damned if I wouldn't charge bayonets on you."[95] By this time Hancock must have had the attention of all within the sound of his voice. As the Nineteenth approached the place near Weir's battery where he thought that it should be, Hancock vaulted from his horse, grabbed the first man on the left of the regiment's front line, and led him a couple of yards forward to the left. He planted the soldier—Pvt. George T. Durgin, a short, heavyset man— firmly on the spot and shouted, "Will you stay here?" Durgin, who probably wished to please the large fellow with the two stars on his shoulder straps who was grasping him and shouting in his face, managed to reply, "I'll stay here, General, until h-ll freezes over." That was long enough to suit the general; Hancock ordered the Nineteenth's colors to align themselves on Durgin and the regiment to form there. He then mounted his horse and rode elsewhere.[96]

Just before McLaws's men struck the Emmitsburg Road line, General

Humphreys sent Lieutenant Christiancy to Hancock to ask for the help of a brigade. Hancock, who was becoming heavily involved in the Third Corps's plight at the time, passed an order down to Gibbon to send Humphreys two regiments. Gibbon referred the matter to Col. Norman J. Hall, commander of his Third Brigade, which was posted south of the Copse of Trees. Hall gave Christiancy the Forty-second New York and the Nineteenth Massachusetts regiments, and Christiancy led them left and into the smoke that hid them from Hall's view, with results that will be recounted below.[97]

General Meade asked Hancock to send a Second Corps brigade to Birney also. In response Hancock selected Willard's brigade of Hays's division. At that time Willard's brigade was in reserve behind Ziegler's Grove. Before Willard's men could get under way General Meade made a second and unusual request of Hancock. He had learned that Sickles had been wounded and wanted Hancock to assume command of the Third Corps in addition to his own.[98]

Hancock certainly had his share of ambition, but it did not lie in the direction suggested by this request. Nevertheless he turned the immediate command of the Second Corps over to Gibbon without delay. Gibbon remarked in later years that he was "not surprised that he [Hancock] should utter some expressions of discontent at being compelled at such a time to give up command of one corps in a sound condition to take command of another which, it was understood, had gone to pieces."[99]

Hancock, accompanied by some of his staff, rode to the left at the head of Willard's brigade. He reached the gap left by Caldwell's division and was going farther when he met Birney. Birney told him that his troops had been driven to the rear and had vacated the position in the Wheatfield area toward which Hancock was moving. Cannon balls were soon whistling around them. Hancock ordered Willard's brigade into line on the ridge beyond the left of the First Minnesota Regiment and sent Maj. William G. Mitchell of his staff to General Meade to get more troops to put in on Willard's right. Willard's regiments formed facing the Plum Run swale and Barksdale's brigade, which was approaching in its smashing drive toward Cemetery Ridge.[100]

Thus, as the brigades of Barksdale, Wilcox, and Perry were driving Humphreys's division back from the Emmitsburg Road and were fighting their way toward Cemetery Ridge, less than half of the Second Corps remained in its position on the ridge ready to meet the Confederate threat. Woodruff's battery was still in position in Ziegler's Grove, and Arnold's battery was behind the wall just north of The Angle. Hays's division had two brigades between the batteries, and its skirmishers were actively engaged to their front at the Bliss farmyard. Cushing's battery was still in The Angle by the Copse of Trees, and Webb's brigade of Gibbon's division was on Cushing's immediate left. Webb had one regiment, the Sixty-ninth Pennsylvania, in front of the copse and behind the wall that ran south from The Angle; his three other regiments remained on the reverse slope of the ridge behind the copse. Hall's

brigade was to Webb's left. Two of its regiments, the Seventh Michigan and the Fifty-ninth New York, were in the front line behind a low breastwork of rails and stone that marked a fence line running south from The Angle, while the Twentieth Massachusetts was behind them in their support. By this time, all of Gibbon's First Brigade, Harrow's, had been distributed to nearby areas on the field.

Most of the dispersal of the Second Corps took place while McLaws's and Anderson's divisions were attacking the Third Corps. Those Confederates who wrote of the assaults by Wilcox's and Perry's brigades used broad terms that portrayed the sweeping character of the attack. Wilcox's brigade allegedly broke two lines, captured six guns, and did not stop until it reached Plum Run's swale. The Floridians swept over a battery, shattered the enemy with crashing fire that threw them into confusion, and charged them with ear-splitting yells. In retrospect, as the details of the assault blurred and some of the unpleasant sights and feelings associated with it were forgotten, it became a glorious event described with hyperbole; the numbers of lines broken and guns captured tended to increase. Wilcox, in calmer times, reflected on the question of objectivity and observed that writers of reports often missed the exact truth. In regard to the numbers of lines broken by the brigade, he said,

> I [am] inclined to believe that in one case referred to, it was part of the same line that had reformed & faced to the front again after having been made to retire; in the case of the artillery captured, the enemy [were] endeavoring to get their guns away and may have had the guns scattered & in the excitement of the battle we mistook [them] for a second battery. It was late and [there was] much smoke; and the brigade rushed over things like a torrent when the turnpike had been crossed & the enemy made to yield.[101]

When the Alabama and Florida brigades reached Plum Run's swale, their ranks were in disorder. Colonel Forney of the Tenth Alabama fell there with his second wound of the day.[102]

Lieutenant Weir saw the enemy advance on his front and right against little or no opposition. The Floridians had outflanked Humphreys's line, and none but skirmishers opposed Wright's brigade beyond the Emmitsburg Road. Weir's guns opened with shot on the lines to the left along the section of the road that they could enfilade and with case and canister on those moving against the battery's position. Soon the battery's canister supply was gone, and when the Floridians neared the guns, Weir ordered their crews to limber up and fall back. As they did so, a regiment, probably the Nineteenth Maine, opened fire from Weir's left and rear. This gave the lieutenant some hope, and he wheeled his battery back into line, dropped trail, and reopened. Weir thought that the enemy was so scattered that they could be driven off readily, but this was not the case. Wright's brigade burst upon the scene from the right about this time in overwhelming strength. Weir tried to withdraw the battery again, but his horse was shot and carried him with it to the ground. When the lieutenant got to his feet, a spent ball hit him and he became confused. As he left the field, he saw to his sorrow that three of his guns were in enemy hands.[103]

Weir never recovered from the misfortunes of that day. He remained in the army, and about twenty-two years later visited the battlefield. After his visit, he wrote to General Hancock about his part in the battle. He conceded that he had left three of his guns in the hands of the enemy and stated that he had never answered his accusers with explanations of how he came to do so. He was absent when the guns were later recovered, and he felt badly because of that. It all preyed upon his mind. On 18 July 1886 at 7:00 P.M., Capt. Gulian V. Weir, Fifth Artillery, Fort Hamilton, New York, "during a temporary aberration of mind," took a rifle and put a bullet through his troubled heart.[104]

The officers and men of the Nineteenth Maine, who were lying in the pasture southeast of Codori's barn and on Weir's battery's left, watched the smoke and heard the noise of battle moving in their direction. They saw some of the Third Corps troops fleeing toward them in a disorganized mass. Colonel Heath walked to the front of his regiment's line and passed along it, cautioning the men to lie still and let the Third Corps fugitives pass over them. The Maine men did so, and they found that some Third Corps people were not careful about where they stepped. In fact, some exhibited "no regard to dignity or military order." Some said that they were whipped and that the Maine men should get out. Others, said to belong to the Excelsior Brigade, yelled as they passed, "Hang on, Boys! we will form in your rear." Those who tried to do so were swept away.[105]

When a segment of the Third Corps line was about 150 yards away, an officer, identified (wrongly perhaps) as General Humphreys, rode up and ordered Colonel Heath to have his regiment stand and stop the fugitives with their bayonets. Heath refused. He feared that if the men of the Nineteenth Maine got to their feet, they might be infected by the disorder, if not swept away by it. He told the general that if the Third Corps men could be gotten out of his way, the Nineteenth would stop their pursuers and that the men of the Third Corps could reform in the Nineteenth's rear. Humphreys, if it was he, was in no mood to argue with a colonel and rode along the Nineteenth's line, ordering it to stand. Heath, who was not about to have his authority usurped by anyone from the Third Corps, followed the general, countermanding his order. The regiment obeyed its colonel. There were sharp words. Heath refused to budge and ended the conversation by saying, "I was placed here by an officer of higher rank for a purpose, and I do not intend to go to the rear. Let your troops form in the rear and we will take care of the enemy in front."[106]

These were bold words to a general, but Heath made them stick. As soon as the regiment's front was clear of fugitives, Heath ordered the Nineteenth to its feet. Then the Confederate line emerged through the smoke about fifty yards away. The Maine men saw a tall color-bearer who jogged ahead of it, tossing his flag several yards to the front and then picking it up as the line advanced. Heath shouted, "Drop that color bearer." A soldier fired and the Floridian dropped. The Nineteenth opened fire and brought the Confederate line to a halt; the two lines traded eight volleys at a range of about thirty yards.[107]

It was nearly dusk, and the biting smoke was so heavy that visibility was very limited in certain areas. Capt. Isaac W. Starbird on the Nineteenth's left reported Confederates off his flank. Heath went over with him for a look, and they saw a double line not more than twenty-five yards away. Starbird refused his company's line, and his forty men poured enfilading fire into the Confederates, who fell back into the smoke and out of sight.[108]

Heath returned to his post behind the center of the Nineteenth's line and learned from Lt. Col. Henry W. Cunningham that Rebels appeared to be passing around the Nineteenth's right. Hell was freezing over! Heath faced the Nineteenth to the rear and marched it back toward the crest of Cemetery Ridge. After going a short distance, the regiment emerged from the smoke, and there were no Rebels on its flank. Since its flank was safe, the Nineteenth faced about and charged.[109]

A short distance from the left of the Nineteenth Maine, Col. Arthur Devereux's Nineteenth Massachusetts Regiment and Col. James Mallon's Forty-second New York Regiment—the former with about four hundred men, the latter with only a hundred—followed Lieutenant Christiancy to the aid of Humphreys's division. The two units filed left at the double-quick about two hundred yards, where they came under some musketry and saw Third Corps troops falling back in great confusion. To avoid enfilading fire, to—in Mallon's words—"infuse confidence in the hearts of those who among those retreating might have some manhood left," and to meet the enemy in a proper sort of formation, the two regiments formed a line. It was at this time, if not slightly earlier, that Devereux asked Christiancy what they were to do and what position they were to take. Christiancy replied, "In support of Humphreys' division." Devereux remarked that it was useless to attempt to form such a small force as theirs in support of a division that was broken and fleeing, and Christiancy made no satisfactory reply. The situation must have changed greatly since Christiancy had left Humphreys, and the lieutenant did not know what to say. Without further ado, the aide galloped off, probably to get instructions, but Devereux and Mallon never saw him again.[110]

At Devereux's suggestion, the two regiments advanced to a slight rise in their front and formed a line. The color sergeant of the Nineteenth removed the cover from his flag, and the men of the two units lay down. In the meantime some Third Corps troops had rallied and formed a line on their left. The colonels conferred and decided that they would wait there for Humphreys's men to clear their front, deliver volleys by rear and front ranks, and then fall back. At that time the smoke was so dense that they could scarcely see. When the enemy appeared, the Third Corps line on their left began to break, and some of the Nineteenth's officers ran over to rally it. Lt. John Adams of the color company received dangerous wounds in the groin and hip. The two Second Corps regiments fired their volleys, which stalled the enemy, and then they fell back, hopefully retaining some of their own manhood as they did so. Colonel Devereux left Maj. Edmund Rice and a line of skirmishers behind to cover their withdrawal. As the Nineteenth moved to the rear, Devereux tried to calm it by clucking, "Steady, boys, steady." They met another line moving forward and, after going about two hundred yards, met Capt. George W. Leach of the brigade staff, who told them to rejoin the brigade.[111]

Wilcox's and Perry's brigades, assisted by Barksdale's, had driven Humphreys's division from the Emmitsburg Road where Sickles had posted it and had eliminated the final segment of Sickles's advanced line. Humphreys, with the help of reinforcements from the Second Corps, had held much of his dwindling force together as it retreated slowly to Cemetery Ridge and rallied it there. Wilcox's and Perry's brigades pursued the Federals to Plum Run at the base of Cemetery Ridge, where they halted to reform their disordered ranks. Both Wilcox and Lang sent to General Anderson, their division commander, for reinforcements and worked to prepare their brigades to continue the assault or to resist the counterattacks that the Federals were certain to deliver against them.

WRIGHT'S AND POSEY'S BRIGADES
ATTACK THE SECOND CORPS

The brigade of Brig. Gen. Ambrose Ransom ("Rans") Wright stood to the left of Perry's brigade on Seminary Ridge north of Spangler's Woods. In later years the Commonwealth of Virginia would erect a memorial there to honor its soldiers at Gettysburg, a large monument surmounted by an equestrian statue of Robert E. Lee. Rans Wright was a heavily bearded man with dark, curly hair, a Georgian thirty-seven years of age. Like most of his fellow Confederate brigadiers on Seminary Ridge that day, Wright had been a lawyer in civilian life. Also like many of them, he had been active in politics, but he had not been a long-time advocate of secession. When Georgia seceded, however, he became colonel of the Third Georgia Regiment, served with it in the Carolinas, became a brigadier general in June 1862, and then joined the Army of Northern Virginia with his brigade. Wright was severely wounded at the Bloody Lane at Antietam but was back with his brigade in time for the battle of Fredericksburg.[112]

Wright's brigade had three Georgia regiments—the Third, Twenty-second, and Forty-eighth—and the Second Georgia Battalion. At the time of its advance the Twenty-second was on the brigade's right, the Third in its

Brig. Gen. Ambrose R. Wright
(Library of Congress)

Brig. Gen. Carnot Posey
(Library of Congress)

center, and the Forty-eighth Regiment was on its left. The Second Battalion stretched across the brigade's front in a skirmish line. Wright's orders were to move forward with Perry's brigade on his right, and he was told that Posey's brigade to his left would advance at the same time. So far, so good; Anderson's division would advance as a single unit. When Wright's three regiments overtook the skirmish line, the Second Battalion would slip, somehow, to the brigade left and continue the assault from there. Wright seems not to have been assigned a specific portion of Cemetery Ridge to strike. Presumably, then, his brigade was simply to advance on Perry's brigade's left and strike that sector of the Union position that happened to be in its front.[113]

Carnot Posey's Mississippi Brigade was to Wright's left, and Anderson ordered Posey to advance after Wright. Posey, age forty-four, was a planter and a lawyer and had been a lieutenant in Jefferson Davis's Mississippi Rifles during the War with Mexico. He commanded the Sixteenth Mississippi in 1861 and fought at Ball's Bluff. He served with Trimble's brigade of Ewell's division in the Valley and on the Peninsula; then he was in Featherston's brigade, which he commanded after Second Manassas. Posey became a brigadier general in November 1862 and died a year later from an infected wound received at Bristoe Station.[114]

Posey's brigade had four regiments: the Twelfth, Sixteenth, Nineteenth, and Forty-eighth Mississippi. They formed on Seminary Ridge south of

McMillan's Woods and fronted toward the Bliss farm buildings and Cemetery Hill beyond. The brigade faced numerous batteries on Cemetery Hill and Cemetery Ridge. The Confederate guns of Pegram's and Lane's battalions on Seminary Ridge within its zone must have attracted numerous rounds in its direction. It is not surprising, then, that the Mississippians sought a measure of safety by piling up a slight breastwork of fence rails and earth.[115]

At some point, probably about midafternoon, before Longstreet's assault began, Generals Hill and Anderson rode into the brigade's area and studied the ground to the front. Soon galloping orderlies and staff officers created a flurry of excitement and caused the Mississippians to "sniff a fight." There were shouted orders to take cover as the nearby batteries opened and, in return, drew fire from the Federal batteries. General Posey received orders to advance after Wright's brigade, but, before Wright moved out, Lt. Samuel D. Shannon of Anderson's staff brought orders for Posey to advance two of his regiments and deploy them "closely as skirmishers" rather than in line of battle. Posey already had parts of the Sixteenth and Nineteenth Mississippi regiments on the skirmish line at a fence about 250 yards to the front, midway to the Bliss farmyard. In response to the order, Posey sent forward the right wing of the Nineteenth to join its comrades at the fence and sent the Forty-eighth Mississippi along with it. Col. Nathaniel H. Harris of the Nineteenth reported that his orders were to advance until he met the enemy's skirmishers and drive them back. Harris double-quicked his men through the wheat field in their front to a fence and found then that the enemy was in the Bliss orchard about two hundred yards ahead, between the fence and the farmyard. Col. Joseph M. Jayne's Forty-eighth Mississippi followed. Although extant accounts do not indicate as much, it is likely that both regiments stirred up a hornet's nest at Bliss's farmyard.[116]

The First Delaware Regiment under Lt. Col. Edward P. Harris and Capt. Henry F. Chew's Company I, Twelfth New Jersey Regiment, both of Smyth's brigade, held the farmyard at that time. Companies A and B of the 106th Pennsylvania Regiment of Webb's brigade prolonged the line to the left on Gibbon's front. The skirmish firing must have been brisk, for some of the Federals believed that the Confederate force was growing stronger and feared that they, in turn, were running out of ammunition. Captain Chew, whose men were in the barn and yard, warned Lieutenant Colonel Harris of the Confederate buildup and became angry when Harris retorted that he knew his business. Shortly afterward the companies on the right wing of the First Delaware did run short of ammunition, and Harris, without authority, withdrew them from the line. This exposed the troops on the remainder of the line and played into the hands of the advancing Mississippians. The Federal skirmish line had to pull back nearer to the Emmitsburg Road, leaving the Bliss farmyard to the Confederates. Hancock, who had a low tolerance for battlefield errors, placed Harris under arrest and removed him from the command of his regiment.[117]

Capt. James C. Lynch, commander of Company B, 106th Pennsylvania, complained of this fiasco to Capt. John J. Sperry of Company A, who commanded the skirmishers of Webb's brigade. Lynch told Sperry that if the Bliss buildings were not retaken, the whole line would have to fall back. Anderson's division had not yet advanced, and there was no other threat to Gibbon's and Hays's divisions from the west. Sperry told Lynch to go ahead and retake the farm buildings, so Lynch took Company B toward the farmyard. The Mississippians let the Pennsylvanians come near and, when they were under the Confederates' guns, ordered Lynch's men to surrender. Lynch had been rash and he was still spoiling for a fight. He refused the surrender demand, and Posey's men shot thirteen of his men before he could pull them back. Clearly the Mississippians were also there to fight.[118]

Company B fell back to a fence line, probably that about midway between the Bliss and Codori buildings. Webb or Gibbon asked for help, and Hancock cantered over to Colonel Smyth and asked him to send a hundred men from his brigade to retake the Bliss farmyard. Smyth turned to Maj. John T. Hill, commander of the Twelfth New Jersey Regiment, who must have been close at hand, and said simply, "Major, send 100 men and take it."[119]

Major Hill asked for volunteers, and the whole regiment responded. Hill then simply ordered the first four companies in the regiment's column to do the job. They were companies B, H, E, and G, and their ranking officer was Capt. Samuel B. Jobes. Jobes marched them in column to the Brian buildings and deployed them into a line forward of the Brian barn. The men of the companies gave three hurrahs for Colonel Smyth and three for New Jersey and advanced to the fields beyond the Emmitsburg Road. There, in the words of Lt. William Potter of Company G, "Bringing their arms to the right shoulder, and taking the double-quick, with ringing cheers they burst through the enemy's skirmish line with the might of a giant, and in one bold mass close down upon, surround and capture the Bliss barn, with the enemy's picket reserve of 92 men and 7 officers, and bringing their prisoners with them, regain our lines."[120]

Potter's description makes Jobe's assault sound like a raid, an attack made without the intention to hold the farmyard area. But the farmyard was taken with the intention of using it as the anchor for the Federal skirmish line. Jobes's force fell back as soon it did because it was forced to do so. Posey's men made the Twelfth New Jersey pay for Hancock's temerity. The Mississippians shot forty-two of the Jerseymen who made the charge; they wounded Jobes and killed Capt. Charles K. Horsfall. By this time Longstreet's assault must have been well under way, and Anderson's division was advancing.[121]

Wright's brigade advanced along with Wilcox's and Perry's brigades to its right. Federal batteries greeted it with "a sheet of fire" and hail of iron when it emerged from the trees on the ridge line. The Georgians double-quicked forward and down into the trough in front of the ridge. They paused there for a moment in defilade to catch their breath and reform. Then they pushed ahead, double-quicking across the folds of ground that gave them particular exposure to the fire of the enemy's batteries. When the Forty-eighth Georgia on the left of Wright's line passed the Forty-eighth Mississippi, which was lying somewhere near the Bliss farmyard and had orders not to go farther forward, the Georgians shouted, "Get up and fight" and "Come forward, Mississippians." This stirred up some of the prone Mississippians; and, in spite of their colonel's orders, a good many advanced with the left of the Georgians' line.[122]

The Second Georgia Battalion, which had led the advance of Wright's brigade from the skirmish line, paused at the fence line about three hundred yards west of the Emmitsburg Road and directly south of the Bliss farmyard and waited there for Wright's main line. Now the smoke of the battle was "extending and ascending until it darkened the rays of the sun," and the Georgians could see scarcely one hundred yards ahead of them. By the time the main line reached the Second Battalion, an important part of Wright's plan went awry. Instead of shifting to the left of the brigade line and forming as a body there, many of the men of the Second Battalion fell in with that portion of the line closest to them. In doing so, they deprived the brigade of a cohesive unit that would give special protection to its left. Some men of the Second, in fact, fell in with Perry's brigade and fought with it.[123]

The fence line taken from Captain Sperry's skirmishers by the Second Georgia Battalion marked the starting place of Wright's actual charge. From that point on the Georgians advanced under small arms fire from the Fifteenth Massachusetts and Eighty-second New York regiments posted along the road to the right of the Codori house, from Brown's battery in its forward position, and from the batteries and riflemen of the Second Corps near the crest of the ridge. Brown's Napoleons were at a disadvantage. They had been posted fronting to the northwest and at a good forty-five-degree angle from Wright's advancing line. Skirmishers harassed Brown's cannoneers, and when Wright's brigade appeared, Brown was able to swing only his four left pieces toward the oncoming Georgians. As the Confederates approached, Brown's cannoneers cut their fuses shorter and shorter—three seconds, two, and then one, until the range was too short for case shot and more suitable for canister.[124]

The men of the Eighty-second New York and the Fifteenth Massachusetts regiments must have waited nervously for the Rebel assault. There were enough of them to put up a delaying fight, but the Confederate shells knocked their flimsy breastworks apart and wounded some of the men behind them. Brown's missiles, particularly the canister, passed close and

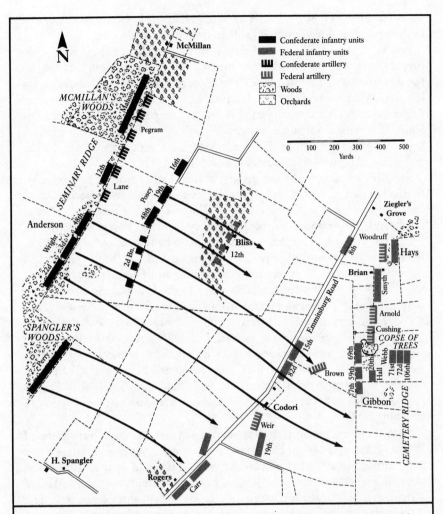

1. Skirmishers from Smyth's brigade, Hays's division, and Posey's brigade, Anderson's division, fight over control of the Bliss buildings. Troops of the Twelfth New Jersey Regiment hold the buildings just prior to Anderson's advance.

2. Wright's brigade advances on Perry's left. Its Second Georgia Battalion, on the skirmish line, is absorbed by its main line. Wright's left wing drives the Eighty-second New York and Fifteenth Massachusetts from their advanced position along the Emmitsburg Road at the Codori buildings.

3. Wright and Perry overrun Weir's battery south of the Codori barn, and Wright captures two guns of Brown's battery midway between the Codori buildings and the Second Corps line on Cemetery Ridge.

4. Wright strikes Hall's brigade on Cemetery Ridge and its right wing enters a gap in the Union line to Hall's left.

5. As Wright advances, Posey's brigade captures the Bliss buildings. Some of Posey's Forty-eighth Mississippi Regiment advances with Wright. Some of Posey's brigade approaches the Emmitsburg Road but does not cross it.

6. Mahone's brigade (the position shown for it is only approximate) does not advance.

Map 15-2. Wright and Posey Attack the Union Center

wounded some of them, and they must have felt very isolated and vulnerable in their position three hundred yards in front of the main line.[125]

But at this time all was not well with the attackers either. As Wright prepared to sweep the two Union regiments along the road from his front, he became painfully aware that Posey's brigade, as a unit, was not advancing on his left. Wright sent Capt. R. H. Bell of his staff back to tell General Anderson of Posey's absence and of Wright's concerns about his brigade's left flank. Bell returned in time with Anderson's reply that Posey already had been ordered forward but that Anderson would repeat the order. In the meantime, Wright's brigade should press forward.[126]

Probably it will never be known with certainty what orders Posey received from Anderson and what his brigade did while Wright's and others attacked the Union positions on Cemetery Ridge. Some time after sending the Nineteenth and Forty-eighth Mississippi regiments forward, Posey dispatched the Sixteenth Mississippi Regiment to their aid. Then, learning of a threat to their flank, he personally led the Twelfth forward as well. When he reached the farmyard area, the Sixteenth, Nineteenth, and Forty-eighth regiments were "well up in advance," probably close to the Emmitsburg Road. They were fighting at long range with the main line of the Second Corps and raked a Federal battery, possibly Brown's, with rifle fire. Before Posey took the Twelfth Mississippi Regiment forward, he sent a request to Brig. Gen. William Mahone, whose brigade was on his left, for a regiment to support his left, but none was sent. As Posey later understood it, Mahone had been ordered to the right with his brigade and could not comply with Posey's request. In his terse report, however, Mahone made no mention of such an assignment.[127]

Something was wrong in Anderson's division that evening. The brigades of Wilcox, Perry, and Wright had attacked as ordered, yet Posey's brigade had gone forward in a piecemeal manner and had frittered away its strength in skirmishing between the Bliss buildings and the Emmitsburg Road. Wilcox, Wright, and Posey each had asked for support, Wilcox three times according to his accounts, but none came, even though Mahone's brigade remained essentially idle on Seminary Ridge. Later there was criticism in the press, and questions were naturally raised, but Generals Anderson and A. P. Hill failed to explain the matter in their reports and made no explanatory statements elsewhere that were recorded.

Wilcox commented that "could the division commander have seen [his brigade's situation and need] with his own eyes, he would have without being asked sent other brigades forward." This suggests that, insofar as Wilcox knew, Anderson had not seen, and therefore was in no position to see, what was taking place on Wilcox's front. This in itself is not condemning, for Anderson could have been with another brigade farther to the left and out of immediate touch with his right. But, when Capt. Walter E. Winn of Wilcox's staff rode to Anderson for aid, he found Anderson and the division's headquarters in a "ravine." Anderson's horse was tied to a tree and the staff was stretched on the ground as though nothing was happening. On the other hand, Lieutenant Shannon, one of Anderson's aides, went to Mahone with orders to advance, but Mahone declined to do so, saying that Anderson had told him to stay in his position. After the battle, when the Southern press voiced criticism of Posey and Mahone for not moving forward, Anderson responded that if there was any blame, it was his—his brigadiers were acting unders his orders. Something was clearly amiss, and Wilcox and Wright always believed that their brigades had not received the support they deserved.[128]

Wright's brigade had a short fight at the Emmitsburg Road. The brigade front extended beyond the right of the short Federal line along the road north of the Codori house and threatened to envelop the Federals' right flank. Colonels Ward and Huston both fell, and in the increasing dusk and smoke Wright's threat was real enough. The men of the Eighty-second New York gave way before the fearsome, yelling Georgians without setting fire to the Codori buildings as they had been ordered to do. When the Eighty-second began to fall back, the men of the Fifteenth saw no use in staying on, and they retired "in some disorder," pressed closely by the enemy, who took more than twenty of them prisoners.[129]

Weir's and Brown's batteries fared no better. Brown's guns were sitting ducks. The Georgians pushed toward Brown's position, peppering its crews with fire that the cannoneers could not stand very long. One bullet struck Lieutenant Brown in the neck, horses fell faster than they could be cut from their harness, and the Rhode Islanders had no recourse but to try to return to the main line. Sgt. Abel Straight's sixth piece was already loaded when the order came for it to get out. He hesitated long enough to fire the gun. Even as he did so, he lost two horses and enough time so that the crew had to abandon the piece. Four of Brown's guns, aided by rifle fire from the Sixty-ninth Pennsylvania and canister from Cushing's battery, raced back to the gap in the wall south of the Copse of Trees with the Georgians in pursuit. The guns jammed up at the wall in such a way as to fire the tempers of old artillerymen like Gibbon and Hall if they saw what was happening, and one gun was still west of the wall as the Georgia line approached. When it appeared that they would not get the gun through the gap, the drivers jumped from their horses and the crew scattered.[130]

Gibbon wrote that Wright's brigade came on with "impetuosity." Webb, who had a perfect view, wrote that the Georgians approached his front in splendid order.[131] And they did. Once the Georgia regiments cleared the obstructions near the Emmitsburg Road, they surged up the slope of Cemetery Ridge like a tide rolling up a beach. Wright's line passed on both sides of the Codori buildings, most of it climbing toward the ridge crest south of the Copse of Trees toward Hall's front and the great gap in the Federal line to Hall's left.

Although Wright's thrust, coupled with that of the brigades on its right, seemed as irresistible as a rolling wave, like a wave, it lost its strength as it climbed the ascending ground. By the time Wilson's Tigers, Company I of the Forty-eighth Georgia, closed on Hall's line, all of its officers were down, and a corporal led the men who were still in ranks. The Third Georgia on the right was "hotly engaged," the Twenty-second "suffered severely," and the ranks of the Second Battalion were "rapidly decreasing."[132] The Second Corps gave Wright's men a warm welcome. Arnold's and Cushing's batteries served canister, but in the smaller doses required by the caliber of three-inch rifles. Cushing's three left guns fired single charges of canister at the Confederates clustered around Brown's abandoned guns so that they could not use them or haul them away.[133]

The Sixty-ninth Pennsylvania Regiment of Webb's brigade assaulted Wright's men from behind the wall in front of the Copse of Trees. It fought with bravery and coolness, as befitted a veteran Irish regiment. Its rifles blazed at the charging Georgians climbing the slope to its front and left. When one Rebel officer climbed upon the Napoleon left by Brown's men in front of the wall, Capt. Michael Duffy became so incensed that he stepped to the top of the wall and shouted for his men to "knock that d—d officer off the gun." General Harrow was standing by him at the wall. Scarcely had Duffy given his order when he fell at Harrow's feet with a minié ball in his head.[134] Webb ordered the other regiments of his brigade forward from the reverse slope of the ridge to the aid of the Sixty-ninth. The Seventy-first hurried to its rear, and the 106th marched to the Sixty-ninth's right behind Cushing's guns so that it might be in a position to advance against Wright's left flank.[135]

Col. Norman J. Hall's brigade was in a desperate situation as Wright's brigade approached its front. The division's reserve, Harrow's brigade, had been parcelled out; Hall's Forty-second New York and Nineteenth Massachusetts regiments had marched to the aid of Humphreys's division and, like that division, been swept back by an enemy whose "advance was irresistible, its regularity surprising, and its rapidity fearful." Hall was well aware of the broad gap on his brigade's left; he thought it was a quarter of a mile across. Some reinforcements came, probably from Webb's brigade, but Hall did not write what troops they were. They tried to form in his support, but Hall tried to send them on to the gap. When Wright's column seemed to be making for his three small regiments, whose men were down behind their paltry works, and the Georgians were but thirty or so yards away, Hall shouted to open fire.[136]

Some thickets and rock outcrops in front of Hall's position gave the Georgians a little shelter from Hall's fire, and they continued to press forward against Hall's front and toward the inviting gap. Wright reported this portion of his charge with high enthusiasm that blurred the accuracy of his statements. He wrote of the rather gentle slope as "so precipitous here that my men could with difficulty *climb* it." The Georgians drove the "Yankee infantry" from behind the stone fence and "then taking cover from the fence we soon *shot all the gunners of the enemy's Artillery*, and rushing over the fence seized their guns." While at the guns, Pvt. William B. Judkins of the Twenty-second used one as a rest and shot a Bluecoat in the arm. The Georgians then charged to the east shoulder of the crest "and drove the enemy's infantry into a rocky gorge on the eastern slope of the heights, and some 80 or 100 yards in rear of the enemy's batteries."[137]

Rans Wright wrote with imagination. His men could not have found too much opposition in the gap itself, and there was no rocky gorge in the ridge's east slope. But, perhaps, he may be pardoned. Visibility was very limited then, and the occasion was dramatic enough to launch recollections into orbits of fancy. Furthermore, Wright himself probably was in no position to see first-hand some of the areas described in his accounts; he probably wrote of what others had told him. In the conditions that existed there, the rock outcrops on the west slope of the ridge might have suggested steep slopes to the Georgians, the flank fire was terrible enough, and in the smoky twilight the gullies on the ridge's east slope might have looked like gorges. The important thing is not Wright's fanciful description of the terrain but that the Georgians did go beyond the wall that marked the main line of Gibbon's division on to the crest of the ridge. At that place and at that time, reported Wright, "We were now complete masters of the field, having gained the key, as it were, of the enemy's whole line."[138]

Wright's brigade had occupied a segment of the ridge crest and pierced the Federal line at the Union center. The question then was, Could the soldiers of the Army of Northern Virginia hold the ground and exploit the penetration, or would their gain quickly be wrested from them?

16

The Repulse

It was sunset. Hood's, McLaws's, and Anderson's divisions had smashed Sickles's advanced line and shattered the units sent to bolster it. Confederate batteries occupied the coveted high ground at the Peach Orchard and along the Emmitsburg Road and fired at fleeing Federal soldiers and at Union batteries on Cemetery Ridge. Confederate brigades, though crippled and fatigued, pursued their adversaries toward Cemetery Ridge and Little Round Top and threatened to seize those dominating heights. Should they be able to do so and demonstrate their ability to hold them, the Army of the Potomac would have to abandon the remainder of its Gettysburg position without delay. Its withdrawal would give General Lee a measure of the victory that he sought when the Army of Northern Virginia crossed the Potomac.

Cemetery Ridge was lightly defended at this time. The Second Corps still held a strong position between the Copse of Trees and Cemetery Hill, and the Fifth Corps was building its strength on Little Round Top. But the mile-wide space between the two corps was manned only by remnants of units driven from the forward line and random regiments and batteries rushed there from the Second Corps and the Artillery Reserve. Other defenders were needed; fortunately for the Union, some of them were nearby, and others were on the way.

It was said that General Lee spent much of the period of the afternoon's battle at his vantage point near the seminary. He watched the course of the fighting as he was able and conversed occasionally with his staff officers and others, particularly Generals Hill and Heth. One man who saw him at this time said that his face betrayed no anxiety, and Colonel Fremantle recalled that he received only one report and sent only one message. Of course, Fremantle was not privy to all that General Lee did during that late afternoon and early evening, but it must be accepted that, in accordance with his concept of command, Lee had given his corps commanders their instructions and was not interfering with their conduct of the battle.[1]

General Meade, in contrast, was actively and directly involved in the events of the late afternoon. Perhaps he had been a division and a corps commander too recently to stand aloof while subordinate generals moved their formations over the field; perhaps his nervous temperament required that he be active; or perhaps the afternoon's surprises made him reluctant to rely too heavily on subordinates at this critical time. Whatever the reason, Meade was in the saddle observing the course of the battle and issuing orders that would send troops to the dangerous gap and was seeing that they were obeyed.

It cannot be known when and where specific orders were issued, for some were more speedily carried out than others. After his 3:00 P.M. meeting with his corps commanders and before he set out for the Third Corps line, Meade asked General Sykes to take his Fifth Corps to the left and hold it "at all hazards." Soon after, while on his way to Sickles's front, he sent General Warren to Little Round Top. Then he ordered Humphreys's division to the left but quickly rescinded that order when the arrival of Fifth Corps troops there rendered Humphreys's movement unnecessary. He must have initiated and called back Caldwell's first shift to the Third Corps front and only a short time later asked General Hancock to send a division, Caldwell's as it turned out, to the aid of Sykes. Soon after his visit to Sickles's line, Meade returned to his headquarters, where he greeted and briefed General Sedgwick and gave him orders for the deployment of the Sixth Corps.[2] While on the portion of his line that was essentially bare of troops, General Meade sent Lt. Paul Oliver of his staff to General Slocum to secure a division of the Twelfth Corps to man the ridge. At about the same time, he asked General Hancock to send a Second Corps brigade to Birney's support, and, on learning that General Sickles had been wounded, asked Hancock to assume command of the Third Corps.[3]

These and later actions by General Meade created a lot of movement within the Army of the Potomac. Sykes's corps came forward on the left. Its divisions approached over two routes, and the operations of the First and Second divisions have been discussed in Chapter 10. Sykes's Third Division, Crawford's, was the ace in the hole. Its two brigades of Pennsylvania Reserves (see Chapter 3) were the last of the corps to reach the field and the last to march from the assembly area along the Baltimore Pike. There was confusion at the outset of the division's move because no staff officer came to guide Crawford to his division's destination. Nevertheless, Crawford started off after Ayres's division with Col. Joseph W. Fisher's brigade in the lead. Crawford halted Fisher at the fork in the road southeast of Powers Hill. Ayres's men had taken the left fork, and Crawford believed it to be the wrong one.[4]

As Crawford paused in a quandary, one of Sickles's ubiquitous aides, Capt. Alexander Moore, rode up to the fork. Moore was searching for reinforcements from the Fifth Corps. Crawford might have assumed that Moore was one of Meade's many staff officers and consented to follow the captain, but Moore was cautious—he would not accept Crawford's help without the approval of General Meade. Meade, of course, was nowhere near Powers Hill, so what was to be done? Crawford remarked that Slocum's headquarters were nearby, and that Slocum commanded the right wing of the army. Surely if Slocum approved, Crawford could follow Moore. This sounded reasonable, though it really was not, so Moore galloped over to Slocum and received his authorization to take Crawford. "Triply armed" with authority to commandeer assistance for the Third Corps wherever he could find it, Moore returned to Crawford and led his two brigades forward toward Little Round Top and the Third Corps front.[5]

The road to Little Round Top by way of the left fork was no more than a narrow country lane. It must have been apparent to Crawford's men that they were approaching the battle area, for they met crowds of wounded headed for the rear. Ambulances and the walking wounded created so much traffic that the Pennsylvanians had to march to the sides of the road, a humanitarian but poor way of doing things for troops who needed to win a battle.[6]

When they neared Little Round Top, Moore went on ahead to report to General Sickles and get instructions from him for Crawford's division. He learned from Captain Poland that Sickles had been wounded. Moore left Crawford to his own devices, apparently rode to army headquarters to report Sickles's condition to General Meade, and then left the field to join Sickles.[7] Fortunately, Crawford met Sykes, who asked him to hold his division on the northeast slope of Little Round Top. The division stopped there briefly. Before it could settle in, Sykes ordered it to the right of Ayres's division on the lower slope of Little Round Top north of the Wheatfield Road.[8]

This stop was a brief one too, for Lt. Col. Frederick T. Locke of Sykes's staff soon brought Crawford an order to shift to the left of the road to Little Round Top's northwest slope, the position vacated by Ayres's division when it advanced across Plum Run toward the Wheatfield. The Reserves did so, and as they formed, the setting sun was a dull, red ball of fire, "wrapped in drifts of lurid smoke." Retreating soldiers filled the fields to their front. Some to their left were coming back at a run, but most retreated at a sullen walk. Hazlett's battery barked slowly on the height to their left, and another battery, either Gibbs's or Walcott's, took position on their right.[9]

Brig. Gen. Samuel W. Crawford had a rather unique background for a division commander in the Army of the Potomac. Born in 1829 in Franklin County, Pennsylvania, across South Mountain from Gettysburg, he had studied medicine at the University of Pennsylvania. He became an army surgeon in 1851 and served at posts in the West. In 1861, he was post surgeon for the garrison at Fort Moultrie and Fort Sumter, South Carolina and, like Doubleday and Hall, was on hand when the Confederates fired on Sumter. A month later Crawford exchanged his scalpel for a sword and received a commission as a major in the Thirteenth Infantry. He became a brigadier general of volunteers in April 1862, commanded a brigade at Cedar Mountain, and commanded both a brigade and a division in the Twelfth Corps at

Antietam, where he was wounded. He recovered in time to take command of the Pennsylvania Reserves in the defenses of Washington in May 1863.[10]

For a Pennsylvanian, Crawford was in the right place at the right time. Not only was he the successor of Gens. George A. McCall, Reynolds, and Meade, illustrious former commanders of the Reserves, he was in his home state on Little Round Top, a place that he described later as the "rocky citadel" that had "become a monument to a rescued Christian civilization; its very name a watchword to every patriotic heart." These exaggerated postwar sentiments suggest that Crawford gloried in his association with the hill.[11]

In this new position William McCandless's First Brigade formed behind Fisher's Third, and both were not far from the left section of Gibbs's battery. Then Sykes ordered Crawford to send a brigade to the left to the aid of Vincent's brigade. For reasons not explained or readily apparent, Crawford sent Fisher's brigade, which must have been settled more firmly into the new position. As Fisher's men filed off to the left, the situation on Crawford's front seemed to grow more ominous. The Regulars were now falling back, followed by a yelling enemy. Crawford permitted Fisher to go along with four of his regiments, but he kept Col. Samuel M. Jackson's Eleventh Reserves with him. At that time also, he sent Capt. Louis Livingston of his staff to Sykes for orders. Sykes, who was off to the right rallying the men of the four brigades of Barnes's and Ayres's divisions, replied that since Crawford was on the ground, he should do as he thought best.[12]

Crawford and Col. William ("Buck") McCandless, commander of the First Brigade, quickly prepared for action. The Reserves formed in two lines. The Eleventh Regiment occupied the center of the first line; the First was on its left; and the Sixth was on its right and probably extended the line across the Wheatfield Road. The Second Reserves formed on the right of the support line, and the Thirteenth (also called the First Rifles and the Buck-tails) was on the left. For reasons not given, the Bucktails, if not the other regiments, went into line in reverse order as Caldwell's regiments had done, and there was some confusion as Col. Charles F. Taylor attempted to correct his regiment's formation.[13]

Crawford's regiments were not the only ones forming in that area. General Meade had ordered Sedgwick to post his corps on the left between the lines of the Third and Fifth corps, and Sedgwick took immediate measures to do so. Lieutenant Colonel McMahon, who had gone with Sedgwick to see General Meade, galloped back to the corps and arrived at the assembly area along the Baltimore Pike waving his hat and shouting, "The General directs the corps toward the heavy firing!" Soon after, Sedgwick reached Wheaton's brigade shouting, "Fall in, boys, move quickly!"[14]

Brig. Gen. Frank Wheaton's and Col. Henry L. Eustis's brigades of Newton's division and Brig. Gens. Joseph J. Bartlett's and Alfred T. A. Torbert's brigades of Wright's division started for the Union left. Wheaton's brigade, under the temporary command of Col. David J. Nevin of the Sixty-second

New York, took the lead.[15] Probably Brig. Gen. Albion P. Howe's division of the Sixth Corps was still approaching over the Baltimore Road when Nevin started Wheaton's brigade toward the Union left. General Sedgwick led the way. Like the Fifth Corps, the Sixth met wounded men and stragglers along the way, but now there were Fifth Corps soldiers to be seen among them. When the Sixth Corps reached the ridge line, Sykes was busy trying to reform some of his units there, and the Reserves were forming up to advance.[16]

Somehow the Ninety-eighth Pennsylvania became separated from the rest of Wheaton's brigade during the approach march. It followed a staff officer, sometimes at a double-quick. After a thirty-mile march, the pace must have occasioned some comment. Its march ended on Little Round Top immediately to the left rear of the Pennsylvania Reserves; the men of the Ninety-eighth fixed bayonets and prepared to charge.[17]

Colonel Nevin led the remaining three regiments of the brigade into line on the Reserves' right, the 139th Pennsylvania in the lead. There are two stories about the brigade's arrival on the ridge. One that seems unlikely held that Nevin, obeying Sedgwick's orders to "hurry up, there; never mind forming your Brigade; pitch in by regiments" found the right of the Reserves' line in his way. At this, the colonel, who was described as "impetuous and fiery," "relieved his mind in language more vehement than elegant" at the expense of General Crawford, whose troops were in his way.[18] The other story held that the Sixty-second New York and the Ninety-third and 139th Pennsylvania regiments were ordered to lie down and hold their fire until the advancing enemy was close at hand. Then they would rise up and capture or kill many of them. But the 139th gave the game away by firing prematurely, warning the Confederates off.[19]

Wheaton's (Nevin's) brigade was the Sixth Corps unit that counted most that afternoon. Bartlett's brigade deployed on its right but had not yet formed when Nevin's men advanced. Bartlett's troops, therefore, were not really engaged. The other units of the Sixth Corps were still strung out in a long line of dusty blue to the rear and would not get up in time to come to grips with the Confederates that day.[20]

As the leading brigades of the Sixth Corps took their positions on the ridge, General Sykes helped rally Ayres's two brigades and posted them between the right of Weed's brigade on Little Round Top and the Wheatfield Road.[21] Barnes's two brigades, back from Trostle's Woods, continued the line to the north. Barnes's men had the protection of a stone wall, probably that along the west edge of the U-shaped woods between the George Weikert house and Little Round Top. Because Sykes could not find Barnes, who had been wounded, he placed Colonel Sweitzer in command of this segment of the new line. Sweitzer's three regiments must have had more than enough fighting for that day, but Tilton's had missed the deadlier action. In Tilton's words, for good reason or bad, he had saved the brigade "from great disaster

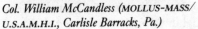

*Col. William McCandless (*MOLLUS-MASS/   *Col. Joseph W. Fisher (*MOLLUS-MASS/
U.S.A.M.H.I., Carlisle Barracks, Pa.)   *U.S.A.M.H.I., Carlisle Barracks, Pa.)*

after it could no longer do any good in front." Having avoided the disaster experienced by others, the men of the brigade were probably a little sensitive to aspersions tossed their way by Zook's troops and by others. Tilton complained somewhat peevishly of being embarrassed by retreating men who had disrupted his line and of fleeing Third Corps troops, who, after his men had taken prone positions behind the wall, blindly jumped over it and landed on them with enough force to cause injuries.[22]

By now there was no more time for preparation. The enemy was coming on in an "irresistible mass of living gray." Lt. Aaron F. Walcott's battery, on the little knoll on the north side of the Wheatfield Road near the lane to the J. Weikert house, made ready to receive them. Gibbs's guns, on higher ground to Walcott's left rear, were ready too. The commanders of both batteries were worried. Walcott termed his position a bad one, and the concerns of Gibbs's battery became part of the lore of the Pennsylvania Reserves. As the Confederates advanced from the Wheatfield, the presumed battery commander, described as a "German captain," approached Colonel Jackson of the Eleventh Reserves. According to Lt. Henry N. Minnigh, a Pennsylvania Dutchman of the First Reserves, the captain said: "Dunder and Blixen, don't let dem repels took my batteries." Jackson tried to calm the worried officer by telling him to double-shot his guns and hold his position and that the Reserves would protect him. Added to this advice came shouts from the ranks, "Stand by your guns, Dutchy, and we will stand by you."[23]

The troops of the Eleventh Reserves took what cover they could while the regiments of McCandless's brigade formed on their line. They could see the Rebels approaching through the fringe of trees east of the Wheatfield and down the slope into Plum Run's valley. The smoke so obscured the attackers there that from their vantage point the Reserves could not distinguish the Confederates from the Federals who were falling back before them. Walcott's artillerymen could see Wofford's men well enough as the Georgians broke from the cover of Trostle's Woods and must have viewed them with apprehension, for the battery had no nearby infantry support. Someone said that Brig. Gen. Charles Griffin, the assigned commander of the First Division, Fifth Corps, personally ordered the battery to displace. Even so, getting away was easier ordered than done. Walcott saw no time to limber up and ordered that the guns be spiked instead. One was, and all six pieces were abandoned.[24]

The retreating Federals swarmed up the slope and through Gibbs's gun line, followed immediately by an "irregular yelling line of the enemy." Gibbs's guns greeted them with double canister, and the Ohio gun crews served their Napoleons so rapidly that they became too hot to touch. Such a reception caused the Confederate line to pause.[25] Gibbs's rapid fire introduced one of the battle's puzzling events and one of its more dramatic counterattacks. According to its accounts, the Ninety-eighth Pennsylvania formed to the left rear of the Reserves' line, probably on the shelf north of Little Round Top's summit and three or four hundred yards to the left of its parent brigade and Colonel Nevin, the brigade's commander. Maj. John B. Kohler, the Ninety-eighth's commander, and his four hundred "German Regulars" (though one company was Irish) from Philadelphia were on their own. Kohler saw the Confederates approach the hill and Gibbs's guns, ordered the men of the Ninety-eighth to fix bayonets, and commanded the regiment to charge.[26]

The Ninety-eighth descended the hill with a "Union hurrah" and passed through the left of the Reserves' forming line down into the valley. It received Confederate fire from Devil's Den, and the marshy ground along Plum Run sucked at the feet of the officers and men so that their line became disordered. But the Ninety-eighth met no serious resistance. The Germans halted when they reached the foot of the slope beyond the run so that those who had mired down could catch up.[27]

At this time, according to Capt. Jacob A. Schmide, the Pennsylvania Reserves began their advance.[28] But Colonel Jackson of the Eleventh Reserves probably would not have agreed with Schmide. In fact, if Jackson knew of the presence of the Ninety-eighth, he chose to ignore it. According to Jackson, the Reserves suffered from long-range fire as the Confederates approached from across the valley below. The Eleventh sustained half its casualties during this waiting period and developed a thirst for revenge. Jackson asked General Crawford's permission to open fire, but Crawford refused it because not all of the retreating Federals had cleared the Reserves' front, and probably all of McCandless's men were not yet in position. Min-

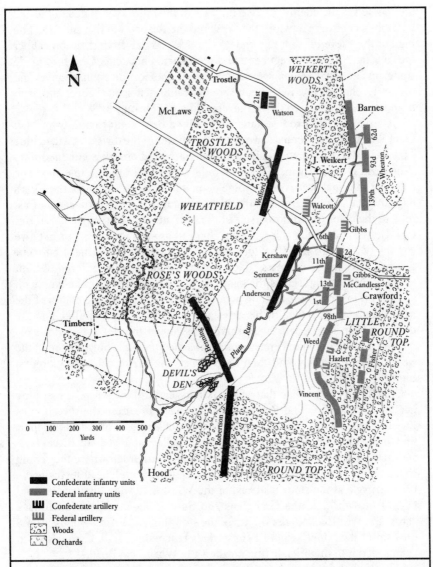

Map 16-1. The Repulse on the Union Left

1. At dusk Vincent's and Weed's brigades have repulsed the attacks against Little Round Top. Wofford's, Semmes's, Anderson's, and Kershaw's brigades have swept the fields west of Little Round Top of Federal units. Their remnants press in some disorder toward Little Round Top and the ridge line to the North.

2. McCandless's brigade, the Eleventh Pennsylvania Reserves, and the Ninety-eighth Pennsylvania form on the north slope of Little Round Top. As soon as troops retreating from the Wheatfield clear their front, these units charge and drive the Confederates beyond the Wheatfield.

3. Wheaton's brigade advances against Wofford. Wofford is ordered back.

4. Additional Sixth Corps units secure this area. Vincent's and Fisher's brigades occupy Round Top.

utes passed as the enemy reached the base of the hill and hesitated in the hail of Gibbs's canister. Crawford then ordered the Reserves to rise and fire. The men of the Eleventh shot two volleys of buck and ball from their .69 caliber muskets, and the other regiments did their part. This done, Crawford made some inspirational remarks, probably about the soil of Pennsylvania, and ordered a charge. The Reserves responded with their special cheer and, with bayonets fixed, bounded down the slope at a double-quick.[29]

General Crawford rode a handsome "blood bay," a gift to him from Maj. Gen. William S. Rosecrans. Two aides, the bearer of the division's flag (a blue Maltese cross on a white field), and some mounted orderlies attended him. When the charge began, Crawford rode to the front of the line near the colors of the First Reserves. At some point a tree or bush snagged the First's flag, and the color-bearer had trouble getting it free. Crawford, seeing this, rode to the colors, bent down, seized the staff, and pulled the flag loose. But Cpl. Bertless Slott, the color-bearer, clung to its staff shouting, "I can't give you my colors." To this Crawford replied, "Don't you know me, I am your general. Give me your colors." Generals often get their way. Corporal Slott let go of the staff but seized the general's pants leg instead and held on with an iron grip through the coming action. Crawford, bearing the colors of the First Reserves and trailed by his aides and orderlies, Corporal Slott, and the division's flag-bearer, led the Reserves' line down the slope. Crawford remained in front until the Pennsylvanians reached the wall along the top of the west side of the valley, and then he returned the First's colors to Corporal Slott.[30]

Crawford's charge, like that of the Ninety-eighth Pennsylvania, met little head-on resistance. The Reserves also received fire from the direction of Devil's Den. In response to this, Colonel McCandless shifted his support line to the brigade's left as they crossed the valley; and Maj. W. Ross Hartshorne took four companies from the Bucktails farther left where they could exchange fire with the Confederates near Devil's Den. The Reserves had a brief struggle at the stone wall east of the Wheatfield with "the bayonet and butt of musket," and the Georgians and South Carolinians there fell back across the Wheatfield to the shelter of the stony hill and Rose's Woods. About dusk, after the Ninety-eighth Pennsylvania reached the wall, Colonel Nevin summoned it to the brigade line north of the Wheatfield Road.[31]

Wheaton's brigade covered the Reserves' right during their charge. Its three regiments fired three volleys before they advanced. They descended the short slope north of the Wheatfield Road on the Reserves' right, passed through Walcott's guns, recovering them for the Army of the Potomac, crossed Plum Run's marsh, and halted near the east tip of Trostle's Woods. They met little or no resistance, and since the marshy area where they halted was no place to establish a line, they fell back a hundred yards or so to the wall along J. Weikert's lane where Walcott's guns were posted. There the Ninety-eighth Pennsylvania joined them, and there they remained. About

Pennsylvania Reserves—the Valley of Death. Painting by F. D. Briscoe (National Archives)

dusk an officer rode up to the Eleventh Reserves' position along the wall west of the Wheatfield. He introduced himself to Colonel Jackson as Col. Frederick H. Collier of the 139th Pennsylvania. He said that in case help was needed, his regiment was to the Reserves' rear. Jackson looked back and saw that the slopes behind were covered with troops. The Sixth Corps had arrived in force, and the Federal left was secure.[32]

Wheaton's brigade was luckier than it knew. Before it began its countercharge, Longstreet had ordered Wofford's brigade back from the area in Wheaton's brigade's front. When he received this order, Col. Goode Bryan of the Sixteenth Georgia saw Longstreet in his rear and walked back to protest it. His regiment had not been attacked in its forward position. If it withdrew, the enemy might recover Walcott's battery and turn it on his men, and his regiment would lose more men in retiring than it had in its advance. But broader considerations had prompted Longstreet's order, and he would not change it.[33]

General McLaws saw Wofford's brigade coming back through Trostle's Woods in line of battle, with Wofford, pistol in hand, following in its rear. McLaws had not known of Longstreet's order and rode quickly to Wofford to learn why his regiments were pulling back. Wofford was angry. His brigade had driven all before it and was resting behind a stone wall when Longstreet's orders came for it to fall back. He saw no necessity for the withdrawal. McLaws observed that Wofford was "very ambitious of military fame and one of the most daring of men and was apprehensive that his coming back might be misconstrued."[34] McLaws posted Wofford's brigade "under the woods" with skirmishers to the front; in reflecting later, he thought that Longstreet's order had been judicious. And judicious it was, for soon, had it not pulled back, much of the Sixth Corps would have been in the brigade's front and the Confederates on its flanks would be falling back.[35]

There was no providential Confederate withdrawal in the Devil's Den area that evening. The Bucktails, on Crawford's left, were targets of Confederates posted there. The Bucktails' lieutenant colonel, Alanson E. Niles, had been shot in the hip when the regiment reached the uphill slope, and his supervision was missed. The fighting at the wall and Colonel Taylor's pursuit of some Confederates beyond the wall caused companies to become mixed and made for confusion. Such was the situation when Lt. John C. Kratzer of K Company talked with Capt. Neri B. Kinsey of Company C about the threat against their left. Kinsey's company, which was on the left, was shooting away, and Kinsey thought that with the help of Kratzer's company he could rout the enemy there. As Kratzer left Kinsey to return to his part of the line to see what might be done, a shell from Gibbs's or Hazlett's battery passed over their heads, and a second burst above them. One of its fragments sliced the arm off a soldier from Company B. The poor fellow jumped up crying, "I won't die, I won't die." He stumbled around in a circle for a brief time, the blood spurting from his stump, and then he fell dead.[36]

The companies on the left of the Bucktails' line were contending with Company C of the First Texas Regiment, commanded by Capt. David K. Rice, plus a body of other men from the First Texas and possibly the Fifteenth Georgia scratched together by Colonel Work. Their job was to cover the Texas Brigade's position at Devil's Den and to guard it from threats from the Plum Run Valley.[37] Rice and his force seemed to be doing a good job, for they had harassed, vexed, and confused the Bucktails. After a discussion by a group of officers on the Bucktails' left, three Bucktails—Capt. Samuel A. Mack, Cpl. Elijah S. Brookins, and Pvt. Abraham S. Davis—scouted to the left and front through the darkening woods to see what they could learn of their enemy. They soon met Confederate soldiers and took cover. They were then joined by Lieutenant Kratzer and Pvt. Ellis J. Hall.[38]

Here the story becomes confused. Accounts agree that Colonel Taylor, who must have been an impetuous fellow, appeared on the left about this time. He came "tearing forward" and asked the small party why it did not fire. Someone replied the rather obvious—their force, having only three rifles, was too weak. Taylor replied that he would order up more men. Before he could say more, someone, probably Kratzer, saw a Confederate raise his rifle and shouted for Taylor to take cover. The Rebel fired. Brookins tried to return the shot, but his rifle misfired. Taylor toppled without a sound, a bullet in his heart. Kratzer was able to catch him, and then, covered by Mack and Davis, he and Brookins carried Taylor back to the stone wall. Unfortunately, Davis was wounded at this time. He called for help but could not get it right away, and he died the next day.[39]

Major Hartshorne took command of the Bucktails after Taylor's death. He realized that the time for aggressive action had passed and formed the regiment behind the stone wall, a practical measure since it was too dark for troops to be moving between the lines. But knowing that there were Confederates to his left and wishing to secure that flank, he sent Kinsey's company in that direction to feel out their position. Kinsey's men advance toward Devil's Den until they were greeted with a volley. This began a brisk fire fight that concerned Hartshorne so much that he sent Kratzer over to look into it. Kratzer talked with Kinsey again. The lieutenant was still optimistic and told Kratzer that, with help, he could take the Confederate position at Devil's Den. Kratzer agreed to help if Hartshorne would permit it. Before Kratzer could pass on Kinsey's request to Hartshorne, shells dropped into the area and Kinsey was wounded. This convinced Hartshorne that the day's adventures were over. He ordered Company C to put out a picket line and fall back to the regiment. Thus, except for occasional firing that lasted until about 9:00 P.M., the battle at Devil's Den and the Wheatfield ended for the day.[40]

General Crawford was in high spirits over the evening's success. To the commander of the Eleventh Reserves, he said with understandable exaggeration, "Colonel Jackson, you have saved the day, your regiment is worth its weight in gold; its weight in gold, sir!"[41] Crawford and McCandless saw that pickets were posted on front and flanks, and Crawford established his headquarters on a small, flat rock just behind the wall that sheltered the Reserves' line.[42] This done, he gave appropriate orders for the care of the wounded and sought some support from Sykes. Sykes had none to give him then but promised him some in the morning.[43]

The Federal accounts of their advance across Plum Run are probably essentially accurate from their point of view, but some Confederates, at least, saw things in a slightly different light. Maj. Henry D. McDaniel reported that the Eleventh Georgia advanced to the foot of the mountain and that nothing prevented the Georgians from carrying it but exhaustion. Captain Hillyer reported that the Ninth Georgia went to the base of Little Round Top and later recalled going up its slope. There, contrary to McDaniel's recollections, Hillyer remembered fifteen or twenty cannon on the crest (he was seeing triple), guarded by Zouaves, but with him there were several Confederate flags guarded by only thirty to forty men each. The Federal position on the hill was so formidable that by common consent the Confederates began to retire. As Hillyer retired, he met a captain of the Eleventh Georgia who said, "If you have been in there any further and could not do anything, there is no use for me to go." They then double-quicked together back to the wall. There the Ninth and the Eleventh, among others, collected together with some of Semmes's and Kershaw's units, reformed, retired with some dignity beyond the Wheatfield, took up a defensive position, and spent the night.[44]

So far things had gone pretty well for Crawford and his two brigades of Pennsylvania Reserves, but the day was not quite over for all of them. When Colonel Rice of the Forty-fourth New York took command of Vincent's brigade, the fighting on the south slope of Little Round Top had not yet slackened, and he had sent for help. The request somehow reached General Crawford as he formed his two brigades on the northwest slope of the hill. Crawford sent Col. John Fisher's Third Brigade to Rice's aid. Its four regiments—the Fifth, Ninth, Tenth, and Twelfth Pennsylvania Reserves—hurried left to Rice's position. Fisher's men arrived as the fighting on Vincent's brigade's front was ending but in time for some of them to fire a few parting shots and in time to assure the Confederates that further assaults on Little Round Top would be futile.[45]

It was then that Colonels Rice and Fisher realized that Round Top ought to be seized quickly and held. The Confederates on Rice's front had retreated in that direction and, though the Union colonels could not have known it, General Law was posting them across the lower slope of the hill south of Devil's Den. The Confederates piled up stone breastworks that may be seen there today.[46]

Expedient measures had saved Little Round Top for the Union but at the cost of organizational fragmentation. The three brigades on the hill, not counting those on its north slope, belonged to each of three different divisions of the Fifth Corps. Two of these three brigade's commanders were colonels, regimental commanders acting in the places of Weed and Vincent, and the third, Colonel Fisher, had just arrived. In short, there was no unifying commander below General Sykes, and he was elsewhere. Under the circumstances it is not at all surprising that Fisher sent for General Crawford, who he knew was not far away. On getting Fisher's summons, Crawford went to the south slope of the hill, where he met with a small group of officers that presumably included Colonel Rice. Fisher asked Crawford's permission to occupy the larger hill with Rice's cooperation. Crawford voiced no objection but said that they should do so at once. Crawford remained on Little Round Top until the effort began, and then he returned to what he must have deemed the place of greatest peril—the wall east of the Wheatfield. There he spent the night.[47]

After receiving Crawford's permission to occupy Round Top, Fisher and Rice took measures to do so. Fisher posted the Ninth and Tenth Reserves across the saddle between the two hills to block it, the right of the Ninth going in where the left of Vincent's brigade had been and the line of the two regiments stretching south from there about halfway to the summit of the larger hill. Then they began the occupation of the summit of Round Top itself. They planned to fight their way there if necessary. The Twentieth Maine, or what was left of it, deployed as skirmishers and moved out first, followed by the Fifth and Twelfth Reserves in line of battle behind it. Fisher was in charge.[48]

Both Cols. Martin D. Hardin of the Twelfth Reserves and Chamberlain of the Twentieth Maine agreed later that the plan resulted in a debacle. It was a graphic illustration of some reasons why Civil War battles usually were not fought at night. The men of the Twentieth Maine, formed as skirmishers, felt their way up the tree-covered and rocky slope as best they could. As they did, small parties of the enemy fell back before them. There was no firing until they neared the crest; then they received some scattered shots, one of which mortally wounded Lt. Arad H. Linscott. In its sweep, the Twentieth claimed the capture of twenty-five enlisted men and an officer said to belong to General Law's staff. After his regiment reached the crest, Chamberlain sent back to Rice for ammunition and support.[49]

Colonel Fisher, in "stentorian tones," ordered the two Reserves regiments forward behind the Twentieth Maine. Because of the darkness and the rocky, tree-covered slope, there was confusion immediately. By the time that the two regiments were a third of the way up the hill all was in chaos. Their once orderly lines were gone, their men scattered over the hillside. The woods resounded with shouts as officers tried to restore the lost formation. In later years, Colonel Hardin wryly expressed the belief that the chaos might have resulted in some good, for the Confederates assumed from all of the racket that the hillside was being occupied in strength by the Sixth Corps, and in trepidation they moved down the hill's slope to get away from it.[50] When the extent of the chaos became apparent, Fisher presumably decided that the two Pennsylvania regiments should return to the saddle, reform, and try again. This was not an easy thing to do; it is not every night that six hundred soldiers stumble around in the darkness in the virtual presence of the enemy, particularly in a place like Round Top's slope. In spite of all the obstacles, the Reserves reformed in the saddle and prepared to try again.[51]

In the meantime, Chamberlain was on the top of the hill and was at a loss to know what was happening below. Thinking that the noisy force there might be the enemy, he prepared to receive him. A tragic exchange of friendly fire was avoided when the Reserves returned to the base of the hill. "Feeling somewhat insecure in this isolated position," Chamberlain sent back to Rice for help, perhaps for a second time, and the Eighty-third Pennsylvania soon joined the Twentieth Maine. Colonel Rice might not have been coordinating well with Fisher, but he was taking care of his own brigade.[52]

By the time the Reserves were ready to try the hill again, the situation had changed. Fisher knew that the crest was in friendly hands and that there was no need to fight for it. Therefore the two regiments, led by a guide, simply filed to the top. There they deployed, the Twelfth on the crest, the Fifth down the slope toward the Tenth, and the Twentieth Maine as skirmishers in their front.[53] Colonel Oates's proposed bastion was now securely held by the Fifth Corps, though its defenders made no attempt to drag artillery to its summit. For all practical purposes, the Confederate threat to the Union left was at an end.

As Wofford's brigade surged toward the north slope of Little Round Top, Barksdale's right regiment, the Twenty-first Mississippi, crossed Plum Run and captured the four guns of Watson's battery that were in position up the slope from the Trostle house. The Mississippians tried to turn the pieces on the troops of Barnes's division, who could be seen rallying to their right in front of Wofford, but they did not have the equipment needed to fire them.[54]

The main line of Barksdale's brigade had not ascended the ridge as far as the Twenty-first, if indeed it scaled any of it at all. As a result of their victorious charge, the Thirteenth, Seventeenth, and Eighteenth Mississippi regiments reached Plum Run's swale fatigued and in some disorder. The swale was a broad trough sprinkled liberally with large, flat rocks and granite boulders and partially covered by a thicket. Although the swale might have provided cover for the first force that reached it, it would bring into disorder and slow any unit that attempted to attack or retreat across it.[55] Col. Thomas M. Griffin of the Eighteenth Mississippi took command of the three regiments there after Barksdale's fall and tried to restore order to the brigade's formation. It was at this time that he saw a Federal force bearing down on the remnant of these three Mississippi regiments.[56]

The approaching Federals were Col. George L. Willard's brigade of Hays's division, led south to support Birney's division. Hancock had brought it there through the "heavy fire of shell and canister . . . commingled with the bullets of a triumphant horde of rebels." Hancock met Birney on the ridge behind Humphreys's division and learned that the Third Corps had been smashed; there was little, then, that he could do as its new overseer but rally the fleeing fragments of Humphreys's division and hope that its men would put up some fight.[57] Hancock halted Willard's brigade on the ridge and ordered Willard to advance down the slope toward the swale and strike the Mississippians there a crippling blow.[58]

Willard's brigade was given an opportunity that its regiments ought to have been seeking for nine months—the chance to redeem themselves from the shame of having been surrendered at Harpers Ferry. A good showing at Gettysburg would do that, and it would also give them acceptance in the Second Corps. When Hancock ordered the brigade forward, it was so new to the corps that it had not yet acquired its brigade pennant, and its men did not have blue trefoil corps badges for their kepis.[59]

George Willard, the brigade's commander, was a New Yorker, thirty-five years old, and a descendant of generals in both the Revolutionary War and the War of 1812. When the Mexican War came, he enlisted in the Fifteenth Infantry and became a first sergeant. He received a commission in 1848, was a captain in the Eighth Infantry when the Civil War began, and in August 1862 took leave of a majority in the Nineteenth Infantry to become colonel of the 125th New York Regiment. One month later he and his regiment were among the Federal troops surrendered at Harpers Ferry, and his career went into limbo. Willard seemed to be an officer of great promise, but fate had given him little opportunity prior to Gettysburg to realize it. Hancock's order meant that a change might be at hand.[60]

Willard quickly deployed the brigade with the 126th New York on the right of the forward line, the 125th on the left, and the 111th in a support line two

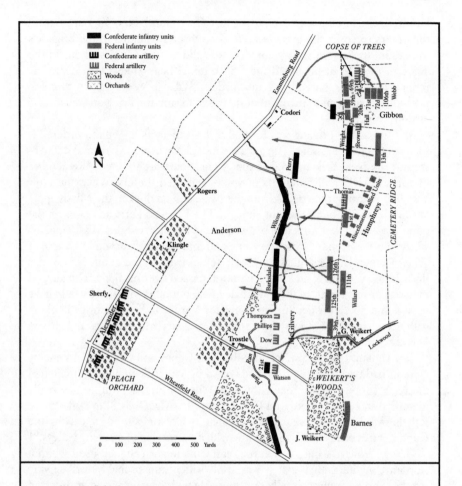

1. At sunset Federal troops are repulsing the Confederate attack in the area of the Round Tops.

2. Col. McGilvery sets up a line of artillery pieces east of the Trostle buildings to delay the Confederate advance there.

3. The Twenty-first Mississippi captures Watson's battery, but the Thirty-ninth New York retakes it.

4. Lockwood's brigade advances to the Trostle buildings and recovers four guns of Bigelow's battery.

5. Willard's brigade drives Barksdale's back beyond the Emmitsburg Road. Willard advances beyond Plum Run and recaptures four guns of Turnbull's battery. Alexander's guns near the Emmitsburg Road force Willard back.

6. The First Minnesota's attack stalls Wilcox's drive. Pressed by Willard's brigade on the right, the fire of Thomas's battery, and rallied troops of Humphreys's division, Wilcox falls back beyond the road.

7. Perry's brigade encounters resistance from troops of Gibbon's and Humphreys's divisions. When Colonel Lang learns of Wilcox's withdrawal, Lang orders the brigade back to Spangler's Woods.

8. The right wing of Wright's brigade reaches the crest of Cemetery Ridge. It is assailed by troops of Hall's and Webb's brigades, the Thirteenth Vermont Regiment, and others and is forced back. Many of Wright's men are captured near the Codori buildings.

9. The Thirteenth Vermont and rallied regiments of Gibbon's and Humphreys's divisions advance to the Emmitsburg Road and recover three guns of Weir's battery.

Map 16-2. The Repulse at the Union Center

hundred yards in the rear. He posted the Thirty-ninth New York apart from the others to cover the brigade's left. The three regiments in the brigade's formation dressed on their colors. As they did so, the Mississippians in the swale in their front peppered them with minié balls. The 125th nervously replied in kind, apparently without orders. Willard ordered them to cease fire, and officers ran to the front of their line to stop the firing and steady the anxious men.[61]

As soon as the brigade was formed to his satisfaction, Willard ordered it forward toward the swale. The advance must have been orderly and deliberate, for the New Yorkers fired as they went. Someone shouted, "Remember Harpers Ferry!" and hundreds of voices repeated the cry. When the New York line was about ten paces from the swale and its thicket, the Mississippians fired a volley, but it was not enough. The Harpers Ferry shoe was on the other foot. The New York line pressed ahead and hurried the Mississippians who did not surrender from the swale and into the fields beyond.[62] Some of Willard's men later said that Barksdale fell in front of the 126th New York's line, frantic with rage, and that a corporal passed over his body. The alleged rage was probably part of the Barksdale myth, but otherwise there would have been some poetic justice in the event, for it was Barksdale's brigade along with Kershaw's that drove the 126th from Maryland Heights at Harpers Ferry.[63]

The vigilant Hancock watched Willard's advance and saw peril. An enemy column had passed a hundred yards or so by Willard's right and threatened the New Yorkers' flank. Likely this was Wilcox's brigade, but no one really identified it. Hancock ordered Col. Clinton D. MacDougall to strike these Rebels with his 111th New York Regiment. MacDougall did so, driving the Confederates back from Willard's line with a succession of crashing volleys.[64]

George Willard's line, now three regiments long, realigned itself without stopping, an indication that it was well drilled and probably was moving slowly. It broke from the thicket of the swale with bayonets fixed and started up the slope toward the Emmitsburg Road after the retreating foe. The New Yorkers recaptured some guns, probably Turnbull's, and then encountered musketry from the right and artillery fire from Alexander's guns near the Emmitsburg Road. There were some who claimed that the 126th left the 111th and 125th regiments at the thicket and pursued the retreating Rebels alone. Perhaps this is true, though there would be disagreement about it. Capt. Orin J. Herendeen received credit for having recaptured one gun, but he had little time to glory in it, for he was killed the next day. Willard led his men 175 yards west of the swale, probably to a fence line that paralleled the Emmitsburg Road about 350 yards to the east. That was close enough to the Confederate batteries just off to the left—in fact, too close. The 126th about faced and marched to the rear, dragging the recaptured guns along. It passed through the swale, and just after Willard crossed Plum Run, a shell fragment tore away his face and a portion of his head. Col. Eliakim Sherrill of the

126th, who had been wounded in the face by a minié ball at Harpers Ferry, then took command of the brigade and returned it to Hays's division. Later, in reporting on the conduct of this brigade at Gettysburg, Alexander Hays wrote: "The history of this brigade's operations is written in blood. . . . The acts of traitors at Harper's Ferry had not tainted their patriotism."[65]

In the meantime, as he paused on the slope above the Trostle farmyard, Col. Benjamin Humphreys believed that his Twenty-first Mississippi Regiment had cut the Federal army in two. He stood at Watson's captured battery and saw no Federal troops in his front, but any feeling of triumph that he might have had was short lived. As he prepared to take the Twenty-first Mississippi to the left to rejoin Barksdale's line, he saw Willard's troops drive it from the swale back toward the Emmitsburg Road. He saw too that Wofford's and Kershaw's brigades were drawing back on his right. Most pressing of all, he saw a Federal force marching in his direction. Therefore, instead of shifting north, he ordered the Twenty-first back to the Trostle farm buildings.[66]

That was the Confederate view of things, but there is more to the story. As Colonel Humphreys reformed the Twenty-first Mississippi and pondered his course of action, Lt. Samuel Peeples, an officer of Watson's battery, tried to find some infantry that would help him recapture Watson's guns. He spoke to two brigade commanders, probably from the Third or Fifth corps, and found that they would not assist him. As Peeples was standing on a boulder to get a better view of what was happening, Capt. John B. Fasset, one of Birney's aides, rode by. Peeples hailed him and pointed to the four three-inch rifles in the Mississippians' hands. He asked Fasset for help in getting some troops to retake them. Fasset asked him how many were needed. Peeples said a regiment, and Fasset galloped off.[67]

Fasset soon met Maj. Hugo Hildebrandt and his Thirty-ninth New York Regiment where Willard had posted it to guard his brigade's left. Fasset pointed to the four cannon and ordered Hildebrandt to retake them in the name of General Birney. Hildebrandt declined, saying that he was not in General Birney's command. Fasset asked him to which command his unit belonged (the men of the Thirty-ninth had no corps badges). Hildebrandt replied Hancock's. Fasset, undaunted, then ordered Hildebrandt to retake the guns by order of General Hancock. That satisfied Hildebrandt's sense of fitness, and he ordered the Garibaldi Guard to march to the left flank. When it reached a point on the ridge above the battery, Hildebrandt deployed the Thirty-ninth's four companies into a line and ordered them to charge. Lt. Samuel Peeples, with a rifle in hand, led the Thirty-ninth's advance.[68]

The New Yorkers believed that they had driven the Twenty-first from Watson's guns, and the Confederates admitted to having received a long-range volley from them.[69] Surely the Twenty-first would have fallen back sooner or later, but the advance of the fresh Thirty-ninth New York must have convinced Colonel Humphreys that the Twenty-first had nothing to gain from tarrying by Watson's guns, which they could neither fire nor readily drag away.[70] Hildebrandt and the Thirty-ninth got little credit for what they had done; in fact, there were those who later confused Watson's guns with Turnbull's and wrote that the Thirty-ninth had recovered only two of them. Fasset received a Medal of Honor thirty years after the battle for his part in the action, and Peeples received more immediate if less distinctive recognition. Sykes wrote in his Fifth Corps report that Peeples "richly deserves promotion for his conduct, and I trust the government will not withhold it." The government did not. In its generosity the War Department made Second Lieutenant Peeples a brevet first lieutenant, a hollow honor at best.[71]

Col. Benjamin Humphreys had a little consolation for his frustrations. Someone gave him a captured horse that he wrongly thought must have belonged to Captain Bigelow but that more likely had been Lieutenant Erickson's. Someone also gave him a spyglass and a satchel that was said to have been taken from the body of an artillery colonel found beside a Napoleon. The satchel contained a photograph of two teenage boys. Humphreys tried to identify the colonel but could not—he could not have known it, but no artillery colonels had fallen on that front. Perhaps it belonged to Erickson too. Humphreys lost the spyglass in Chickamauga Creek, and after the battle of Chickamauga someone stole the satchel.[72]

As Willard's brigade advanced against Barksdale's, the First Division of the Twelfth Corps marched from Culp's Hill toward the left center of the Union line. General Meade had asked for Williams's division, and Slocum sent it.[73] Brig. Gen. Alpheus S. Williams, the division's commander, believed that he was still the acting corps commander, as Slocum still considered himself the commander of the army's right wing. Williams therefore ordered Brig. Gen. Thomas H. Ruger to take the division left to Cemetery Ridge. To avoid any question of rank that might develop between Ruger and Lockwood, Williams went along. Lockwood's two regiments led the way, and the division's Third and First brigades followed in that order.[74]

Lockwood's two regiments were large ones (the 150th New York had about six hundred officers and men) and were new to battle. Their uniforms were in a respectable condition, and their equipment was little worn. They set off promptly and, having no guide, followed Granite Schoolhouse Lane toward the sound of battle. They hiked along in a column of fours, cartridge boxes full and blanket rolls slung across their shoulders. But the evening was warm, the men of the brigade were new to soldiering in the field, and their excitement mounted as they heard the growing sound of gunfire in their front and met a growing stream of wounded men and stragglers heading toward the rear. Some, fellow New Yorkers without doubt, greeted the 150th with shouts of "Go in, Dutchess County! Give it to them, boys! Give it to them!" Excitement bred carelessness, and soon the men of the 150th were tossing their blanket rolls away along the road.[75] The column turned south along the Taneytown Road, and soon after, Maj. William G. Mitchell, Hancock's senior aide, rode up to General Meade with a request for troops to go in on Willard's left. Meade apparently offered him the Twelfth Corps division and asked him where it should go. Mitchell replied that if it moved by the right flank, it would be in the right spot to strike the enemy. This was done.[76]

There were those who wrote later that General Meade had personally led Lockwood's brigade to its position. They included Major Biddle, his aide, Hancock, and Captain Meade, the general's aide. Meade could have done this, or at least directed Lockwood's brigade on its way, but General Williams and other Twelfth Corps officers made no mention of Meade's doing so in their reports and writings. Williams did write of arriving on Cemetery Ridge, seeing signs of battle, and following a line of woods, perhaps the north edge of Weikert's Woods, until an artillery officer rode up to him and asked him for his help. This officer, of course, was Lieutenant Colonel McGilvery, who had known Williams during previous campaigns and was delighted to see him there. McGilvery knew that his thrown-together line of guns had disintegrated, leaving only Dow's battery and a section of Thompson's battery in action there. In response to McGilvery's hurried briefing, Williams ordered Lockwood to deploy and "occupy the woods," the woods in this instance probably being the west end of Trostle's Woods and the orchard beside it, where Bigelow's guns had been.[77]

Lockwood sent his regiments forward immediately. The leading regiment, the First Maryland, Potomac Home Brigade, did not even take the time to deploy from column into line. The 150th, which had fallen behind, followed in the Marylanders' support. They advanced at the double-quick, part of the way at least, down to the Trostle farmyard and perhaps a little beyond. While the First Maryland kept its attention to the front, the 150th collected three of Bigelow's captured guns. The infantrymen received help later when the limbers of Seeley's battery sent down by McGilvery brought off the fourth piece. It was fortunate that Lockwood's charge met little resistance, for it was conducted with the bravery and the skill of the inexperienced. A veteran Confederate unit might have given it a long and sadly remembered initiation into the art of war. As it was, the charges by Willard's and Lockwood's brigades must have been a bitter pill for McLaws's men to swallow, for they signaled the end of an opportunity that would never come again.[78]

Williams deployed his remaining two brigades on Lockwood's left, probably fronting Weikert's Woods, in "lines of masses." He prepared to send them forward, but by the time they were ready, it was apparent that the enemy had pulled back and that an advance in the growing darkness would be folly. The Twelfth Corps had provided impressive insurance for a brief time, but Williams learned from both Sedgwick and Sykes that his division was no longer required on the left. It was well that this was the case, because trouble had developed on Culp's Hill, and the division was needed badly in the position that it had vacated.[79]

To the north Hancock met General Humphreys on the slope of the ridge and directed him to reform his retreating division where Caldwell's had been. Humphreys reported that this was done. In Hancock's recollection, Humphreys's small force was "scarcely equal to an ordinary battalion, but with many colors," the small command being composed of many shattered regiments.[80] Hancock rode north a little farther and saw a line of infantry stumbling through the thicket of the swale, an indistinct line blurred by the darkness and the smoke. He took it for a Union regiment in retreat, and with Capt. William D. Miller, his remaining aide, Hancock spurred forward to rally it. Its men greeted him with shots fired at close range that luckily missed him but that wounded Miller in two places. Hancock shouted for Miller to get out of there and quickly reined his horse into a somewhat sheltered place that gave him a little cover. Both officers got away.[81]

Hancock's flight carried him to one of his own Second Corps regiments, the First Minnesota of Harrow's brigade, which was posted in support of Thomas's battery. Thomas's was probably the "lower" battery that had been pounding away at Wilcox's brigade.[82] Wilcox's Tenth, Eleventh, and Fourteenth regiments were to charge it, but by the time they had passed through the swale, their lines were jumbled and they had lost their momentum. They were taking fire from Thomas's guns, from the rifles of the 111th New York Regiment, and possibly from Third Corps troops rallying on their right. Colonel Forney of the Tenth Alabama fell just short of the swale with his second wound of the afternoon, and Lt. Col. Lucius Pinckard and Col. John C. C. Sanders of the Fourteenth and Eleventh Alabama regiments also suffered severe wounds. Capt. J. Horace King, commander of the Ninth Alabama had a finger shot away. Lieutenant Colonel Herbert of the Eighth Alabama was the only regimental commander of Wilcox's brigade to emerge unscathed that day, and he was not initially on this line. By the time the Eighth Alabama closed up on the brigade's right, Herbert saw a horseman who he believed, upon later reflection, was Hancock and engaged some attacking troops at the range of forty yards. Some of Wilcox's men passed beyond the swale and began to ascend the slope, but theirs was a forlorn hope. Wilcox sent back to General Anderson for help, but none came.[83]

Col. William Colvill, Jr., and the officers and men of the First Minnesota Regiment must have watched the oncoming Confederates with great foreboding. By then a red setting sun glowed dimly over the smoke-covered field and the Third Corps retreat. They saw first an orderly withdrawal that disintegrated progressively to fleeing clusters and then to individuals harried back to the thickety swale by yelling Rebels. It seemed to them that only they and Thomas's battery stood against the entire Army of Northern Virginia. Then General Hancock appeared out of the smoke, followed by the wounded Captain Miller. Hancock reined in his horse and looked at the 262 officers and enlisted men in the eight-company line and bellowed in disbelief, "My God! Are these all of the men we have here? What regiment is this?" "First Minnesota," Colvill replied. Pointing toward Wilcox's line and a flag that led it, probably that of the Eleventh Alabama, Hancock shouted, "Advance, Colonel, and take those colors!"[84]

There was no time for delay, no time for the field officers to get their horses that were waiting only a short distance off. The First was already in line, bayonets fixed and rifles at right shoulder shift.[85] Colvill ordered the Minnesotans forward at the double-quick, and the regiment jogged off at a slow trot, carefully preserving its line as it descended the slope toward the Alabamians in the thicket 150 yards away. The First received a galling fire, and it was apparent to each man that there were long odds against his coming through the fight unscathed. The pace picked up as the First's line neared the thicket, and at Colvill's command to charge, the regiment covered the last few yards with bayonets leveled.[86]

The sight of a well-disciplined line approaching almost relentlessly with bayonets fixed was more than the men of Wilcox's scrambled line could bear. They broke and fell back on their better-ordered support line, halting its advance and throwing it too into some disorder. Colvill halted the First when it reached the stream bed, and the First Minnesota fired a volley into the very faces of the Confederates in its front. This won the Minnesotans a temporary advantage. The firing became general, and the men of the First took cover behind rocks and in Plum Run's shallow bed. They loaded and fired at will. The longer lines of the Alabamians gradually enfolded the men in blue. As one wing encircled the First's right, Company I swung back to face it. Lt. Waldo Farrar reported his company's move to Colonel Colvill, who told him to have his men lie down. They did, but it is likely that Farrar remained standing, for he was soon killed. A ball hit Colonel Colvill in the foot; and Lt. Col. Charles P. Adams, Maj. Mark N. Downie, and numerous company-grade officers and enlisted men fell.[87]

Fortunately for the First Minnesota, Wilcox could not or did not organize a counterattack. Colvill's onslaught, the lesser assaults, and the threat of more attacks loomed large in Wilcox's mind. He sent for aid and none came. With a little support, and perhaps some luck, as he concluded after the battle, his brigade might have pushed on to the crest. But there was no additional support, and he saw no Confederates advancing to cover his brigade's flanks. So he ordered his regiments back to avoid their destruction or capture. In his report of the battle General Lee said that Wilcox's brigade had been "compelled" to retire, but the punctilious Wilcox would not accept that phraseology. Like Wofford's, his men were not "compelled" to fall back; he had ordered them back because he saw no hope of their going forward or of their staying where they were.[88]

Sensing a reduction in pressure on the First Minnesota, Colonel Colvill ordered Capt. Nathan N. Messick to take the regiment back to the crest of the ridge. It would have to be a hurried retreat, and Colvill could not go. Messick rushed those who could run back to the crest. When they collected there, only forty-seven officers and men were with the colors. In an action

Col. George L. Willard (MOLLUS-MASS/
U.S.A.M.H.I., *Carlisle Barracks, Pa.)*

Col. William Colvill, Jr. (MOLLUS-MASS/   Col. Francis V. Randall
U.S.A.M.H.I., Carlisle Barracks, Pa.)

lasting fifteen minutes, 215 of the First Minnesota's 262 officers and men—
82 percent of those who had charged—had fallen on the slope or in the swale
among the Alabamians. Most, like Colvill, were wounded and would survive,
but forty died. The First Minnesota had not captured the Alabama battle flag
as Hancock had ordered it to do, but it had stalled Wilcox's attack and kept it
from the ridge. In doing so the First Minnesota had "sustained the greatest
percentage of loss of any Union regiment at Gettysburg, or during the war."[89]
Hancock wrote later that he could not "speak too highly of this regiment and
its commander in its attack," but it is unlikely that the general tarried long to
see the outcome of its effort. He hurried off to take care of the other threats
that demanded his attention.[90]

The Florida Brigade advanced on Wilcox's left. The seven hundred Floridians had driven all before them on their narrow front and had bashed in
Humphreys's right. When the Floridians reached "a small eminence" at the
foot of the ridge—the brush and rocks of the swale did not reach north into
their zone—they paused to get their second breath and reform their lines. As
they did this, some Union troops, probably remnants of Humphreys's division, gathered in a grove on the crest about fifty yards to their front. The
Bluecoats poured a heavy fire down on the Floridians, and the Floridians
returned it. At this time an aide told Colonel Lang that a heavy force was
advancing against Wilcox. A little later Lang heard that Wilcox's brigade was
falling back and that the enemy was advancing beyond his right. Lang walked
to the right to see for himself. Yes, the enemy (perhaps Willard) had passed
his right flank about a hundred yards and threatened to surround his little
force. Considering discretion the better part of valor, Lang ordered the
Floridians to fall back to the Emmitsburg Road. Finding no suitable cover
there, he ordered the brigade back to its starting place in Spangler's Woods.[91]

In his report of the day's fighting, General Wright complained that when
his brigade reached the ridge crest to the left of Perry's brigade, he found that
the Floridians had not crossed the road and were falling back, that Posey's
brigade had not advanced, and that his Georgians were entirely unsupported
on both right and left. He was wrong about the Floridians' not having crossed
the road, but he was basically correct on other counts. What had happened to
Anderson's alleged promise that Posey would support the Georgians' left?
Unfortunately, Anderson's report gives no clue. It does not acknowledge that
Posey's brigade failed to cross the road, and suggests that Posey's was the
last brigade to fall back from the front. A. P. Hill's report recognized that
Wright's, Perry's, and Wilcox's brigades advanced and had some success but
that, having received no reinforcements, they had to fall back. But Hill too
failed to state why reinforcements were not sent.[92]

Hill's role in the battle of Gettysburg is an enigma, and none of his actions
are more enigmatic than those of the late afternoon of 2 July. His headquarters were at the Emanuel Pitzer farmhouse, a large brick building behind the
center of his line and about four hundred yards west of Seminary Ridge. But

if Colonel Fremantle is correct, Hill spent a lot of time that afternoon in the company of General Lee. Hill gave General Anderson his division's orders about noon and later asked Colonel Walker to have his corps's artillery aid Longstreet's attack as much as possible. Just what General Hill did during Longstreet's assault is recorded only in a fragmentary way. After McLaws's division had advanced and gone beyond the Peach Orchard and when Anderson's brigades must have been advancing, Hill rode down the front of Pegram's battalion to the rear of McLaws's division. Capt. William W. Chamberlaine, who was with him, reported only that they had an exciting gallop and that they rallied some Confederates who were falling back in twos and threes.[93] There must have been more to this ride than Chamberlaine recorded, but we do not know what it was.

In contrast to Generals Lee, Hill, and Anderson, who seemed to remain essentially passive, General Meade and his principal commanders continued to be very active. Sometime after seeing General Sickles, Meade replaced General Pleasonton's horse with his own mount, Baldy, and Baldy was shot.[94] After arranging for the security of the Union left, Meade returned to the Leister house. It was during Anderson's assault that Capt. John C. Tidball, commander of the Second Brigade, Horse Artillery, saw him there. For reasons not clear, Tidball had been on Cemetery Ridge and had seen Union soldiers fleeing over it while First Corps units sat quietly behind Cemetery Hill. This seemed wrong to him. He found General Meade at his headquarters, temporarily alone, seemingly awaiting news of the battle's progress. Tidball spoke to the general of what he had seen. Meade said something to Tidball that led the captain to believe that he thought the Sixth Corps would take care of the matter. But it seems unlikely that Meade would have believed this—perhaps he was referring to Williams's division. Tidball called Meade's attention to the First Corps troops nearby, and the general told Tidball to ask General Newton to send them to Cemetery Ridge, where they were needed. As Tidball crossed the Taneytown Road to find Newton, he saw General Meade riding south toward the danger point on the ridge.[95]

Tidball found General Newton without delay, and soon Newton sent orders to both Generals Doubleday and Robinson to shift their divisions from the reverse slope of Cemetery Hill to the Second Corps front on Cemetery Ridge.[96] The Thirteenth Vermont Regiment was the first to get orders to move. This was the high point in the regiment's nine months of service, and it was recalled and recounted with relish in later years. The Thirteenth's men had been disturbed by Confederate shelling that day, but Generals Doubleday and Stannard rode among them calmly and had spent some time nearby, standing on a wall, watching the battle's progress through their binoculars. As the fighting spread toward the Union center, Col. Francis Randall mounted his horse and was ready for action.[97] Randall was not disappointed. An officer rode in his direction "with all speed." It was General Doubleday. Said Doubleday, "Colonel what regiment do you command?"

"The 13th Vermont, Sir," replied Randall. "Where is General Stannard?" asked Doubleday. Randall pointed to a clump of trees in the distance, too far for Doubleday to reach in a short time. Doubleday, who did not yet know the Vermonters, then asked, "Colonel will your regiment fight?" Randall answered, "I believe they will sir." He then went on to say that he had been in a number of battles but that the Thirteenth had been in none. However, he had great confidence in it. Doubleday asked Randall to introduce him to the five companies at hand. He did so, and Doubleday gave them a pep talk. The Vermonters responded with cheers. Doubleday then ordered Randall to take his men and report to General Hancock. After Randall was on his way, Doubleday went on to give Stannard orders for the rest of the brigade to follow.[98]

As the Thirteenth Vermont filed into the Taneytown Road and headed south, General Meade and some of his staff officers were nearing the danger point. (Apparently Meade had not been so alone as Tidball thought.) Some of the staff had ridden on ahead, and those with the general were about to gallop off when he stopped them. "Not so fast, gentlemen, not so fast," said the general as he rode along at a sedate pace. When they reached the endangered portion of the line, they saw Floridians and Georgians coming in their direction. It would be touch and go. Who would arrive first in strength, the enemy or the numerous reinforcements that had been ordered up? In the meantime only the army commander and a few members of his staff seemed to be plugging the gap. The general was anxious; he nervously straightened himself in the saddle as though to ride against the advancing line, and his staff mirrored his attitude. As they awaited the onslaught, one officer wondered why the enemy did not shoot them down.[99]

The scene that filled the general's eyes must be beyond the imagination of twentieth-century man, for he has never seen anything like it. Peter F. Rothermel and other artists have tried to depict such events, but the scale of their works is small, and they can appeal only to the sense of sight. The viewers of these paintings cannot feel the fear, excitement, anger, and responsibility of those who were a part of the actual scene. There was the ever-present bitter smoke that blanketed the area, blurring and obscuring features that ought to have been clearly seen. It was evening and the sun was setting behind South Mountain to the west in the attackers' rear, adding its reddish glow to the flashes of rifles and cannons. There was ear-splitting booming and barking from nearby artillery, duller thumping by the Confederate guns in the distance, and a roar produced by thousands of muskets near and far. There were individual and mass Federal cheers, as in a stadium, competing with high-pitched, distant Rebel yells and the screams of wounded horses. There was all of this and more. Whether it deadened or quickened the senses is hard to say.

More to the point, Wright's Georgians surged behind their red battle flags over the wall and across the broad crest. In his report, Wright wrote of driving

Federals from the heights and into a rocky gorge eighty to a hundred yards east of the batteries. That was not exactly true. When Hancock later read that Wright's men had crossed the crest, he jotted a marginal notation, "Not quite! I think!"[100]

Veterans and battlefield commissioners did not mark the point of Wright's penetration on 2 July as they marked the site of Pickett's "high water mark" on 3 July. But some conclusions may be drawn about its location from the fragmentary information at hand. First of all, the main line of Hall's brigade on the north shoulder of the gap consisted of the Fifty-ninth New York and the Seventh Wisconsin regiments; and, according to the regiments' flank markers, their line extended along the ridge's forward slope about ninety yards south from the Copse of Trees. The Fifty-ninth, with a front of about forty yards, was on the right, the Seventh on the left.

Since Wright's brigade had a strength of about 1,450, it seems safe to assume that its three regiments and scattered portions of the Second Battalion had a cumulative strength of at least 1,000 as they assaulted the ridge and that each regiment had a front of about a hundred yards. Wright's left regiment, the Forty-eighth Georgia, apparently struck the front of the Fifty-ninth New York, for Sgt. James Wiley of the Fifty-ninth captured its colors and received a Medal of Honor for doing so.[101] If the Forty-eighth's colors were near the center of its line, the regiment's right flank, fifty yards away, could have been opposite almost any portion of the Seventh Wisconsin's line but was probably somewhere near its left and the edge of the gap. If this were so, the Third and Twenty-second Georgia regiments, on the Georgia brigade's right, were opposite the gap and had little opposition in their front. They could have charged onto the ridge somewhere between one and three hundred yards south of the Copse of Trees, and many of them would have penetrated much further than Pickett's men did on the following day.

The reaction of Gibbon's division to Wright's assault was positive and violent. Arnold's and Cushing's batteries raked the Georgians' left with shell and canister after Brown's battery and the men from Harrow's advanced line moved from their fields of fire. Lt. Samuel Canby of Cushing's battery received a hand wound and 1st Sgt. Frederick Fuger took command of Canby's section, a significant step up for Fuger, who commanded the battery after Cushing's death the next day. In a short time the gunners' visibility became so poor that Gibbon ordered his batteries to cease fire for fear that they might hit his infantrymen.[102]

When Wright's brigade pressed on to the ridge, it presented its right flank to some of Humphreys's men who had rallied and its left to Webb's brigade. Webb's men had no major pressures in their front to distract them and had a field day tearing at Wright's left flank. Once Brown's battery had cleared its front, the Sixty-ninth Pennsylvania "receive[d] the advancing foe . . . with a defiant shout, as they shake out the folds of their green flag and pour a withering fire at short range into the faces of their adversaries." They fired

Brig. Gen. William Harrow
(National Archives)

Col. Norman J. Hall (MOLLUS-MASS/ U.S.A.M.H.I., Carlisle Barracks, Pa.)

Brig. Gen. Alexander S. Webb (National Archives)

volley after volley, impeded only by their excitement, the smoke, and the thickets to their left front, which must have concealed portions of the Rebel column from their view.[103]

The fire of the Sixty-ninth made the Confederate line waver, and Webb ordered his three remaining regiments forward from their positions behind the crest of the ridge. The Seventy-first Pennsylvania went ahead to the left of the Sixty-ninth and recaptured the gun from Brown's battery that had been left in front of the wall. The Seventy-second remained in a support line, probably behind the Copse of Trees. Its commander, Col. DeWitt C. Baxter was wounded there. Companies A and B of the 106th Pennsylvania were on the skirmish line firing at Posey's men, but the rest of the regiment advanced through Cushing's guns at Webb's order and fired several volleys at a range of about sixty yards. When the Confederate line in its front wavered, the 106th fixed bayonets and charged.[104] The men of the 106th went over the wall with a cheer and double-quicked down the slope toward Brown's captured Napoleons and the Emmitsburg Road. They drove the Confederates in their front back beyond the road, captured about twenty of them, and recovered Brown's three guns. While the 106th was at the gun position, Companies A and B, which had been off to the right in front of Posey's brigade, passed back by its right to the rear.[105]

Lt. Col. William L. Curry halted the 106th at the road. It was alone there except for a remnant of the Eighty-second New York off to its right that Wright's brigade had brushed aside. As the men of the 106th approached the road, they spied a Confederate officer at the Codori buildings to their left waving a white handkerchief. Curry asked Capt. Robert H. Ford to take his company over to the Codori buildings and see what the Confederates wanted. Ford stuck a sheet of newspaper on a bayonet, and, under that flag of truce, Ford and his company approached the Confederate officer for a parley. The officer, Capt. Claiborne Snead of the Third Georgia, told Ford that Col. William Gibson of the Forty-eighth Georgia had been wounded badly. Gibson was at the Codori farmyard, and if he did not get immediate medical attention would surely die. Snead said also that much of that regiment was there. Ford demanded their surrender, but Snead refused—he wanted to march those able to walk back to the Confederate line.[106] Ford insisted on their surrender. Snead, knowing that he had no other alternative, capitulated. With Snead's surrender, the 106th claimed to have captured Colonel Gibson and over two hundred other Georgians, including twenty captains and lieutenants. Even if enlarged by the excitement of the hour, it was a big take that probably deserves more attention than it has received.[107]

Colonel Curry sent an officer back to General Webb for orders. When that officer did not return, Curry went himself. He asked for support if the 106th was to remain at the road. Webb told him to post a skirmish line there and return the regiment to the crest. Ten minutes or so after the 106th reached the crest, Webb sent it to assist the Eleventh Corps on Culp's Hill, and it remained there for the duration of the battle.[108]

As the 106th Pennsylvania was advancing against Wright's flank, Hall's two little regiments blasted away at the head of the column. The Georgians had had some cover when they were behind the thickets in front of Hall's line, but when they emerged from cover, they received Hall's regiments's scathing fire. Some of the Georgians reached Brown's guns thirty yards to the left of the Seventh Michigan. A color-bearer planted his flag there, and the men of the Seventh later found his body pierced by a dozen minié balls. Like many others that day, some of Hall's men believed that General Barksdale had fallen in their front. When it became apparent to some of the Georgians that they could neither advance nor retreat, they threw down their rifles and crawled toward Hall's line and capture.[109] But the casualties were not all on the Confederate side. One of Hall's brigade's major losses was Lt. Col. Max Thoman, commander of the Fifty-ninth New York, who was nicknamed "Jack of Diamonds." Thoman lived long enough to request that he be buried on the field.[110]

The Twentieth Massachusetts, in Hall's support line, found Brown's three guns to be almost as troublesome as the Georgians. First, after they returned through the gap in the wall, the guns ran through the Twentieth's line. Then one went into position so close behind the Twentieth that its muzzle blasts burned the infantrymen in its front. The support of Brown's guns here was a mixed blessing.[111]

As Wright's brigade surged into the gap on the left of Hall's brigade, General Meade

> straightens himself in his stirrups, as do also the aides who now ride closer to him, bracing themselves to meet the crisis. It is in the minds of those who follow him that he is going to throw himself into the breach— anything to gain a few moments' time. Suddenly someone cries out, "There they come, general!" and looking to the right, Newton is seen galloping in advance of Doubleday's division, followed by Robinson.[112]

No one shouted, "General Meade to the rear!" or if anyone did, no one mentioned it. General Newton drew rein beside Meade and asked for orders. There was a hurried conversation; then Newton pulled out a flask and offered it to the commanding general. As he did so, a shell burst in the earth nearby and showered them with dirt, but this sprinkling "did not seem to interfere in any way with the important duty under consideration."[113]

As the generals conversed in the enemy's presence, the First Corps came on "in close column by division, at a sharp double quick, with muskets at right shoulder, the two divisions sweep down the Taneytown Road, swing around to the right, and as, amid the wildest excitement and shouting, they press forward to the line of battle, Meade rides ahead with the skirmish line, waving his hat, saying to those about him, 'Come on, gentlemen.' "[114] General Meade did not ride very far. An officer from the staff of the provost marshal rode up with the erroneous report that a strong Confederate force was massing in their front, presumably beyond the general's view. General Meade ordered the First Corps units to halt on the ridge crest.[115] Meade might have halted the First Corps reinforcements for that reason, of course, but Wright's troops were falling back by this time, and it seems likely that he would have halted Newton's men on the ridge instead of letting them assume the risk of a counterattack in the growing darkness.

Newton's order, however, did not affect Colonel Randall of the Thirteenth Vermont, whose battalion had preceded the remainder of the First Corps units and who reported to General Hancock. Hancock pointed across the fields to Weir's captured guns and, in the manner of his order to Colonel Colvill, shouted to Randall, "The enemy are pressing me hard—they have just captured that battery yonder . . . and are dragging it from the field. Can you retake it?" The irrepressible Randall replied, "I can, and damn quick too, if you will let me." Randall thought that Hancock was reluctant to let him, but the general said that Randall could try. That was enough for Randall, who could not have been more pleased.[116]

By this time, Randall's five companies of the Thirteenth Vermont had arrived. Randall deployed them into line, told his company commanders what he intended to do, rode to the front, and ordered them forward.[117] The Thirteenth Vermont went off at the double-quick, Randall leading the way on his gray horse. They jogged down the slope toward Weir's guns at the left of the Codori barn. Capt. John Lonergan's Company A was giving an "Irish yell." A bullet hit Randall's horse in the neck, and the animal fell, pinning the colonel to the ground. Randall must have sworn vigorously, and when he saw that the Thirteenth's line had paused, he shouted, "Go on boys I'll be at your head as soon as I get out of this damned saddle." The line continued on, but some men broke ranks to pull the horse off the colonel's leg. Randall jumped quickly to his feet and ran to catch up with his five companies, which must have slowed their pace by now. Randall rounded the flank of the line, limping, hat off, and waving his sword around his head. When he had the breath to do so, he shouted, "I am all right. Come on boys, follow me." The Thirteenth obeyed.[118]

An enemy line fired a volley at the Thirteenth but did it little injury. The Vermonters' charge was so sudden and overpowering that some of the Georgians threw themselves to the ground in surrender, and the Fifteenth's line passed over them. The ubiquitous Hancock, who was following in the Thirteenth's wake, shouted for Randall to go on ahead and said that he would take care of the prisoners. The Thirteenth charged on to Weir's guns with more enthusiasm than order, at least on the part of Colonel Randall and Captain Lonergan. Randall later wrote a letter on behalf of Lonergan's getting the Medal of Honor for the capture of the guns. In it he stated that Randall was the first to reach the guns and that he grabbed hold of one with one hand and wielded his sword with the other. Captain Lonergan, whose bravery he commended, was the first man, then, to reach his side![119]

After retaking Weir's guns, Randall led his men on to the Emmitsburg Road. He then sent his adjutant, Lt. James S. Peck, to tell Hancock where the Thirteenth was to be found. Before Peck returned, two pieces of artillery began to shell Randall's line from the high ground along the Emmitsburg Road to the left. Randall sent Lonergan and his company to capture them, which he claimed that they did. (This is a very dubious claim. What guns would they have been? The Confederates lost none.) Randall claimed also that Lonergan's company captured three officers and eighty men from the Rogers, or perhaps the Klingle, farmyard. Randall identified the Confederates as being from a "rebel picket reserve." As the Confederates were taken into custody, Randall advised them to "remember you were captured by Colonel Randall of the 13th Vermont."[120]

After the action at the Rogers house, Randall received Hancock's orders for him to return his companies to the main line. He complied, but only up to a point. It was now practically dark, but Randall halted his men about a hundred yards from the Union line and told them to lie down and rest. In due course, a staff officer appeared, and Randall reportedly said to him, "Captain, report to your General what we have done. We have recaptured six guns, taken two from the enemy, driven him a half mile and taken a hundred prisoners. Also tell him we propose staying here until he acknowledges our achievements." With that modest declaration by a colonel from a state known for its taciturn inhabitants, the captain rode away. Randall saw fit not to wait for his return because word came, wrongly, that the enemy was trying to flank them. Preferring to "loose [*sic*] his laurels rather than spend the Fall in Libby prison," Randall led his force back to the main line. They were welcomed there by the cheers of the Vermonters left behind and received the thanks of General Doubleday. Doubleday testified later that "they apologized to me for not halting, and I accepted the apology."[121]

Randall's advance had signaled a change in the flow of battle at the Union center. The remnants of Humphreys's division, the Nineteenth Maine, and two regiments of Col. Roy Stone's brigade, First Corps, which were in the rear of Humphreys's line, perceived the change and advanced. Humphreys testified that they did so without orders, at least without his, and Carr and Brewster were noncommittal about any orders that they gave. Colonel Heath of the Nineteenth Maine ordered his regiment forward, and the Nineteenth charged "like a tornado let loose." The Excelsiors raised the spontaneous shout, "Boys, let's go back and get those guns!" and they advanced with cheers and in disorder.[122]

Carr's brigade, now on the left, went back to the Emmitsburg Road to the position it occupied before the Confederate assault began. Brewster's Excelsiors, the Nineteenth Maine, and Stone's 149th and 150th Pennsylvania regiments charged into the area south of the Codori barn. All claimed the capture of Weir's guns, which must already have been retaken by Randall's men. Sgt. Thomas Hogan of the Seventy-second New York somehow secured the colors of the Eighth Florida, which he presented to General Humphreys.[123]

The counterattacking regiments halted their advance near the road. When the Nineteenth Maine reached a point in that area, a staff officer rode up and asked Colonel Heath where the Nineteenth Maine was going. Heath replied, "We are chasing the 'rebs,' " and the officer advised him to go no farther. The First and Second corps laid tenuous claim to the area retaken with a picket line, and most of the attacking regiments returned to Cemetery Ridge.[124]

Brewster's Excelsiors started to haul Weir's three guns to the rear, dragging them with prolonges. They reached a ditch that was hard to cross and found two Confederates, a captain and a private, lying in it. Captain Rafferty of the Seventy-first New York pointed his revolver at them and ordered them to their feet. The Confederate captain asked what he wanted them to do. "Do?" replied Rafferty, "do anything to make yourself useful. There, take hold and help drag out that gun."[125]

The fighting in front of Cemetery Ridge was over for the day, and the terrain gained by the Confederates through their assault had been limited to that held by Sickles's advanced line. Essentially all of the Army of the

Potomac was on the field, its line on Cemetery Ridge was still intact, and its position was stronger than it had been when the Confederate assault began. After his division halted its movement near the George Weikert house, Brig. Gen. Alpheus Williams rode along the ridge in search of someone who could give him further orders. He found General Meade surrounded by a large number of officers. He learned from them that the Army of the Potomac had repelled enemy attacks all along the line and had punished the Confederate attackers severely. All were greatly relieved. In Williams's recollection, "gratification and gratulation abounded." It was at about this time, perhaps, that someone remarked to General Meade that things had been pretty desperate at one time. "Yes," replied the general, "but it is all right now, it is all right now."[126]

17

Epilogue

General Longstreet pronounced his corps's assault of 2 July to be the "best three hours' fighting ever done by any troops on any battle-field."[1] Colonel Alexander wrote that the Confederate assault of 2 July "not only contests with Pickett's Charge the palm of being the most brilliant & desperate part of the whole battle of Gettysburg, but that it is not excelled in these qualities by any record of our war."[2] These were testimonials to the Confederate effort; the performance of the Union forces mirrored it, but less brightly. The number of Federal participants had greatly exceeded the number of Confederates involved. Eleven Confederate brigades fought twenty-two Federal brigades, exclusive of those of the First, Sixth, and Twelfth corps whose participation had been limited. The Confederates smashed the Third Corps line and met and defeated many of its piecemeal reinforcements one by one. Yet each sapped some of the Confederates' finite strength, and the Confederate assault failed to achieve its objective.

General Sickles increased the odds of Confederate success when he advanced his Third Corps from its important and relatively secure position on Cemetery Ridge. In doing so he had abandoned vital terrain, isolated his corps, and put the entire army at special risk. It was a grievous error mitigated only by the hard and costly fighting of his corps and by the assistance given it by the corps of Hancock and Sykes. Sykes secured the Little Round Top area with the Fifth Corps, and Hancock, as usual, conducted himself magnificently. It was through Hancock's efforts in great part that the Federals were able to reestablish their position on Cemetery Ridge.

Hancock, Sykes, and their fellow corps commanders were General Meade's deputies, and the responsibility for the conduct of the battle that day was his alone. It was Meade who had ordered the concentration of the Army of the Potomac at Gettysburg, approved the Gettysburg position, and assigned his corps to their positions on the field. When he belatedly became aware of Sickles's advance, he took immediate measures to make the best of the situation and ordered Sykes to reinforce the endangered left. When the

Confederate assault began, he took great risks to shift additional troops from his reserve and other portions of his line to bolster the Federal left and center. General-in-Chief Halleck, in his report of the campaign, wrote that to "General Meade belongs the honor of a well-earned victory in one of the greatest and best-fought battles of the war." To Meade he wrote, "You handled your troops in that battle as.well, if not better, than any general has handled his army during the war. You brought all your forces into action at the right time and place, which no commander of the Army of the Potomac has done before. You may well be proud of that battle."[3]

George G. Meade was a competent army commander, and Gettysburg was his finest battle. Robert E. Lee was a great commander, and Gettysburg must have ranked among the saddest events of his long military career. The Confederate soldiers, inspired by his leadership, fought splendidly on 2 July, but victory escaped them. Not only did their enemy fight well, but also flaws in Confederate planning and conduct of the battle created handicaps that they could not overcome.

A lot of the Confederates' difficulties that day originated with General Lee himself and with his staff and top commanders. Lee decided to assault the strong Federal position in his front on 2 July because he had to maintain the initiative. Unfortunately, the absence of Stuart and his cavalry and the presence of his large trains limited Lee's potential for manuever, and an attack against the Federal position seemed his best alternative. Because of faulty intelligence concerning the position and strength of the Union left, he ordered an assault in accordance with a plan that did not comport with reality. It was only when Longstreet and his divisions reached the attack area that the Confederates realized that Lee's orders were impractical and had to be changed. Lee, with Longstreet's help, no doubt, hastily modified the plan in being, for it was too late to make any major changes in it. Longstreet then attacked.

It seems apparent today that General Lee erred greatly when he permitted Ewell's corps to remain east of Gettysburg in strength. Hindsight tells us that much of it would have been better used to strengthen the Confederate force on Seminary Ridge. It ought to have been as apparent to the Confederate commanders as it was to the Federals that the terrain on Ewell's front was unsuited to offensive operations. Ewell's continued presence there meant that a third of Lee's outnumbered infantry was relegated to a secondary mission. Had a substantial portion of Ewell's corps been shifted to Seminary Ridge, the 2 July attack against the Union left and center could have been delivered in greater strength and with a greater chance of success.

The extent to which General Lee delegated authority and his reluctance to be abrupt with his subordinates permitted problems to develop on 2 July. He was patient with Longstreet's dissent and delays on the morning of 2 July and seems not to have hurried him along. He did not rectify Hill's faulty deployment of Anderson's division or his inadequate measures to sustain Anderson's attack, and he allowed both corps commanders to conduct their assaults without interference. Perhaps he saw no cause for alarm, but his toleration of the shortcomings of his subordinates that day lessened the chances of Confederate success.

As night fell and the fighting ended, a New York soldier remembered that "silence followed the roar and tumult of battle. Through the darkness the rifles of the distant pickets flashed like fire flies, while, nearer by, the night air was burdened with the plaintive moans of wounded men who were lying between the lines and begging for water. About 10 o'clock the full moon rose from behind Culp's Hill, and in its light the field took on a weird and ghastly aspect."[4] Colonel Alexander recalled that with the moon's rise came a "glorious moonlight night," one that helped with preparations for the following day. He wrote:

> The first thing was to care for the wounded of both sides for there were many of the enemy's within our lines beside all of our own. Most of our own dead, too, were promptly buried; but the enemy's dead were left where they lay. Then our poor horses needed to be taken off somewhere & watered & brought back & fed. The crippled ones killed, & harness taken from the dead, & fresh ones scuffled for with the quartermasters. Then limbers & caissons of all guns must rendezvous with ordnance wagons containing the particular kind and calibre of ammunition which its gun needs, & the boxes must be opened & cartridges, shell, fuses, primers etc. be packed in the ammunition chests replacing all expenditures of the afternoon. The men must get something to eat—not only for tonight but tomorrow too. And then the scattered batteries & battalions must all be gotten together & in hand. And when it is sure, that all are fit & ready to resume action at dawn, they must be put near their probable positions, & some chance given the men to get a little sleep.[5]

The artillerymen of Alexander's battalion finished their work by 1:00 A.M. Part of the battalion was in the Peach Orchard, which was on the right of Alexander's gun line, and "what with deep dust & blood, & filth of all kinds, the trampled & wrecked Peach Orchard was a very unattractive place." But Alexander made a bed there on two fence rails, using his saddle for a pillow, and got two hours of sleep.[6]

Over to the Confederate right Law's and Robertson's brigades occupied a line across the west slope of Round Top about halfway up from Plum Run. These Confederates built a wall for their protection, a wall that is there still. They took care of their wounded and brought up ammunition for the next day. Benning's and Anderson's brigades were back near Devil's Den and the Wheatfield and continued the Confederate line from there to McLaws's position west of the Wheatfield.[7] As darkness fell, the troops at Devil's Den heard a commotion in the Federal position close by, suggesting that the Bluecoats were about to attack. Men of the First Texas and the Fifteenth

Georgia made ready to receive them under Old Rock Benning's eye. His instructions, as remembered, were, "Hold your fire until they come right up. Then pour a volley into them, and, if they don't stop, run your bayonets into their bellies." The charge never came, and the bayonets remained in their scabbards.[8]

The Confederates at Devil's Den had rival claims over the three ten-pounder Parrotts that had been captured from Smith's Fourth New York Battery. A Texan wrote that Benning honored the claims of the First Texas over those of the Twentieth Georgia, remarking, "Ah, Boys, those Texans had captured this battery before you were in a quarter of a mile from here." That was a Texan's recollection and probably appropriately modest, but the Texans were given the job of removing the pieces from the Devil's Den area. It fell to Companies F and I of the First Texas. The darkness, the rough terrain, and the Federal threat combined to make the task rather difficult. To avoid making noise that might draw fire, the Texans plotted their route carefully and wrapped the guns' wheels in blankets. After the Texans got the guns away, they turned them over to the corps ordnance officer. He issued them to Henry's battalion to replace three damaged during the battle.[9]

McLaws's four brigades occupied the west end of Rose's Woods and the stony hill and supported the batteries posted north of the Peach Orchard by Colonel Alexander. Although McLaws's men might have found some satisfaction in occupying captured ground, such a pleasure was denied the troops of Anderson's division, most of whom reformed back along Seminary Ridge about where they had been when the attack began.[10]

From their position on Round Top's west slope soldiers of Hood's division could hear the troops of Vincent's and Fisher's brigades of the Fifth Corps piling up walls on the hill above them. Fifth Corps regiments also held Little Round Top in strength. Sweitzer's and Tilton's brigades, together with the brigades of the First and Third divisions of the Sixth Corps, held the ground between Little Round Top and the George Weikert house that Sickles vacated before the fight began. McCandless's brigade of the Pennsylvania Reserves stayed in its advanced position behind the wall between Plum Run and the Wheatfield.[11]

After the firing stopped and the moon appeared, there was an informal truce in the Wheatfield area that permitted stretcher-bearers and ambulances to collect the wounded there. One of McLaws's men sang hymns to comfort the wounded who were near enough to hear him. His impromptu recital lasted quite awhile, and soldiers from both sides listened to him attentively and in silence. After he closed with a rendition of "When This Cruel War Is Over," he received cheers and applause from his audience along the Union line.[12]

Birney's shattered division assembled and bivouacked east of the Taneytown Road. De Trobriand met Birney there at dusk and found him to be a dejected man, who believed that the Confederates had won the day. As they talked, Birney remarked that his horse had been killed and muttered that he wished he had shared his horse's fate. But when they learned that the Confederate assault on Little Round Top and Cemetery Ridge had been repulsed, the future seemed brighter, and Birney set to work to get his division ready for more fighting.[13]

Humphreys's division reformed on the ridge crest north of the George Weikert house, put out pickets, collected some of its wounded, and prepared to resume the battle. Possibly because some of its regiments had joined in the counterattack against the brigades of Anderson's division, the morale of its men seemed high enough to promise good performance when the battle reopened. Colonel Bailey, whose Second New Hampshire Regiment's casualties topped 50 percent, wrote that the Second was "fearfully diminished in numbers, yet firm and fearless still."[14]

Caldwell's mauled division assembled somewhere near the Taneytown Road and then returned to the segment of the ridge that it had occupied when the battle opened. Gibbon's division, which had fought at or near its position close to the Union center, held its ground there at the end of the fight. Its men worked to strengthen that position. The Twentieth Massachusetts had only one shovel, and other units were probably no better off, so they had to dig with bayonets and boards. The men of the Twentieth piled up a mound only a foot high, but it was better than nothing. The soldiers of the Fifty-ninth New York and Sixty-ninth Pennsylvania regiments near the Copse of Trees collected small arms and cartridges dropped by Wright's Georgians in the field in front of them. Many were .69 caliber muskets that fired buck and ball. The Federals loaded the big guns with a dozen buckshot pellets each and propped them along the wall where they would be handy when needed. Some men had as many as five pieces at their disposal when Pickett charged next day.[15]

It had been a costly three hours for both armies. We cannot be certain of the human cost, for the accuracy of the casualty figures depended on the correctness of the count and the criteria used by those recording it. Furthermore, the casualties reported for some units are those sustained on both 2 and 3 July, and we cannot separate the figures for each day with accuracy. All in all it seems fair to assume on the basis of the reports made that the three Confederate divisions that attacked on 2 July lost about 6,000 officers and enlisted men who were killed, missing, or wounded badly enough to render them unfit for immediate service. Hood's and McLaws's divisions each had about 2,200 casualties, a rate of about 30 percent; Anderson's had about 1,600, or 40 percent in Wilcox's, Perry's, and Wright's brigades.[16]

It is more difficult to assess Federal casualties from the published reports because some of the reports make no distinction between those sustained on 2 and 3 July. Sickles's two divisions reported 593 officers and enlisted men killed, 3,029 wounded, and 589 missing. This suggests a rate of more than 30 percent. That is comparable to the losses of Hood's and McLaws's divisions,

Union dead. Photograph by Timothy H. O'Sullivan (National Archives)

Dead horses of Bigelow's battery in the Trostle farmyard. Photograph by Timothy H. O'Sullivan (National Archives)

which, of course, fought with units of the Fifth and Second corps as well as the Third. Second Corps casualties for the day numbered 2,800, Caldwell's division sustaining 1,275 of them. The Fifth Corps had 2,187 for the entire battle, but essentially all of them must have been sustained on 2 July.[17] Federal casualties for the afternoon's battle, therefore, probably numbered about 9,000—an indication of the lethal character of the Confederate assault and testimony to the accuracy of Longstreet's boast.

These figures indicate some of the damage done to units, but they can only suggest its full extent. They fail to show clearly the numbers of men who became separated from their regiments in the course of the fight but rejoined them before the count upon which the report was based was made. They do not reveal the number of men who were still with their colors but who were partially unfit for duty because of minor wounds or shattered nerves. They can only suggest the disorganization created by the fall of key personnel in the chain of command and in the lines of battle.

The Army of Northern Virginia lost only one division commander that day, John Bell Hood, but his loss at the beginning of the Confederate assault may well have been the difference between its success and failure. In addition, the removal of G. T. Anderson, Barksdale, and Semmes—not to mention Law— from the heads of their brigades, together with the fall of numerous regimental commanders, must have lessened significantly the tactical efficiency of Longstreet's corps. All of the brigade commanders of Anderson's division were unscathed, but Wilcox's and Wright's brigades each lost three of their four regimental commanders.

It was fortunate for the Third Corps that Sickles was shot at the close of its fight, and his fall probably had but minimal effect on its outcome. Sickles, as a corps commander, was not quite the peer of either John F. Reynolds or Hancock, who fell on 1 and 3 July respectively; but he was competent, and his aggressive spirit, like theirs, was sadly lacking among the corps commanders of the Army of the Potomac in the closing half of the campaign. Zook, Cross, Willard, Graham, Weed, and Vincent were all brigade commanders of promise. Graham was exchanged and returned to active service in the spring of 1864, but the others were gone forever and were difficult to replace. Like Sickles, four of the brigade commanders—Willard, Graham, Weed, and Vincent—became casualties in the closing stages of the day's action. Their loss probably had little effect on their brigades' performances that day. But, who can say what more Caldwell's division might have accomplished had its two senior brigade commanders, Zook and Cross, not fallen in the opening of its fight?

The battlefield of 2 July was a ghastly place. Captain Cavada observed that the air of early evening there was "laden with mist and pervaded by that strange musty smell peculiar to battlefields immediately after a battle." Cavada had a slight wound and was fatigued, but he could not relax. He worried about his brother Fred, who had been seen last when Barksdale's brigade smashed into the 114th Pennsylvania at the Sherfy buildings. He was worried also about his friend Capt. William H. Chester of Humphreys's staff, who had not been seen since he received a severe wound and was taken from the firing line. When he could rest no longer, Cavada, along with some other men, walked from the division's position on the ridge out toward the Emmitsburg Road.[18]

Cavada's party crossed the swale, probably where the First Minnesota regiment had fought. Cavada saw that

> on every side lay the cold stiffened bodies of our dead soldiers, sometimes two or three forming ghastly groups together—in most unnatural attitudes—Sometimes lying naturally and as if asleep—occasionally a wounded man [not] able to move would draw our attention by plaintive moans or a request for water. These we comforted with the assurance that the ambulances would find them in a few minutes. We found but few Rebel dead or wounded on this side of the hollow—but on crossing it they became very numerous, even moreso than our own.[19]

Plum Run's valley in front of Little Round Top must have resembled the shambles seen by Cavada at the swale. The corpses of Georgians and Alabamians lay thickly in the Slaughter Pen and gorge. Union soldiers, alive and dead, crowded the marshy west bank of Plum Run, and Confederates lay along its eastern bank. Some had fallen there, but others, who had been wounded, had gotten that far in trying to reach the shelter of their lines and could not cross. The dead and wounded mingled along the banks for a while with soldiers of the Fifth Corps who filled their canteens from the bloody stream.[20]

The ambulance corps of both armies worked hard that night, but only one corps ambulance officer, Capt. James A. Bates, chief ambulance officer of the Fifth Corps, made a report that was published. He wrote that eighty-one of that corps's ambulance crews labored throughout the night until 4:00 A.M. and that they had recovered all of the wounded behind the picket line. By this time they had transported 1,300 wounded to hospitals beyond the Taneytown Road.[21]

The wounded at Gettysburg must have gotten along as well or better than the wounded on most other fields of the war. Both armies had field hospitals close to the battlefield; there was water available, particularly after the armies moved away; and both armies had access to numerous public and private buildings in the area. The wounded of both sides benefited from aid furnished by civilians and civilian organizations. After the battle, when the time came for the wounded to be taken elsewhere, there was a railroad connection reopened between Gettysburg and the outer world. But still, individual soldiers suffered the universal discomforts and horrors experienced by the battle casualties of the Civil War. They feared particularly the prospect of being wounded and alone, of falling helplessly into the hands of the enemy and being mistreated.

One wounded Confederate was Sgt. William Johns of Colonel Oates's Fifteenth Alabama Infantry Regiment. Johns fell somewhere in the Round Top area, immobilized by wounds in the hip and thigh, and lay in the open with his face to the sky. He suffered first from the burning thirst common to badly wounded men and could not quench it. Then on 4 July heavy rains fell. The downpour relieved his thirst, but it nearly drowned him. He believed that he had saved himself from drowning only by covering his face with his hat. Union soldiers found him on the night of 4 July and carried him to a hospital where he received care. Johns was crippled for the rest of his life.[22]

Lt. Barzilia J. Inman of the 148th Pennsylvania Regiment had a uniquely terrifying experience. Inman fell wounded and unconscious, probably in Trostle's Woods, and was left there for dead. He awakened during the night and found that he was lying among some corpses and was unable to stand. Then he heard the grunting of hogs and by the moon's light saw them rooting and tearing at some bodies nearby. One fearsome swine, grunting loudly, approached him. Inman grasped his sword firmly, and when the beast came near, he jammed the sword's point into the hog's belly. The hog squealed and backed away, but Inman had to force himself to stay awake the rest of the night out of fear of being eaten alive.[23]

The looting of corpses was a common thing, for it was an excusable way of getting shoes and items of clothing and personal equipment. But it was also thievery for personal gain. The soldiers of the Army of the Potomac had been paid on 30 June, and some of its fallen must have been lucrative plucking for friend and foe alike. It is not surprising, then, to read that after troops were able to wander through the Round Tops area, it was rare to find a body there that had not been robbed. And those robbed need not have been dead. Rebel soldiers in the Peach Orchard robbed Lt. Charles Vickery of the Second New Hampshire, who had a mortal wound and was defenseless, "with their customary dexterity." Later an officer had the lieutenant carried to a barn and given water. Vickery died on 10 July.[24]

Cavada and his comrades did not find Captain Chester on the field. They found the carcass of his gray horse, which had the lower part of its head shot away. Beside the horse was the headless body of the faithful sergeant who had been taking Chester to the rear, and nearby they saw the corpse of a Confederate whose brains oozed from a hole in his forehead. Somehow they learned that Chester had already been taken to the rear. Cavada found Chester the next morning at the Third Corps hospital. Chester was lying in a row of seriously wounded men who "merely gazed around with a quiet beseeching look, following the movements of the busy surgeons with the hope that their turn will come next." In contrast, not far away were men who were less seriously wounded and who cheerfully compared their damages and speculated on the amount of furlough time that each of them would get.[25]

Chester told Cavada of his ordeal. After an artillery round killed his sergeant and the horse, he had lain stranded near their bodies. The advancing Confederate line passed by him, its soldiers paying him no heed, but it drew some Federal fire in his direction. At this time, though, Chester worried less about being shot than he did about falling into Confederate hands. After the attacking line had passed, a straggler appeared. The straggler was no more a Good Samaritan than he was a good soldier, and, as Chester recounted, "brutally endeavored to wrench the watch and chain from off my person." Chester threatened to shoot the thief, but the looter, who was intent upon his thievery, ignored the threat. Chester raised a small pistol that he had hidden until then and shot the fellow in the head. The robber uttered a deep groan and rolled dead at Chester's feet. Fortunately, other Confederates did not noticed the shooting. Another "d—d rebel" appeared a short time later. He ignored Chester as he stripped the saddle from his horse and along with it took a silver flask, his saddle holsters, and the pistols in them. As Chester spoke to Cavada of this last indignity, he "expressed a determination to pay those thieving rascals off as he had served the one who tried for his watch." But it was not to be. Chester died in the hospital.[26]

Amid the inhumanity there were soldiers who showed much kindness and compassion for their helpless enemies. When Union soldiers on Little Round Top found Pvt. John H. Roberts of the Fifth Texas and saw that they could not move him at that time, they piled up a stone wall beside him to protect him from Confederate rifle and artillery fire.[27] And Lt. Thomas Oliver of the Twenty-fourth Georgia Regiment dragged the wounded Lt. J. Jackson Purman of the 140th Pennsylvania Regiment from the open in the Wheatfield to some shelter and possibly saved his life. Purman lost his wounded leg but found and married Mary Witherow, who was one of his nurses at Gettysburg. After the war, when Purman became a Washington attorney and G.A.R. official, he rejoiced to learn that Oliver had become mayor of Atlanta and took pleasure one day in introducing him to Theodore Roosevelt.[28]

The fates of General Sickles and General Barksdale created a lot of immediate interest among those who fought at Gettysburg. Many Union soldiers at varied places on the field claimed that they had seen Barksdale shot or had seen him after he was shot. In fact, Union soldiers found him somewhere west of Plum Run after Willard's brigade's counterattack and carried him to the Second Corps aid station at the Hummelbaugh house near the Taneytown Road. Assistant Surgeon Alfred T. Hamilton of the 148th Pennsylvania Regiment ran the station and Musician Robert A. Cassidy was one of Hamilton's helpers. Because of its central location and the nearby fighting, Hamilton's station was a busy one, and Barksdale was just one of the many wounded treated there.[29]

Both Hamilton and Cassidy wrote of Barksdale's presence at their station in a convincing manner. Stretcher-bearers carried Barksdale to the station for treatment and to await ambulance transportation to a hospital. Because the house was full, someone made a bed of blankets for the general in the yard. Cassidy looked at the patient by candlelight and saw that he was an officer of high rank. He attempted to give him water from a canteen, but the general could not sit up enough to drink that way. Cassidy had someone hold the candle for him, and he gave Barksdale water with a spoon. Barksdale identified himself, and Cassidy called Surgeon Hamilton over to see his famous patient.[30]

Hamilton examined Barksdale and found a wound in the left side of his chest and a fracture and two wounds in the general's left leg. Cassidy recalled that the chest wound looked too large to have been made by a minié ball, but perhaps it was an exit wound. Barksdale's left lung must have been punctured badly because blood sprayed from the wound with every breath.[31]

Hamilton was undoubtedly impressed by his patient, for he recalled him in a detailed way. He described Barksdale as a corpulent, bald man who was refined in appearance. Barksdale seemed to Hamilton to be a man of vigor and endurance, firmness, quick perception, and ability. The general wore trousers trimmed with gold braid, a short round jacket trimmed with gold braid on its sleeves and closed by Mississippi buttons bearing a star. The jacket's collar had three stars, as Hamilton recalled it, but he made no mention of whether the stars were embraced by a general's wreath. The general's shirt was of cotton or fine linen, and Barksdale fastened it with studs bearing Masonic emblems.[32]

Hamilton prescribed morphine for Barksdale to ease his pain, and Cassidy gave it to him. Barksdale asked both Hamilton and Cassidy several times if his wound was mortal and how long he had to live. Both assured him that the wound was mortal, and Cassidy told him that soon he would be standing "in the presence of the final judge." Barksdale told Hamilton that he wanted peace but only on terms that would recognize the Confederacy's independence. He warned Cassidy, "Beware! You will have Longstreet thundering in your rear in the morning!" As time passed, Barksdale lost consciousness, and Cassidy left him to attend to others.[33]

Cassidy saw Barksdale's body the next morning. Souvenir hunters had picked over it. One of them, Pvt. William C. Myers of the 148th Pennsylvania, took some gold braid; others, almost everything else of interest. Cassidy took one remaining button from the general's coat and a strap from his sword belt. (He offered these items to Mrs. Barksdale in 1866.) It was at about this time that Lt. George G. Benedict of the Twelfth Vermont Regiment saw the general. He recognized him because he had seen him on the floor of the House of Representatives in better days. Benedict wrote that Barksdale's "bald head and broad face, with open unblinking eyes, lay uncovered in the sunshine. There he lay alone, without a comrade to brush the flies from his corpse." Someone buried the general that day in a temporary grave near the Hummelbaugh house.[34]

General Sickles had a different fate. Someone—Dr. Sim himself or Sickles with Dr. Sim's concurrence—decided that Sickles should leave the Third Corps's hospital immediately and go to Washington. In retrospect, this seems like a foolish and dangerous decision, but Major Tremain and others made hurried preparations for the journey. Sickles and his retinue left Gettysburg on the morning of 3 July, hardly more than twelve hours after the general had been shot and his leg amputated. The first stage of the journey was to Littlestown, Pennsylvania, just eight miles to the southeast on the Baltimore Pike. A journey to Littlestown seems simple enough, but it did not prove so. Dr. Sim ruled out Sickles's riding there in an ambulance, probably because he thought that its jolting would cause Sickles's stump to hemorrhage. General Pleasonton introduced another complication when he urged that the party avoid the pike in favor of country roads, probably those southwest of it, because he could not guarantee that users of the pike would be safe from Confederate cavalry.[35]

Sickles departed Gettysburg in a manner reminiscent of a wounded medieval lord. His aides had assembled a force of forty Third Corps soldiers to serve as stretcher-bearers and to provide an escort, a squad of cavalrymen to serve as couriers, and a couple of wagons to carry baggage and supplies. The party also included Dr. Sim, who left the remainder of the Third Corps wounded in other hands, and Sickles's three aides: Major Tremain, Captain Moore, and Captain Fry. Four soldiers carried the stretcher at a time, and they changed shifts frequently to avoid fatigue and lessen the probability of an accident that would injure the general. Sickles himself cautioned the bearers on each side to walk in opposite step and not to let him fall, for "It would be the last of me." Once started, the party traveled at a walking pace of about 1½ miles per hour and encountered no special problems. Sim gave the general a sedative. Sickles was "serene," lying on the stretcher, hat over his eyes, and smoking a cigar. The party stopped at a farmhouse for the night. Sickles pleased his companions next morning by showing them that he was able to shave himself, and all were cheered when a courier brought them news of the repulse of Pickett's Charge. Indignation tempered their joy, though, when their host demanded payment for the sheets they had used and the food and forage that the party had consumed.[36]

Sickles and his retinue reached Littlestown on 4 July. Captain Fry had ridden on ahead and had a railroad car waiting for the general, and the bearers placed him in it. Then the soldiers returned to Gettysburg while Dr. Sim, the aides, and perhaps some orderlies or hospital stewards accompanied the general to Washington. The train ride via Baltimore must have been a painful ordeal for Sickles, for stretchers make uncomfortable railroad berths for badly wounded men. After the party reached Washington on 5 July, they took Sickles to a residence at 248 F Street, near the Ebbitt house. Even then Sim would not allow Sickles to be transferred from his stretcher to a bed.[37]

Sickles's arrival was no secret, and he had numerous visitors as the days passed. Among the first was Lt. Col. James F. Rusling, the quartermaster of the Third Corps, who had been on sick leave and had missed the Gettysburg campaign. Rusling and Sickles had not talked long when President Lincoln arrived with his son Tad, a pair of guests that would have disturbed the calm in any invalid's room. After the natural greetings and discussion about the general's health, the president and the general talked about the battle of Gettysburg. Rusling was present and listened to their conversation. In reporting it he seemed to catch the essence of Daniel Sickles, the soldier-politician. According to Rusling:

> Sickles, recumbent on his stretcher, with a cigar between his fingers, puffing it leisurely, answered Mr. Lincoln in detail, but warily, as became so astute a man and soldier; and discussed the great battle and its probable consequences with a lucidity and ability remarkable in his condition then—enfeebled and exhausted as he was by the shock and danger of such a wound and amputation. Occasionally he would wince with pain, and call sharply to his orderly to wet his fevered stump with water. But he never dropped his cigar, nor lost the thread of his narrative, nor missed the point of their discussion. . . . He certainly got his side of the story of Gettysburg well into the President's mind and heart that Sunday afternoon; and this doubtless stood him in good stead afterward, when Meade proposed to court-martial him for fighting so magnificently, if unskillfully (which remains to be proved), on that bloody and historic July 2d.[38]

There is no indication that General Meade ever intended or seriously considered to court-martial General Sickles,[39] but Sickles told his story, probably a revised version of that told President Lincoln, until his death in 1914. In substance Sickles held that General Meade had not intended to concentrate his army at Gettysburg and that on 2 July, even after his army was concentrated there, Meade still intended to withdraw it from the Gettysburg position. In his version, General Sickles's decision to post the Third Corps's main line on the high ground west of the Cemetery Ridge line had disrupted and frustrated the Confederate plan of attack and Meade's planned withdrawal. The Third Corps sacrifice on 2 July led, then, to a Federal victory at Gettysburg in spite of the alleged ineptness of General Meade and the poor support provided the gallant Third Corps by General Sykes and some craven Fifth Corps officers and units.[40]

Seven days after the battle on Little Round Top's slope, Pvt. John C. West of the Fourth Texas Regiment concisely summed up the battle as he saw it. In a letter to his wife West wrote: "I started from Texas to find a fight, and I have made a success of it." The Confederates of Hood's, McLaws's, and Anderson's divisions had found a fight indeed. Although they could take great pride in the fighting they had done, they must have taken little satisfaction in its results. At day's end the Army of the Potomac still held its position on Cemetery Ridge, and it had been given time to assemble its scattered corps and to strengthen that position. Yet, somehow General Lee was able to look at the Confederates' limited success with optimism. He believed that with the elusive "proper concert of action" and with the "increased support that the positions gained on the right would enable the artillery to render the assaulting columns," his army would "ultimately succeed." Therefore, he decided to continue the attack on the following morning. The general plan would be unchanged except that Longstreet would have the use of the three fresh brigades of Pickett's division and the help of a division and two additional brigades of Hill's corps. General Ewell would assail the enemy's right as Longstreet attacked his left.[41]

Unlike General Lee, General Meade had much to be pleased about after the battle of 2 July. But past encounters with the Army of Northern Virginia had taught him caution. He wrote to Mrs. Meade on the morning of 3 July that all was going well, that they had had "a great fight" on 2 July, and that the enemy had attacked and had been repulsed completely. He stated, with some exaggeration perhaps, that both armies had been shattered, but that the Army of the Potomac was in fine spirits and very determined.[42]

General Meade might not have realized it fully then, but he could hardly have asked for better results from the battle of 2 July. The Confederate assault that he had feared would take place before his army was assembled had been delivered and repulsed. The casualties had been heavy—heavier probably than they ought to have been—but that was the price of waging war, and they could not be recovered. Furthermore, by the end of that day's battle practically the entire Army of the Potomac was at hand and available for use. Its brigades occupied Culp's Hill, Cemetery Hill, Cemetery Ridge, and both Round Tops, and it had ample reserves of men and ammunition. Its corps commanders were united in the belief that the army should hold its position and fight. By the morning of 3 July, the Confederate penetration on Culp's Hill, which was already sealed off, would be eliminated, brigades of the Sixth Corps would guard against Confederate flank attacks from positions on Wolf Hill and behind Round Top, and Federal cavalry pickets and patrols would watch for Confederate turning movements far beyond the infantry's flanks. General Newton summed up the situation quite well in a comment that he made to Meade sometime that evening, perhaps at the Council of War. Said Newton, "General Meade, I think you ought to feel much gratified with to-day's results." "In the name of common sense, Newton, why?" was the inquiry in reply. "Why," said Newton, with a pleasant expression and smile, "they have hammered us into a solid position they cannot whip us out of."[43]

General Butterfield recounted this conversation, possibly in an attempt to show that General Meade had not really comprehended the army's situation and therefore merited little credit for it. And yet Meade had laid out its position with Captain Paine and others early that morning, and many of the Federal movements made that day were made at his personal direction.

Newton was right, the Federal position was secure. General Lee's opportunity to win a decisive victory at Gettysburg had all but passed when complete success had eluded his attacking divisions on the afternoon and evening of 2 July. General Lee still hoped for ultimate success on 3 July. That hope would rest in Pickett's Charge.

Order of Battle

Army of the Potomac and Army of Northern Virginia, 1–3 July 1863

The Order of Battle is reproduced from U.S. War Department, *The War of the Rebellion: A Compilation of the Official Records of the Union and Confederate Armies*, 128 vols. (Washington, D.C.: U.S. Government Printing Office, 1880–1901), ser. 1, 27 (1):155–68, and (2):283–91.

No. 9.

Organization of the Army of the Potomac, Maj. Gen. George G. Meade, U. S. Army, commanding, at the battle of Gettysburg, July 1–3, 1863.

GENERAL HEADQUARTERS.

COMMAND OF THE PROVOST-MARSHAL-GENERAL.

Brig. Gen. MARSENA R. PATRICK.

93d New York,* Col. John S. Crocker.
8th United States (eight companies),* Capt. Edwin W. H. Read.
2d Pennsylvania Cavalry, Col. R. Butler Price.
6th Pennsylvania Cavalry, Companies E and I, Capt. James Starr.
Regular cavalry (detachments from 1st, 2d, 5th, and 6th Regiments).

SIGNAL CORPS.

Capt. LEMUEL B. NORTON.

GUARDS AND ORDERLIES.

Oneida (New York) Cavalry, Capt. Daniel P. Mann.

ARTILLERY.†

Brig. Gen. HENRY J. HUNT.

ENGINEER BRIGADE.‡

Brig. Gen. HENRY W. BENHAM.

15th New York (three companies), Maj. Walter L. Cassin.
50th New York, Col. William H. Pettes.
United States Battalion, Capt. George H. Mendell.

FIRST ARMY CORPS.§

Maj. Gen. ABNER DOUBLEDAY.
Maj. Gen. JOHN NEWTON.

GENERAL HEADQUARTERS.

1st Maine Cavalry, Company L, Capt. Constantine Taylor.

FIRST DIVISION.

Brig. Gen. JAMES S. WADSWORTH.

First Brigade.

Brig. Gen. SOLOMON MEREDITH.
Col. WILLIAM W. ROBINSON.

19th Indiana, Col. Samuel J. Williams.
24th Michigan:
    Col. Henry A. Morrow.
    Capt. Albert M. Edwards.
2d Wisconsin:
    Col. Lucius Fairchild.
    Maj. John Mansfield.
    Capt. George H. Otis.
6th Wisconsin, Lieut. Col. Rufus R. Dawes.
7th Wisconsin:
    Col. William W. Robinson.
    Maj. Mark Finnicum.

Second Brigade.

Brig. Gen. LYSANDER CUTLER.

7th Indiana, Col. Ira G. Grover.
76th New York:
    Maj. Andrew J. Grover.
    Capt. John E. Cook.
84th New York (14th Militia), Col. Edward B. Fowler.
95th New York:
    Col. George H. Biddle.
    Maj. Edward Pye.
147th New York:
    Lieut. Col. Francis C. Miller.
    Maj. George Harney.
56th Pennsylvania (nine companies), Col. J. William Hofmann.

---

* Not engaged.
† See artillery brigades attached to army corps and the reserve.
‡ Not engaged. With exception of the regular battalion, it was, July 1, and while at Beaver Dam Creek, Md., ordered to Washington, D. C., where it arrived July 3.
§ Maj. Gen. John F. Reynolds, of this corps, was killed July 1, while in command of the left wing of the army; General Doubleday commanded the corps July 1, and General Newton, who was assigned to that command on the 1st, superseded him July 2.

SECOND DIVISION.

Brig. Gen. JOHN C. ROBINSON.

First Brigade.

Brig. Gen. GABRIEL R. PAUL.
Col. SAMUEL H. LEONARD.
Col. ADRIAN R. ROOT.
Col. RICHARD COULTER.
Col. PETER LYLE.
Col. RICHARD COULTER.

16th Maine:
  Col. Charles W. Tilden.
  Maj. Archibald D. Leavitt.
13th Massachusetts:
  Col. Samuel H. Leonard.
  Lieut. Col. N. Walter Batchelder.
94th New York:
  Col. Adrian R. Root.
  Maj. Samuel A. Moffett.
104th New York, Col. Gilbert G. Prey.
107th Pennsylvania:
  Lieut. Col. James MacThomson.
  Capt. Emanuel D. Roath.

Second Brigade.

Brig. Gen. HENRY BAXTER.

12th Massachusetts:
  Col. James L. Bates.
  Lieut. Col. David Allen, jr.
83d New York (9th Militia), Lieut. Col. Joseph A. Moesch.
97th New York:
  Col. Charles Wheelock.
  Maj. Charles Northrup.
11th Pennsylvania:*
  Col. Richard Coulter.
  Capt. Benjamin F. Haines.
  Capt. John B. Overmyer.
88th Pennsylvania:
  Maj. Benezet F. Foust.
  Capt. Henry Whiteside.
90th Pennsylvania:
  Col. Peter Lyle.
  Maj. Alfred J. Sellers.
  Col. Peter Lyle.

THIRD DIVISION.

Brig. Gen. THOMAS A. ROWLEY.
Maj. Gen. ABNER DOUBLEDAY.

First Brigade.

Col. CHAPMAN BIDDLE.
Brig. Gen. THOMAS A. ROWLEY.
Col. CHAPMAN BIDDLE.

80th New York (20th Militia), Col. Theodore B. Gates.
121st Pennsylvania:
  Maj. Alexander Biddle.
  Col. Chapman Biddle.
  Maj. Alexander Biddle.
142d Pennsylvania:
  Col. Robert P. Cummins.
  Lieut. Col. A. B. McCalmont.
151st Pennsylvania:
  Lieut. Col. George F. McFarland.
  Capt. Walter L. Owens.
  Col. Harrison Allen.

Second Brigade.

Col. ROY STONE.
Col. LANGHORNE WISTER.
Col. EDMUND L. DANA.

143d Pennsylvania:
  Col. Edmund L. Dana.
  Lieut. Col. John D. Musser.
149th Pennsylvania:
  Lieut. Col. Walton Dwight
  Capt. James Glenn.
150th Pennsylvania:
  Col. Langhorne Wister.
  Lieut. Col. H. S. Huidekoper.
  Capt. Cornelius C. Widdis.

Third Brigade.

Brig. Gen. GEORGE J. STANNARD.
Col. FRANCIS V. RANDALL.

12th Vermont,† Col. Asa P. Blunt.
13th Vermont:
  Col. Francis V. Randall,
  Maj. Joseph J. Boynton.
  Lieut. Col. William D. Munson.
14th Vermont, Col. William T. Nichols.
15th Vermont,† Col. Redfield Proctor.
16th Vermont, Col. Wheelock G. Veazey.

---

* Transferred, in afternoon of July 1, to the First Brigade.
† Guarding trains, and not engaged in the battle.

ARTILLERY BRIGADE.

Col. CHARLES S. WAINWRIGHT.

Maine Light, 2d Battery (B), Capt. James A. Hall.
Maine Light, 5th Battery (E):
  Capt. Greenleaf T. Stevens.
  Lieut. Edward N. Whittier.
1st New York Light, Battery L:*
  Capt. Gilbert H. Reynolds.
  Lieut. George Breck.
1st Pennsylvania Light, Battery B, Capt. James H. Cooper.
4th United States, Battery B, Lieut. James Stewart.

SECOND ARMY CORPS.†

Maj. Gen. WINFIELD S. HANCOCK.
Brig. Gen. JOHN GIBBON.

GENERAL HEADQUARTERS.

6th New York Cavalry, Companies D and K, Capt. Riley Johnson.

FIRST DIVISION.

Brig. Gen. JOHN C. CALDWELL.

First Brigade.

Col. EDWARD E. CROSS.
Col. H. BOYD McKEEN.

5th New Hampshire,Lieut. Col. Charles
  E. Hapgood.
61st New York, Lieut. Col. K. Oscar
  Broady.
81st Pennsylvania :
  Col. H. Boyd McKeen.
  Lieut. Col. Amos Stroh.
148th Pennsylvania, Lieut. Col. Robert
  McFarlane.

Second Brigade.

Col. PATRICK KELLY.

28th Massachusetts, Col. R. Byrnes.
63d New York (two companies) :
  Lieut.Col. Richard C. Bentley.
  Capt. Thomas Touhy.
69th New York (two companies) :
  Capt. Richard Moroney.
  Lieut. James J. Smith.
88th New York (two companies), Capt.
  Denis F. Burke.
116th Pennsylvania (four companies),
  Maj. St. Clair A. Mulholland.

Third Brigade.

Brig. Gen. SAMUEL K. ZOOK.
Lieut. Col. JOHN FRASER.

52d New York:
  Lieut. Col. C. G. Freudenberg.
  Capt. William Scherrer.
57th New York, Lieut. Col. Alford B.
  Chapman.
66th New York:
  Col. Orlando H. Morris.
  Lieut. Col. John S. Hammell.
  Maj. Peter Nelson.
140th Pennsylvania:
  Col. Richard P. Roberts.
  Lieut. Col. John Fraser.

Fourth Brigade.

Col. JOHN R. BROOKE.

27th Connecticut (two companies) :
  Lieut. Col. Henry C. Merwin.
  Maj. James H. Coburn.
2d Delaware:
  Col. William P. Baily.
  Capt. Charles H. Christman.
64th New York:
  Col. Daniel G. Bingham.
  Maj. Leman W. Bradley.
53d Pennsylvania, Lieut. Col. Richards
  McMichael.
145th Pennsylvania (seven companies) :
  Col. Hiram L. Brown.
  Capt. John W. Reynolds.
  Capt. Moses W. Oliver.

---

* Battery E, 1st New York Light Artillery, attached.
† After the death of General Reynolds, General Hancock was assigned to the command of all the troops on the field of battle, relieving General Howard, who had succeeded General Reynolds. General Gibbon, of the Second Division, assumed command of the corps. These assignments terminated on the evening of July 1. Similar changes in commanders occurred during the battle of the 2d, when General Hancock was put in command of the Third Corps, in addition to that of his own. He was wounded on the 3d, and Brig. Gen. William Hays was assigned to the command of the corps.

SECOND DIVISION.

Brig. Gen. JOHN GIBBON,
Brig. Gen. WILLIAM HARROW.

First Brigade.

Brig. Gen. WILLIAM HARROW.
Col. FRANCIS E. HEATH.

19th Maine:
Col. Francis E. Heath.
Lieut. Col. Henry W. Cunningham.
15th Massachusetts:
Col. George H. Ward.
Lieut. Col. George C. Joslin.
1st Minnesota:*
Col. William Colvill, jr.
Capt. Nathan S. Messick.
Capt. Henry C. Coates.
82d New York (2d Militia):
Lieut. Col. James Huston.
Capt. John Darrow.

Second Brigade.

Brig. Gen. ALEXANDER S. WEBB.

69th Pennsylvania:
Col. Dennis O'Kane.
Capt. William Davis.
71st Pennsylvania, Col. Richard Penn Smith.
72d Pennsylvania:
Col. De Witt C. Baxter.
Lieut. Col. Theodore Hesser.
106th Pennsylvania, Lieut. Col. William L. Curry.

Third Brigade.

Col. NORMAN J. HALL.

19th Massachusetts, Col. Arthur F. Devereux.
20th Massachusetts:
Col. Paul J. Revere.
Lieut. Col. George N. Macy.
Capt. Henry L. Abbott.
7th Michigan:
Lieut. Col. Amos E. Steele, jr.
Maj. Sylvanus W. Curtis.
42d New York, Col. James E. Mallon.
59th New York (four companies):
Lieut. Col. Max A. Thoman.
Capt. William McFadden.

Unattached.

Massachusetts Sharpshooters, 1st Company:
Capt. William Plumer.
Lieut. Emerson L. Bicknell.

THIRD DIVISION.

Brig. Gen. ALEXANDER HAYS.

First Brigade.

Col. SAMUEL S. CARROLL.

14th Indiana, Col. John Coons.
4th Ohio, Lieut. Col. Leonard W. Carpenter.
8th Ohio, Lieut. Col. Franklin Sawyer.
7th West Virginia, Lieut. Col. Jonathan H. Lockwood.

Second Brigade.

Col. THOMAS A. SMYTH.
Lieut. Col. FRANCIS E. PIERCE.

14th Connecticut, Maj. Theodore G. Ellis.
1st Delaware:
Lieut. Col. Edward P. Harris.
Capt. Thomas B. Hizar.
Lieut. William Smith.
Lieut. John T. Dent.
12th New Jersey, Maj. John T. Hill.
10th New York (battalion), Maj. George F. Hopper.
108th New York, Lieut. Col. Francis E. Pierce.

---

* 2d Company Minnesota Sharpshooters attached.

Third Brigade.

Col. GEORGE L. WILLARD.
Col. ELIAKIM SHERRILL.
Lieut. Col. JAMES M. BULL.

39th New York (four companies), Maj. Hugo Hildebrandt.
111th New York:
    Col. Clinton D. MacDougall.
    Lieut. Col. Isaac M. Lusk.
    Capt. Aaron P. Seeley.
125th New York, Lieut. Col. Levin Crandell.
126th New York:
    Col. Eliakim Sherrill.
    Lieut. Col. James M. Bull.

ARTILLERY BRIGADE.

Capt. JOHN G. HAZARD.

1st New York Light, Battery B:*
    Lieut. Albert S. Sheldon.
    Capt. James McKay Rorty.
    Lieut. Robert E. Rogers.
1st Rhode Island Light, Battery A, Capt. William A. Arnold.
1st Rhode Island Light, Battery B:
    Lieut. T. Fred. Brown.
    Lieut. Walter S. Perrin.
1st United States, Battery I:
    Lieut. George A. Woodruff.
    Lieut. Tully McCrea.
4th United States, Battery A:
    Lieut. Alonzo H. Cushing.
    Sergt. Frederick Fuger.

THIRD ARMY CORPS.

Maj. Gen. DANIEL E. SICKLES.
Maj. Gen. DAVID B. BIRNEY.

FIRST DIVISION.

Maj. Gen. DAVID B. BIRNEY.
Brig. Gen. J. H. HOBART WARD.

First Brigade.

Brig. Gen. CHARLES K. GRAHAM.
Col. ANDREW H. TIPPIN.

57th Pennsylvania (eight companies):
    Col. Peter Sides.
    Capt. Alanson H. Nelson.
63d Pennsylvania, Maj. John A. Danks.
68th Pennsylvania:
    Col. Andrew H. Tippin.
    Capt. Milton S. Davis.[?]
105th Pennsylvania, Col. Calvin A. Craig.
114th Pennsylvania:
    Lieut. Col. Frederick F. Cavada.
    Capt. Edward R. Bowen.
141st Pennsylvania, Col. Henry J. Madill.

Second Brigade.

Brig. Gen. J. H. HOBART WARD.
Col. HIRAM BERDAN.

20th Indiana:
    Col. John Wheeler.
    Lieut. Col. William C. L. Taylor.
3d Maine, Col. Moses B. Lakeman.
4th Maine:
    Col. Elijah Walker.
    Capt. Edwin Libby.
86th New York, Lieut. Col. Benjamin L. Higgins.
124th New York:
    Col. A. Van Horne Ellis.
    Lieut. Col. Francis M. Cummins.
99th Pennsylvania, Maj. John W. Moore.
1st United States Sharpshooters:
    Col. Hiram Berdan.
    Lieut. Col. Casper Trepp.
2d United States Sharpshooters (eight companies), Maj. Homer R. Stoughton.

*Transferred from Artillery Reserve, July 1; 14th New York Battery attached.

Third Brigade.

Col. P. Regis de Trobriand.

17th Maine, Lieut. Col. Charles B. Merrill.
3d Michigan:
 Col. Byron R. Pierce.
 Lieut. Col. Edwin S. Pierce.
5th Michigan, Lieut. Col. John Pulford.
40th New York, Col. Thomas W. Egan.
110th Pennsylvania (six companies):
 Lieut. Col. David M. Jones.
 Maj. Isaac Rogers.

SECOND DIVISION.

Brig. Gen. Andrew A. Humphreys.

First Brigade.

Brig. Gen. Joseph B. Carr.

1st Massachusetts, Lieut. Col. Clark B. Baldwin.
11th Massachusetts, Lieut. Col. Porter D. Tripp.
16th Massachusetts:
 Lieut. Col. Waldo Merriam.
 Capt. Matthew Donovan.
12th New Hampshire, Capt. John F. Langley.
11th New Jersey:
 Col. Robert McAllister.
 Capt. Luther Martin.
 Lieut. John Schoonover.
 Capt. William H. Lloyd.
 Capt. Samuel T. Sleeper.
 Lieut. John Schoonover.
26th Pennsylvania, Maj. Robert L. Bodine.
84th Pennsylvania,* Lieut. Col. Milton Opp.

Second Brigade.

Col. William R. Brewster.

70th New York, Col. J. Egbert Farnum.
71st New York, Col. Henry L. Potter.
72d New York:
 Col. John S. Austin.
 Lieut. Col. John Leonard.
73d New York, Maj. Michael W. Burns.
74th New York, Lieut. Col. Thomas Holt.
120th New York:
 Lieut. Col. Cornelius D. Westbrook.
 Maj. John R. Tappen.

Third Brigade.

Col. George C. Burling.

2d New Hampshire, Col. Edward L. Bailey.
5th New Jersey:
 Col. William J. Sewell.
 Capt. Thomas C. Godfrey.
 Capt. Henry H. Woolsey.
6th New Jersey, Lieut. Col. Stephen R. Gilkyson.
7th New Jersey:
 Col. Louis R. Francine.
 Maj. Frederick Cooper.
8th New Jersey:
 Col. John Ramsey.
 Capt. John G. Langston.
115th Pennsylvania, Maj. John P. Dunne.

*Guarding corps trains, and not engaged in the battle.

ARTILLERY BRIGADE.

Capt. GEORGE E. RANDOLPH.
Capt. A. JUDSON CLARK.

New Jersey Light, 2d Battery:
Capt. A. Judson Clark.
Lieut. Robert Sims.
1st New York Light, Battery D, Capt. George B. Winslow.
New York Light, 4th Battery, Capt. James E. Smith.
1st Rhode Island Light, Battery E:
Lieut. John K. Bucklyn.
Lieut. Benjamin Freeborn.
4th United States, Battery K:
Lieut. Francis W. Seeley.
Lieut. Robert James.

FIFTH ARMY CORPS.

Maj. Gen. GEORGE SYKES.

GENERAL HEADQUARTERS.

12th New York Infantry, Companies D and E, Capt. Henry W. Rider.
17th Pennsylvania Cavalry, Companies D and H, Capt. William Thompson.

FIRST DIVISION.

Brig. Gen. JAMES BARNES.

First Brigade.

Col. WILLIAM S. TILTON.

18th Massachusetts, Col. Joseph Hayes.
22d Massachusetts, Lieut. Col. Thomas Sherwin, jr.
1st Michigan:
Col. Ira C. Abbott.
Lieut. Col. William A. Throop.
118th Pennsylvania, Lieut. Col. James Gwyn.

Second Brigade.

Col. JACOB B. SWEITZER.

9th Massachusetts, Col. Patrick R. Guiney.
32d Massachusetts, Col. G. L. Prescott.
4th Michigan :
Col. Harrison H. Jeffords.
Lieut. Col. George W. Lumbard.
62d Pennsylvania, Lieut. Col. James C. Hull.

Third Brigade.

Col. STRONG VINCENT.
Col. JAMES C. RICE.

20th Maine, Col. Joshua L. Chamberlain.
16th Michigan, Lieut. Col. Norval E. Welch.
44th New York :
Col. James C. Rice.
Lieut. Col. Freeman Conner.
83d Pennsylvania, Capt. Orpheus S. Woodward.

SECOND DIVISION.

Brig. Gen. ROMEYN B. AYRES.

First Brigade.

Col. HANNIBAL DAY.

3d United States (six companies):
Capt. Henry W. Freedley.
Capt. Richard G. Lay.
4th United States (four companies),
Capt. Julius W. Adams, jr.
6th United States (five companies),
Capt. Levi C. Bootes.
12th United States (eight companies),
Capt. Thomas S. Dunn.
14th United States (eight companies),
Maj. Grotius R. Giddings.

Second Brigade.

Col. SIDNEY BURBANK.

2d United States (six companies):
Maj. Arthur T. Lee.
Capt. Samuel A. McKee.
7th United States (four companies),
Capt. David P. Hancock.
10th United States (three companies),
Capt. William Clinton.
11th United States (six companies), Maj. De Lancey Floyd-Jones.
17th United States (seven companies),
Lieut. Col. J. Durell Greene,

Third Brigade.

Brig. Gen. STEPHEN H. WEED.
Col. KENNER GARRARD.

140th New York:
Col. Patrick H. O'Rorke.
Lieut. Col. Louis Ernst.
146th New York:
Col. Kenner Garrard.
Lieut. Col. David T. Jenkins.
91st Pennsylvania, Lieut. Col. Joseph H. Sinex.
155th Pennsylvania, Lieut. Col. John H. Cain.

THIRD DIVISION.*

Brig. Gen. SAMUEL W. CRAWFORD.

First Brigade.	*Third Brigade.*
Col. WILLIAM MCCANDLESS.	Col. JOSEPH W. FISHER.
1st Pennsylvania Reserves (nine companies), Col. William C. Talley.	5th Pennsylvania Reserves, Lieut. Col. George Dare.
2d Pennsylvania Reserves, Lieut. Col. George A. Woodward.	9th Pennsylvania Reserves, Lieut. Col. James McK. Snodgrass.
6th Pennsylvania Reserves, Lieut. Col. Wellington H. Ent.	10th Pennsylvania Reserves, Col. Adoniram J. Warner.
13th Pennsylvania Reserves: Col. Charles F. Taylor. Maj. William R. Hartshorne.	11th Pennsylvania Reserves, Col. Samuel M. Jackson.
	12th Pennsylvania Reserves (nine companies), Col. Martin D. Hardin.

ARTILLERY BRIGADE.

Capt. AUGUSTUS P. MARTIN.

Massachusetts Light, 3d Battery (C), Lieut. Aaron F. Walcott.
1st New York Light, Battery C, Capt. Almont Barnes.
1st Ohio Light, Battery L, Capt. Frank C. Gibbs.
5th United States, Battery D:
Lieut. Charles E. Hazlett.
Lieut. Benjamin F. Rittenhouse.
5th United States, Battery I:
Lieut. Malbone F. Watson.
Lieut. Charles C. MacConnell.

SIXTH ARMY CORPS.

Maj. Gen. JOHN SEDGWICK.

GENERAL HEADQUARTERS.

1st New Jersey Cavalry, Company L,
1st Pennsylvania Cavalry, Company H, } Capt. William S. Craft.

FIRST DIVISION.

Brig. Gen. HORATIO G. WRIGHT.

Provost Guard.

4th New Jersey (three companies), Capt. William R. Maxwell.

First Brigade.	*Second Brigade.*
Brig. Gen. A. T. A. TORBERT.	Brig. Gen. JOSEPH J. BARTLETT.†
1st New Jersey, Lieut. Col. William Henry, jr.	5th Maine, Col. Clark S. Edwards.
2d New Jersey, Lieut. Col. Charles Wiebecke.	121st New York, Col. Emory Upton.
3d New Jersey, Lieut. Col. Edward L. Campbell.	95th Pennsylvania, Lieut. Col. Edward Carroll.
15th New Jersey, Col. William H. Penrose.	96th Pennsylvania, Maj. William H. Lessig.

---

* Joined corps June 28. The Second Brigade left in the Department of Washington.
† Also in command of the Third Brigade, Third Division, on July 3.

Third Brigade.

Brig. Gen. DAVID A. RUSSELL.

6th Maine, Col. Hiram Burnham.
49th Pennsylvania (four companies), Lieut. Col. Thomas M. Hulings.
119th Pennsylvania, Col. Peter C. Ellmaker.
5th Wisconsin, Col. Thomas S. Allen.

SECOND DIVISION.*

Brig. Gen. ALBION P. HOWE.

<table>
<tr><td>

Second Brigade.

Col. LEWIS A. GRANT.

2d Vermont, Col. James H. Walbridge.
3d Vermont, Col. Thomas O. Seaver.
4th Vermont, Col. Charles B. Stoughton.
5th Vermont, Lieut. Col. John R. Lewis.
6th Vermont, Col. Elisha L. Barney.

</td><td>

Third Brigade.

Brig. Gen. THOMAS H. NEILL.

7th Maine (six companies), Lieut. Col. Selden Connor.
33d New York (detachment), Capt. Henry J. Gifford.
43d New York, Lieut. Col. John Wilson.
49th New York, Col. Daniel D. Bidwell.
77th New York, Lieut. Col. Winsor B. French.
61st Pennsylvania, Lieut. Col. George F. Smith.

</td></tr>
</table>

THIRD DIVISION.

Maj. Gen. JOHN NEWTON.†
Brig. Gen. FRANK WHEATON.

<table>
<tr><td>

First Brigade.

Brig. Gen. ALEXANDER SHALER.

65th New York, Col. Joseph E. Hamblin.
67th New York, Col. Nelson Cross.
122d New York, Col. Silas Titus.
23d Pennsylvania, Lieut. Col. John F. Glenn.
82d Pennsylvania, Col. Isaac C. Bassett.

</td><td>

Second Brigade.

Col. HENRY L. EUSTIS.

7th Massachusetts, Lieut. Col. Franklin P. Harlow.
10th Massachusetts, Lieut. Col. Joseph B. Parsons.
37th Massachusetts, Col. Oliver Edwards.
2d Rhode Island, Col. Horatio Rogers, jr.

</td></tr>
</table>

Third Brigade.

Brig. Gen. FRANK WHEATON.
Col. DAVID J. NEVIN.

62d New York:
    Col. David J. Nevin.
    Lieut. Col. Theodore B. Hamilton.
93d Pennsylvania, Maj. John I. Nevin.
98th Pennsylvania, Maj. John B. Kohler.
102d Pennsylvania,‡ Col. John W. Patterson.
139th Pennsylvania:
    Col. Frederick H. Collier.
    Lieut. Col. William H. Moody.

ARTILLERY BRIGADE.

Col. CHARLES H. TOMPKINS.

Massachusetts Light, 1st Battery (A), Capt. William H. McCartney.
New York Light, 1st Battery, Capt. Andrew Cowan.
New York Light, 3d Battery, Capt. William A. Harn.
1st Rhode Island Light, Battery C, Capt. Richard Waterman.
1st Rhode Island Light, Battery G, Capt. George W. Adams.
2d United States, Battery D, Lieut. Edward B. Williston.
2d United States, Battery G, Lieut. John H. Butler.
5th United States, Battery F, Lieut. Leonard Martin.

---

* No First Brigade in division.
† See foot note (§), p. 155.
‡ Guarding wagon train at Westminster, and not engaged in the battle.

ELEVENTH ARMY CORPS.*

Maj. Gen. OLIVER O. HOWARD.

GENERAL HEADQUARTERS.

1st Indiana Cavalry, Companies I and K, Capt. Abram Sharra.
8th New York Infantry (one company), Lieut. Hermann Foerster.

FIRST DIVISION.

Brig. Gen. FRANCIS C. BARLOW.
Brig. Gen. ADELBERT AMES.

First Brigade.	*Second Brigade.*
Col. LEOPOLD VON GILSA.	Brig. Gen. ADELBERT AMES. Col. ANDREW L. HARRIS.
41st New York (nine companies), Lieut. Col. Detleo von Einsiedel. 54th New York: Maj. Stephen Kovacs. Lieut. Ernst Both [?]. 68th New York, Col. Gotthilf Bourry. 153d Pennsylvania, Maj. John F. Frueauff.	17th Connecticut: Lieut. Col. Douglas Fowler. Maj. Allen G. Brady. 25th Ohio: Lieut. Col. Jeremiah Williams. Capt. Nathaniel J. Manning. Lieut. William Maloney. Lieut. Israel White. 75th Ohio: Col. Andrew L. Harris. Capt. George B. Fox. 107th Ohio: Col. Seraphim Meyer. Capt. John M. Lutz.

SECOND DIVISION.

Brig. Gen. ADOLPH VON STEINWEHR.

First Brigade.	*Second Brigade.*
Col. CHARLES R. COSTER.	Col. ORLAND SMITH.
134th New York, Lieut. Col. Allan H. Jackson. 154th New York, Lieut. Col. D. B. Allen. 27th Pennsylvania, Lieut. Col. Lorenz Cantador. 73d Pennsylvania, Capt. D. F. Kelley.	33d Massachusetts, Col. Adin B. Underwood. 136th New York, Col. James Wood, jr. 55th Ohio, Col. Charles B. Gambee. 73d Ohio, Lieut. Col. Richard Long.

THIRD DIVISION.

Maj. Gen. CARL SCHURZ.

First Brigade.	*Second Brigade.*
Brig. Gen. ALEX. SCHIMMELFENNIG. Col. GEORGE VON AMSBERG.	Col. W. KRZYZANOWSKI.
82d Illinois, Lieut. Col. Edward S. Salomon. 45th New York : Col. George von Amsberg. Lieut. Col. Adolphus Dobke. 157th New York, Col. Philip P. Brown, jr. 61st Ohio, Col. Stephen J. McGroarty. 74th Pennsylvania: Col. Adolph von Hartung. Lieut. Col. Alexander von Mitzel. Capt. Gustav Schleiter. Capt. Henry Krauseneck.	58th New York: Lieut. Col. August Otto. Capt. Emil Koenig. 119th New York: Col. John T. Lockman. Lieut. Col. Edward F. Lloyd. 82d Ohio: Col. James S. Robinson. Lieut. Col. David Thomson. 75th Pennsylvania: Col. Francis Mahler. Maj. August Ledig. 26th Wisconsin: Lieut. Col. Hans Boebel. Capt. John W. Fuchs.

---

* During the interval between the death of General Reynolds and the arrival of General Hancock, on the afternoon of July 1, all the troops on the field of battle were commanded by General Howard, General Schurz taking command of the Eleventh Corps, and General Schimmelfennig of the Third Division.

ARTILLERY BRIGADE.

Maj. THOMAS W. OSBORN.

1st New York Light, Battery I, Capt. Michael Wiedrich.
New York Light, 13th Battery, Lieut. William Wheeler.
1st Ohio Light, Battery I, Capt. Hubert Dilger.
1st Ohio Light, Battery K, Capt. Lewis Heckman.
4th United States, Battery G:
    Lieut. Bayard Wilkeson.
    Lieut. Eugene A. Bancroft.

TWELFTH ARMY CORPS.

Maj. Gen. HENRY W. SLOCUM.*
Brig. Gen. ALPHEUS S. WILLIAMS.

PROVOST GUARD.

10th Maine (four companies), Capt John D. Beardsley.

FIRST DIVISION.

Brig. Gen. ALPHEUS S. WILLIAMS.
Brig. Gen. THOMAS H. RUGER.

First Brigade.	*Second Brigade.†*
Col. ARCHIBALD L. McDOUGALL.	Brig. Gen. HENRY H. LOCKWOOD.
5th Connecticut, Col. W. W. Packer.	1st Maryland, Potomac Home Br. gade, Col. William P. Maulsby.
20th Connecticut, Lieut. Col. William B. Wooster.	1st Maryland, Eastern Shore, C . James Wallace.
3d Maryland, Col. Jos. M. Sudsburg.	150th New York, Col. John H. Ketcham.
123d New York:	
Lieut. Col. James C. Rogers.	
Capt. Adolphus H. Tanner.	
145th New York, Col. E. L. Price.	
46th Pennsylvania, Col. James L. Selfridge.	

Third Brigade.

Brig. Gen. THOMAS H. RUGER.
Col. SILAS COLGROVE.

27th Indiana:
    Col. Silas Colgrove.
    Lieut. Col. John R. Fesler.
2d Massachusetts:
    Lieut. Col. Charles R. Mudge.
    Maj. Charles F. Morse.
13th New Jersey, Col. Ezra A. Carman.
107th New York, Col. Nirom M. Crane.
3d Wisconsin, Col. William Hawley.

SECOND DIVISION.

Brig. Gen. JOHN W. GEARY.

First Brigade.	*Second Brigade.*
Col. CHARLES CANDY.	Col. GEORGE A. COBHAM, Jr.
5th Ohio, Col. John H. Patrick.	Brig. GEN. THOMAS L. KANE.
7th Ohio, Col. William R. Creighton.	Col. GEORGE A. COBHAM, Jr.
29th Ohio:	29th Pennsylvania, Col. William Rickards, jr.
Capt. Wilbur F. Stevens.	109th Pennsylvania, Capt. F. L. Gimber.
Capt. Edward Hayes.	111th Pennsylvania:
66th Ohio, Lieut. Col. Eugene Powell.	Lieut. Col. Thomas M. Walker.
28th Pennsylvania, Capt. John Flynn.	Col. George A. Cobham, jr.
147th Pennsylvania (eight companies),	Lieut. Col. Thomas M. Walker.
Lieut. Col. Ario Pardee, jr.	

* Exercised command of the right wing of the army during a part of the battle. But see Slocum to Meade, December 30, 1863, p. 763, and Meade to Slocum, February 25, 1864, p. 769.
† Unassigned during progress of battle; afterward attached to First Division, as Second Brigade. The command theretofore known as the Second (or Jackson's) Brigade had previously been consolidated with the First Brigade.

Third Brigade.

Brig. Gen. GEORGE S. GREENE.

60th New York, Col. Abel Godard.
78th New York, Lieut. Col. Herbert von Hammerstein.
102d New York:
    Col. James C. Lane.
    Capt. Lewis R. Stegman.
137th New York, Col. David Ireland.
149th New York:
    Col. Henry A. Barnum.
    Lieut. Col. Charles B. Randall.

ARTILLERY BRIGADE.

Lieut. EDWARD D. MUHLENBERG.

1st New York Light, Battery M, Lieut. Charles E. Winegar.
Pennsylvania Light, Battery E, Lieut. Charles A. Atwell.
4th United States, Battery F, Lieut. Sylvanus T. Rugg.
5th United States, Battery K, Lieut. David H. Kinzie.

CAVALRY CORPS.

Maj. Gen. ALFRED PLEASONTON.

FIRST DIVISION.

Brig. Gen. JOHN BUFORD.

First Brigade.

Col. WILLIAM GAMBLE.

8th Illinois, Maj. John L. Beveridge.
12th Illinois (four cos.), ⎱ Col. George H.
3d Indiana (six cos.), ⎰   Chapman.
8th New York, Lieut. Col. William L. Markell.

Second Brigade.

Col. THOMAS C. DEVIN.

6th New York, Maj. Wm. E. Beardsley.
9th New York, Col. William Sackett.
17th Pennsylvania, Col. J. H. Kellogg.
3d West Virginia (two companies), Capt. Seymour B. Conger.

Reserve Brigade.

Brig. Gen. WESLEY MERRITT.

6th Pennsylvania, Maj. James H. Haseltine.
1st United States, Capt. Richard S. C. Lord.
2d United States, Capt. T. F. Rodenbough.
5th United States, Capt. Julius W. Mason.
6th United States:
    Maj. Samuel H. Starr.
    Lieut. Louis H. Carpenter.
    Lieut. Nicholas Nolan.
    Capt. Ira W. Claflin.

SECOND DIVISION.

Brig. Gen. DAVID McM. GREGG.

Headquarters Guard.

1st Ohio, Company A, Capt. Noah Jones.

First Brigade.

Col. JOHN B. McINTOSH.

1st Maryland (eleven companies), Lieut. Col. James M. Deems.
Purnell (Maryland) Legion, Company A, Capt. Robert E. Duvall.
1st Massachusetts,* Lieut. Col. Greely S. Curtis.
1st New Jersey, Maj. M. H. Beaumont.
1st Pennsylvania, Col. John P. Taylor.
3d Pennsylvania, Lieut. Col. E. S. Jones.
3d Pennsylvania Heavy Artillery, Section Battery H,† Capt. W. D. Rank.

Second Brigade.‡

Col. PENNOCK HUEY.

2d New York, Lieut. Col. Otto Harhaus.
4th New York, Lieut. Col. Augustus Pruyn.
6th Ohio (ten companies), Maj. William Stedman.
8th Pennsylvania, Capt. William A. Corrie.

---

* Served with the Sixth Army Corps, and on the right flank.
† Serving as light artillery.
‡ At Westminster, etc., and not engaged in the battle.

Third Brigade.

Col. J. IRVIN GREGG.

1st Maine (ten companies), Lieut. Col. Charles H. Smith.
10th New York, Maj. M. Henry Avery.
4th Pennsylvania, Lieut. Col. William E. Doster.
16th Pennsylvania, Lieut. Col. John K. Robison.

THIRD DIVISION.

Brig. Gen. JUDSON KILPATRICK.

Headquarters Guard.

1st Ohio, Company C, Capt. Samuel N. Stanford.

First Brigade.	*Second Brigade.*
Brig. Gen. ELON J. FARNSWORTH. Col. NATHANIEL P. RICHMOND.	Brig. Gen. GEORGE A. CUSTER.
5th New York, Maj. John Hammond. 18th Pennsylvania, Lieut. Col. William P. Brinton. 1st Vermont, Lieut. Col. Addison W. Preston. 1st West Virginia (ten companies): Col. Nathaniel P. Richmond. Maj. Charles E. Capehart.	1st Michigan, Col. Charles H. Town. 5th Michigan, Col. Russell A. Alger. 6th Michigan, Col. George Gray. 7th Michigan (ten companies), Col. William D. Mann.

HORSE ARTILLERY.

First Brigade.	*Second Brigade.*
Capt. JAMES M. ROBERTSON.	Capt. JOHN C. TIDBALL.
9th Michigan Battery, Capt. Jabez J. Daniels. 6th New York Battery, Capt. Joseph W. Martin. 2d United States, Batteries B and L, Lieut. Edward Heaton. 2d United States, Battery M, Lieut. A. C. M. Pennington, jr. 4th United States, Battery E, Lieut. Samuel S. Elder.	1st United States, Batteries E and G, Capt. Alanson M. Randol. 1st United States, Battery K, Capt. William M. Graham. 2d United States, Battery A, Lieut. John H. Calef. 3d United States, Battery C, Lieut. William D. Fuller.*

ARTILLERY RESERVE.

Brig. Gen. ROBERT O. TYLER.
Capt. JAMES M. ROBERTSON.

Headquarters Guard.

32d Massachusetts Infantry, Company C, Capt. Josiah C. Fuller.

First Regular Brigade.	*First Volunteer Brigade.*
Capt. DUNBAR R. RANSOM.	Lieut. Col. FREEMAN McGILVERY.
1st United States, Battery H: Lieut. Chandler P. Eakin. Lieut. Philip D. Mason. 3d United States, Batteries F and K, Lieut. John G. Turnbull. 4th United States, Battery C, Lieut. Evan Thomas. 5th United States, Battery C, Lieut. Gulian V. Weir.	Massachusetts Light, 5th Battery (E),† Capt. Charles A. Phillips. Massachusetts Light, 9th Battery: Capt. John Bigelow. Lieut. Richard S. Milton. New York Light, 15th Battery, Capt. Patrick Hart. Pennsylvania Light, Batteries C and F, Capt. James Thompson.

---

* With Huey's Cavalry Brigade, and not engaged in the battle.
† 10th New York Battery attached.

Second Volunteer Brigade.

Capt. ELIJAH D. TAFT.

1st Connecticut Heavy, Battery B,* Capt. Albert F. Brooker.
1st Connecticut Heavy, Battery M,* Capt. Franklin A. Pratt.
Connecticut Light, 2d Battery, Capt. John W. Sterling.
New York Light, 5th Battery, Capt. Elijah D. Taft.

Third Volunteer Brigade.

Capt. JAMES F. HUNTINGTON.

New Hampshire Light, 1st Battery, Capt. Frederick M. Edgell.
1st Ohio Light, Battery H, Lieut. George W. Norton.
1st Pennsylvania Light, Batteries F and G, Capt. R. Bruce Ricketts.
West Virginia Light, Battery C, Capt. Wallace Hill.

Fourth Volunteer Brigade.

Capt. ROBERT H. FITZHUGH.

Maine Light, 6th Battery (F), Lieut. Edwin B. Dow.
Maryland Light, Battery A, Capt. James H. Rigby.
New Jersey Light, 1st Battery, Lieut. Augustin N. Parsons.
1st New York Light, Battery G, Capt. Nelson Ames.
1st New York Light, Battery K,† Capt. Robert H. Fitzhugh.

Train Guard.

4th New Jersey Infantry (seven companies), Maj. Charles Ewing.

No. 124.

Organization of the Army of Northern Virginia at the battle of Gettysburg, July 1–3. *

FIRST ARMY CORPS.

Lieut. Gen. JAMES LONGSTREET.

M'LAWS' DIVISION.

Maj. Gen. LAFAYETTE MCLAWS.

Kershaw's Brigade.

Brig. Gen. J. B. KERSHAW.

2d South Carolina :
  Col. J. D. Kennedy.
  Lieut. Col. F. Gaillard.
3d South Carolina :
  Maj. R. C. Maffett.
  Col. J. D. Nance.
7th South Carolina, Col. D. Wyatt Aiken.
8th South Carolina, Col. J. W. Henagan.
15th South Carolina :
  Col. W. D. De Saussure.
  Maj. William M. Gist.
3d South Carolina Battalion, Lieut. Col. W. G. Rice.

Semmes' Brigade.†

Brig. Gen. P. J. SEMMES.
Col. GOODE BRYAN.

10th Georgia, Col. John B. Weems.
50th Georgia, Col. W. R. Manning.
51st Georgia, Col. E. Ball.
53d Georgia, Col. James P. Simms.

Barksdale's Brigade.

Brig. Gen. WILLIAM BARKSDALE.
Col. B. G. HUMPHREYS.

13th Mississippi, Col. J. W. Carter.
17th Mississippi :
  Col. W. D. Holder.
  Lieut. Col. John C. Fiser.
18th Mississippi :
  Col. T. M. Griffin.
  Lieut. Col. W. H. Luse.
21st Mississippi, Col. B. G. Humphreys.

Wofford's Brigade.

Brig. Gen. W. T. WOFFORD.

16th Georgia, Col. Goode Bryan.
18th Georgia, Lieut. Col. S. Z. Ruff.
24th Georgia, Col. Robert McMillan.
Cobb's (Georgia) Legion, Lieut. Col. Luther J. Glenn.
Phillips (Georgia) Legion, Lieut. Col. E. S. Barclay.

Artillery.

Col. H. G. CABELL.

1st North Carolina Artillery, Battery A, Capt. B. C. Manly.
Pulaski (Georgia) Artillery :
  Capt. J. C. Fraser.
  Lieut. W. J. Furlong.
1st Richmond Howitzers, Capt. E. S. McCarthy.
Troup (Georgia) Artillery :
  Capt. H. H. Carlton.
  Lieut. C. W. Motes.

---

*The actual commanders are indicated as far as practicable.
†No reports on file for this brigade. Bryan was in command July 7, and was probably Semmes' immediate successor. The commanders of the Tenth, Fifty-first, and Fifty-third Georgia are given as reported for June 22 and July 31. Manning reported in command of Fiftieth Georgia, June 22. No commander reported on return for July 31.

PICKETT'S DIVISION.

Maj. Gen. GEORGE E. PICKETT.

Garnett's Brigade.

Brig. Gen. R. B. GARNETT.
Maj. C. S. PEYTON.

8th Virginia, Col. Eppa Hunton.
18th Virginia, Lieut. Col. H. A. Carrington.
19th Virginia:
    Col. Henry Gantt.
    Lieut. Col. John T. Ellis.
28th Virginia:
    Col. R. C. Allen.
    Lieut. Col. William Watts.
56th Virginia:
    Col. W. D. Stuart.
    Lieut. Col. P. P. Slaughter.

Kemper's Brigade.

Brig. Gen. J. L. KEMPER.
Col. JOSEPH MAYO, Jr.

1st Virginia:
    Col. Lewis B. Williams.
    Lieut. Col. F. G. Skinner.
3d Virginia:
    Col. Joseph Mayo, jr.
    Lieut. Col. A. D. Callcote.
7th Virginia:
    Col. W. T. Patton.
    Lieut. Col. C. C. Flowerree.
11th Virginia, Maj. Kirkwood Otey.
24th Virginia, Col. William R. Terry.

Armistead's Brigade.

Brig. Gen. L. A. ARMISTEAD.
Col. W. R. AYLETT.

9th Virginia, Maj. John C. Owens.
14th Virginia:
    Col. James G. Hodges.
    Lieut. Col. William White.
38th Virginia:
    Col. E. C. Edmonds.
    Lieut. Col. P. B. Whittle.
53d Virginia, Col. W. R. Aylett.
57th Virginia, Col. John Bowie Magruder.

Artillery.

Maj. JAMES DEARING.

Fauquier (Virginia) Artillery, Capt. R. M. Stribling.
Hampden ((Virginia) Artillery, Capt. W. H. Caskie.
Richmond Fayette Artillery, Capt. M. C. Macon.
Virginia Battery, Capt. Joseph G. Blount.

HOOD'S DIVISION

Maj. Gen. JOHN B. HOOD.
Brig. Gen. E. M. LAW.

Law's Brigade.

Brig. Gen. E. M. LAW.
Col. JAMES L. SHEFFIELD.

4th Alabama, Lieut. Col. L. H. Scruggs.
15th Alabama:
    Col. William C. Oates.
    Capt. B. A. Hill.
44th Alabama, Col. William F. Perry.
47th Alabama:
    Col. James W. Jackson.
    Lieut. Col. M. J. Bulger.
    Maj. J. M. Campbell.
48th Alabama:
    Col. James L. Sheffield.
    Capt. T. J. Eubanks.

Robertson's Brigade.

Brig. Gen. J. B. ROBERTSON.

3d Arkansas:
    Col. Van H. Manning.
    Lieut. Col. R. S. Taylor.
1st Texas, Lieut. Col. P. A. Work.
4th Texas:
    Col. J. C. G. Key.
    Maj. J. P. Bane.
5th Texas:
    Col. R. M. Powell.
    Lieut. Col. K. Bryan.
    Maj. J. C. Rogers.

Anderson's Brigade.

Brig. Gen. GEORGE T. ANDERSON.
Lieut. Col. WILLIAM LUFFMAN.

7th Georgia, Col. W. W. White.
8th Georgia, Col. John R. Towers.
9th Georgia :
   Lieut. Col. John C. Mounger.
   Maj. W. M. Jones.
   Capt. George Hillyer.
11th Georgia :
   Col. F. H. Little.
   Lieut. Col. William Luffman.
   Maj. Henry D. McDaniel.
   Capt. William H. Mitchell.
59th Georgia :
   Col. Jack Brown.
   Capt. M. G. Bass.

Benning's Brigade.

Brig. Gen. HENRY L. BENNING.

2d Georgia :
   Lieut. Col. William T. Harris.
   Maj. W. S. Shepherd.
15th Georgia, Col. D. M. DuBose.
17th Georgia, Col. W. C. Hodges.
20th Georgia :
   Col. John A. Jones.
   Lieut. Col. J. D. Waddell.

Artillery.

Maj. M. W. HENRY.

Branch (North Carolina) Artillery, Capt. A. C. Latham
German (South Carolina) Artillery, Capt. William K. Bachman.
Palmetto (South Carolina) Light Artillery, Capt. Hugh R. Garden.
Rowan (North Carolina) Artillery, Capt. James Reilly.

ARTILLERY RESERVE.

Col. J. B. WALTON.

Alexander's Battalion.

Col. E. P. ALEXANDER.

Ashland (Virginia) Artillery :
   Capt. P. Woolfolk, jr.
   Lieut. James Woolfolk.
Bedford (Virginia) Artillery, Capt. T. C.
   Jordan.
Brooks (South Carolina) Artillery, Lieut.
   S. C. Gilbert.
Madison (Louisiana) Light Artillery, Capt.
   George V. Moody.
Virginia Battery, Capt. W. W. Parker.
Virginia Battery, Capt. O. B. Taylor.

Washington (Louisiana) Artillery.

Maj. B. F. ESHLEMAN.

First Company, Capt. C. W. Squires.
Second Company, Capt. J. B. Richardson.
Third Company, Capt. M. B. Miller.
Fourth Company :
   Capt. Joe Norcom.
   Lieut. H. A. Battles.

SECOND ARMY CORPS.

Lieut. Gen. RICHARD S. EWELL.

Escort.

Randolph's Company Virginia Cavalry, Capt. William F. Randolph.

EARLY'S DIVISION.

Maj. Gen. JUBAL A. EARLY.

Hays' Brigade.

Brig. Gen. HARRY T. HAYS.

5th Louisiana :
   Maj. Alexander Hart.
   Capt. T. H. Biscoe.
6th Louisiana, Lieut. Col. Joseph Hanlon.
7th Louisiana, Col. D. B. Penn.
8th Louisiana :
   Col. T. D. Lewis.
   Lieut. Col. A. de Blanc.
   Maj. G. A. Lester.
9th Louisiana, Col. Leroy A. Stafford.

Smith's Brigade.

Brig. Gen. WILLIAM SMITH.

31st Virginia, Col. John S. Hoffman.
49th Virginia, Lieut. Col. J. Catlett Gibson.
52d Virginia, Lieut. Col. James H. Skinner.

Hoke's Brigade.

Col. ISAAC E. AVERY.
Col. A. C. GODWIN.

6th North Carolina, Maj. S. McD. Tate.
21st North Carolina, Col. W. W. Kirkland.
57th North Carolina, Col. A. C. Godwin.

Gordon's Brigade.

Brig. Gen. J. B. GORDON.

13th Georgia, Col. James M. Smith.
26th Georgia, Col. E. N. Atkinson.
31st Georgia, Col. Clement A. Evans.
38th Georgia, Capt. William L. McLeod.
60th Georgia, Capt. W. B. Jones.
61st Georgia, Col. John H. Lamar.

Artillery.

Lieut. Col. H. P. JONES.

Charlottesville (Virginia) Artillery, Capt. James McD. Carrington.
Courtney (Virginia) Artillery, Capt. W. A. Tanner.
Louisiana Guard Artillery, Capt. C. A. Green.
Staunton (Virginia) Artillery, Capt. A. W. Garber.

JOHNSON'S DIVISION.

Maj. Gen. EDWARD JOHNSON.

Steuart's Brigade.

Brig. Gen. GEORGE H. STEUART.

1st Maryland Battalion Infantry :
    Lieut. Col. J. R. Herbert.
    Maj. W. W. Goldsborough.
    Capt. J. P. Crane.
1st North Carolina, Lieut. Col. H. A. Brown.
3d North Carolina, Maj. W. M. Parsley.
10th Virginia, Col. E. T. H. Warren.
23d Virginia, Lieut. Col. S. T. Walton.
37th Virginia, Maj. H. C. Wood.

Stonewall Brigade.

Brig. Gen. JAMES A. WALKER.

2d Virginia, Col. J. Q. A. Nadenbousch.
4th Virginia, Maj. William Terry.
5th Virginia, Col. J. H. S. Funk.
27th Virginia, Lieut. Col. D. M. Shriver.
33d Virginia, Capt. J. B. Golladay.

*Nicholls' Brigade.**

Col. J. M. WILLIAMS.

1st Louisiana, Capt. E. D. Willett.
2d Louisiana, Lieut. Col. R. E. Burke.
10th Louisiana, Maj. T. N. Powell.
14th Louisiana, Lieut. Col. David Zable.
15th Louisiana, Maj. Andrew Brady.

Jones' Brigade.

Brig. Gen. JOHN M. JONES.
Lieut. Col. R. H. DUNGAN.

21st Virginia, Capt. W. P. Moseley.
25th Virginia :
    Col. J. C. Higginbotham.
    Lieut. Col. J. A. Robinson.
42d Virginia :
    Lieut. Col. R. W. Withers.
    Capt. S. H. Saunders.
44th Virginia :
    Maj. N. Cobb.
    Capt. T. R. Buckner.
48th Virginia :
    Lieut. Col. R. H. Dungan.
    Maj. Oscar White.
50th Virginia, Lieut. Col. L. H. N. Salyer.

Artillery.

Maj. J. W. LATIMER.
Capt. C. I. RAINE.

1st Maryland Battery, Capt. William F. Dement.
Alleghany (Virginia) Artillery, Capt. J. C. Carpenter.
Chesapeake (Maryland) Artillery, Capt. William D. Brown.
Lee (Virginia) Battery :
    Capt. C. I. Raine.
    Lieut. William W. Hardwicke.

* The regimental commanders are given as reported for June 14,

RODES' DIVISION.

Maj. Gen. R. E. RODES.

Daniel's Brigade.

Brig. Gen. JUNIUS DANIEL.

32d North Carolina, Col. E. C. Brabble.
43d North Carolina :
    Col. T. S. Kenan.
    Lieut. Col. W. G. Lewis.
45th North Carolina :
    Lieut. Col. S. H. Boyd.
    Maj. John R. Winston.
    Capt. A. H. Gallaway.
    Capt. J. A. Hopkins.
53d North Carolina, Col. W. A. Owens.
2d North Carolina Battalion :
    Lieut. Col. H. L. Andrews.
    Capt. Van Brown.

Iverson's Brigade.

Brig. Gen. ALFRED IVERSON.

5th North Carolina :*
    Capt. Speight B. West.
    Capt. Benjamin Robinson.
12th North Carolina, Lieut. Col. W. S.
    Davis.
20th North Carolina :†
    Lieut. Col. Nelson Slough.
    Capt. Lewis T. Hicks.
23d North Carolina :‡
    Col. D. H. Christie.
    Capt. William H. Johnston.

Doles' Brigade.

Brig. Gen. GEORGE DOLES.

4th Georgia :
    Lieut. Col. D. R. E. Winn.
    Maj. W. H. Willis.
12th Georgia, Col. Edward Willis.
21st Georgia, Col. John T. Mercer.
44th Georgia :
    Col. S. P. Lumpkin.
    Maj. W. H. Peebles.

Ramseur's Brigade.

Brig. Gen. S. D. RAMSEUR.

2d North Carolina :
    Maj. D. W. Hurtt.
    Capt. James T. Scales.
4th North Carolina, Col. Bryan Grimes.
14th North Carolina :
    Col. R. Tyler Bennett.
    Maj. Joseph H. Lambeth.
30th North Carolina :
    Col. Francis M. Parker.
    Maj. W. W. Sillers.

O'Neal's Brigade.

Col. E. A. O'NEAL.

3d Alabama, Col. C. A. Battle.
5th Alabama, Col. J. M. Hall.
6th Alabama :
    Col. J. N. Lightfoot.
    Capt. M. L. Bowie.
12th Alabama, Col. S. B. Pickens.
26th Alabama, Lieut. Col. John C. Goodgame.

Artillery.

Lieut. Col. THOMAS H. CARTER.

Jeff. Davis (Alabama) Artillery, Capt. W. J. Reese.
King William (Virginia) Artillery, Capt. W. P. Carter.
Morris (Virginia) Artillery, Capt. R. C. M. Page.
Orange (Virginia) Artillery, Capt. C. W. Fry.

---

* The four captains present (West, Robinson, James M. Taylor, Thomas N. Jordan), were reported as wounded July 1; Robinson and Taylor as having rejoined July 2, but it does not appear who commanded during Robinson's absence.
  † Lieutenant-Colonel Slough and Maj. John S. Brooks reported as wounded at 4 p. m. July 1.
  ‡ Colonel Christie, Lieut. Col. R. D. Johnston, Maj. C. C. Blacknall, and the senior captain (Abner D. Peace), reported as wounded early in the fight, July 1.

ARTILLERY RESERVE.

Col. J. THOMPSON BROWN.

First Virginia Artillery.

Capt. WILLIS J. DANCE.

2d Richmond (Virginia) Howitzers, Capt.
David Watson.
3d Richmond (Virginia) Howitzers, Capt.
B. H. Smith, jr.
Powhatan (Virginia) Artillery, Lieut.
John M. Cunningham.
Rockbridge (Virginia) Artillery, Capt. A.
Graham.
Salem (Virginia) Artillery, Lieut. C. B.
Griffin.

Nelson's Battalion.

Lieut. Col. WILLIAM NELSON.

Amherst (Virginia) Artillery, Capt. T. J.
Kirkpatrick.
Fluvanna (Virginia) Artillery, Capt. J. L.
Massie.
Georgia Battery, Capt. John Milledge, jr.

THIRD ARMY CORPS.

Lieut. Gen. AMBROSE P. HILL.

ANDERSON'S DIVISION.

Maj. Gen. R. H. ANDERSON.

Wilcox's Brigade.

Brig. Gen. CADMUS M. WILCOX.

8th Alabama, Lieut. Col. Hilary A. Her-
bert.
9th Alabama, Capt. J. H. King.
10th Alabama:
Col. William H. Forney.
Lieut. Col. James E. Shelley.
11th Alabama:
Col. J. C. C. Sanders.
Lieut. Col. George E. Tayloe.
14th Alabama:
Col. L. Pinckard.
Lieut. Col. James A. Broome.

Wright's Brigade.

Brig. Gen. A. R. WRIGHT.
Col. WILLIAM GIBSON.
Brig. Gen. A. R. WRIGHT.

3d Georgia, Col. E. J. Walker.
22d Georgia:
Col. Joseph Wasden.
Capt. B. C. McCurry.
48th Georgia:
Col. William Gibson.
Capt. M. R. Hall.
Col. William Gibson.
2d Georgia Battalion:
Maj. George W. Ross.
Capt. Charles J. Moffett.

Mahone's Brigade.

Brig. Gen. WILLIAM MAHONE.

6th Virginia, Col. George T. Rogers.
12th Virginia, Col. D. A. Weisiger.
16th Virginia, Col. Joseph H. Ham.
41st Virginia, Col. William A. Parham.
61st Virginia, Col. V. D. Groner.

Perry's Brigade.

Col. DAVID LANG.

2d Florida, Maj. W. R. Moore.
5th Florida, Capt. R. N. Gardner.
8th Florida, Col. David Lang.

Posey's Brigade.

Brig. Gen. CARNOT POSEY.

12th Mississippi, Col. W. H. Taylor.
16th Mississippi, Col. Samuel E. Baker.
19th Mississippi, Col. N. H. Harris.
48th Mississippi, Col. Joseph M. Jayne.

Artillery (Sumter Battalion).

Maj. JOHN LANE.

Company A, Capt. Hugh M. Ross.
Company B, Capt. George M. Patterson.
Company C, Capt. John T. Wingfield.

HETH'S DIVISION.

Maj. Gen. HENRY HETH.
Brig. Gen. J. J. PETTIGREW.

First Brigade.

Brig. Gen. J. J. PETTIGREW.
Col. J. K. MARSHALL.

11th North Carolina, Col. Collett Leven-
thorpe.
26th North Carolina:
Col. Henry K. Burgwyn, jr.
Capt. H. C. Albright.
47th North Carolina, Col. G. H. Fari-
bault.
52d North Carolina:
Col. J. K. Marshall.
Lieut. Col. Marcus A. Parks.

Second Brigade.

Col. J. M. BROCKENBROUGH.

40th Virginia:
Capt. T. E. Betts.
Capt. R. B. Davis.
47th Virginia, Col. Robert M. Mayo.
55th Virginia, Col. W. S. Christian.
22d Virginia Battalion, Maj. John S.
Bowles.

Third Brigade.

Brig. Gen. JAMES J. ARCHER.
Col. B. D. FRY.
Lieut. Col. S. G. SHEPARD.

13th Alabama, Col. B. D. Fry.
5th Alabama Battalion, Maj. A. S.
Van de Graaff.
1st Tennessee (Provisional Army), Maj.
Felix G. Buchanan.
7th Tennessee, Lieut. Col. S. G. Shepard.
14th Tennessee, Capt. B. L. Phillips.

Fourth Brigade.

Brig. Gen. JOSEPH R. DAVIS.

2d Mississippi, Col. J. M. Stone.
11th Mississippi, Col. F. M. Green.
42d Mississippi, Col. H. R. Miller.
55th North Carolina, Col. J. K. Connally.

Artillery.

Lieut. Col. JOHN J. GARNETT.

Donaldsonville (Louisiana) Artillery, Capt. V. Maurin.
Huger (Virginia) Artillery, Capt. Joseph D. Moore.
Lewis (Virginia) Artillery, Capt. John W. Lewis.
Norfolk Light Artillery Blues, Capt. C. R. Grandy.

PENDER'S DIVISION.

Maj. Gen. WILLIAM D. PENDER.
Brig. Gen. JAMES H. LANE.
Maj. Gen. I. R. TRIMBLE.
Brig. Gen. JAMES H. LANE.

First Brigade.

Col. ABNER PERRIN.

1st South Carolina (Provisional Army),
Maj. C. W. McCreary.
1st South Carolina Rifles, Capt. William
M. Hadden.
12th South Carolina, Col. John L. Miller.
13th South Carolina, Lieut. Col. B. T.
Brockman.
14th South Carolina, Lieut. Col. Joseph
N. Brown.

Second Brigade.

Brig. Gen. JAMES H. LANE.
Col. C. M. AVERY.
Brig. Gen. JAMES H. LANE.
Col. C. M. AVERY.

7th North Carolina:
Capt. J. McLeod Turner.
Capt. James G. Harris.
18th North Carolina, Col. John D. Barry.
28th North Carolina:
Col. S. D. Lowe.
Lieut. Col. W. H. A. Speer.
33d North Carolina, Col. C. M. Avery.
37th North Carolina, Col. W. M. Bar-
bour.

Third Brigade.

Brig. Gen. EDWARD L. THOMAS.

14th Georgia.
35th Georgia.
45th Georgia.
49th Georgia, Col. S. T. Player.

Fourth Brigade.

Brig. Gen. A. M. SCALES.
Lieut. Col. G. T. GORDON.
Col. W. LEE J. LOWRANCE.

13th North Carolina :
    Col. J. H. Hyman.
    Lieut. Col. H. A. Rogers.
16th North Carolina, Capt. L. W. Stowe.
22d North Carolina, Col. James Conner.
34th North Carolina :
    Col. William Lee J. Lowrance.
    Lieut. Col. G. T. Gordon.
38th North Carolina :
    Col. W. J. Hoke.
    Lieut. Col. John Ashford.

Artillery.

Maj. WILLIAM T. POAGUE.

Albemarle (Virginia) Artillery, Capt. James W. Wyatt.
Charlotte (North Carolina) Artillery, Capt. Joseph Graham.
Madison (Mississippi) Light Artillery, Capt. George Ward.
Virginia Battery, Capt. J. V. Brooke.

ARTILLERY RESERVE.

Col. R. LINDSAY WALKER.

McIntosh's Battalion.

Maj. D. G. McINTOSH.

Danville (Virginia) Artillery, Capt. R. S. Rice.
Hardaway (Alabama) Artillery, Capt. W. B. Hurt.
2d Rockbridge (Virginia) Artillery, Lieut. Samuel Wallace.
Virginia Battery, Capt. M. Johnson.

Pegram's Battalion.

Maj. W. J. PEGRAM.
Capt. E. B. BRUNSON.

Crenshaw (Virginia) Battery.
Fredericksburg (Virginia) Artillery, Capt. E. A. Marye.
Letcher (Virginia) Artillery, Capt. T. A. Brander.
Pee Dee (South Carolina) Artillery, Lieut. William E. Zimmerman.
Purcell (Virginia) Artillery, Capt. Joseph McGraw.

CAVALRY.

STUART'S DIVISION.

Maj. Gen. J. E. B. STUART.

Hampton's Brigade.

Brig. Gen. WADE HAMPTON.
Col. L. S. BAKER.

1st North Carolina, Col. L. S. Baker.
1st South Carolina.
2d South Carolina.
Cobb's (Georgia) Legion.
Jeff. Davis Legion.
Phillips (Georgia) Legion.

Robertson's Brigade.

Br'g. Gen. BEVERLY H. ROBERTSON.*

4th North Carolina, Col. D. D. Ferebee.
5th North Carolina.

Fitz. Lee's Brigade.

Brig. Gen. FITZ. LEE.

1st Maryland Battalion :†
    Maj. Harry Gilmor.
    Maj. Ridgely Brown.
1st Virginia, Col. James H. Drake.
2d Virginia, Col. T. T. Munford.
3d Virginia, Col. Thomas H. Owen.
4th Virginia, Col. Williams C. Wickham.
5th Virginia, Col. T. L. Rosser.

Jenkins' Brigade.

Brig. Gen. A. G. JENKINS.
Col. M. J. FERGUSON.

14th Virginia.
16th Virginia.
17th Virginia.
34th Virginia Battalion, Lieut. Col. V. A. Witcher.
36th Virginia Battalion.
Jackson's (Virginia) Battery, Capt. Thomas E. Jackson.

---

* Commanded his own and W. E. Jones' brigade.   † Serving with Ewell's corps.

Jones' Brigade.	*W. H. F. Lee's Brigade.*
Brig. Gen. WILLIAM E. JONES.	Col. J. R. CHAMBLISS, Jr.
6th Virginia, Maj. C. E. Flournoy. 7th Virginia, Lieut. Col. Thomas Marshall. 11th Virginia, Col. L. L. Lomax.	2d North Carolina. 9th Virginia, Col. R. L. T. Beale. 10th Virginia, Col. J. Lucius Davis. 13th Virginia.

Stuart Horse Artillery.

Maj. R. F. BECKHAM.

Breathed's (Virginia) Battery, Capt. James Breathed.
Chew's (Virginia) Battery, Capt. R. P. Chew.
Griffin's (Maryland) Battery, Capt. W. H. Griffin.
Hart's (South Carolina) Battery, Capt. J. F. Hart.
McGregor's (Virginia) Battery, Capt. W. M. McGregor.
Moorman's (Virginia) Battery, Capt. M. N. Moorman.

IMBODEN'S COMMAND.

Brig. Gen. J. D. IMBODEN.

18th Virginia Cavalry, Col. George W. Imboden.
62d Virginia Infantry,* Col. George H. Smith.
Virginia Partisan Rangers, Capt. John H. McNeill.
Virginia Battery, Capt. J. H. McClanahan.

ARTILLERY.†

Brig. Gen. W. N. PENDLETON.

NOTES

ABBREVIATIONS

The following abbreviations are used in the notes.

BC   Robert L. Brake Collection. United States Army Military History Institute. Carlisle Barracks, Pennsylvania.

BP   John B. Bachelder Papers. New Hampshire Historical Society. Concord, New Hampshire.

CCW   U.S. Congress. *Report of the Joint Committee on the Conduct of the War. . . .* Washington, D.C.: U.S. Government Printing Office, 1865.

DAB   Johnson, Allen, and Dumas Malone, eds. *Dictionary of American Biography.* 20 vols. New York: Charles Scribner's Sons, 1928–36.

GL   Gettysburg Letterbook. George Gordon Meade Collection. The Historical Society of Pennsylvania. Philadelphia, Pennsylvania.

GNMP   Gettysburg National Military Park.

HSP   The Historical Society of Pennsylvania. Philadelphia, Pennsylvania.

LC   Library of Congress. Washington, D.C.

Me at Gbg   Maine Gettysburg Commission. *Maine at Gettysburg: Report of the Maine Commissioners.* Portland, Me.: Lakeside Press, 1898.

NY at Gbg   New York Monuments Commission for the Battlefields of Gettysburg and Chattanooga. *Final Report on the Battlefield of Gettysburg.* [Cover title, *New York at Gettysburg.*] 3 vols. Albany, N.Y.: J. B. Lyon Company, Printers, 1900.

OR   U.S. War Department. *The War of the Rebellion: A Compilation of the Official Records of the Union and Confederate Armies.* 128 vols. Washington, D.C.: U.S. Government Printing Office, 1880–1901.

Pa at Gbg   Nicholson, John P., ed. *Pennsylvania at Gettysburg: Ceremonies at the Dedication of the Monuments Erected by the Commonwealth of Pennsylvania.* 2 vols. Harrisburg: Wm. Stanley Ray, State Printer, 1904.

SHC   Southern Historical Collection. University of North Carolina. Chapel Hill, North Carolina.

CHAPTER I

1. *OR* 27 (3):369.

2. Ibid. (1):61; Benjamin, "Hooker's Appointment and Removal," p. 243; Cleaves, *Meade*, p. 124. A marker at the side of the old road between Frederick and Harpers

Ferry, at the base of the east slope of Braddock Heights, indicates that Meade received G.O. 194 and the command of the army at a point about seven hundred yards north of the marker. His predecessors technically had been McClellan, Burnside, and Hooker; Pope's command had been the Army of Virginia.

3. *OR* 27 (1):60, (3):369.

4. Smart, *A Radical View* 2:17.

5. Cleaves, *Meade*, is a useful biography. For specific comments on Meade see de Trobriand, *Four Years*, p. 519; Duff to Harriet, 29 June 1863, in Duff, "Family History," personal collection of Samuel E. Duff (photocopy of letter in David Birney Folder, Box 4, BC); Grant, *Personal Memoirs* 2:538; Lyman, *Meade's Headquarters*, p. 188; and Hunt to Gantt, 27 Oct. 1886, Hunt Papers, LC.

6. *OR* 27 (1):61.

7. Meade to Mrs. Meade, 29 June 1863, "Letters to Mrs. Meade," Meade Collection, HSP.

8. Coddington, *Gettysburg Campaign*, pp. 180–81, 188–89, 651; Sorrel, *Recollections*, p. 155; Hall, "Harrison," pp. 22–24.

9. Warner, *Generals in Gray*, p. 181; Boatner, *Civil War Dictionary*, pp. 476–77.

10. Freeman, *R. E. Lee* 3:54, 4:521; Lord, *Fremantle Diary*, p. 198.

11. G. Tucker, *High Tide*, p. 222.

12. Freeman, *R. E. Lee* 4:521–22, 525.

13. *OR* 27 (2):307, 316–17, 444.

14. Freeman, *Lee's Lieutenants* 3:147.

15. *OR* 27 (2):305, 313.

16. Ibid.; see also discussions in Freeman, *R. E. Lee* 3:18–28 and Coddington, *Gettysburg Campaign*, pp. 8–9.

17. *OR* 27 (2):306, 315.

18. Ibid., p. 443.

19. Ibid., pp. 321–22, 679–84, 687–97.

20. The standard shoulder weapon in both armies was a muzzle-loading rifle-musket that was fired with a percussion cap. It had the long barrel of a musket but was rifled and fired lead bullets with conoidal heads called minié balls. The prototypes of this weapon were the Springfield rifle-musket, .58 caliber, and the Enfield rifle-musket, .577 caliber. Similar weapons of French and Austrian manufacture were used also. A few units were armed with breech-loading, single-shot Sharps rifles, .52 caliber; others with .69 caliber smoothbore muskets. To avoid the use of the cumbersome term "rifle-musket" in this study I have elected to refer to rifled pieces as rifles, smoothbores as muskets. The above terms are defined in several sources including Boatner, *Civil War Dictionary*, and Coggins, *Arms*, pp. 26–33.

21. W. C. Ward, "Incidents," p. 345; Barziza, *Adventures*, p. 41; Dickert, *Kershaw's Brigade*, p. 229.

22. Owen, *In Camp*, p. 240.

23. McLaws, "Gettysburg," p. 65.

24. Barziza, *Adventures*, pp. 41–42; Fletcher, *Rebel Private*, p. 66; Collier, *"They'll Do,"* p. 127; W. R. and M. B. Houghton, *Two Boys*, p. 85; Polley, *Hood's Texas Brigade*,

pp. 146–47; Simpson, *Gaines' Mill to Appomattox*, p. 132; Lasswell, *Rags and Hope*, p. 176.

25. J. C. West, *A Texan*, p. 89.

26. Lord, *Fremantle Diary*, pp. 186–87, 190–91; *OR* 51 (2):725; Ross, *Cities and Camps*, p. 42; Lawley, "Battles of Gettysburg."

27. Alexander, "Battle of Gettysburg," p. 19, Alexander Papers, SHC. Lt. Donnell Smith described a similar incident: see Colston, "The Campaign of Gettysburg," Campbell-Colston Papers, SHC.

28. Fletcher, *Rebel Private*, pp. 67–68; F. P. Fleming, *Memoir*, p. 146.

29. *OR* 51 (2):728–29.

30. Ibid. 27 (2):606–7, 637.

31. Alexander, "Battle of Gettysburg," pp. 20–21, Alexander Papers, SHC.

32. *OR* 27 (1):64–69, 114, 144.

33. Ibid., pp. 114, 144.

34. Ibid. (3):416–17, (1):221–22. In a letter dated 8 March 1895 the quartermaster general wrote Gen. Alexander S. Webb that "as a rule" the trains moved with each corps until they reached Edwards Ferry. Then they moved as a single train to Frederick, where they rejoined their respective corps. Finally, they concentrated at Westminster, where they remained until after the battle. The combined trains contained approximately 4,000 six-mule wagons and 1,000 ambulances. See Box 4, Folder 004-0072, Webb Papers, Yale University Library.

35. *OR* 27 (3):416–17.

36. Ibid. (1):68, (3):420, 424.

37. Ibid. (3):416–17.

38. *NY at Gbg* 3:1340. The corps badges for the Army of the Potomac are depicted in *Battles and Leaders of the Civil War* 3:154. Although Butterfield designed the badge system for that army, he must have been influenced by the Kearny Patch.

39. Hanifen, *Battery B*, p. 65; Rauscher, *Music on the March*, p. 80; Marbaker, *Eleventh New Jersey*, p. 89.

40. Marbaker, *Eleventh New Jersey*, p. 89.

41. *NY at Gbg* 3:1289; K. M. Scott, *One Hundred and Fifth Regiment*, p. 82; de Trobriand, *Four Years*, pp. 479–80.

42. W. Clark, *Hampton Battery F*, p. 140.

43. J. L. Smith, *118th Pennsylvania*, pp. 231–32; Sturtevant, *Thirteenth Vermont*, p. 197; *OR* 27 (3):398; Marsena R. Patrick Journal, 30 June 1863, Patrick Papers, LC.

44. *OR* 27 (3):398; Smart, *A Radical View* 2:12–15.

45. Smart, *A Radical View* 2:12–15; *Pa at Gbg* 2:802. The latter source indicates that three companies of the Second Pennsylvania Volunteer Cavalry were sent to Frederick by Patrick.

46. Rauscher, *Music on the March*, p. 81; Hays, *Red Patch*, p. 191; Cavada Diary, 30 June 1863, HSP.

47. J. R. C. Ward, *One Hundred and Sixth*, p. 152; Woodward, *Our Campaigns*, p. 262; *Pa at Gbg* 1:227.

48. *OR* 27 (1):547, 595; Hamilton, "History of the 110th Pennsylvania," p. 106,

Miltary Order of the Loyal Legion of the United States, The Civil War Library and Museum.

49. *OR* 27 (3):395–96.

50. B. Thompson, "This Hell," p. 16.

51. Muffly, *148th Pennsylvania*, p. 716; J. R. C. Ward, *One Hundred and Sixth*, pp. 149–50.

52. Holcombe, *First Minnesota*, pp. 348–50; Imholte, *First Volunteers*, pp. 114–15.

53. B. Thompson, "This Hell," p. 16; Frederick, *Fifty-seventh New York*, p. 164; Hancock Testimony, *CCW*, p. 403.

54. Favill, *Diary*, p. 241.

55. Cole, *Under Five Commanders*, p. 190.

CHAPTER 2

1. *OR* 27 (2):443, 466.

2. Ibid., pp. 307, 317, 444.

3. Ibid., p. 444; "Personal Narrative, G. Campbell Brown," May–August 1885 Folder, Box 3, Hunt Papers, LC.

4. *OR* 27 (2):317, 444.

5. Ibid., pp. 613, 616, 622; Wilcox, "Annotations," 1 July, Box 1, Wilcox Papers, LC; Lawley, "Battles of Gettysburg."

6. *OR* 27 (2):613, 631; Long, *Memoirs of Lee*, p. 275; Longstreet, *From Manassas to Appomattox*, pp. 351–53; Lord, *Fremantle Diary*, p. 202.

7. *OR* 27 (2):613, 616. At this time the basic artillery unit technically was designated a "company," though the term "battery" was in common and official use and will be used in this text.

8. "Personal Narrative, G. Campbell Brown," May–August 1885 Folder, Box 3, Hunt Papers, LC.

9. *OR* 27 (2):503, (3):943–44.

10. Law, "Struggle," p. 319; *OR* 51 (2):731.

11. McLaws, "Gettysburg," p. 67; Polley, *Hood's Texas Brigade*, p. 154; J. C. West, *A Texan*, p. 84; *OR* 51 (2):732. Since Johnson's division passed McLaws's early in the morning and did not reach Gettysburg until evening, after the fighting was over, it is obvious that the march was a slow one, less than two miles per hour on a turnpike. Johnson complained in his report that his march was slowed by Longstreet's train, but Hill's must have been the culprit. Whatever the desire to have the trains forward, there seems to be little doubt that the wagons clogged the roads and interfered with the movement of the infantry.

12. McLaws, "Gettysburg," p. 67.

13. Abernathy, *Our Mess*, pp. 29–30; R. M. Powell, "With Hood."

14. J. C. West, *A Texan*, p. 84; Polley, *Hood's Texas Brigade*, p. 154; McLaws, "Gettysburg," p. 64; R. M. Powell, "With Hood."

15. Dickert, *Kershaw's Brigade*, pp. 232–33.

16. Alexander, "Gettysburg," pp. 21, 29, Alexander Papers, SHC; *OR* 51 (2):733.

17. Longstreet, *From Manassas to Appomattox*, p. 352; Lord, *Fremantle Diary*, p. 202.

18. *DAB* 2:391; Boatner, *Civil War Dictionary*, p. 490.

19. G. Tucker, *Lee and Longstreet*, p. 164.

20. Lawley, "Battles of Gettysburg"; Freeman, *Lee's Lieutenants* 1:164–66; G. Tucker, *Lee and Longstreet*, p. 166; Lord, *Fremantle Diary*, p. 198.

21. Lord, *Fremantle Diary*, pp. 202–3.

22. Ibid.

23. Longstreet to A. B. Longstreet, 24 July 1863, in Longstreet, "Account of the Campaign," p. 55.

24. Long, *Memoirs*, p. 277.

25. Longstreet, "Lee's Invasion," pp. 246–47; Longstreet, "Lee's Right Wing," pp. 339–40.

26. Longstreet, "Campaign of Gettysburg." E. P. Alexander reports this conversation in his *Military Memoirs of a Confederate*, p. 381, but it is unlikely that he heard any of the conversation firsthand. See discussions of this also in Freeman, *R. E. Lee* 3:72–76, and *Lee's Lieutenants* 3:106–10.

27. Lawley, "Battles of Gettysburg."

28. Ibid.

29. *OR* 27 (2):308, 318.

30. Long to Longstreet, 19 Apr. 1876, Long Papers, SHC; Long, *Memoirs*, p. 277; Longstreet, "Account of the Campaign," p. 62.

31. Longstreet, "Lee in Pennsylvania," pp. 437–38. See also Marshall to Longstreet, 7 May 1875, and Taylor to Longstreet, 18 Apr. 1875, in Longstreet Papers, Duke University, William R. Perkins Library; Long to Longstreet, 31 May 1876, Long Papers, SHC. This criticism of Longstreet was made initially by General Early in an address delivered at Washington and Lee University on 19 January 1873 and was taken up by General Pendleton and others. By this time Longstreet was quite vulnerable in the South because he had become a Republican and accepted a Federal appointment from his old friend, President Grant. Although Longstreet was able to refute the charges of failing to make an attack ordered for sunrise, many people continued to assume that they had validity. In addition many of his own criticisms of the conduct of the battle were not presented tactfully, and some were considered to reflect in a derogatory manner on General Lee. Longstreet did not regain his credibility in his lifetime. This feuding is discussed at some length in G. Tucker, *Lee and Longstreet*, and Connelly, *The Marble Man*.

32. Freeman, *Lee's Lieutenants* 3:100–103. The Blocher house, which is located north of Gettysburg, just east of the junction of the Carlisle and Table Rock roads, was said to have been the meeting place of Lee and Ewell.

33. *OR* 27 (2):308.

CHAPTER 3

1. The First Corps was between Emmitsburg and Gettysburg, the Eleventh at Emmitsburg, the Third east of Emmitsburg, the Second at Uniontown, the Fifth at Union Mills, and the Sixth at Manchester. Their movements will be discussed below. See *OR* 27 (1):144.

2. *OR* 27 (3):416–18, 422.

3. Ibid., p. 460.

4. Ibid., pp. 458–59.

5. Butterfield Testimony, *CCW*, p. 423. In his testimony before the Committee on the Conduct of the War Butterfield in effect claimed not to know Meade's intentions regarding the circular, an inference that Meade might have intended it as a withdrawal order. Previously Sickles had testified that from information that he had received he was satisfied that Meade had intended to retreat from Gettysburg (see Sickles Testimony, *CCW*, p. 298). Gibbon, however, insisted that when Butterfield showed him a draft of the circular, Butterfield indicated that Meade did not intend to leave; he only intended to be prepared to do so. Meade in his testimony stated that he told Butterfield that the circular was precautionary and that the idea of his leaving Gettysburg after going to the trouble of concentrating the army there was absurd (see Gibbon and Meade Testimony, *CCW*, pp. 442, 436–38). This charge that Meade intended to retreat from Gettysburg became a principal accusation against Meade in the so-called Meade-Sickles Controversy, in which Meade had little or no direct involvement.

6. Hancock Testimony, *CCW*, p. 409; *OR* 27 (3):461.

7. Meade, *With Meade*, p. 63; *OR* 27 (1):924.

8. Meade, *With Meade*, p. 64; Warren Testimony, *CCW*, p. 377; Hancock Testimony, *CCW*, p. 404; *OR* 27 (3):461.

9. *OR* 27 (3):461; Meade Testimony, *CCW*, p. 348. In his testimony Butterfield stated that Meade had told him that he could not spare Butterfield to go to Gettysburg and that he could not go himself. Butterfield then suggested that Hancock go, and Meade accepted his suggestion. See Butterfield Testimony, *CCW*, p. 423.

Caldwell, not Gibbon, was second in rank to Hancock in the Second Corps and would have been expected to take command in Hancock's absence. However, Meade and Hancock trusted Gibbon's ability more than Caldwell's and, therefore, appointed Gibbon over him.

10. *DAB* 4:221–22; Boatner, *Civil War Dictionary*, p. 372; Warner, *Generals in Blue*, pp. 203–4.

11. G. Tucker, *Hancock*, p. 89; Boatner, *Civil War Dictionary*, p. 372; Lyman, *Meade's Headquarters*, p. 372; Grant, *Personal Memoirs* 2:539–40. In a letter to Peter F. Rothermel, the artist, dated 31 December 1868, Hancock stated that he wore at Gettysburg a black felt slouch hat stiff enough for the brim and crown to hold their shapes, an officer's undress uniform coat buttoned at the top and open at the waist, a sword belt under the coat, and a staff officer's sword. Neither he nor other officers

wore sashes. See Folder 2, Box 1, Peter F. Rothermel Papers, Pennsylvania Historical and Museum Commission.

12. Meade Testimony, *CCW*, pp. 330, 348; Hancock Testimony, *CCW*, p. 404.

13. Hancock, *Reminiscences*, pp. 188–89; Hancock Testimony, *CCW*, p. 405; *OR* 27 (1):367–68.

14. *OR* 27 (1):277. This does not include Calef's battery (A–2d U.S.) of horse artillery, which was also in the area.

15. Ibid., pp. 368, 704, 758, 927.

16. Ibid., pp. 368, 696–97; Doubleday to Bates, 4 Feb. 1874, Abner Doubleday Folder, Box 4, BC.

17. *OR* 27 (3):457, (1):696. Pvt. Daniel M. Connor, Company K, 1st Indiana Volunteer Cavalry, claimed to have carried the first dispatch from Howard to Meade concerning the battle and to have returned to the battlefield with the headquarters staff. See Connor, "At Gettysburg."

18. *OR* 27 (1):366.

19. Ibid., pp. 368–69, 704.

20. Meade Testimony, *CCW*, p. 348; *OR* 27 (3):464, 466.

21. *OR* 27 (1):71–72, 366, 696.

22. Ibid. (3):467; Hunt, "Second Day," p. 291.

23. *OR* 27 (3):462.

24. Biddle to Meade, 18 Aug. 1880, GL, p. 27. We do not know the route taken by the various couriers between Taneytown and Manchester. As the crow flies, the distance is about sixteen miles; but by the better roads through Westminster, it is about twenty miles.

25. *OR* 27 (3):465, 484; Hyde, "Recollections"; Hyde, *Greek Cross*, p. 142. Herein lies a minor puzzle. Butterfield, in a dispatch timed at 5:30 on the following morning, wrote that Oliver had been sent with the 7:30 P.M. dispatches directing the Sixth Corps to march to Gettysburg rather than Taneytown. It is likely, however, that it was Oliver who carried the 4:30 dispatches, those that put the Sixth Corps on the road, for such orders came at dusk and were being followed as darkness fell. In later years Oliver wrote that he had been sent to the Sixth Corps with orders and had stayed with the corps until it was well under way. There were also those who wrote that the corps march began when Oliver arrived. See *OR* 27 (3):484; Oliver to Meade, 16 May 1882, GL, p. 89; *Pa at Gbg* 2:652.

26. Hyde, "Recollections," pp. 194–95.

27. *OR* 27 (3):484–85.

28. Waters to Meade, 21 June 1888, GL, p. 123; Paine to Meade, 10 May 1886, GL, p. 77; Hunt, "Second Day," p. 291. General Hunt seems to say that he went forward with the Meade party also. Waters is termed a "tall orderly" in McEneany, "Gettysburg."

29. Paine to Meade, 20 June 1886, GL, p. 77; Meade, *Life and Letters* 2:62; Meade, *With Meade*, p. 95.

30. The Twelfth Corps marched about five miles from Littlestown to Two Taverns

on the Baltimore Pike, where it halted until late afternoon. It was when Slocum was at Two Taverns that he yielded to Howard's requests that he come forward. The Sixth Corps march, which did not begin until dusk, is described in Chapter 4.

31. *OR* 27 (1):129, 482.

32. Ibid., p. 531; Humphreys Testimony, *CCW*, p. 389; Cavada Diary, 1 July 1863, HSP. The route of Longstreet's proposed march around the Union left is not known. However, it seems probable that any such movement would have been into the area posted here by Humphreys's division.

33. Sickles Testimony, *CCW*, p. 296.

34. *OR* 27 (1):531; H. H. Humphreys, *Humphreys*, p. 187; Cavada Diary, 1 July 1863, HSP.

35. Haynes, *Second Regiment Camps and Marches*, p. 136; Marbaker, *Eleventh New Jersey*, p. 91; Lewis, *Battery E*, p. 181.

36. Tremain, *Two Days*, p. 14.

37. Ibid., pp. 18–19; *OR* 27 (3):463.

38. *OR* 27 (3):463–64.

39. Ibid.

40. Birney Testimony, *CCW*, p. 366; *OR* 27 (3):465, (1):482.

41. *Pa at Gbg* 1:356, 2:685; *OR* 27 (1):493; Craft, *One Hundred Forty-first*, p. 119.

42. Weygant, *One Hundred Twenty-fourth*, p. 171; *NY at Gbg* 3:67; *Me at Gbg*, p. 160; Craft, *One Hundred and Forty-first*, p. 117; *Pa at Gbg* 2:685; J. E. Smith, *A Famous Battery*, p. 139.

43. No one explained why these particular brigades were left at Emmitsburg. Each was commanded only by a colonel, and Burling was acting only in place of Brig. Gen. Gershom Mott, who had been wounded at Chancellorsville. Three other brigades of the corps were commanded by brigadier generals and it would seem logical for one of them to have been left at Emmitsburg.

44. There were two doctors named Anan at Emmitsburg—Andrew, who was middle aged, and Robert L., who was a younger man. See Williams and McKinsey, *Frederick County* 2:59.

45. *OR* 27 (1):531, 543; Humphreys Testimony, *CCW*, pp. 388–89; Cavada Diary, 1 July 1865, HSP. Probably the division turned left from the Emmitsburg Road about three miles north of Emmitsburg.

46. Musgrove, *Autobiography*, p. 85; Robertson, *McAllister*, p. 332; Blake, *Three Years*, p. 203; Marbaker, *Eleventh New Jersey*, p. 94.

47. *OR* 27 (1):531. Probably the First Corps unit referred to was Biddle's brigade, Doubleday's division, which apparently approached Gettysburg over a route similar to that followed by Humphreys's division. See ibid., pp. 315, 323, 326.

48. Musgrove, *Autobiography*, p. 86.

49. H. H. Humphreys, *Humphreys*, pp. 188, 191; *OR* 27 (1):531, 543; Humphreys to Campbell, 6 Aug. 1863, A. A. Humphreys Folder, Box 4, BC. Humphreys went forward with three members of his staff—Capt. Carswell McClellan, Lt. Henry H. Humphreys, and Pvt. James E. Dimond, a staff orderly—together with Colonel Hayden and Dr. Anan.

50. A. A. Humphreys, "Pennsylvania Campaign," pp. 1–2; "Memo of a Visit to Gettysburg," p. 57, Box 22, A. A. Humphreys Papers, HSP.

51. H. H. Humphreys, *Humphreys*, p. 188; Rafferty, "Third Corps' Great Battle."

52. Musgrove, *Autobiography*, p. 86; *Pa at Gbg* 1:196; Marbaker, *Eleventh New Jersey*; *OR* 27 (1):531, 543.

53. Coyne, "Fourth Excelsior"; Cavada Diary, 1 July 1863, HSP.

54. H. H. Humphreys, *Humphreys*, p. 191; Cavada Diary, 1 July 1863, HSP.

55. *OR* 27 (1):129; Tremain, *Two Days*, p. 31.

56. *NY at Gbg* 3:1336–37.

57. Swanberg, *Sickles*, pp. 47–76.

58. Ibid., pp. 116–23; *NY at Gbg* 3:1337–38.

59. Swanberg, *Sickles*, pp. 165–66, 169, 171–74.

60. Ibid., p. 174.

61. Warren Testimony, *CCW*, p. 384.

62. Tremain, *Two Days*, pp. 32–33.

63. *OR* 27 (3):468.

64. Ibid., p. 467.

65. Ibid., p. 464. Ready records do not state what Graham did with the Third Corps train. Presumably the ammunition and headquarters wagons went up to Gettysburg, the others back to Westminster. The presence of numerous wagons in the column might account for the slowness of the march to Gettysburg.

66. *Pa at Gbg* 1:79–85.

67. *OR* 27 (3):424.

68. Carter, "Reminiscences," p. 158.

69. Woodward, *Our Campaigns*, p. 202; Campbell, "Pioneer Memories," p. 568.

70. T. M. Anderson, "Fourteenth Regiment," p. 685.

71. Hardin, *Twelfth Regiment*, p. 144; Brainard, *Campaigns*, p. 110. The feared Confederate cavalry had fought at Hanover on June 30 and was pushing on to Carlisle on July 1.

72. Carter, *Four Brothers*, p. 297; Porter, *Maltese Cross*, p. 163.

73. *Pa at Gbg* 1:227.

74. Judson, *83d Regiment*, p. 66; Woodward, *Our Campaigns*, p. 263.

75. Hardin, *Twelfth Regiment*, p. 144; Carter, *Four Brothers*, p. 297.

76. *Pa at Gbg* 1:462; Norton, *Attack*, p. 285; Nash, *Forty-fourth*, p. 141.

77. J. L. Smith, *118th Pennsylvania*, p. 236; Woodward, *Our Campaigns*, p. 263; Carter, *Four Brothers*, p. 297; Brainard, *Campaigns*, p. 110.

78. Mason to Meade, 13 Aug. 1886, GL, p. 46. There seems to be no reason for believing that Sykes knew of the battle prior to Mason's arrival. Yet Slocum, Sykes's wing commander, had heard of it from Howard early in the afternoon and had written Howard at 3:35 P.M. that the Twelfth Corps would be coming up. Butterfield, in a letter to Sykes timed at 7:00 P.M., ordered the Fifth Corps to Gettysburg. This dispatch contained the sentence, "The general had supposed that General Slocum would have ordered you up." If Mason's recollections were correct, this message must have arrived after Mason had been there. See *OR* 27 (3):463, 467.

79. *OR* 27 (1):600.

80. "Report of Col. Jacob B. Sweitzer," Box 1, Chamberlain Papers, LC.

81. J. L. Smith, *118th Pennsylvania*, p. 237; Brainard, *Campaigns*, p. 111.

82. O. S. Barrett, *Reminiscences*, p. 21; Carter, "Reminiscences," p. 161.

83. J. L. Smith, *118th Pennsylvania*, p. 237; "Report of Col. Jacob B. Sweitzer," Box 1, Chamberlain Papers, LC; "Extract from the Private Journal of Col. Joseph Hayes," Box 4, Chamberlain Papers, LC; Hunt to Gantt, 3 Sept. 1866, Box 4, Hunt Papers, LC.

84. *OR* 27 (1):595, 652, (3):483.

85. Imholte, *First Volunteers*, p. 115; B. Thompson, "This Hell," p. 16.

86. *OR* 27 (3):422–23.

87. B. Thompson, "This Hell," p. 16.

88. *OR* 27 (1):367–69; Hancock Testimony, *CCW*, p. 405.

89. *OR* 27 (1):367–69; Hancock Testimony, *CCW*, p. 405; Gibbon, *Personal Recollections*, p. 132; Walker, *Second Army Corps*, p. 268; *Pa at Gbg* 2:727.

90. Bruce, *Twentieth Regiment*, p. 269; *OR* 27 (1):411; *Pa at Gbg* 1:330, 2:728; Gibbon, *Personal Recollections*, p. 132.

91. *OR* 27 (1):403, 407; Muffly, *148th Pennsylvania*, p. 461; Ford, *Fifteenth*, p. 264; Diary of Patrick H. Taylor, 1 July 1863, BP.

92. *OR* 27 (1):400, 411. The Second Corps picket line probably connected with that of Geary's division, which Hancock and Slocum had posted on and north of Little Round Top.

93. *Pa at Gbg* 2:621. Mulholland did not say why he received the assignment; perhaps he was field officer of the day for the division. It seems likely that Mulholland's party would have followed lanes connecting the Taneytown and Emmitsburg roads and would have reached the latter at the house marked "E. Trostle" on the Warren Map.

94. Favill, *Diary*, p. 242.

CHAPTER 4

1. Cavada Diary, 1 July 1863, HSP.

2. Ibid. The flag of Humphreys's division, the Second Division, Third Corps, measured 4½ by 6 feet. It had a blue field with a white diamond in its center.

3. Ibid.

4. Jacobs, "Meteorology"; J. L. Smith, *118th Pennsylvania*, p. 238; Jacobs, *Notes*, p. 28. In his article on meteorology Jacobs referred to the clouds as "cumulo stratus."

5. Hunt, "Second Day," p. 297.

6. *OR* 27 (1):349; Paine to Colonel Meade, 20 May 1886, GL, p. 77.

7. Meade, *Life and Letters*, p. 63; Meade, *With Meade*, p. 96; McCullough, *The Great Bridge*, p. 86.

8. Smart, *A Radical View* 2:23.

9. *OR* 27 (1):773–77.

10. Ibid., pp. 233, 749, 760; Hunt, "Second Day," p. 297. Twenty years later General Hunt had a slightly different recollection of events at daybreak. After the ride to the left, in all probability, Hunt and Seth Williams rested beneath a tree in the cemetery a few yards from General Meade. As the day dawned, General Slocum came up and stated that because of the absence of a division (Geary's?), there was a gap in his line between Culp's Hill and Cemetery Hill. Meade asked immediately, "Where is Gen. Hunt?" Williams, who had walked over to where Meade was standing, pointed to Hunt's tree and said that he was lying beneath it. Meade said, "It is no time to sleep now," to which Hunt responded, "I am not asleep, and heard all that Gen. Slocum said." "Very well," General Meade replied, "you must see to this as it is your affair. See that the line is made good with artillery until the infantry is in position." Because the Artillery Reserve was not yet up, Hunt took batteries from the Eleventh Corps and posted them so that they would cover the gap if the enemy approached it. See Hunt to Meade, 14 Aug. 1886, GL, p. 26.

In his report (*OR* 27 [1]:749) Major Osborn stated that he placed three batteries to the right of the Baltimore Pike before Slocum placed infantry there. He later removed the batteries.

11. It is doubtful that there was any great strength on Little Round Top. The 147th Pennsylvania's position is marked near the base of the hill's north slope, but it is unclear whether or not the Fifth Ohio was on its left on the hill's north slope or downslope to the right.

12. *OR* 27 (1):759, 773, 825.

13. Meade Testimony, *CCW*, pp. 331, 349; Warren Testimony, *CCW*, p. 377; Taylor, *Warren*, p. 123; *OR* 27 (3):486. Warren had returned to the field that morning from Taneytown.

14. *OR* 27 (3):487; Warren Testimony, *CCW*, p. 377; Meade Testimony, *CCW*, p. 331.

15. *OR* 27 (1):825.

16. Imholte, *First Volunteers*, p. 115; *Pa at Gbg* 2:727.

17. Gibbon, *Personal Recollections*, p. 133; Bruce, *Twentieth*, p. 273.

18. Gibbon to Colonel Meade, 24 July 1886, GL, p. 95.

19. *OR* 27 (1):381, 407, 413–14, 442; *Pa at Gbg* 1:550, 2:727; Hancock Testimony, *CCW*, p. 406.

20. *OR* 27 (3):415; Diary of Patrick H. Taylor, 2 July 1863, BP.

21. J. R. C. Ward, *One Hundred and Sixth*, p. 157. No executions authorized by Circular 30 were reported; probably none took place.

22. *OR* 27 (1):515, 562, (3):483.

23. Ibid. (1):592, 600, 610, 634, 778.

24. Ibid., pp. 600, 662.

25. Ibid., pp. 600, 610; Carter, *Four Brothers*, p. 299.

26. *OR* 27 (1):644; Wright, "Second Regiment," p. 451.

27. *OR* 27 (1):592; Carter, "Reminiscences," p. 162.

28. On his map for 2 July Bachelder shows the Ninth Massachusetts in position in the open fields south of the E. Deardorff and S. Heck buildings.

29. The most likely route from this area to the Federal rear passed the Deardorff buildings and zigzagged by a succession of farm buildings to the Baltimore Pike at the S. W. Horn [Horner] farmhouse, a distance of 1½ miles. The Horn buildings were about 1,000 yards south of the pike's crossing of Rock Creek, or just inside the present U.S. 15 Bypass. This bypass bisects the area occupied by the Fifth Corps and the Federal picket line east to the Hanover and York roads.

30. *OR* 27 (1):592, 600, 610.

31. Crawford Testimony, *CCW*, p. 469; Crawford, "Pennsylvania Reserves"; *Pa at Gbg* 1:294.

32. *OR* 27 (1):773, 778, 811.

33. *NY at Gbg* 3:1030.

34. Ibid., p. 1039; *OR* 27 (3):68–69.

35. *OR* 27 (1):755–66. This awkward arrangement existed because Slocum, who had been designated commander of the army's right wing, had in turn designated Williams acting commander of the Twelfth Corps. But, after the Fifth and Sixth corps reached the field and were posted, the right wing, for all practical purposes, did not exist, and Slocum commanded only his corps. Slocum, however, considered himself a wing commander throughout the battle, though his wing and his corps were essentially one and the same. See *OR* 27 (1):165, 764, 769.

36. The supposition that the arrival of the Fifth Corps freed the Second to take position on Cemetery Ridge seems valid but was not stated by the principals.

37. Benedict, *Army Life*, p. 165. Many believe that Rowley was drunk and might have been sleeping it off. See Coddington, *Gettysburg Campaign*, p. 308.

38. *OR* 27 (1):156, 258, 349. The Twelfth and Fifteenth Vermont regiments were guarding the train.

39. Sturtevant, *Thirteenth Vermont*, p. 245.

40. Benedict, *14th Reg't*, p. 10.

41. *OR* 27 (1):151.

42. Confederate batteries posted immediately southwest of the town fronting toward Cemetery Hill and the north end of Cemetery Ridge would have been very vulnerable to fire from the batteries on Cemetery Hill. But if well handled and well supported by other batteries that could be brought to bear on Cemetery Hill, they probably could have been very effective and helpful to troops assaulting the Union center.

The name "Bryan" appears on the Warren Map as the name of the family who lived at the house by Ziegler's Grove during the battle period. I understand that it has been determined recently that the name should more properly be "Brian."

43. *NY at Gbg* 2:780; *OR* 27 (1):465; Haskin, *First Regiment*, p. 170.

44. *OR* 27 (1):467–71.

45. Ibid., p. 461.

46. Ibid., p. 369.

47. Ibid., pp. 472, 474, 475; *NY at Gbg* 2:800; Willson, *Disaster*, p. 168.

48. U.S. War Department, *U.S. Infantry Tactics*, pp. 155–56.

49. *OR* 27 (1):453, 464–65. The 1860 census for Cumberland Township, Adams

County, Pennsylvania, indicates that the Bliss buildings were the home of William and Adelina Bliss, their two daughters, and a hired man.

50. B. Thompson, "This Hell," p. 17.

51. *NY at Gbg* 1:282–83; Waring, "Garibaldi Guard," pp. 568–70. The names "Garibaldi Guard" and "Garibaldi Guards" were both used. "Garibaldi Guards" appears on the regiment's memorial.

52. *NY at Gbg* 1:282–83; Waring, "Garibaldi Guard," pp. 568–72, 575.

53. *OR* 27 (1):472.

54. Simons, *One Hundred and Twenty-fifth*, p. 109; *NY at Gbg* 2:884–85.

55. G. T. Fleming, *Alexander Hays*, p. 431.

56. *OR* 27 (1):453, 465, 469, 472; Richardson to Bachelder, 18 Aug. 1869, BP.

57. *OR* 27 (1):454–55, 469.

58. B. Thompson, "This Hell," pp. 17–18. The monument of the First Company, Massachusetts Sharpshooters, located on this portion of Cemetery Ridge, has a bas-relief of a soldier aiming such a rifle.

59. R. S. Thompson, "A Scrap," p. 98.

60. *OR* 27 (1):478–79; Warren Map. See also G. R. Stewart, *Pickett's Charge*, p. 67, for a description of this area.

61. Rhodes, *Battery B*, p. 203.

62. A diagram in *OR* 27 (3):1087 shows the lineup of batteries given here, including Rorty's, which is shown further left, amid Caldwell's division, as described below.

63. *DAB* 4:237; Lyman, *Meade's Headquarters*, pp. 103, 107; Gibbon to Mrs. Gibbon, 3 July 1863, Civil War Letters, Gibbon Papers, HSP; G. R. Stewart, *Pickett's Charge*, p. 64.

64. *OR* 27 (1):427, 431.

65. *Pa at Gbg* 1:402–4.

66. J. R. C. Ward, *One Hundred and Sixth*, p. 158; *Pa at Gbg* 1:550.

67. *DAB* 10:571; Lydecker, "Webb," June 1911, Folder 008–0132, Box 8, Webb Papers, Yale University Library; Nevins, *Wainwright*, p. 333.

68. Cullum, *Biographical Register* 2:726–27.

69. *OR* 27 (1):416, 435. The Fifty-ninth's commander was Lt. Col. Max A. Thoman; the Seventh was commanded by Lt. Col. Amos E. Steele, Jr.

The position of Brown's battery was not well described in reports regarding its location with respect to Hall's brigade. Hall reported it as being on the brigade's left, but the report of the Seventh Michigan suggested that the Seventh supported the battery whose guns were to both its right and left. See *OR* 27 (1):435, 447.

70. Ibid., pp. 447, 449.

71. Ibid., pp. 445, 451; Bruce, *Twentieth Regiment*, p. 283.

72. *NY at Gbg* 1:313. In later years the Forty-second's association with Tammany Hall inspired the regiment's memorial committee to select the design of a life-size bronze Indian standing in front of a much less than full-size tepee. General Sickles and Colonel Eli Parker, who was an Indian, spoke at the monument's dedication. Both said a lot about Tammany Hall but little about the Forty-second's participation in the battle.

73. Warner, *Generals in Blue*, p. 211; Holcombe, *First Minnesota*, p. 339.

74. *OR* 27 (1):423; Bachelder Map; Holcombe, *First Minnesota*, p. 339.

75. Warner, *Generals in Blue*, p. 64; Young, *Battle of Gettysburg*, p. 391.

76. *OR* 27 (1):379, 381, 391, 400, (3):1087.

77. Ibid. (1):478, (3):1087; *NY at Gbg* 3:1182, 1324. Captain Pettit commanded the battery from the time of its organization in August 1861 until the Gettysburg Campaign. Sometime shortly prior to the campaign, Battery B's strength was increased by the addition of men from two sections of the Fourteenth New York Battery, formerly Hogan's battery, which had begun its service with the Irish Brigade. Capt. James McKay Rorty had been assigned to the Fourteenth Battery, but when it was broken up, he served temporarily on the Second Corps staff. Thus it was that he was in a position to take over the battery when it was assigned to that corps.

78. Col. John Fraser, reporting for Zook's brigade, stated that Zook formed in Kelly's rear. See *OR* 27 (1):384.

79. Ibid., pp. 384, 391, 394, 397, 403, 414. The alignment of the regiments of the brigades was, from front to rear, as follows: Cross's brigade, Sixty-first New York, Eighty-second Pennsylvania, 148th Pennsylvania in two lines, Fifth New Hampshire; Kelly's brigade, Twenty-eighth Massachusetts and 116th Pennsylvania in first line, Sixty-third, Sixty-ninth, and Eighty-eighth New York regiments in second line; Zook's brigade, 140th Pennsylvania in two lines, Fifty-second, Fifty-seventh, and Sixty-sixth New York regiments in lines to the rear; Brooke's brigade, not recorded but possibly Second Delaware, Sixty-fourth New York, Fifty-third Pennsylvania, Twenty-seventh Connecticut, and 145th Pennsylvania from front to rear.

80. *NY at Gbg* 1:420–21, 3:1358.

81. Child, *Fifth Regiment*, p. 312.

82. Ibid.; Livermore, *Days*, p. 256; Charles A. Hale, "With Cross in the Gettysburg Campaign," p. vii, Brooke Papers, HSP; *Pa at Gbg* 2:733. Hale's account was written in 1883 for inclusion in the regiment's history but was not used. It was revised and typed on 10 August 1894. A copy is also in the Rothermel Papers, Pennsylvania Historical and Museum Commission.

83. Livermore, *Days*, pp. 756–57.

84. *Pa at Gbg* 2:732–33; Muffly, *148th Pennsylvania*, p. 461.

85. Charles A. Hale, "With Cross in the Gettysburg Campaign," pp. v–vi, Brooke Papers, HSP.

86. *NY at Gbg* 2:481, 515.

87. Ibid., pp. 475, 491.

88. Ibid., pp. 491–92, 510–11.

89. Ibid., pp. 491–92.

90. Ibid., pp. 506–7. The Sixty-ninth New York State Militia actually continued in existence throughout the war as a New York National Guard unit and had three additional short periods of federal service. The Sixty-ninth New York Volunteer Infantry and the Sixty-ninth New York National Guard Artillery, which became the 182d New York Volunteer Infantry, were all reorganized as the Sixty-ninth Infantry Regiment, New York National Guard, in the fall of 1865 and continued to exist with

this designation until 1917 when it was given the designation, 165th Infantry Regiment. It served then as an integral part of the Forty-second (Rainbow) Division in World War I and with the Twenty-seventh Infantry Division in World War II. See U.S., Department of the Army, *Army Lineage Book* 2:477–79.

91. Ibid., p. 488.

92. *OR* 27 (1):387; *Pa at Gbg* 2:1134.

93. Meagher's resignation was rescinded, and he was assigned to command a military district in the Chattanooga area. See Boatner, *Civil War Dictionary*, p. 540.

94. Livermore, *Days*, p. 243; *OR* 27 (3):1087.

95. Livermore, *Days*, p. 248.

96. *OR* 27 (1):167–68, 241, 872.

97. Ibid., pp. 873, 878–79.

98. Ibid., p. 72.

99. Ibid., pp. 389, 423, 449.

100. Carter, "Reminiscences," p. 163.

101. William Wright, "Recollections of the War of the Rebellion, 146th Regiment," p. 80, New-York Historical Society; Farley, "Bloody Round Top"; *NY at Gbg* 3:955.

102. Porter, *Maltese Cross*, p. 162.

103. Minnigh, *Company K*, pp. 23, 26.

104. Hardin, *Twelfth Regiment*, p. 152; *Pa at Gbg* 1:294.

105. Statement of Captain Joseph Leeper, 140th N.Y.I., n.d., BP; Porter, *Maltese Cross*, p. 165. Stephen H. Weed was born in New York City in 1834 and graduated from West Point in 1854. He then served as an artillery officer against the Seminoles and in the West. Weed commanded Battery I, Fifth U.S. Artillery, in the Army of the Potomac through Antietam and the artillery of the Fifth Corps at Chancellorsville. He was promoted to brigadier general and command of his brigade in June 1863. See *NY at Gbg* 3:1364.

106. *Pa at Gbg* 2:677.

107. Best, *121st New York*, pp. 86–87. The returns of the Army of the Potomac indicate that the Sixth Corps had 15,679 officers and men "present for duty equipped" on 30 June 1863 and 12,832 infantry and artillery on 4 July 1863. See *OR* 27 (1):151–53.

108. Best, *121st New York*, p. 87; *Pa at Gbg* 2:653; G. T. Stevens, *Three Years*, p. 239.

109. Sedgwick Testimony, *CCW*, p. 460; *OR* 27 (1):665, (3):467–68.

110. *Pa at Gbg* 1:505–6; Mark, *Red, White, and Blue*, p. 212; Bowen, "Marching"; J. S. Anderson, "March of the Sixth Corps," p. 78.

111. *OR* 27 (1):665, 684.; Sedgwick Testimony, *CCW*, p. 460.

112. Bowen, "Marching."

113. Mark, *Red, White, and Blue*, p. 216.

114. *OR* 27 (1):665, 668, 669.

115. *Pa at Gbg* 2:653.

116. Ibid. 1:506, 2:677–78; Mark, *Red, White, and Blue*, p. 213.

117. *Pa at Gbg* 2:654; J. S. Anderson, "March of the Sixth Corps," p. 82; Bowen, "Marching"; G. T. Stevens, *Three Years*, p. 240.

118. *OR* 27 (1):665; *Pa at Gbg* 1:506.

119. *Pa at Gbg* 1:378. It seems highly unlikely that infantry marched with fixed bayonets.

120. Sedgwick Testimony, *CCW*, p. 460.

121. Hyde, "Recollections," p. 197.

122. *Pa at Gbg* 2:654.

123. Ibid., p. 678.

124. *OR* 27 (1):663, 665, 673, 678. Sedgwick reported that the Sixth Corps marched over 30 miles, Wright reported 32–35, Upton 32, and Grant about 30. Since we do not know the route followed between Manchester and Littlestown, we cannot improve on these estimates.

CHAPTER 5

1. Sickles Testimony, *CCW*, p. 297. In 1885, in spite of all that had been written and probably said about the elements of the Meade-Sickles Controversy, Colonel (Captain) Meade wrote General Webb that he did not know how General Meade had given his orders on 2 July. He thought that they might have been given orally to Sickles in the cemetery lodge after Meade's arrival there. See: Colonel Meade to Webb, 2 Dec. 1885, Folder 0055, Box 3, Webb Papers, Yale University Library.

2. Meade, *Life and Letters*, p. 66; Meade, *With Meade*, p. 106; Colonel Meade to Webb, 8 Sept. 1875, Folder 0053, Box 3, Webb Papers, Yale University Library.

3. Meade, *Life and Letters*, p. 66; Meade, *With Meade*, pp. 106–7. Capt. George G. Meade, Jr., had been a West Point cadet until he left the Academy in 1862 because of an excess of demerits. Soon afterward he became a lieutenant in the Sixth Pennsylvania Volunteer Cavalry (Rush's Lancers). He became an aide to his father at the outset of the Gettysburg campaign.

Capt. George E. Randolph was born in Quincy, Illinois, in March 1840 and moved to Rhode Island in 1846. He was a descendant of the Virginia Randolphs and a nephew of President William Henry Harrison. He worked in the wool and leather business and, when the war came, became first sergeant of Battery A, First Rhode Island Light Artillery. He was wounded in both legs at Bull Run, but became a second lieutenant in August 1861 and a first lieutenant in September. One month later he was promoted to captain and given command of Battery E. He became chief of artillery for Birney's division in December 1862 and the Third Corps's chief of artillery in April 1863. He left the army in January 1864, moved to Colorado and, in due course, became the general manager of the Denver Railroad Company. See Lewis, *Battery E*, pp. 260–61.

4. Meade, *Life and Letters*, p. 67; Meade, *With Meade*, p. 101; Meade Testimony, *CCW*, p. 338.

5. Meade, *Life and Letters*, pp. 66–67; Meade, *With Meade*, p. 103.

6. *DAB* 2:290.

7. Ibid.; Warner, *Generals in Blue*, p. 34.

8. Lyman, *Meade's Headquarters*, p. 266.

9. Warner, *Generals in Blue*, p. 34; Young, *Battle of Gettysburg*, p. 48; Nevins, *Wainwright*, p. 228.

10. *OR* 27 (1):513, 581; Craft, *One Hundred Forty-first*, p. 118; *Pa at Gbg* 1:537. Only one history, that of the Ninety-ninth Pennsylvania Regiment, mentions the bivouac area, and it stated that it was in a peach orchard. Bachelder's map for 2 July shows Graham's brigade in column south of the G. Weikert house about a hundred yards. Ward's brigade is shown parallel to it but to the front. There is no peach orchard shown nearby. Randolph reported that his batteries were near the Taneytown Road.

11. *OR* 27 (1):498, 501, 513; *Me at Gbg*, p. 180. In his report of the battle, Lt. Charles F. Sawyer said that the Fourth Maine's left was on the Ninety-ninth Pennsylvania, but Colonel Walker later said that it connected with the cavalry. Since the report of the Ninety-ninth states that it did not advance until 2 July, it appears that Walker was correct.

12. *OR* 27 (1):482.

13. Ibid., pp. 482, 531, 825; Birney Testimony, *CCW*, p. 366. If Birney did not occupy Little Round Top until 7:00 A.M., not to mention 9:00 A.M., and if Geary's brigades left at 5:00 A.M. or soon after, Captain Johnston might well have found it unoccupied at the time of his reconnaissance. This will be discussed in Chapter 6.

14. *OR* 27 (1):507, 511, 513; *Pa at Gbg* 1:538; *NY at Gbg* 2:701; A. W. Tucker, "124th New York."

15. Lewis, *Battery E*, p. 194. Battery E, First Rhode Island Light Artillery, was still popularly called Randolph's battery, though Randolph was no longer its commander. Its assigned commander was Lt. John K. Bucklyn. It will be referred to below as Bucklyn's battery.

16. *OR* 27 (1):581.

17. Ibid., pp. 497, 498, 500, 502, 504; *Pa at Gbg* 2:610, 685.

18. *OR* 27 (1):500, 513, 525.

19. Ibid., pp. 927, 939; Cheney, *Ninth Regiment*, p. 114. Moyer, *Seventeenth Regiment*, p. 398, indicates that the Seventeenth was in line on the "left" of the Peach Orchard and that its men exchanged some shots with the enemy. Buford and others also suggest that the area was heavily picketed by his cavalry and this must be so. And yet, Humphreys's division apparently did not encounter any cavalry pickets until it reached the Peach Orchard area after dark over the very road that the cavalry was supposedly guarding. In addition, as will be seen in Chapter 6, the Federal cavalry did not intercept the small Confederate reconnaissance parties led by Captain Johnston and General Pendleton on the morning of 2 July.

20. Cheney, *Ninth Regiment*, p. 114; *OR* 27 (1):914, 927–28, 935, 939.

21. Calef to Colonel Meade, 24 Jan. 1887, GL, p. 103. In this letter Calef wrote, "Those were whirling days for such a boy as I was, and I would be more careful now as to time and location." Apparently he referred to his lack of precision in noting his position.

22. C. A. Stevens, *Berdan's Sharpshooters*, pp. 2–5.

23. Ibid.

24. The state origins of the sharpshooter companies were:

First United States Sharpshooters		Second United States Sharpshooters	
A. N.Y.	F. Vt.	A. Minn.	E. Vt.
B. N.Y.	G. Wis.	B. Mich.	F. N.H.
C. Mich.	H. N.Y.	C. Pa.	G. N.H.
D. N.Y.	I. Mich.	D. Me.	H. Vt.
E. N.H.	K. Mich.		

In addition to the above companies within the two sharpshooter regiments there were separate companies including two companies of Andrew Sharpshooters from Massachusetts in the Second and Fifth corps and a Minnesota company assigned to the First Minnesota Regiment. See C. A. Stevens, *Berdan's Sharpshooters*, p. 5.

25. C. A. Stevens, *Berdan's Sharpshooters*, pp. 4–7.

26. *NY at Gbg* 3:1074–75; *Me at Gbg*, p. 354.

27. *OR* 27 (1):518.

28. *Me at Gbg*, p. 180; *OR* 27 (1):515. We know today that any force in Spangler's Woods prior to the arrival there of the Florida brigade must have consisted of skirmishers and been very small.

29. Sickles had three aides: Maj. Henry E. Tremain, Capt. Alexander Moore, and Capt. Thomas W. A. Fry.

30. After Sickles became incapacitated and no longer required his services, Tremain served on the staffs of generals Hooker and Butterfield in Tennessee. He was awarded the Medal of Honor for riding between two Federal forces that were exchanging fire at Resaca in order to stop them from doing so. Later he served on the staffs of generals D. McM. Gregg and George Crook. After the war his service was recognized by a brevet to the grade of brigadier general of volunteers, and he returned to the profession of law. His service with Sickles, Hooker, and Butterfield suggests that he would not have been a partisan of General Meade, and in 1867 Meade believed that Tremain was the author of an article critical of him that appeared in the *New York Times* of 1 June 1867 and was signed "a Staff Officer." One must wonder what Tremain might have had to do with the HISTORICUS articles. See Meade to Webb, 13 Mar. 1867, Folder 0018, Webb Papers, Yale University Library.

31. Tremain, *Two Days*, p. 42.

32. Humphreys Testimony, *CCW*, p. 391.

33. Ibid.; *OR* 27 (1):532, 556.

34. Cavada Diary, 2 July 1863, HSP.

35. *OR* 27 (1):519, 570.

36. Haley to Bachelder, 27 Feb. 1882, BP.

37. Hamilton, "110th Regiment."

38. Hamilton, "History of the 110th Pennsylvania," p. 110, Military Order of the Loyal Legion of the United States, The Civil War Library and Museum.

39. Haynes, *Second Regiment Camps and Marches*, p. 37; Haynes, *Second Regiment in*

the War, p. 167; *OR* 27 (1):519, 522, 570, 587; *NY at Gbg* 3:1289; de Trobriand, *Four Years*, p. 487.

40. Tremain, *Two Days*, p. 42.

41. *OR* 27 (1):130.

42. Meade, *With Meade*, p. 106; Meade Testimony, *CCW*, p. 328; Sickles Testimony, *CCW*, p. 298.

43. Sickles Testimony, *CCW*, p. 298; Hunt, "Second Day," p. 301.

44. Hunt Testimony, *CCW*, p. 449; Tremain, "Letter to General Sickles."

45. Warren Map. Although the Warren Map shows a number of orchards along the Emmitsburg Road, and some of them were peach orchards, the War Department recognized only the one southeast of the Emmitsburg Road–Wheatfield Road intersection as "the Peach Orchard." In commenting on a number of assertions that certain units were in the Peach Orchard, Capt. Henry N. Minnigh of the First Pennsylvania Reserves, a native of Gettysburg, wrote that much confusion came about because there were two orchards in the area of concern—The Peach Orchard in the southeast corner of the intersection of the Emmitsburg and Wheatfield roads and another orchard area north of the Wheatfield Road, around the Wentz house. The latter orchard contained both peach and apple trees. See Minnigh, "Gettysburg."

46. The Warren Map shows the elevations at the Peach Orchard and Spangler's lane to be 467 and 463 feet, respectively, but the modern United States Geological Survey Map places both above the 580-foot contour. Most of Cemetery Ridge south of the Copse of Trees has an elevation of about 560 feet.

47. Hunt Testimony, *CCW*, p. 449; Hunt, "Second Day," p. 302.

48. Hunt, "Second Day," pp. 301–2.

49. Ibid.

50. Ibid., p. 302; Sickles Testimony, *CCW*, p. 298.

51. *OR* 27 (1):914; Pleasonton Testimony, *CCW*, p. 359. These two brigades suffered 127 casualties, a low figure when compared with those sustained by the infantry brigades of the First and Eleventh corps.

52. *OR* 27 (1):131.

53. Meade, *With Meade*, p. 107; *OR* 27 (3):490. In his report (*OR* 27 [1]:914) Pleasonton ignored the misunderstanding that permitted Buford to leave the field, writing only that on 2 July Buford's division held a position on the left until it was relieved by the Third Corps. This paucity of reporting suggests that the cavalry did not patrol or scout aggressively on 2 July, for it did not disturb the Confederates or embarrass their movements sufficiently to receive mention in the Confederate accounts, and it seems not to have provided any significant information to Meade, Pleasonton, or Sickles.

54. *OR* 27 (1):515; C. A. Stevens, *Berdan's Sharpshooters*, p. 303; Hunt, "Second Day," p. 302; Clipping, "The Second Day's Fight," Scrapbook, Box 1, Twichell Papers, Yale University, The Beinecke Rare Book and Manuscript Library.

55. *NY at Gbg* 3:1067; *OR* 27 (1):507, 517; *Me at Gbg*, pp. 127–28.

56. *NY at Gbg* 3:1067, 1078; *OR* 27 (1):515; C. A. Stevens, *Berdan's Sharpshooters*,

p. 303; Jonathan Newcomb, "A Soldier's Story of Personal Experiences in the Battle of Gettysburg," *Maine Bugle* 3 (April 1896): 100 (photocopy in BC).

57. Wilcox, "Letter," p. 114; Bachelder Map, 2 July 1863.

58. *OR* 27 (2):613–14, 617; Bachelder Map, 2 July 1863.

59. *OR* 27 (2):617; Wilcox to Johnson, 9 Feb. 1889, in H. A. Johnson, "What Regiment?"

60. *OR* 27 (2):617.

61. *NY at Gbg* 3:1079; C. A. Stevens, *Berdan's Sharpshooters*, p. 304; Newcomb, "Soldier's Story," p. 100. Berdan's story of the Pitzer's Woods fight was told after he would have been aware of Longstreet's movements and the later controversy over the events of the day. This suggests that his comments on delaying Wilcox stemmed more from hindsight than any orders that he probably had that day.

62. G. Clark, "Wilcox's Alabama Brigade," p. 229; G. Clark, *A Glance*, p. 36; Herbert to Bachelder, 9 July 1884, BP; *OR* 27 (2):617. With some advantages of hindsight there were those who believed that McLaws's and Hood's divisions were at least a portion of the three columns seen by Berdan. This is highly unlikely, for, as discussed in Chapter 6, these divisions were nowhere near Pitzer's Woods or within Berdan's range of vision at this time.

63. Allen, "Berdan's Sharpshooters."

64. *OR* 27 (1):507; G. Clark, "Wilcox's Alabama Brigade," p. 229; *Me at Gbg*, pp. 128–29; Herbert to Bachelder, 9 July 1884, BP.

65. C. A. Stevens, *Berdan's Sharpshooters*, p. 305.

66. Ibid., p. 312.

67. *OR* 27 (1):507, 517; *Me at Gbg*, p. 130.

68. *NY at Gbg* 3:1068–69, 1079, 1:38. In 1886 Nathaniel Sessions of Company I, First United States Sharpshooters, maintained that the fire of a whole Confederate division had been concentrated on Berdan's force and that the Federals had held it off for two hours. The *National Tribune* was not averse to printing such imaginative claims. See Sessions, "Gettysburg."

69. The Leister house had two small rooms on its ground floor and a loft above them. The outer door and the porch were on the south side of the house. This door opened into the kitchen, a room with a fireplace and stairs that led to the loft. An inner door in the partition between the two rooms was near the outer door. Both rooms were small. According to the 1860 census for Cumberland Township, Adams County, three adults and three children lived there.

70. Tremain, *Two Days*, p. 50; Sickles, "Gettysburg." The map that General Meade was studying could have been a wall map that was made commercially in 1858.

71. *OR* 27 (1):482–83.

72. Sickles Testimony, *CCW*, p. 298.

CHAPTER 6

1. Lord, *Fremantle Diary*, p. 257; Ross, *Cities and Camps*, p.48; Longstreet, *From Manassas to Appomattox*, p. 384. Probably Longstreet's headquarters at this time was somewhere along the Chambersburg Pike near Marsh Creek.

2. Ross, *Cities and Camps*, p. 42. An upright cannon barrel marks the headquarters site.

3. Lord, *Fremantle Diary*, p. 198; Hood, "Letter," p. 147; Johnston to McLaws, 27 June 1892, Civil War Sources and Photostats III, Container 173, Freeman Papers, LC. The location of Lee's log and observation point was never identified. If Alexander's statement that from it they could see the town and "the enemy's line above it" can be taken literally (and Alexander might not have intended that it be taken so), it seems likely that the site was north of the seminary dormitory. See Alexander, "Gettysburg," p. 29, Alexander Papers, SHC.

4. Reports fail to state at what hour of the morning Anderson's division relieved Heth's.

5. Hood, "Letter," p. 147; McSwain, *Crumbling Defenses*, p. 37. John L. Black was a thirty-two-year-old former West Pointer who did not graduate from the academy. Probably most of the troops with him belonged to the First South Carolina Cavalry. See: Krick, *Lee's Colonels*, p. 48.

6. Long, "Letter," pp. 67–68; Venable, "Letter," p. 289; "Personal Narrative, C. Brown," Folder 1885, Hunt Papers, LC.

7. Freeman, *Lee's Lieutenants* 3:101; Long, "Letter," p. 67; Long, *Memoirs of Lee*, p. 277.

8. *OR* 27 (2):350.

9. Ibid.; Coupland to Pendleton, 22 Feb. 1878, and Randolph to Pendleton, 11 Mar. 1878, Folder 61, Pendleton Papers, SHC. It is likely that those involved in this reconnaissance included Thomas H. B. Randolph and Coupland R. Page, who was probably the "Coupland" who wrote this letter. In the postwar years a Coupland R. Page was an Episcopal priest at St. Andrew's Church in Clear Spring, Maryland.

10. Long, *Memoirs of Lee*, pp. 280–81; Long, "Letter," p. 67; Long to Longstreet, 19 Apr. 1875, Long Papers, SHC. A. P. Hill's headquarters were at the Emanuel Pitzer farmhouse about five hundred yards west of Seminary Ridge and northwest of Spangler's Woods. A tablet on an upright cannon barrel near the present North Carolina Memorial site on Seminary Ridge indicates this location.

11. Johnston to Fitzhugh Lee, 16 Feb. 1878, and Johnston to McLaws, 27 June 1892, Civil War Sources and Photostats III, Container 173, Freeman Papers, LC. Johnston stated specifically that he told General Lee he had gone to Little Round Top. Since his writings indicate that he became familiar with the Gettysburg terrain, there seems to be little doubt that he was really on that hill. He denied a statement by McLaws that he had an escort of two hundred men. He wrote McLaws that he had "only three or four men. I had been told by General Lee that while in Mexico he found that he could get nearer the enemy and do more with a few men than with many."

12. Johnston to McLaws, 27 June 1892, and Johnston to Peterkin, n.d., Civil War Sources and Photostats III, Container 173, Freeman Papers, LC.

13. Johnston to McLaws, 27 June 1892, and Johnston to Peterkin, n.d., Civil War Sources and Photostats III, Container 173, Freeman Papers, LC.

14. *OR* 27 (1):519, 570, 927, 939.

15. Hood, "Letter," p. 147; McLaws, "Gettysburg," p. 68. Freeman, *R. E. Lee* 3:552–54 (app. 3), discusses the time of the arrival of Longstreet and his divisions on Cemetery Ridge. He concluded that Longstreet joined General Lee at 5:15 A.M. and that one division arrived between 7:00 and 7:30 A.M., the other between 8:00 and 8:30. These times could be accurate, but they seem to be based on questionable statements.

16. McLaws, "Gettysburg," p. 68. In this account McLaws states that Lee might have said, "No, General, I wish it placed just perpendicular to that."

17. Kershaw, "Kershaw's Brigade," p. 331.

18. W. C. Storrick of Gettysburg wrote that Lee was seen taking the stated route. See W. C. Storrick Notes, Civil War Sources and Photostats III, Container 173, Freeman Papers, LC. If Lee had also ridden to the almshouse and back to Ewell's headquarters, he would have traveled well over six miles by the time he returned to Seminary Ridge. The length of the trip, together with his conversations, suggests that Lee must have been gone as long as two hours.

There were cupolas also on the main dormitory buildings at the college and the seminary, and there were church steeples and other more convenient observation points within the town, such as the roof of the Fahnstock building, which had been used earlier by Howard. Why Trimble and Lee went back to the almshouse, therefore, is hard to understand.

19. Trimble, "Campaign and Battle," p. 212; Trimble, "Battle and Campaign," p. 125.

20. Longstreet, "Lee in Pennsylvania," p. 438; Longstreet, quoted in Early, "Supplement to General Early's Review," p. 289.

21. Long, *Memoirs of Lee*, p. 281.

22. Ibid.; Lawley, "Battles of Gettysburg"; Hood, "Letter," p. 148.

23. Hood, "Letter," p. 148; Longstreet, "Lee's Right Wing," p. 340; Longstreet, "Lee in Pennsylvania," p. 422.

24. Longstreet, "Lee in Pennsylvania," p. 422; Law, "Struggle," p. 319. Pickett's division did not march from Chambersburg until the morning of 2 July and did not reach the Gettysburg area, perhaps Marsh Creek, until late in the afternoon. It bivouacked there for the night, for Lee stated on its arrival that he would have no need for it that day. See *OR* 27 (2):385, 999; G. R. Stewart, *Pickett's Charge*, p. 3.

25. *OR* 27 (2):308, 318–19.

26. Hood, "Letter," pp. 149–50; McLaws, "Gettysburg," p. 71; Kershaw, "Kershaw's Brigade," p. 332; Longstreet, "Lee's Right Wing," p. 341; *OR* 27 (2):614, 618.

27. *OR* 27 (2):613, 617; Bachelder Map, 2 July.

28. *OR* 27 (2):607, 613, 617.

29. Ibid., pp. 613, 617. Wilcox wrote that his brigade took position at 9:00 A.M. and

that nothing happened until 2:00 P.M., a five-hour period. This seems an excessive wait. Wilcox was probably on line by 1:00 P.M. and Longstreet's corps filed by his rear about 3:00 or 3:30 P.M.

30. Law, "Struggle," p. 319; Oates, *The War*, p. 206; Longstreet, *From Manassas to Appomattox*, p. 365.

31. Polley, *Hood's Texas Brigade*, p. 155. Polley identified the soldier who overheard Lee's conversation as Ferdinand Hahn. However, I found no one of that name in the brigade's rosters. There was a Pvt. John Hahn in Company F, Fourth Texas.

32. Dickert, *Kershaw's Brigade*, p. 236.

33. McSwain, *Crumbling Defenses*, p. 38.

34. Ibid., pp. 38–39. Horsey probably rode south before the fight in Pitzer's Woods, after Buford's brigades had pulled off and before the arrival of the Third Corps brigades from Emmitsburg.

35. Ibid.

36. Alexander, "Gettysburg," p. 30, Alexander Papers, SHC.

37. *DAB* 1:165; Boatner, *Civil War Dictionary*, p. 7.

38. Alexander, "Gettysburg," p. 30, Alexander Papers, SHC; *OR* 27 (2):350. Alexander stated that he did not remember looking at his watch all the while but believed that by 11:00 A.M. his battalion had moved down to Pitzer's Schoolhouse. Since it is likely that he was with Pendleton about noon, it is probable that his battalion did not reach Pitzer's Schoolhouse before 1:30 or so.

39. Ibid. Apparently excessive rivalry, if not bad feeling, had developed between the battalions of Longstreet's Artillery Reserve because Walton, who had commanded the Washington Artillery, was thought by some to have given that battalion precedence in the march column too often.

40. Ibid., p. 31; Alexander, "Letter," p. 101; Alexander, "Artillery Fighting," p. 359. Alexander wrote that he turned left off the road to avoid the crest, but it seems more practical for his battalion to have turned out to the right. In "Artillery Fighting" Alexander implies that Cabell's and Henry's battalions were with him during this march, but the other sources cited here indicate otherwise. It is probable that the other two battalions marched with their divisions. Certainly, as indicated in Chapter 8, they deployed with them.

41. Storrick, *Battle of Gettysburg*, pp. 52–53. The 1860 census records of Adams County, Pennsylvania, show three occupants at the Wentz property in that year: John, age 73; Mary, age 72; and Susan, age 24.

42. Alexander, "Gettysburg," pp. 31–32, Alexander Papers, SHC; Alexander, "Letter," p. 102. In his manuscript Alexander cited this event as an example of the need for additional staff officers. He said that scarcely any of the generals had half the number needed to keep constant supervision over the execution of their orders.

43. McLaws, "Gettysburg," p. 70.

44. Kershaw, "Kershaw's Brigade," p. 331; Kershaw to Bachelder, 26 Mar. 1876, BP; Abernathy, *Our Mess*, p. 30.

45. McLaws, "Gettysburg," p. 69; Abernathy, *Our Mess*, p. 31; McLaws to Longstreet, 12 June 1873, McLaws Papers, SHC. Captain Johnston's role in this is not at

all clear. In later years Longstreet wrote that Johnston was ordered by General Lee to conduct the column and that he, Longstreet, rode in the rear with General Hood until things went wrong at the crest (Longstreet, "Lee in Pennsylvania," pp. 422–23; Longstreet, "Lee's Right Wing," p. 340.). Johnston, in a letter to Fitzhugh Lee, denied this and wrote that he had ridden most of the march with Longstreet *except* for the short distance "from the bend in the road to the top of the hill" when he rode with McLaws (F. Lee, "A Review," pp. 183–84; Johnston to Fitz Lee, 11 Feb. 1878, Civil War Sources and Photostats III, Container 173, Freeman Papers, LC). In a letter to McLaws, Johnston wrote that Lee sent him to Longstreet without instructions and that, as the head of the column passed the Fairfield Road, he warned Longstreet that it would be disclosed to the enemy. See Johnston to McLaws, 27 June 1892, Civil War Sources and Photostats III, Container 173, Freeman Papers, LC.

Since all of these statements were made long after the battle, they must be viewed with some skepticism. Common sense suggests that Johnston was sent to Longstreet as an adviser, as he indicated, and there is no reason for thinking that he was not with McLaws at the time the division halted. He might well have been with Longstreet earlier and later. Longstreet's being with Hood rather than at the head of the column in itself had no particular significance and obtained some only when Longstreet implied that he was there because he was displaced as corps commander, a seemingly foolish observation probably stemming from the quarreling of later years. But another question still remains—where was Major Clarke, Longstreet's engineer, all this while, and had he no useful advice?

It must be assumed that officers like Longstreet, McLaws, and Kershaw were practical men who must have noted the route of Alexander's battalion and avoided it for what they deemed to be a good reason. Unfortunately, we do not know the reason.

46. Longstreet, "Lee in Pennsylvania," pp. 422–23.

47. McLaws, "Gettysburg," p. 69; McLaws to Longstreet, 12 June 1873, McLaws Papers, SHC; McLaws, "Federal Disaster"; Kershaw, "Kershaw's Brigade," p. 331. McLaws had two accounts of this matter published and wrote another friendly account to Longstreet. All seem reasonable.

48. Kershaw, "Kershaw's Brigade," p. 332.

49. McLaws, "Gettysburg," p. 69; Warren Map.

50. McLaws, "Gettysburg," p. 69; Peterkin to Pendleton, 6 Dec. 1875, Folder 58, Pendleton Papers, SHC; Strider, *Peterkin*, p. 63; *OR* 27 (2):350–51; S. P. Lee, *Memoirs of Pendleton*, p. 292.

51. McLaws, "Gettysburg," pp. 69–70.

52. Ibid.; Kershaw, "Kershaw's Brigade," p. 332.

53. Longstreet, "Lee's Right Wing," p. 340.

54. Longstreet, "Lee in Pennsylvania," p. 423.

55. *OR* 27 (2):367; Kershaw, "Kershaw's Brigade," p. 333.

56. Hood, "Letter," p. 148. President Eisenhower's farm included these two properties, and he lived in the enlarged John Biesecker house. The farm extended from the boundary of Gettysburg National Military Park, near the crest of Seminary Ridge on the east, where the Confederates formed their line, west almost to Willoughby

Run. The president's farm operation also included the Samuel Pitzer farm north of the western extension of the Wheatfield Road (now the Water Works Road), which also extended from the ridge line west to Willoughby Run. Pitzer's Schoolhouse was at the junction of the present Water Works Road and the Black Horse Tavern Road, opposite the later schoolhouse site. In effect that portion of Longstreet's corps west of the Emmitsburg Road was deployed along or by the east edge of the Eisenhower farm.

CHAPTER 7

1. Sickles Testimony, *CCW*, p. 298.

2. Although the slight ridge north of Devil's Den had no known name at the time of the battle, it was later identified on some maps as Houck's Ridge, after the owner of that area at the time of the battle. This name has never gained wide use. The ridge is referred to as Devil's Den Ridge in the text simply as a matter of convenience. As a terrain feature per se, it is probably not prominent enough to bear a name. The topographical features in the Devil's Den area are discussed in Georg, "Our Principal Loss," p. 1.

3. This portion of the ridge line extending north into Pitzer's Woods has been called Warfield's Ridge. However, because it is, in location if not in geological fact, an extension of Seminary Ridge, that is what it will be called in the text.

4. In aiming, the gunner sighted through a detachable rear sight, a brass instrument called a pendulum hausse, that was temporarily affixed to a seat at the top of the gun's breech. He sighted down the barrel over the front sight, a wedge-shaped piece of metal that was screwed into the top of the muzzle. The range was set by moving a slider on the pendulum hausse to its proper place, much as an infantryman would adjust the rear sight on his rifle, and the muzzle of the gun was raised or lowered accordingly. The gunner aimed his piece laterally simply by having cannoneers shift its trail to the right or left.

The pendulum hausse and its service in general, together with infantry and cavalry tactics, is described in Gilham, *Manual of Instruction* and the much more recent Coggins, *Arms*. There also are other volumes, both official and unofficial, that deal with these matters, of course.

5. We shall never really know what the ground surface was at Devil's Den at the time of the battle. The avenue placed there by the various park developers and the wear of heavy visitation have altered it considerably. Unfortunately, this is also true of other areas where there were gun positions, particularly along the two ridge lines and on Little Round Top.

6. Gilham, *Manual of Instruction*, p. 53; Coggins, *Arms*, pp. 64–65. The prescribed distance between the end of the trail handspike and the noses of the lead horses of the limber team when a gun was firing was six yards.

7. *OR* 27 (1):588; Bradley and Ayars, "At Gettysburg."

8. *OR* 27 (1):588; J. E. Smith, *A Famous Battery*, p. 102.

9. *NY at Gbg* 3:1356; Kearny to Secretary of War, 9 June 1862, Ward Papers, New

York Public Library, Astor, Lenox and Tilden Foundation, Rare Books and Manuscripts Division. Ward commanded a brigade through Spotsylvania, where he received a head wound. He had some problems because of alleged intoxication during the Wilderness campaign, but the secretary of war refused to bring him to trial—perhaps long service and wounds spoke in his favor. After leaving the army, he was clerk of the superior court and the state supreme court of New York and lived until 1904, when he was hit by a train. See Warner, *Generals in Blue*, pp. 537–38.

10. *OR* 27 (1):493, 506, 511, 513.

11. Ibid., pp. 493, 506, 510, 511, 513; *Me at Gbg*, p. 160; *NY at Gbg* 3:868.

12. Warren Map. The Wheatfield was roughly trapezoidal in shape, about 300 yards wide on its northern and southern sides, 250 on the east, and 400 on the west. The Wheatfield Road and Trostle's Woods (a large, triangular wooded plot) bounded its north side. A worm fence at the west edge of the Wheatfield separated it from the woods and bald knob that formed the stony hill and from the wet ground at the southwest corner of the Wheatfield (see map on p. 251, *Me at Gbg*). A stone wall separated the Wheatfield from Rose's Woods on the south.

13. *NY at Gbg* 3:1194, 1198, 1204.

14. Ibid. The Napoleon properly was a "12 pounder, Field Gun, Light, Model 1857." See Hazlett, Olmstead, and Parks, *Field Artillery*, and Gibbon, *Artillerist's Manual*, for information on the Napoleon and other field guns.

15. Warren Map. This map, published in the atlas volume of *OR* as "Map of the Battle-Field of Gettysburg, Surveyed and drawn under the direction of Bvt. Maj. Gen. G. K. Warren," was revised and presumably refined by the Gettysburg National Park Commission (John P. Nicholson, Chairman) and is at Gettysburg National Military Park. The revised version of the map was used as the base map for this study; for convenience it will be referred to as the 1901 Commission/Cope Map.

16. De Trobriand, *Four Years*, p. 495; E. B. Houghton, *Seventeenth Maine*, p. 91; *Me at Gbg*, p. 192; Hamilton, "110th Pennsylvania," p. 121.

17. De Trobriand, *Four Years*, p. 495.

18. Pulford to Bachelder, 20 Dec. 1863, BP; *Pa at Gbg* 1:590; Hamilton, "110th Regiment"; *Me at Gbg*, p. 193; *OR* 27 (1):520–24; de Trobriand, *Four Years*, p. 495. Col. John Pulford of the Fifth Michigan recalled that the brigade was in two lines, one in the road to the right of the Wheatfield and the other in the woods to the right of the field.

19. *OR* 27 (1):526; *Me at Gbg*, p. 193; Verrill, "Seventeenth Maine," p. 261.

20. *OR* 27 (1):507, 523; *Me at Gbg*, p. 130. Because the Third Maine and the Third Michigan shared the numeral "3," were posted in the same area, and were detached from their parent brigades, it appears that the identities of the two regiments have merged in accounts of the battle. If so, the Third Michigan must take much of the blame, for its terse report was never supplemented by a readily found unofficial account of its efforts. Both regiments have memorials on the south side of the Peach Orchard, the Third Maine near the road, the Third Michigan to its left.

21. *NY at Gbg* 3:1360; Swanberg, *Sickles*, pp. 10–12, 34. After being captured at Gettysburg on 2 July, Graham was exchanged in 1864 and returned to duty. Possibly

because of his naval experience, he was given command of a naval brigade including a flotilla of gunboats on the James River. He commanded the assault and the reembarkation of troops in the first expedition against Fort Fisher. After the war, he became surveyor of the port of New York and served on the New York Monuments Commission for Gettysburg from 1883 until his death in 1886.

22. *OR* 27 (1):498; *Pa at Gbg* 1:356, 387; Hays, *Red Patch*, pp. 194–95.

23. *OR* 27 (1):500.

24. Ibid., p. 497; *Pa at Gbg* 1:345, 356. For brief information on Marie Tebe see Boatner, *Civil War Dictionary*, p. 828.

25. *OR* 27 (1):502; *Pa at Gbg* 2:606, 610; Babcock, "114th Regiment." Charles H. T. Collis became colonel of the 114th Pennsylvania Volunteer Infantry, Collis's Zouaves, when that regiment was organized. He received a brevet to brigadier general as of 28 October 1864 and to major general for war service. He received a Medal of Honor in 1893 for service at the battle of Fredericksburg. See Boatner, *Civil War Dictionary*, p. 166.

Sometime in the postwar years Collis, a Philadelphian, built a rather luxurious cottage that he called "Red Patch" on Seminary Ridge just south of the Fairfield Road. Here, it was said, he entertained less sedately than his Gettysburg neighbors. The house's various bedrooms were named for Union generals. After Collis's death in 1902, a monument to him, complete with bust, was erected among the graves in the national cemetery, though the general's remains molder elsewhere.

26. *OR* 27 (1):498–99; *Pa at Gbg* 1:393–94.

27. *OR* 27 (1):504; *Pa at Gbg* 2:686.

28. Hunt, "Second Day," p. 303; Hunt Testimony, *CCW*, p. 450.

29. Hunt, "Second Day," pp. 304–5. Hunt stated that, after the firing began and Smith's guns were not heard, he rode to Devil's Den and found that Smith had just been able to get his guns up over the rocks one by one. After Smith opened, Hunt left. He was alone and was frightened by an encounter with a herd of terrified cattle running about wildly in the Plum Run Valley.

30. *OR* 27 (1):585.

31. Ibid., pp. 583, 585; Hanifen, *Battery B*, p. 68. Shell was simply a shell casing filled with powder that was exploded by either impact or time fuse. Case, or shrapnel, was a shell casing containing both a bursting charge and a mass of lead balls. It was exploded by a time fuse and was intended for personnel.

32. *OR* 27 (1):590; Bucklyn to Bachelder, 31 Dec. 1863, BP; Lewis, *Battery E*, p. 206.

33. Ames, *Battery G*, pp. 27, 61–62. A battery wagon was a long-bedded, roofed cart that, like a caisson, was hooked to a limber. One was alloted for each battery, and it carried tools, spare parts, and equipment. Each battery also had a traveling forge—a fire box, bellows, and vise drawn by a limber and intended for use by the farrier in shoeing horses and for repairing equipment. See Hazlett, Olmstead, and Hume, *Field Artillery*, p. 219; *OR*, Atlas, pl. 173.

34. Ames, *Battery G*, pp. 64, 66; *OR* 27 (1):900. An artillery section had two guns and was commanded by a lieutenant called a chief of section. Each gun's crew was

commanded by a sergeant who was called a chief of piece. The right section contained the No. 1 and No. 2 pieces. In a six-gun battery the center section contained Nos. 3 and 4, and the left section Nos. 5 and 6; but in a four-gun battery Nos. 3 and 4 were in the left section. Each gun was served by the limber that towed it together with a second limber and a caisson.

35. Ames, *Battery G*, p. 66. The lieutenant was a veteran who had performed well in previous battles and apparently did so in this one after the firing began. In his report (*OR* 27 [1]:901) Ames wrote, "My lieutenants and men, one and all, performed their duties with that alacrity and promptness that shows them possessed of the qualities that make the patriot soldier." Patriotism is no guarantee against nervousness under fire; in fact it might increase it.

36. Ames, *Battery G*, p. 69.

37. Humphreys Testimony, *CCW*, p. 391.

38. Dana, *Recollections*, p. 173. There is a bronze statue of Humphreys beside the Emmitsburg Road north of the Klingle house. Another stands at the focal point of the national cemetery on Marye's Heights in Fredericksburg, Virginia.

39. Bardeen, *Fifer's War Diary*, p. 216.

40. Dana, *Recollections*, p. 174; Lyman, *Meade's Headquarters*, pp. 6–7, 78, 243.

41. *OR* 27 (1):509, 543, 547.

42. Ibid., p. 531.

43. Ibid., p. 532; Humphreys Testimony, *CCW*, p. 390.

44. *OR* 27 (1):532, 558.

45. Durboraw, "Big Battle."

46. Ibid. Klingle returned to his house after the battle and found it a shambles. After the war he submitted a claim for his household goods, shoes, and shoe leather (which were probably taken), damages done to his crops and buildings, and damage to his fields from rifle pits. He served later in the Union army. For his claim see Daniel Klingle, Claim 214-772, Claims Branch, Office of the Quartermaster General, Record Group 92, National Archives.

47. *OR* 27 (1):532, 570; Humphreys Testimony, *CCW*, p. 390; Cavada Diary, 2 July 1863, HSP.

48. Tremain, *Two Days*, pp. 54–55. HISTORICUS attributed the statement, "O, generals are all apt to look for the attack to be made where they are," to General Meade but stated that it was made at the time of Sickles's morning visit to Meade's headquarters (see *OR* 27 [1]:130). Tremain must have been aware of the HISTORICUS account when he wrote *Two Days*.

49. Ibid., pp. 55–56.

50. *OR* 27 (1):131; Tremain, *Two Days*, p. 61; Sickles Testimony, *CCW*, p. 299.

51. *OR* 27 (3):1086; Sickles, "Gettysburg." Sickles was listed as one to whom this circular was sent. There is no knowing if he received it, but it seems likely that he did.

52. Meade, *Life and Letters*, pp. 71–72; *OR* 27 (1):72. Although Meade stated that he would fall back if he learned that the enemy was trying to move to his rear and get between his army and Washington, it seems unlikely that he would have done this had Lee attempted to turn his left. To have fallen back to the Pipe Creek line under such

circumstances would have uncovered Monterey Pass and Frederick and thrown away an obvious opportunity to strike Lee's army when it was highly vulnerable. Had Lee turned Meade's right, however, a retreat to the Pipe Creek line might have been a logical response.

53. *OR* 27 (1):592; Warren Testimony, *CCW*, p. 377; Meade, *With Meade*, p. 108; Sykes to Editor, *The Chronicle*, 9 Dec. 1865, in Gross, *Battlefield of Gettysburg*, p. 26.

54. Sickles Testimony, *CCW*, p. 299; Tremain, *Two Days*, p. 61; Meade, *With Meade*, p. 108; Fasset, "Letter"; Paine to Meade, 22 May 1886, GL, p. 78.

55. Sickles, "Gettysburg."

56. Ibid.

57. *OR* 27 (3):487. In response to Meade's circular requesting a report and position sketch for each corps, Lt. Col. Nelson H. Davis made one for the Second Corps. Of those submitted, it alone was published in *OR*.

58. Meade to Webb, 7 Dec. 1885, Folder 0055, Box 3, Webb Papers, Yale University Library.

59. *OR* 27 (3):488.

60. Ibid.

61. Ibid. (1):72.

62. Tremain, *Two Days*, p. 65.

63. Taylor, *Warren*, p. 122.

64. Biddle to Meade, 18 Aug. 1880, GL, p. 27, and 10 July 1886, GL, p. 33; Starr to Meade, 7 Feb. 1880, GL, p. 81; Oliver to Meade, 16 May 1882, GL, p. 89.

65. Cavada Diary, 2 July 1863, HSP.

66. Oliver to Meade, 16 May 1882, GL, p. 89; Barclay to Sickles, 12 June 1886, in Sickles, "Gettysburg."

67. *OR* 27 (1):131–32.

68. Sickles Testimony, *CCW*, p. 299.

69. Biddle to Meade, 18 Aug. 1880, GL, p. 27; Meade, *With Meade*, p. 114.

70. Tremain, *Two Days*, p. 70; Starr to Meade, 7 Feb. 1880, GL, p. 33.

71. H. H. Humphreys, *Humphreys*, p. 193; Warren Testimony, *CCW*, p. 377; Meade, *With Meade*, p. 119; Meade, *Life and Letters*, p. 82; *OR* 27 (1):532.

72. H. H. Humphreys, *Humphreys*, pp. 193–94.

73. Ibid.

74. Ibid., p. 194; G. Tucker, *High Tide*, p. 240.

75. *Pa at Gbg* 2:622.

76. *NY at Gbg* 1:40.

77. Twichell to Sis, 5 July 1863, Twichell Papers, Collection of American Literature, The Beinecke Rare Book and Manuscript Library, Yale University (photocopy in Folder, New York, Seventy-first Infantry, Box 10, BC).

78. *Pa at Gbg* 1:196.

79. *OR* 27 (1):549; Blake, *Three Years*, p. 206; Storrick, *Battle of Gettysburg*, p. 32.

80. *OR* 27 (1):584, 589, 590; Seeley to Bachelder, 23 May 1878, BP.

81. *OR* 27 (1):532, 543, 551, 553; Bartlett, *Twelfth Regiment*, p. 328; Marbaker, *Eleventh New Jersey*, pp. 96–97.

82. Baldwin to Bachelder, 20 May 1865, BP.

83. *NY at Gbg* 3:1352–53; Blake, *Three Years*, p. 200.

84. *NY at Gbg* 2:605.

85. *OR* 27 (1):532, 558, 566; 41 (1):203. Most of the reports of the Excelsior Brigade are so uninformative as to be almost useless, and its memorials and the texts in *NY at Gbg* are equally disappointing. This is ironic because its organizer, General Sickles, was chairman of the New York Monuments Commission. One would expect that this brigade above all others would have benefited historically from the New York memorialization project.

CHAPTER 8

1. Young, *Battle of Gettysburg*, pp. 368–69; Warner, *Generals in Gray*, p. 204; Freeman, *Lee's Lieutenants* 2:270–72, 389, 661–62, 665, 694; Evans, *Confederate Military History* 6:431.

2. Freeman, *Lee's Lieutenants* 3:xxviii.

3. McLaws, "Gettysburg," pp. 70–71; McLaws to wife, 7 July 1863, Folder 7, McLaws Papers, SHC.

4. McLaws, "Gettysburg," pp. 70–71.

5. Ibid.; Kershaw, "Kershaw's Brigade," p. 332; *OR* 27 (2):367.

6. Kershaw, "Kershaw's Brigade," p. 332; *OR* 27 (2):367; Kershaw to Bachelder, 6 Apr. 1876, BP.

7. McLaws, "Gettysburg," p. 70; Kershaw, "Kershaw's Brigade," p. 332; *OR* 27 (2):367.

8. Warner, *Generals in Gray*, p. 171; McLaws, "Gettysburg," p. 70; Freeman, *Lee's Lieutenants* 3:343. Kershaw succeeded McLaws in command of the division prior to the Wilderness campaign and commanded it until his capture at Sayler's Creek on 6 April 1865. After the war he was a judge and a postmaster at Camden, South Carolina.

9. *OR* 27 (2):380.

10. McLaws, "Gettysburg," p. 70.

11. Ibid.; Kershaw to Bachelder, 3 Apr. 1876, BP; Sutton, *Grandpa's War Stories*, p. 40.

12. *OR* 27 (2):367; Kershaw, "Kershaw's Brigade," pp. 322–23; McLaws, "Gettysburg," p. 70. In the above-mentioned 3 April 1876 letter to Bachelder, Kershaw wrote that the Fifteenth South Carolina was on Cabell's right. Thus, there was a gap in the brigade line the width of a regimental front (perhaps a hundred yards) behind the right of Cabell's guns, and the Seventh and Third were next in line. It was said that the Third was in a wooded lot behind the artillery, probably in Biesecker's Woods. If so, it is likely that the Seventh would also have been in Biesecker's Woods. The Second was in open ground and had large trees in front of its left. These were at the top of the ridge between Biesecker's and Pitzer's woods and probably at the position of Manly's battery. The six companies of the Third South Carolina Battalion and the

ten of the Eighth Regiment were to the left but were also south of the road. All of Barksdale's brigade was north of the road in Pitzer's Woods. The order of its Mississippi regiments from the right was Twenty-first, Seventeenth, Thirteenth, and Eighteenth.

The order in line, from the right, of the regiments of the two rear Georgia brigades as depicted on the Bachelder Map for 2 July was as follows: Fifty-third, Fifty-first, Fiftieth, and Tenth in Semmes's brigade, and Sixteenth, Eighteenth, Twenty-fourth, Cobb's Legion, and Phillips's Legion in Wofford's brigade. Bachelder's sources for these alignments are not known.

13. Kershaw, "Kershaw's Brigade," p. 333; *OR* 27 (2):367; McLaws, "Gettysburg," p. 70.

14. McLaws, "Gettysburg," p. 72; "Major Raphael Moses Journal," Typescript, p. 5, Civil War Sources and Photostats III, Container 173, Freeman Papers, LC.

15. McLaws, "Gettysburg," p. 72.

16. Ibid.

17. Ibid.

18. Ibid.

19. Coddington, *Gettysburg Campaign*, p. 384.

20. McLaws, "Gettysburg," pp. 68–69.

21. Hood, "Letter," p. 149.

22. Longstreet, "Lee's Right Wing," pp. 340–41. There seems to be no other direct evidence that Lee himself modified the attack plan, but two things suggest that he might have. As seen in Chapter 15, Wilcox claimed that Lee and he talked at about this time somewhere off Barksdale's left. Therefore, Lee was in the area and accessible. In addition, as also described below, Longstreet refused a change in Hood's orders because the revised orders had come from General Lee. See Wilcox, "General Wilcox to the Rescue," and below.

23. McLaws, "Gettysburg," pp. 72–73. There seems to be no other mention of a battery's having been in the road itself. Alexander did not mention it. See below.

24. Ibid., p. 73.

25. Sorrel, *Recollections*, p. 157.

26. McLaws to wife, 7 July 1863, McLaws Papers, SHC; Coddington, *Gettysburg Campaign*, p. 381.

27. *OR* 27 (2):429; Alexander, *Military Memoirs*, p. 395.

28. "Position of Troops," pp. 9–11, GNMP. The number and type of guns in Confederate batteries indicated here, later in this chapter, and in Chapter 15 are taken from the tablets placed on the battlefield by the War Department.

29. Krick, *Parker's Virginia Battery*, p. 146; Figg, *Boy Company*, p. 139.

30. *OR* 27 (2):429; Alexander, "Gettysburg," p. 35, Alexander Papers, SHC.

31. Alexander, "Gettysburg," pp. 21–22, Alexander Papers, SHC.

32. McNeily, "Barksdale's Brigade," p. 238.

33. Sutton, *Grandpa's War Stories*, p. 40.

34. McLaws, "Gettysburg," pp. 70, 73.

35. Kershaw, "Kershaw's Brigade," pp. 333–34; *OR* 27 (2):367. The stony hill in

Kershaw's front in later years was labeled and designated by a tablet as "The Loop." The origin of this name is unknown; it seems not to go back to the battle. Possibly the name is derived from the fact that Sickles Avenue loops in a switchback as it climbs the hillside from the lower ground in the southwest corner of the Wheatfield to the crest of the stony hill. Because the Loop designation has no battle connotation, I have elected to refer to the area as "the stony hill," as Kershaw did.

36. *OR* 27 (2):368; Kershaw, "Kershaw's Brigade," pp. 333–34.

37. *OR* 27 (2):368; Kershaw, "Kershaw's Brigade," pp. 333–34; Law, in "Struggle," p. 325, stated that after Hood's division was engaged and McLaws did not advance, he went over to McLaws's front. He spoke with Kershaw who was awaiting orders to move. He showed Kershaw where his right flank should go, and Kershaw promptly moved out, according to Law. Kershaw said nothing of this conversation. It rings false as stated, for it has Kershaw moving out at his own volition rather than McLaws's and contradicts Kershaw's own statement in "Kershaw's Brigade," p. 334.

38. *OR* 27 (2):397, 414; Law, "Struggle," p. 320.

39. Warner, *Generals in Gray*, p. 175; "General E. M. Law," pp. 49–50; Oates, *The War*, pp. 261, 777; Evans, *Confederate Military History* 7:423–24.

40. Warner, *Generals in Gray*, p. 261; Evans, *Confederate Military History* 11:253–54. Jerome B. Robertson's son was Felix H. Robertson.

41. *OR* 27 (2):392–95; Oates, *The War*, p. 207; Oates, *Gettysburg*. In the Forty-seventh Regiment's report Maj. James Campbell wrote that the three companies were detached to guard the road to the regiment's right rear. This would seem conclusive except that Oates claims to have spoken with Capt. James Q. Burton of the Forty-seventh about the route followed by the three companies of the Forty-seventh that were on the skirmish line. It seems unlikely that the regiment's line would have been reduced by six companies, thus the three detached to the right rear and the three on the skirmish line were probably one and the same.

42. *OR* 27 (2):407–8, 411–12. The brigade tablet, located on Confederate Avenue south of the Emmitsburg Road, states that the brigade formed fifty yards west of it. At that point the tablet is about one hundred yards both east and south of the Emmitsburg Road, which crosses the ridge diagonally.

43. *OR* 27 (2):414, 420–21, 426; Oates, *The War*, p. 207; Bachelder Map, 2 July 1863.

44. *OR* 27 (2):396–97, 399, 401, 403. Anderson's brigade's tablet, which is along West Confederate Avenue near the Philip Snyder house, indicates that the brigade formed at 4:00 P.M. one hundred yards west of the tablet's location. This seems too close, because Robertson's brigade tablet, on line with Anderson's to the south beyond the road, indicates that that brigade, which was in the forward line, was fifty yards to the west. This would imply that the two brigade lines were only fifty yards apart. Anderson's tablet's inscription indicates that his brigade would have been in Biesecker's Woods. This would have been true also if the distance given on the tablet was 150 yards.

45. Young, *Battle of Gettysburg*, p. 382; Krick, *Lee's Colonels*, p. 172.

46. *OR* 27 (2):428. The batteries' armament is taken from their tablets.

47. Ibid.; Hood, "Letter," p. 148; Krick, *Death Roster*, p. 8. There is some question as to whether Major Henry or Maj. John C. Haskell commanded this battalion, but Henry is listed as its commander in *OR* and signed its report as the battalion commander.

48. Freeman, *Lee's Lieutenants* 2:xxvii, xxx; Young, *Battle of Gettysburg*, p. 369; Lord, *Fremantle Diary*, p. 193.

49. Hood, "Letter," p. 148; Simpson, *Lee's Grenadier Guards*, p. 267; Chilton, *Unveiling*, p. 339. Maj. Henry Tremain sent General Sickles an extract of a eulogy by Congressman Alexander W. Gregg for the late Congressman John M. Pinckney of Texas. In it Gregg stated that Pinckney and four others of the Fourth Texas were sent on a scout to Little Round Top. See Sickles Correspondence, New-York Historical Society.

50. Law, "Struggle," p. 321. The early morning reconnaissance was headed by officers of engineers. It appears that both Law's and Hood's parties were composed of enlisted men. Law's men were not named.

51. *OR* 27 (2):393, 395, 410; W. C. Ward, "Incidents," p. 346; Oates, *The War*, p. 212. A regiment's pioneers carried and used axes and shovels.

52. J. C. West, *A Texan*, p. 93.

53. Ibid., p. 85; Polley, *Hood's Texas Brigade*, pp. 167, 176.

54. Polley, *Hood's Texas Brigade*, p. 168; *OR* 27 (2):410.

55. Barziza, *Adventures*, p. 44.

56. Collier, *"They'll Do,"* p. 139.

57. Polk, *Memories*, p. 15.

58. Law, "Struggle," p. 321.

59. Ibid.

60. Ibid., pp. 321–22.

61. Ibid., p. 322.

62. Hood, "Letter," p. 148.

63. Ibid., pp. 149–50.

64. Sorrel, *Recollections*, p. 169.

65. "Journal of Raphael J. Moses, C.S.A.," p. 5, Civil War Sources and Photostats III, Container 173, Freeman Papers, LC.

66. Fairfax to Longstreet, 12 Nov. 1877, in Longstreet, *From Manassas to Appomattox*, p. 381.

67. Ibid.

68. Hood, "Letter," p. 150; Chilton, *Unveiling*, p. 339. Chilton quoted Colonel Work of the First Texas, who said that Hood was heard to say, "Very well; when we get under fire, I will have a digression." These seem unlikely words from a professional soldier of Hood's stature even under trying circumstances. Though in hindsight they might have pleased the Texans, they diminished Hood.

69. Hood, "Letter," p. 150.

70. Longstreet, *From Manassas to Appomattox*, p. 381; Barziza, *Adventures*, p. 46.

71. Longstreet, *From Manassas to Appomattox*, pp. 367–69. In these statements Longstreet displayed the lack of objectivity that characterized some of his later views of the battle.

72. Chilton, *Unveiling*, p. 350. Colonel Work recalled that Hood commanded, "Forward, my Texans, and win this battle or die in the effort!" (see Chilton, *Unveiling*, p. 339). John West of the Fourth Texas recalled Hood's shouting, "Forward—steady—forward," which is more cautionary in tone and sounds like the coaching of a company officer (see J. C. West, *A Texan*, p. 94).

73. Fletcher, *Rebel Private*, p. 73.

74. R. M. Powell, "With Hood."

75. W. C. Ward, "Incidents," p. 346. The commands given in the text are changed slightly from those given in the article to bring them into closer conformity with the drill manual.

76. Ibid., p. 347; Oates, *The War*, p. 228. Col. William F. Perry of the Forty-fourth Alabama wrote that both Little Round Top and Devil's Den looked like volcanoes. Little Round Top might have given that appearance after Hazlett's battery began to fire from it, but that would have been a short while later in the day, as described in Chapter 10.

77. Oates, *The War*, pp. 207–8. Oates wrote that the skirmish line had three companies of the Forty-seventh and two of the Forty-eighth, each under the command of a captain. He wrote later that the whole line should have been under the command of a major.

78. Ibid.; *OR* 27 (2):391, 393; W. C. Ward, "Incidents," p. 347.

79. *OR* 27 (2):392–93; Oates, *The War*, p. 207.

80. Law, "Struggle," p. 324; Oates to Robbins, 14 Feb. 1903, Oates Correspondence, GNMP.

81. Oates, *The War*, p. 210; Oates to Robbins, 14 Feb. 1903, Oates Correspondence, GNMP. In a letter to Colonel Stoughton of the Second United States Sharpshooters Oates wrote that he was to find the Federal left, "turn it if possible, and to go as far as I could." See Oates, *Gettysburg*.

82. Oates, *The War*, p. 210. A worm fence paralleled Plum Run at the base of Round Top's west slope, separating the woods on the slope from the cleared fields at and west of the run. Although this fence seems like the likely place for the sharpshooters to have made a stand, various Confederates involved wrote that the Federal stand was made from behind a stone wall. Therefore, the sharpshooters must have been behind a wall that bordered the farm lane connecting the Slyder farmyard with a cleared area on the west slope of Round Top. This cleared area was about two hundred yards east of Plum Run and forty feet higher than the run. The wall bordered the west side of the cleared field. The memorial of the First Vermont Volunteer Cavalry Regiment was later placed in this field.

83. Oates, *The War*, pp. 207–8.

84. W. C. Ward, "Incidents," p. 347; *OR* 27 (2):391, 394, 395; Krick, *Death Roster*, pp. 35, 42.

85. *OR* 27 (2):404, 407; Robertson to Bachelder, 11 May 1882 and 30 Apr. 1876, BP.

86. Robertson to Bachelder, 30 Apr. 1876, BP; Hood, "Letter," p. 150; Dyer, *Gallant Hood*, p. 194.

87. Colston, "The Campaign of Gettysburg," p. 12, Campbell-Colston Papers, SHC.

88. Oates, *The War*, pp. 210, 212; *OR* 27 (2):405. Law's successor as acting brigade commander, Col. James L. Sheffield, was not told to take command of the brigade until the fighting was over for the day. See *OR* 27 (2):396.

89. *OR* 27 (2):404, 407, 411, 412; Robertson to Bachelder, 30 Apr. 1876, BP. Robertson, like Benning, reported being fired on by a battery on the "mountain"— apparently Little Round Top—during his advance. He wrote also that it was held by the enemy in heavy force. Although Hazlett's battery was on the hill later in the day, it is unlikely that the battery was there during the advance. See Chapter 10.

90. *OR* 27 (2):393, 396; Oates, *The War*, p. 228. The whereabouts of the Forty-eighth are difficult to discern from Colonel Sheffield's report. Colonel Perry's report presents the Forty-fourth's position more clearly, and we can tell from it that the Forty-fourth was on the left of the Forty-eighth and on the left of the brigade line. Possibly Perry did not know that the Fourth and Fifth Texas regiments were in Law's line.

91. Warner, *Generals in Gray*, pp. 25–26; Evans, *Confederate Military History* 6:395–96.

92. *OR* 27 (2):414.

93. Ibid., pp. 415, 421, 424.

94. Anderson to Bachelder, 4 Dec. 1884, BP.

95. Hillyer, *Battle of Gettysburg*, p. 5.

96. Ibid.; Anderson to Bachelder, 15 Mar. 1876 and 4 Dec. 1894, BP. In the 1894 letter Anderson wrote that he was ordered in on Law's left rather than Robertson's. It is likely that his 1876 recollections are more accurate.

97. Hillyer, *Battle of Gettysburg*, pp. 5–6; *OR* 27 (2):399.

CHAPTER 9

1. Hunt, "Second Day," pp. 305–6.

2. *OR* 27 (1):509, 588; *NY at Gbg* 3:1290; *Me at Gbg*, pp. 162, 181. The term "gorge" was used for the ravine between Devil's Den and Round Top in the reports of both Colonel Shepherd of the Second Georgia and Colonel Hodges of the Seventeenth Georgia. Colonel Walker of the Fourth Maine and Captain Smith of the Fourth New York also used "gorge" in their accounts (see *OR* 27 [2]:420, 425; *Me at Gbg*, p. 63; *NY at Gbg* 3:1291). Although the term has not been commonly used outside these reports, it seems like an appropriate one, and I have used it here.

In his report for the Fourth Maine, Lt. Charles F. Sawyer stated that Company F was left on the brow of the hill (Devil's Den) when the regiment went into the valley. It seems likely, therefore, that this was the force deployed in the Den as skirmishers. See *OR* 27 (1):509.

3. A. W. Tucker, "124th New York"; J. E. Smith, *A Famous Battery*, p. 139.

4. *NY at Gbg* 3:1290; J. E. Smith, *A Famous Battery*, p. 104; *OR* 27 (1):588; A. W. Tucker, "124th New York."

5. *OR* 27 (1):506, 510, 513; *Me at Gbg*, p. 162.

6. *OR* 27 (1):493.

7. Ibid. (2):404, 407, 408.

8. The acreages, elevations, and distances given here were scaled from the 1901 Commission/Cope Map and should be considered only approximate.

9. *OR* 27 (1):493.

10. Ibid. (2):407; Robertson to Bachelder, 30 Apr. 1876, BP.

11. *OR* 27 (1):506, 511, 513, (2):407–8.

12. Collier, *"They'll Do,"* p. 142.

13. *OR* 27 (2):407–8.

14. Ibid. (1):592–93; Norton, *Attack*, pp. 293–94; Sykes to Editor, *The Chronicle*, 9 Dec. 1865, in Gross, *Battlefield of Gettysburg*, pp. 26–27; Sykes to Editor, *The Tribune*, 24 July 1876, "Battle of Gettysburg Letterbook," p. 165, Doubleday Papers, New-York Historical Society.

15. *OR* 27 (1):506, 512, 513; Osbourn, *Twentieth Indiana*.

16. "Account of Erasmus C. Gilbreath, Co. I," Gilbreath Manuscripts, Indiana Division, Indiana State Library (photocopy in Folder, Indiana, Twentieth Regiment, Box 16, BC).

17. *Me at Gbg*, pp. 193, 212; *OR* 27 (2):407.

18. "Recollections of Private A. C. Sims," Confederate Research Center (photocopy in Folder, Texas, Infantry, First Regiment, Box 8, BC).

19. *OR* 27 (2):408.

20. Ibid., pp. 394–95; Oates, *The War*, p. 228.

21. *OR* 27 (2):394–95; Oates, *The War*, p. 228.

22. *Me at Gbg*, pp. 163, 181.

23. *OR* 27 (1):509; *Me at Gbg*, p. 163.

24. *OR* 27 (2):396.

25. *Me at Gbg*, pp. 163–64.

26. *NY at Gbg* 2:876.

27. Ibid., p. 868; Weygant, *One Hundred Twenty-fourth*, pp. 172–73.

28. *NY at Gbg* 2:869; Weygant, *One Hundred Twenty-fourth*, p. 175; J. E. Smith, *A Famous Battery*, p. 137.

29. *NY at Gbg* 3:1290; Polk, *Memories*, p. 15; J. E. Smith, *A Famous Battery*, p. 139.

30. Polley, *Hood's Texas Brigade*, p. 172; *OR* 27 (2):410; Law, "Struggle," p. 324; Simpson, *A Compendium*, p. 79. In his report Colonel Work praised Barbee for his bravery but wrote only that he was shot in the thigh. In later years Law mentioned several wounds. Barbee was listed on the Confederate Roll of Honor for his bravery at Gettysburg; he was killed in Tennessee in January 1864.

31. *NY at Gbg* 2:869; Weygant, *One Hundred Twenty-fourth*, p. 176; A. W. Tucker, "124th New York"; J. E. Smith, *A Famous Battery*, p. 137. During the loading process the No. 1 cannoneer swabbed the barrel with a wet sponge before loading to extinguish any sparks that might be there. From the time the sponge entered the muzzle of the gun until the charge was inserted by the No. 2, the No. 3 cannoneer closed the vent by pressing his left thumb over it. (He wore a thumbstall to keep from being burned by the hot barrel.) The vent was closed to keep any sparks in it from being fanned and igniting the powder charge prematurely. See Gilham, *Manual of Instruction*, pp. 494–96; Coggins, *Arms*, p. 70. At times when the danger of a premature explosion was surpassed by that of an enemy assault—when the barrel was hot and the gun crew was firing canister—the crew sometimes tried to increase its rate of fire by omitting sponging. At this time the No. 3 was often able to fire the piece simply by removing his thumb from the vent.

32. *NY at Gbg* 2:867; Weygant, *One Hundred Twenty-fourth*, p. 176; Polley, *Hood's Texas Brigade*, p. 170; A. W. Tucker, "124th New York."

33. *NY at Gbg* 2:869; Weygant, *One Hundred Twenty-fourth*, p. 176.

34. *NY at Gbg* 2:869; Weygant, *One Hundred Twenty-fourth*, p. 176; A. W. Tucker, "124th New York."

35. *NY at Gbg* 2:869; Weygant, *One Hundred Twenty-fourth*, p. 176.

36. *NY at Gbg* 2:869; Weygant, *One Hundred Twenty-fourth*, p. 176.

37. *NY at Gbg* 2:869–70. The quotation is from an unidentified article by Capt. William Silliman.

38. Polley, *Hood's Texas Brigade*, p. 171.

39. *NY at Gbg* 2:870; Weygant, *One Hundred Twenty-fourth*, p. 176.

40. Weygant, *One Hundred Twenty-fourth*, p. 177.

41. Polley, *Hood's Texas Brigade*, p. 170; OR 27 (2):408–9, 421.

42. *OR* 27 (2):420–26.

43. *NY at Gbg* 2:870; OR 27 (1):589.

44. *NY at Gbg* 3:1293.

45. J. E. Smith, *A Famous Battery*, pp. 104, 137–39; Bradley and Ayars, "At Gettysburg"; *NY at Gbg* 3:1291.

46. Weygant, *One Hundred Twenty-fourth*, p. 178; Hanford, "Gettysburg"; J. E. Smith, *A Famous Battery*, p. 139; *NY at Gbg* 2:872; Birney Testimony, *CCW*, p. 367; Sykes to Editor, *The Chronicle*, 9 Dec. 1865, in Gross, *Battlefield of Gettysburg*, p. 26.

47. *NY at Gbg* 2:871.

48. Ibid., p. 872; Weygant, *One Hundred Twenty-fourth*, pp. 178–79.

49. *OR* 27 (1):520, 526, 571, 577.

50. Ibid. (2):394, 396; Oates, *The War*, p. 228.

51. *Me at Gbg*, pp. 166, 182; Walker to Bachelder, 6 Jan. 1886, BP; J. E. Smith, *A Famous Battery*, p. 141.

52. *OR* 27 (2):394; Oates, *The War*, p. 228. Perry's account in Oates, *The War*, states that the Forty-fourth captured several artillerymen. This is unlikely since Smith's casualties included only one man missing who might have been captured apart from Private Broderick, who was captured and escaped. Perry also wrote that a "spherical

case-shot" exploded near his head. If Perry was correct, which is not at all certain, the round could have come only from a smoothbore piece in Gibbs's, Winslow's, or Latham's battery.

53. Oates, *The War*, pp. 228–29.

54. *OR* 27 (2):415, 424, 426; "Journal of Private John Malachi Bowden," Special Collections Department, Robert W. Woodruff Library, Emory University (photocopy in Folder, Georgia, Second Regiment, Box 7, BC).

55. *OR* 27 (2):421.

56. *Me at Gbg*, p. 164.

57. *OR* 27 (2):422; Chilton, *Unveiling*, pp. 192, 339. It was said that the Federal infantry passed the word along the line not to fire at Branard. If so, this might account for his not being shot earlier.

58. *OR* 27 (2):409, 422.

59. Ibid. (1):494, 506, 512; Weygant, *One Hundred Twenty-fourth*, p. 180; *NY at Gbg* 2:872; Osbourn, *Twentieth Indiana.*

60. *OR* 27 (2):426; Chilton, *Unveiling*, p. 340.

61. Lokey, "Wounded at Gettysburg"; *OR* 27 (2):426. In a letter dated 27 December 1865, to C. L. Bedinger, Samuel Weaver, a native of Virginia who was a Gettysburg physician, described the need for as much information as possible on circumstances of the deaths of Confederates killed at Gettysburg if he was to locate and identify their bodies. He wrote, as an example, that he had recently been asked to recover the body of Colonel Jones. He stated that Mrs. Jones had written that

> Col. Jones fell while making a charge on little Round Top—on Snyder farm & was buried about 150 yds from the house under a Cherry tree & was wounded in or through the left side of his head, I went out to examine the graves on Mr. Snyders farm but I couldent find such a location as she described on Mr. Snyders place. I then went on to the next farm a Mr Slyders. There I found a cherry tree about 150 yards from the house with two graves under it. I opened them both and in the one I found the remains of a soldier to answer the description Mrs. Jones sent me, wounded in the left side of his head and the left lower jaw broken.

This letter is from the Papers of the Bedinger-Dandridge Family, Box 5, Correspondence, 1863–75, Manuscripts Department, William R. Perkins Library, Duke University (photocopies on file at Fredericksburg and Spotsylvania . . . National Military Park).

62. *Me at Gbg*, p. 182; Bradley and Ayars, "At Gettysburg."

63. *OR* 27 (2):426, (1):513; *Pa at Gbg* 1:540. On 13 March 1863 General Birney, who succeeded to the command of Philip Kearny's division, directed that a "cross of valor" be awarded to enlisted men who distinguished themselves in battle. It was a bronze cross with the inscription "Kearny Cross" on the front and "Birney's Division" on the back. Presumably, this was comparable to the Kearny Medal, an award for officers, established on 29 November 1862, in Kearny's honor. See Boatner, *Civil War Dictionary*, p. 449.

64. *Me at Gbg*, p. 182; *OR* 27 (2):427.

65. *OR* 27 (1):526; *NY at Gbg* 1:46, 109. The reports do not state positively whether the Fortieth New York Volunteer Infantry or the Sixth New Jersey Volunteer Infantry arrived in Plum Run Valley first, and the regimental account of each fails to mention the presence of the other. However, since the Fortieth advanced almost to the gorge and further than the Sixth New Jersey, and the Sixth was the last out of the valley, it seems likely that the Fortieth was there first.

66. *NY at Gbg* 1:297, 300.

67. *OR* 27 (1):526, (2):420, 424–25.

68. Ibid. (1):526.

69. Ibid. (2):420, 425.

70. Ibid. (1):526, (2):420, 425.

71. Ibid. (1):589.

72. Ibid. Smith did not state where his sections were posted and did not name their chiefs.

73. Ibid. (2):415. Benning described the artillery fire in his report. The regimental reports did not mention it specifically.

74. J. E. Smith, *A Famous Battery*, pp. 143–44.

75. *OR* 27 (1):589.

76. Ibid., pp. 577–78; New Jersey Gettysburg Battlefield Commission, *Final Report*, p. 101; Toombs, *New Jersey*, p. 212. In Burlington to Bachelder, 18 Feb. 1884, BP, Burling wrote that he followed the Sixth New Jersey to its position, but he did stay with it.

77. *OR* 27 (1):526–27.

78. *NY at Gbg* 3:1292–93; *OR* 27 (1):178.

79. *NY at Gbg* 3:1292; J. E. Smith, *A Famous Battery*, p. 106; *OR* 27 (1):589.

80. *OR* 27 (1):236, 583.

81. Polley, *Hood's Texas Brigade*, p. 169.

CHAPTER 10

1. Roebling to Smith, 5 July 1913, Roebling Letters Typescript, Roebling Collections, Rutgers University Libraries. This was Roebling's recollection at this date. Yet, in 1877 Warren wrote that he suggested Meade send him to the left. The accounts need not be exclusive. See: Hunt, "Second Day," p. 307.

2. *NY at Gbg* 3:979–81.

3. Taylor, *Warren*, pp. 119–20; Meade, "Letter," p. 413.

4. Hunt, "Second Day," p. 307; *NY at Gbg* 3:977. The verse is from the "Dedicatory Poem" by Maj. Andrew Coats for the Warren Monument on Little Round Top. Some officers at Gettysburg, and others, have said that if the Confederates had occupied Little Round Top, they would have placed artillery there and with it driven the Federal forces from the field. This is an attractive supposition, but it is unlikely that artillery *itself* would have accomplished this. The number of pieces that could have been

placed on the hill in position to enfilade Cemetery Ridge is quite limited due to the conformation of the hill's crest and its surface—it would have accommodated a battery at most. So few guns so far from their prime targets probably would not have driven off the Army of the Potomac.

5. Warren to Farley, 13 July 1872, in Norton, *Attack*, p. 309 and Hunt, "Second Day," p. 307. The quotation is from the Hunt account. In the light of other events, Warren's story seems somewhat romantic, but there is no reason to doubt his truthfulness in the matter.

6. Hunt to Gantt, 21 Oct. 1886, Box 4, Hunt Papers, LC.

7. Hunt, "Second Day," pp. 307–8; Meade, *Life and Letters*, p. 82; Meade, *With Meade*, p. 119. Chauncey B. Reese (1837–70), a graduate of West Point in 1859, like Mackenzie and Roebling, was a young officer of promise and was breveted a brigadier general of volunteers in recognition of his Civil War service. However, his career was cut short by death from yellow fever while on duty in Mobile.

8. OR 27 (1):138, 600; Norton, *Attack*, p. 264. Ranald S. Mackenzie (1840–89), an 1862 West Point graduate, served as an officer of engineers until the fall of 1863, when he became colonel of the Second Connecticut Heavy Artillery. He commanded a brigade in the Sixth Corps in the Valley in the fall of 1864 and during the Petersburg campaign. He led the cavalry division of the Army of the James during the Appomattox campaign. He was appointed a brigadier general in October 1864 and subsequently breveted a major general. He was a prominent commander in the Indian Wars in the Southwest and in 1872 became a brigadier general in the Regular Army. He was disabled and retired in 1884. General Grant regarded Mackenzie as the most promising officer in the army. See Boatner, *Civil War Dictionary*, p. 499.

9. Young, *Battle of Gettysburg*, p. 344; Hill, "Lee Attacks," p. 359; Lyman, *Meade's Headquarters*, p. 9; Wright, "Recollections of the War of the Rebellion, 146th Regiment," p. 75, New-York Historical Society.

10. Jay to Ingham, 9 Feb. 1893, GL, p. 147.

11. OR 27 (1):592; Sykes to Editor, *Tribune*, 29 July 1876, "Battle of Gettysburg Letterbook," p. 184, Doubleday Papers, New-York Historical Society; Sykes to Editor, *The Chronicle*, 9 Dec. 1866, in Gross, *Battlefield of Gettysburg*, p. 27; Locke to Chamberlain, 5 July 1886, Box 3, Apr.–Dec. 1886 Folder, Frost Family Collection, Yale University Library.

12. Ingham to Sykes, 28 Jan. 1873, "Meade Letterbook," Meade Collection, HSP; OR 27 (1):592; Sykes to Editor, *The Chronicle*, 9 Dec. 1886, in Gross, *Battlefield of Gettysburg*, p. 27.

13. OR 27 (1):592; Sykes to Editor, *Tribune*, 29 July 1876, "Battle of Gettysburg Letterbook," Doubleday Papers, New-York Historical Society; Jay to Ingham, 9 Feb. 1893, GL, p. 142.

14. OR 27 (1):600; *Pa at Gbg* 1:461.

15. Norton, *Attack*, p. 264. The Eighty-third Pennsylvania Volunteer Infantry's memorial at Gettysburg is surmounted by a statue of Vincent.

16. Ibid., p. 285; *Pa at Gbg* 1:461.

17. Norton, *Attack*, pp. 281–84.

18. Ibid.; *Pa at Gbg* 1:460.

19. *Pa at Gbg* 1:460–61.

20. Norton, *Army Letters*, p. 167.

21. The memorial of the Forty-fourth New York is probably the largest regimental monument on the battlefield. It stands at the south end of Little Round Top's crest, above and behind the Forty-fourth's position. Its large size is due in part to its also being the monument of the Twelfth New York Volunteer Infantry. The Twelfth had distinguished service but had only two companies at Gettysburg, which acted as the provost guard at Fifth Corps headquarters. The two regiments were once brigaded under Butterfield, who had commanded the Twelfth and is memorialized by a plaque within the memorial.

22. *OR* 27 (1):623; *Me at Gbg*, p. 253; Warren to Farley, 13 July 1872, in Norton, *Attack*, p. 311.

23. *Me at Gbg*, p. 254.

24. The right flank marker of the Twentieth Maine is near the crest of the spur between the regiment's memorial and the main hill. The Twentieth's companies were formed, from left to right, in the following order: A, C, H, F, D, K, I, and E. Company B was off to the left. See *Me at Gbg*, p. 254.

25. Norton, *Attack*, p. 265. In reporting this conversation Norton must have assumed that Vincent posted the Sixteenth Michigan on the right of the line before posting the other regiments. Since Chamberlain reported otherwise, and since it would have been desirable to post the left of the line first on the spur if the spur was to be defended, it seems likely that Chamberlain rather than Norton was correct.

26. *OR* 27 (1):616, 618, 628; Graham, "On to Gettysburg," p. 10. The shelf below that occupied by the Sixteenth Michigan, as described here and marked by that regiment's memorial, would have served as a logical position for Vincent's right for many reasons. It would have been at the same elevation as the line of the Eighty-third Pennsylvania Volunteer Infantry and would have permitted a straighter brigade line. If occupied, it would have denied the Confederates the defilade in its front. However, it would have been difficult to reach from the rear with any safety and more vulnerable to snipers from the Devil's Den–Slaughter Pen area. Since it was lower, it probably could have been turned more easily than a position on the higher shelf, a crucial consideration as things turned out.

27. *NY at Gbg* 1:365.

28. Nash, *Forty-fourth Regiment*, p. 144.

29. Morrill to Chamberlain, 8 July 1863, BP; *Me at Gbg*, p. 254. The granite marker indicating Company B's position is on the west side of a north-south stone wall, near the south end of that wall. It is in the woods about two hundred yards east of the Twentieth Maine's memorial.

30. *OR* 27 (1):617, 628, 630; Graham, "On to Gettysburg," p. 10.

31. *NY at Gbg* 1:359–63.

32. Nash, *Forty-fourth Regiment*, p. 154; *OR* 27 (1):630.

33. *OR* 27 (2):391, 411–12; W. C. Ward, "Incidents," p. 349; J. W. Stevens, *Reminiscences*, p. 114.

34. J. W. Stevens, *Reminiscences*, p. 114.

35. M. V. Smith, *Reminiscences*, p. 36. Smith's account of what he saw at Devil's Den, though he confused that place with Little Round Top, seems quite credible. The irony is that at the time of writing he seemed to see nothing wrong with straggling from his place in the regiment's line, where men were needed badly, and fighting his own battle.

36. *OR* 27 (2):392.

37. Ibid., p. 271; Oates, *The War*, p. 211.

38. *OR* 27 (2):392; Oates, *The War*, p. 212. Oates wrote that the men sent for the canteens went astray in the woods and were captured.

39. Oates, *The War*, p. 212; Oates to Bachelder, 29 Mar. 1876, BP.

40. Oates, *The War*, p. 212. Oates's stated desire to turn the crest of Round Top into a strongpoint does not seem to reflect his character. Law's brigade was in the attack and not on the defensive; any time spent on the hill was time lost, though a pause for rest there might have been justified. Round Top had little or no value as an artillery position in the attack that afternoon. One can easily assume that the fighting for that day would have been over before any guns could have been dragged to the top of the hill. And, if a suitable place could have been found for them there, they still could not have been used unless trees were felled to clear a field of fire. One can, then, wonder what targets would have been fired at that could not have been assailed equally effectively from guns in other positions. Assuming that Hazlett's battery, seven hundred yards away, would have been a target, Federal fortunes most likely would not have been affected seriously even if it had been taken under fire before the fighting of the day ended.

41. Oates's biography is summed up by Robert K. Krick in his introduction to the 1974 edition of Oates, *The War*. (This introductory section is not paginated.)

42. Ibid. Because, for reasons we do not know, the Confederate Senate did not confirm Oates's commission as colonel, he did not have that grade technically, though he certainly was so recognized by the Army of Northern Virginia. Therefore, when another officer of the regiment, Alexander A. Lowther, who as a major had outranked Oates, succeeded in getting a confirmed commission and appeared with it to take command, the army and Oates had to recognize his claim. Oates was then reduced to the grade of major but was given command of the Forty-eighth Georgia Regiment. He was shot in the right arm in June 1864, and that arm had to be amputated. After the war Oates practiced law, became active in Alabama politics, served as a congressman from 1880 to 1894, and was elected to one term as governor in 1895–96. He was a brigadier general during the War with Spain. See also: Krick, *Lee's Colonels*, pp. 225, 268.

43. Oates, *The War*, p. 212. Norton, in *Attack*, p. 258, wrote that Oates's force descended Round Top by a path. This would suggest an approach in a single or double file, an unlikely formation in the presence of the enemy.

44. Oates, *The War*, pp. 207, 214, 221, 586.

45. R. M. Powell, "With Hood."

46. J. C. West, *A Texan*, pp. 86, 95.

47. *OR* 27 (2):412; Typescript of letter of J. Mark Smither to mother, n.d., Folder, Texas, Fifth Infantry, Box 8, BC.

48. Fletcher, *Rebel Private*, p. 74; *OR* 27 (2):413.

49. *OR* 27 (2):413; Fletcher, *Rebel Private*, p. 75. Pvt. J. Mark Smither wrote that Law ordered the second advance. How he knew this is not clear. See Typescript, Letter of J. Mark Smither to mother, Folder, Texas, Fifth Infantry, Box 8, BC.

50. *OR* 27 (2):391, 411–12. Major Rogers reported that he was ordered to make second and third assaults against Vincent's line and implied that both Texas regiments received such an order. He did not say who gave the orders. Certainly it was not Robertson, who was in front of Devil's Den. Major Bane, in his report, did not indicate who ordered the attacks but stated that Law ordered the regiment to take up the defensive position on Round Top.

51. There seems to be no reason for thinking that the Texans and the Fourth Alabama did not go directly to the saddle, whereas Oates's force went to the crest of Round Top and rested there. In his account Oates stated twice that the battle was "raging below" before his command started down the hill, although he was not specific about where it was raging. Perhaps he did not know (see Oates, *The War*, pp. 211, 213). Oates was the ranking officer present opposite Vincent's line but made no claim to directing the Fourth. In fact, he wrote of the Fourth's isolation from the Forty-seventh, a thing that Major Robbins of the Forty-seventh denied. Robbins wrote that the Fourth and Forty-seventh were connected but wrote nothing of coordination between them. See Oates, *The War*, p. 217; Oates to Bachelder, 29 Mar. 1876, BP; Robbins to Nicholson, 26 Feb. 1903, Oates Correspondence, GNMP.

52. Oates, *The War*, p. 214.

53. Ibid., p. 755.

54. *OR* 27 (1):628, 631, 632.

55. Bean, "Fall of General Zook."

56. Judson, *83d Regiment*, p. 68.

57. *OR* 27 (1):620.

58. Partridge to Bachelder, 31 Mar. 1866, BP.

59. Gerrish, "Battle of Gettysburg."

60. General Warren's probable location on the hill is marked by his statue at the signal station site near the north end of the crest.

61. Warren to Farley, 13 July 1872, in Norton, *Attack*, p. 311; Hunt, "Second Day," p. 307.

62. Warren to Farley, 13 July 1872, in Norton, *Attack*, p. 311.

63. *OR* 27 (1):659; A. P. Martin, "Little Round Top."

64. A. P. Martin, "Little Round Top"; Augustus P. Martin, "Artillery Brigade in the Battle of Gettysburg," Box 1, Chamberlain Papers, LC.

65. Taylor, *Warren*, p. 129.

66. A. P. Martin, "Little Round Top"; Rittenhouse, "Little Round Top," p. 312. It seems unlikely that the guns were disassembled. Manhandling was probably confined to pushing and lifting them over the rocks.

67. E.C.C., "Battery D, 5th Artillery."

68. Taylor, *Warren*, p. 129.

69. Rittenhouse, "Little Round Top," p. 6.

70. Ibid.; T. Scott, "On Little Round Top."

71. Norton, *Attack*, p. 311.

72. Hunt, "Second Day," p. 309.

73. *OR* 27 (1):651.

74. Brainard, *Campaigns*, p. 112.

75. *NY at Gbg* 3:970; Norton, *Attack*, p. 316; *OR* 27 (1):634, 645; E. Warren to [?], 15 Nov. 1877, and Marvin to Warren, 29 Oct. 1877, BP; *OR* 41 (1):201.

76. Norton, *Attack*, pp. 288, 290, 320.

77. Statement of Joseph M. Leeper, n.d., BP; Farley, "Bloody Round Top"; Marvin to Warren, 29 Oct. 1877, BP; Norton, *Attack*, pp. 311, 330; Leeper "Gettysburg."

78. Ingham to Sykes, 28 Jan. 1893, GL, p. 42.

79. E. Warren to [?], 15 Nov. 1877, BP; Sickles et al., "Further Recollections," p. 266.

80. E. Warren to [?], 15 Nov. 1877, BP.

81. *OR* 27 (1):593, 651, 652.

82. Ibid., p. 593.

83. Ibid. (2):396, 411, 413. In his report of the Forty-eighth Alabama's operations Colonel Sheffield wrote nothing of this specific assault. However, the report of Maj. J. P. Bane of the Fourth Texas states that both the Forty-fourth and Forty-eighth Alabama reinforced the Texans on their left. Since the Forty-eighth was on the Fourth Texas's immediate left, Bane could be expected to know what it was doing; he would have been less knowlegeable of the operations of the Forty-fourth.

84. Fletcher, *Rebel Private*, p. 75; *OR* 27 (2):411.

85. *OR* 27 (1):617, 628. The Sixteenth's action here is hard to explain by the little known about the incident. In spite of the adverse criticism given Lieutenant Kydd in the regiment's report—no small punishment in itself—the regiment's returns suggest that no further disciplinary action was taken against him. After the fighting of that day, Norton, who was sent to the rear on an errand, claimed to have seen Lieutenant Colonel Welch and members of the Sixteenth far in the rear, and at that time Welch seemed to know nothing of the brigade's location. See Norton, "Strong Vincent," pp. 506–7.

86. *NY at Gbg* 1:371; *Pa at Gbg* 1:462; *OR* 27 (1):603, 620, 1041. Vincent received a hurried promotion to brigadier general on 3 July and died on 7 July. A marker, purporting to mark where he fell, was placed downslope from the site of the Forty-fourth New York's memorial. The marker was erected in 1877 and was the first placed on the battlefield outside of the national cemetery.

87. Farley, "Letter"; *NY at Gbg* 3:956–57; Farley, "Bloody Round Top."

88. Farley, "Bloody Round Top"; Leeper, "Gettysburg"; Hazen, "140th New York"; *NY at Gbg* 3:957; Farley, "Reminiscences," p. 221; Farley, "Letter." Leeper stated that Warren was on the hill and told O'Rorke not to form the 140th New York in a line but to go right in. This seems unlikely in the light of other accounts.

89. Farley, "Bloody Round Top"; Leeper, "Gettyburg"; Hazen, "140th New York."

The 140th New York's battle casualties numbered 133. They were treated initially at an aid station just behind the crest of Little Round Top.

90. In later years Chamberlain declared that he had seen neither Vincent nor Rice during the fight. See Chamberlain to Bachelder, n.d., BP.

91. *OR* 27 (1):616–18; Norton, *Army Letters*, p. 167. Colonel Rice continued to command the brigade and was promoted to brigadier general. He commanded the Second Brigade, Fourth Division, Fifth Corps, in the Wilderness. This brigade was composed of former First Corps units and did not include the Forty-fourth New York. He was mortally wounded at Spotsylvania. It was said that his last words were, "Tell the Forty-fourth I am done fighting. Turn me over and let me die with my face to the enemy." See *NY at Gbg* 1:367.

92. In 1903 Major Robbins, Fourth Alabama, maintained that the alleged gap that permitted Vincent's brigade to enfilade the Forty-seventh Alabama had not existed. He stated that the Fourth Alabama had fought the right companies of the Twentieth Maine and that it was in touch with the Forty-seventh Alabama on its right. See Robbins to Nicholson, 26 Feb. 1903, Oates Correspondence, GNMP, and n. 51, this chapter.

93. *OR* 27 (2):395; Oates, *The War*, p. 217.

94. Oates, *The War*, pp. 218–19.

95. Ibid., pp. 612–13.

96. Ibid., p. 688.

97. Ibid., p. 674.

98. Ibid., p. 226. Toward the end of the century Colonel Oates sought the Gettysburg Battlefield Commission's permission to erect a monument on Little Round Top's slope where Lt. John Oates fell. In keeping with its policies, the commission refused Oates's request. Major Robbins was a member of the commission at this time. If Oates had really known the correct spot, the placement of such a marker would have added a great deal to the understanding of this portion of the battle.

99. *OR* 27 (1):623; Spear to Bachelder, 15 Nov. 1872, and Chamberlain to Bachelder, n.d., BP.

100. *OR* 27 (1):623; Chamberlain to Barnes, n.d., Barnes Manuscripts, New-York Historical Society; Chamberlain to Bachelder, n.d., BP.

101. *Me at Gbg*, pp. 273, 276.

102. *OR* 27 (1):623–24; Chamberlain to Barnes, n.d., Barnes Manuscripts, New-York Historical Society; Chamberlain to Nicholson, 14 Aug. 1903, Oates Correspondence, GNMP.

103. *Me at Gbg*, p. 256. Both Colonel Chamberlain and Sergeant Tozier received the Medal of Honor for their heroism at Gettysburg.

104. Oates, *The War*, pp. 219, 711, 756. John G. Archibald, the Fifteenth's color-bearer, was forty-six years old when he enlisted in Company H. Although seriously wounded at both Antietam and the Wilderness, he was present at Appomattox and had the rank of ensign. At Appomattox he hid the Fifteenth's flag by wrapping it around his body, and he carried it home. He told Oates that it was his intention to have it folded and placed beneath his head in his coffin when he was buried.

Pat O'Connor was the first sergeant of Company K, became a lieutenant in December 1863, and was killed near Ashland, Virginia, in June 1864.

105. *OR* 27 (1):624.

106. Oates, *The War*, p. 221.

107. Chamberlain to Barnes, n.d., Barnes Manuscripts, New-York Historical Society; *Me at Gbg*, p. 257; *OR* 27 (1):624.

108. Oates, *The War*, pp. 219–20.

109. Ibid.

110. *OR* 27 (1):624.

111. *Me at Gbg*, p. 257; Spear to Bachelder, 15 Nov. 1892, BP.

112. *Me at Gbg*, pp. 257–58; *OR* 27 (1):624.

113. Oates, *The War*, pp. 220–21, 717. Private Keel's throat wound was mortal, and he died in a hospital a few hours after receiving it.

114. Morrill to Chamberlain, 8 July 1863, BP; *OR* 27 (2):393.

115. *OR* 27 (1):179, 625; *Me at Gbg*, p. 261.

116. Oates, *The War*, pp. 216, 221–22; Jordan, *Some Events*, pp. 43–45; *OR* 27 (2):339.

117. Oates, *The War*, p. 217.

118. Chamberlain to Nicholson, 19 Aug. 1903, Oates Correspondence, GNMP. Oates obtained his information about this incident from Colonel Bulger. Rice was killed in 1864; and by the time that Oates's published account appeared, Bulger too was dead. Oates mentioned Chamberlain's denial in a footnote.

119. J. W. Stevens, *Reminiscences*, p. 114.

120. Lasswell, *Rags and Hope*, p. 182.

121. Ibid., p. 180.

122. R. M. Powell, "With Hood."

123. Nash, *Forty-fourth*, p. 300.

124. J. W. Stevens, *Reminiscences*, pp. 114–15.

125. Nash, *Forty-fourth*, p. 300.

126. Lasswell, *Rags and Hope*, pp. 180–81.

127. Brainard, *Campaigns*, p. 118; Williamson, "At Gettysburg"; Porter, *Maltese Cross*, p. 170.

128. Brainard, *Campaigns*, pp. 118–19.

129. Ibid., p. 118; Wright, "Recollections of the War of the Rebellion, 146th Regiment," p. 85, New-York Historical Society; Porter, *Maltese Cross*, p. 174; Williamson, "At Gettysburg." The probable involvement of Weed's four regiments is indicated by their casualties or the lack thereof. The numbers available are for both 2 and 3 July. The 140th New York had 183 casualties, and the 146th New York, 28; the Ninety-first and 155th Pennsylvania regiments had but 19 each. See *OR* 27 (1):180.

130. *OR* 27 (1):652; Porter, *Maltese Cross*, p. 174.

131. *OR* 27 (1):661–62. Captain Gibbs reported that all of his battery's sections were posted on 2 July. However, Captain Martin wrote that only two sections, those of Lts. H. F. Guthrie and William Walworth, were posted on 2 July. Gibbs should have known.

132. *OR* 27 (1):661; *NY at Gbg* 3:1189.

133. *OR* 27 (1):660; J. Parker, *Twenty-second Massachusetts*, p. 313.

134. A. P. Martin, "Little Round Top"; E. Warren to [?], BP. Col. Kenner Garrard was from Cincinnati, Ohio, and was the stepson of Associate Justice of the Supreme Court John McLain. He graduated from West Point in 1851 and was a captain in the Second Cavalry in San Antonio when the war began. He became a prisoner of war there and was paroled. His parole permitted assignments at the War Department and West Point but not in the field until he was exchanged in September 1862. He then became a colonel of volunteers and was given command of the newly organized 146th New York Volunteer Infantry Regiment. He led that regiment at Fredericksburg and Gettysburg. Although his career had been delayed, he became a brigadier general on 23 July and continued to serve with the Fifth Corps until January 1864, when he was placed in charge of the Cavalry Bureau. In February he took command of the Second Cavalry Division, Army of the Cumberland, and in November of the Second Division, Sixteenth Corps, which he commanded at the Battle of Nashville. See Reid, *Ohio*, p. 852.

135. A. P. Martin, "Little Round Top"; Ingham to Sykes, 28 Jan. 1873, GL, p. 142.

136. Rittenhouse, "Little Round Top," p. 7.

137. Ibid. Thomas Scott, a cannoneer on Hazlett's No. 2 piece, wrote that Hazlett was shot as he dismounted to go to Weed. See T. Scott, "On Little Round Top." The Rittenhouse story has been the traditional one.

138. Rittenhouse "Little Round Top"; Warren to Bachelder, 15 Nov. 1877, BP.

139. This is the Porter Farley account. Farley, if not present, could have gotten the story directly from Crennell, with whom he served. Since Rittenhouse succeeded Hazlett to the command of the battery, he should have been busy with it. Furthermore, his account does not indicate that he actually heard Weed's words. Rittenhouse's account of this is as follows: Weed's adjutant general said to him, "You will be all right soon, General." Weed replied, "By sundown I will be as dead as Julius Caesar." See Farley, "Bloody Round Top"; Rittenhouse, "Little Round Top," p. 8.

CHAPTER 11

1. *DAB* 3:258–59.

2. *OR* 27 (1):571; Toombs, *New Jersey*, pp. 219–20. Burling's report suggests that the Eighth New Jersey Regiment was the last taken from him. Apparently it was in position before the Seventeenth Maine was sent to the stone wall. The rather copious accounts of the Seventeenth's fight make no mention of the Eighth New Jersey and the 115th Pennsylvania regiments until 1880. This suggests that during the battle they confused them with the 110th Pennsylvania and the Fifth Michigan and continued to do so until 1880. See Verrill, "Seventeenth Maine," p. 261, and Dunne to Bachelder, 30 June 1884, BP.

3. *OR* 27 (1):520, 522–23.

4. Tilton to Barnes, 16 Apr. 1864, Barnes Manuscripts, New-York Historical Society; *OR* 27 (1):593, 601, 613; Bennett, *Musket*, pp. 140–41.

5. This rough estimate of column length is based on McLaws's statement in "Gettysburg," p. 70; the source for pace in formation is Wagner, *Organization*, p. 46.

6. James Houghton Journal, Michigan Historical Collection, Bentley Historical Library, University of Michigan (photocopy in Folder, Michigan, Fourth Infantry, Box 16, BC).

7. Warner, *Generals in Blue*, pp. 17–20; *DAB* 1:630–31; J. L. Smith, *118th Pennsylvania*, p. 272.

8. Young, *Battle of Gettysburg*, p. 59; *Pa at Gbg* 1:385–86.

9. *OR* 27 (1):610; "Sweitzer Report," Box 1, Chamberlain Papers, LC; John Milton Bancroft Diary, pp. 48–49, Michigan Historical Collection, Bentley Historical Library, University of Michigan (photocopy in Folder, Michigan, Fourth Infantry, Box 16, BC). In his official report (see *OR* 27 [1]:610–11) Sweitzer wrote that the brigade was in a

> wood fronting an open field, the woods bordering two sides of the field, the side in which we were and also that extending at right angles from our left toward the enemy, and in the last-mentioned wood the First Brigade was posted, connecting with our left . . . this formation threw the Thirty-second Massachusetts, which was on the left, into an exposed position beyond the woods in low, cleared ground, I directed Colonel Prescott to change his front to the rear, so as to give him the benefit of the elevated ground and the cover of the woods, which movement he executed.

10. *OR* 27 (1):601, 607; J. L. Smith, *118th Pennsylvania*, p. 242; Wert, *Complete Handbook*, p. 113.

11. De Trobriand, *Four Years*, p. 498; *OR* 27 (1):520, 526.

12. Barnes to Editor, *The Herald*, 16 March 1864, in Meade, *Life and Letters*, p. 334; *OR* 27 (1):607, 611.

13. *OR* 27 (1):520, 525, 528. George Verrill and other spokesmen for the Seventeenth Maine's veterans developed a rather pat story of their fight in the Wheatfield, which is probably substantially accurate as far as it goes. However, it was not until 1880 that they appreciated that the troops on the right belonged to Burling's brigade as well as de Trobriand's. See n. 2, this chapter. The rail fence near the right of the Seventeenth Maine is not shown on the Warren Map. It is shown on the maps in *Me at Gbg*, pp. 194, 251.

14. Evans, *Confederate Military History* 6:391–92; Warner, *Generals in Gray*, pp. 6–7; Heitman, *Historical Register*, p. 88.

15. *OR* 27 (2):399, 401; Anderson to Bachelder, 15 Mar. 1876, BP; Hillyer, *Battle of Gettysburg*.

16. Hamilton, "History of the 110th Pennsylvania," p. 121, Military Order of the Loyal Legion of the United States, The Civil War Library and Museum; Verrill, "Seventeenth Maine," p. 264.

17. Verrill, "Seventeeth Maine," p. 265; *Me at Gbg*, p. 212; Verrill to Bachelder, 15

Aug. 1884 and 22 Aug. 1884, BP; Dunne to Bachelder, 30 June 1881, BP. The presence of Burling's brigade on this part of the field was noted by Captain Winslow, who wrote in "On Little Round Top" that "while the fight was raging the hottest I noticed a mounted officer galloping back and forth along the rear of the line of infantry in my front, exposed to both the enemy's and our own fire, and I expected every moment to see him fall. Inquiry proved this officer to have been Captain Tommy Ayres [Thomas W. Eayre] . . . of General Mott's staff, who fearlessly ran the gauntlet of the fire of friend and foe bearing orders to different portions of the line."

Dunne wrote that the 115th formed behind the stone wall, but it seems unlikely that the wall itself extended beyond the right of the Seventeenth Maine. See the Warren Map.

18. *OR* 27 (1):587; Winslow to Bachelder, 17 May 1878, BP; Verrill to Merrill, 11 Feb. 1884, BP. Hunt was usually careful about discipline in firing and the needless expenditure of ammunition.

19. Winslow to Bachelder, 17 May 1878, BP; *OR* 27 (1):583; Winslow, "On Little Round Top."

20. Verrill, "Seventeenth Maine," pp. 264–65. In a letter to Colonel Merrill, 11 Feb. 1884 (BP), Verrill wrote that those shooting were from the 110th Pennsylvania Volunteer Infantry—perhaps so, perhaps not.

21. Toombs, *New Jersey*, pp. 219–20; Dunne to Bachelder, 30 June 1884, BP; Bates, *Pennsylvania Volunteers* 3:1211. The Eighth New Jersey Volunteer Infantry had 49 casualties, a rate of a little less than 30 percent. This was quite comparable to the casualty rate of the nearby 110th Pennsylvania Volunteer Infantry—53 of 152—which was better posted and was fighting with its brigade.

22. *Me at Gbg*, pp. 195, 212; Verrill, "Seventeenth Maine," p. 266; Verrill to Merrill, 11 Feb. 1884, BP.

23. *OR* 27 (2):401; Verrill, "Seventeenth Maine," p. 266; E. B. Houghton, *Seventeenth Maine*, p. 92.

24. *Me at Gbg*, p. 195.

25. *OR* 27 (2):397, 399, 403.

26. Anderson to Bachelder, 15 Mar. 1876 and 4 Dec. 1894, BP. The Army of Northern Virginia's order of battle (*OR* 27 [2]:285) suggests that Col. John R. Towers of the Eighth Georgia was the ranking officer present but that he did not take command. Col. William W. White and the Seventh Georgia were in the rear at the time watching for Federal cavalry on the Emmitsburg Road. White took command of the brigade on 3 July.

The ball struck Anderson between the femoral artery and the bone. He was taken first to one of the Plank family's houses, back toward the Black Horse Tavern, and then back to Virginia. He returned to the army in time to participate in the Wilderness campaign and was at Appomattox.

27. Carter, "Reminiscences," p. 165; Bennett, *Musket*, p. 140.

28. O. W. West, "On Little Round Top."

29. *OR* 27 (1):593, 601.

30. De Trobriand, *Four Years*, pp. 497–98.

31. Kershaw, "Kershaw's Brigade," p. 334; *OR* 27 (2):367–68; see also Chapter 8. Kershaw gave his time of arrival opposite the Peach Orchard as 3:00 P.M. and the time of attack as 4:00 P.M. He probably was about an hour early on both counts.

32. Law, "Struggle," p. 325; McLaws, "Gettysburg," p. 73.

33. Kershaw, "Kershaw's Brigade," p. 334; Kershaw to Bachelder, 6 Apr. 1876, BP; Dickert, *Kershaw's Brigade*, pp. 237, 255. The brigade strength is taken from the brigade's battlefield tablet.

34. Kershaw, "Kershaw's Brigade," p. 334; *OR* 27 (2):368–69.

35. *OR* 27 (1):508; *Me at Gbg*, p. 145; Coxe, "Battle of Gettysburg," p. 434; *Pa at Gbg* 1:394; Shumate, "With Kershaw."

36. Kershaw, "Kershaw's Brigade," p. 335; Kershaw to Bachelder, 3 Apr. 1876, BP.

37. Baruch, *Confederate Surgeon*, p. 3; Coxe, "Battle of Gettysburg," p. 434; Alex. McNeil to wife, n.d., Folder, South Carolina, Second Infantry, Box 8, BC.

38. *OR* 27 (2):372; J. B. Suddath to brother, 9 July 1863, in Suddath, "Letters," pp. 98–99; Dickert, *Kershaw's Brigade*, p. 238.

39. Kershaw, "Kershaw's Brigade," p. 335; *OR* 27 (2):368; Kershaw to Bachelder, 26 Mar. 1876, BP.

40. J. L. Smith, *118th Pennsylvania*, p. 265. Smith quotes a letter from General McLaws dated 16 Oct. 1886. The rabbit remark was apparently not unique to Gettysburg.

41. Kershaw to Bachelder, 26 Mar. 1876, BP.

42. Ibid., p. 438.

43. *OR* 27 (2):368; Kershaw, "Kershaw's Brigade," p. 335.

44. Shumate, "With Kershaw." Shumate saw the wounded officer after the war, after he had become a man of some local distinction. Said Shumate, "When I jestingly reminded him of the great speed he made through the oatfield he did not seem to relish being reminded of the race with grape and canister."

45. Dickert, *Kershaw's Brigade*, pp. 252–53.

46. Kershaw to Bachelder, 26 Mar. 1876, BP; Alex. McNeil to wife, n.d., Folder, South Carolina, Second Infantry, BC. John D. Kennedy received his second wound of the war at Gettysburg. He became a brigadier general and took command of Kershaw's brigade in December 1864.

47. Carter, *Four Brothers*, p. 334; Carter, "Reminiscences," pp. 166–67; J. L. Parker, *Twenty-second Massachusetts*, p. 334.

48. J. L. Smith, *118th Pennsylvania*, p. 265. In a postwar exchange of letters General McLaws and F. A. Donaldson agreed that the two rabbits were one and the same. McLaws observed that the fleeing rabbit must have learned from other rabbits of the condition of the Confederate commissariat and feared that, if caught by the Confederates, he would be eaten. McLaws then ceded all claim to the rabbit and generously wrote that thereafter it could be referred to as the "Rabbit of the 118th Pennsylvania Volunteers."

49. J. L. Smith, *118th Pennsylvania*, p. 243; Henry T. Peck to mother, 7 July 1863, Folder, Pennsylvania, 118th Infantry, Box 11, BC; Carter, *Four Brothers*, p. 308; Abbott to Bachelder, 14 June 1880, BP.

50. J. L. Smith, *118th Pennsylvania*, p. 243.

51. Carter, *Four Brothers*, p. 309.

52. *OR* 27 (1):611; "Report of Col. Jacob B. Sweitzer," Box 1, Chamberlain Papers, LC.

53. O. W. West, "On Little Round Top."

54. *OR* 27 (1):611.

55. *Me at Gbg*, p. 196; Verrill, "Seventeenth Maine," p. 267. Probably the fighting on the right of the Seventeenth Maine was given greater coverage in postwar accounts because the men who prepared those accounts were on that wing of the regiment's line.

56. De Trobriand, *Four Years*, p. 498; de Trobriand, "Battle of Gettysburg."

57. Dickert, *Kershaw's Brigade*, p. 241; *OR* 27 (2):368, 372; Kershaw, "Kershaw's Brigade," p. 336.

58. Kershaw to Bachelder, 6 Apr. 1876, BP.

59. *OR* 27 (1):601, 607, 610.

60. Ibid., p. 601; J. L. Smith, *118th Pennsylvania*, pp. 243, 246.

61. Carter, *Four Brothers*, pp. 309–10; Carter, "Reminiscences," p. 167; J. L. Smith, *118th Pennsylvania*, p. 334.

62. *OR* 27 (1):611.

63. Massachusetts Adjutant General's Office, *Massachusetts Soldiers* 2:651; *OR* 27 (1):602; J. L. Smith, *118th Pennsylvania*, p. 279.

64. *OR* 27 (1):483, 520.

65. HISTORICUS to Editor, *New York Herald*, 4 Apr. 1864, reprinted in Meade, *Life and Letters*, p. 339; Sedgwick to Barnes, 10 Apr. 1864, and Sweitzer to Barnes, 8 Apr. 1864, Barnes Manuscripts, New-York Historical Society.

66. *OR* 27 (1):132.

67. Barnes to Editor, *New York Herald*, 16 Mar. 1864, in Meade, *Life and Letters*, p. 333; Barnes to Editor, *New York Herald*, 21 Mar. 1864.In a letter to his wife dated 27 Mar. 1864, A. A. Humphreys wrote of "the pleasurable sensation" he received when he read a copy of Barnes's letter in reply to HISTORICUS. See A. A. Humphreys Folder, Box 4, BC.

68. Tilton to Barnes, 14 Mar. 1864, Barnes Manuscripts.

69. *OR* 27 (1):133.

70. J. L. Smith, *118th Pennsylvania*, pp. 272–73; *DAB* 1:630–31.

71. *OR* 27 (1):520, 525, 528; de Trobriand, *Four Years*, pp. 495–99.

72. De Trobriand, *Four Years*, p. 500.

73. *OR* 27 (1):520; de Trobriand, *Four Years*, p. 500.

74. *OR* 27 (1):520, 522, 525, 528.

75. *Me at Gbg*, p. 196; Verrill, "Seventeenth Maine," p. 268.

76. Haley to Bachelder, 2 Feb. 1887, BP.

77. Winslow, "On Little Round Top." A Napoleon's shell was a hollow iron ball filled with black powder; spherical case (shrapnel) was a hollow ball packed with powder and small balls. Both were designed to be exploded by a time fuse, a Borman Fuse, which was a pewter disc enclosing a graduated powder train. The fuse time was

set by puncturing the fuse at a proper place along the powder train. The flame from the propelling charge, when the piece was fired, ignited the powder train at the puncture point. This was far from a reliable system, and many shells were duds; but even these then had an effect similar to solid shot. See Gilham, *Manual of Instruction*, pp. 76–80; Coggins, *Arms*, pp. 67, 82–83.

78. *OR* 27 (1):587; Winslow to Bachelder, 17 May 1878, BP.

79. *OR* 27 (1):587. In *NY at Gbg* 3:1206, Thomas Osborn, in his dedication address at the battery's memorial, stated that Ames's left section retired first, Crego's right section second, and Lt. Lester Richardson's center section last. It is likely that the right section would have been the last away only if it had infantry support. Osborn, of course, was not there, and we do not know the source of his information.

80. Dunne to Bachelder, 30 June 1884, BP.

81. *OR* 27 (1):587–88; Winslow, "On Little Round Top."

82. Ibid.; Winslow to Bachelder, 17 May 1878, BP.

83. *Me at Gbg*, pp. 196–97. It was written that Sgt. Gustavus Pratt of Company C carried eighty rounds into the fight and fired about sixty of them while at the wall. This was thought to indicate that the Seventeenth Maine was at the wall about two hours.

84. *Me at Gbg*, pp. 197–98; Verrill, "Seventeenth Maine," p. 268; Roberts, "At Gettysburg," p. 52; Verrill to Bachelder, 11 Feb. 1884, BP.

85. De Trobriand suggested that a New Jersey regiment and the Third Michigan might have been involved in the action, but the records do not seem to support this. See de Trobriand, *Four Years*, p. 501.

86. Roberts, "At Gettysburg," pp. 52–53; Pulford to Bachelder, 20 Dec. 1863, BP; Verrill to Merrill, 11 Feb. 1884, BP. Surgeons amputated Lieutenant Roberts's leg, and he was placed in the Henry Gerlach home at 319 Baltimore Street. His article tells of a pleasant return visit to Gettysburg and to the Gerlachs in 1868.

The red patch worn by the troops that Verrill saw could have been a red Maltese Cross worn by the troops of Barnes's First Division, Fifth Corps; the red clover leaf or trefoil of Caldwell's First Division, Second Corps; or the red diamond of Birney's First Division, Third Corps. Since Verrill wore the latter and would have known it, the patch must have been one of the other two, probably that of Caldwell's division.

87. De Trobriand, *Four Years*, pp. 500–501; *OR* 27 (1):484–85, 520, 523, 525.

CHAPTER 12

1. Gibbon to Meade, 24 July 1886, GL, p. 95; Gibbon Testimony, *CCW*, p. 440.

2. Walker, *Great Commanders*, p. 125; Hancock Testimony, *CCW*, p. 406.

3. *OR* 27 (1):369, 379, 386, 398, 414; Hancock Testimony, *CCW*, p. 406. Caldwell's report states that his division was ordered to support the Second Corps, which had moved forward. Surely he meant the Third Corps rather than the Second.

4. *Pa at Gbg* 2:623. Hancock wrote that he carried a staff officer's light sword. He stated also that he wore a black felt slouch hat stiff enough in top and brim to hold its

shape. On it he wore a general officer's cord. He wore the coat for the undress uniform, buttoned at the top and open toward the waist. He wore his sword belt under his coat, and he and other general officers did not wear sashes. See Hancock to Rothermel, 31 Dec. 1868, Folder 2, Box 1, Rothermel Papers, Pennsylvania Historical and Museum Commission.

Major Mulholland, the source of this Hancock quotation, plainly indicates that the statement was made in the presence of Caldwell's officers and not elsewhere.

5. *OR* 27 (1):369, 379; Hunt, "Second Day," p. 304; Meade, *With Meade*, p. 116; Hancock, Testimony, *CCW*, p. 406.

6. *Pa at Gbg* 2:623.

7. *OR* 27 (1):379.

8. *Pa at Gbg* 2:623–24; *NY at Gbg* 2:479, 515; Notes of a conversation with Col. Mulholland, n.d., BP. A life-size bronze statue of Father Corby, right hand raised, stands on the rock on Cemetery Ridge where he presumably stood at this solemn time.

9. Hale, "With Colonel Cross," p. vii, Miscellaneous Papers, Brooke Papers, HSP. The most quoted version of the exchange between Hancock and Cross is that given by Major Mulholland in his address at the dedication of the memorial of the 116th Pennsylvania Volunteer Infantry on the stony hill. According to Mulholland, Hancock haled Cross, as his brigade passed near the Wheatfield Road, with the comment, "Cross, this is the last fight you'll fight without a star." To this Cross replied, "Too late, too late, general, this is my last battle." Mulholland's version seems more dramatic than Hale's, perhaps, and has been quoted more often, but I have selected Hale's because Hale could have witnessed the conversation, whereas Mulholland was in no position to do so. In addition, Mulholland's oratorical flair suggests that he might have improved on what was originally said. See *Pa at Gbg* 2:624.

10. Hale, "With Colonel Cross," p. 7.

11. *OR* 27 (1):398; *Pa at Gbg* 2:624; Mulholland, *116th Pennsylvania*, p. 135; R. L. Stewart, *One Hundred and Fortieth Regiment*, p. 102; Fuller, *Personal Recollections*, p. 93. Anna Etheridge was a nurse from Wisconsin. She joined the Second Michigan in Detroit, but she then transferred her allegiance to the Third Michigan and went to the field with it. She never carried a rifle, of course, but it was said that she carried pistols. She was wounded in the hand at Chancellorsville. General Birney gave her the Kearny Cross, an award that he instituted for enlisted personnel who distinguished themselves in battle. She was sometimes called "Michigan Annie" and "Gentle Anna." See Brockett and Vaughn, *Woman's Work*, pp. 747–53, and Boatner, *Civil War Dictionary*, p. 267.

12. Paxton, *Sword and Gown*, p. 324.

13. Favill, *Diary*, pp. 245–46. Favill said that Tremain was the aide who spoke to Zook, but Tremain said not. In 1895, however, Tremain wrote that he had conducted Zook's brigade (see: Tremain to Mulholland, 7 July 1875, File, 116th Pennsylvania Volunteer Infantry vs. 140th Pennsylvania Volunteer Infantry, GNMP). Bean gives a slightly different version of this in "The Fall of General Zook." According to Bean an aide intercepted Zook as the brigade passed near Trostle's farmyard. He told Zook

that there was an emergency off to the right and asked Zook to take his brigade there. Then, as Bean has it, " 'Sir,' said Zook with a calm, firm look, full of significance, 'if you will give me the order of General Sickles, I will obey it.' 'Then,' was answered: 'General Sickles' order is, General, that you file your brigade to the right and move into action here.' " Zook then gave the command, "File right," and marched his brigade into the line of battle.

14. *Pa at Gbg* 2:728. This deployment was considered so important in the events of the day that Maj. Robert H. Forster of the 140th Pennsylvania Volunteer Infantry described it in detail.

Trostle's Woods was shaped rather like a right triangle. It extended along the north side of the Wheatfield Road for about 1,300 feet. On its west side the woods extended north from the road toward the Trostle farmyard a distance of about about 500 feet. It contained approximately fifteen acres. The floor of the woods sloped northeast into a marshy area west of the J. Weikert house.

15. *OR* 27 (1):386, 394, 400.

16. *Pa at Gbg* 2:728; *NY at Gbg* 2:460; Muffly, *148th Pennsylvania*, pp. 245, 682, 703; Hale, "With Colonel Cross," p. vii, Brooke Papers, HSP; *OR* 27 (1):384.

17. Hale, "With Colonel Cross," p. viii, Brooke Papers, HSP.

18. Muffly, *148th Pennsylvania*, pp. 439, 536; Hale, "With Colonel Cross," p. viii, Brooke Papers, HSP.

19. Hale, "With Colonel Cross," p. ix, Brooke Papers, HSP.

20. Fuller, *Personal Recollections*, p. 94.

21. *OR* 27 (1):385.

22. Fuller, *Personal Recollections*, p. 94.

23. Hale, "With Colonel Cross," p. x, Brooke Papers, HSP.

24. Ibid. The boulder that sheltered the Confederate sniper is about ten feet high and has a horizontal cleft about two feet below its top. It is in the southwest corner of the junction of Sickles and Brooke avenues. See Hale, "With Colonel Cross," p. xiii, Brooke Papers, HSP.

Sergeant Phelps was killed later that afternoon.

25. Child, *Fifth Regiment*, pp. 208–12. A similar but longer statement was attributed to Cross by Howard in "After the Battle."

26. Muffly, *148th Pennsylvania*, p. 603; *OR* 27 (2):401, 404, 422.

27. *Pa at Gbg* 2:729; Muffly, *148th Pennsylvania*, pp. 537, 877; *OR* 27 (1):381, 384–85.

28. Muffly, *148th Pennsylvania*, p. 537.

29. Ibid., p. 682.

30. Ibid., p. 603.

31. *OR* 27 (1):394–98; *NY at Gbg* 1:394, 426; Freudenberg to Bachelder, 16 June 1880, and Hamel to Bachelder, n.d., BP. In the brigade report Lieutenant Colonel Fraser stated that the Fifty-second was on the brigade left and the Sixty-sixth in its center. Since others stated otherwise and the Sixty-sixth's memorial is to the left of the Fifty-second's in the line of memorials on the field, it seems likely that Fraser, who was on the right with the 140th, was wrong.

32. Paxton, *Sword and Gown*, p. 325.

33. Carter, "Reminiscences," p. 167; *OR* 27 (1):133.

34. *Pa at Gbg* 2:684; Thomas B. Rogers Account, *St. Louis Globe Democrat*, 9 Mar. 1913, Folder, Pennsylvania 140th Infantry, Box 11, BC.

35. Enclosure, Purman to Bachelder, 3 Nov. 1871, BP.

36. R. L. Stewart, *One Hundred and Fortieth Regiment*, pp. 363–64.

37. *OR* 27 (1):394, 396, 398; *Pa at Gbg* 2:1137; *NY at Gbg* 1:108.

38. Favill, *Diary*, p. 246; *Pa at Gbg* 2:684; Bachelder to Nicholson, 8 July 1899, File, 116th Pennsylvania Volunteer Infantry vs. 140th Pennsylvania Volunteer Infantry, GNMP.

39. Purman, "Gen. Zook." Gilbert Frederick stated that Zook was hit when his horse jumped a stone wall (see Frederick, *Fifty-seventh New York*, p. 169, and *NY at Gbg* 1:420). The site of Zook's fall, as marked, is well within the Wheatfield. Capt. James D. Brady of Zook's staff, who claimed to have been with Zook when he was shot, however, wrote that Zook was hit by a bullet that ricocheted off a boulder. This, he wrote, happened to the right of where the stone shaft that marks the site of Zook's fall is located. Brady wrote that they were among boulders at the time. If so, Zook was probably on the knoll west of the Wheatfield. See Brady to Mulholland, 18 Apr. 1898, File, 116th Pennsylvania Volunteer Infantry vs. 140th Pennsylvania Volunteer Infantry, GNMP.

40. Favill, *Diary*, p. 246; *NY at Gbg* 1:421; Bean, "Fall of General Zook."

41. *NY at Gbg* 1:421; Favill, *Diary*, pp. 244–48; Bean, "Fall of General Zook." According to Favill they packed Zook's body in ice and took it to Baltimore in a railroad car filled with corpses: "The stench was prodigious." The body was embalmed there, taken to Port Kennedy, Pennsylvania, for two days, and then transported to New York City, where it lay in state until 10 July.

42. Favill, *Diary*, p. 246.

43. The Order of Battle of the Army of the Potomac lists only Zook and Lieutenant Colonel Fraser as the brigade's commanders. Yet, in his report of the battle for the 140th Pennsylvania Volunteer Infantry, Fraser stated that he sought orders from Zook and his staff during the battle but could not find them. He also said that he did not know Zook had been mortally wounded until after the fight was over. In addition, Colonel Roberts would have been Zook's successor before Fraser at the time that Zook was wounded. Further, Fraser would have been posted behind the right of the 140th and probably would have been unable to see Zook leave the field. See *OR* 27 (1):157, 395.

44. Freudenberg to Bachelder, 16 June 1880, BP.

45. *Pa at Gbg* 2:625.

46. This verse is from the poem "Our Fallen Comrades" by William Collins and is printed in *NY at Gbg* 2:483.

47. *OR* 27 (2):368; Kershaw, "Kershaw's Brigade," p. 336. Paul J. Semmes entered the Confederate service as colonel of the Second Georgia Infantry Regiment in 1861. He fought in the Peninsula campaign and became a brigadier general on 11 March 1862. His brigade was in McLaws's division during and after the Maryland campaign

of 1862. Prior to the war Semmes had been a businessman in Columbus, Georgia, active in militia affairs. He was the brother of Adm. Raphael Semmes.

48. *OR* 27 (2):368; Kershaw, "Kershaw's Brigade," p. 336; Dickert, *Kershaw's Brigade*, p. 250. The loss of Colonel De Saussure was a heavy one. The forty-three-year-old colonel had served in the Mexican War and had been an officer in the Regular Army until he resigned his captaincy in the First Cavalry in 1861. Some called him the "Bayard of South Carolina." There were those who believed that this small-statured man with a stentorian voice had military talents on a par with Kershaw's. This comparison was great praise, and his talent would be sorely missed.

49. Kershaw, "Kershaw's Brigade," p. 336.

50. *OR* 27 (1):396, 398.

51. Ibid., p. 395.

52. *Pa at Gbg* 2:684; R. L. Stewart, *One Hundred and Fortieth Regiment*, p. 105.

53. R. L. Stewart, *One Hundred and Fortieth Regiment*, pp. 104–6. Purman, in "Gen. Zook," said that Zook and Roberts had eaten together before the battle and said goodbye to one another. When found after the battle, Roberts's body had been stripped of its uniform and sword. The sword was found a year later by Capt. D. R. P. Neeley of the 149th Pennsylvania Volunteer Infantry in the Wilderness on the body of a dead Confederate captain.

54. R. L. Stewart, *One Hundred and Fortieth Regiment*, p. 106; Paxton, *Sword and Gown*, p. 325.

55. *OR* 27 (1):395.

56. Notes of a conversation with Mulholland, n.d., BP; Kershaw to Bachelder, 26 Mar. 1876, BP.

57. Mulholland, *116th Pennsylvania*, p. 136; *OR* 27 (1):392; *Pa at Gbg* 2:625.

58. *Pa at Gbg* 2:625; Notes of a conversation with Mulholland, n.d., BP.

59. *Pa at Gbg* 2:625.

60. Kershaw, "Kershaw's Brigade," p. 336; *OR* 27 (2):368–69.

61. *OR* 27 (2):372.

62. Kershaw's staff, according to Dickert, *Kershaw's Brigade*, p. 221, consisted of the following officers (the comments are a paraphrase of Dickert's):

Capt. Charles R. Holmes, AAG	One of the very best staff officers in the army.
Capt. William M. Dwight, AIG	Cool and collected in battle.
Capt. Alfred E. Doby, Aide	Brave, reckless and daring.
Lt. John A. Myers, Ordnance Officer	His duties did not call him to the firing line.

63. *OR* 27 (2):369; Kershaw, "Kershaw's Brigade," p. 337.

64. Coxe, "Battle of Gettysburg," pp. 434–35.

65. *OR* 27 (1):379, 400.

66. Warner, *Generals in Blue*, p. 46; Boatner, *Civil War Dictionary*, p. 88. Brooke recovered from his wound and commanded his brigade in the Virginia campaign of 1864 until he was wounded at Cold Harbor. In the meantime he was promoted to a

brigadier general of volunteers in May 1864 and later was breveted a major general. Brooke secured a commission in the Regular Army after the war in the comparatively high grade of lieutenant colonel in the Thirty-seventh Infantry, and in 1897 he became a major general. He served as a military governor in both Puerto Rico and Cuba. When he died on 5 September 1926, he was survived by only one other general officer of the Union army—Adelbert Ames, who lived until 1933.

67. These strength figures are from Busey and Martin, *Regimental Strengths at Gettysburg*, p. 238. They indicate the authors' estimate of the number of troops actually engaged.

68. *OR* 27 (1):409, 414; "B. J. Worden's Gettysburg Experience," Indiana Division, Indiana State Library (photocopy in Folder, Pennsylvania, Fifty-third Infantry, Box 11, BC).

69. *OR* 27 (1):379, 400.

70. Ibid., pp. 400–401.

71. Brooke to Walker, 14 Nov. 1885 and 18 Mar. 1886, BP; Walker, *Second Army Corps*, p. 280; *Pa at Gbg* 2:331. But, as indicated above, Freudenberg stated that he took command of the brigade and was shot almost immediately. He wrote nothing of talking with Brooke and yielding command to him. Perhaps Brooke saw Freudenberg after Freudenberg was wounded.

72. *OR* 27 (1):379, 400.

73. Ibid., p. 414; Sheldon, *"Twenty-Seventh,"* p. 77; Ellis, *Cattaraugus Co.*, p. 105. The site of Captain Merwin's fall is indicated by a stone marker in the Wheatfield.

74. *OR* 27 (1):403.

75. Brooke to Walker, 18 Mar. 1886, BP; *OR* 27 (1):400, 403, 407, 412.

76. *OR* 27 (2):409, 422.

77. Ibid.

78. Ibid. (1):401, 402; Kershaw to Bachelder, 26 Mar. 1876 and 6 Apr. 1876, BP. In "Death of Semmes," Capt. Howard Prince of the Twentieth Maine refuted an earlier article (dated 26 May 1883) by William Brown. Brown's article held that Semmes was shot in front of Vincent's line. As support Prince enclosed a copy of a letter by Col. D. W. Aiken of the Seventh South Carolina published in the Charleston *News and Courier* of 22 June 1882. In it Aiken stated that Semmes was hit by a shell fragment while standing near him as their brigades rested in Biesecker's Woods prior to the assault. He stated that, with his help, Bachelder marked the spot with a stake on 7 June 1882.

Aiken would usually be considered a reliable witness, except that Kershaw, as reported above, wrote that he talked with Semmes, who then was 150 yards in the rear of Kershaw's brigade when it was near the Rose buildings. This would place Semmes and his brigade east of the Emmitsburg Road. Kershaw's statement was made in his report that was written three months after the battle.

In 1876 Kershaw wrote Bachelder that he believed that Semmes was shot down beside a fence in an open field. See Kershaw to Bachelder, 6 Apr. 1876, BP.

Aiken's credibility is strained further by the statement attributed to him in the Prince letter that Semmes died on the field. Instead the general was transported to

Martinsburg, where he died on 10 July. Among his last words was said to be the statement, "I consider it a privilege to die for my country." See Evans, *Confederate Military History* 6:436.

79. Brooke Notes, "Position of Troops," pp. 25–26, GNMP. The boulder on which Brooke stood was marked by a cross. It might still be there, but I have not found it.

80. Sheldon, *"Twenty-Seventh,"* p. 77.

81. *OR* 27 (1):400–401; Brooke to Walker, 14 Nov. 1885, BP.

82. Wilson to Bachelder, 25 Mar. 1881, BP; *OR* 27 (1):379, 611.

83. *OR* 27 (1):401; Brooke to Walker, 14 Nov. 1885, BP; Whipple, "Memories," p. 21, Typescript, Fredericksburg and Spotsylvania . . . National Military Park.

84. McLaws, "McLaws' Division"; Pendleton, *Confederate Memoirs*, p. 35. In this article McLaws quoted a "Colonel McGlosbin," who was undoubtedly Capt. Peter Alexander Selkirk McGlashan of the Fiftieth Georgia. McGlashan apparently commanded the Fiftieth Georgia after Lieutenant Colonel Kearse was shot. Yet Col. W. R. Manning is listed as the Fiftieth's only commander in the Order of Battle in *OR*. See *OR* 27 (2):283; Krick, *Lee's Colonels*, pp. 210, 234, 242.

85. Mulholland, *116th Pennsylvania*, p. 136. The monument of the 116th Pennsylvania Regiment, which is on the stony hill, is surmounted by a life-size recumbent figure of a dead soldier, similar to the young man described by Mulholland.

86. *Pa at Gbg* 2:625.

87. Ibid.; Notes on a conversation with Col. Mulholland, n.d., BP. Major Mulholland's story about getting a regiment of Zook's brigade to escort him seems improbable, but Mulholland did not let that daunt him. In his address at the dedication of the 116th Pennsylvania Volunteer Infantry's memorial Mulholland made veiled references to the escorting unit, saying that its officers had made claims about the regiment's role in the battle that were not true. In later talks with Col. John Bachelder, Mulholland identified the regiment as the 140th Pennsylvania Volunteer Infantry. Mulholland is not recorded as having said why it took a regiment to escort him on his little reconnaissance or why, if it was the large 140th, he believed that it was without field officers. He also did not say why the 140th, which was on the right of Zook's line, was convenient to him or why its officers should have been persuaded to accompany a strange officer on a reconnaissance. Nothing is mentioned of this in the 140th's report. It must be assumed that if Mulholland had such an escort for a brief time, it was not the 140th Pennsylvania Volunteer Infantry.

88. *NY at Gbg* 2:476. This is the first stanza of a poem, "The Irish Brigade," by William Geoghegan.

89. *Pa at Gbg* 2:627.

90. *OR* 27 (1):395.

91. Ibid., p. 398.

92. Ibid, pp. 396–97. The many regimental monuments, or memorials, on the Gettysburg battlefield are helpful sources of information on the battle, particularly in locating positions. Those of the Irish Brigade and Zook's brigade are exceptions. They are placed in two lines on the south end of the stony hill (the Loop) fronting south, those of the Irish Brigade in the first line, those of Zook's brigade behind them.

The monument of the Fifty-seventh New York, which was apparently always in Zook's support line, is marked on the left of Zook's line with its left flank marker in the Wheatfield, its right in the trees. While it is conceivable that the Irish Brigade did some fighting on the line marked by its memorials, the memorials of Zook's brigade might represent only the position that it occupied before it retreated from the area.

93. Statement of Col. C. H. Morgan, n.d., BP.

94. Ibid.

95. "Report of Col. Jacob B. Sweitzer," Box 1, Chamberlain Papers, LC; *OR* 27 (1):611.

96. "Report of Col. Jacob B. Sweitzer," Box 1, Chamberlain Papers, LC; *OR* 27 (1):611.

97. *OR* 27 (1):382, 384.

98. "Report of Col. Jacob B. Sweitzer," Box 1, Chamberlain Papers, LC; *OR* 27 (1):611.

99. "Report of Col. Jacob B. Sweitzer," Box 1, Chamberlain Papers, LC; *OR* 27 (1):611–12.

100. *OR* 27 (2):369; Kershaw, "Kershaw's Brigade," p. 337.

101. "Report of Col. Jacob B. Sweitzer," Box 1, Chamberlain Papers, LC; *OR* 27 (1):611–12; James Houghton Journal, Michigan Historical Collection, Bentley Historical Library, University of Michigan (photocopy in Folder, Michigan, 4th Infantry, Box 16, BC). The flag of Sweitzer's brigade was a white pennant bearing a red maltese cross and a red band along its pole edge.

102. *OR* 27 (1):612; "Report of Col. Jacob B. Sweitzer," Box 1, Chamberlain Papers, LC.

103. *OR* 27 (1):612; "Report of Col. Jacob B. Sweitzer," Box 1, Chamberlain Papers, LC; Hull to Bachelder, 24 Mar. 1864, BP; *Pa at Gbg* 1:383.

104. *OR* 27 (1):612; O. W. West, "On Little Round Top."

105. F. Parker, *Thirty-second Regiment*, p. 171; Stephenson, *Thirty-second Regiment*, p. 11.

106. *OR* 27 (1):612; "Report of Col. Jacob B. Sweitzer," Box 1, Chamberlain Papers, LC; Stephenson, *Thirty-second Regiment*, p. 12. In *Pa at Gbg* 1:383, this quotation is attributed to General Barnes rather than to Lieutenant Ross.

107. *OR* 27 (1):612; "Report of Col. Jacob B. Sweitzer," Box 1, Chamberlain Papers, LC.

108. Campbell, "Pioneer Memories," p. 568.

109. Ibid., p. 579; Seage to Bachelder, 23 Sept. 1884, BP. An article in the *Detroit Free Press*, 8 July 1863, stated that Colonel Jeffords shot the Confederate grasping the flag with his revolver, held the flag aloft, and shouted, "Rally round the flag, boys." Lt. Robert Campbell, the regiment's quartermaster, claimed that this could not have happened in this way, because Jeffords had given Campbell his revolver at Union Mills, Maryland, on July 1, saying that it was a heavy load and that Campbell had more use for it than he. See Campbell, "Pioneer Memories," p. 569. Jeffords's funeral was held in Dexter, Michigan, on 10 July. See *Detroit Free Press*, 11 July 1863.

References are made to Colonel Jeffords's brother in the accounts of this action. Yet no other Jeffords is listed on the roll of the Fourth Michigan. Perhaps the lieutenant in question was a half brother or stepbrother and had a different surname.

The memorial to the Fourth Michigan is in the southern portion of the Wheatfield on or near the spot where Jeffords fell. It includes a bas-relief of an officer holding a flag. On the plinth, beneath a summary of the regiment's accomplishments, is the verse:

> From his bosom that heaved, the last torrent that was streaming
> And pale was his visage, deep marked with a scar.
> And dim was that eye, once expressively beaming
> That melted in love, and that kindled in war.

110. Stephenson, *Thirty-second Regiment*, p. 12; F. J. Parker, *Thirty-second Regiment*, p. 171; O. W. West, "On Little Round Top."

111. The brigade reported 466 casualties out of 1,010 officers and men who were in the Wheatfield that afternoon. See: *OR* 27 (1):613.

112. *OR* 27 (2):397, 399, 401, 403.

113. Hillyer, *Battle of Gettysburg*, p. 10. Captain Hillyer pressed a boy who usually did camp chores into service as a gun bearer. He carried and loaded a rifle for the captain and held the captain's sword when he shot. With this arrangement Hillyer believed that he fired more than forty rounds that day.

114. *NY at Gbg* 3:1362; Obituary of Gen. Romeyn B. Ayres, *National Tribune*, 18 Dec. 1888; Warner, *Generals in Blue*, pp. 13–14; Boatner, *Civil War Dictionary*, p. 36.

115. General Sedgwick's equestrian statue is now in this area. Robbins, "Regular Troops," states that the order of regiments, from right to left, in Burbank's line was Second, Seventh, Tenth, Eleventh, and Seventeenth and in Day's was Third, Fourth, Sixth, Twelfth, and Fourteenth.

116. *OR* 27 (1):634, 645. The commanders of the two regular brigades were Col. Hannibal Day and Col. Sidney Burbank. Both were officers of long service, but neither had achieved any distinction or fame in the Civil War. Day was born in Vermont in 1804 and graduated from West Point in 1823. He served with the Second Infantry in the Black Hawk Expedition, the Seminole Wars of 1838–39 and 1841–42, and the War with Mexico. He was appointed to the colonelcy of the Sixth U.S. Infantry in June 1862 but apparently did administrative duties and did not take to the field. After seeing field service in the Gettysburg campaign, he retired on 1 August 1863 with forty years of service. He was breveted a brigadier general of volunteers in 1865 for long and faithful service. Day died in 1891. See Cullum, *Biographical Register* 1:313, and Boatner, *Civil War Dictionary*, p. 228.

Colonel Burbank was a native of Massachusetts who graduated from West Point in 1829 along with James Barnes and Robert E. Lee. Burbank's career, superficially at least, was a typical one that included service on the western frontier and against the Seminoles. After becoming a major in 1855, Burbank served a brief tour with the First Infantry; he became a lieutenant colonel in May 1861 and colonel of the Second Infantry in September 1862. Burbank was involved with recruiting and administrative duties until April 1863, when he took command of the Second Brigade, Second

Division, Fifth Corps, which he held until June 1864. This was followed by administrative assignments until he retired in 1870. Burbank was breveted a brigadier general
of the Regular Army, and he died in 1882. See Cullum, *Biographical Register* 1:432–33,
and Boatner, *Civil War Dictionary*, pp. 105–6.

117. *OR* 27 (1):593.

118. Ibid., pp. 634, 640, 645, 646, 649; Chase, "Gettysburg," pp. 301, 303.

119. Chase, "Gettysburg," p. 303.

120. *OR* 27 (1):634, 646; Chase, "Gettysburg," pp. 301–2.

121. *OR* 27 (1):641, 643; W. H. Powell, *Fifth Army Corps*, p. 535. Day's brigade is
depicted in column on p. 534 of W. H. Powell's *Fifth Army Corps*.

122. W. H. Powell, *Fifth Army Corps*, pp. 534–35; *OR* 27 (1):634.

123. W. H. Powell, *Fifth Army Corps*, p. 535.

124. *OR* 27 (1):592–93; Jay to Ingham, 9 Feb. 1883, GL, p. 142.

125. Ingham to Sykes, 28 Jan. 1873, GL, p. 142. Apparently by this time the
Regular Army brigades had advanced beyond Plum Run to the wall.

126. Ibid.

127. *OR* 27 (1):634, 645. Maj. Richard Cross, reporting for the Fifth New Hamp-
shire, stated that that regiment was relieved by the Fifth Corps; Col. H. Boyd
McKeen, reporting for the brigade, stated that it was relieved by Barnes's division
(Sweitzer's brigade); and Lt. Col. Oscar Broady, reporting for the Sixty-first New
York, wrote that it was relieved by a brigade of the Fifth Corps. It is unlikely that
Sweitzer's brigade would have relieved the Fifth New Hampshire. However it seems
likely that it would have relieved the regiments to the right of Cross's brigade. See *OR*
27 (1):382–84.

128. *OR* 27 (1):634, 635, 645, 646.

129. Ibid., pp. 646, 649; Shaw, *Service in Peace and War*, p. 322. Robbins in "Regular
Troops," wrote that Ayres's order was to "face about and wheel to the right at the
double-quick and form on the general line of battle."

130. *OR* 27 (1):646, 648, 650.

131. W. H. Powell, *Fifth Army Corps*, p. 535.

132. *OR* 27 (1):641.

133. W. H. Powell, *Fifth Army Corps*, p. 535.

134. *NY at Gbg* 1:55.

135. *OR* 27 (1):159.

CHAPTER 13

1. Alexander, "Gettysburg," p. 36, Alexander Papers, SHC. Alexander wrote here
that the battalion's losses at Antietam were 85 men and 60 horses, at Gettysburg 144
men and 116 horses. In his report he stated that the Gettysburg losses were 139 men,
not including the 8 Mississippi infantrymen, and 116 horses (see *OR* 27 [2]:430).

2. See Chapters 5 and 7.

3. See Chapter 7.

4. *OR* 27 (1):570; Haynes, *Second Regiment in the War*, p. 169; Haynes, *Second Regiment Camps and Marches*, p. 138.

5. *OR* 27 (1):570; Haynes, *Second Regiment in the War*, p. 169.

6. *OR* 27 (1):570–71.

7. Ibid., p. 578.

8. Ibid., pp. 573–74; Haynes, *Second Regiment in the War*, p. 171.

9. *OR* 27 (2):380–81. Manly did not state whether Thain's heroic act took place on 2 or 3 July. I have arbitrarily selected 2 July as the date.

10. Ibid., pp. 384–85; Letter of Andrew W. Reese in the *Southern Banner*, Athens, Ga., 26 Aug. 1863, Folder, Troup Artillery, Box 7, BC.

11. *OR* 27 (2):338, 379.

12. Fraser's battery, like the others of the battalion, was marked and commemorated by the War Department behind the stone wall that ran along the ridge line. Although Lt. William Furlong reported that the battery had been behind a loose rock fence and on the battalion's right, Cabell described Little Round Top as having been on the battalion's right and slightly to its front. He termed the fire received from guns on it as flanking fire. If placed behind the wall, the guns in the area marked might have been too low to have a field of fire, and they could not have fired efficiently at Federal batteries along the Wheatfield Road, which would have been to their left. Cabell's report and an examination of the ground suggest that Fraser's guns were fronting the Peach Orchard in the field between Biesecker's Woods and the Emmitsburg Road about two hundred yards north of the P. Snyder buildings. See *OR* 27 (2): 375, 382.

13. *OR* 27 (2):375–82.

14. Ibid., p. 382. Cabell reported that the shell that killed Captain Fraser also killed two sergeants and a private. A table with his report states that the battery had 6 killed and 13 wounded. Furlong, however, reported 3 killed and 12 wounded. Krick, *Death Roster*, lists at least 5 dead from Fraser's battery.

15. *OR* 27 (2):382.

16. Ibid., p. 375.

17. Ibid. (1):586; New Jersey Gettysburg Battlefield Commission, *Final Report*, p. 51; Hanifen, *Battery B*, p. 68. It seems appropriate to wonder why Clark's battery was withdrawn from the Peach Orchard and Ames's battery placed essentially where it had been. This was probably done because Ames's Napoleons were deemed more suited to short-range fire against infantry that might soon attack the Peach Orchard and because Clark's rifled guns were better suited to counterbattery fire against Cabell's guns. Both batteries could better perform these missions in the positions assigned them.

18. *OR* 27 (1):585–86; Hanifen, *Battery B*, p. 69. Confederate reports do not indicate the loss of a limber in Clark's target area.

19. *OR* 27 (1):881.

20. The Ninth Massachusetts Battery was organized on 1 July 1862. Capt. Achille de Vecchi, an officer on leave from the Italian army, served as its commander until June 1863. Then Capt. John Bigelow took command. Bigelow had been a lieutenant in the Second Massachusetts Battery and was wounded at Malvern Hill. In its year of

service prior to Gettysburg the battery had seen no combat. See Baker, *Ninth Mass. Battery*, pp. 8–16, 44–45.

21. Ibid., p. 56; Bigelow to Bachelder, n.d., BP; Reed to mother and sister, 6 July 1863, Folder, Massachusetts, Ninth Battery, Box 16, BC; Bigelow, *Peach Orchard*, p. 52.

22. Baker, *Ninth Mass. Battery*, pp. 56–57.

23. Bigelow, *Peach Orchard*, pp. 52, 59; Bigelow to Bachelder, n.d., BP. Only Manly's battery would have fired spherical case.

24. Baker, *Ninth Mass. Battery*, p. 79; Bigelow to Bachelder, n.d., BP.

25. Capt. Charles A. Phillips was the son of a congressman, a resident of Salem, and a twenty-two year old. He had been a student at Harvard, and when war came, he joined the Fifth Massachusetts Battery. After the war he finished his studies, presumably became a lawyer, and died of lung congestion in 1876 in Gold Hill, Nevada. See Appleton et al., *Fifth Massachusetts Battery*, p. 970.

26. The seats of the gunner and the No. 5 and No. 6 cannoneers were on the chest of the gun limber; those of cannoneers 1, 2, and 7 on the caisson limber, and those of Nos. 3, 4, and 8 on the middle chest of the caisson. They took their seats at the command, "Cannoneers, mount," and left them at the command, "Cannoneers, dismount," or at a command for action. The officers, sergeants, bugler, and guidon bearer rode individual horses; the drivers rode the near horses in each pair of a team. See: Gilham, *Manual of Instruction*, pp. 517–18; Coggins, *Arms*, p. 71.

27. Phillips to Bachelder, n.d., BP; Appleton et al., *Fifth Massachusetts Battery*, pp. 626, 629–30, 637.

28. Appleton et al., *Fifth Massachusetts Battery*, pp. 636–37.

29. Ibid., pp. 630, 636.

30. Alexander, "Gettysburg," pp. 36–37, Alexander Papers, SHC; Colston, "Gettysburg," p. 555; Colston, "The Campaign of Gettysburg," p. 12, Campbell-Colston Papers, SHC.

31. Alexander later marked what he recalled to be the locations of the batteries' centers at points about 40 and 95 yards south of the Wheatfield Road. Thus, their combined fronts occupied a space between points about 20 and 120 yards south of the road. See "Position of Troops," pp. 9–11, GNMP.

32. "Position of Troops," pp. 9–11, GNMP.

33. *OR* 27 (2):432.

34. Figg, *Boy Company*, pp. 138–39; Krick, *Parker's Virginia Battery*, p. 155. Capt. William W. Parker was a Richmond physician, age 39; he was, therefore, older than most battery commanders and ten years older than his battalion commander. He received permission to recruit a company in February 1862 and within a month had obtained enough young men to form a company. It had a cast sufficiently youthful that it was nicknamed "the Boy Company." It fought from Second Manassas to Appomattox.

35. Alexander, "Gettysburg," p. 37, Alexander Papers, SHC; Alexander, "Artillery Fighting," p. 360. The twenty-four-pounder howitzer barrels weighed more than 1,300 pounds each.

36. Alexander, "Gettysburg," pp. 21, 36, Alexander Papers, SHC.

37. Ibid., p. 43; Alexander, "Artillery Fighting," p. 359; *OR* 27 (1):429–30.

38. *OR* 27 (1):589–90.

39. Ibid., p. 900.

40. *Pa at Gbg* 2:909–12.

41. *OR* 27 (1):890; *Pa at Gbg* 2:910.

42. *Pa at Gbg* 2:910; *OR* 27 (1):235, 881, 890.

43. *NY at Gbg* 3:1327–28.

44. Craig to Hunt, 17 July 1879, Box 2, Hunt Papers, LC. Hart served in the Second Artillery from 1845 to 1850 and rose to the grade of first sergeant. He apparently served for some of that time with General Hunt. He served with the Ordnance Department from 1850 to 1854 and then in the Marine Corps until July 1862. Hart was wounded at Gettysburg on 3 July, injured near Brandy Station by an exploding shell fuse in April 1864, and shot in the right shoulder near Petersburg in June 1864. He received a brevet as major to date from 12 July 1864. In 1867 he reenlisted in the Forty-fourth Infantry but was soon discharged to become the Superintendent of the national cemetery at Point Lookout, Maryland. Subsequently he was superintendent of the national cemeteries at Port Hudson, Louisiana, and Salem, New Jersey. He died in 1892. See Biographical Statement, Adjutant General's Office, Miscellaneous Records Division, 15 July 1887, in Pension File, Cert. #340116, Catherine Hart, Widow of Patrick Hart, Record Group 15, National Archives.

45. *OR* 27 (1):881; Hart to Bachelder, 24 Jan. 1891, BP. In Hart's 1891 letter his account of his arrival is different from that recited here. He wrote that on his arrival he saw a party of officers under a tree. He rode to it and found General Sickles there. Hart reported to Sickles, who told him in which direction to go. Hunt reached him after that.

Capt. Nathaniel Irish was apparently assigned to Battery F, Pennsylvania Light Artillery, but was serving as a temporary aide to Lieutenant Colonel McGilvery.

46. Alexander, "Artillery Fighting," p. 359; Alexander, "Gettysburg," pp. 35–36, Alexander Papers, SHC. The number of Confederate guns given here was taken from the War Department tablets at the battery positions.

47. *Pa at Gbg* 1:387, 2:611.

48. *OR* 27 (1):500, 573, 578; *Pa at Gbg* 1:356, 394.

49. Haynes, *Second Regiment Camps and Marches*, p. 139; Haynes, *Second Regiment in the War*, pp. 173–74; Howard, "After the Battle."

50. *OR* 27 (1):502; *Pa at Gbg* 2:610–11; Bloodgood, *Personal Reminiscences*, p. 138.

51. *OR* 27 (2):368; Kershaw, "Kershaw's Brigade," pp. 334–35.

52. *OR* 27 (1):881.

53. Ibid., pp. 881–82; Kershaw to Bachelder, 26 Mar. 1876, BP.

54. *OR* 27 (1):901.

55. Hanifen, *Battery B*, pp. 74–75.

56. Ibid., p. 72; Timm, "Clark's N.J. Battery."

57. Hanifen, *Battery B*, p. 74; Timm, "Clark's N. J. Battery."

58. Hanifen, *Battery B*, pp. 75–76.

59. Phillips to Bachelder, n.d., BP.

60. Bigelow, *Peach Orchard*, pp. 53–54; Bigelow to Bachelder, n.d., BP. It seems impossible to identify the horseman. Since all regimental officers were dismounted, he must have been from a brigade, division, or corps staff.

61. *OR* 27 (1):601.

62. Carter, *Four Brothers*, p. 311; Col. Joseph Hayes Sketch and Map, Barnes Manuscripts, New-York Historical Society. From left to right Tilton's regiments occupied the wall in the following order: Twenty-second Massachusetts, Fifteenth Massachusetts, First Michigan, and 118th Pennsylvania Volunteer Infantry.

63. *OR* 27 (1):901; Martin Report, Box 1, Chamberlain Papers, LC; Ames, *Battery G*, p. 73.

64. Ames, *Battery G*, p. 75.

65. Ibid., p. 76; *OR* 27 (1):901.

66. *OR* 27 (1):574; Haynes, *Second Regiment in the War*, p. 176.

67. *OR* 27 (1):574; Haynes, *Second Regiment in the War*, p. 176; Howard, "After the Battle"; Bailey to Bachelder, 29 Mar. 1882, BP. This pile of rails, which probably came from the fence at the Peach Orchard, and another pile along the Emmitsburg Road apparently were among the few defensive works erected by Birney's division and must have been minimal at best. Their contents must have been lethal when hit by an artillery round.

68. *OR* 27 (1):499, 505; Howard, "After the Battle"; Haynes, *Second Regiment in the War*, p. 172; Bailey to Bachelder, 29 Mar. 1882, BP.

69. Bailey to Bachelder, 29 Mar. 1882, BP; Howard, "After the Battle"; *OR* 27 (1):499.

70. Warner, *Generals in Gray*, p. 16; McNeily, "Barksdale's Brigade," p. 236; Evans, *Confederate Military History* 7:239–40; McLaws, "Gettysburg," p. 70.

71. McNeily, "Barksdale's Brigade," pp. 236–38; Ross, *Cities and Camps*, p. 55; McLaws, "Gettysburg," p. 73; Owen, *In Camp*, p. 245.

72. Although the incident described by Duke must have taken place, his narration does not seem to fit any house on Barksdale's front. Apart from the Sherfy house, which ought to have been well within the Federal position, there were three houses between Barksdale's line and the Emmitsburg Road—the Staub, Snyder, and Warfield houses. The Staub house seems to have been too far north to be the one described, and the Snyder and Warfield houses seem too close to the Confederate position to have afforded the sort of danger suggested by Duke's account.

73. Duke, "Mississippians," p. 216. This story was printed about forty-five years after the battle. Although it is probably basically true, the dialogue must be taken with at least a grain of salt. One portion of it that includes an alleged conversation between Duke and Longstreet seems so fanciful that I have omitted it.

Pvt. Woods B. Mears was mortally wounded in the thigh later in the battle. See Service Record, Woods B. Mears, 11th Mississippi Infantry Regiment, Record Group 94, National Archives.

74. B. G. Humphreys, "Sunflower Guards," p. 11, Claiborne Papers, SHC; McNeily, "Barksdale's Brigade," pp. 237–38.

75. *OR* 27 (2):368–69; Kershaw, "Kershaw's Brigade," p. 334.

76. McLaws, "Gettysburg," p. 73.

77. Ibid., p. 74.

78. McNeily, "Barksdale's Brigade," p. 236.

79. "Battle-Field Reminiscences," *Lebanon Herald and Register*, 15 May 1866, Ethelbert Barksdale Papers, Mississippi Department of Archives and History.

80. "Biographical Sketch of William Barksdale," pp. 29–30, Claiborne Papers, SHC.

81. McLaws, "Gettysburg," p. 74.

82. Ibid.; "Biographical Sketch of William Barksdale," pp. 29–30, Claiborne Papers, SHC.

83. *OR* 27 (1):498.

84. The width of the front embracing the space between the left of the Peach Orchard and the Sherfy house is at least 1,200 feet, and the combined strength of the 68th and 114th Pennsylvania Volunteer Infantry was a maximum of 695, including file closers, musicians, and others not normally in line. Although some of the front was taken up by the Sherfy barn and Bucklyn's battery, it is apparent that the line was weak. It seems logical to assume that its principal weakness lay between the regiments—the area near the Wentz buildings and the Wheatfield Road.

85. Lewis, *Battery E*, p. 208.

86. Ibid., pp. 211, 216.

87. Probably Bucklyn referred to Company B, Second New Hampshire Volunteer Infantry, and Company A, Third Michigan Volunteer Infantry regiments.

88. *OR* 27 (1):502, 590; Bucklyn to Bachelder, 31 Dec. 1863, BP; Lewis, *Battery E*, pp. 208–9. In his history of the battery, Lewis wrote that the center and left sections, those south of Sherfy's barn, retired to the crest behind them by prolonge. This is not mentioned elsewhere. If they did retire by prolonge, it was not necessarily because they were firing, for the 114th Pennsylvania Volunteer Infantry was in front of some of them.

89. *OR* 27 (1):178; Lewis, *Battery E*, pp. 209–11; Bucklyn to Bachelder, 31 Dec. 1863, BP. Three of Bucklyn's battery's thirty casualties were killed.

Bucklyn was twenty-nine years old at the time of the battle. A native of Rhode Island, he was a graduate of Brown University and a teacher by profession. He enlisted as a private in September 1861, became a quartermaster sergeant, and then became a second lieutenant in March 1862. He commanded the battery as a first lieutenant from May 1863 until April 1864, when a captain elsewhere within the regiment was given command of the battery. Bucklyn then went to the staff of Col. Charles Tompkins, commander of the Sixth Corps's artillery. He became a captain finally in January 1865. After the war he founded the Mystic Valley English and Classical Institute. See Lewis, *Battery E*, p. 402.

90. Nelson, *Battles*, pp. 150–51; J. M. Martin et al., *Fifty-seventh Regiment*, p. 88; *OR* 27 (1):500.

91. Moran, "A New View"; Moran, "About Gettysburg"; *NY at Gbg* 2:605. The memorial of the Seventy-third New York Volunteer Infantry, which purports to mark

the regiment's position, is about one hundred yards east of the Emmitsburg Road.

92. *OR* 27 (1):499, 574; Bailey to Bachelder, 29 Mar. 1882, BP. To strike the Peach Orchard, the Twenty-first Mississippi would have had to cross the Wheatfield Road somewhere between Seminary Ridge and the orchard. It is likely that Colonel Tippin would have ordered the Sixty-eighth Pennsylvania to hold its fire until the Confederate line was within two hundred yards. This would have been at the junction of two fences with the road about two hundred yards west of the Emmitsburg Road. The Twenty-first Mississippi would have approached the orchard, then, at an angle from the northwest.

93. *OR* 27 (2):429–30; Alexander, "Artillery Fighting," p. 360.

94. Haynes, *Second Regiment in the War*, p. 186; W. W. Holden, "Gettysburg."

95. The chimney mentioned by Holden might have been an outdoor oven or fireplace that stood alone, rather than a chimney attached to a building.

96. In spite of the title headlining Holden's account—"Gettysburg: An Infantryman Confirms Captain Hart's Story"—he did not confirm Hart's story. He did not know the identity of the battery in the Peach Orchard and near the Wentz house, which certainly must have been Ames's and not Hart's.

The unharmed condition of the house might have resulted from its being more removed than the barn from the Federal guns that were drawing Confederate artillery fire. In later years Holden heard that Henry Wentz, ordnance sergeant of Taylor's battery, had lived there and that the Confederates had spared the house in deference to him. This seems improbable.

97. Haynes, *Second Regiment in the War*, pp. 186–87; Haynes, *Second Regiment Camps and Marches*, pp. 141–43; *OR* 27 (1):574.

98. "Biographical Sketch of William Barksdale," p. 29, Claiborne Papers, SHC; McNeily, "Barksdale's Brigade," pp. 236–38; B. Humphreys, "The Sunflower Guards," pp. 11–13, Claiborne Papers, SHC.

99. Written sources do not define the position except to say that the Sixty-eighth was in the orchard and the 114th in the rear of Bucklyn's battery. Their monuments are in the Peach Orchard and the Sherfy yard. See *OR* 27 (1):499; *Pa at Gbg* 1:394, 2:611.

100. Bryan to McLaws, 10 Dec. 1877, McLaws Papers, SHC.

101. Warner, *Generals in Gray*, pp. 343–44; McLaws, "McLaws' Division."

102. Figg, *Boy Company*, p. 140; Krick, *Parker's Virginia Battery*, p. 156.

103. Krick, *Parker's Virginia Battery*, p. 156.

104. McLaws, "Gettysburg," p. 74; Lawley, "Battles of Gettysburg."

105. McLaws, "Federal Disaster."

106. *OR* 27 (1):499; *Pa at Gbg* 1:394; Bailey to Bachelder, 29 Mar. 1882, BP.

107. *OR* 27 (1):505, 508, 524; Kilmer, "The Stand"; Bloodgood, *Personal Reminiscences*, p. 140; Craft, *One Hundred Forty-first*, p. 122.

108. *OR* 27 (1):574; Haynes, *Second Regiment in the War*, p. 179; Bailey to Bachelder, 29 Mar. 1882, BP.

109. *OR* 27 (1):505; *Pa at Gbg* 2:686.

110. *OR* 27 (1):890.

111. Ibid., p. 887; *NY at Gbg* 3:1329; Hart to Bachelder, 23 Aug. 1891, BP.

112. *OR* 27 (1):503; *Pa at Gbg* 2:612.

113. Moran, "About Gettysburg." The Sherfy barn burned on 3 July.

114. Moran, "A New View."

115. Ibid.; *OR* 27 (1):890; Moran, "A New View." Major Burns denied later that he had given Moran permission to try to recapture the gun.

116. McNeily, "Barksdale's Brigade," p. 238.

117. Nelson, *Battles*, pp. 150–51; J. M. Martin et al., *Fifty-seventh Regiment*, pp. 88–89. Possibly the fence referred to was the east-west fence south of the Sherfy buildings rather than the more distant fence west of them.

118. Nelson, *Battles*, pp. 150–51; J. M. Martin et al., *Fifty-seventh Regiment*, p. 89.

119. *OR* 27 (1):500–501; K. Scott, *One Hundred and Fifth Regiment*, pp. 82–83.

120. Haynes, *Second Regiment in the War*, p. 180; *OR* 27 (1):574.

121. Bailey to Bachelder, 29 Mar. 1882, BP; *OR* 27 (1):574.

122. *OR* 27 (1):499.

123. Ibid., pp. 177–78, 574; Haynes, *Second Regiment in the War*, pp. 180–81.

124. Craft, *One Hundred Forty-First*, p. 122; Bloodgood, *Personal Reminiscences*, p. 141. Bloodgood reported the same conversation but with a slight difference in words.

125. Bloodgood, *Personal Reminiscences*, p. 141; *OR* 27 (1):505; Kilmer, "The Stand."

126. Craft, *One Hundred Forty-first*, p. 123.

127. Randolph to Bachelder, 4 Mar. 1866, BP; "Condition of General Sickles," *New York Sun*, 8 July 1863; Tremain, *Two Days*, p. 89. The *Sun*'s account of Sickles's wounding held that Sickles leaned forward in the saddle and with his right hand pulled his foot from the stirrup and lifted his leg over the horse without assistance. It did not say how he got off the horse.

128. Bullard to Sickles, 13 Sept. 1897, Sickles Correspondence, New-York Historical Society.

129. Tremain, *Two Days*, p. 89.

130. Bullard to Sickles, 13 Sept. 1897, Sickles Correspondence, New-York Historical Society.

131. Ibid.

132. Tremain, *Two Days*, pp. 89–90; Twichell to Sis, 5 July 1863, John Hopkins Twichell Papers, Collection of American Literature, The Beinecke Rare Book and Manuscript Library, Yale University (photocopy in Folder, New York, Seventy-first Infantry, Box 10, BC).

133. Tremain, *Two Days*, p. 90.

134. Sickles's leg bones, encased in a glass casket, are in the Armed Forces Medical Museum, Armed Forces Institute of Pathology, at Walter Reed Army Hospital in Washington, D.C. There is a photograph of them in Swanberg, *Sickles*, p. 307.

135. *OR* 27 (1):177–78; McNeily, "Barksdale's Brigade," p. 237; Abernathy, *Our Mess*, pp. 14, 34. James Ramsaur was a recently appointed third lieutenant in Company B, Seventeenth Mississippi. The wounds mentioned apparently were not serious, for his service record mentions no hospitalization.

136. Duke, "Mississippians," p. 216.

137. Moran, "A New View."

CHAPTER 14

1. Alexander, "Artillery Fighting," p. 360; Alexander, "Gettysburg," p. 37, Alexander Papers, SHC.

2. Alexander, "Gettysburg," p. 37, Alexander Papers, SHC.

3. Ibid.; Alexander, "Artillery Fighting," p. 360.

4. Colston, "The Campaign of Gettysburg," p. 12, Campbell-Colston Papers, SHC; Colston, "Gettysburg," p. 552; Alexander, *Military Memoirs*, p. 399. Maj. James Dearing commanded a battalion of four batteries that was with Pickett's division. Dearing resigned from West Point in April 1861 to enter the Confederate service. He commanded a cavalry brigade during the last year of the war, was wounded at High Bridge, Virginia, on 6 April 1865, and died shortly after Lee's surrender.

5. *OR* 27 (2):432.

6. *Pa at Gbg* 2:613.

7. Alexander Interview, 30 May 1894, "Position of Troops," pp. 10–12, GNMP. Alexander identified points as the centers of batteries as he could recall them after thirty-six years, and they were recorded with reference to "a point in the Emmitsburg Road and the center of the Wheatfield Road." Alexander stated that his battalion was on line between Moody's and Taylor's batteries, that the center of Moody's was 100 feet south of the center of the Wheatfield Road, and that Taylor's center was 500 feet from Moody's stake and 420 feet southeast of the Emmitsburg Road.

8. Alexander, "Gettysburg," p. 38, Alexander Papers, SHC.

9. Ibid.; *OR* 27 (2):430.

10. Krick, *Parker's Virginia Battery*, p. 158; Figg, *Boy Company*, p. 140; *OR* 27 (2):432.

11. McLaws, "Battle of Gettysburg"; "Biographical Sketch of William Barksdale," pp. 30–31, Claiborne Papers, SHC.

12. Warner, *Generals in Gray*, pp. 145–46; Freeman, *Lee's Lieutenants* 3:199.

13. Hanifen, *Battery B*, pp. 76–77.

14. Ibid., pp. 77–78; *OR* 27 (1):586; Bonnell to Bachelder, 24 Mar. 1882, BP.

15. *OR* 27 (1):890; G. Clark, *A Glance*, pp. 63–64.

16. *OR* 27 (1):890; U.S. Department of the Army, *Medal of Honor*, p. 138.

17. Phillips to Bachelder, n.d., BP; *OR* 27 (1):882; Appleton et al., *Fifth Massachusetts Battery*, p. 630.

18. Appleton et al., *Fifth Massachusetts Battery*, p. 627; Phillips to Bachelder, n.d., BP.

19. Appleton et al., *Fifth Massachusetts Battery*, pp. 624, 637; *OR* 27 (1):885.

20. Appleton et al., *Fifth Massachusetts Battery*, pp. 634, 631, 639–40.

21. Ibid., pp. 637–41; Phillips to Bachelder, n.d., BP; *OR* 27 (1):882.

22. Appleton et al., *Fifth Massachusetts Battery*, pp. 624, 638, 640. Scott made his

way to Baltimore, got a pass, and on 8 July went by train to New York. He went from New York to Newport, Rhode Island. A local physician treated him, and he returned to his battery when his leave expired on 25 September.

23. *OR* 27 (1):882, 885; Appleton et al., *Fifth Massachusetts Battery*, pp. 624, 628, 637. In 1879 Hart wrote General Hunt that Phillips's sergeants had told him their officers had deserted them, and, on hearing that, he led them from the field. In later years he maintained also that Phillips and his officers had deserted their guns, but he did not say when this was done or how he knew of it. Although Hart's act was probably well intentioned, it apparently deprived McGilvery of two guns that might have been useful at a critical time. See Hart to Hunt, 30 June 1879, and 15 July 1879, Box 2, Hunt Papers, LC; Hart to Bachelder, 24 Jan. 1891, BP.

24. Bigelow, *Peach Orchard*, p. 56.

25. Baker, *Ninth Mass. Battery*, p. 60; Bigelow, *Peach Orchard*, p. 56.

26. Baker, *Ninth Mass. Battery*, pp. 75, 77.

27. Bigelow to Bachelder, n.d., BP.

28. Herbert to Bachelder, 9 July 1884, BP; J. L. Smith, *118th Pennsylvania*, pp. 246–47; *Pa at Gbg* 2:636.

29. Baker, *Ninth Mass. Battery*, p. 60; Bigelow, *Peach Orchard*, p. 56; Bigelow to Bachelder, n.d., BP; *OR* 27 (1):882, 886. The fence corner in which Bigelow's battery made its stand has changed considerably, in great part because of the conversion of the Trostle lane into United States Avenue. Two photographs taken by Timothy Sullivan juxtaposed with modern photographs in Frassanito, *Gettysburg, A Journey in Time*, pp. 148–49, indicate some of the changes in that area. The ground must have been altered also by the digging of a drainage ditch along the wall that was along the lane to the battery's right.

30. Bigelow to Nicholson, 20 Feb. 1901, "Position of Troops," pp. 20–21, GNMP; Bigelow to Bachelder, n.d., BP.

31. Bigelow to Bachelder, n.d., BP; Baker, *Ninth Mass. Battery*, p. 61; Bigelow, *Peach Orchard*, p. 57; Bigelow to Nicholson, 20 Feb. 1901, "Position of Troops," p. 33, GNMP.

32. Bigelow to Bachelder, n.d., BP; Bigelow, *Peach Orchard*, p. 58; Bigelow to Nicholson, 20 Feb. 1901, "Position of Troops," pp. 33–34, GNMP; Bigelow to the Adjutant General, 19 June 1895, Medal of Honor Application, Charles W. Reed, Record Group 94, National Archives. In a sketch map with his letter to Nicholson, Bigelow indicates that the No. 3 piece upset at a point east of the Trostle house rather than at the gate. The gate was southwest of the house, opposite the yard between the house and barn.

33. Bigelow to Bachelder, n.d., BP.

34. Bigelow to the Adjutant General, 19 June 1895, Medal of Honor Application, Charles W. Reed, Record Group 94, National Archives.

35. *OR* 27 (1):882, 886; Bigelow, *Peach Orchard*, p. 60; Baker, *Ninth Mass. Battery*, p. 227.

36. McNeily, "Barksdale's Brigade," p. 249.

37. Baker, *Ninth Mass. Battery*, p. 227; Bigelow to the Adjutant General, 19 June 1895, Medal of Honor Application, Charles W. Reed, Record Group 94, National Archives; Bigelow, *Peach Orchard*, p. 60.

38. Bigelow to the Adjutant General, 19 June 1895, and Dow to the Adjutant General, 3 Aug. 1895, Medal of Honor Application, Charles W. Reed, Record Group 94, National Archives.

39. *OR* 27 (1):882; Hunt, "Second Day," p. 302.

40. *OR* 27 (1):882–83, 885, 890, 897; Appleton et al., *Fifth Massachusetts Battery*, p. 628; Bigelow Letter, *Minneapolis Journal*, 31 Aug. 1897; Phillips to Bachelder, n.d., BP. The War Department marked the position of Watson's battery and a portion, therefore, of McGilvery's line about a hundred yards north of Weikert's Woods and three hundred yards west of Hancock Avenue. This is about three hundred yards north of the position shown by Bachelder on his 1876 map and seems too far north and east. It must be noted that the present right-of-way of the avenue east of the Trostle buildings was not that of Trostle's lane—as shown on the Warren Map. The lane ran southeast from Trostle's farmyard to a point about midway down the west front of Weikert's Woods. It seems likely that Bigelow would have ridden south of the lane to Dow's battery, which was just right of Watson's. If so, the position indicated on the Bachelder Map for McGilvery's line on 2 July is closer to correct than that implied by the marking of Watson's position.

41. B. Humphreys, "The Sunflower Guards," pp. 11–13, Folder 27, Claiborne Papers, SHC; B. Humphreys to Bachelder, 1 May 1876, BP.

42. *OR* 27 (1):660.

43. McLaws, "McLaws' Division"; McNeily, "Barksdale's Brigade," p. 249.

44. McNeily, "Barksdale's Brigade," p. 249; B. Humphreys to Bachelder, 1 May 1876, BP.

45. McLaws, "Gettysburg"; McLaws, "McLaws' Division."

46. *OR* 27 (1):483, 533; Humphreys Testimony, *CCW*, p. 392; H. H. Humphreys, *Humphreys*, p. 195.

47. *OR* 27 (1):553, 559, 566; Marbaker, *Eleventh New Jersey*, p. 98; Westbrook, "On the Firing Line."

48. Marbaker, *Eleventh New Jersey*, p. 98; Toombs, *New Jersey*, p. 239.

49. Rafferty, "Gettysburg," p. 27; Cavada Diary, 2 July 1863, HSP.

50. McClellan to Humphreys, 21 Sept. 1864, Box 22, p. 8, Humphreys Papers, HSP.

51. *OR* 27 (1):568; *NY at Gbg* 2:819; Westbrook, "On the Firing Line"; Van Santvoord, *One Hundred and Twentieth*, p. 74.

52. *NY at Gbg* 2:819, 822.

53. Wilcox, "General C. M. Wilcox," p. 99.

54. McNeily, "Barksdale's Brigade," pp. 238, 243; "Biographical Sketch of William Barksdale," pp. 30–31, Claiborne Papers, SHC; Love, "Mississippi," p. 32.

55. "Biographical Sketch of William Barksdale," p. 31, Claiborne Papers, SHC.

56. McNeily, "Barksdale's Brigade," p. 240; Love, "Mississippi," p. 33.

57. McNeily, "Barksdale's Brigade," p. 240; Love, "Mississippi," p. 33. Private Lloyd's arm was amputated, and he was left in a hospital at Gettysburg to become a prisoner of war.

58. "Biographical Sketch of William Barksdale," p. 32, Claiborne Papers, SHC.

CHAPTER 15

1. G. Clark, *A Glance*, p. 37; G. Clark, "Wilcox's Alabama Brigade," p. 229.

2. The Bachelder Map for 2 July places the three regiments of Perry's brigade along a north-south track that ran diagonally through Spangler's Woods. However, the Florida Commission located the three regiments in a line about 730 feet long that ran along the east edge of the woods southwest from its northeast corner. The commission's location appears the more likely of the two.

Bachelder's 2 July map locates Wright's brigade in the north end of Spangler's Woods and to the north of it, Posey's in the area presently occupied by the North Carolina Memorial, and Mahone's at the McMillan farmyard. Their War Department tablets, however, are located south of the Bachelder locations, with Mahone's near the North Carolina Memorial and Posey's near the Virginia Memorial. Their subsequent movements seem to support the Bachelder location.

3. Freeman, *Lee's Lieutenants* 1:157–58.

4. Freeman, *Lee's Lieutenants* 2:655, 665, 695; Evans, *Confederate Military History* 1:692.

5. Freeman, *Lee's Lieutenants* 1:xlix, 159, 664–68, 2:691, 696–97; Warner, *Generals in Gray*, p. 134.

6. Chamberlaine, *Memoirs*, pp. 70–71.

7. *OR* 27 (2):610.

8. Ibid., pp. 610, 652. Richardson had three pieces from Maurin's battery, two from Lewis's, two from Moore's, and two from Grandy's. Seven were three-inch Ordnance rifles and two were ten-pounder Parrotts.

9. Ibid., p. 675, (1):457, 460, 467. According to War Department tablets Hurt had two Whitworth guns and two three-inch Ordnance rifles, and Johnson had two Napoleons and two three-inch Ordnance rifles. Although the battalion's report states that Rice's battery was in reserve, the tablet states that it had two Napoleons in position. Johnson's battery had two Napoleons and two three-inch Ordnance rifles.

10. According to War Department tablets Marye had two Napoleons and two ten-pounder Parrotts, Crenshaw two Napoleons and two twelve-pounder howitzers, Zimmerman four three-inch Ordnance rifles, and McGraw four Napoleons.

11. *OR* 27 (2):678. War Department tablets indicate that McGraw's and Crenshaw's batteries also fired at sharpshooters, perhaps the skirmishers at the Bliss buildings. Lt. Andrew B. Johnston commanded the Crenshaw battery.

12. *OR* 27 (2):635. Patterson's position is marked to the left of Gilbert's (Rhett's) just about opposite the Staub house site, the Klingle house, and Seeley's battery. Wingfield's battery is marked near the North Carolina Memorial and Ross's battery

to its right. The obvious difference between the navy Parrotts and those made for army use is that the navy guns have a ring for breeching tackle as part of the cascabel. The battlefield tablets make a distinction between the ten-pounder Parrotts and the three-inch navy Parrotts.

13. *OR* 27 (2):618, 635.

14. Ibid., pp. 613–14. The statement that Longstreet's line would be "in a direction nearly at right angles with mine" could have at least two interpretations. It could be assumed that this would be so had Longstreet's units been able to deploy across the Emmitsburg Road, but they did not do this. Wilcox did not state why his brigade's alignment was not adjusted to conform with Longstreet's to his right. See *OR* 27 (2):617.

15. Wilcox, "General Wilcox." If Wilcox recalled Lee's visit to his brigade correctly, Lee must have been aware of the deployment of Wilcox's brigade. Perhaps, if it did concern him, Lee considered it a matter of prerogative for subordinate commanders and did not interfere.

16. *OR* 27 (2):617. Wilcox stated here that the Tenth Alabama was at right angles to the rest of his line. This, presumably, would have included the Eighth Alabama.

17. Herbert to Bachelder, 9 July 1884, BP; Herbert Statement, Position of 8th Alabama, "Position of Troops," p. 30, GNMP; Fortin, "Herbert's 'History,'" p. 115. Hilary A. Herbert was a congressman from 1877 to 1893 and secretary of the navy from 1893 to 1897. His account of the Eighth's role in the battle does not coincide with Wilcox's accounts, but it seems creditable, and I have accepted it with some reservations.

18. G. Clark, *A Glance*, p. 37; G. Clark, "Wilcox's Alabama Brigade," p. 229; Bachelder Map, 2 July 1863. Bachelder's map shows the Tenth Alabama in Pitzer's Woods and the Ninth on the left of the line, with its left abutting Spangler's Woods. Between them in a concave arc are the Eleventh, Fourteenth, and Eighth regiments, in order from the right. According to Herbert in his 1884 letter to Bachelder, the Eighth happened to be on the Tenth's left because it advanced there after the Eleventh was driven back. In a letter from Bachelder to Humphreys, 25 Mar. 1876, Box 26, Humphreys Papers, HSP, Bachelder described a later formation, dealt with below, that placed the Fourteenth to the left of the Eleventh in the brigade line. Thus, that order here. Bachelder's locations of Wilcox's two left center regiments on his map do not appear to take the terrain into account; thus, I assume that they were intended to be general in nature.

19. J. G. Barrett, *Yankee Rebel*, p. 115; "Where Honor Is Due."

20. *OR* 27 (2):631. Col. David Lang was born in Camden County, Georgia, in 1838. He graduated from the Georgia Military Institute in 1857. He enlisted as a private in the First Florida Regiment and was a sergeant when his enlistment expired. He then raised Company C, Eighth Florida, and five months later became colonel of that regiment. See Krick, *Lee's Colonels*, pp. 210–11; Groene, "Colonel David Lang," pp. 340–41.

21. McClellan to Humphreys, 21 Sept. 1864, Book 22, p. 8, Humphreys Papers, HSP; *OR* 27 (1):553, 584, 590.

22. Hulen, "Gettysburg"; *OR* 27 (1):532, 873, 875.

23. McClellan to Humphreys, 21 Sept. 1864, Book 22, p. 8, Humphreys Papers, HSP. Capt. Carswell McClellan and Maj. H. B. McClellan of Gen. J. E. B. Stuart's staff were brothers.

24. Humphreys Testimony, *CCW*, pp. 391, 393; *OR* 27 (1):532; "Humphreys Narrative," Box 26, Humphreys Papers, HSP.

25. *OR* 27 (1):532, 575, 576.

26. Ibid. (2):532–33; Humphreys Testimony, *CCW*, p. 392; McClellan to Humphreys, 21 Sept. 1864, Book 22, p. 8, Humphreys Papers, HSP.

27. Cavada Diary, 2 July 1863, HSP.

28. Ibid.; Humphreys to wife, 4 July 1863, Book 33, p. 36, Humphreys Papers, HSP.

29. Blake, *Three Years*, p. 207; Bartlett, *Twelfth Regiment*, pp. 415–16.

30. Van Santvoord, *One Hundred and Twentieth*, p. 75.

31. Marbaker, *Eleventh New Jersey*, p. 97; Robertson, *McAllister*, p. 238.

32. Twichell to Sis, 5 July 1863, Twichell Papers, Collection of American Literature, The Beinecke Rare Book and Manuscript Library, Yale University (photocopy in Folder, New York, 71st Infantry, Box 10, BC).

33. Auchmoedy to father, 10 Aug. 1863, Auchmoedy Papers, New-York Historical Society.

34. *OR* 27 (1):590, (2):636.

35. Ibid (1):590; Cavada Diary, 2 July 1863, HSP.

36. *OR* 27 (1):577; W. W. Holden, "Gettysburg."

37. G. Clark, "Wilcox's Alabama Brigade," pp. 229–30; Young, *Battle of Gettysburg*, p. 378; Freeman, *Lee's Lieutenants* 3:202–3.

38. *OR* 27 (2):618.

39. Fortin, "Herbert's 'History,'" p. 116.

40. J. G. Barrett, *Yankee Rebel*, p. 116.

41. *OR* 27 (2):618; Wilcox, "Annotations to Official Report, 17 July 1863," Box 1, Wilcox Papers, LC.

42. *OR* 27 (2):631; Lang, "Letter," p. 195.

43. *OR* 27 (1):576–77.

44. Humphreys Testimony, *CCW*, p. 392; *OR* 27 (1):533; Humphreys to Campbell, 6 Aug. 1863, A. A. Humphreys Folder, Box 4, BC.

45. *OR* 27 (1):533. Birney reported that he visited Humphreys's division, and, finding a gap in the line of his own division that the enemy could advance through and take Humphreys in reverse, he ordered a change in front. This suggests that the break was at the Peach Orchard. Humphreys's comments suggest that he received Birney's order through a staff officer who McClellan believed was Captain Fasset. And yet there is no doubt that Birney did visit Humphreys's front and speak to Carr and some of the regimental commanders on Humphreys's left. See *OR* 27 (1):483.

46. Humphreys to Bachelder, 14 Nov. 1865, Box 20, Humphreys Papers, HSP.

47. Humphreys Narrative, p. 9, Box 26, Humphreys Papers, HSP.

48. Humphreys to Campbell, 6 Aug. 1863, A. A. Humphreys Folder, Box 4, BC; Humphreys Testimony, *CCW*, p. 392.

49. Cavada Diary, 2 July 1863, HSP.

50. L. D. Holden, *My First*, p. 75; Cudworth, *First Regiment*, p. 397.

51. Baldwin to Bachelder, 20 May 1865, BP; "Where Honor is Due." We can only speculate on the identity of the three heavy lines. Perhaps they were the three regiments of the Florida Brigade.

52. *OR* 27 (1):576; Baldwin to Bachelder, 20 May 1865, BP. Probably General Carr wanted the First Massachusetts on his right simply because that flank was vulnerable. Companies B and C of the First United States Sharpshooters also fell back at this time. See C. A. Stevens, *Berdan's Sharpshooters*, p. 317.

53. Wilcox, "Annotations to Official Report, 17 July 1863," Box 1, Wilcox Papers, LC. Unless there was a Federal skirmish line west of the road, the 80 yards estimated by Wilcox seems too short. The fence was about 250 yards west of the road.

54. Cavada Diary, 2 July 1863, HSP.

55. Blake, *Three Years*, pp. 208–10.

56. Bartlett, *Twelfth Regiment*, pp. 122–24.

57. *OR* 27 (1):584, 591; Cavada Diary, 2 July 1863, HSP.

58. *OR* 27 (1):873; Humphreys Narrative, p. 13, Box 26, Humphreys Papers, HSP; Report, Turnbull to Thomas, 12 July 1863, Hunt Papers, LC; Humphreys to Hancock, 2 Oct. 1863, A. A. Humphreys Folder, Box 4, BC.

59. *OR* 27 (1):178, 591.

60. Ibid., p. 553; Marbaker, *Eleventh New Jersey*, p. 99; Robertson, *McAllister*, p. 333; New Jersey Gettysburg Battlefield Commission, *Final Report*, p. 55.

61. Marbaker, *Eleventh New Jersey*, p. 99; *OR* 27 (1):553; Robertson, *McAllister*, p. 333; New Jersey Gettysburg Battlefield Commission, *Final Report*, pp. 55, 106.

62. Baldwin to Bachelder, 20 May 1865, BP; *Pa at Gbg* 1:197; *OR* 27 (1):203.

63. *OR* 41 (1):202.

64. *Pa at Gbg* 1:197; Baldwin to Bachelder, 20 May 1865, BP.

65. Humphreys to Wilcox, 30 Nov. 1877, Box 27, Humphreys Papers, HSP.

66. Humphreys Narrative, Box 26, Humphreys Papers, HSP.

67. *OR* 27 (1):533, 543.

68. Humphreys to wife, 4 July 1863, Book 33, p. 36, Humphreys Papers, HSP.

69. Bartlett, *Twelfth Regiment*, p. 328; Langley to Bachelder, 24 Mar. 1864, BP.

70. Bartlett, *Twelfth Regiment*, p. 376; Langley to Bachelder, 24 Mar. 1864, BP.

71. *NY at Gbg* 2:606.

72. Rafferty, "Gettysburg"; Rafferty, "Third Corps' Great Battle," p. 27.

73. *OR* 27 (1):533; New Jersey Gettysburg Battlefield Commission, *Final Report*, p. 56.

74. *OR* 27 (1):554.

75. McClellan to Humphreys, 21 Sept. 1864, Book 22, p. 8, Humphreys Papers, HSP; Humphreys to Birney, 4 Oct. 1863, A. A. Humphreys Folder, Box 4, BC.

76. Bartlett, *Twelfth Regiment*, p. 127; H. H. Humphreys, *Humphreys*, p. 197;

Humphreys to Hammond, 15 Aug. 1863, A. A. Humphreys Folder, Box 4, BC. Humphreys wrote Hammond, the surgeon general, in an effort to locate the wounded Dimond. Apparently Dimond never reached a hospital.

77. H. H. Humphreys, *Humphreys*, p. 196; Bartlett, *Twelfth Regiment*, p. 127; Cavada Diary, 2 July 1863, HSP.

78. *OR* 27 (1):533.

79. *NY at Gbg* 2:820.

80. Young, *Battle of Gettysburg*, p. 257; *NY at Gbg* 2:821; *OR* 27 (1):544.

81. Humphreys to wife, 4 July 1863, Book 33, p. 36, Humphreys Papers, HSP; H. H. Humphreys, *Humphreys*, p. 198; Bardeen, *Fifer's War Diary*, p. 216; Humphreys to Hancock, 2 Dec. 1863, A. A. Humphreys Folder, Box 4, BC.

82. Bachelder to Humphreys, 25 Mar. 1876, Book 26, p. 618, Humphreys Papers, HSP. William H. Forney, age thirty-nine, had attended the University of Alabama, served in the War with Mexico, and was a lawyer who had been active in politics. He entered the Confederate service as a captain in the Tenth Alabama Regiment. He later led a brigade in Mahone's division, and in February 1865 he became a brigadier general. Forney served in Congress from 1875 to 1893. He died in 1898.

83. Freeman, *Lee's Lieutenants* 3:203; Wilcox, "Annotations to Official Report, 17 July 1863," Box 1, Wilcox Papers, LC.

84. Herbert to Bachelder, 9 July 1884, BP; Fortin, "Herbert's 'History,'" pp. 116–17. In about 1902, when Hilary Herbert visited the battlefield, he tried to convince John Bachelder that the Tenth Alabama advanced as indicated in this text and not with the main line of Wilcox's brigade. Bachelder seemed to have become convinced of the veracity of Herbert's description when he related his brigade's movement across Trostle's lane. Bachelder and the military park staff had heard previously of a Confederate unit's doing this from Colonel Sewell of the Fifth New Jersey, and the maneuver was deemed worthy of comment.

Sergeant Ragsdale was listed on the Confederate Roll of Honor for his courage and good conduct at Gettysburg. See *OR* 27 (2):775.

The presence of the Fifth New Jersey at the Trostle buildings, however, suggests that it did not retire with Humphreys's division when attacked by Barksdale but instead probably had fallen back initially to Trostle's Woods where it had been for a brief time earlier with Burling's brigade.

85. Fortin, "Herbert's 'History,'" p. 117.

86. James McClure Scott, "Confederate War Reminiscences," p. 13, Fredericksburg and Spotsylvania . . . National Military Park. James McC. Scott was assigned to the Tenth Virginia Cavalry Regiment and was on his way to join it. He became involved with the Ninth Alabama Regiment at Gettysburg because he happened to be visiting a brother who was serving with Anderson's division.

87. *OR* 27 (2):632; Lang, "Letter," p. 195; Humphreys to Wilcox, 30 Nov. 1877, Box 27, Humphreys Papers, HSP.

88. Wilcox, "Letter."

89. Bachelder to Humphreys, 25 Mar. 1896, Box 26, Humphreys Papers, HSP.

90. *OR* 27 (1):423, 426; *NY at Gbg* 1:663.

91. Rhodes, *Battery B*, pp. 201–2; C. H. Morgan Statement, n.d., BP.

92. *OR* 27 (1):235, 419, 424–25; Colvill to Bachelder, 9 July 1866, BP; Holcombe, *First Minnesota*, p. 344.

93. *OR* 27 (1):880.

94. Craig to Hunt, n.d., Box 2, Hunt Papers, LC.

95. Heath to Bachelder, 12 Oct. 1887, BP.

96. J. D. Smith, *Nineteenth Regiment*, p. 70.

97. *OR* 27 (1):370, 417, 436, 533.

98. Ibid., pp. 370, 453, 473.

99. Gibbon, *Personal Recollections*, p. 137; Gibbon to Hunt, 31 May 1879, Box 2, Hunt Papers, LC.

100. *OR* 27 (1):370; Hancock to Humphreys, 11 Mar. 1878, Box 27, Humphreys Papers, SHC; Hancock to Bachelder, 11 July 1885, BP.

101. Wilcox, "Annotations to Official Report, 17 July 1863," Box 1, Wilcox Papers, LC; *OR* 27 (2):618, 632; Lang, "Letter," p. 195.

102. *OR* 27 (2):619, 631; G. Clark, "Wilcox's Alabama Brigade," p. 229.

103. Bachelder to Humphreys, 25 Mar. 1876, Box 26, Humphreys Papers, SHC ; *OR* 27 (1):880.

104. Weir to Hancock, 25 Nov. 1885, BP; ACP File, Gulian W. Weir, Record Group 94, National Archives.

105. *Me at Gbg*, p. 292; J. D. Smith, *Nineteenth Regiment*, p. 71; Adams, "Nineteenth Maine," pp. 251–53.

106. *Me at Gbg*, p. 292; Heath to Bachelder, 12 Oct. 1887, BP; Adams, "Nineteenth Maine," p. 254. Adams indicated that there were those who believed that the general was not Humphreys. Humphreys wrote of being with Turnbull's battery during the retreat. At that time, at least, he would have been some distance to the south of the Nineteenth Maine. See Humphreys to Birney, 4 Oct. 1863, A. A. Humphreys Folder, Box 4, BC.

107. *Me at Gbg*, p. 293; Heath to Bachelder, 12 Oct. 1887, BP; J. D. Smith, *Nineteenth Maine*, p. 71.

108. Heath to Bachelder, 12 Oct. 1887, BP.

109. Ibid.; *Me at Gbg*, p. 295.

110. *OR* 27 (1):442–43, 451.

111. Waitt, *Nineteenth Regiment*, pp. 230–31; *OR* 27 (1):443, 451; Purcell, "Nineteenth Massachusetts," p. 280. Waitt stated that the two regiments, the Nineteenth Massachusetts and Forty-second New York Volunteer Infantry, crossed Plum Run before taking their position. Neither Mallon nor Devereux mentions doing so in his report.

112. Warner, *Generals in Gray*, p. 345; Evans, *Confederate Military History* 6:456–57. Wright was promoted to major general on 16 November 1864 and ordered to Georgia. After the war he was editor of the Augusta *Chronicle and Sentinel*. He died in 1872.

113. *OR* 27 (2):622–23.

114. Ibid., p. 633; Warren, *Generals in Gray*, p. 244.

115. Capt. J. S. Lewis to mother, 31 July 1863, Lewis Papers, SHC; Foote,

"Marching in Clover." Foote mentioned that a red barn, presumably the Bliss barn, was in their front.

116. *OR* 27 (2):633–34; Foote, "Marching in Clover"; James J. Kirkpatrick Diary, 2 July 1863, Barker Texas History Center, University of Texas at Austin (photocopy in Folder, Mississippi, Sixteenth Infantry, Box 17, BC). In his report Col. N. H. Harris of the Nineteenth Mississippi said that the Forty-eighth Mississippi advanced with Wright's brigade. In his diary Harris wrote that the Nineteenth and Forty-eighth Mississippi regiments advanced to "threaten the enemy, in support of a movement made by the brigades of Wilcox and Perry further to the right." See Harris, *Diary of Gen. Nat. H. Harris*, p. 22.

117. *OR* 27 (1):469; New Jersey Gettysburg Battlefield Commission, *Final Report*, p. 110; J. R. C. Ward, *One Hundred and Sixth*, p. 162.

118. J. R. C. Ward., *One Hundred and Sixth*, p. 160.

119. Ibid.; New Jersey Gettysburg Battlefield Commission, *Final Report*, p. 108.

120. *OR* 27 (1):465–70; New Jersey Gettysburg Battlefield Commission, *Final Report*, pp. 108, 110; Haines, *Men of Co. F*, p. 38.

121. *OR* 27 (2):633–34; Haines, *Men of Co. F*, pp. 38–39.

122. *OR* 27 (2):623; Snead, *Address*, p. 9; Foote, "Marching in Clover"; Wright to wife, 7 July 1863. A copy of the Wright letter was obtained by the author from John E. Divine of Leesburg, Virginia, but Mr. Divine did not know then the location of the original. However, it could be the same letter as that cited in Freeman, *Lee's Lieutenants* 3:127. Freeman stated that it was placed at his disposal by A. R. Wright of Atlanta, Georgia, a grandson of the general.

123. *OR* 27 (2):623, 630; Snead, *Address*, p. 9.

124. Rhodes, *Battery B*, pp. 201–2; *OR* 27 (1):423, 426. In his report Lieutenant Colonel Joslin, Fifteenth Massachusetts Infantry, used the pronoun "their" when referring to batteries firing canister from his rear. The word "their" would imply Confederate and, in this instance, should have been "the," meaning Federal. This is one of the rare typographical errors found in this publication.

125. *OR* 27 (1):423; *NY at Gbg* 2:664.

126. *OR* 27 (2):624; Wright to wife, 7 July 1863, in private collection of John E. Divine.

127. *OR* 27 (2):621, 633–34; James J. Kirkpatrick Diary, 2 July 1863, Barker Texas History Center, University of Texas at Austin (photocopy in Folder, Mississippi, Sixteenth Infantry, Box 17, BC).

128. Freeman, *R. E. Lee* 3:555; "Annotations to Official Report, 17 July 1863," Box 1, Wilcox Papers, LC; Wilcox, "General Wilcox." Wilcox is the principal source of this information, and he probably had some bias in the matter.

129. *OR* 27 (1):423; *NY at Gbg* 2:664; *OR* 27 (2):629–30.

130. *OR* 27 (1):478, 481; Rhodes, *Battery B*, p. 203.

131. *OR* 27 (1):417; Webb to wife, 6 July 1863, BP.

132. *OR* 27 (2):628–630; Paul, "Severe Experiences," p. 85.

133. Frederick Fuger, "Battle of Gettysburg: Recollections of the Battle," pp. 20–21, Typescript, Box 7, Folder 007 0110, Webb Papers, Yale University Library.

134. *OR* 27 (1):431; McDermott to Bachelder, 2 July 1886, BP; McDermott, *69th Regiment*, p. 29. General Harrow might have been the acting division commander at this time.

135. *OR* 27 (1):432, 434.

136. Ibid., pp. 436, 445, 447.

137. Ibid. (2):623; Wright to wife, 7 July 1863, in private collection of John E. Divine; Private William B. Judkins Narrative, The Georgia Room, Sara Hightower Regional Library (photocopy in Folder, Georgia, Twenty-second Infantry, Box 7, BC).

138. *OR* 27 (2):623.

CHAPTER 16

1. General Lee's activities after leaving Longstreet and Wilcox are summarized in Coddington, *Gettysburg Campaign*, pp. 444–45. Colonel Fremantle and General Heth were Coddington's principal sources.

2. General Meade's activities have been described in Chapters 6, 7, 10, and 15.

3. Oliver to Meade, 16 May 1882, GL, p. 89.

4. Crawford was on what today is called Granite Schoolhouse Lane. The lane connects with the Baltimore Pike east of Powers Hill and passes south around the base of Powers Hill to the Taneytown Road at a point about midway between Cemetery Hill and Little Round Top. The assembly areas for the Fifth and Sixth Corps and the park of the Artillery Reserve were located near it. The fork at which Crawford halted was southeast of Powers Hill. Granite Schoolhouse Lane continued west from it. The road to its left, which had been used by Ayres's division also, ran south, and not toward the battlefield, for about seven hundred yards and by the G. Spangler farmyard to a second fork, the right branch of which led to the J. Eckenrode farmyard and to the Wheatfield Road at Little Round Top.

5. *OR* 27 (1):653; 41 (1):201; Crawford Testimony, *CCW*, p. 469.

6. Hardin, *Twelfth Regiment*, p. 153.

7. *OR* 41 (1):201. Moore wrote nothing of attempting to contact Birney or of returning to Crawford. Perhaps his conversation with Poland was tantamount to one with Birney.

8. Crawford Testimony, *CCW*, p. 469; Sykes to Farley, 5 Aug. 1872, in Norton, *Attack*, p. 294.

9. Crawford to Jacobs, Dec. 1863, III, Crawford Papers, LC; Hardin, *Twelfth Regiment*, p. 153; *Pa at Gbg* 1:258, 295.

10. Warner, *Generals in Blue*, pp. 99–100.

11. Crawford to Stover, 14 May 1867, Case 5, Box 2, Autograph Collection of Simon Gratz, HSP.

12. Jackson to Rothermel, 5 July 1877, Rothermel Papers, Pennsylvania Historical and Museum Commission; Crawford to Jacobs, Dec. 1863, III, Crawford Papers, LC; Crawford, "Pennsylvania Reserves."

13. *OR* 27 (1):653, 657; *Pa at Gbg* 1:301; Glover, *Bucktailed Wildcats*, p. 205. The

Sixth Reserves's memorial is north of the Wheatfield Road near Plum Run. Its inscription indicates that it moved to that position from the rear.

The various regiments of the Pennsylvania Reserves used their reserves designations with pride, but they, like the Pennsylvania cavalry regiments, had numerical listings as Pennsylvania Volunteers. In this numerical sequence the First Reserves was the Thirtieth Pennsylvania Volunteer Infantry, and the numbers ran in sequence so that the Thirteenth Reserves was the Forty-second Pennsylvania Volunteer Infantry.

14. Hyde, *Greek Cross*, p. 148; Sedgwick Testimony, *CCW*, p. 460; *Pa at Gbg* 2:678.

15. When Newton took command of the First Corps, Brig. Gen. Frank Wheaton took command of the Third Division, Sixth Corps. Colonel Nevin then took command of Wheaton's brigade.

16. Hyde, *Greek Cross*, p. 198; *Pa at Gbg* 1:506–7.

17. *Pa at Gbg* 1:526.

18. Ibid. 2:679; Mark, *Red, White and Blue*, p. 217.

19. *Pa at Gbg* 1:507; Mark, *Red, White, and Blue*, p. 218. Nevin's brigade was formed, from right to left: Sixty-second, Ninety-third, 139th.

20. *OR* 27 (1):663, 671.

21. Ibid., pp. 635, 639, 641, 646, 648, 650; Jay to Ingham, 9 Sept. 1893, GL, p. 142.

22. *OR* 27 (1):608, 609; Report, Sweitzer to Chamberlain, Box 1, Chamberlain Papers, LC.

23. J. L. Parker, *Twenty-second Massachusetts*, p. 313; *Pa at Gbg* 1:278; Minnigh, *Company K*, p. 26. The story of the German captain creates a mystery because Gibbs's battery was recruited in Portsmouth, Ohio, an area not generally associated with German immigrants. In addition, the surnames of Frank Gibbs and Lt. Herbert F. Guthrie do not suggest that either would have had a German accent.

24. J. L. Parker, *Twenty-second Massachusetts*, p. 313. Gen. Charles Griffin had been on sick leave and was absent. However, in his report Griffin stated that he returned to the army on 3 July.

If Walcott made a report for his battery, it was not published, and neither Captain Martin nor General Hunt mentioned anything of Walcott's battery's operations per se. Since Martin had been the battery's commander, he might have been disposed to ignore the loss and recovery of the guns.

25. *OR* 27 (1):662.

26. *Pa at Gbg* 1:525–26, 530.

27. Ibid., pp. 526, 530.

28. Only members of the Ninety-eighth Pennsylvania Volunteer Infantry, like Schmide and Sgt. F. J. Loeble, spoke of this assault by the regiment. Although not supported by the testimony of others, it appears reasonable. Unfortunately, Major Kohler's report (*OR* 27 [1]:686) is terse and does not support it, and Colonel Nevin was in no position to observe it. This account is given some credibility, however, by the fact that the regiment's memorial was erected on Little Round Top rather than on the brigade line along Weikert's lane, though Schmide complained that the monument was not far enough forward. See *Pa at Gbg* 1:524.

29. *Pa at Gbg* 1:75, 113, 224, 278, 283, 301; *OR* 27 (1):653, 657; Crawford to Jacobs, Dec. 1863, III, Crawford Papers, LC; Sypher, *Pennsylvania Reserve Corps*, p. 460. In his address at the dedication of the memorial of the Eleventh Reserves, Jackson said that it was he who ordered the volley fired and the charge, not Crawford. His earlier letters state otherwise.

30. Crawford to Rothermel, 8 Mar. 1870, Rothermel Papers, Pennsylvania Historical and Museum Commission; Dobson to Crawford, 16 Jan 1882, IV, Crawford Papers, LC; Spear to McCoy, 22 June 1871, Rothermel Papers, Pennsylvania Historical and Museum Commission.

31. *Pa at Gbg* 1:113, 227, 228, 301, 526; Thomson and Rauch, *"Bucktails,"* p. 269. Col. William McCandless, commander of the First Brigade, was overshadowed in the Gettysburg accounts by General Crawford, who stayed with the brigade. McCandless started with the Second Reserves as a private, but when the regiment was reorganized in June 1861, he became its major. He became its colonel in August 1862. He commanded the brigade at Fredericksburg and Gettysburg and in the Wilderness. General Grant requested that he be promoted to the grade of brigadier general in May 1864, but McCandless declined the promotion and was mustered out with the Second Reserves as its colonel in June 1864.

On 3 July two men of the Sixth Reserves found a horse. Then, "A youngster named Dan Cole, to relieve the monotony of picket-firing, mounted the animal and rode down the front of the brigade line, playing 'Buck McCandless.' He appealed in the most pathetic tones to the boys to remember their 'daddies' and 'mammies' and 'best gal,' and never to desert the old flag as long as there was a ration left. He created much amusement until the horse bounced him off and scampered over to the rebels, when the cheers and shouts of both lines caused us to forget for the moment we were enemies" (*Pa at Gbg* 1:116).

32. *OR* 27 (1):685, 688; *Pa at Gbg* 1:279–80, 2:679. Colonel Nevin, reporting for the brigade, stated that it had recovered two Napoleons. The Sixty-second New York Volunteer Infantry claimed on its monument the capture of two, as did the 139th Pennsylvania also.

33. McLaws, "McLaws' Division."

34. McLaws, "Federal Disaster."

35. McLaws, "Battle."

36. Thomson and Rauch, *"Bucktails,"* p. 268. The nucleus of the Bucktails, 315 men, was recruited from lumbermen in the mountains of central Pennsylvania. They assembled at Sinnamahoning, Pennsylvania, and rafted from there via Sinnamahoning Creek and the West Branch of the Susquehanna River to Harrisburg. They flew a buck's tail from a pole on one of their rafts, and this became their symbol. After the regiment, the Thirteenth Reserves, was organized in June 1861, its men wore bucks' tails on their caps. They were rather unique at Gettysburg in that they were one of the few regiments that carried Sharps rifles. See Bates, *Pennsylvania Volunteers*, 906.

37. *OR* 27 (2):409.

38. Thomson and Rauch, *"Bucktails,"* pp. 269–70; *Pa at Gbg* 2:302.

39. Thomson and Rauch, "*Bucktails*," pp. 269–70; *Pa at Gbg* 2:302.

In the dedication address for the regiment's memorial, Capt. John P. Bond stated that someone demanded that the Confederates surrender. Many of them—Bond thought that there were some two to three hundred—threw down their arms, but one shouted, "I'll never surrender to a corporal's guard," and the Rebels went for their rifles. At this Lieutenant Kratzer shouted, "Tree, every man of you," and just as Taylor stepped to Kratzer's tree, he fell with a bullet in his heart. A marker beside Ayres Avenue indicates where Taylor is supposed to have fallen.

40. *Pa at Gbg* 1:113, 302.

41. Ibid., p. 279.

42. *OR* 27 (1):653, 657.

43. Crawford Testimony, *CCW*, p. 470. In 1897 six members of the Sixth Reserves received the Medal of Honor. The citations indicate simply that the six men charged a log house near Devil's Den and forced a squad of Confederates there to surrender. The house is not identified, and there is no further statement of what occurred. Nor is the incident related in the appropriate published reports and writings relating to the regiment. The men were Chester S. Furman, John Hast, George Mears, Wallace Johnson, Levi Roach, and Thaddeus Smith. From the location of the regiment north of the Wheatfield Road, one must assume that the building charged was the J. Weikert house, though this might not have been the case. If this was the case, the charge must have taken place before Wofford's men had retired from that area. See Department of the Army, *Medal of Honor*, p. 139.

44. *OR* 27 (2):399, 401–3; Hillyer, *Battle*, p. 9; McLaws, "McLaws' Division"; Suddath to brother, 9 July 1863, "Letters," p. 99.

45. *OR* 27 (1):618, 658; *Pa at Gbg* 1:295–96.

46. *OR* 27 (1):618; Law, "Struggle," p. 326.

47. *OR* 27 (1):654, 658; Crawford Testimony, *CCW*, p. 470; Crawford to Jacobs, Dec. 1863, III, Crawford Papers, LC. Col. Joseph W. Fisher is the subject of no readily available biographies. He began his Civil War service as lieutenant colonel of the Fifth Reserves in June 1861 and became its colonel in July 1862. He was mustered out with the Fifth Reserves in June 1864, but in March 1865 he became the colonel of the 195th Pennsylvania Volunteer Infantry. He was brevetted a brigadier general of volunteers in November 1865 in recognition of his war service. See Boatner, *Civil War Dictionary*, p. 280.

48. *OR* 27 (1):618, 625, 654, 658; Fisher, "Round Top Again." Fisher stated that the Twentieth Maine formed the skirmish line because it was armed with Springfield rifles, whereas the reserves had Harpers Ferry "altered muskets."

49. *OR* 27 (1):625; *Me at Gbg*, p. 259.

50. *Pa at Gbg* 1:296. Col. Martin D. Hardin (1837–1923), a graduate of West Point in 1858, was a native of Illinois. He was commissioned in the artillery and had been an aide to General Hunt on the Peninsula. He was wounded twice at Second Bull Run, lost an arm from a bushwhacker's shot near Catlett's Station, and was wounded again at North Anna. He was appointed lieutenant colonel of the Twelfth Reserves in July 1862 and became its colonel in September of the same year. He commanded the

defenses of Washington north of the Potomac at the time of Early's raid. He became a brigadier general of volunteers on 2 July 1864. After the war he served as a major in the Forty-third Infantry until he retired from the Regular Army in 1870 in the grade of brigadier general. Following retirement he practiced law in St. Augustine. See Boatner, *Civil War Dictionary*, pp. 374–75, and Warner, *Generals in Blue*, p. 205.

51. *Pa at Gbg* 1:296.

52. *OR* 27 (1):625, 632.

53. *Pa at Gbg* 1:296.

54. McNeily, "Barksdale's Brigade," p. 249.

55. The deciduous thicket that grew in the swale has grown into mature trees, and cattle pastured there have kept down the undergrowth. The rocks and stream bed are still visible.

56. Humphreys to Bachelder, 1 May 1876, BP.

57. Hancock Testimony, *CCW*, p. 407; *OR* 27 (1):370, 475.

58. Hancock to Humphreys, 11 Mar. 1878, Box 27, Humphreys Papers, HSP; Hancock to Bachelder, 7 Nov. 1885, BP; *OR* 27 (1):370.

59. Richardson to Bachelder, 8 May 1868, BP.

60. *NY at Gbg* 2:888.

61. Simons, *One Hundred and Twenty-fifth*, pp. 111–12; *NY at Gbg* 1:886; Willson, *Disaster*, p. 168; *OR* 27 (1):474.

62. Willson, *Disaster*, p. 169; *NY at Gbg* 2:906; Richardson to Bachelder, 8 May 1868, BP.

63. Richardson to Bachelder, 8 May 1868 and 18 May 1869, BP.

64. *OR* 27 (1):474–75.

65. Simons, *One Hundred and Twenty-fifth*, p. 113; *NY at Gbg* 2:887, 906; Willson, *Disaster*, p. 171; Richardson to Bachelder, 8 May 1868, BP; *OR* 27 (1):453. A granite marker located about three hundred yards southwest of the Pennsylvania State Memorial in the thicket on the east side of Plum Run marks the place where Willard is supposed to have fallen. It was said that his body was carried to the Fry house along the Taneytown Road, wrapped in linen, and sent home for burial.

66. B. Humphreys to Bachelder, 1 May 1876, BP; B. Humphreys, "The Sunflower Guards," p. 13, Claiborne Papers, SHC; McLaws, "McLaws' Division."

67. Peeples to Fasset, 15 Aug. 1870, Medal of Honor File, John B. Fasset, F 446 VS 1864, Box 4, Record Group 94, National Archives; Fasset to Bachelder, 27 Oct. 1894, BP.

68. Deposition, Hugo B. Hildebrandt, 9 Jan. 1894, Medal of Honor File, John B. Fasset, F 446 VS 1864, Box 4, Record Group 94, National Archives; *OR* 27 (1):660; *NY at Gbg* 1:279.

69. McNeily, "Barksdale's Brigade," p. 249.

70. McLaws, "McLaws' Division."

71. *OR* 27 (1):594, 660; Heitman, *Historical Register*, p. 514. Peeples was also brevetted a captain for gallantry at the battle of Winchester. He was a first lieutenant in the Nineteenth Infantry when he died in 1870.

72. Humphreys to Bachelder, 1 May 1876, BP.

73. Oliver to Meade, 16 May 1882, GL, p. 89.

74. *OR* 27 (1):774, 778, 783, 804, 812.

75. *OR* 27 (1):810; *NY at Gbg* 3:1033; Quaife, *Cannon's Mouth*, p. 228.

76. Hancock to Humphreys, 11 Mar. 1878, Box 27, Humphreys Papers, LC.

77. *OR* 27 (1):116, 765–66, 774, 778, 804; Quaife, *Cannon's Mouth*, p. 228; James C. Biddle, "General Meade at Gettysburg," in *Annals of the War*, p. 212; Meade, *Life and Letters*, p. 88; Meade, *With Meade*, p. 127.

78. *OR* 27 (1):804, 806, 809, 883; *NY at Gbg* 3:1022, 1042.

79. *OR* 27 (1):774, 778, 783, 804.

80. Hancock to Bachelder, 7 Nov. 1885, BP; Hancock to Humphreys, 11 Mar. 1878, Humphreys Papers, HSP; *OR* 27 (1):371.

81. *OR* 27 (1):371; Walker, *Great Commanders*, p. 127.

82. Bachelder to Humphreys, 25 Mar. 1876, Box 26, Humphreys Papers, HSP.

83. *OR* 27 (2):618; Bachelder to Humphreys, 26 Mar. 1876, Box 26, Humphreys Papers, HSP; G. Clark, *A Glance*, p. 38; G. Clark, "Wilcox's Alabama Brigade," p. 229; Herbert to Bachelder, 9 July 1884, BP; Fortin, "Herbert's 'History,'" p. 117.

84. The exchange between Colvill and Hancock is a composite of two accounts, Colonel Colvill's and Lt. William Lochren's. Lochren wrote that Hancock's order was, "Charge those lines," which seems more realistic, but Colvill received the order and ought to have known what it was. See Colvill to Bachelder, 9 July 1866, BP; Holcombe, *First Minnesota*, p. 344; Lochren, "1st Minnesota."

85. Company C was the division's provost guard; Company F was off to the left serving as skirmishers. Neither, then, was in the line. Company L, a supernumerary unit called the Second Minnesota Sharpshooters, was in the Ziegler's Grove area. The position "right shoulder shift" was similar to the later "right shoulder arms" except that the rifle butt was held parallel to the chest front with the lock plate up.

86. Colvill to Bachelder, 9 July 1866 and 30 Aug. 1866, BP; Holcombe, *First Minnesota*, p. 344; Lochren, "1st Minnesota"; Searles, "First Minnesota," p. 105.

87. Searles, "First Minnesota," pp. 105–6; Colvill to Bachelder, 9 July 1866, BP; Holcombe, *First Minnesota*, p. 346; Lochren, "1st Minnesota"; Lochren, "First Minnesota," p. 50.

88. *OR* 27 (2):319, 618; Wilcox, "General C. M. Wilcox," p. 103.

89. Holcombe, *First Minnesota*, p. 346; *NY at Gbg* 1:58.

90. *OR* 27 (1):371.

91. Ibid. (2):631–32; Lang, "Letter," pp. 195–96.

92. *OR* 27 (2):608, 614.

93. Lord, *Fremantle Diary*, p. 208; Chamberlaine, *Memoirs*, pp. 70–71.

94. Meade purchased Baldy from Gen. David Hunter in September 1861 for 150 dollars. Baldy was apparently so named because of a white blaze on his face. Although Baldy's gait bothered those who had to ride with the general, Meade became attached to him. Baldy was wounded in the leg at Second Bull Run, in the neck at Antietam, and in the right side at Gettysburg. After recuperating from the latter wound, he rejoined Meade, who rode him in the Virginia campaigns of 1864 until Weldon Railroad in August 1864, when a twelve-pounder ball struck Baldy a glancing blow.

Although he was not injured severely, Meade sent him back to Pennsylvania, a seasoned veteran with fourteen assorted wounds. He lived until 16 December 1882, when he was too feeble to stand and had to be put down. His head was mounted and hangs today in The Civil War Library and Museum, Military Order of the Loyal Legion, in Philadelphia. See Cavanaugh, " 'Old Baldy,' " pp. 2–4.

95. Tidball to Meade, 31 Mar. 1882, GL, p. 50. In a letter to S. P. Bates, 5 Apr. 1874 (MG-17, Box 2, Bates Papers, Pennsylvania Historical and Museum Commission), Doubleday recounted the above story, obviously from Tidball, but gave it a different twist. In the Doubleday account, Tidball found Meade "shut up in a little room walking up and down with his staff around him." Meade is depicted as having been at a loss until Tidball arrived and made his suggestion. Colonel Meade wrote to Tidball about this account, and Tidball gave the colonel the slightly different version given in this text. In a letter to Meade he expressed regret that Doubleday must have misunderstood him and placed him in the "light of a detractor." I have accepted the version supplied to Meade because it is direct from Tidball and seems to comport better with the situation and with the character of Meade displayed elsewhere.

96. *OR* 27 (1):258, 290, 294, 308.

97. Ibid., p. 351; Sturtevant, *Thirteenth Vermont*, pp. 263, 269; G. H. Scott, "Vermont," p. 62. Colonel Randall had Companies A, B, C, E, and G with him. The other five were with Lt. Col. William Munson and were posted in support of a battery on Cemetery Hill.

98. G. H. Scott, "Thirteenth Vermont," pp. 62–63.

99. Oliver to Meade, 16 May 1882, GL, p. 89; Meade, *Life and Letters*, p. 89; Meade, *With Meade*, p. 128.

100. *OR* 27 (2):623; "Chancellorsville and Gettysburg," p. 111.

101. *OR* 27 (1):441, 453.

102. Ibid., p. 417; Fuger, "Cushing's Battery," p. 407.

103. McDermott and Reilly, *69th Regiment*, p. 28.

104. *OR* 27 (1):427, 434; *Pa at Gbg* 1:551; J. R. C. Ward, *One Hundred and Sixth*, p. 161. Accounts do not indicate where on the crest the 106th stood on 2 July, but it is likely that it was at or near the site of its memorial.

105. *OR* 27 (1):434; J. R. C. Ward, *One Hundred and Sixth*, p. 161.

106. *Pa at Gbg* 1:551; J. R. C. Ward, *One Hundred and Sixth*, pp. 161–62.

107. *OR* 27 (1):434. In his report Ford claimed the capture of about 250 prisoners, including Colonel Gibson and 20 company grade officers. Wright's brigade had 333 officers and enlisted men reported captured or missing at Gettysburg. The number captured by the 106th Pennsylvania Volunteer Infantry, if correct, therefore, was a sizable portion of the total. Webb mentioned the 106th's feat in his report, but Gibbon did not. And yet no other Union regiment on the field must have captured so many Confederates.

Colonel Gibson of the Forty-eighth Georgia on 30 July sent Captain Ford a letter of thanks for the care that he received from Ford and the 106th. See J. R. C. Ward, *One Hundred and Sixth*, p. 162.

Captain Snead was exchanged in April 1864 and became lieutenant colonel of the

Third Georgia Regiment in July of that year (see Krick, *Lee's Colonels*, p. 329). In a speech about Wright and the Third Georgia at a reunion in 1874 Snead spoke of the charge but made no mention of this incident (see Snead, *Address*, pp. 9–10).

108. *OR* 27 (1):434; *Pa at Gbg* 1:551.

109. *OR* 27 (1):436, 447.

110. *NY at Gbg* 1:440.

111. *OR* 27 (1):436.

112. Meade, *Life and Letters*, p. 89.

113. Oliver to Meade, 16 May 1882, GL, p. 89.

114. Meade, *Life and Letters*, p. 89. Some shells fell near First Corps troops during their march to Cemetery Ridge. One struck near the battalion of the Thirteenth Vermont commanded by Lt. Col. William D. Munson, and a fragment tore a 3-by-5-inch piece from one of the pants legs of Capt. George Blake of Company K. Blake was proud of the tear and wore the pants home in that condition. For many years he displayed the torn pants along with sword and sash on the wall of a room in his house. See Sturtevant, *Thirteenth Vermont*, p. 275.

115. Oliver to Meade, 16 May 1882, GL.

116. *OR* 27 (1):351–52; Benedict, *Army Life*, p. 168; G. H. Scott, "Vermont," p. 64; Hancock to Humphreys, 11 Mar. 1878, Box 27, Humphreys Papers, HSP.

117. *OR* 27 (1):352.

118. G. H. Scott, "Vermont," p. 64; Benedict, *Army Life*, pp. 168–69.

119. *OR* 27 (1):352; G. H. Scott, "Vermont," p. 64, Sturtevant, *Thirteenth Vermont*, p. 271; Randall to Lonergan, 15 July 1869, Application of John Lonergan, Medal of Honor File, 326 VS 1882, Box 1732, Record Group 94, National Archives. Sturtevant stated that he believed Sgt. George Scott reached the guns first.

120. *OR* 27 (1):352; G. H. Scott, "Vermont," p. 65; Lonergan to Proctor, n.d., Application of John Lonergan, Medal of Honor File, 326 VS 1882, Box 1732, Record Group 94, National Archives. There were no Confederate guns captured on 2 July. The only Federal pieces recovered in this area were Weir's.

121. G. H. Scott, "Vermont," p. 65; Doubleday Testimony, *CCW*, p. 309.

122. *OR* 27 (1):261, 336, 348, 422, 533; Rafferty, "Gettysburg," p. 28; Adams, "Nineteenth Maine," p. 256; *Pa at Gbg* 2:741, 755; Ramsey to Bachelder, n.d., BP; Humphreys Testimony, *CCW*, p. 392; J. D. Smith, *Nineteenth Regiment*, p. 72.

123. *OR* 27 (1):261, 336, 348, 422, 542, 551, 553, 554, 558; Bartlett, *Twelfth Regiment*, p. 329; *Pa at Gbg* 2:741, 755; Marbaker, *Eleventh New Jersey*, p. 398; Adams, "Nineteenth Maine," p. 257.

124. Adams, "Nineteenth Maine," p. 257.

125. Rafferty, "Third Corps' Great Battle."

126. Quaife, *Cannon's Mouth*, p. 228; Meade, *With Meade*, p. 128; Meade, *Life and Letters*, p. 89.

CHAPTER 17

1. Longstreet, "Mistakes of Gettysburg"; Longstreet, "Lee in Pennsylvania," p. 424.

2. Alexander, "Gettysburg," p. 38, Alexander Papers, SHC.

3. OR 27 (1):16, 104.

4. NY at Gbg 2:664.

5. Alexander, "Gettysburg," p. 43, Alexander Papers, SHC.

6. Ibid., p. 44. Perhaps in this instance Alexander used the name "Peach Orchard" in a broad sense rather than that specially defined above. Since the left of his battalion's line was at the Peach Orchard, it seems likely that he would have bivouacked in another orchard closer to his battalion's center, possibly that opposite the Sherfy house.

7. OR 27 (2):369, 391, 396, 406, 413, 416, 422, 426; Law, "Struggle," pp. 326, 337.

8. "Recollections of Pvt. A. C. Sims, Co. F," Confederate Research Center (photocopy in Folder, Texas, 1st Infantry, Box 8, BC).

9. OR 27 (2):355, 409, 426, 428; Chilton, Unveiling, p. 340; "Recollections of Pvt. A. C. Sims, Co. F," Confederate Research Center (photocopy in Folder, Texas, 1st Infantry, Box 8, BC). In his report Benning was not so generous and gave most of the credit for the capture of the guns to the Twentieth Georgia. However, the fact that the Texans were given the responsibility of moving the guns away from Devil's Den seems to confirm their claim that they captured them.

Latham's battery turned in a six-pounder gun and a twelve-pounder howitzer that were disabled. A three-inch rifle of Reilly's battery burst. Presumably Smith's guns replaced these guns.

10. OR 27 (2):614, 618, 624, 632.

11. Ibid. (1):593, 604, 608, 613, 618, 635, 645, 654, 657, 658.

12. Hillyer, "Battle," p. 10.

13. OR 27 (1):497–98, 522–23, 527–28; de Trobriand, Four Years, pp. 506–7.

14. OR 27 (1):535, 553, 559, 571, 576, 579.

15. Ibid., pp. 437, 445, 552; Buckley to Bachelder, n.d., BP.

16. OR 27 (2):338–40, 343, 619, 624, 632. The strength of Wilcox's, Wright's, and Perry's brigades together was 3,927 according to their battlefield tablets. Their losses, according to their reports, totaled 1,565. Wilcox's and Perry's brigades suffered additional casualties in Pickett's Charge.

The tablets of the brigades of McLaws's division show a combined strength of 5,948, and those of Hood's division 5,900. Their reported casualties were 2,141 and 2,261 respectively.

The losses of Henry's, Cabell's, and Alexander's battalions for the battle were 37, 27, and 139 respectively. There was no breakdown of figures between 2 July and 3 July. See OR 27 (2):338–40.

17. OR 27 (1):175–80. The Third and Fifth corps casualty figures were taken directly from the "Return of Casualties in the Union Forces ... July 1–3, 1863," because the casualties of each were essentially that for the battle. The same was true

of Caldwell's division of the Second Corps. The estimate for the entire Second Corps is that of Caldwell's division together with half those reported for Hays's and Gibbon's divisions and the corps artillery.

18. Cavada Diary, 2 July 1863, HSP.

19. Ibid.

20. *Pa at Gbg* 1:228.

21. *OR* 27 (1):597.

22. Oates, *The War*, pp. 597–98.

23. J. L. Smith, *118th Pennsylvania*, p. 249.

24. Muffly, *148th Pennsylvania*, p. 465; Haynes, *Second Regiment in the War*, p. 82.

25. Cavada Diary, 2 and 3 July 1863, HSP.

26. Ibid., 3 July 1863.

27. Simpson, *Lee's Grenadier Guards*, p. 286.

28. R. L. Stewart, *One Hundred and Fortieth Regiment*, pp. 425–29. J. Jackson Purman and Ord. Sgt. James M. Piper of the 140th Pennsylvania received the Medal of Honor for trying to help a wounded comrade in the Wheatfield. Both were shot while doing so. See Department of the Army, *Medal of Honor*, p. 140.

29. Muffly, *148th Pennsylvania*, pp. 172–73. The Hummelbaugh house is a small two-story frame building that sits along the present Pleasonton Avenue just west of the Taneytown Road. In 1860 Jacob Hummelbaugh, a shoemaker, and his house-keeper resided there. See Bureau of the Census, Adams County, Pennsylvania, 1860—Cumberland Township.

30. Cassidy to Mrs. Barksdale, n.d., *Mississippi Index*, 13 June 1866, Ethelbert Barksdale Papers, Mississippi Department of Archives and History.

31. Ibid.

32. Muffly, *148th Pennsylvania*, p. 173.

33. Ibid.; Cassidy to Mrs. Barksdale, n.d., *Mississippi Index*, 13 June 1866, Ethelbert Barksdale Papers, Mississippi Department of Archives and History.

34. Cassidy to Mrs. Barksdale, n.d., *Mississippi Index*, 13 June 1866, Ethelbert Barksdale Papers, Mississippi Department of Archives and History; Benedict, *Army Life*, p. 170; Muffly, *148th Pennsylvania*, p. 245. Somehow General Sykes received a sword that was said to have been Barksdale's. He forwarded it to General Meade on 5 July. See *OR* 27 (1):596.

In 1882 a David Parker, formerly of the Fourteenth Vermont, wrote to Mrs. Barksdale. He stated that he and others volunteered to search for General Barksdale and that they found him. Parker wrote that he held the general's head and gave him coffee with a spoon. He reported that Barksdale had lost his left foot and that he had another leg wound and a chest wound. He asked that messages be given to his family and then became unconscious. Parker said that they carried him to Cemetery Hill, where the general died (see Parker to Mrs. Barksdale, 11 March 1882, and 22 March 1882, Ethelbert Barksdale Papers, Mississippi Department of Archives and History). The account given in the text and the Parker accounts can be reconciled generally if it is assumed that some of the discrepancies arise from the haziness of Parker's memory with the passing of time and his lack of familiarity with the battlefield's terrain.

Yet another account that cannot be reconciled with the others was written by none other than Humphreys's staff officer—Carswell McClellan. McClellan wrote in 1890 that he had come upon Barksdale while looking for a wounded comrade (Chester, perhaps?) and that he was probably the last officer to whom Barksdale spoke. One man in McClellan's group held Barksdale's head while another moistened his lips with water. McClellan wrote that Barksdale said, "Oh! how kind you are—how kind you are!" McClellan then observed, "One need not fight any the less stoutly because of being a *gentleman*." See McClellan to Munford, 7 Jan. 1890, Munford Division, Box 26, Letters, 1776–1895, File 1886–1891, Munford-Ellis Family Papers, Duke University, William R. Perkins Library.

35. Tremain, *Two Days*, pp. 93–95. Tremain wrote that Sim decided that Sickles should go to Washington. However, considering Sickles's nature, it seems in character for him to have advocated the early trip. It appears that the dangers of the journey would have far outweighed any benefits to Sickles's health that would have been derived from it. If this is so, nonmedical considerations must have prompted the trip. However, to put the move in some context, it would be well to remember that while Sickles was traveling to Washington, hundreds of wounded Confederates were being carted in wagons back to Virginia.

36. Ibid., pp. 93–98; Swanberg, *Sickles*, p. 221; "Condition of General Sickles," *New York Sun*, 8 July 1863. The route followed by the Sickles party is not known. It is likely that it would have taken roads southwest of the Baltimore Pike, between the Pike and the Taneytown Road.

It is safe to say that most of the men of the Third Corps were Sickles partisans and found little fault with him. An exception was Capt. Carswell McClellan of Humphreys's staff, who wrote, "I can't forget that the same spirit that carried off to Washington the Corps Surgeon to watch over one wounded leg when some three thousand poor fellows lay in that horrid field hospital needing far more his care put us where we stood that day and left us unaided as a result of his folly" (McClellan to Humphreys, 21 Sept. 1864, Book 22, p. 8, Humphreys Papers, HSP).

37. Tremain, *Two Days*, pp. 96–100; Rusling, *Men and Things*, p. 12; Swanberg, *Sickles*, p. 221.

38. Rusling, *Men and Things*, p. 13.

39. In his report General Meade stated only that Sickles, "not fully apprehending the instructions in regard to the position to be occupied, had advanced." General Halleck wrote in his report that Sickles, "misinterpreting his orders, instead of placing the Third Corps on the prolongation of the Second, had moved it nearly three-quarters of a mile in advance—an error which nearly proved fatal in the battle." The wording of these reports does not suggest a desire to court-martial Sickles; nor is that intention suggested elsewhere in the official writings of Meade and Halleck. In fact, both men probably would have regarded a court-martial as impractical, if nothing else, and not worth the time it would have taken from their duties. Halleck's attitude is probably suggested in his advice to Meade to ignore the charges made by Sickles against Meade in the HISTORICUS letter unless Sickles made them officially. Both officers must have believed that a court-martial would not have been counte-

nanced by President Lincoln and would have created an awful row. Sickles's wound had removed him from command of the Third Corps, and that solved the problems that his presence with the corps created. See *OR* 27 (1):16, 116, 127, 139.

40. Sickles must have told President Lincoln this story many times in the months after the battle. Sickles told it also when he testified before the Joint Commitee on the Conduct of the War in January 1864 and was supported then by the testimony of General Butterfield and some others. However, most of the officers who testified did not support the story. Sickles then made his views public through letters written by Historicus to the editor of the *New York Herald* and published on 12 March and 4 April 1864. His efforts to unseat General Meade from command of the Army of the Potomac and return to the command of the Third Corps were not successful.

Sickles renewed his campaign for vindication of his actions of 2 July in a speech made to veterans at Gettysburg in July 1886 and continued in these efforts until he died. Meade never responded to Sickles's charges, for he was advised by both President Lincoln and General Halleck not to. After Sickles's 1886 speech, long after Meade's death, G. G. Benedict responded by releasing a letter written in 1870 by General Meade, and Francis Walker wrote an article defending General Meade (see Walker, "Meade," pp. 406–12). General Meade was defended also in biographies written by his son and former aide, which have been cited above.

41. J. C. West, *A Texan*, p. 88; *OR* 27 (2):320.

42. Meade to Mrs. Meade, 3 July 1863, "Letters to Mrs. Meade," Meade Collection, HSP.

43. Sickles et al., "Further Recollections," p. 284.

BIBLIOGRAPHY

A bibliography of sources cited appears below. It includes a variety of unpublished items, a few maps, numerous books and pamphlets, and articles from newspapers and periodicals. Another source, not listed of course, is the battlefield itself and its scores of markers and monuments. A comment on some of these sources seems in order.

Two manuscript collections are particularly worthy of notice. One is the John B. Bachelder Papers. Although the original items of this collection are in the custody of the New Hampshire State Historical Society, I saw microfilm copies of them at Gettysburg National Military Park. Bachelder amassed this treasure trove of information on the battle through interviews and correspondence with officers of the two armies that began soon after the battle and continued into the 1880s, the period of the battlefield's memorialization. This source is priceless, and it is diminished only by its paucity of Confederate entries. Bachelder used some of the information that he obtained prior to 1876 in making his published maps of the battlefield, which are themselves a source of information. He was the S. L. A. Marshall of his era. The other collection meriting special comment is the Robert L. Brake Collection at the U.S. Army Military History Institute at Carlisle Barracks, Pennsylvania. Brake, a commander in the navy, was an ardent gleaner of Gettysburg materials and visited scores of repositories in search of them. It is my understanding that he hoped to use these materials in preparing a study of the battle but that his death prevented this. Thanks to Commander Brake, copies of these once-scattered Gettysburg sources are now conveniently available to students of the battle at a single place.

One newspaper requires some special comment. This is the *National Tribune*, a Washington, D.C., weekly that was published for Union veterans. It featured articles and letters on Civil War battles written by Union veterans of all ranks. Although these accounts vary greatly in quality and credibility, they are a valuable source of information that cannot be ignored.

I have listed together the various books and pamphlets cited because some do not lend themselves readily to separate classification. Almost all of them are either unit histories or accounts of veterans, but there are a few biographies and other secondary works, those of Douglas Southall Freeman and Edwin B. Coddington being the most notable. By far the most important title in this listing is *The War of the Rebellion: Official Records of the Union and Confederate Armies*. Its Series 1, Volume 27, contains official correspondence and reports of the Gettysburg campaign. The *Official Records*, as it is commonly called, contains reports for most units; and although the reports vary in quality and some are rather difficult reading, they have the advantage of having been written immediately after the battle, when their authors' memories were fresh if not always objective. They are *the* indispensable source.

Unit histories, the good ones at least, were almost as valuable as the *Official*

Records. I was familiar with many of them before beginning this study but found that Charles E. Dornbusch's monumental compilation, *Military Bibliography of the Civil War*, and Richard Allen Sauers's *The Gettysburg Campaign, June 3–August 1, 1863: A Comprehensive, Selectively Annotated Bibliography* were quite helpful in identifying publications to examine and for reviewing to see that I had used all sources reasonably available. For locating unit histories these bibliographies are useful tools indeed. Still, one of the frustrating and regrettable aspects of Gettysburg research is the lack of material available on many units, particularly those of the Army of Northern Virginia. For instance, there are no reports of Semmes's, Wofford's, or Barksdale's brigades published in the *Official Records*, and I found but a few unofficial accounts relating to Semmes's and Wofford's brigades that had any substance to them. This means that we know of these brigades and others like them only what we are told in the often casual references of others, including the enemy. On the Union side, the Regular Army units, especially the artillery batteries, also suffer from this deficiency. One lesson that the Civil War should have for modern military personnel is that immortality can be obtained only through good reports and unit histories.

The battlefield itself and its monuments and markers stand side by side with the written word as sources of information on this battle. The Gettysburg battlefield is no pool table—an appreciation of its terrain was of utmost importance to those who fought there, and it must be understood as much as possible by students of the battle today. Unfortunately, few reports and personal accounts related terrain and terrain features to operations except in the most general way; and even some of those accounts are hard to understand, partly because the writers sometimes had vague recollections of the field. Difficulties arise also because some portions of the field have been changed in the normal course of farming and by the construction of memorials, avenues, and other facilities. Although the later additions are an intrusion on the historic scene, the memorials are interesting and provide information on troop positions that would be impossible to determine from the written accounts of the battle. Sad to say, for a variety of reasons, their locations are not always correct and can be misleading.

MANUSCRIPT SOURCES

Confederate Research Center. Hill College, Texas.
  "Recollections of Private A. C. Sims."
Duke University. William R. Perkins Library, Manuscript Department.
    Durham, North Carolina.
  Bedinger-Dandridge Papers.
  James Longstreet Papers.
  Munford-Ellis Family Papers.
Emory University. Robert W. Woodruff Library, Special Collections
    Department. Atlanta, Georgia.
  "Journal of Private John Malachi Bowden."

Fredericksburg and Spotsylvania . . . National Military Park. Fredericksburg, Virginia.
    James McClure Scott, "Confederate War Reminiscences."
    "Memories of George W. Whipple."
Gettysburg National Military Park. Gettysburg, Pennsylvania.
    Letter, Alexander McNeil to wife, 7 July 1863.
    William C. Oates Correspondence.
    U.S. Gettysburg Battlefield Commission, Engineers Department, "A Record of the Position of Troops on the Battlefield."
The Historical Society of Pennsylvania. Philadelphia, Pennsylvania.
    Autograph Collection of Simon Gratz.
    John Rutter Brooke Papers.
    Adolpho Fernandez de la Cabada [Cavada] Diary, 1861–63.
    John Gibbon Papers.
    Major General A. A. Humphreys Papers.
    George Gordon Meade Collection.
Indiana State Library, Indiana Division. Indianapolis, Indiana.
    Gilbreath Manuscripts—"Account of Erasmus C. Gilbreath."
    Benson J. Worden, "B. J. Worden's Gettysburg Experience."
Library of Congress, Manuscript Division. Washington, D.C.
    Burbank-Van Voorhis Family Papers—Diary of Sidney Burbank.
    Joshua L. Chamberlain Papers.
    Samuel W. Crawford Papers.
    Douglas S. Freeman Papers.
    Henry J. Hunt Papers.
    Marsena R. Patrick Papers.
    Cadmus M. Wilcox Papers.
Military Order of the Loyal Legion of the United States. The Civil War Library and Museum. Philadelphia, Pennsylvania.
    James C. Hamilton, "History of the 110th Pennsylvania Infantry Regiment."
Mississippi Department of Archives and History. Jackson, Mississippi.
    Ethelbert Barksdale Papers.
National Archives. Washington, D.C.
    Record Groups 15, 21, 22, 92, 94.
New Hampshire Historical Society. Concord, New Hampshire.
    John B. Bachelder Papers.
The New-York Historical Society. New York, New York.
    Silas Auchmoedy Papers.
    General James Barnes Manuscripts.
    Abner Doubleday Papers.
    Daniel E. Sickles Correspondence.
    William Wright, "Recollections of the War of the Rebellion, 146th Regiment."
The New York Public Library. Astor, Lenox and Tilden Foundation, Rare Books and Manuscripts Division. New York, New York.

John Henry Hobart Ward Papers.
Pennsylvania Historical and Museum Commission, Division of Archives and
     Manuscripts. Harrisburg, Pennsylvania.
     MG-17, Samuel Penniman Bates Papers, 1853–95.
     MG-108, Peter F. Rothermel Papers, 1864–80.
Personal Collections.
     Edith D. Bancroft, M.D., Bryn Athyn, Pennsylvania.
     John Milton Bancroft Diary.
     William H. Brown, Madison, New Jersey.
     Letter, Henry T. Peck to mother, 7 July 1863.
     John E. Divine, Leesburg, Virginia.
     Letter, A. R. Wright to wife, 7 July 1863.
     Levi Bird Duff III, Pittsburgh, Pennsylvania.
     Samuel E. Duff, "Family History, Volume I, Ancestors of Levi Bird
          Duff III." (December 1941).
Rutgers University Libraries, Special Collections and Archives. New
     Brunswick, New Jersey.
     Roebling Collections.
Sara Hightower Regional Library, The Georgia Room. Rome, Georgia.
     Private William B. Judkins Narrative.
United States Army Military History Institute, United States Army Military
     History Collection. Carlisle Barracks, Pennsylvania.
     Robert L. Brake Collection.
University of Michigan. Bentley Historical Library, Michigan Historical
     Collection. Ann Arbor, Michigan.
     John Milton Bancroft Diary.
     James Houghton Journal.
University of North Carolina. Southern Historical Collection.
     Chapel Hill, North Carolina.
     E. P. Alexander Papers.
     Campbell-Colston Papers.
     J. F. H. Claiborne Papers.
     Henry Lewis Papers.
     Armistead L. Long Papers.
     Lafayette McLaws Papers.
     William Nelson Pendleton Papers.
University of Texas at Austin. Barker Texas History Center. Austin, Texas.
     James J. Kirkpatrick Diary.
Yale University. The Beinecke Rare Book and Manuscript Library, Collection
     of American Literature. New Haven, Connecticut.
     Joseph Hopkins Twichell Papers.
Yale University Library. New Haven, Connecticut.
     Frost Family Papers.
     Alexander Stewart Webb Papers.

NEWSPAPERS

Army and Navy Journal
Boston Sunday Herald
Detroit Free Press
Gettysburg Compiler
Minneapolis Journal
National Tribune
The News and Courier (Charleston)

New York Herald
New York Sun
New York Times
Philadelphia Weekly Press
Philadelphia Weekly Times
The Times (London)

MAPS

Bachelder, John B. *Position of Troops, Second Day's Battle*. New York: Office of the Chief of Engineers, U.S. Army, 1876.

Gettysburg National Park Commission. *Map of the Battlefield of Gettysburg*, NMP-GET-8447 (referred to in text and notes as "1901 Commission/Cope Map").

United States Army. Engineer Department. *Map of the Battle-Field of Gettysburg, Surveyed and drawn under the direction of Bvt. Maj. Gen. G. K. Warren* (popularly called "The Warren Map"). (See pl. 95 of the Atlas to U.S. Department of War, *War of the Rebellion: Official Records of the Union and Confederate Armies*.)

BOOKS, ARTICLES, AND PAMPHLETS

Abernathy, William M. *Our Mess: Southern Gallantry and Privations*. McKinney, Tex.: McKintex Press, 1977.

Adams, Silas. "The Nineteenth Maine at Gettysburg." Military Order of the Loyal Legion of the United States, Maine Commandery, *War Papers* 4 (1915): 249–63.

Alexander, Edward Porter. "The Great Charge and Artillery Fighting at Gettysburg." In *Battles and Leaders of the Civil War*, edited by Robert U. Johnson and Clarence C. Buel, 3:357–68.

_____. "Letter from General E. P. Alexander." *Southern Historical Society Papers* 4 (1877): 97–111.

_____. *Military Memoirs of a Confederate*. New York: Charles Scribner's Sons, 1907.

Allen, Lewis Y. "Berdan's Sharpshooters." *National Tribune*, 12 August 1886.

Ames, Nelson. *History of Battery G, First Regiment, New York Light Artillery*. Marshalltown, Iowa: Marshall Printing Co., 1900.

Anderson, James S. "The March of the Sixth Corps to Gettysburg." Military Order of the Loyal Legion of the United States, Wisconsin Commandery, *War Papers* 4 (1914): 75–84.

Anderson, Thomas M. "The Fourteenth Regiment of Infantry." *Journal of the Military Service Institution of the United States* 11 (1890): 673–96.

The Annals of the War, Written by Leading Participants North and South. Philadelphia: Times Publishing Company, 1879.

Appleton, Nathan, et al. *History of the Fifth Massachusetts Battery*. Boston: Luther Cowles, Publishers, 1902.

Babcock, William A. "The 114th Regiment, Pennsylvania Volunteers." *Philadelphia Weekly Times*, 24 April 1886.

Baker, Levi W. *History of the Ninth Mass. Battery*. Framingham, Mass.: Lakeview Press, 1888.

Bandy, Ken, and Florence Freeland. *The Gettysburg Papers*. 3 vols. Dayton: Press of Morningside Bookshop, 1978.

Bardeen, Charles W. *A Little Fifer's War Diary*. Syracuse: C. W. Bardeen, Publisher, 1910.

Barrett, John G., ed. *Yankee Rebel: The Civil War Journal of Edmund DeWitt Patterson*. Chapel Hill: University of North Carolina Press, 1966.

Barrett, Orvey S. *Reminiscences, Incidents, Battles, Marches and Camp Life of the Old 4th Michigan Infantry in the War of the Rebellion, 1861–1864*. Detroit: W. S. Ostler, 1888.

Bartlett, Asa W. *History of the Twelfth Regiment, New Hampshire Volunteers in the War of the Rebellion*. Concord, N.H.: Ira C. Evans, Printer, 1897.

Baruch, Simon. *Reminiscences of a Confederate Surgeon*. New York: n.p., 1915.

Barziza, Decimus et Ultimus. *The Adventures of a Prisoner of War, 1863–1864*. Edited by R. Henderson Shuffler. Austin: University of Texas Press, 1964.

Bates, Samuel P. *History of Pennsylvania Volunteers, 1861–1865*. 5 vols. Harrisburg: D. Singerly, State Printer, 1869.

Bean, Theodore. "Fall of General Zook." *Philadelphia Weekly Times*, 6 January 1883.

Benedict, George G. *Army Life in Virginia*. Burlington, Vt.: Free Press Association, 1895.

———. *A Short History of the 14th [Vermont] Reg't*. Bennington, Vt.: Press of C. A. Pierce, 1887.

Benjamin, Charles F. "Hooker's Appointment and Removal." In *Battles and Leaders of the Civil War*, edited by Robert U. Johnson and Clarence C. Buel, 3:239–43.

Bennett, Edwin C. *Musket and Sword*. Boston: Coburn Publishing Co., 1900.

Best, Isaac O. *History of the 121st New York State Infantry*. Chicago: James H. Smith, 1921.

Bigelow, John. *The Peach Orchard, Gettysburg, July 2, 1863*. Minneapolis: Kimball-Storer Co., 1919.

Blake, Henry N. *Three Years in the Army of the Potomac*. Boston: Lee and Shepard, 1865.

Bloodgood, J. D. *Personal Reminiscences of the Civil War*. New York: Hunt and Eaton, 1893.

Boatner, Mark Mayo. *The Civil War Dictionary*. New York: David McKay Company, 1959.

Bowen, James L. "Marching to Gettysburg." *Philadelphia Weekly Times*, 27 May 1882.

Bradley, Thomas W., and Peter B. Ayars. "At Gettysburg." *National Tribune*, 4 February 1886.

Brainard, Mary G. G. *Campaigns of the One Hundred and Forty-sixth Regiment, New York State Volunteers*. New York: G. P. Putnam's Sons, 1915.

Brockett, Linus P., and Mary C. Vaughn. *Woman's Work in the Civil War*. Philadelphia: Ziegler, McCurdy & Co., 1867.

Bruce, George A. *The Twentieth Regiment of Massachusetts Volunteer Infantry*. Cambridge: Houghton-Mifflin & Company, 1906.

Busey, John W., and David G. Martin. *Regimental Strengths at Gettysburg*. Baltimore: Gateway Press, Inc., 1982.

Campbell, Robert. "Pioneer Memories of the War Days of 1861–1865." *Collection and Remarks Made by the Michigan Pioneers and Historical Society* 30 (1906): 562–72.

Carter, Robert G. *Four Brothers in Blue*. Washington, D.C.: Press of Gibson Bros., 1913.

_____. "Reminiscences of the Gettysburg Campaign." Military Order of the Loyal Legion of the United States, Maine Commandery, *War Papers* 2 (1902): 149–83.

Cavanaugh, Michael A., Jr. " 'Old Baldy,' General George Gordon Meade's Veteran War Horse." *Loyal Legion Historical Journal* 37 (1981): 2–4.

Chamberlaine, William W. *Memoirs of the Civil War*. Washington, D.C.: Press of Byron S. Adams, 1912.

"Chancellorsville and Gettysburg. Extracts from General Doubleday's Monograph, with General Hancock's Autograph Notes Thereon." *Journal of the Military Service Institute of the United States* 47 (1911): 101–17.

Chase, Dudley H. "Gettysburg." Military Order of the Loyal Legion of the United States, Indiana Commandery, *War Papers* 1 (1898): 293–309.

Cheney, Newel. *History of the Ninth Regiment, New York Cavalry*. Jamestown, N.Y.: Martin Merz and Son, 1901.

Child, William A. *A History of the Fifth Regiment, New Hampshire Volunteers in the American Civil War*. Bristol, N.H.: R. W. Musgrove, Printer, 1893.

Chilton, F. B. *Unveiling and Dedication of Monument to Hood's Texas Brigade*. Houston: F. B. Chilton, 1911.

Clark, George. *A Glance Backward, or Some Events in the Past History of My Life*. Houston: Press of Rein & Sons Company, 1914.

_____. "Wilcox's Alabama Brigade at Gettysburg." *Confederate Veteran* 17 (1909): 229–30.

Clark, William. *History of Hampton Battery F, Independent Pennsylvania Light Artillery*. Pittsburgh: Werner Company, 1909.

Cleaves, Freeman. *Meade of Gettysburg*. Norman: University of Oklahoma Press, 1960.

Coddington, Edwin B. *The Gettysburg Campaign*. Dayton: Press of Morningside Bookshop, 1979.

Coggins, Jack. *Arms and Equipment of the Civil War*. New York: Fairfax Press, 1983.

Cole, Jacob H. *Under Five Commanders*. Paterson, N.J.: News Printing Co., 1906.

Collier, Calvin L. *"They'll Do to Tie To!" The Story of the Third Regiment, Arkansas Infantry, C.S.A.* Little Rock: Pioneer Press, 1959.

Colston, Frederick M. "Gettysburg as We Saw It." *Confederate Veteran* 5 (1897): 551–53.

Connelly, Thomas L. *The Marble Man: Robert E. Lee and His Image in American Society.* Baton Rouge: Louisiana State University Press, 1977.

Connor, Daniel M. "At Gettysburg: The Experiences and Sights of an Indiana Cavalryman." *National Tribune*, 27 July 1922.

Coxe, John. "The Battle of Gettysburg." *Confederate Veteran* 21 (1913): 433–36.

Coyne, John M. "The Fourth Excelsior." *National Tribune*, 5 January 1893.

Craft, David. *History of the One Hundred Forty-first Regiment Pennsylvania Volunteers.* Towanda, Pa.: Reporter-Journal Printing Company, 1885.

Crawford, Samuel W. "The Pennsylvania Reserves at the Battle of Gettysburg." *Philadelphia Weekly Press*, 8 September 1886.

Cudworth, Warren H. *History of the First Regiment Massachusetts Infantry.* Boston: Walker, Fuller and Company, 1866.

Cullum, George W. *Biographical Register of the Officers and Graduates of the U.S. Military Academy, at West Point, N.Y.* 3 vols. Boston: Houghton-Mifflin & Company, 1891.

Dana, Charles A. *Recollections of the Civil War.* New York: D. Appleton & Company, 1902.

de Trobriand, P. Regis. "The Battle of Gettysburg." *New York Herald*, 29 March 1864.

———. *Four Years with the Army of the Potomac.* Boston: Ticknor and Company, 1889.

Dickert, D. August. *History of Kershaw's Brigade.* Newberry, S.C.: Elbert H. Hull Company, 1899.

Dornbusch, Charles E. *Military Bibliography of the Civil War.* 3 vols. New York: New York Public Library, 1967.

Duke, J. W. "Mississippians at Gettysburg." *Confederate Veteran* 14 (1906): 216.

Durboraw, I. N. "The Big Battle: A Comrade Sends Reminiscences of Gettysburg." *National Tribune*, 8 December 1892.

Dyer, John P. *The Gallant Hood.* Indianapolis: Bobbs-Merrill Company, 1950.

E. C. C. "Battery D, 5th Artillery." *National Tribune*, 10 December 1891.

Early, Jubal A. "Supplement to General Early's Review, Reply to General Longstreet." *Southern Historical Society Papers* 4 (1877): 282–302.

Ellis, Franklin, ed. *History of Cattaraugus Co., N.Y.* Philadelphia: L. H. Everts, 1879.

Evans, Clement A., ed. *Confederate Military History: A Library of Confederate States History . . . Written by Distinguished Men of the South.* 12 vols. Atlanta: Confederate Publishing Co., 1889.

Farley, Porter. "Bloody Round Top." *National Tribune*, 3 May 1883.

———. "Letter to Editor, 10 March 1899." *Army and Navy Journal*, 22 April 1899.

———. "Reminiscences of the 140th Regiment, New York Volunteer Infantry." *Rochester Historical Society Publications* 22 (1944): 199–252.

Fasset, J. Barclay, "Letter to General Sickles, 12 June 1886," in "Gettysburg: Great Speech of Gen. Sickles on the Battlefield, July 2." *National Tribune*, 15 July 1886.

Favill, Josiah M. *The Diary of A Young Officer*. Chicago: R. R. Donnelly & Sons, Company, 1909.

Figg, Royall W. *"Where Men Only Dare Go!" or the Story of a Boy Company by an Ex-boy*. Richmond: Whittet & Shepperson, 1885.

Fisher, Joseph W. "Round Top Again." *National Tribune*, 16 April 1885.

Fleming, Francis P. *Memoir of Capt. C. Seton Fleming of the Second Florida Infantry, C.S.A.* Jacksonville, Fla.: Times Union Publishing House, 1884.

Fleming, George T., ed. *Life and Letters of Alexander Hays*. Pittsburgh: n.p., 1919.

Fletcher, William Andrew. *Rebel Private Front and Rear*. Beaumont, Tex.: Press of the Greer Print, 1908.

Foote, Frank. "Marching in Clover." *Philadelphia Weekly Times*, 8 October 1881.

Ford, Andrew E. *The Story of the Fifteenth Regiment, Massachusetts Volunteer Infantry in the Civil War*. Clinton: Press of W. J. Coulter, 1898.

Fortin, Maurice S., ed. "Colonel Hilary A. Herbert's 'History of the 8th Alabama Volunteer Regiment, C.S.A.'" *Alabama Historical Quarterly* 39 (1977): 5–321.

Frassanito, William A. *Gettysburg: A Journey in Time*. New York: Charles Scribner's Sons, 1975.

Frederick, Gilbert. *The Story of A Regiment, . . . the Fifty-seventh New York Volunteeer Infantry in the War of the Rebellion*. Chicago: C. H. Morgan Company, Printers, 1895.

Freeman, Douglas S. *Lee's Lieutenants*. 3 vols. New York: Charles Scribner's Sons, 1949–51.

_____. *R. E. Lee: A Biography*. 4 vols. New York: Charles Scribner's Sons, 1934–35.

Fuger, Frederick. "Cushing's Battery at Gettysburg." *Journal of the Military Service Institution of the United States* 40 (1907): 405–10.

Fuller, Charles A. *Personal Recollections of the War of 1861 . . . in the 61st New York Volunteer Infantry*. Sherburne, N.Y.: News Job Printing House, 1906.

"General E. M. Law at Gettysburg." *Confederate Veteran* 30 (1922): 49–50.

Georg, Kathleen R. "Our Principal Loss Was in This Place." *The Morningside Notes*, 12 June 1984.

Gerrish, Theodore. "Battle of Gettysburg." *National Tribune*, 23 November 1882.

Gibbon, John. *The Artillerist's Manual, Compiled from Various Sources, and Adapted to the Service of the United States*. New York: D. Van Nostrand, 1860. Reprint. Westport, N.Y.: Greenwood Press, 1971.

_____. *Personal Recollections of the Civil War*. New York: G. P. Putnam's Sons, 1928.

Gilham, William. *Manual of Instruction for the Volunteers and Militia of the United States*. Philadelphia: Charles DeSilver, 1861.

Glover, Edwin A. *Bucktailed Wildcats*. New York: Thomas Yoseloff, 1960.

Graham, Ziba B. "On to Gettysburg." Military Order of the Loyal Legion of the United States, Michigan Commandery, *War Papers* 1 (1893): 1–16.

Grant, U. S. *Personal Memoirs of U. S. Grant.* 2 vols. New York: Charles L. Webster & Company, 1886.

Groene, Bertram H., ed. "Civil War Letters of Colonel David Lang." *Florida Historical Quarterly* 54 (1976): 340–66.

Gross, George J. *The Battlefield of Gettysburg.* Philadelphia: Collins, Printer, 1866.

Haines, William P. *History of the Men of Co. F with Description of the Marches and Battles of the 12th New Jersey Vols.* Camden, N.J.: C. S. McGrath Printer, 1897.

Hall, James O. "A Modern Hunt for a Fabled Agent: The Spy Harrison," *Civil War Times Illustrated,* 24, no. 10 (1986): 18–25.

Hamilton, James C. M. "The 110th Regiment in the Gettysburg Campaign." *Philadelphia Weekly Press,* 24 February 1886.

Hancock, Almira Russell. *Reminiscences of Winfield Scott Hancock.* New York: Charles L. Webster & Company, 1887.

Hanford, J. Harvey. "Gettysburg: The Experiences of a Private in the 124th New York in the Battle." *National Tribune,* 24 September 1885.

Hanifen, Michael. *History of Battery B, First New Jersey Artillery.* Ottawa, Ill.: Republican Times Printers, 1905.

Hardin, Martin D. *History of the Twelfth Regiment, Pennsylvania Reserves Volunteer Corps.* New York: Published by the Author, 1890.

Harris, W. M., comp. *Movements of the Confederate Army in Virginia and the Part Taken Therein by the Nineteenth Mississippi Regiment. From the Diary of Gen. N. H. Harris.* Duncanby, Miss.: n.p., 1901.

Haskin, William L. *The History of the First Regiment of Artillery.* Portland, Me.: B. Thurston and Company, 1879.

Haynes, Martin A. *A History of the Second Regiment, New Hampshire Volunteer Infantry in the War of the Rebellion.* Lakeport, N.H.: n.p., 1896.

————. *History of the Second Regiment, New Hampshire Volunteers: Its Camps and Marches.* Manchester, N.H.: Charles F. Livingston Printer, 1865.

Hays, Gilbert Adams. *Under the Red Patch: Story of the Sixty-third Regiment, Pennsylvania Volunteers.* Pittsburgh: Sixty-third Pennsylvania Volunteers Regimental Association, 1908.

Hazen, Samuel R. "'Fighting the Good Fight': the 140th New York and Its Work on Little Round Top." *National Tribune,* 13 September 1894.

Hazlett, James C., Edwin Olmstead, and M. Hume Parks. *Field Artillery Weapons in the Civil War.* Newark: University of Delaware Press, 1983.

Heitman, Francis B. *Historical Register of the United States Army.* Washington: *National Tribune,* 1890.

Hill, Daniel H. "Lee Attacks North of the Chickahominy." In *Battles and Leaders of the Civil War,* edited by Robert U. Johnson and Clarence C. Buel, 2:347–62.

Hillyer, George. *Battle of Gettysburg: Address before the Walton County, Georgia, Confederate Veterans, August 2d, 1904.* Walton County, Ga: *Walton Tribune,* 1904.

Holcombe, Return I. *History of the First Regiment, Minnesota Volunteer Infantry.* Stillwater, Minn.: Easton & Masterson, 1916. (Completed by Jasper N. Searles and Matthew W. Taylor and sometimes attributed to them.)

Holden, Leverett D. *My First and Last Fights and Fredericksburg to Gettysburg Memories of the Civil War.* Malden, Mass.: Samuel Tilden Printer, n.d.

Holden, Wyman W. "Gettysburg: An Infantryman Confirms Captain Hart's Story." *National Tribune,* 26 March 1891.

Hood, John B. "Letter from General John B. Hood." *Southern Historical Society Papers* 4 (1877): 145–50.

Howard, Oliver O. "After the Battle." *Philadelphia Weekly Times,* 31 October 1885, and *National Tribune,* 31 December 1885.

Houghton, Edwin B. *The Campaigns of the Seventeenth Maine.* Portland, Me.: Short and Loring, 1866.

Houghton, William R., and Mitchell B. Houghton. *Two Boys in the Civil War.* Montgomery: Paragon Press, 1912.

Hulin, Charles, "Gettysburg: Batteries That Did Fight in the Peach Orchard." *National Tribune,* 29 January 1891.

Humphreys, Andrew A. "The Pennsylvania Campaign of 1863." *Historical Magazine,* 2d ser. 6 (July 1869): 1–8.

Humphreys, Henry H. *Andrew Atkinson Humphreys: A Biography.* Philadelphia: John C. Winston Company, 1924.

Hunt, Henry J. "The Second Day at Gettysburg." In *Battles and Leaders of the Civil War,* edited by Robert U. Johnson and Clarence C. Buel, 3:290–313.

Hyde, Thomas W. *Following the Greek Cross or Memories of the Sixth Army Corps.* Cambridge: Houghton, Mifflin and Company, 1894.

––––––. "Recollections of the Battle of Gettysburg." Military Order of the Loyal Legion of the United States, Maine Commandery, *War Papers* 1 (1898): 189–206.

Imholte, John Quinn. *The First Volunteers: History of the First Minnesota Volunteer Regiment.* Minneapolis: Ross and Haines, 1963.

Jacobs, Michael. "Meteorology of the Battle." *Gettysburg Star and Sentinel,* 11 August 1885.

––––––. *Notes on the Rebel Invasion of Maryland and Pennsylvania and the Battle of Gettysburg.* Gettysburg: Times Printing House, 1909.

Johnson, Allen, and Dumas Malone, eds. *Dictionary of American Biography.* 20 vols. New York: Charles Scribner's Sons, 1928-36.

Johnson, H. A. "What Regiment Supported Berdan's Sharpshooters?" *National Tribune,* 16 May 1889.

Johnson, Robert U., and Clarence C. Buel, eds. *Battles and Leaders of the Civil War.* 4 vols. New York: Century Company, 1884–89. Reprint. New York: Thomas Yoseloff, 1956.

Jordan, William C. *Some Events and Incidents during the Civil War.* Montgomery: Paragon Press, 1909.

Judson, Amos M. *History of the 83d Regiment Pennsylvania Volunteers.* Erie: B. F. H. Lynn Publishers, 1865.

Kershaw, Joseph B. "Kershaw's Brigade at Gettysburg." In *Battles and Leaders of the Civil War,* edited by Robert U. Johnson and Clarence C. Buel, 3:331–38.

Kilmer, George W. "The Stand at the Peach Orchard: The 141st Pennsylvania at Gettysburg." *National Tribune*, 27 December 1923.

Krick, Robert K. *The Gettysburg Death Roster: The Confederate Dead at Gettysburg*. Dayton: Press of the Morningside Bookshop, 1981.

_____. *Lee's Colonels: A Biographical Register of the Field Officers of the Army of Northern Virginia*. Dayton: Press of the Morningside Bookshop, 1979.

_____. *Parker's Virginia Battery, C.S.A*. Berryville, Va.: Virginia Book Company, 1975.

Lang, David. "Letter to General Edward A. Perry, 19 July 1863," in "Gettysburg. The Courageous Part Taken in the Desperate Conflict 2–3, July, 1863, by the Florida Brigade." *Southern Historical Society Papers* 27 (1899): 192–205.

Lasswell, Mary, ed. *Rags and Hope: The Recollections of Val C. Giles, Four Years with Hood's Brigade*. New York: Coward-McCann, 1961.

Law, Evander M. "The Struggle for 'Round Top.'" In *Battles and Leaders of the Civil War*, edited by Robert U. Johnson and Clarence C. Buel, 3:318–30.

Lawley, Francis. "The Battles of Gettysburg." *The Times* (London), 18 August 1863.

Lee, Fitzhugh. "A Review of the First Two Days' Operations at Gettysburg and A Reply to General Longstreet." *Southern Historical Society Papers* 5 (1878): 162–94.

Lee, Susan P. *Memoirs of William Nelson Pendleton, D.D*. Philadelphia: J. B. Lippincott Company, 1893.

Leeper, Joseph M. "Gettysburg: The Part Taken in the Battle by the Fifth Corps." *National Tribune*, 30 April 1885.

Lewis, George. *The History of Battery E, First Regiment, Rhode Island Light Artillery*. Providence: Snow and Farnham Printers, 1892.

Livermore, Thomas L. *Days and Events*. Cambridge: Houghton, Mifflin Company, 1920.

Lochren, William. "The First Minnesota at Gettysburg." In Military Order of the Loyal Legion of the United States, Minnesota Commandery, *Glimpses of the Nation's Struggle*, 3d ser., 1890, pp. 41–56.

_____. "1st Minnesota at Gettysburg." *National Tribune*, 23 October 1890.

Lokey, J. W. "Wounded at Gettysburg." *Confederate Veteran* 22 (1914): 400.

Long, Armistead L. "Letter, A. L. Long to Early, 5 April 1876." *Southern Historical Society Papers* 4 (1877): 66–68.

_____. *Memoirs of Robert E. Lee*. New York: J. M. Stoddart & Company, 1887.

Longstreet, James. "The Campaign of Gettysburg." *Philadelphia Weekly Times*, 3 November 1877.

_____. *From Manassas to Appomattox*. Philadelphia: J. B. Lippincott, 1896.

_____. "General Longstreet's Account of the Campaign and Battle." *Southern Historical Society Papers* 5 (1878): 54–85.

_____. "Lee in Pennsylvania." In *Annals of the War*, pp. 414–46. Philadelphia: Times Publishing Company, 1879.

_____. "Lee's Invasion of Pennsylvania." In *Battles and Leaders of the Civil War*, edited by Robert U. Johnson and Clarence C. Buel, 3:244–51.

————. "Lee's Right Wing at Gettysburg." In *Battles and Leaders of the Civil War*, edited by Robert U. Johnson and Clarence C. Buel, 3:339–54.

————. "Letter from General Longstreet." *Southern Historical Society Papers* 5 (1878): 52–53.

————. "The Mistakes of Gettysburg." *Philadelphia Weekly Times*, 23 February 1878.

Lord, Walter L., ed. *The Fremantle Diary*. Boston: Little, Brown and Company, 1954.

Love, William. "Mississippi at Gettysburg." *Publications of the Mississippi Historical Society* 9 (1906): 25–51.

Lydecker, Charles E. "General Alexander S. Webb." *City College Quarterly* 7, no. 2 (June 1911): 5–22.

Lyman, Theodore. *Meade's Headquarters, 1863–1865*. Boston: Atlantic Monthly Press, 1922.

McCullough, David. *The Great Bridge*. New York: Simon and Schuster, 1972.

McDermott, Anthony W., and John E. Reilly. *A Brief History of the 69th Regiment, Pennsylvania Veteran Volunteers. . . .* Philadelphia: D. J. Gallagher & Company, Printers, 1889.

McEneany, Patrick. "Gettysburg: Snapshot Impressions of a Great Battle as Told by a Chief of Orderlies." *National Tribune*, 22 March 1900.

McLaws, Lafayette. "The Battle of Gettysburg." *Philadelphia Weekly Press*, 21 April 1886.

————. "The Federal Disaster on the Left." *Philadelphia Weekly Press*, 4 August 1886.

————. "Gettysburg." *Southern Historical Society Papers* 7 (1879): 64–90.

————. "McLaws' Division and the Pennsylvania Reserves." *Philadelphia Weekly Press*, 20 October 1886.

McNeily, J. S. "Barksdale's Mississippi Brigade at Gettysburg." *Publications of the Mississippi Historical Society* 14 (1914): 231–65.

McSwain, Eleanor D. *Crumbling Defenses or Memoirs and Reminiscences of John Logan Black, Colonel, C.S.A.* Macon: Eleanor D. McSwain, 1960.

Maine Gettysburg Commission. *Maine at Gettysburg: Report of the Maine Commissioners*. Portland, Me.: Lakeside Press, 1898.

Marbaker, Thomas D. *History of the Eleventh New Jersey Volunteers*. Trenton: MacCrellish and Quigley, 1898.

Mark, Penrose G. *Red, White, and Blue Badge*. Harrisburg: Aughinbaugh Press, 1911.

Martin, Augustus P. "Little Round Top." *Gettysburg Compiler*, 24 October 1899.

Martin, James M., et al. *History of the Fifty-seventh Regiment, Pennsylvania Veteran Volunteer Infantry*. Meadville, Pa.: McCoy and Calvin, n.d.

Massachusetts Adjutant General's Office. *Massachusetts Soldiers, Sailors and Marines in the Civil War*. 9 vols. Norwood, Mass.: Norwood Press, 1931.

Meade, George G. "Letter to G. G. Benedict, 16 March 1870," in "The Meade-Sickles Controversy." In *Battles and Leaders of the Civil War*, edited by Robert U.

Johnson and Clarence C. Buel, 3:413–14.

Meade, George G. [Jr.], ed. *The Life and Letters of George Gordon Meade.* 2 vols. New
York: Charles Scribner's Sons, 1913.

———. *With Meade at Gettysburg.* Philadelphia: John C. Winston Company, 1930.

Minnigh, H. N. "Gettysburg: What Troops Fought in the Peach Orchard?" *National
Tribune,* 2 July 1891.

———. *History of Company K, 1st (Inft.) Penn'a Reserves, "The Boys Who Fought at
Home."* Duncansville, Pa.: Home Print Publisher, 1891.

Moran, Francis E. "About Gettysburg." *National Tribune,* 6 November 1890.

———. "A New View of Gettysburg." *Philadelphia Weekly Times,* 22 April 1882.

Moyer, Henry P. *History of the Seventeenth Regiment, Pennsylvania Volunteer Cavalry.*
Lebanon, Pa.: Sowers Printing Company, 1911.

Muffly, Joseph W., ed. *The Story of Our Regiment: A History of the 148th Pennsylvania
Vols.* Des Moines: Kenyon Printing & Manufacturing Company, 1904.

Mulholland, St. Clair A. *The Story of the 116th Regiment Pennsylvania Infantry.* Philadelphia: F. McManus Jr. & Company Printers, 1899.

Musgrove, Richard W. *Autobiography of Capt. Richard W. Musgrove.* N.p.: Mary D.
Musgrove, 1921.

Nash, Eugene Arius. *A History of the Forty-fourth Regiment, New York Volunteer Infantry in the Civil War.* Chicago: R. R. Donnelly & Sons Company, 1911.

Nelson, Alanson H. *The Battles of Chancellorsville and Gettysburg.* Minneapolis:
Alanson H. Nelson, 1899.

Nevins, Allan, ed. *A Diary of Battle: The Personal Journals of Colonel Charles S. Wainwright, 1861–1865.* New York: Harcourt, Brace & World, 1962.

New Jersey Battlefield Commission. *Final Report of the Gettysburg Battle-field Commission of New Jersey.* Trenton: John L. Murphy Publishing Company, 1891.

New York Monuments Commission for the Battlefields of Gettysburg and
Chattanooga. *Final Report on the Battlefield of Gettysburg.* [Cover title, *New York at
Gettysburg.*] 3 vols. Albany, N.Y.: J. B. Lyon Company, Printers, 1900.

Nicholson, John P., ed. *Pennsylvania at Gettysburg: Ceremonies at the Dedication of the
Monuments Erected by the Commonwealth of Pennsylvania.* 2 vols. Harrisburg:
Wm. Stanley Ray, State Printer, 1904.

Norton, Oliver W. *Army Letters, 1861–1865.* Chicago: O. L. Deming, 1903.

———. *The Attack and Defense of Little Round Top.* New York: Neale Publishing
Company, 1913.

———. "Strong Vincent and His Brigade at Gettysburg, July 2, 1863." In *The Gettysburg Papers,* edited by Ken Bandy and Florence Freeland, 2:499–516. Dayton: Press of the Morningside Bookshop, 1978.

Oates, William C. *Gettysburg, July 2, 1863, Col. William C. Oates to Col. Homer R.
Stoughton.* N.p., 1888.

———. *The War between the Union and the Confederacy . . . History of the 15th Alabama
Regiment. . . .* New York: Neale Publishing Company, 1905. Reprint. Dayton:
Press of the Morningside Bookshop, 1974.

Osbourn, Francis A. *One of the "Fighting Three Hundred," the Twentieth Indiana Infantry.* N.p., n.d.

Owen, William Miller. *In Camp and Battle with the Washington Artillery of New Orleans.* Boston: Ticknor and Company, 1885.

Parker, Francis J. *The Story of the Thirty-second Regiment, Massachusetts Infantry.* Boston: C. W. Calkins & Company, Publishers, 1880.

Parker, John Lord. *Henry Wilson's Regiment: History of the Twenty-second Massachusetts Infantry, the Second Company Sharpshooters, and the Third Light Battery. . . .* Boston: Press of Rand Avery Company, 1887.

Paul, William. "Severe Experiences at Gettysburg." *Confederate Veteran* 19 (1912): 85.

Paxton, John R. *Sword and Gown.* Edited by Calvin D. Wilson. New York: Knickerbocker Press, 1926.

Pendleton, Constance, ed. *Confederate Memoirs, Early Life and Family History, William Frederic Pendleton, Mary Lawson Young Pendleton.* Bryn Athyn, Pa.: n.p., 1958.

Polk, J. M. *Memories of the Lost Cause.* Austin: J. M. Polk, 1905.

Polley, J. B. *Hood's Texas Brigade: Its Marches, Its Battles, Its Achievements.* New York: Neale Publishing Company, 1910.

Porter, John T., ed. *Under the Maltese Cross: Antietam to Appomattox . . . Campaigns 155th Pennsylvania Regiment.* Pittsburgh: 155th Regimental Association, 1910.

Powell, R. M. "With Hood at Gettysburg." *Philadelphia Weekly Times,* 13 December 1884.

Powell, William H. *The Fifth Army Corps. . . .* New York: G. P. Putnam's Sons, 1896.

Prince, Howard J. "Death of Semmes." *Philadelphia Weekly Times,* 2 June 1883.

Purcell, Hugh D. "The Nineteenth Massachusetts at Gettysburg." *Essex Institute Historical Collections* 99 (1963): 277–88.

Purman, J. Jackson. "Gen. Zook at Gettysburg." *National Tribune,* 25 March 1909.

Quaife, Milo M., ed. *From the Cannon's Mouth: The Civil War Letters of General Alpheus S. Williams.* Detroit: Wayne State University Press, 1959.

Rafferty, Thomas. "Gettysburg." In Military Order of the Loyal Legion of the United States, New York Commandery, *Personal Recollections of the War of the Rebellion,* 1st ser., 1891, pp. 1–32.

————. "Gettysburg: The Third Corps' Great Battle on July 2." *National Tribune,* 2 and 9 February 1888.

Rauscher, Frank. *Music on the March . . . 114th Regt., P. V., Collis' Zouaves.* Philadelphia: Press of Wm. F. Fell & Co., 1892.

Reichardt, Theodore. *Diary of Battery A, First Regiment, Rhode Island Light Artillery.* Providence: N. Bangs Williams, 1865.

Reid, Whitelaw. *Ohio in the War.* 2 vols. Columbus, Ohio: Eclectic Publishing Company, 1893.

Rhodes, John H. *The History of Battery B, First Regiment, Rhode Island Artillery.* Providence: Snow & Farnham, Printers, 1914.

Rittenhouse, Benjamin F. "The Battle of Gettysburg as Seen from Little Round

Top." Military Order of the Loyal Legion of the United States, District of Columbia Commandery, *War Papers* 3 (1887): 1–14.

Robbins, Richard. "The Regular Troops at Gettysburg." *Philadelphia Weekly Times*, 4 January 1879.

Roberts, Charles. "At Gettysburg." Military Order of the Loyal Legion of the United States, Maine Commandery, *War Papers* 1 (1898): 47–57.

Robertson, James I., Jr., ed. *The Civil War Letters of General Robert McAllister*. New Brunswick: Rutgers University Press, 1965.

Ross, Fitzgerald. *A Visit to the Cities and Camps of the Confederate States*. Edited by Richard B. Harwell. Urbana: University of Illinois Press, 1958.

Rusling, James Fowler. *Men and Things I Saw in Civil War Days*. New York: Methodist Book Concern, 1914.

Scott, George H. "Vermont at Gettysburg." *Proceedings of the Vermont Historical Society* 1 (1930): 51–74.

Scott, Kate M. *History of the One Hundred and Fifth Regiment of Pennsylvania Volunteers*. Philadelphia: New-World Publishing Company, 1877.

Scott, Thomas. "On Little Round Top: A Batteryman's Reminiscences of Gettysburg." *National Tribune*, 2 August 1894.

Searles, Jasper N. "The First Minnesota Infantry." In Military Order of the Loyal Legion of the United States, Minnesota Commandery, *Glimpses of the Nation's Struggle*, 2d ser., 1890, pp. 80–113.

Searles, Jasper N., and Matthew F. Taylor. *History of the First Minnesota Volunteer Infantry. . . .* Stillwater, Minn.: Easton & Masterson, 1916. (*See* Holcombe, Return I.)

Sessions, Nathaniel. "Gettysburg: A Skirmish Which Had an Important Bearing on That Great Victory." *National Tribune*, 15 April 1886.

Shaw, Frederick B. *One Hundred and Forty Years of Service in Peace and War: History of the Second Infantry, United States Army*. Detroit: Strathmore Press, 1930.

Sheldon, Winthrop D. *The "Twenty-Seventh" [Connecticut]: A Regimental History*. New Haven: Morris & Benham, 1866.

Shumate, W. T. "With Kershaw at Gettysburg." *Philadelphia Weekly Times*, 6 May 1882.

Sickles, Daniel E. "Comment—The Meade-Sickles Controversy." In *Battles and Leaders of the Civil War*, edited by Robert U. Johnson and Clarence C. Buel, 3:414–19.

———. "Gettysburg: Great Speech of Gen. Sickles on the Battlefield, July 2." *National Tribune*, 22 July 1886.

Sickles, Daniel E., et al. "Further Recollections of Gettysburg." *North American Review* 152 (1891): 257–86.

Simons, Ezra D. *A Regimental History: The One Hundred and Twenty-fifth New York State Volunteers*. New York: Judson Printing Company, 1888.

Simpson, Harold B. *Gaines' Mill to Appomattox*. Waco: Texian Press, 1963.

———. *Hood's Texas Brigade: A Compendium*. Hillsboro, Tex.: Hill Junior College Press, 1977.

———. *Hood's Texas Brigade: Lee's Grenadier Guards*, Waco: Texian Press, 1970.

Smart, James G., ed. *A Radical View: The Agate Dispatches of Whitelaw Reid*. 2 vols. Memphis: Memphis State University Press, 1976.

Smith, James E. *A Famous Battery and Its Campaigns*. Washington, D.C.: W. H. Lowdermilk & Company, 1892.

Smith, John Day. *The History of the Nineteenth Regiment of Maine Volunteer Infantry*. Minneapolis: Great Western Printing Company, 1909.

Smith, John L., comp. *History of the 118th Pennsylvania Volunteers, Corn Exchange Regiment*. Philadelphia: J. L. Smith, Publisher, 1905.

Smith, M. V. *Reminiscences of the Civil War*. [Co. D, 4th Texas Infantry Regiment.] N.p., n.d.

Snead, Claiborne. *Address of Col. Claiborne Snead . . . On the 31st of July, 1874: History of the 3d Georgia Regiment and the Career of . . . Gen. Ambrose R. Wright*. Augusta: Chronicle and Sentinel Job Printing Establishment, 1874.

Sorrell, G. Moxley. *Recollections of a Confederate Staff Officer*. New York: Neale Publishing Company, 1905.

Stephenson, Luther. *A Sketch Giving Some of the Incidents during the Service of the Thirty-second Regiment, Massachusetts Volunteer Infantry*. Boston: Wheelman Press, 1900.

Stevens, Charles A. *Berdan's Sharpshooters in the Army of the Potomac*. St. Paul: The Price McGill Company, 1892.

Stevens, George T. *Three Years in the Sixth Corps*. Albany, N.Y.: S. R. Gray Publisher, 1866.

Stevens, John W. *Reminiscences of the Civil War*. Hillsboro, Tex.: Hillsboro Mirror Print, 1902.

Stewart, George R. *Pickett's Charge*. Boston: Houghton Mifflin Company, 1959.

Stewart, Robert L. *History of the One Hundred and Fortieth Regiment, Pennsylvania Volunteers*. N.p.: Regimental Association, 1912.

Storrick, W. C. *The Battle of Gettysburg*. Harrisburg: McFarland Company, 1969.

Strider, Robert E. L. *The Life and Work of George William Peterkin*. Philadelphia: George W. Jacobs & Company, 1929.

Sturtevant, Ralph O. *Pictorial History, Thirteenth Vermont Volunteers*. Burlington, Vt.: Regimental Association, 1910.

Suddath, James B. "From Sumter to the Wilderness: Letters of Sergeant James Butler Suddath." Edited by Frank B. Williams, Jr. *South Carolina Historical Magazine* 63 (April 1962): 93–104.

Sutton, Elijah H. *Grandpa's War Stories*. Demorest, Ga.: n.p., n.d.

Swanberg, W. A. *Sickles the Incredible*. New York: Charles Scribner's Sons, 1956.

Sypher, J. R. *History of the Pennsylvania Reserve Corps*. Lancaster: Elias Barr & Co., 1865.

Taylor, Eugene, G. *Gouveneur Kemble Warren: The Life and Letters of an American Soldier*. Boston: Houghton-Mifflin Company, 1932.

Thompson, Benjamin. "This Hell of Destruction." Part 2. *Civil War Times Illustrated* 12, no. 6 (1973): 12–23.

Thompson, Richard S. "A Scrap of Gettysburg." Military Order of the Loyal Legion of the United States, Illinois Commandery, *Military Essays and Recollections* 3 (1893): 95–109.

Thomson, O. R. Howard, and William H. Rauch. *History of the "Bucktails."* Philadelphia: Eclectic Printing Company, 1906.

Timm, Elias H. "Clark's N.J. Battery." *National Tribune*, 8 January 1891.

Toombs, Samuel. *New Jersey in the Gettysburg Campaign.* Orange, N.J.: Evening Mail Publishing House, 1888.

Tremain, Henry E. "Letter to General Sickles, 26 June 1880," in "Gettysburg: Great Speech of Gen. Sickles on the Battlefield, July 2." *National Tribune*, 15 July 1886.

———. *Two Days of War: A Gettysburg Narrative and Other Experiences.* New York: Bonnell, Silver and Bowers, 1905.

Trimble, Isaac. "The Battle and Campaign of Gettysburg." *Southern Historical Society Papers* 26 (1898): 116–28.

———. "The Campaign and Battle of Gettysburg." *Confederate Veteran* 25 (1917): 209–13.

Tucker, A. W. " 'Orange Blossoms': Services of the 124th New York at Gettysburg." *National Tribune*, 21 January 1886.

Tucker, Glenn. *Hancock the Superb.* Indianapolis: Bobbs-Merrill Company, 1960.

———. *High Tide at Gettysburg.* Indianapolis: Bobbs-Merrill Company, 1958.

———. *Lee and Longstreet at Gettysburg.* Indianapolis: Bobbs-Merrill Company, 1968.

U.S. Bureau of the Census. *Records of the Bureau of Census, Population Schedules, 1860, Pennsylvania.* Vol. 1, *Adams County, Cumberland Township.*

U.S. Congress. *Report of the Joint Committee on the Conduct of the War at the Second Session, Thirty-Eighth Congress, Army of the Potomac, General Meade. . . .* Washington, D.C.: U. S. Government Printing Office, 1865.

U.S. Department of the Army. *The Army Lineage Book.* Vol. 2, *Infantry.* Washington, D.C.: U. S. Government Printing Office, 1953.

U.S. Department of the Army. *The Medal of Honor of the United States Army.* Washington, D.C.: U. S. Government Printing Office, 1948.

U.S. War Department. *U.S. Infantry Tactics. . . .* Philadelphia: J. B. Lippincott & Company, 1862.

U.S. War Department. *The War of the Rebellion: A Compilation of the Official Records of the Union and Confederate Armies.* 128 vols. Washington, D.C.: U.S. Government Printing Office, 1880–1901.

Van Santvoord, Cornelius. *The One Hundred and Twentieth Regiment, New York State Volunteers.* Rondout, N.Y.: Press of the Kingston Freeman, 1894.

Venable, Charles S. "Letter, Venable to Longstreet, 11 May 1875," in "Supplement to General Early's Review, Reply to General Longstreet." *Southern Historical Society Papers* 4 (1877): 282–302.

Verrill, George W. "The Seventeenth Maine." Military Order of the Loyal Legion of the United States, Maine Commandery, *War Papers* 1 (1898): 259–82.

Wagner, Arthur L. *Organization and Tactics*. Kansas City, Mo.: Franklin Hudson Publishing Co., 1906.

Waitt, Ernest L. *History of the Nineteenth Regiment, Massachusetts Volunteer Infantry*. Salem, Mass.: Salem Press Company, 1906.

Walker, Francis A. *Great Commanders: General Hancock*. New York: D. Appleton and Company, 1898.

———. *History of the Second Army Corps*. New York: Charles Scribner's Sons, 1886.

———. "Meade at Gettysburg." In *Battles and Leaders of the Civil War*, edited by Robert U. Johnson and Clarence C. Buel, 3:406–12.

Ward, Joseph R. C. *History of the One Hundred and Sixth Regiment, Pennsylvania Volunteers*. Philadelphia: Grant, Faires & Rodgers, 1883.

Ward, W. C. "Incidents and Personal Experiences on the Battlefield of Gettysburg." *Confederate Veteran* 8 (1900): 345–49.

Waring, George E., Jr. "The Garibaldi Guard." In *The First Book of the Author's Club, Liber Scriptorum*. New York: Author's Club, 1893.

Warner, Ezra J. *Generals in Blue*. Baton Rouge: Louisana State University Press, 1964.

———. *Generals in Gray*. Baton Rouge: Louisiana State University Press, 1959.

Wert, J. Howard. *A Complete Handbook of the Monuments and Indications and Guide to the Positions on the Gettysburg Battle-field*. Philadelphia: R. M. Sturgeon & Company, 1886.

West, John C. *A Texan in Search of a Fight*. Waco: Press of J. S. Hill & Company, 1901.

West, Oscar W. "On Little Round Top." *National Tribune*, 22 November 1906.

Westbrook, Cornelius D. "On the Firing Line." *National Tribune*, 20 September 1900.

Weygant, Charles H. *History of the One Hundred and Twenty-fourth Regiment, N.Y.S.V.* Newburgh, N. Y.: Journal Printing House, 1877.

"Where Honor is Due." *Boston Herald*, 23 July 1899.

Wilcox, Cadmus M. "General C. M. Wilcox on the Battle of Gettysburg." *Southern Historical Society Papers* 6 (1878): 97–104.

———. "General Wilcox to the Rescue." *Philadelphia Weekly Times*, 24 November 1877.

———. "Letter from General C. M. Wilcox, 26 March 1877," in "Causes of the Confederate Defeat at Gettysburg." *Southern Historical Society Papers* 4 (1877): 111–17.

Williams, Thomas J. C., and Folger McKinsey, eds. *History of Frederick County*. 2 vols. Baltimore: Regional Publishing Company, 1967.

Williamson, R. L. "At Gettysburg. Another of Weed's Brigade Tells What They Did on Round Top." *National Tribune*, 1 September 1892.

Willson, Arabella M. *Disaster, Struggle, Triumph: The Adventures of 1,000 "Boys in Blue."* Albany, N.Y.: Argus Company, Printers, 1870.

Winslow, George B. "On Little Round Top." *National Tribune*, 26 July 1879.

Woodward, E. M. *Our Campaigns*. Philadelphia: John E. Potter and Company, 1865.

Wright, William M. "The Second Regiment of Infantry." *Journal of the Military Service Institution of the United States* 16 (1895): 438–55.

Young, Jesse Bowman. *The Battle of Gettysburg*. New York: Harper & Brothers Publishers, 1913.